EP.TH4D

Toyota Hi-Lux / 4 Runner

1979-1997
Diesel LN

ISBN 9780958727877

ELLERY PUBLICATIONS
VEHICLE REPAIR MANUAL SERIES

This repair and maintenance manual has been published to help provide vehicle owners and enthusiasts with an invaluable, comprehensive and thorough guide in all aspects of restoration, maintenance and mechanical repair work.

The manual is published from the latest information obtained at our factory. Where extensive research is undertaken to obtain the information for the benefit of people who purchase this manual.

DISCLAIMER

Every endeavour has been made to ensure all information in this manual is accurate. Mistakes and omissions can always occur, and the publisher does not assume any duty or care, or legal responsibility in relation to the contents of this book.

Maintenance, repair and tune-up are essential for safe and reliable use of all motor vehicles. These operations should be undertaken in such a manner as to eliminate the possibility of personal injury or in such a way that could damage the vehicle or compromise the safety of the vehicle, driver, passenger or a third party.

Ellery Publications,

Imprint of Renniks Publications Pty Ltd,
Unit 3, 37/39 Green Street,
Banksmeadow NSW 2019
Australia

Phone   61 2 9695 7055
Fax   61 2 9695 7355
Web   www.ellery.com.au

Product #	EP.TH4D
Title	Hi-Lux / 4 Runner 1979-1997 Diesel LN
ISBN	9780958727877
	(also National Library of Australia Card number)

Composition & Printing: nitrro.com

Max Ellery's Toyota Hilux and 4 Runner 1979 - 1997 Diesel - Automoble Repair Manual

INDEX

CONTENTS   **Page**

CONTENTS

Page

CONTENTS   **Page**

GENERAL INFORMATION -- MODEL IDENTIFICATION

RN 20(upto 1977 Hilux), RN 30 & RN 40 SERIES - Up To 1983 Hilux

Engine Data
Petrol / Gasoline

8R OHV	3.38in Bore x 3.15in Stroke	1858cc (113.4cu.in)	Max Power 108hp@5500
12R OHV			
18R SOHC	3.48in Bore x 3.15in Stroke	1980cc (120.7cu.in)	Max Power 97@5500
20R DOHC	88.5mm Bore x 89.0mm Stroke	2189cc (133.6cu.in)	Max Power 95@4800

Transmission Data
Manual Transmissions

Type	L42, 40 & 43	4 Speed Manual
	W50	4 Speed Manual

Cold Tyre Pressure
RN 30, 40, 31 and 41

Tyre Size	Unloaded - slow driving				Unloaded - faster driving			
	Front		Rear		Front		Rear	
	kg/cm2	Psi	kg/cm2	Psi	kg/cm2	Psi	kg/cm2	Psi
6.00-14, 6PR 1.6	23	2.4	34	2.1	30	2.9	41	
6.50-14, 8PR 2.4	34	2.4	34	2.9	41	2.4	34	
185R 14(C), 8PR	1.8	26	1.8	26	2.3	33	2.3	33
185SR 14	1.4	20	1.4	20	1.7	24	1.7	24

LN 30 and 40

Tyre Size	Unloaded - slow driving				Unloaded - faster driving			
	Front		Rear		Front		Rear	
	kg/cm2	Psi	kg/cm2	Psi	kg/cm2	Psi	kg/cm2	Psi
6.00-14, 6PR 1.8 and 6.50-14, 8PR	26	2.4	34	2.3	33	2.9	41	

RN 32 and 42

Tyre Size	Unloaded - slow driving				Unloaded - faster driving			
	Front		Rear		Front		Rear	
	kg/cm2	Psi	kg/cm2	Psi	kg/cm2	Psi	kg/cm2	Psi
185SR 14, 4PR	1.4	20	1.4	20	1.7	24	1.7	24
7.00 14, 6PR	1.4	20	1.4	20	1.7	24	1.7	24
E78 14, (B)	1.4	20	1.4	20	1.7	24	1.7	24
ER78 14, (B)	1.4	20	1.4	20	1.7	24	1.7	24
7.50 14, 6PR	1.4	20	1.4	20	1.7	24	1.7	24
185SR 14, 4PR	1.4	20	1.4	20	1.7	24	1.7	24
185SR 14, 4PR	1.4	20	1.4	20	1.7	24	1.7	24
185SR 14, 4PR	1.4	20	1.4	20	1.7	24	1.7	24

YN, LN 50's and 60's SERIES 1983-1988 Hilux

Engine Data

Petrol / Gasoline   1Y, 1Y-C, 2Y, 2Y-C, 3Y and 3Y-C OHV Engines

1Y (1.6litre)	86.0mm Bore x 70.0mm Stroke	1626cc	Max Power 55kw@4800rpm
2Y (1.8litre)	86.0mm Bore x 78.0mm Stroke	1812cc	Max Power 58kw@4800rpm
3Y (2.0litre)	86.0mm Bore x 86.0mm Stroke	1998cc	Max Power 65kw@4600rpm

Diesel   l, 2L and 2L-T (turbo) Engines

L (2.2litre)	3.54in Bore x 3.38in Stroke	2188cc (133.5cu.in)	Max Power 62hp@4200rpm
2L (2.4litre)	92.0mm Bore x 92.0mm Stroke	2446cc	Max Power 55kw@4000rpm
2L-T (2.4litre)	92.0mm Bore x 92.0mm Stroke	2446cc	Max Power 64kw@3500rpm

Transmission Data

Automatic Transmission

Type	A43D	4 Speed including Overdrive

Manual Transmissions

Type	L40 and 42	4 Speed Manual
	W52	4 Speed Manual
	G40, 52 and 54	4 and 5 Speed Manaul

Cold Tyre Inflation Pressure

2 Wheel Drive

Tyre Size	Front		Rear	
	kg/cm2	Psi	kg/cm2	Psi
6.00-14, 6PR and 6.50-14, 8PR	1.6	23	2.4	34
185R14C-8PR	1.8	26	1.8	26
185R14-8PRLT	1.8	26	2.4	34
6.50-14-8PRLT	1.8	26	2.4	34
185SR 14	1.7	24	2.2	31

4 Wheel Drive

Tyre Size	Front		Rear	
	kg/cm2	Psi	kg/cm2	Psi
7.00-15, 6PR	1.8	26	2.4	34
7.00-15, 8PR	1.8	26	2.4	34
7.00-16, 8PR	2.4	34	3.0	43
205 SR 16	1.7	24	2.4	34
205R 16C 6PR	1.7	24	2.4	34

YN, RN, VZN and LN 120's and 130's SERIES 1989 0n - Hilux

Engine Data

Petrol / Gasoline   3Y, 3Y-C, 4Y 4Y-C and 4Y-E OHV engines

3Y (2.0litre)	86.0mm Bore x 86.0mm Stroke	1998cc	Max Power 65kw@4600rpm
4Y-C (2.2litre)	91.0mm Bore x 86.0mm Stroke	2237cc	Max Power 71kw@4600rpm
4Y-E (2.2litre)	91.0mm Bore x 86.0mm Stroke	2237cc	Max Power 74kw@4400rpm

21R and 22R

21R	84mm Bore x 91mm Stroke	2002cc	Max Power 70kw@4800rpm
22R	92mm Bore x 91mm Stroke	2367cc	Max Power 75kw@4800rpm

3V-ZE Engine

3VZ-E(3.0litre)	87.5mm Bore x 82.0mm Stroke	2959cc	Max Power 105kw@4600rpm

Diesel   2L, 2L-T(turbo) and 3L Engines

2L (2.4litre)	92.0mm Bore x 92.0mm Stroke	2446cc	Max Power 55kw@4000rpm
2L-T (2.4litre)	92.0mm Bore x 92.0mm Stroke	2446cc	Max Power 64kw@3500rpm
3L (2.8litre)	96.0mm Bore x 96.0mm Stroke	2779cc	Max Power 60kw@4000rpm

Transmission Data
Automatic Transmission

Type	A43D, A40H, A343H 4 Speed including Overdrive

Manual Transmissions

Type		
	G40, G52, G54 & G58	4 and 5 Speed Manaul
	W56	4 Speed
	L40	4 Speed

2 Wheel Drive

Tyre Size	Front		Rear	
	kg/cm2	Psi	kg/cm2	Psi
6.00-14LT, 6PR Middle East	1.6	23	4.25	62
6.50-14LT, 8PR Middle East	1.6	23	4.25	62
195SR14, 6PR Middle East	1.8	26	3.75	54
195SR14C, 6PR Thailand	1.8	26	1.8	26
6.00-14LT, 6PR Other Countries	1.6	23	2.4	35
6.50-14LT, 8PR Other Countries	1.6	23	2.4	35
185R14C, 8PR Other Countries	1.8	26	2.4	35
195SR14 Other Countries	1.7	25	2.3	33
195R14C-8PR	1.8	26	1.8	26
1991 on				
185R 14C, 8PR Europe	2.2	32	4.5	65
195R 14C, 8PR Europe	2.2	32	4.5	65
195SR14 Europe	1.7	25	2.3	33
185R 14, 8PR Australia	1.8	26	2.4	35
195R 14C, 8PR Austalia	1.8	26	2.4	35
195SR14 Australia	1.7	25	2.3	33
6.00-14LT, 6PR Middle East	1.6	23	4.25	62
6.50-14LT, 8PR Middle East	1.6	23	4.25	62
195SR14, 6PR Middle East	1.8	26	3.75	54
195SR14C, 6PR Thailand	1.8	26	1.8	26
6.00-14LT, 6PR Other Countries	1.6	23	2.4	35
6.50-14LT, 8PR Other Countries	1.6	23	2.4	35
185R14C, 8PR Other Countries	1.8	26	2.4	35
195SR14 Other Countries	1.7	25	2.3	33

4 Wheel Drive - Independant Front Suspension

Tyre Size	Front		Rear	
	kg/cm2	Psi	kg/cm2	Psi
205R 16	1.7	25	2.4	35
205SR 16R	1.7	25	2.0	29
205R 16R/F Europe	1.7	25	2.6	38
215R 15 6PR	1.9	28	2.3	33
265/75R 15	1.9	28	1.9	28

4 Wheel Drive - Leaf Spring Front Suspension

Tyre Size	Front kg/cm2	Psi	Rear kg/cm2	Psi
7.00-15, 6PR	1.8	26	--	--
7.00-15, 8PR	--	--	4.25	62
7.00-16, 8PR	2.4	35	4.25	62
205R16C-6PR	1.7	25	3.0	44
205R 16 Reinforced	1.7	25	2.4	35
205R 16R/F Europe	1.7	25	3.0	44

YN, RN, VZN and LN 120's and 130's SERIES 1989 to 1997 - 4 Runner

Engine Data
Petrol / Gasoline   3Y, 3Y-C, 4Y 4Y-C and 4Y-E OHV Engines

3Y (2.0litre)	86.0mm Bore x 86.0mm Stroke	1998cc	Max Power 65kw@4600rpm
4Y-C (2.2litre)	91.0mm Bore x 86.0mm Stroke	2237cc	Max Power 71kw@4600rpm
4Y-E (2.2litre)	91.0mm Bore x 86.0mm Stroke	2237cc	Max Power 74kw@4400rpm

21R and 22R

21R	84mm Bore x 91mm Stroke	2002cc	Max Power 70kw@4800rpm
22R	92mm Bore x 91mm Stroke	2367cc	Max Power 75kw@4800rpm

3VZ-E engine

3VZ-E(3.0litre)	87.5mm Bore x 82.0mm Stroke	2959cc	Max Power 105kw@4600rpm
Diesel	2L, 2L-T(turbo) and 3L Engines		
2L (2.4litre)	92.0mm Bore x 92.0mm Stroke	2446cc	Max Power 55kw@4000rpm
2L-T (2.4litre)	92.0mm Bore x 92.0mm Stroke	2446cc	Power 64kw@3500rpm
3L (2.8litre)	96.0mm Bore x 96.0mm Stroke	2779cc	Power 65kw@4000rpm

Transmission Data
Automatic Transmission
Type   A43D,A340H, A343H   4 Speed including Overdrive
Manual Transmissions
Type   G40, G52, G54 & G58   4 and 5 Speed Manaul
                    W56   4 Speed
                    L40   4 Speed
                    G52 and R150F   4 and 5 Speed Manaul

Cold Tyre Inflation Pressures

Tyre Size	Front kg/cm2	Psi	Rear kg/cm2	Psi
185R 14C, 8PR Europe	2.2	32	4.5	65
195R 14C, 8PR Europe	2.2	32	4.5	65
195SR14 Europe	1.7	25	2.3	33
185R 14, 8PR Australia	1.8	26	2.4	35
195R 14C, 8PR Austalia	1.8	26	2.4	35
195SR14 Australia	1.7	25	2.3	33
6.00-14LT, 6PR Middle East	1.6	23	4.25	62
6.50-14LT, 8PR Middle East	1.6	23	4.25	62
195SR14, 6PR Middle East	1.8	26	3.75	54
195SR14C, 6PR Thailand	1.8	26	1.8	26
6.00-14LT, 6PR Other Countries	1.6	23	2.4	35
6.50-14LT, 8PR Other Countries	1.6	23	2.4	35
185R14C, 8PR Other Countries	1.8	26	2.4	35
195SR14 Other Countries	1.7	25	2.3	33
205R16C-6PR	1.7	25	3.0	44
205R 16 Reinforced	1.9	28	2.3	33
215SR 15	1.9	28	2.3	33

ENGINE TUNE-UP & MAINTENANCE

ENGINE TUNE-UP & MAINTENANCE

* for a complete in depth listing of oil levels please see page 409

SERVICE OPERATIONS

CHECK OIL LEVEL.

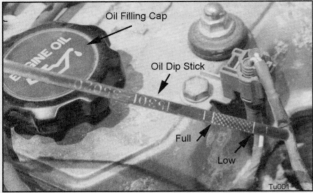

The oil level should be between the L & F marks on the level gauge. Inspect for leakage, and fill oil up to the F mark if level is low.

Oil Capacity, Oil Quality & Oil Pressure
"L" Engine Lubricant Quantity Specification:
L, 2L, & 2L-T Hilux & 4 Runner (1984) w/o new oil filter:
4.3 Litres, 5.1 US qts, 4.2 Imp qts.
L, 2L, & 2L-T Hilux & 4 Runner (1984) new oil filter:
5.8 Litres, 6.1 US qts, 5.1 Imp qts.
L, 2L, & 2L-T Hilux & 4 Runner (1984) dry fill:
6.5 Litres, 6.9 US qts, 5.7 Imp qts
2L & 3L Hilux (1988 on) w/o new oil filter:

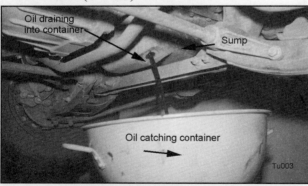

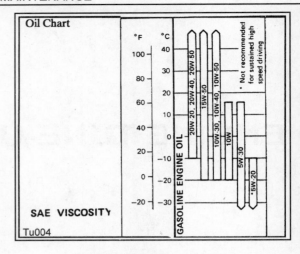

Oil Chart

SAE VISCOSITY

Tu004

GASOLINE ENGINE OIL

5.0 Litres, 5.3 US qts, 4.4 Imp qts.
2L & 3L Hilux & 4 Runner (1988) new oil filter:
6.0 Litres, 6.3 US qts, 5.3 Imp qts.
2L & 3L Hilux & 4 Runner (1988) dry fill:
6.5 Litres, 6.9 US qts, 5.7 Imp qts.

Lubricant Quality:
Engine Oil Grade API grade:
SC, SD, SE, SF (Australia & Europe SE & SF)

"R" Engine Lubricant Quantity Specification:
12R & 18R Hilux & 4Runner w/o new oil filter:
3.2 Litres, 3.4 US qts, 2.8 Imp qts
12R & 18R Hilux & 4Runner with new oil filter:
3.8 Litres, 4.0 US qts, 3.3 Imp qts
20R,21R,22R,22R-E&22R-TE Hilux & 4Runner w/o new oil filter:
3.8 Litres, 4.0 US qts, 3.3 Imp qts
20R,21R,22R,22R-E&22R-TE Hilux & 4Runner with new oil filter: 4.3 Litres, 4.5 US qts, 3.8 Imp qts
12R, & 18R Hilux & 4Runner dry fill:
4.2 Litres, 4.4 US qts, 3.7 Imp qts
20R,21R,22R,22R-E&22R-TE Hilux & 4Runner dry fill:
4.8 Litres, 5.1 US qts, 4.2 Imp qts

Lubricant Quality:
Engine Oil Grade API grade:
SC, SD, SE, SF (Australia & Europe SE & SF)

"R" Series Engines
Lubricant Quantity Specification:
Hilux 2WD w/o new oil filter:
3.0 Litres, 3.2 US qts, 2.6 Imp qts
Hilux 2WD with new oil filter:
3.5 Litres, 3.7 US qts, 3.1 Imp qts
Hilux & 4 Runner 4WD w/o new oil filter:
3.5 Litres, 3.7 US qts, 3.1 Imp qts
Hilux & 4 Runner 4WD with new oil filter:
4.0 Litres, 4.2 US qts, 3.5 Imp qts
Hilux 2WD dry fill:
4.2 Litres, 4.4 US qts, 3.7 Imp qts

Hilux & 4 Runner 4WD dry fill:
>4.6 Litres, 4.8 US qts, 4.0 Imp qts

Lubricant Quality:
Engine Oil Grade API grade: SD, SE, SF

"Y" Engine Lubricant Quantity Specification:
All Ex YN 4WD Hilux & 4Runner w/o new oil filter:
>3.0 Litres, 3.2 US qts, 2.6 Imp qts

All Ex YN 4WD Hilux & 4Runner with new oil filter:
>3.5 Litres, 3.7 US qts, 3.1 Imp qts

YN 4WD Hilux & 4Runner w/o new oil filter:
>3.5 Litres, 3.7 US qts, 3.1 Imp qts

YN 4WD Hilux & 4Runner with new oil filter:
>4.0 Litres, 4.2 US qts, 3.5 Imp qts

All EX YN 4WD Hilux & 4Runner dry fill:
>4.2 Litres, 4.4 US qts, 3.7 Imp qts

YN 4WD Hilux & 4Runner dry fill:
>4.6 Litres, 4.9 US qts, 4.0 Imp qts

Lubricant Quality:
Engine Oil Grade API grade:
>SC, SD, SE, SF (Australia & Europe SE & SF)

3VZ-E
Lubricant Quantity Specification:
With out new oil filter:
>4.2 Litres, 4.4 US qts, 3.7 Imp qts

With new oil filter:
>4.5 Litres, 4.8 US qts, 4.0 Imp qts

Dry fill:
>5.3 Litres, 5.6 US qts, 4.7 Imp qts

Lubricant Quality:
Engine Oil Grade: API grade SD, SE, SF

OIL PRESSURE
"L" series engines L, 2L & 2L-T up to 60's series
3000 rpm plus 2.5 - 6.0 kg/cm 36-85psi 245-588 kPa
"L" series 2L & 3L 80's to 130's
3000 rpm plus 3.0 - 5.5 kg/cm 43-78psi 294-539kPa
"R" series engines 18R, 20R, 21R, 22R, 22R-E & 22R-TE
3000 rpm plus: 2.5-5.0kg/cm 36-71psi, 245-490kPa(min)
"Y" series engines
3000 rpm plus: 2.5-5.0kg/cm 36-71psi, 245-490kPa(min).
3VZ-E
3000 rpm plus: 2.5-5.3kg/cm 36-75psi, 245-520kPa(min).

CHECKING AND FILLING COOLING SYSTEM
If the cooling system needs to drained, the following instructions should be obeyed when refilling the cooling system to ensure that the block is drained fully.
1. Adjust heater control to maximum.
2. Have a coolant mixture such as Tectaloy coolant on hand to fill system.
Coolant Specification: e.g.
Cast Iron Head Models: Tectaloy 60+

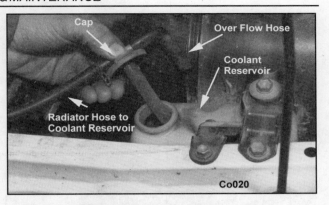

Co020

Aluminium Head Models: Tectaloy Optimal
* Do not combine different types of antifreeze or corrosion inhibitors as they may be incompatible. If a different type has been used in the cooling system rinse the system with clean water.
3. Remove radiator cap and fill cooling system with coolant mixture.
4. Remove top from coolant reservoir and top up system.
5. When the coolant is cold the coolant level should be at the FULL mark. Depending on the engine temperature the level will vary.
6. Start engine and run it at 2000 rpm for 10 minutes to open thermostat and purge air from system. Fill supply tank to "FULL/MAX" mark.

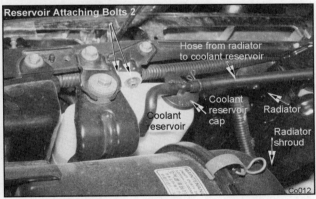

Co012

7. Replace cap.
Coolant
LN:
L, 2L & 2L-T up to 60's:
>10.6 litres, 11.2 US qts, 9.3 Imp qts

2L 80's series on:
>9.2 litres, 9.7US qts, 8.1 Imp qts

3L: 9.0 litres, 9.5US qts, 8.0 Imp qts.
RN:
18R: 9.0 litres, 9.5US qts, 8.0 Imp qts.
20R: 7.0 litres 7.4US qts, 6.25Imp qts
18R-G, 21R, 22R, 22R-E & 22R-TE:
>8.4 litres, 8.9US qts, 7.4 Imp qts.

YN:
Y & 1Y-C: 7.3 litres, 7.7US qts, 6.4 Imp qts.

2Y: 7.0 litres, 7.4US qts, 6.2 Imp qts.
3Y, 4Y, 4Y-C & 4Y-E: 7.0 litres, 7.4US qts, 6.2 Imp qts.
3VZN
3VZ-E: 10.5 litres, 11.1 US qts, 9.2 Imp qts.

INSPECT AIR FILTER

(a) Inspect the air cleaner element to ensure is not excessively damaged, dirty or oily.

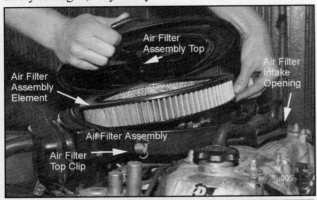

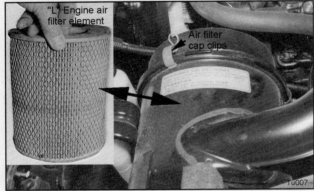

(b) Clean the element with compressed air. First clean the inside thoroughly, then clean the outside of the element.

Inspection of High Tension Lead. (Petrol / Gasoline Engines)

1. Carefully Remove High Tension Lead by Rubber Boot from Spark Plugs.
* Pulling on or bending the cords may damage the conductor

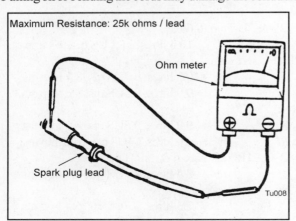

inside.
2. Examine Resistance of High Tension Lead with Distributor Cap.
Check that the resistance does not exceed the maximum using an ohmmeter.
Maximum resistance: 25 k ohms / cord.
Inspect the terminals, and replace the high tension lead and/or distributor cap if more than maximum specified.

OIL FILTER

* The oil filter should be replaced every 10,000 Kilometres or 6 months which ever occurs first, or when the engine oil is contaminated in any way.

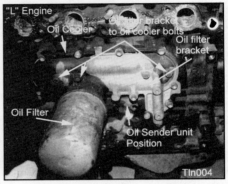

Replacement
1. Unscrew oil filter with a suitable oil filter wrench, then remove and discard.

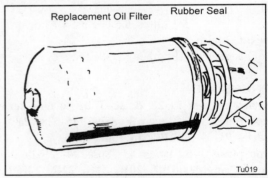

2. (a) Make sure seal is placed correctly in recess in new filter.
(b) Pour some clean engine oil into filter until level is approximately 2 cms below top of filter.
3. (a) Smear some engine oil over filter seal.
(b) Screw filter into place until seal contacts mating surface of adaptor, then tighten through a further 2/3 of a turn.
4. (a) Clean any excess oil from filter and adaptor.
(b) Check oil level, then start engine and check for oil leaks.
(c) Repair as necessary.
* After running the engine, the oil level must be rechecked and oil added as necessary, to compensate for oil used to refill the oil filter.

COMPRESSION CHECK "R" Engines

1. Make sure of the following:
(a) Engine is at operating temperature;
(b) Battery is at (or near) full charge;
(c) Spark plugs are removed;
(d) Remove the coil distributor connector (and cold start injector connector plus solenoid resistor if EFI) (this stops both fuel injection and ignition during engine cranking).
2. (a) Install suitable compression tester into spark plug hole, screw in type are more accurate. Depress accelerator pedal to fully open position and crank engine.

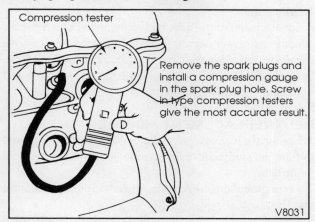

Compression tester

Remove the spark plugs and install a compression gauge in the spark plug hole. Screw in type compression testers give the most accurate result.

V8031

(b) Read compression gauge indication.
3. Check remaining cylinders.
Specified Compression:
12R, 18R, 20R, 21R :11.0 kg/cm, 156pis, 1,079kPa.
22R's :   12.0 kg/cm, 171pis, 1,177kPa.
Minimum Specified Compression:
12R, 18R, 20R, 21R: 9.0 kg/cm, 128pis, 883kPa.
22R's: 10.0 kg/cm, 142pis, 981kPa.
* If cylinder compression in 1 or more cylinders is low, pour a small amount of engine oil into the cylinders through the spark plug holes and test compression.

COMPRESSION CHECK "L" Engines

1. Make sure of the following:
(a) Engine is at operating temperature.
(b) Battery is at (or near) full charge.
(c) Remove glow plugs.
(d) Remove the fuel pump solenoid connector (this stops both fuel injection and ignition during engine cranking).
2. (a) Install suitable compression tester into spark plug hole, screw in type are more accurate. Depress accelerator pedal to fully open position and crank engine.
(b) Read compression gauge indication.
3. Check remaining cylinders.
Specified Compression:
32.0 kg/cm, 455pis, 3,138kPa.
Minimum Specified Compression:
20.0 kg/cm, 284pis, 1,961kPa.

* If cylinder compression in 1 or more cylinders is low, pour a small amount of engine oil into the cylinders through the spark plug holes and test compression.

COMPRESSION CHECK "Y" Engines

1. Make sure of the following:
(a) Engine is at operating temperature;
(b) Battery is at (or near) full charge;
(c) Spark plugs are removed;
(d) Remove the coil distributor connector (and cold start injector connector plus solenoid resistor if EFI) (this stops both fuel injection and ignition during engine cranking).
2. (a) Install suitable compression tester into spark plug hole, screw in type are more accurate. Depress accelerator pedal to fully open position and crank engine.
(b) Read compression gauge indication.
3. Check remaining cylinders.
Specified Compression:
12.5 kg/cm, 178pis, 1,226kPa.
Minimum Specified Compression:
9.0 kg/cm, 128pis, 883kPa.
* If cylinder compression in 1 or more cylinders is low, pour a small amount of engine oil into the cylinders through the spark plug holes and test compression.

COMPRESSION CHECK 3VZ-E

1. Make sure of the following:
(a) Engine is at operating temperature;
(b) Battery is at (or near) full charge;
(c) Spark plugs are removed;
(d) Remove the coil igniter connector and cold start injector connector plus solenoid resistor. This stops both fuel injection and ignition during engine cranking.
2. (a) Install suitable compression tester into spark plug hole, screw in type are more accurate. Depress accelerator pedal to fully open position and crank engine.
(b) Read compression gauge indication.
3. Check remaining cylinders.
Specified Compression:
12.0 kg/cm, 171pis, 1,177kPa.
Minimum Specified Compression:
10.0 kg/cm, 142pis, 981kPa.
* If cylinder compression in 1 or more cylinders is low, pour a small amount of engine oil into the cylinders through the spark plug holes and test compression.

Compression Test Results

NORMAL Compression builds up quickly and evenly on each cylinder.
PISTON RINGS Compression low on 1st stroke, tending to build up on following strokes, but does not reach normal. Improves considerably with addition of oil.
VALVES Low on 1st stroke and does not tend to build up on following strokes. Do not improve much with addition of oil.

HEAD GASKET If cylinder compression in any 2 adjacent cylinders is low (and if adding oil does not help compression), cylinder head gasket has blown out.

DRIVE BELTS

Inspection
* Some belt squeal when the engine is started or stopped is normal and has no effect on durability of drive belt.

Visual Inspection
* Condition of the belt is best judged by twisting the belt so as to see the "V" surfaces.

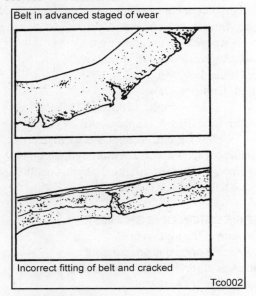

Belt in advanced staged of wear

Incorrect fitting of belt and cracked

Tco002

Stages of Belt Wear:
1. NEW BELT: Cracks or chunks.
2. MODERATELY USED BELT: Few cracks; some wear on surfaces. Replacement not required.
3. SEVERELY USED BELT: Several cracks per inch. Should be replaced before chunking occurs.
4. FAILED BELT: Separation of belt material from backing (chunking). Replace belt immediately.

ALTERNATOR WATER PUMP.
NEW BELT DEFLECTION (mm) 7-8
USED BELT DEFLECTION (mm) 9-10

POWER STEERING PUMP

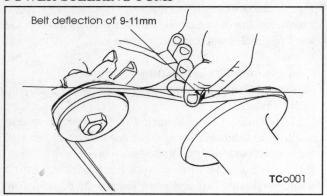

Belt deflection of 9-11mm

TCo001

NEW BELT DEFLECTION (mm) 8-9
USED BELT DEFLECTION (mm) 10-11

AIRCONDITIONING
NEW BELT DEFLECTION (mm) 8-9
USED BELT DEFLECTION (mm) 10-11

To adjust the tension: Check for a belt tensioner pulley, if one present adjust by turning adjuster bolt, or loosen alternator mounting bolts and adjusting arm pivot bolt. Then turn adjusting nut on alternator upper mounting bolt to achieve correct tension.

Tighten mounting bolts and adjusting arm pivot bolt.

Replacement
Release tension of the belts by loosening the alternator, air conditioner, power steering pump adjustment bolts. Remove drive belts from drive pulleys. Replace belts, taking care the belts are fitted correctly. Tension belts by adjusting and tightening alternator, air conditioner etc.

BELT REPLACEMENT with IDLER PULLEY
1. Loosen the locknut on the idler pulley mounting stud and turning the stud, relieve the tension on the power steering pump belt.
2. Loosen the alternator mounting bolts and the adjusting arm pivot bolt.
3. To loosen the belt, turn the adjusting nut on the alternator upper mounting bolt.
4. Remove the belt.
5. Install fan belt on crankshaft, alternator and water pump pulleys.
6. As previously described, adjust belt. Install power steering pump belt.
7. Turn the idler pulley mounting stud to adjust to specified tension. Tighten the lock nut.

Idler pulley adjusting bolt

Idler pulley

Tu010

INSPECT VALVE CLEARANCE
Tappet (Valve) clearance 18R[20R, 21R,22R,22R-E & 22R-TE] 18R-G
1. i) Adjust tappet clearance (valve clearance) by turning engine to number 1 cylinder TDC compression.
Adjust valves as shown:
1.ii) Adjust tappet clearance (valve clearance) by turning

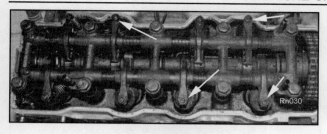

engine 360^0 from step number 1.1.

(a) Adjust valves as shown:

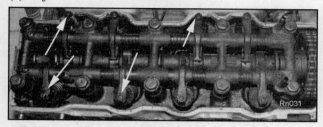

(a) Loosen lock nut.

(b) Adjust clearance with a feeler gauge to the hot specified gap.

(c) Tighten lock nut.

If assembling a cold engine allow another extra 0.10mm, only to allow engine to be started and warmed up to operating temperature, then adjust valve gap at engine hot temperature.

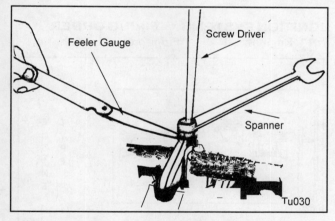

Tappet (Valve) clearance Hot, engine running temp 18R:

Intake valve clearance:	**0.18mm, 0.0071in**
Exhaust valve clearance:	**0.33mm, 0.0130in**

[20R, 21R,22R,22R-E & 22R-TE]:

Intake valve clearance:	**0.20mm, 0.0079in**
Exhaust valve clearance:	**0.30mm, 0.012in**

5. (b) Check valve clearance between valve pad and cam while turn cam with a spanner. If not within specification replace valve pad.

18R-G Specified Valve Pad to Cam Clearance:

Intake valve clearance:

　　　0.24-0.34mm, 0.0094-0.0134in

Exhaust valve clearance:

　　　0.29-0.39mm, 0.0114-0.0154in

6. Install the rubber plug at the front of the head for 18R engines and at the front and rear of the engine for [18R-G, 20R, 21R,22R,22R-E & 22R-TE]. Use a sealant on the rubber plug to stop oil leaks.

7. Install rocker cover and gasket as previously described, tighten to specification.

VALVE ROCKER TAPPET CLEARANCE ADJUSTMENT [L, 2L & 2L-T Up to 60's Series]

1. Disconnect battery earth lead.

2. Remove rocker cover as previously described.

3. Turn the engine over so the crankshaft is at TDC/ compression on number 1 cylinder.

4.1. Adjust tappet clearance (valve clearance) by turning engine to number 1 cylinder TDC compression.

Adjust valves as shown:

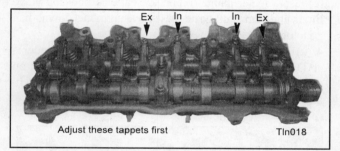

Adjust these tappets first　　　Tln018

4.11. Adjust tappet clearance (valve clearance) by turning engine 360^0 from step number 4.1.

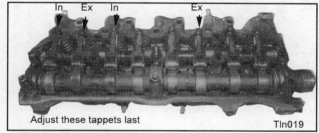

Adjust these tappets last　　　Tln019

Adjust valves as shown:

(a) Loosen lock nut.

(b) Adjust clearance with a feeler gauge to the hot specified gap.

(c) Tighten lock nut.

Tappet (Valve) clearance. Cold engine.

Intake valve clearance:	**0.27mm, 0.0106in**
Exhaust valve clearance:	**0.38mm, 0.0150in**

5. Install rocker cover and gasket as previously described, tighten to specification.

Rocker Cover Bolts Torque:

　　　60kg-cm, 4.5ft-lb, 6Nm

VALVE to CAM CLEARANCE ADJUSTMENT [2L & 3L 80's Series on]

1. Disconnect battery earth lead.

2. Remove rocker cover as previously described.

3. (a) Turn the engine over so the crankshaft is at TDC/ compression on number 1 cylinder, check position of timing mark on crankshaft balancer. (Both lifters on number 1 cylinder will have no tension on them, if they do turn engine 360^0, now they should have no tension).

(b) Check valve lifters as shown.

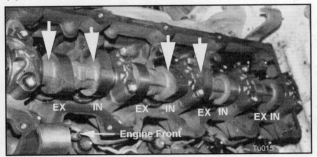

(c) Use a feeler gauge to check clearance between valve lifters and camshaft, write these measurements down, then go to next step.

4. (a) Turn the engine over 360^0 so that number 4 cylinder is at TDC/ compression, check position of timing mark on crankshaft balancer. (Both lifters on number 4 cylinder will have no tension on them).

(b) Check valve lifters as shown.

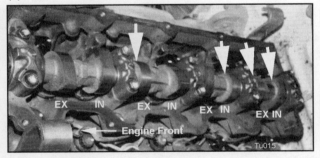

(c) Use a feeler gauge to check clearance between valve lifters and camshaft, write these measurements down, then go to next step.

5. Use a lifter compressor to allow the removal of the old adjusting shim, measure this shim, compare the difference with the written down measurement.

6. Install the correct adjusting shim to obtain the specified valve clearance.

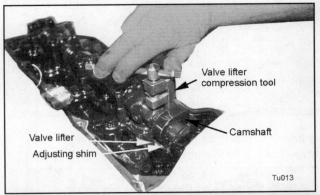

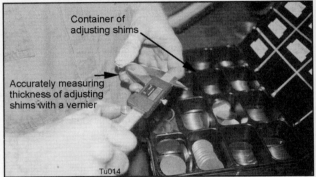

2L & 3L 80's series on Valve Clearance cold
Intake Valves 0.20 - 0.30mm (0.008-0.012in)
Exhaust 0.40 - 0.50mm (0.016-0.020in)

IGNITION SYSTEMS FIRING ORDER

"R" Engines: Firing order is 1-3-4-2.

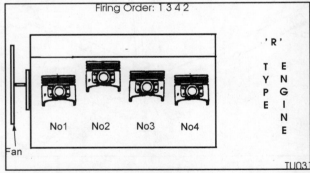

"Y" Engines: Firing order is 1-3-4-2.

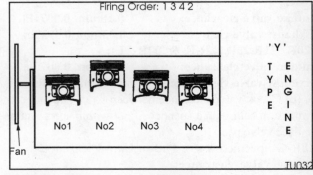

"3VZ-E" Engines: Firing order is 1-2-3-4-5-6

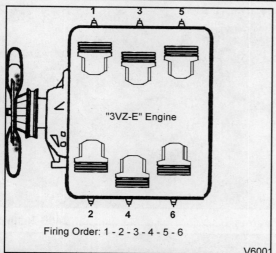

Firing Order: 1 - 2 - 3 - 4 - 5 - 6

V6001

INSPECTION OF SPARK PLUGS

1. Remove, Clean & Inspect Spark Plugs.

(a) Clean the spark plugs with a spark plug cleaner or wire brush..

(b) Examine the spark plugs for electrode wear, thread damage and insulator damage. Replace the plugs if worn or damaged.

2. Adjust Electrode Gap. Gently bend the outer electrode to obtain the correct electrode gap.

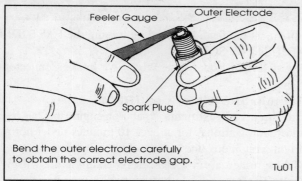

Bend the outer electrode carefully to obtain the correct electrode gap.

Tu01

Type and Grade:

"R" Engines:

12R ND: W16EP or NGK: BP5ES-L

18R ND: W16ER-U or NGK: BP5EA-L

20R ND: W16EP or NGK: BP5ES-L

21R & 22R ND: W16ER-U or NGK: BP5EY

"Y" Engines:

All countries not Europe-ND W16EX-U or NGK BP5EY

Europe-ND W16EXR-U or NGK BPR5EY

3VZ-E engines: ND: K16R-U or NGK: BKR5EYA

Correct electrode gap:

"R" Engines: 0.8 mm (0.031 in.)

"Y" Engines: 0.8 mm (0.031 in.)

"3VZ-E" Engines: 0.8 mm (0.031 in.)

3. Install Spark Plugs.

Torque:

"R" Engines: 180 kg-cm (13 ft-lb, 18 N·m).

"Y" Engines: 180 kg-cm (13 ft-lb, 18 N·m).

"3VZ-E" Engines   180 kg-cm (13 ft-lb, 18 N·m).

INSPECTION & ADJUSTMENT - IGNITION TIMING.

1. Connect Tachometer and Timing Light to engine.

"Y" & "R" Engines

(Conventional Type):

Connect the tachometer positive (+) terminal to the ignition coil negative (-) terminal.

(11A Distributor with service terminal):

Connect the tachometer positive (+) terminal to the distributor service terminal.

(11B Distributor without service terminal):

Connect the tachometer positive (+) terminal to the distributor black wire.

"3VZ-E" engines

Connect the tachometer positive (+) terminal to the distributor black wire.

2. Check dwell angle. (Conventional Type Only)

Dwell angle at idle speed:

R Engines	**52^0 plus or minus 6^0**
Y except 4Y-E Engine	**52^0 plus or minus 6^0**

(a) With the engine idling ensure the dwell angle is within specified range, if applicable.

(b) Set the rubbing block gap closer, if angle is too large and if too small, increase the gap.

3. Check Ignition Timing.

(a) Disconnect the vacuum hose from the distributor vacuum advance then block the end of the hose.

4Y-E use a wire and connect the E1 and T terminals of check wiring plug.

3VZ-E use a wire and connect the E1 and T terminals of check wiring plug.

(b) Use a timing light to check the timing.

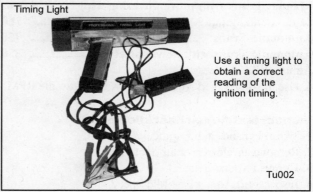

Use a timing light to obtain a correct reading of the ignition timing.

Tu002

(c) Loosen the distributor bolt and turn the distributor to line up the marks if necessary. Check the timing again after tightening the distributor. Specified timing listed below.

Distributor Locking Bolt Specified Torque:

185kg-cm, 13ft-lb, 18Nm

(d) Reconnect the vacuum hose, 4Y-E & 3VZ-E disconnect the wire from the check wiring plug.

IGNITION TIMING:

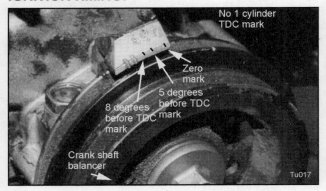

R engines: 8^0 +/ 1^0 @ Idle rpm.
Y engines: 8^0 +/ 1^0 @ Idle rpm.
4Y & 4Y-C: 4^0 +/- 1^0 @ Idle rpm.
4Y South Africa: 8^0 +/- 1^0 @ Idle rpm.
4Y-E: 12^0 +/- 1^0 @ Idle rpm.
3VZ-E: 10^0 +/- 1^0 @ Idle rpm.

IDLE RPM

"R" series and "Y" series other than 4Y-E Engine Idle RPM

Hot Engine: That is an engine that has been allowed to warm up for at least 10 minutes under normal driving conditions, and with the choke fully open.

Make sure there are no accessories operating as this will give a false RPM reading, also the transmission must be in neutral:
1. Connect a tachometer.
2. Check engine RPM and specified RPM.

Specified Engine Idle RPM:

Manual Trans	**700**
Manual Trans Australia except NSW & Vic	**650**
Manual Trans with power steering	**800**
Manual Trans with power steering expt NSW & Vic	**750**
Automatic Trans	**750**
Automatic Trans with power steering	**850**

Adjust RPM if necessary.
4. Use the idle speed adjusting screw to adjust idle RPM.

Inspect and Adjust Fast Idle Speed

1. Warm Up and Stop Engine.
2. Remove air cleaner or air duct tube.
3. Connect Tachometer.
4. Inspect and Adjust Fast Idle Speed.
(a) Start the engine.
(b) Fully turn the choke lever counter-clockwise, and fully open the choke valve, with the fast idle cam is set at the first stage.
(c) Check the fast idle speed.

Fast Idle Speed for carburettor engines:
R Engines **2400-2600rpm**

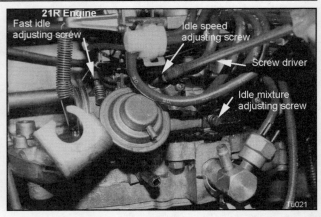

Y Engines **2400-2600rpm**

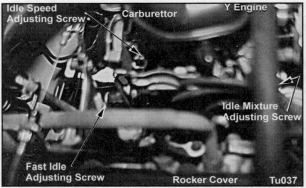

(d) Adjust the fast idle speed by turning the FAST IDLE ADJUSTING SCREW.
5. Install Air Cleaner Assembly or Air Intake Connector.

Fuel Mixture & Idle Speed RPM

Hot Engine Adjustments: That is an engine that has been allowed to warm up for at least 10 minutes under normal driving conditions, and with the choke fully open.

Make sure there are no accessories operating as this will give a false RPM reading, also the transmission must be in neutral:
1. Connect a tachometer to the engine to check engine RPM.
2. Check engine RPM, if not with in specification adjust idle speed.

Fuel Mixture and Idle RPM:
YN Series

Manual	685-715
Manual Australia except Vic & NSW	635-665
Manual W/- P.Steer	785-815
Manual W/- P.Steer Australia except Vic & NSW.	735-765
Automatic	725-750
Automatic W/- P.Steer	825-850

RN Series

Manual	675-700
Automatic	700-725

3. With idle speed adjusted as above.

"4Y-E" Engine Idle RPM

Hot Engine: That is an engine that has been allowed to

warm up for at least 10 minutes under normal driving conditions, and with the choke fully open.

Make sure there are no accessories operating as this will give a false RPM reading, also the transmission must be in neutral:

1. Connect a tachometer.

2. With engine at normal hot condition as above, and with engine operating..

3. With a aid of pliers restrict the flow of air in the air hose shown. Check engine RPM, it should not drop by more than 50RPM.

4. Disconnect electrical wire to idle speed control valve, as shown.

5. Check engine RPM and specified RPM.

Specified Engine Idle RPM:

M/T 700RPM   A/T 750RPM

Adjust RPM if necessary.

6. Use the throttle by-pass screw which is called the idle speed adjusting screw to adjust idle RPM.

7. Reconnect wire to the idle speed control valve.

8. Adjust idle mixture screw for correct CO reading as described in fuel or emission control chapter.

"3VZ-E" Engine Idle RPM

Hot Engine: That is an engine that has been allowed to warm up for at least 10 minutes under normal driving conditions, and with the choke fully open.

Make sure there are no accessories operating as this will give a false RPM reading, also the transmission must be in neutral:

1. Connect a tachometer.

2. With engine at normal hot condition as above, and with engine operating..

3. Screw the idle speed adjusting screw all the way in, idle rpm should be lower than specified rpm as listed below.

4. Adjust rpm by turning the idle speed screw out until rpm is within specified RPM.

Specified Engine Idle RPM:

Australia 650-750RPM   Europe 750-850RPM

Use the throttle by-pass screw which is called the idle speed adjusting screw to adjust idle RPM.

5. Adjust idle mixture screw for correct CO reading as described in fuel or emission control chapter.

"L" series Engine Idle RPM Adjustment

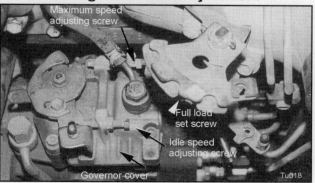

Maximum speed adjusting screw
Full load set screw
Idle speed adjusting screw
Governor cover
Tu018

FUEL MIXTURE & IDLE SPEED

Method with CO Meter

1. Visually Inspect Carburettor or E.F.I. system

(a) Check for loose screws or a loose mounting to the manifold.

(b) Check for wear in the linkage, missing snap rings or excessive looseness in the throttle shaft. Correct any problems found.

2. Initial Conditions:

(a) Air cleaner and air ducting installed.

(b) Normal operating coolant temperature.

(c) Choke fully open.

(d) All accessories and lights switched off.

(e) All vacuum lines connected.

(f) Ignition timing set as specified.

(g) Transmission in the "N" range.

(h) Carburettor models - float level should be correct.

E.F.I. models all wiring looms properly connected.

(i) CO meter operating normally.

(j) If there is an idle limiter cap on the idle mixture adjusting screw, remove it.

3. Adjust Idle Speed and Idle Mixture.

(a) Start the engine.

(b) Using a CO meter to measure the CO concentration in the exhaust, turn the idle speed and idle mixture adjusting screws to obtain the specified CO value at idle speed.

Idle speed:

Idle mixture speed RPM:

4Y-E Engines manual trans	**700**
4Y-E Engines automatic trans	**750**
3VZ-E Engines	**800**

(c) Remove CO tester for next test.

4. Inspect CO Concentration.

(a) Check that the CO meter is properly calibrated.

(b) Race the engine 60 seconds at about 2,500 rpm before measuring concentration.

(c) Wait 1-3 minutes after racing the engine to allow the concentration to stabilize.

(d) Insert a testing probe at least 40 cm (1.3 ft) into the tailpipe, and measure concentration within a short time.

Idle CO concentration:

R Engines	**2.5% or less**
Y Engines Europe, Australia, GCC countries & Singapore not listed	**1.0%-2.0%**
Y Engines other countries	**2.5% or less**
2Y-C(U) & 3Y-C(U)	**0.5%-1.5%**
4Y-E	**0.0%-0.5%**
3VZ-E	**0.0%-0.5%**

* If the CO concentration is within specification this adjustment is complete.

* If the CO concentration is not within specification, turn the idle mixture adjusting screw to obtain the specified concentration value.

* If the CO concentration cannot be corrected by adjusting

the idle mixture, see for other possible causes.

CO PROBLEM SOLVING:

1) Rough Idle - CO Normal:
Causes:
* Faulty ignition system:
  - Timing needs adjusting
  - Spark plugs need cleaning or gap adjusting
  - Spark plug leads need checking
  - Faulty distributor cap
* Exhaust valves need attention.
* Blown head gasket
* Faulty EGR valve or pipe.

2) Rough Idle (fluctuating HC reading) - CO Low:
Causes:
* Vacuum system has a leak:
  - Vacuum hoses are not connected or cracked
  - Intake manifold gasket leaking
  - PCV line
  - Carburettor loose on manifold
  - EFI throttle body loose on intake chamber.

3) Rough Idle (black smoke from exhaust) - CO High:
Causes:
* Air filter needs replacing
* PCV valve and or PCV pipe blocked
* Carburettor needs adjusting or replacing:
  - Faulty choke action
  - Incorrect float setting
  - Leaking needle or seat
  - Leaking power valve
* EFI components needs adjusting or replacing:
  - Pressure regulator
  - Air flow meter
  - Water and Air temperature sensors
  - Injectors including cold start injectors

. [w/ Idle Limiter Cap] Install New Idle Limiter Cap.
After this adjustment is completed, install a new idle limiter cap on the mixture adjusting screw.
* After completing adjustment, perform a road test to make certain engine performance has not changed.

B. Alternative Method
* To be used only if CO meter is not available.
1. Visually Inspect Carburettor.
(a) Check for loose screws or loose mountings to the manifold.
(b) Check for wear in the linkage, missing snap rings or excessive looseness in the throttle shaft. Correct any problems found.
2. Initial Conditions.
(a) Air cleaner installed.
(b) Normal operating coolant temperature.

(c) Choke fully open.
(d) All accessories switched off.
(e) All vacuum lines connected.
(f) Ignition timing set correctly.
(g) Transmission in the "N" range.
(h) Fuel level should be about even with the correct level in the sight glass.
(i) If there is an idle limiter cap on the idle mixture adjusting screw, remove it.
3. Adjust Idle Speed and Idle Mixture.
(a) Start the engine.
(b) Set to the maximum speed by turning the IDLE MIXTURE ADJUSTING SCREW.
(c) Set to the idle mixture speed by turning the IDLE SPEED ADJUSTING SCREW.
(d) Before moving to the next step, continue adjustments (b) and (c) until the maximum speed will not rise any further, no matter how much the IDLE MIXTURE ADJUSTING SCREW is adjusted.
(e) Set to the idle speed by screwing in the IDLE MIXTURE ADJUSTING SCREW.

Specified Engine Idle RPM:

Idle speed for R carburettor engines:	
Manual and Automatic Trans	**750**
Idle speed for Y carburettor engines:	
Manual Trans	**700**
Manual Trans Australia except NSW & Vic	**650**
Manual Trans with power steering	**800**
Manual Trans with power steering except Australia NSW & Vic	**750**
Automatic Trans	**750**
Automatic Trans with power steering	**850**

This is a lean Drop Method for setting idle speed and mixture.
4. [w/ Idle Limiter Cap] Install New Idle Limiter Cap.
After this adjustment is completed, install a new idle limiter cap on the idle mixture adjusting screw.
* After completing adjustment, perform a road test to make certain engine performance has not changed.

Problem Diagnosis:

See ENGINE and EMISSION Chapters for additional Problem Diagnosis.

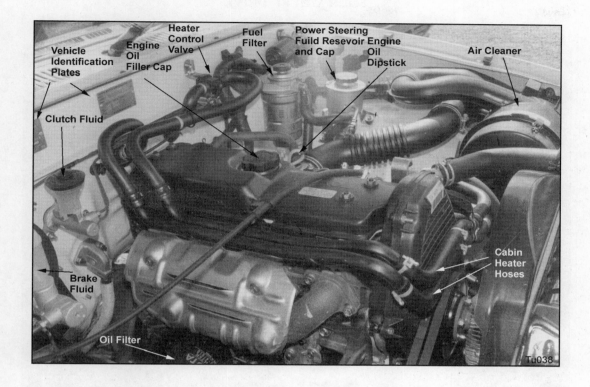

TWO WHEEL DRIVE

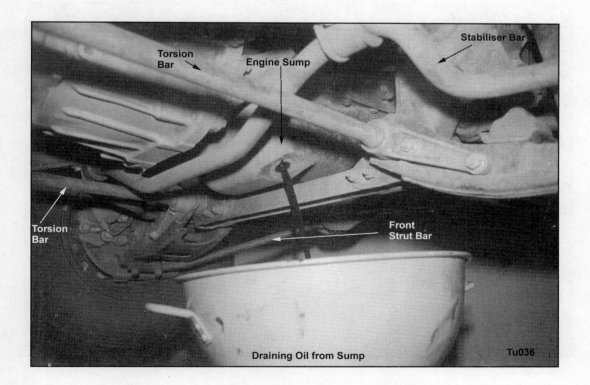

Draining Oil from Sump

FOUR WHEEL DRIVE

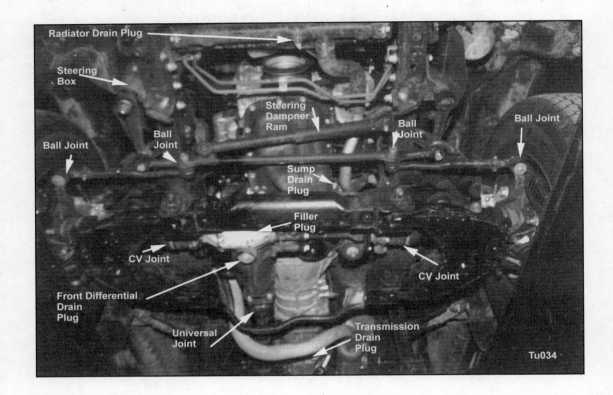

Radiator Drain Plug

Steering Box

Steering Dampner Ram

Ball Joint

Ball Joint

Ball Joint

Ball Joint

Sump Drain Plug

Filler Plug

CV Joint

CV Joint

Front Differential Drain Plug

Universal Joint

Transmission Drain Plug

Tu034

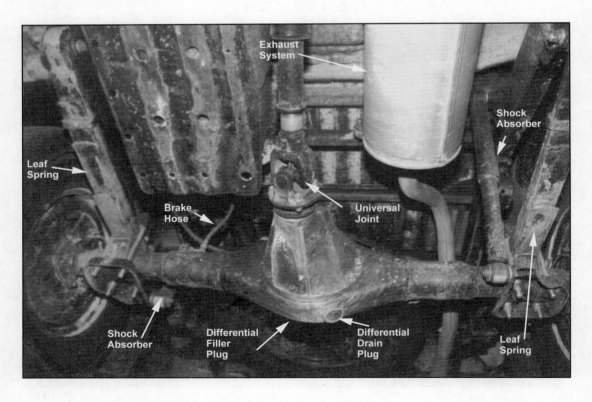

Exhaust System

Shock Absorber

Leaf Spring

Brake Hose

Universal Joint

Shock Absorber

Differential Filler Plug

Differential Drain Plug

Leaf Spring

EMISSION CONTROL

GENERAL PRECAUTIONS.

1. Know the importance of periodical maintenance.

a) Every service item in the periodic maintenance list must be performed.

b) Failing to do even one item can cause the engine to run poorly and increase exhaust emission.

2. Determine if you have an engine or emission system problem.

a) Engine problems are usually not caused by the emission control systems.

b) When troubleshooting, always check the engine and the ignition system first.

3. Check hose and wiring connections first.

The most frequent cause of problems is simply a bad wiring or vacuum hose connection. Always make sure that all connections are secure and correct.

4. Observe the following precautions to avoid damage to the parts:

a) To disconnect vacuum hoses, pull on the end, not the middle of the hose.

b) To pull apart electrical connectors, pull on the end, not the middle of the hose.

c) Be careful not to drop electrical components, such as sensors or relays. If they are dropped on a hard surface, they should be replaced and not reused.

d) When steam cleaning an engine, protect the distributor, crank sensor, coil, air filter, air intake.

e) Never use an impact wrench to remove or install thermo switches, thermo sensors or other sensors.

f) When checking continuity at a wire connector, insert the tester probe carefully to prevent terminals from bending.

g) When using a vacuum gauge, never force the hose onto a connector that is too large. Use a step-down adaptor instead. Once the hose has been stretched, it may leak.

5. Tag hoses before disconnecting them:

a) When disconnecting vacuum hoses, use tags to identify hoses and mark how they should be reconnected.

b) After completing a job, double check that the vacuum hoses are properly connected.

6. When replacing components use a new component if a second-hand component cannot be tested.

7. Perform work safely.

a) If the vehicle is to be jacked up only at the front or rear end, be sure to block the wheels.

b) After the vehicle is jacked up always support it on stands. It is extremely dangerous to do any work on the vehicle raised on a jack alone, even for jobs that can be finished quickly.

c) Disconnect the battery cable from the negative terminal of the battery to make work safer when replacing electrical parts or working on parts near an electrical source.

PRECAUTIONS WITH A CATALYTIC CONVERTER

WARNING: If large amounts of unburnt petrol flow into the catalytic converter, it may overheat and create a fire hazard. To prevent this, observe the following precautions and explain them to your customer.

1. Use only unleaded petrol.

2. Avoid prolonged idling.

Avoid running the engine at fast idle speed for more than 10 minutes and at idle speed for more than 20 minutes.

3. Avoid spark jump test.

a) Perform spark jump test only when absolutely necessary and as quickly as possible.

b) Never race the engine while testing.

4. Avoid prolonged engine compression measurement. Engine compression tests must be made as quickly as possible.

5. Do not run engine when fuel tank is nearly empty.

This may cause the engine to misfire and create an extra load on the catalytic converter.

6. Avoid coasting with ignition turned off and prolonged engine braking.

7. Do not dispose of used catalytic converter along with parts contaminated with petrol or oil.

PROBLEM SOLVING.

OIL CONSUMPTION TO HIGH
High Oil Loss

(1) Tighten bolts and/or replace gaskets and seals as required for external leaks.

(2) Check oil with car on a level surface and allow drain down time to ensure a correct reading of dipstick.

(3) Severe usage such as towing or continuous high speed driving will normally cause oil consumption to increase.

(4) PCV system failure.

(5) Use recommended S.A.E viscosity.

(6) Valve guides and/or valve stem seals worn, or seals omitted. Ream guides and install oversize service valves and/or new valve stem seals.

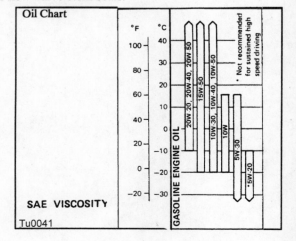

EMISSION CONTROL

PROBLEM	POSSIBLE CAUSES	REMEDY
Excessive Oil Consumption	Oil Leak	Repair oil leak
	PCV line blocked	Check and clean PCV system
	Piston rings worn or broken	Install new piston rings
	Valve stem oil seal worn / faulty	Check and replace oil valve seals
Excessive Fuel Consumption	Fuel leak	Damaged fuel tank
		Damaged fuel lines
	Air cleaner clogged	Check and replace air cleaner
	Ignition timing	Test "Electric spark timing"
	Spark plugs faulty	Replace spark plugs
	Spark plug leads	Replace spark plug leads
	Carbon canister system faulty	Check and repair carbon canister system
	Brake drag	Check and repair brakes
	Slipping clutch	Check clutch, replace if necessary
Emoo1ch	Automatic Tranmission slipping	Check transmission adjust and repair if necessary

PROBLEM	POSSIBLE CAUSES	REMEDY
Engine will not crank or cranks slowly	Starting system faulty	Check starting system forelectrical faults
	Ignition system faulty	Check ignition system in this manual
	Electric spark timing	Check and adjust ignition timing
Engine will not start, cranks over OK	No fuel at carburettor or injectors	Check fuel lines
		Check fuel filter
		Check operation of fuel pump
		Faulty fuel regulator
	Spark plugs faulty	Replace spark plugs
	Spark plug leads faulty	Test and replace leads if necessary
Em002ch	Elecrtical system faulty	Pull apart plugged connections, clean terminal contacts, assemble connections

PROBLEM	POSSIBLE CAUSES	REMEDY
Rough Idle	Spark plugs faulty	Replace spark plugs
	Sparl plug leads faulty	Replace sparl plug leads
	Fuel problems	Check fuel lines
		Check fuel filter
		Check operation of fuel pump
	Faulty oxygen sensor	Test sensor or replace sensor
	Ignition timing	Check and adjust timing
	Engine over hot	Check engine cooling, repair system
	Engine valves faulty	Remove cylinder head, repair valves
Em003ch	Compression low	Check compression, repair fault

PROBLEM	POSSIBLE CAUSES	REMEDY
Poor acceleration	Spark plugs faulty	Replace spark plugs
	Spark plugs leads faulty	Replace spark plug leads
	Fuel problems	Check fuel lines
		Check fuel filter
		Check operation of fuel pump
	Fuel injectors If applicable	Test and replace faulty injectors
	Carburettor faulty	Check and repair carburettor
	Faulty oxygen sensor	Test and replace oxygen sensor
	Ignition timing	Adjust ignition timing
	Ignition system faulty	Check and replace faulty components
	Engine over hot	Check cooling system and repair
	Exhaust system	Check exhaust system and repair
Em004ch		Faulty catalytic converter

PROBLEM	POSSIBLE CAUSES	REMEDY
Engine backfires or muffler explosion	Insufficient fuel flow	Fuel mix is to lean
		Fuel pump faulty
		Blocked fuel filter
		Fuel pipes damaged
	Incorrect ignition timing	Check and adjust ignition timing
Em005ch	Restricted air flow	Check and replace air cleaner element

(7) Allow enough time for the piston rings to seat. Replace worn or broken rings as needed, if rings have been incorrectly installed, worn or broken, or not seated.

(8) Piston incorrectly installed or misfitted.

Gaskets.

(1) Incorrectly tightened fasteners or damaged/dirty threads.

(2) Worn or damaged gasket (cracking or porosity).

(3) Fluid pressure/level too high.

(4) Incorrect sealant used (when required)

Inspection of Seals.

(1) Damaged seal bore (burred, nicked, scratched)

(2) Worn or loose bearing which causes excessive seal wear.

(3) Worn or damaged seal or incorrect installation.

(4) Fluid pressure/level too high.

Oil Leak Investigation

Oil leaks are easily located and repaired by visually finding the leak, replacing or repairing the required parts. (1) Determine whether the fluid is transmission lubricant, engine oil, power steering fluid etc.

(2) Run the car at normal operating temperature and park the car over a large sheet of paper. After a few minutes, you should be able to find the approximate location of the leak by drippings on the paper.

(3) Using a degreaser or steam to clean the area of the leak, drive the car for a few kilometres. The visually inspect the suspected part.

Dye & Light Oil Leak Detection.

Purchase a commercially available kit.

(a) Follow kit directions and add required amount of dye into leaking component oil.

(b) Drive the vehicle under normal operating conditions to allow the oil leak to be detected.

(c) As the kit light is shone onto the suspected area. The dyed oil will allow you to detect exactly where the leak is occurring.

Low Oil Pressure

(1) Blocked oil filter.

(2) Incorrect oil viscosity for expected temperature, or oil diluted with moisture or unburned fuel mixtures.

(3) Excessive bearing clearance.

(4) If the oil level is low, fill to mark on dipstick.

(5) Oil pump dirty/worn, or oil pump suction pipe screen blocked, or hole in oil pump suction pipe.

(6) Incorrect or failing oil pressure sender.

ENGINE KNOCKS

Try to detect if the noise comes from within the engine. This should be able to be detected by holding a long screw driver handle to your ear (preferably a screw driver that the steel shaft goes all the way through the handle). Hold the other end of the screw driver against the engine block, you should be able to detect a louder and sharper knock if the problem is within the engine.

Light engine knock as engine is warming up only.

Piston knock will give a particular knock and disappear as the engine warms up. This could be acceptable, however it can be eliminated by honing cylinder bore and replacing piston if the piston to cylinder gap is over specification. Excessive piston pin clearance can also give a light engine knock.

Hydraulic valve lifters will give a light knock if they are allowing the oil to leak from them, this will usually disappear as they prime themselves with engine oil.

Check for loose pulleys on water pump, alternator, power steering pump or air conditioner compressor.

Loud knock and is worse with increased RPM

If the noise comes from within the engine it could be a bearing that is in the process of failing, this could be a connecting rod bearing or crankshaft bearing. The engine should be pulled down and all bearings and journals inspected. Inspect for wear and clearance.

Check for loose or cracked flexiplate/flywheel bolts. Also check for broken or loose pulleys at the front of the engine.

EMISSION CONTROL SYSTEMS.

Positive Crankcase Ventilation (PCV valve):
Reduces blow-by fumes(HC)

Fuel Evaporative Emission Control - Carbon Canister (Evaporative system): Reduces evaporative HC

Oxygen Sensor system: Monitors oxygen to reduce NOx

Spark Control System (EST System - Electronic spark timing): Reduces NOx and HC

Idle Air Control (IAC) Valve(petrol EFI):Reduces HC&CO

Catalytic Converter:Reduces HC and CO

POSITIVE CRANKCASE VENTILATION (PCV) SYSTEM.

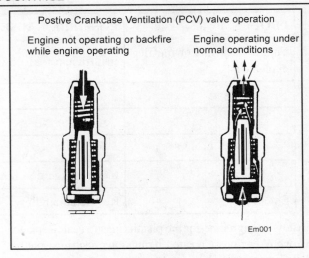

Postive Crankcase Ventilation (PCV) valve operation

Engine not operating or backfire while engine operating

Engine operating under normal conditions

Em001

INSPECTION OF PCV VALVE

1. Remove PCV valve from rocker cover.
2. Attach clean hose to PCV valve.
3. Blow from cylinder head side.

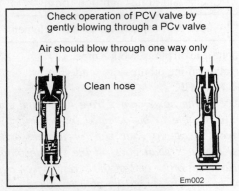

Check operation of PCV valve by gently blowing through a PCv valve

Air should blow through one way only

Clean hose

Em002

Check that air passes through easily.

WARNING: Do not suck air through the valve.
Petroleum substances inside the valve are harmful.

4. Blow from intake manifold side.
Check that air passes through with difficulty.
If the PCV valve fails either of these checks, replace it.
5. **Reinstall PCV valve into rocker cover.**
INSPECTION OF PCV HOSES AND CONNECTIONS.
Visually inspect hoses, connections and gaskets.
Check for cracks, leaks or damage.

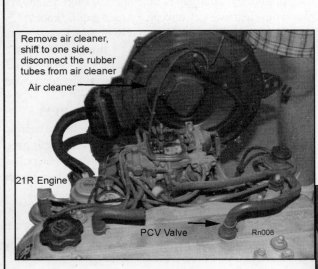

Remove air cleaner, shift to one side, disconnect the rubber tubes from air cleaner

Air cleaner

21R Engine

PCV Valve

Rn008

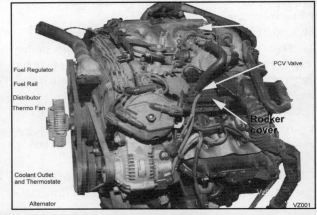

Fuel Regulator
Fuel Rail
Distributor
Thermo Fan

Coolant Outlet and Thermostate
Alternator

PCV Valve

Rocker cover

VZ001

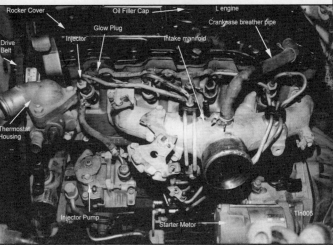

Rocker Cover
Oil Filler Cap
L engine
Glow Plug
Crankease breather pipe
Injector
Intake manifold
Drive Belt

Thermostat Housing

Injector Pump
Starter Motor

TIn005

FUEL EVAPORATIVE EMISSION CONTROL SYSTEM.

INSPECTION OF FUEL VAPOUR LINES, FUEL TANK AND TANK CAP.

1. Visually Inspect Lines And Connections.
Look for loose connection, kinks or damage.
2. Visually Inspect Fuel Tank.
Look for deformation, cracks or fuel leakage.
3. Visually Inspect Fuel Filler Cap.
Look for a damaged or deformed gasket and cap.
If necessary, repair or replace the cap.

INSPECTION OF CARBON CANISTER.
1. Remove Carbon Canister.
2. Visually Inspect Carbon Canister.
Look for cracks or damage.
3. Check for clogged filter and stuck check valve.
a) Using low-pressure compressed air, blow into the tank pipe and check that the air flows without resistance from the other pipes
b) If a problem is found, replace the charcoal canister.
 4. Clean Filter In Canister
 Clean the filter by blowing 3 kg/cm sq. (43 psi, 294kPa) of compressed air into the pipe to the outer vent control valve

while holding the other upper canister pipes closed.
NOTE:
Do not attempt to wash the canister.
No activated carbon should come out.
5. Install Carbon Canister.

INSPECTION OF PURGE CONTROL VALVE
Check Purge Control Valve Operation.
a) Disconnect the hoses from the valve.
b) Check that the valve is open when a vacuum is applied to the vacuum control connection.
c) Check that the valve is closed when there is no vacuum present.
d) Reconnect the hoses to the proper locations.
If the valve does not operate, replace the valve.

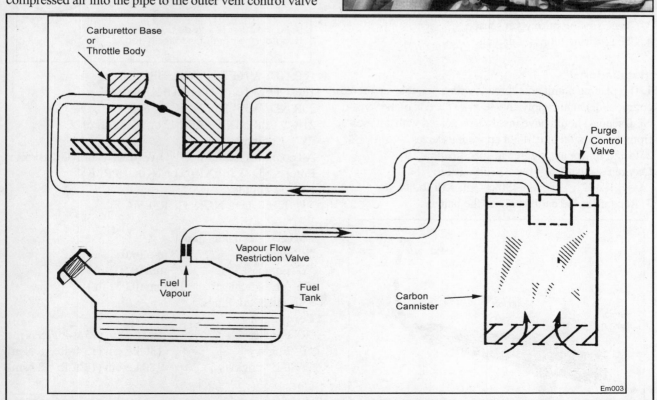

OXYGEN SENSOR SYSTEM.

Removal

1. Disconnect the battery earth cable.

2. Remove the sensor from the left side manifold or exhaust pipe. Care must be used while unscrewing sensor, as the senor will not operate if damaged.

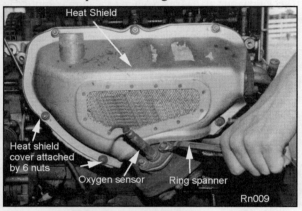

Heat Shield

Heat shield cover attached by 6 nuts

Oxygen sensor

Ring spanner

Rn009

Inspection of Oxygen Sensor.

1. Check and clean Oxygen Sensor.

a) Check for contamination or damage, the end must be kept free of grease, dirt or other contaminates.

2. a) Cold test with a volt metre should read 0.35 - 0.45 Volt.

b) Hot test.

Engine running and engine at operating temperature the voltage should vary between 0.010 - 1.000 of a volt.

3. Check seating of oxygen sensor.

4. Check wiring loom for damage.

Installation

1. If replacing a unit coat threads with a suitable anti-seize compound. Do not apply anti-seize to the end of the sensor. New senors should have the threads coated with anti-seize from the manufacture, if not apply anti-seize.

2. Install sensor and tighten to specification.

Oxygen Sensor tighten specification:

450kg-cm, 33ft.lb, 44Nm

3. Reconnect the earth cable to the battery.

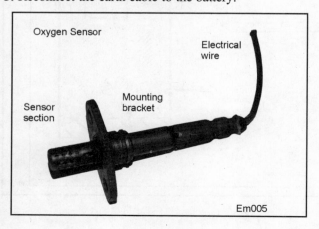

Oxygen Sensor

Electrical wire

Mounting bracket

Sensor section

Em005

SPARK CONTROL SYSTEM.

FIRING ORDER

"L" Engines	Firing order is 1-3-4-2.
"R" Engines	Firing order is 1-3-4-2.
"Y" Engines	Firing order is 1-3-4-2.
"3VZ-E" Engines	Firing order is 1-2-3-4-5-6

INSPECTION OF SPARK PLUGS

1. Remove, Clean & Inspect Spark Plugs.

a) Clean the spark plugs with a spark plug cleaner or wire brush..

b) Examine the spark plugs for electrode wear, thread damage and insulator damage. Replace the plugs if worn or damaged.

2. Adjust Electrode Gap. Gently bend the outer electrode to obtain the correct electrode gap.

Type and Grade:

"R" Engines:

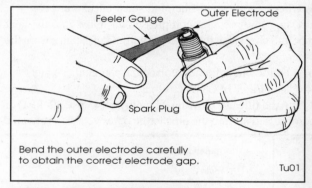

Feeler Gauge

Outer Electrode

Spark Plug

Bend the outer electrode carefully to obtain the correct electrode gap.

Tu01

12R ND: W16EP or NGK: BP5ES-L

18R ND: W16ER-U or NGK: BP5EA-L

20R ND: W16EP or NGK: BP5ES-L

21R & 22R ND: W16ER-U or NGK: BP5EY

"Y" Engines:

All countries not Europe-ND W16EX-U or NGK BP5EY

Europe-ND W16EXR-U or NGK BPR5EY

3VZ-E engines:

ND: K16R-U or NGK: BKR5EYA

Correct electrode gap:

"R" Engines:	0.8 mm (0.031 in.)
"Y" Engines:	0.8 mm (0.031 in.)
"3VZ-E" Engines:	0.8 mm (0.031 in.)

3. Install Spark Plugs.

Torque:

"R" Engines:	180 kg-cm (13 ft-lb, 18 N·m).
"Y" Engines:	180 kg-cm (13 ft-lb, 18 N·m).
"3VZ-E" Engines	180 kg-cm (13 ft-lb, 18 N·m).

INSPECTION & ADJUSTMENT - IGNITION TIMING.

1. Connect Tachometer and Timing Light to engine.
"Y" & "R" Engines
(Conventional Type):
Connect the tachometer positive (+) terminal to the ignition coil negative (-) terminal.
(11A Distributor with service terminal):
Connect the tachometer positive (+) terminal to the distributor service terminal.
(11B Distributor without service terminal):
Connect the tachometer positive (+) terminal to the distributor black wire.
"3VZ-E" engines
Connect the tachometer positive (+) terminal to the distributor black wire.

2. Check dwell angle. (Conventional Type Only)

Dwell angle at idle speed:

R Engines	52^0 **plus or minus** 6^0.
Y except 4Y-E Engine	52^0 **plus or minus** 6^0

a) With the engine idling ensure the dwell angle is within specified range, if applicable.
b) Set the rubbing block gap closer, if angle is too large and if too small, increase the gap.

3. Check Ignition Timing.
a) Disconnect the vacuum hose from the distributor vacuum advance then block the end of the hose.
4Y-E use a wire and connect the E1 and T terminals of check wiring plug.
3VZ-E use a wire and connect the E1 and T terminals of check wiring plug.
b) Use a timing light to check the timing.
c) Loosen the distributor bolt and turn the distributor to line up the marks if necessary. Check the timing again after tightening the distributor. Specified timing listed below.

Distributor Locking Bolt Specified Torque:
185kg-cm, 13ft-lb, 18Nm

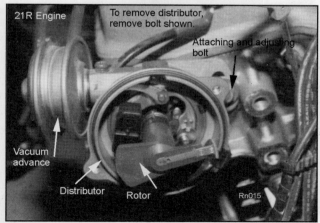

d) Reconnect the vacuum hose, 4Y-E & 3VZ-E disconnect the wire from the check wiring plug.

IGNITION TIMING:

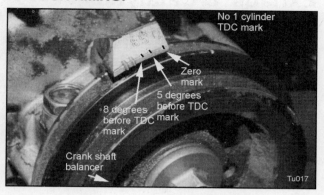

R engines:	8^0 +/ 1^0 @ Idle rpm.

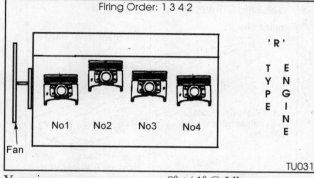

Y engines:	8^0 +/ 1^0 @ Idle rpm.
4Y & 4Y-C	4^0 +/- 1^0 @ Idle rpm.
4Y South Africa	8^0 +/- 1^0 @ Idle rpm.
4Y-E	12^0 +/- 1^0 @ Idle rpm.

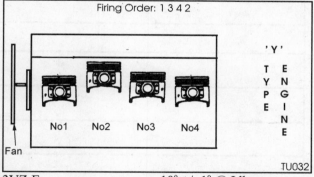

3VZ-E	10^0 +/- 1^0 @ Idle rpm.

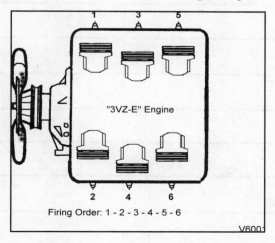

Exhaust & Catalytic Converter

INSPECTION OF EXHAUST PIPE ASSEMBLY.

1. Check Connection For Looseness or Damage.
2. Check Clamps For Weakness, Cracks, or Damage.

INSPECTION OF CATALYTIC CONVERTER.

Check For Dents or Damage.
If any part of protector is damaged or dented to the extent that it contacts the catalyst, repair it or replace it.

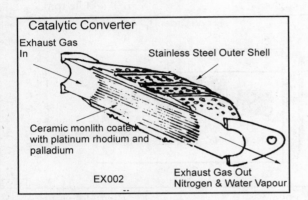

Catalytic Converter
Exhaust Gas In
Stainless Steel Outer Shell
Ceramic monlith coated with platinum rhodium and palladium
Exhaust Gas Out Nitrogen & Water Vapour
EX002

INSPECTION OF HEAT INSULATOR.

1. Check Heat Insulator For Damage.
2. Check For Adequate Clearance Between Catalytic Converter And Heat Insulator.

REPLACEMENT OF CATALYTIC CONVERTER.

1. Remove Catalytic Converter.
a) Jack up the vehicle.
b) Check that the converter is cool.
c) Remove the bolts at the front and rear of the converter.
d) Remove the converter and gaskets.
2. Install Catalytic Converter.
a) Place new gaskets on the converter front and rear pipes, and connect the converter to the exhaust pipes.
b) Tighten the bolts.
Torque: Catalyst - Exhaust Pipe:
450kg-cm, 33ft.lb, 44Nm
c) Reinstall the bracket bolts and tighten them.

Memo

"L" ENGINE MAINTENANCE & REBUILD

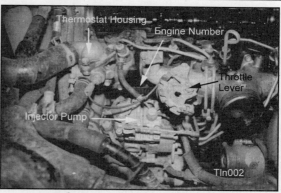

TIn002

"L" ENGINE MAINTENANCE & REBUILD

GENERAL DESCRIPTION

The "L" series engines are an in line 4 cylinder single overhead cam engine (SOHC) with the cylinder block made of cast iron. The cylinder head has 2 valves per cylinder.

The standard L engine bore of 90.00mm (3.5433in), 2L engine has a bore and stroke of 92.00mm x 92.00, 3L engines have a bore and stroke of 96.00mm x 96.00. 2L-T engines are turbo charged.

Five main bearings support the crankshaft.

The engines are designed to run on diesel fuel.

ENGINE SERIAL NUMBER

Engine No. Location: The engine number is as illustrated located high on the left side of the block, towards the front of the engine block.

MAINTENANCE HINTS

1. a) When any internal engine parts are serviced, care and cleanliness are important.

b) An engine is a combination of many machined, honed, polished and lapped surfaces with tolerances that are measured in thousandths of a millimetre.

c) Friction areas should be coated liberally with engine oil during assembly to protect and lubricate the surfaces on initial operation.

d) Proper cleaning and protection of machined surfaces and friction areas is part of the repair procedure and is considered standard workshop practice.

2. When valve train components are removed for service, they should be kept in order and should be installed in the same locations (with the same mating surfaces) as when removed.

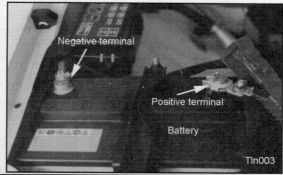

TIn003

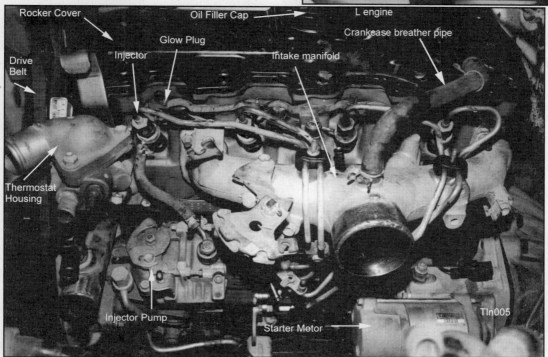

TIn005

3. Battery terminals should be disconnected before any major work is begun. If not, damage to wiring harnesses or other electrical components could result.

4. When raising or supporting the engine for any reason, do not use a jack under the oil pan. There are small clearances between the oil pan and the suction pipe screen, so jacking may cause the oil pan to be bent against the screen, with damage being done to the oil suction pipe assembly.

5. If the air flow ducting is removed or disconnected, the intake opening should be covered to avoid accidental entrance of foreign material (which could follow the intake passage into a cylinder and cause extensive damage when the engine is started).

GENERAL MAINTENANCE

CHECKING ENGINE OIL PRESSURE

1. Ensure the engine is at operating temperature and disconnect wiring harness connector from oil pressure sender unit.
2. Loosen and remove oil pressure sender unit.
3. Install a suitable oil pressure gauge assembly into oil filter adaptor oil pressure sender unit position.

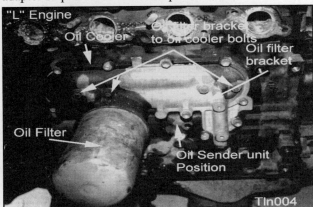

4. Start engine and check oil pressure reading with engine running under no load.

Oil pressure: 3000 rpm plus:
2.5-6.0kg/cm 36-85psi, 245-588kPa(min).

5. a) After completing test, apply LOCTITE 243 sealant or equivalent to sender unit threads.
b) Install and torque sender unit.

Oil Pressure Sender Unit
Torque: 55kg-cm, 4.8ft-lb, 5.4Nm

c) Install wiring harness connector, start engine and check for oil leaks.

OIL FILTER

* The oil filter should be replaced every 10,000 Kilometres or 6 months which ever occurs first, or when the engine oil is contaminated in any way.

Replacement

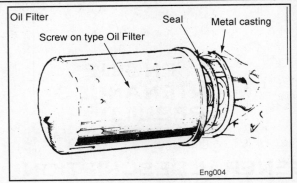

1. Unscrew oil filter with a suitable oil filter wrench, then remove and discard.
2. a) Seal must be placed correctly in recess in new filter.
b) Pour some clean engine oil into filter until level is approximately 2 cms (1.0 in) below top of filter.
3. a) Smear some engine oil over filter seal.
b) Screw filter into place until seal contacts mating surface of adaptor, then tighten through a further 2/3 of a turn.
4. a) Clean any excess oil from filter and adaptor.
b) Check oil level, then start engine and check for oil leaks.
c) Repair as necessary.
* After running the engine, the oil level must be rechecked and oil added as necessary, to compensate for oil used to refill the oil filter.

COMPRESSION CHECK

1. Make sure of the following:
a) Engine is at operating temperature;
b) Battery is at (or near) full charge;
c) Glow plugs are removed;
d) Remove the fuel cut solenoid wire connector, (this stops fuel injection during engine cranking).
2. a) Install suitable compression tester into glow plug hole, screw in type is more accurate. Depress accelerator pedal

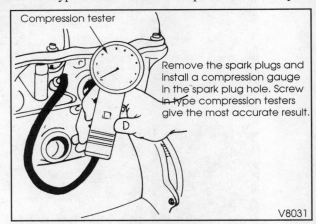

to fully open position and crank engine.
(b) Read compression gauge indication.
3. Check remaining cylinders.
Specified Compression:
L & 2L-T 30.0 kg/cm, 427pis, 2,942kPa.

2L & 3L   **32.0 kg/cm, 455pis, 3,138kPa.**
Minimum Specified Compression:
                    20.0 kg/cm, 284pis, 1,961kPa.
* If cylinder compression in 1 or more cylinders is low, pour a small amount of engine oil into the cylinders through the spark plug holes and test compression.

Compression Test Results
NORMAL Compression builds up quickly and evenly on each cylinder.
PISTON RINGS Compression low on 1st stroke, tending to build up on following strokes, but does not reach normal. Improves considerably with addition of oil.
VALVES Low on 1st stroke and does not tend to build up on following strokes. Do not improve much with addition of oil.
HEAD GASKET If cylinder compression in any 2 adjacent cylinders is low (and if adding oil does not help compression), cylinder head gasket has blown out.

DRIVE BELTS
Inspection
* Some belt squeal when the engine is started or stopped is possible and has no effect on durability of drive belt.
Visual Inspection
* Condition of the belt is best judged by twisting the belt so as to see the "V" surfaces.

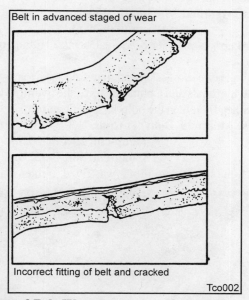

Belt in advanced staged of wear

Incorrect fitting of belt and cracked

Tco002

Stages of Belt Wear:
1. NEW BELT: No cracks or chunks.
2. MODERATELY USED BELT: Few cracks; some wear on surfaces. Replacement not required.
3. SEVERELY USED BELT: Several cracks per inch. Should be replaced before chunking occurs.
4. FAILED BELT: Separation of belt material from backing (chunking). Replace belt immediately.
Replacement

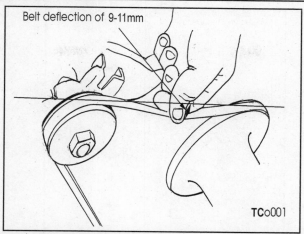

Belt deflection of 9-11mm

TCo001

Idler pulley adjusting bolt

Idler pulley

Tu010

Release tension of the belts by loosening the alternator, air conditioner, power steering pump adjustment bolts. Remove drive belts from drive pulleys. Replace belts, taking care the belts are fitted correctly. Tension belts by adjusting and tightening alternator, idler pulley etc.

INTAKE MANIFOLD [All engines except turbo

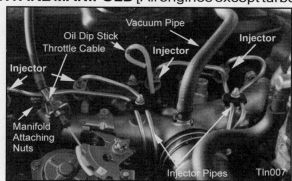

Vacuum Pipe
Oil Dip Stick
Throttle Cable
Injector
Injector
Injector
Injector
Manifold Attaching Nuts
Injector Pipes
Tln007

eng.]
Remove
1. Remove the air cleaner intake shroud if fitted.
2. Remove the air cleaner and air duct.
3. Disconnect the vacuum hoses from the manifold.
4. Disconnect the fuel pipes from the fuel pump to the injectors
5. Disconnect the accelerator connecting rod attaching nuts

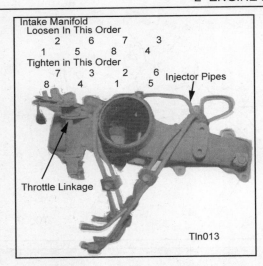

Intake Manifold
Loosen In This Order
Tighten in This Order
Injector Pipes
Throttle Linkage
Tln013

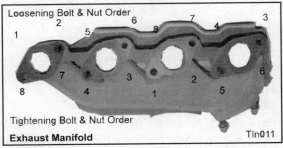

Loosening Bolt & Nut Order
Tightening Bolt & Nut Order
Exhaust Manifold
Tln011

and remove the rod attachments.

6. Remove the 2 nuts 6 bolts attaching the manifold to the cylinder head. As required remove the fittings from the manifold, such as engine hanger. Discard the old intake manifold gasket.

Install

1. Ensure that the surfaces of manifold and cylinder head are clean and free of any burrs.

2. Use a straight edge to check the surface of the intake manifold is flat, if over maximum warpage specification, machine the surface or replace the manifolds.

Intake Manifold Maximum Warpage:
        0.20mm (0.0079in)

3. Using Permabond A168 or equivalent install fittings on the threads.

4. Fit the manifold gasket to the cylinder head and install the manifold.

5. Apply Permabond A115 or equivalent to the bolt threads. Place the bolts and nuts, tighten in sequence to specification.

Intake Manifold Bolts Torque:
        240kg-cm, 17ft-lb, 24Nm

6. Connect the accelerator connecting rod and install the rod attaching nuts.

7. Install the fuel pipe from the injector pump to the injectors.

Injector Pipes Nut Specified Torque:
        250kg-cm, 18ft-lb, 25Nm

8. Connect the vacuum hoses to the vacuum hose outlets.

9. Install the air cleaner and air ducting.

10. Install the heat shield and the air cleaner intake shroud if fitted.

EXHAUST MANIFOLD [All engines except turbo eng]

Remove

1. Remove the heat shield if fitted.

2. Remove the two nuts from the manifold studs, attaching the front exhaust pipe to exhaust manifold.

3. Remove the 2 nuts and 6 bolts attaching the manifold to the

cylinder head.

4. Remove the exhaust manifold and old gasket.

Install

1. Ensure that the surfaces of manifold and cylinder head are clean and free from of any burrs.

2. Use a straight edge to check the surface of the exhaust manifold is flat, if over maximum warpage specification,

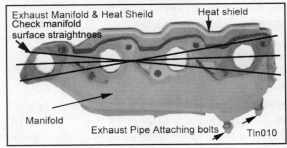

Exhaust Manifold & Heat Sheild
Check manifold surface straightness
Heat shield
Manifold
Exhaust Pipe Attaching bolts
Tln010

machine the surface or replace the manifolds.

Exhaust Manifold Maximum Warpage:
        0.20mm (0.0079in)

3. Using Permabond A168 or equivalent install fittings on the threads.

4. Install the exhaust gasket and manifold.

5. Install the 2 nuts and 6 bolts attaching the manifold to the cylinder head. Tighten the bolts to specification.

Exhaust Manifold Bolts Torque:

L & 2L	**400kg-cm, 29ft-lb, 39Nm**
3L	**530kg-cm, 38ft-lb, 52Nm**

6. Install the heat shield if one was fitted, tighten bolts to

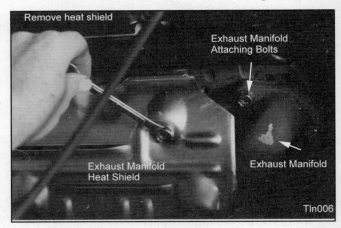

Remove heat shield
Exhaust Manifold Attaching Bolts
Exhaust Manifold Heat Shield
Exhaust Manifold
Tln006

specification.

Exhaust Manifold Heat Shield Bolts Torque:

195kg-cm, 14ft-lb, 19Nm

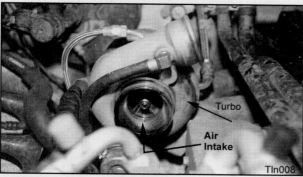

INTAKE MANIFOLD [2L-T]

1. Disconnect the accelerator cable and bracket.
2. Remove the air cleaner support brackets.
3. Remove the air cleaner and air duct pipe.
4. Remove 2 bolts and 3 clamps attaching the air duct intake pipe from the turbo charger to the intake manifold, remove the pipe.
5. Disconnect the vacuum hoses from the manifold.
6. Disconnect the fuel pipes from the fuel pump to the injectors
7. Remove the 2 nuts 6 bolts attaching the manifold to the cylinder head. As required remove the fittings from the manifold, such as engine hanger. Discard the old intake manifold gasket.

Install
1. Ensure that the surfaces of manifold and cylinder head are clean and free from of any burrs.
2. Use a straight edge to check the surface of the intake manifold is flat, if over maximum warpage specification, machine the surface or replace the manifolds.
Intake Manifold Maximum Warpage:
0.20mm (0.0079in)
3. Using Permabond A168 or equivalent install fittings on the threads.
4. Fit the manifold gasket to the cylinder head and install the manifold.
5. Apply Permabond A115 or equivalent to the bolt threads. Place the bolts and nuts, tighten in sequence to specification.
Intake Manifold Bolts Torque:
240kg-cm, 17ft-lb, 24Nm
7. Install the fuel pipes from the injector fuel pump to the injectors.
Injector Pipes Nut Specified Torque:
250kg-cm, 18ft-lb, 25Nm
8. Connect the vacuum hoses to the vacuum hose outlets.
9. Install the air duct intake pipe and replace the 2 bolts and 3 clamps attaching the air duct intake pipe from the air cleaner to the turbo charger. Tighten bolts to specification.
Turbocharger Air Duct Intake Pipe Bolts Torque:
120kg-cm, 9ft-lb, 12Nm
10. Reconnect the accelerator cable and bracket.

EXHAUST MANIFOLD [2L-T Eng]
Remove
1. Remove the accelerator cable and bracket.
2. Remove 2 bolts and 3 clamps attaching the air duct intake pipe from the turbo charger to the intake manifold, remove the pipe.
3. Remove the 2 bolts attaching the turbocharger intake pipe flange from air cleaner, remove the flange.
4. Remove turbocharger heat shield.
5. Remove the two oil pipe nuts at the turbocharger, disconnect the oil pipe from the turbocharger.
6. Remove the 4 nuts attaching the turbocharger to the exhaust manifold, remove the turbocharger, old gasket and the gasket from the oil pipe.
7. Remove the 4 nuts attaching the turbocharger to the exhaust pipe.
8. Remove the 2 nuts and 6 bolts attaching the manifold to the cylinder head.
9. Remove the exhaust manifold and old gasket.

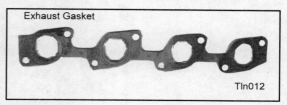

Install
1. Ensure that the surfaces of manifold and cylinder head are clean and free from of any burrs.
2. Use a straight edge to check the surface of the exhaust manifold is flat, if over maximum warpage specification, machine the surface or replace the manifolds.
Exhaust Manifold Maximum Warpage:
0.20mm (0.0079in)
3. Using Permabond A168 or equivalent install fittings on the threads.
4. Install the exhaust manifold.
5. Install the 2 nuts and 6 bolts attaching the manifold to the cylinder head. Tighten the bolts to specification.
Exhaust Manifold Bolts Torque:
530kg-cm, 38ft-lb, 52Nm
6. Install the heat shield if one was fitted, tighten bolts to specification.
Exhaust Manifold Heat Shield Bolts Torque:
195kg-cm, 14ft-lb, 19Nm
7. Install the turbocharger to the exhaust manifold, replace the 4 nuts, tighten to specification. Install a new gasket and position a new gasket between the oil pipe flange and turbocharger.
Turbocharger to Exhaust Manifold Nuts Torque:
530kg-cm, 38ft-lb, 52Nm
8. Install the 4 nuts attaching the turbocharger to the exhaust pipe.
Turbocharger to Exhaust Pipe Nuts Torque:

280kg-cm, 19ft-lb, 25Nm

9. Install the two oil pipe nuts at the turbocharger, tighten to specification.

Oil Pipe to Turbocharger Nuts Torque:
120kg-cm, 9ft-lb, 12Nm

10. Replace turbocharger heat shield.

11. Install the turbocharger intake pipe flange (from the air cleaner), replace and tighten to specification the two bolts.

Turbocharger Intake Pipe Flange Bolts Torque:
120kg-cm, 9ft-lb, 12Nm

12. Install the air duct intake pipe to the intake manifold and replace the 2 bolts and 3 clamps attaching the air duct intake pipe to the turbo charger. Tighten bolts to specification.

Turbocharger Air Duct Intake Pipe Bolts Torque:
120kg-cm, 9ft-lb, 12Nm

13. Reconnect the accelerator cable and bracket.

TURBOCHARGER

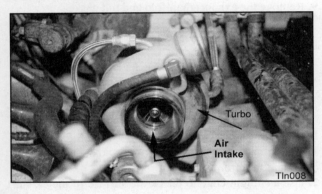

TIn008

Remove

1. Remove the accelerator cable and bracket.

2. Remove 2 bolts and 3 clamps attaching the air duct intake pipe from the turbo charger to the intake manifold, remove the pipe.

3. Remove the 2 bolts attaching the turbocharger intake pipe flange from air cleaner, remove the flange.

4. Remove turbocharger heat shield.

5. Remove the two oil pipe nuts at the turbocharger, disconnect the oil pipe from the turbocharger.

6. Remove the 4 nuts attaching the turbocharger to the exhaust manifold, remove the turbocharger, old gasket and the gasket from the oil pipe.

7. Remove the 4 nuts attaching the turbocharger to the exhaust pipe.

8. Remove the 2 nuts and 6 bolts attaching the manifold to the cylinder head.

9. Remove the exhaust manifold and old gasket.

Inspection

1. Inspect the turbocharger fins for damage, such as fins broken, fractured or bent, if damaged replace turbocharger.

2. Spin the turbocharger centre shaft and impeller, if the shaft and impeller will not spin freely replace the turbocharger.

3. Install a micrometer gauge at the intake hole against the

end of the turbocharger impeller, from the other end slide the shaft back ward and forwards. Check for shaft and impeller movement, if not within specification, replace the turbocharger.

Turbocharger Shaft and Impeller Free Play:
0.13mm, 0.0051in

Install

1. Install the turbocharger to the exhaust manifold, replace the 4 nuts, tighten to specification. Install a new gasket and position a new gasket between the oil pipe flange and turbocharger.

Turbocharger to Exhaust Manifold Nuts Torque:
530kg-cm, 38ft-lb, 52Nm

2. Install the 4 nuts attaching the turbocharger to the exhaust pipe.

Turbocharger to Exhaust Pipe Nuts Torque:
280kg-cm, 19ft-lb, 25Nm

3. Install the two oil pipe nuts at the turbocharger, tighten to specification.

Oil Pipe to Turbocharger Nuts Torque:
120kg-cm, 9ft-lb, 12Nm

4. Replace turbocharger heat shield.

5. Install the turbocharger intake pipe flange (from the air cleaner), replace and tighten to specification the two bolts.

Turbocharger Intake Pipe Flange Bolts Torque:
120kg-cm, 9ft-lb, 12Nm

6. Install the air duct intake pipe to the intake manifold and replace the 2 bolts and 3 clamps attaching the air duct intake pipe to the turbo charger. Tighten bolts to specification.

Turbocharger Air Duct Intake Pipe Bolts Torque:
120kg-cm, 9ft-lb, 12Nm

8. Reconnect the accelerator cable and bracket.

ROCKER COVER AND/OR SEAL

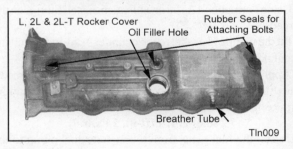

TIn009

Remove

1. Disconnect battery earth lead.

2. [2L-T] a) Remove the accelerator cable and bracket.

b) Remove 2 bolts and 3 clamps attaching the air duct intake pipe from the turbo charger to the intake manifold, remove the pipe.

2. Remove breather hose from the rocker cover to inlet manifold, if fitted.

3. a) Unscrew rocker cover to cylinder head fastening bolts and remove rocker cover from cylinder head.

b) If replacing rocker cover seal, remove seal from recess in

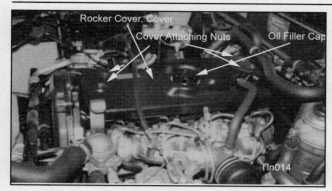

Rocker Cover, Cover
Cover Attaching Nuts
Oil Filler Cap
Tln014

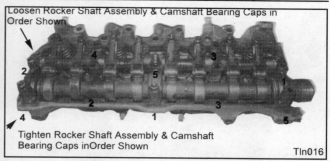

Loosen Rocker Shaft Assembly & Camshaft Bearing Caps in Order Shown

Tighten Rocker Shaft Assembly & Camshaft Bearing Caps inOrder Shown
Tln016

rocker cover to cylinder head.

Install

1. a) If necessary, install seal in rocker cover recess.

b) Install rocker cover and new seal assemblies.

* Make sure seal is correctly installed in rocker cover.

2. Install rocker cover to cylinder head and torque bolts to specification.

Rocker Cover Bolts Torque:

60kg-cm, 4.5ft-lb, 6Nm

3. [2L-T] a) Install the accelerator cable and bracket.

b) Install intake pipe from turbocharger to intake manifold and the 2 bolts and 3 clamps attaching the air duct intake pipe.

4. Install breather hose to rocker cover from intake manifold, if fitted.

5. Connect battery earth lead.

6. Start engine and check for oil leaks.

ROCKER ARMS AND ROLLER ASSEMBLY [L, 2L & 2L-T 50's & 60's Series]

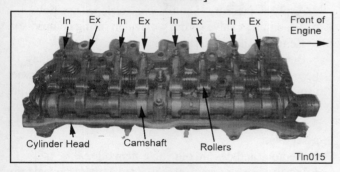

In Ex In Ex In Ex In Ex Front of Engine

Cylinder Head   Camshaft   Rollers
Tln015

It is important that the original location of all pivots and arms is retained during assembly, so place components on a suitable rack.

Remove

1. a) Disconnect battery earth lead.

b) Remove rocker cover as described above.

c) Loosen the rocker assembly bolts in the order shown working from the front and rear of the engine to the centre of the assembly. Loosen a little each pass until the bolts are loose. Remove rocker arm assembly 10 bolts, washers and rocker arms.

2. Slide rocker arm shaft from rocker arms and rocker shaft

springs if required, otherwise leave the arms and shaft as an assembly.

* When you lift the rocker assembly the camshaft upper bearings will be in the rocker assembly, take care if they fall out as they must remain with the bearing they belong to unless new camshaft bearings are being fitted.

Clean & Inspect

1. Clean all components in a suitable cleaning solvent, then dry with clean dry compressed air.

2. Clean rocker arm bolts threads.

3. Inspect all components for wear and replace as necessary.

4. Inspect condition of the rocker arm rollers for wear, replace if any flat spots or badly scoured.

Install

1. Before assembly wipe the rocker shaft, rocker arms and contact surfaces with a engine oil.

2. Coat rocker arm bolt threads with LOCTITE 243 sealant or equivalent.

3. Assembly rockers arm bolts, shaft, rocker arm shaft springs and rocker arms in their original positions on cylinder head.

4. Torque rocker arm assembly 10 bolts, at the same time make sure the rollers remain in contact cam lobes. Tighten in 2 to 3 passes and gradually tighten to specification..

Rocker Arm Assembly Bolts Specified Torque:

195kg-cm, 14ft-lb, 19Nm

5. Adjust rocker tappet clearances as described below.

6. Install rocker cover and gasket as previously described, tighten to specification.

Rocker Cover Nuts Torque:

60kg-cm, 4.5ft-lb, 6Nm

7. a) Connect battery earth lead.

b) Start engine and check for oil leaks or valve train noise.

VALVE ROCKER TAPPET CLEARANCE ADJUSTMENT [L, 2L & 2L-T 50's & 60's Series]

1. Disconnect battery earth lead.

2. Turn the engine over so the crankshaft is at TDC/compression on number 1 cylinder.

3. Remove rocker cover as previously described.

4.1. Adjust tappet clearance (valve clearance) by turning engine to number 1 cylinder TDC compression.

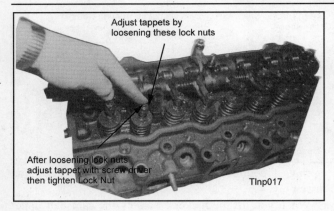

Adjust valves as shown:

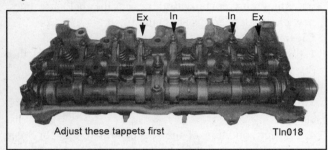

4.11. Adjust tappet clearance (valve clearance) by turning engine 360⁰ from step number 6.1.

Adjust valves as shown:

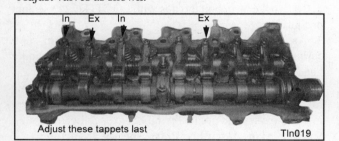

a) Loosen lock nut.

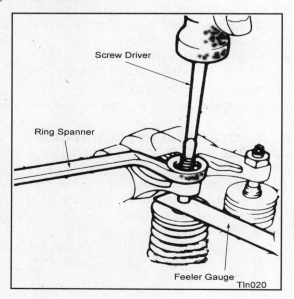

b) Adjust clearance with a feeler gauge to the hot specified gap.

c) Tighten lock nut.

Tappet (Valve) clearance. Cold engine.

Intake valve clearance: **0.27mm, 0.0106in**

Exhaust valve clearance: **0.38mm, 0.0150in**

5. Install rocker cover and gasket as previously described, tighten to specification.

Rocker Cover Bolts Torque:

         60kg-cm, 4.5ft-lb, 6Nm

VALVE STEM OIL SEALS [L, 2L & 2L-T 50's & 60's Series]

Replacement

1. Disconnect battery earth lead.

2. Remove the following:

a) Rocker cover as previously described in this Chapter.

b) Rocker arms as previously described in this Chapter.

c) Remove injector from relevant cylinder and screw air adaptor into injector plug hole.

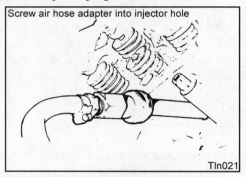

3. Apply air pressure to hold valves in closed position.

4. a) Compress valve spring with valve spring compressor.

b) Remove valve collets.

* Before installing valve spring compressor, it may be necessary to tap top of valve cap with a soft-faced hammer to overcome the binding of the valve collets in the valve spring cap.

5. a) Remove spring cap, spring and valve compressor as an assembly.

b) Remove and discard old valve stem oil seal.

6. Install new valve stem oil seal and make sure the seal fully seats on top of the valve guide.

* Make sure the correct type of seal is fitted to the appropriate valve, based on part No. and package description.

7. a) Install spring, cap and valve compressor as an assembly on the valve stem.

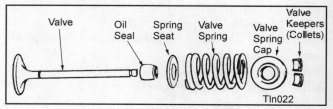

b) Install valve collets and slowly release spring compressor, then remove spring compressor.

c) Disconnect air line to special tool.

8. Install the following:

a) Rocker arms as previously described in this Chapter.

b) Rocker cover as previously described in this Chapter.

9. Remove special tool and install and torque injector.

Injector Torque Specification:
>700kg-cm, 51ft-lb, 69Nm

10. Install injector fuel pipes.

Injector Pipe Torque Specification:
>250kg-cm, 18ft-lb, 25Nm

Injector Leakage Pipe Torque Specification:
>500kg-cm, 36ft-lb, 49Nm

11. Start engine and check for fuel leaks, oil leaks and valve train noise.

CYLINDER HEAD[L, 2L & 2L-T 50's & 60'sSeries]

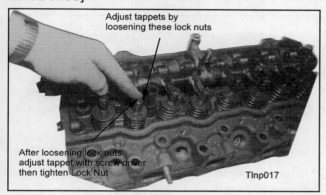

Make sure that all valve train components are kept in order so they can be installed in their original locations.
* [2L-T engines see Turbocharger - Remove and Install in this chapter for details.]

Remove

1. Disconnect battery earth lead.

2. Remove the 4 glow plugs and wiring loom.

3. Remove alternator.

a) Remove nuts from alternator adjuster bracket studs and remove engine harness earth wire connection and wiring harness retainer bracket.

b) Remove alternator, remove alternator support bolts, then remove support assembly.

4. Drain coolant from engine at radiator lower hose and remove top radiator hose.

5. a) Remove the two bracket nuts supporting the fuel injection pipes.

b) Loosen the four injector pipes at the injector and fuel pump.

c) Remove the four injector pipes and brackets. Cover the four injector pump outlet nozzles with some tape, to stop dust contaminating the fuel.

6. Remove the right side engine lifting bracket and exhaust manifold attaching 4 bolts plus 2 heat insulators, remove the

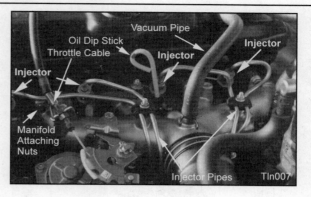

exhaust manifold.

* If you wish you may leave the exhaust manifold attached to the exhaust pipe. Disconnect the exhaust pipe front bracket, then allow the manifold to move to one side allowing you access to remove the cylinder head.

7. Remove the intake manifold 2 nuts and 6 bolts attaching the intake manifold and left side engine lifting bracket from the cylinder head.

8. Remove the attaching bolts and coolant thermostat housing and water outlet assembly.

9. Remove the timing belt cover 12 bolts and cover as previously described.

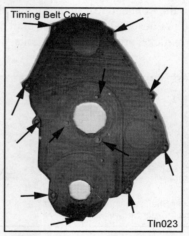

10. Remove the 3 bolts securing the rocker cover, and rocker cover as previously described in this chapter.

11. Rotate the crankshaft so the crankshaft is at TDC/compression on number 1 cylinder. Check for alignment mark on camshaft gear in line with cylinder head.

12. Use an oil based crayon, place alignment marks the timing belt and cam shaft gear, injection pump gear and crankshaft gear. Also draw an arrow showing direction of rotation of timing belt, if the belt is to reinstalled on the engine.

** *Timing belts do have a life span, and the average life of a timing belt should be 100,000 kilometres, 62,138mile for normal driving conditions.*

13. Remove the tension spring.

14. Remove the timing pulley belt from the 3 pulleys.

15. Remove the bolt attaching the camshaft gear to the cam

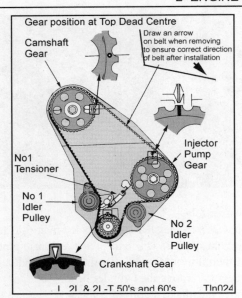

Gear position at Top Dead Centre

Camshaft Gear

Draw an arrow on belt when removing to ensure correct direction of belt after installation

Injector Pump Gear

No1 Tensioner

No 1 Idler Pulley

No 2 Idler Pulley

Crankshaft Gear

L, 2L & 2L-T 50's and 60's   Tln024

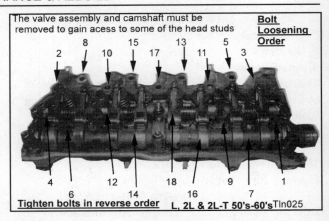

The valve assembly and camshaft must be removed to gain acess to some of the head studs

Bolt Loosening Order

2 8 10 15 17 13 11 5 3

4 12 18 9 1

6 14 16 7

Tighten bolts in reverse order   L, 2L & 2L-T 50's-60's Tln025

shaft, remove the gear.

17. Remove the 6 bolts attaching the plate at the front of the cylinder head which contains the camshaft front oil seal, remove the front plate. Remove the camshaft oil seal, with a screw driver, do not damage oil seal housing.

18. Loosen the rocker assembly bolts in the order shown working from the front and rear of the engine to the centre of the assembly. Loosen a little each pass until the bolts are loose. Remove rocker arm assembly 10 bolts, washers and rocker arms.

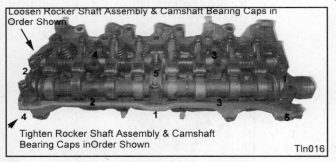

Loosen Rocker Shaft Assembly & Camshaft Bearing Caps in Order Shown

2 4 3 1

2 5 3 5

4 1

Tighten Rocker Shaft Assembly & Camshaft Bearing Caps inOrder Shown   Tln016

19. Slide rocker arm shaft from rocker arms and rocker shaft springs if required, otherwise leave the arms and shaft as an assembly.

* When you lift the rocker assembly the camshaft upper bearings will be in the rocker assembly, take care if they fall out as they must remain with the bearing they belong to unless new camshaft bearings are being fitted.

20. Remove the camshaft from the cylinder head.

21. Loosen the 18 cylinder head bolts in the order shown working from the front and rear of the engine to the centre of the assembly. Loosen a little each pass until the bolts are loose. Remove cylinder head 18 bolts.

22. Lift the cylinder head and gasket from the engine block.

Inspection

1. Taking care not to scratch machined surfaces, clean

mating surfaces of cylinder head and cylinder block.

* Do not use a motorised wire brush on any gasket sealing surface.

2. Check cylinder head deck, intake and exhaust manifold mating surfaces for distortion. These surfaces may be refaced **once only** by parallel grinding.

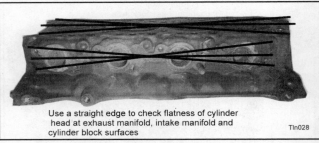

Use a straight edge to check flatness of cylinder head at exhaust manifold, intake manifold and cylinder block surfaces   Tln028

* Head to block surface if more than .15mm (0.0059in) must be removed from any surface, replace cylinder head.

* Head to manifold surface if more than .20mm (0.0079in) must be removed from any surface, replace cylinder head.

3. Inspect the following:

a) Cylinder head for cracks, especially between valve seats or exhaust ports.

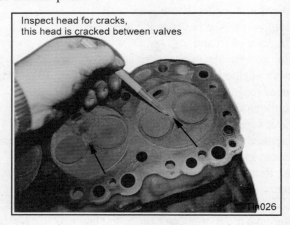

Inspect head for cracks, this head is cracked between valves   Tln026

b) Cylinder head deck surface for corrosion, casting sand inclusions or blow holes.

c) Cylinder block deck surface with a suitable straight edge.

4. Clean cylinder head bolts and replace any bolt that has suspect threads, or stretched or damaged heads caused by improper use of tools.

5. a) Clean cylinder head bolt hole threads in cylinder block using an appropriate size thread tap.

b) If necessary, threads may be reconditioned with suitable thread inserts.

* Clean out bolt holes with an air hose.

Installation

1. Place head gasket in position over dowel pins on cylinder block.

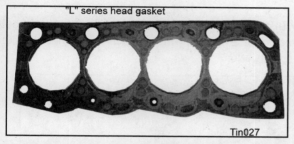

"L" series head gasket

Tin027

2. a) Carefully guide cylinder head into place over dowel pins and gasket.

b) Coat threads of cylinder head bolts with LOCTITE 243 sealant or equivalent and tighten with finger.

3. Tighten the head bolts to the following sequence and in the order shown.

* It is important to follow the given procedure to avoid head gasket failure and possible engine damage.

Cylinder Head Bolt Torque:
1,200kg-cm, 87ft-lb, 118Nm

4. Replace camshaft and cam shaft bearings No 1 bearing use thrust bearings.

* Inspection of camshaft and camshaft bearings are detailed under Camshaft section in this chapter.

5. Install rocker arm assembly (previously described in this Chapter), tighten bolts in order shown and to specification.

Rocker Arm and Shaft Assembly Bolt Specified Torque: **195kg-cm, 14ft-lb, 19Nm**

6. a) Install a new camshaft oil seal into the plate at the front of the cylinder head which contains the camshaft front oil seal if new has not been installed. Tap oil seal home with a oil seal insertion tool or circular object same size as seal, do not damaged oil seal lips.

b) Install the plate at the front of the cylinder head which contains the camshaft front oil seal, install the 6 bolts attaching the front plate and tighten to specification.

Front Camshaft Oil Seal Retainer Plate Bolt Specified Torque: **185kg-cm, 13ft-lb, 18Nm**

7. Turn the engine over so the crankshaft is at TDC/compression on number 1 cylinder, the engine should be in this position from removing the cylinder head.

8. Install the camshaft gear on the camshaft, tighten the attaching bolt to specification.

Camshaft Gear Attaching Bolt Specified Torque:

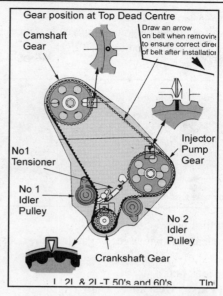

Gear position at Top Dead Centre

Camshaft Gear

Draw an arrow on belt when removing to ensure correct direction of belt after installation

Injector Pump Gear

No1 Tensioner

No 1 Idler Pulley

No 2 Idler Pulley

Crankshaft Gear

L, 2L & 2L-T 50's and 60's   Tin

1000kg-cm, 72ft-lb, 98Nm

9. Install the timing belt to the original position aligning the timing marks made when removing the timing belt. Taking not that the belt is rotating the same direction as previously, check for direction arrow made when removing belt.

* **New Timing Belt:** (a) Position the camshaft gear, injection pump gear and crankshaft gear into the correct position.

Camshaft gear mark is to aligned with the cylinder head and cylinder block joining line.

Injection pump gear alignment mark at the highest position. Crankshaft gear at the highest position.

Install timing belt onto the lower section of the crankshaft gear, around the inside of the 2 idler pulleys and over the camshaft gear.

* Keep the timing belt tight and meshed into the grooves on the gears

Ensure the alignment marks on the injection pump gear and pump body are aligned.

Slide the timing belt onto the injection pump gear.

10. Install the tension spring for the timing belt.

11. Temporally install the crankshaft pulley bolt so the engine can be turned over, check the timing belt runs correctly and that the timing marks on the camshaft gear, injection pump gear and crankshaft gear are in the correct position at TDC compression on No 1 cylinder.

12. (1) Adjust tappet clearance (valve clearance). Engine must be at number 1 cylinder TDC compression.

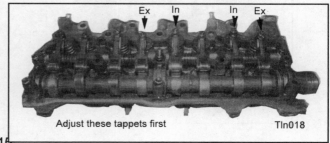

Ex   In   In   Ex

Adjust these tappets first   Tln018

Adjust valves as shown:

12.(11) Adjust tappet clearance (valve clearance) by turning engine 360^0 from step number 12.(1).

Adjust valves as shown:

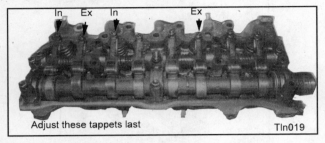

In   Ex   In   Ex

Adjust these tappets last   TIn019

a) Loosen lock nut.

b) Adjust clearance with a feeler gauge to the hot specified gap.

c) Tighten lock nut.

Tappet (Valve) clearance. Cold engine.

Intake valve clearance: **0.27mm, 0.0106in**

Exhaust valve clearance: **0.38mm, 0.0150in**

13. a) Install a new timing cover oil seal into the timing belt cover if new has not been installed. Tap oil seal home with a oil seal insertion tool or circular object same size as seal, do not damaged oil seal lips.

b) Install timing belt front cover and tighten the 12 bolts to specification.

Timing Belt Cover Bolts Specified Torque:
60kg-cm, 4.5ft-lb, 6Nm

14. Install the crankshaft pulley, tighten attaching bolt to specification.

Crankshaft Pulley Attaching Bolt:
1400kg-cm, 101ft-lb, 137Nm

15. Install the rubber plug at the rear of the head. Use a sealant on the rubber plug to stop oil leaks, also at the front oil seal retaining plate joins.

16. Install rocker cover and gasket as previously described, tighten to specification.

Rocker Cover Nuts Torque:

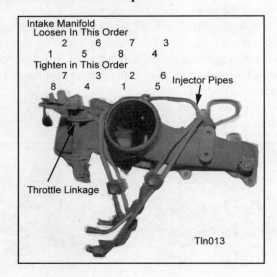

Intake Manifold
Loosen In This Order
2   6   7
1   5   8   4   3
Tighten in This Order
7   3   2   6   Injector Pipes
8   4   1   5

Throttle Linkage

TIn013

60kg-cm, 4.5ft-lb, 6Nm

17. Replace the intake manifold and new gasket, install the 2 nuts and 6 bolts attaching the intake manifold and left side engine lifting bracket to the cylinder head. Tighten to specification.

Intake Manifold Nuts and Bolts Specified Torque:
240kg-cm, 17ft-lb, 24Nm

18. Install the coolant thermostat housing and water outlet assembly, new gasket and attaching bolts, tighten to specification.

Coolant Outlet / Thermostat Housing Attaching Bolt
195kg-cm, 14ft-lb, 19Nm

19. Install the exhaust manifold. Install the 2 nuts and 6 bolts attaching the manifold to the cylinder head. Tighten the bolts to specification.

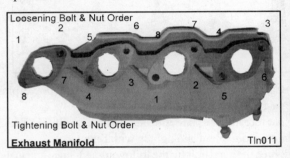

Loosening Bolt & Nut Order
2   6   7   4   3
1   5   8
7   3   2   6
8   4   1   5
Tightening Bolt & Nut Order
Exhaust Manifold   TIn011

Exhaust Manifold Bolts Torque:

L & 2L	400kg-cm, 29ft-lb, 39Nm
2L-T & 3L	530kg-cm, 38ft-lb, 52Nm

20. Install the heat shield if one was fitted, tighten bolts to specification.

Exhaust Manifold Heat Shield Bolts Torque:
195kg-cm, 14ft-lb, 19Nm

21. Install injector fuel pipes.

Injector Pipe Torque Specification:
250kg-cm, 18ft-lb, 25Nm

Injector Leakage Pipe Torque Specification:
500kg-cm, 36ft-lb, 49Nm

22. Install vacuum hoses to intake manifold.

23. Install breather hoses from rocker cover to intake manifold.

24. Install alternator.

a) Install mounting bracket bolts.

b) Install adjusting bracket bolt.

c) Install alternator and wiring loom.

25. Install the 4 glow plugs and wiring loom.

26. a) Fit radiator hose.

b) Fill radiator with appropriate coolant.

Coolant

LN:

10.6 litres, 11.2 US qts, 9.3 Imp qts.

27. Install the earth cable to the battery.

28. Start engine and check for oil, coolant, fuel and exhaust leaks.

CYLINDER HEAD [2L & 3L 80's Series on]

Make sure that all valve train components are kept in order so they can be installed in their original locations.
* [2L-T engines see Turbocharger - Remove and Install in this chapter for details.]

Remove

1. Disconnect battery earth lead.

2. Remove the 4 glow plugs and wiring loom.

3. Remove alternator.

a) Remove nuts from alternator adjuster bracket studs and remove engine harness earth wire connection and wiring harness retainer bracket.

b) Remove alternator, remove alternator support bolts, then remove support assembly.

4. Drain coolant from engine at radiator lower hose and remove top radiator hose.

5. a) Remove the two bracket nuts supporting the fuel injection pipes.

b) Loosen the four injector pipes at the injector and fuel pump.

c) Remove the four injector pipes and brackets. Cover the four injector pump outlet nozzles with some tape, to stop dust contaminating the fuel.

6. Remove the 4 bolts attaching the heat shield and heat shield from the exhaust manifold.

7. Remove the right side engine lifting bracket and exhaust manifold attaching 6 bolts plus 2 nuts, remove the exhaust

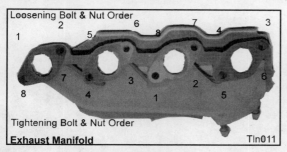

manifold.

* If you wish you may leave the exhaust manifold attached to the exhaust pipe. Disconnect the exhaust pipe front

bracket, then allow the manifold to move to one side allowing you access to remove the cylinder head.

8. Remove the intake manifold 2 nuts and 6 bolts attaching the intake manifold and left side engine lifting bracket from the cylinder head.

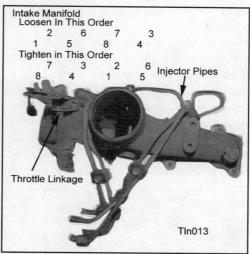

9. Remove the attaching bolts and coolant thermostat housing and water outlet assembly.

10. Remove the crankshaft balancer pulley bolt, use a pulley remover to remove the pulley, as described in this chapter.

11. Remove the timing belt cover 11 bolts and cover as previously described.

12. Remove the 8 bolts and 2 nuts securing the rocker cover, rocker cover and gasket as previously described in this chapter.

13. Rotate the crankshaft (it may be necessary to temporally install the crankshaft balancer pulley bolt) so the crankshaft is at TDC/ compression on number 1 cylinder. Check for alignment mark on camshaft gear in line with cylinder head / back of camshaft gear cover.

14. Use an oil based crayon, place alignment marks the timing belt and cam shaft gear, injection pump gear and

crankshaft gear. Also draw an arrow showing direction of rotation of timing belt, if the belt is to reinstalled on the engine.
** *Timing belts do have a life span, and the average life of a timing belt should be 100,000 kilometres, 62,138mile for normal driving conditions.*

15. Loosen the idler pulley bolts and remove the idler pulley tension spring.

16. Remove the timing pulley belt from the 4 pulleys.

17. Remove the bolt attaching the camshaft gear to the cam shaft, remove the gear with a pulley remover.

18. Remove the bolts attaching the plate at the front of the cylinder head which contains the camshaft front oil seal, remove the front plate. Remove the camshaft oil seal, with a screw driver, do not damage oil seal housing.

19. Loosen the 18 cylinder head bolts in the order shown working from the front and rear of the engine to the centre

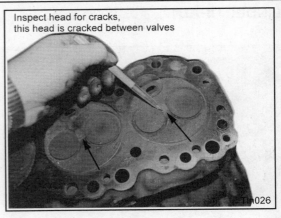

Inspect head for cracks, this head is cracked between valves

Tln026

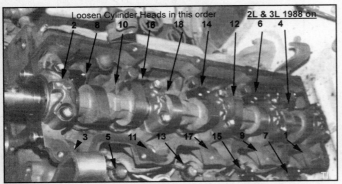

Loosen Cylinder Heads in this order   2L & 3L 1988 on

of the assembly. Loosen a little each pass until the bolts are loose. Remove cylinder head 18 bolts.

20. Lift the cylinder head and gasket from the engine block.

Cylinder Head Inspection

1. Taking care not to scratch machined surfaces, clean mating surfaces of cylinder head and cylinder block.
* Do not use a motorised wire brush on any gasket sealing surface.

2. Check cylinder head deck, intake and exhaust manifold mating surfaces for distortion. These surfaces may be refaced **once only** by parallel grinding.

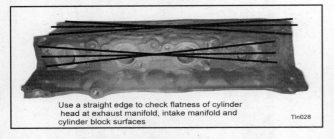

Use a straight edge to check flatness of cylinder head at exhaust manifold, intake manifold and cylinder block surfaces

Tln028

* Head to block surface if more than .15mm (0.0059in) must be removed from any surface, replace cylinder head.
* Head to manifold surface if more than .20mm (0.0079in) must be removed from any surface, replace cylinder head.

3. Inspect the following:

a) Cylinder head for cracks, especially between valve seats or exhaust ports.

b) Cylinder head deck surface for corrosion, casting sand inclusions or blow holes.

c) Cylinder block deck surface with a suitable straight edge.

4. Clean cylinder head bolts and replace any bolt that has suspect threads, or stretched or damaged heads caused by improper use of tools.

Cylinder Block and Piston Height Inspection

1. a) Clean cylinder head bolt hole threads in cylinder block using an appropriate size thread tap.

b) If necessary, threads may be reconditioned with suitable thread inserts.

* Clean out bolt holes with an air hose.

2. Check cylinder block deck surface with a suitable straight edge and compare with measurements and directions above in Cylinder Head Inspection.

3. Measure the height of the piston above the cylinder block surface for head gasket selection.

a) Install a digital or very accurate micrometer on the cylinder block surface so piston height can be measured.

b) Slowly turn the crankshaft while measuring the maximum height of each piston as it protrudes out of the engine block. Measure each piston twice 180^0 apart, record each measurement. If the piston exceeds specified measurements remove and reinstall piston & connecting rod assembly, or replace piston and connecting rod assembly.

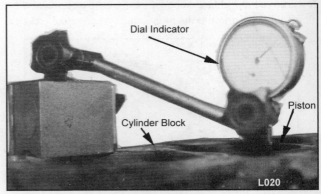

Dial Indicator

Cylinder Block

Piston

L020

Piston Height Protrusion above Cylinder Block:
0.68 - 0.97mm, 0.0268 - 0.0382in

c) The above measurement is required for the selection of

head gasket to be used.

Installation

1. Select a head gasket to suit piston height protrusion as described above in Cylinder Block and Piston Height Inspection. Use the highest piston protrusion measurement to select the gasket in the chart below.

Gaskets come in 3 option thicknesses and are identified by a stamped mark or a section of the gasket removed.

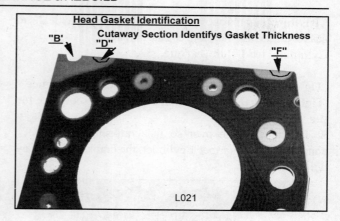

Head Gasket Identification
Cutaway Section Identifys Gasket Thickness
L021

Piston Height Protrusion	Gasket Identification	Gasket Thickness
0.68-0.77mm	B	1.40-1.50mm
0.78-0.87mm	D	1.50-1.60mm
0.88-0.97mm	F	1.60-1.70mm

2. Place head gasket in position over dowel pins on cylinder block.

3. a) Carefully guide cylinder head into place over dowel pins and gasket.

b) Install the correct length bolts to the correct position the shorter bolts are tightening numbers 11, 3, 5 & 13.

c) Coat threads of cylinder head bolts with LOCTITE 243 sealant or equivalent and tighten with finger.

4. Tighten the head bolts to the following sequence and in the order shown.

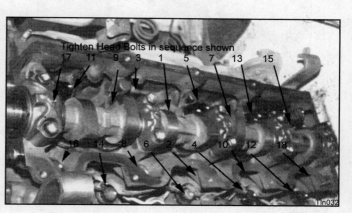

Tighten Head Bolts in sequence shown
TIn032

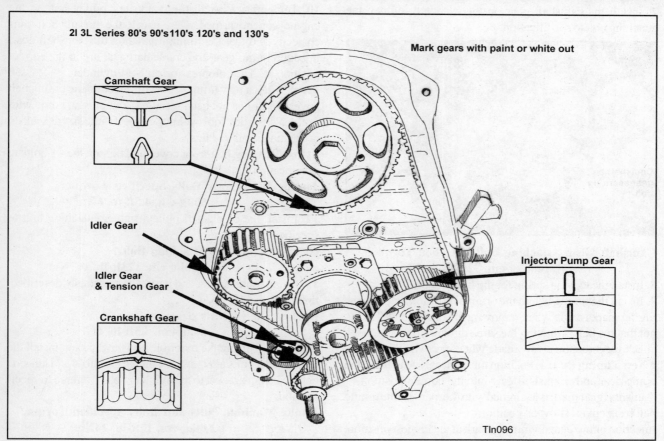

2l 3L Series 80's 90's 110's 120's and 130's

Mark gears with paint or white out

Camshaft Gear

Idler Gear

Idler Gear & Tension Gear

Crankshaft Gear

Injector Pump Gear

TIn096

49

* It is important to follow the given procedure to avoid head gasket failure and possible engine damage.

Cylinder Head Bolt Torque:
800kg-cm, 58ft-lb, 78Nm
Tighten a further 90⁰ turn of each bolt in sequence
Tighten a further 90⁰ turn of each bolt in sequence for the second time.

5. Turn the engine over so the crankshaft is at TDC/ compression on number 1 cylinder, the crankshaft keyway will be at the top.

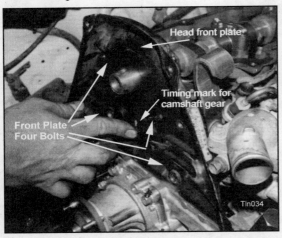

6. Turn the cam shaft to TDC/ compression on number 1 cylinder, the camshaft keyway will be at the top.

7. Install the camshaft gear on the camshaft, tighten the attaching bolt to specification.

Camshaft Gear Attaching Bolt Specified Torque:
1000kg-cm, 72ft-lb, 98Nm

8. Install the tension spring for the timing belt.

9. Install the timing belt to the original position aligning the timing marks made when removing the timing belt. Taking not that the belt is rotating the same direction as previously, check for direction arrow made when removing belt.

* New Timing Belt: a) Position the camshaft gear, injection pump gear and crankshaft gear into the correct position. Camshaft gear mark is to aligned with the mark on the timing belt back cover, (Lowest position).

Injection pump gear alignment mark at the highest position.

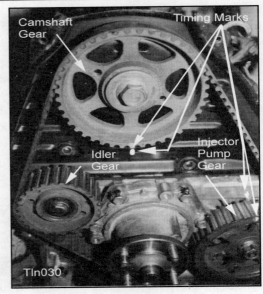

Crankshaft gear at the highest position.

Install timing belt onto the lower section of the crankshaft gear, around the inside of the lowest idler pulley, over the camshaft gear and injection pump gear.

* Keep the timing belt tight and meshed into the grooves on the gears

Ensure the alignment marks on the injection pump gear and pump body are aligned.

Slide the timing belt onto the higher idler pulley/gear.

10. Temporarily install the crankshaft pulley bolt so the engine can be turned over, check the timing belt runs correctly and that the timing marks on the camshaft gear, injection pump gear and crankshaft gear are in the correct position at TDC compression on No 1 cylinder.

11. a) Install a new timing cover oil seal into the timing belt cover if new has not been installed. Tap oil seal home with a oil seal insertion tool or circular object same size as seal, do not damaged oil seal lips.

b) Install timing belt front cover and tighten the 11 bolts to specification.

Timing Belt Cover Bolts Specified Torque:
60kg-cm, 4.5ft-lb, 6Nm

12. Install the crankshaft pulley, tighten attaching bolt to specification.

Crankshaft Pulley Attaching Bolt:
1700kg-cm, 123ft-lb, 167Nm

13. Install rocker cover and gasket as previously described, tighten to specification.

Rocker Cover Nuts Torque:
60kg-cm, 4.5ft-lb, 6Nm

14. Replace the intake manifold and new gasket, install the 2 nuts and 6 bolts attaching the intake manifold and left side engine lifting bracket to the cylinder head. Tighten to specification.

Intake Manifold Nuts and Bolts Specified Torque:
240kg-cm, 17ft-lb, 24Nm

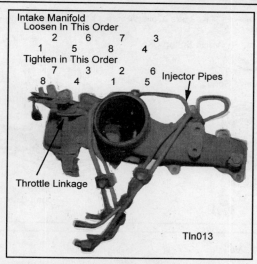

Intake Manifold
Loosen In This Order

Throttle Linkage

Injector Pipes

TIn013

15. Install the coolant thermostat housing and water outlet assembly, new gasket and attaching bolts, tighten to specification.

Coolant Outlet / Thermostat Housing Attaching Bolt
195kg-cm, 14ft-lb, 19Nm

16. Install the exhaust manifold. Install the 2 nuts and 6 bolts attaching the manifold to the cylinder head. Tighten the bolts to specification.

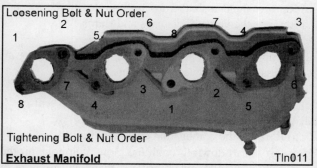

Loosening Bolt & Nut Order

Tightening Bolt & Nut Order

Exhaust Manifold　　　　　　　　　　　　TIn011

Exhaust Manifold Bolts Torque:
530kg-cm, 38ft-lb, 52Nm

17. Install the heat shield if one was fitted, tighten bolts to specification.

Exhaust Manifold Heat Shield Bolts Torque:
195kg-cm, 14ft-lb, 19Nm

18. Install injector fuel pipes.

Injector Pipe Torque Specification:
250kg-cm, 18ft-lb, 25Nm

Injector Leakage Pipe Torque Specification:
500kg-cm, 36ft-lb, 49Nm

19. Install vacuum hoses to intake manifold.

20. Install breather hoses from rocker cover to intake manifold.

21. Install alternator.

a) Install mounting bracket bolts.

b) Install adjusting bracket bolt.

c) Install alternator and wiring loom.

22. Install the 4 glow plugs and wiring loom.

23. a) Fit radiator hose.

b) Fill radiator with appropriate coolant.

Coolant

LN:

2L	**9.2 litres, 9.7 US qts, 8.1 Imp qts.**
3L	**9.0 litres, 9.5 US qts, 8.0 Imp qts.**

24. Install the earth cable to the battery.

25. Start engine and check for oil, coolant, fuel and exhaust leaks.

Cylinder Head Assembly

1. Replace camshaft and cam shaft bearings No 1 bearing use thrust bearings.

* Inspection of camshaft and camshaft bearings as detailed under Camshaft section in this chapter.

2. Install camshaft bearing caps, tighten bolts in order shown and to specification.

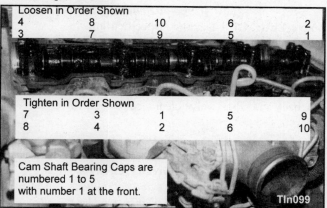

Loosen in Order Shown

Tighten in Order Shown

Cam Shaft Bearing Caps are numbered 1 to 5 with number 1 at the front.

TIn099

Camshaft Bearing Caps Bolt Specified Torque:
195kg-cm, 14ft-lb, 19Nm

3. a) Install a new camshaft oil seal into the plate at the front of the cylinder head. Tap oil seal home with a oil seal insertion tool or circular object same size as seal, do not damaged oil seal lips.

b) Install the plate at the front of the cylinder head which contains the camshaft front oil seal, install the bolts attaching the front plate and tighten to specification.

Front Camshaft Oil Seal Retainer Bolt Specified Torque: **185kg-cm, 13ft-lb, 18Nm**

Front Plate Bolt Torque: **185kg-cm, 13ft-lb, 18Nm**

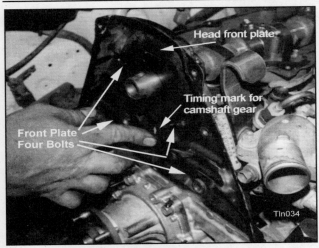

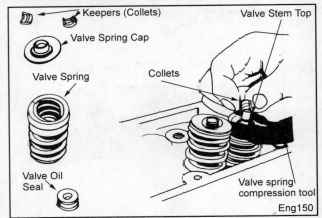

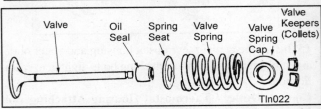

4. Check for oil clearance of valve lifters. Measure the valve lifter bore and the diameter of valve lifter. If not within specification replace valve lifter, in extreme cases it may be necessary to replace cylinder head.

Valve Lifter Diameter Specification
        40.892-40.902mm, 0.0023-0.0039in
Valve Lifter Bore Diameter specification.
        40.960-40.980mm, 1.6126-1.6134in
Valve Lifter Oil Clearance Specification.
0.058-0.088mm, 0.0023-0.0035in -
        Max 0.10mm, 0.0157in

5. Install valve lifters.
6. Install valves
7. Check and adjust valve clearance of each valve.

CYLINDER HEAD RECONDITIONING

* Make sure that all valve train components are kept together and identified so that they can be installed in their original locations.

Dismantle

1. Remove glow plugs if not removed.
2. Remove fuel injectors if not removed.
3. [L, 2L & 2L-T 50's & 60's Series] Compress valve springs in turn with a conventional spring compressor and remove valve collets.
4. [L, 2L & 2L-T 50's & 60's Series] Remove the following:
a) Valve spring caps, springs and valve stem oil seals.
b) Valves from cylinder head.

Caution: *Do not force valves out of guides, as mushroomed valve ends, due to rocker arm wear or dirt in the guide, will damage guide. Remove burrs by chamfering valve stem with an oil stone or file.*

5. [2L & 3L 80's Series on]
a) Loosen and remove the camshaft bearing cap bolts, remove the bearing caps.

* When you lift the camshaft bearing caps, take care as the upper bearing caps may fall out. The caps must remain with the bearing they belong to unless new camshaft bearings are being fitted.
b) Remove the camshaft from the cylinder head.
c) Remove the valve lifters caps and shims.
6. [2L & 3L 80's Series on]
a) Compress valve springs in turn with a valve spring compressor and remove valve collets.
b) Remove the following:
c) Valve spring caps, springs and valve stem oil seals.
d) Valves from cylinder head.
7. a) Remove the combustion chambers from the head.
b) Insert a drift down through the glow plug hole, hit the combustion chamber out of the head, there may be shims in with the combustion chamber.

Clean

1. a) Clean all carbon from combustion chambers, valve ports, etc., with a rotary-type carbon removing wire brush.
* Do not wire brush on any gasket sealing surface.
b) Clean cylinder head gasket surface of cylinder head.
2. Thorough clean valve guides with a suitable cleaning solvent or a wire brush.
3. Clean valve heads with a drill and wire brush.
* Do not scratch the valve stem.
4. Wash all components in a suitable cleaning solvent and air dry with dry compressed air.

Cylinder Head Inspection

1. Cylinder heads should be inspected for cracks in valve seats and combustion chambers, and for external cracks to water jackets.
2. Check cylinder head deck surface for corrosion.

3. Using a straight edge and feeler gauge, check cylinder head deck, intake and exhaust manifold surfaces for distortion. Check cylinder head deck surface diagonally, longitudinally and transversely.

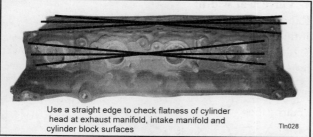

Use a straight edge to check flatness of cylinder head at exhaust manifold, intake manifold and cylinder block surfaces

Tln028

These surfaces may be refaced **once only** by parallel grinding.

* Head to block surface if more than .15mm (0.0059in) must be removed from any surface, replace cylinder head.

* Head to manifold surface if more than .10mm (0.004in) must be removed from any surface, replace cylinder head.

4. Inspect the following:

a) Cylinder head for cracks, especially between valve seats or exhaust ports.

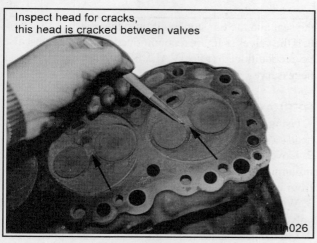

Inspect head for cracks, this head is cracked between valves

Tln026

b) Cylinder head deck surface for corrosion, casting sand inclusions or blow holes.

c) Cylinder block deck surface with a suitable straight edge.

5. Use a micrometer to measure the protrusion of the combustion chamber, if not within specification place shims

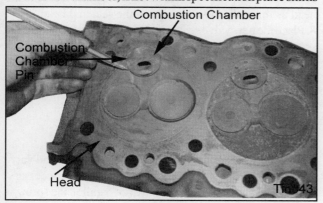

Combustion Chamber

Combustion Chamber Pin

Head

Tln043

behind combustion chamber, shims available in 0.05mm thickness.

Combustion Chamber Protrusion Specification:
0.01 - 0.07mm, 0.0004 - 0.0028in

VALVE GUIDES
Clearance Checking

1. Excessive valve stem to guide bore clearance will cause lack of power, rough idling and noisy valve operation.

2. Insufficient clearance will result in noisy and sticking of the valve and will interfere with smoothness of operation of engine.

3. Measure the inside diameter of the valve guide with an inside measuring micrometer. Then measure the diameter of the valve stem. Subtract the valve stem diameter from the inside diameter of the valve guide to obtain clearance measurement.

OR

* Use a dial gauge on a valve stem in the valve guide, measure

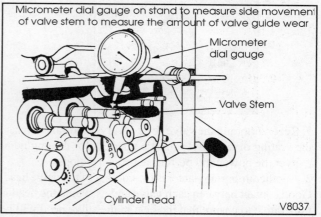

Micrometer dial gauge on stand to measure side movement of valve stem to measure the amount of valve guide wear

Micrometer dial gauge

Valve Stem

Cylinder head

V8037

movement of valve, to indicate valve stem clearance.

* It is important to check the clearance with a new standard valve before attempting to ream the valve guide.

Maximum Clearance - Valve stem to Valve Guide:
[L, 2L & 2L-T 50's & 60's Series]
Intake - 0.021 - 0.057 mm   Maximum 0.10mm
Exhaust - 0.040 - 0.076 mm Maximum 0.12mm
[2L & 3L 80's Series on]
Intake - 0.020 - 0.055 mm   Maximum 0.08 mm
Exhaust - 0.035 - 0.070 mm Maximum 0.10 mm

4. When using a new valve, if valve stem to valve guide clearance is within specification, check original valve stem diameter (refer VALVES) and replace any worn valves as necessary.

5. If necessary replace the valve guide.

Use a hammer and flat end rod to drive the old valve guide down and out of the head.

Use a hammer and flat end rod to drive the new valve guide into the head.

[L, 2L & 2L-T 50's & 60's Series]

Ream bush out to specified diameter with an 8.5mm reamer.

[2L & 3L 80's Series on]

Ream bush out to specified diameter with an 8.0mm reamer.

Intake - 0.021 - 0.057 mm   Maximum 0.10mm

Exhaust - 0.040 - 0.076 mm Maximum 0.12mm

[2L & 3L 80's Series on]

Valve Guide Bush Inside Diameter:

[L, 2L & 2L-T 50's & 60's Series]

   8.51-8.53mm (0.3350-0.3358in)

[2L & 3L 80's Series on]

   8.010 - 8.030 mm

VALVE SEATS

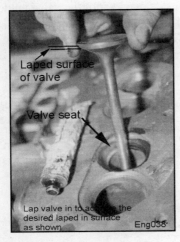

Laped surface of valve

Valve seat

Lap valve in to achieve the desired laped in surface as shown

Eng038

1. Reconditioning the valve seats is very important because the seating of the valves must be perfect for the engine to deliver the power and performance its develops.

2. Another important factor is the cooling of the valve head. Good contact between each valve and its seat in the head is imperative to ensure that the heat in the valve head will be properly carried away.

3. Several different types of equipment are available for reconditioning valve seats. The recommendations of the manufacturer of the equipment being used should be carefully followed to attain proper results.

4. Check valve seats for any evidence of pitting or damage at valve contact surface. If pitting is evident, the valve seats will need to be reconditioned.

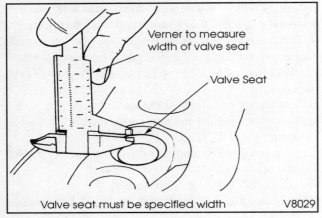

Verner to measure width of valve seat

Valve Seat

Valve seat must be specified width   V8029

* Because the valve guide serves to support and centre the valve seat grinder, it is essential that the valve guide is serviced before reconditioning the valve seats.

* **Valve seat angles are 45°.**

* **Valve seat width:**

Exhaust 1.2 - 1.6mm (0.047-0.063in)

Intake   1.2 - 1.6mm (0.047-0.063in)

5. If the seat is too wide after grinding, it may be narrowed by using a 30° or 65° grinding stone. The 30° stone will lower

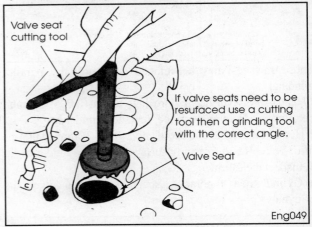

Valve seat cutting tool

If valve seats need to be resufaced use a cutting tool then a grinding tool with the correct angle.

Valve Seat

Eng049

the seat and the 65° stone will raise the seat.

6. If the valves seats are reconditioned, the valves must also be reconditioned (refer VALVES) or replace valves as necessary.

REPLACING VALVE SEAT

1. Using a lathe, turn down the out side diameter of a valve head so it fill fit neatly into inside of the valve seat.

2. Cover the head that surrounds the valve seat with an inflammable paste, such as soap paste. This will stop damage from weld spatter.

3. Weld a continuous run of weld around the edge of the valve, so it is welded to the inside of the valve seat.

4. Lift the head so the top of the valve can be tapped to free the valve seat.

5. Slide the machined valve and valve seat out of the head.

6. Machine the head as the new valve seat is over size by 0.38mm diameter and depth.

7. The new valve seat should not to be hit or forced into the head as this will cause damage to the seat and head.

8. Place the new valve seat in liquid nitrogen or dry ice so the seat will shrink in size.

9. Carefully place the valve seat into position with an old valve (converted into a special tool as shown in diagram) positioned through the seat into the valve guide. Gently tap the special tool to position and centre the valve seat

VALVE SPRINGS

1. Inspect valve spring surfaces on cylinder head and valve cap for wear or gouging. Replace components as necessary.

2. a) Check spring ends. If they are not parallel, the spring is bent.

b) Replace valve springs that do not meet specification.

Maximum allowable variance in spring end length: 2.00 mm, while rotating spring on level desk.
[L, 2L & 2L-T 50's & 60's Series]
Valve Spring Free length: 47.98mm (1.8890in)
  [2L & 3L 80's Series on]
Valve Spring Free length:
Blue Paint Identification Mark   49.14mm (1.9346in)
Yellow Paint Identification Mark   46.20mm (1.8189in)
3. a) Check valve spring load with a spring tester.

b) Springs should be compressed to the specified height and checked against specifications.

Valve spring compressed height/load:
Also Valve Spring Install Height
Valve spring height:
  [L, 2L & 2L-T 50's & 60's Series]

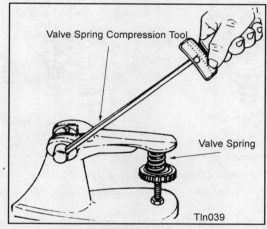

Tln039

Spring   Compressed height   39.3mm (1.547in)
            Compression pressure 29.2kg, 64.4lb, 286 N
  [2L & 3L 80's Series on]
Spring   Compressed height   30.7mm (1.457in)
            Compression pressure 32.0kg, 71.0lb, 315 N
c) Replace any valve spring if not to specification.

VALVES

1. a) Inspect valve stem for burrs and scratches. (Burrs and minor scratching may be removed with an oil stone.)

b) Valves with excessive stem wear or that are warped should be replaced.

c) Inspect valve stem tip for wear. The valve tip may be reconditioned by grinding.

d) Follow the grinder manufacturers instructions. Make sure the new tip surface is at right-angles to the valve stem.

e) Measure length of valve if not within specification, replace with a new valve.

[L, 2L & 2L-T 50's & 60's Series]
New Valve Length
Intake Valve: 122.95 mm (4.8405in)
Exhaust Valve: 122.75 mm (4.8327in)

Eng039

Minimum Valve Length
Intake Valve: 122.45 mm (4.8209in)
Exhaust Valve: 122.25 mm (4.8130in)
[2L & 3L 80's Series on]
New Valve Length
Intake Valve: 103.29 - 103.69 mm (4.0665 - 4.0823in)
Exhaust Valve:103.14 - 103.54 mm (4.0606 - 4.0764in)
Minimum Valve Length
Intake Valve: 102.79 mm (4.0468in)
Exhaust Valve: 102.64 mm (4.0409in)
2. Inspect valve stem collet groove for damage.

3. a) Check valve face for burning or cracking.

b) If pieces have broken off, inspect corresponding piston and cylinder head area for damage.

4. a) Inspect valve stem for straightness and valve head for bending or distortion using 'V' blocks.

b) Bent or distorted valves must be replaced.

5. Valves with pitted or grooves faces can be reconditioned with a valve refacing machine, ensuring correct relationship between head and stem.

Valve face angle: 44.5°.
* If pitting or grooving is so deep that refacing would result in a 'knife' edge at the valve head, valve must be replaced.
* Measure valve margin after refacing valves. If margin is less than minimum specified, the valve must be replaced.

Minimum valve head margin thickness:
[L, 2L & 2L-T 50's & 60's Series]
Intake Valve: 0.9 mm (0.035in)
Exhaust Valve: 1.0 mm (0.039in)
[2L & 3L 80's Series on]
Intake Valve: 1.1 mm (0.043in)

Exhaust Valve: **1.2 mm (0.047in)**

6. Lightly lap reconditioned valves into valve seat.

* New valves must not be lapped. Lapping destroys the protective coating on the valve face.

7. After refacing or installing a new valve, check for correct seating as follows:

a) Lightly coat valve face with bearing blue.

b) Insert valve and rotate about 1/6 of a revolution.

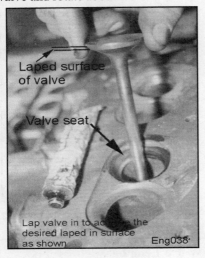

c) Remove valve and check for full contact with seat.

i) If partial contact is indicated, insert valve again and turn through a full revolution.

ii) If blue on seat indicates full contact, reface valve.

iii) If partial contact is still indicated, regrind cylinder head valve seat.

d) Clean all traces of bearing blue from valves and seats.

VALVE SPRING INSTALLED HEIGHT
[L, 2L & 2L-T 50's & 60's Series]

Excessive valve spring installed height, caused by valve seat wear or valve and seat reconditioning, has to be compensated for, by adding shims under the valve springs.

1. Place valve in its guide, then install valve spring cap and collets.

2. Pull up on valve spring cap to seat collet and valve.

3. Measure from machined spring seat to spring side of cap, using a vernier calliper. Valve spring installed height should be as follows:

Valve Spring Install Height
39.3mm (1.547in)

Shim valve spring seat as needed if any measurement is not as indicated.

CYLINDER HEAD ASSEMBLY ASSEMBLE

1. Dry and clean all components thoroughly.

2. Using clean engine oil, lubricate valve stems and valve guides

3. Install valves in corresponding guides.

4. Make sure that seals fully seat on top of guide, install valve stem oil seals. The original seals may not be the same colour as the replacement seals.

5. Install the valve spring seat over the valve guide onto the cylinder head.

6. Place valve springs (springs are painted white or yellow on base) and cap over valve stem.

5. Using a suitable spring compressor, compress valve springs.

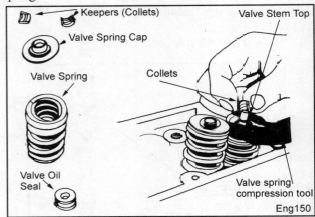

* Excess compression could cause spring cap to damage valve stem oil seal, ensure to compress valve springs only enough to install valve collets.

6. Install valve collets, making sure that they locate accurately in groove in top end of valve stem. Release the valve spring compressor slowly ensuring that the collets sit properly. Grease may be used to hold collets in place.

7. a) 2L & 3L 80's series on. Install valve lifters and adjusting shims, and camshaft, camshaft bearings and front retainer.

b) Use a feeler gauge to check clearance between valve lifters and camshaft, install correct adjusting shim to obtain specified clearance. (Check tune-up chapter for details).

2L & 3L 80's series on Valve Clearance cold
Intake Valves   0.20 - 0.30mm (0.008-0.012in)
Exhaust 0.40 - 0.50mm (0.016-0.020in)

8. a). Install combustion chamber, align the knock pin with the cylinder head caverty.

b) Use a micrometer to measure the protrusion of the combustion chamber, if not within specification place shims behind combustion chamber, shims available in 0.05mm thickness.

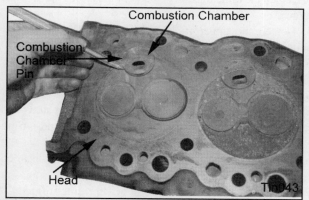

Combustion Chamber Protrusion Specification:
0.01 - 0.07mm, 0.0004 - 0.0028in

CAMSHAFT BEARINGS

Care must be taken during bearing removal and installation, not to damage bearings that are not being replaced.

Each camshaft bearing journal has 2 bearing halves, the front camshaft bearing is the thrust bearing.

1. Remove the camshaft as previously described in Cylinder Head section if not removed.

2. Wipe oil from both inner and outer surfaces of bearing shells.

3. Inspect inner surface of bearing shells for gouges, wear or embedded foreign matter.

If foreign matter is found, determine its nature and source. Inspect outer surface of bearing shell for surface wear (indicates movement of shell or high spot in surrounding material), looseness or turning (flattened tangs and wear grooves), or overheating (discoloration).

The camshaft may be bent or have tapered bearing journals if uneven side to side wear is found.

* Bearing failure, other than normal wear, must be examined carefully.

4. Install bearing shells in original positions in cylinder head and bearing cap if inspection reveals that crankshaft is OK.

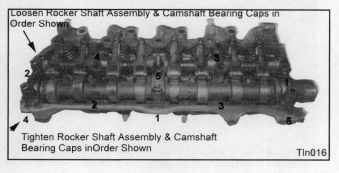

5. Place a piece of plastigage across width of bearing journal, parallel to camshaft centreline.

6. [L, 2L & 2L-T 50's & 60's series] Install rocker assembly in original position, tighten bolts as specified.
[2L & 3L 80's Series on] Install bearing caps in original position, tighten bolts as specified.

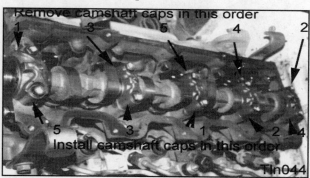

* Make sure that camshaft does not rotate with plastigage installed.

[L, 2L & 2L-T 50's & 60's series]
Rocker Assembly Bolts Specification:
195kg-cm, 14ft-lb, 19Nm
[2L & 3L 80's Series on]
Bearing Cap Bolts Specification:
255kg-cm, 18ft-lb, 25Nm

7. [L, 2L & 2L-T 50's & 60's series] Remove rocker assembly and bolts. Inspect for flattened plastigage sticking to either camshaft or bearing shell in cap.
[2L & 3L 80's series on] Remove bearing caps and bolts. Inspect for flattened plastigage sticking to either camshaft or bearing shell in cap.

8. Determine bearing clearance by comparing width of flattened plastigage at widest point with graduation on plastigage envelope. The number within the graduation on the envelope indicates the clearance.

Clearance between camshaft bearings and camshaft should not exceed specification.

Specified Oil Clearance:
0.022 - 0.074mm, 0.0009 - 0.0029in
Maximum Oil Clearance:
0.1mm, 0.004in

9. It is advisable to install new bearing shells if bearing clearance exceeds specification and recheck clearance as previously described.

10. Remove all remains of plastigage after measuring. Using clean engine oil, lubricate bearing shells and journal. Install rocker assembly in original position as described in step 6. Finally tighten cap bolts as specified.

Rocker Assembly Bolts Specification:
195kg-cm, 14ft-lb, 19Nm

11. With bearing shells installed and rocker assembly bolts tightened, it should be possible to turn camshaft without binding.

**Remove drive belt pulley install pulley
puller to drive belt pulley bolt holes.**

Tln045

CRANKSHAFT BALANCER

Remove

1. Disconnect battery earth lead and remove drive belts as shown in the **BELT DRIVE** section.

2. Pull park brake fully on, chock rear wheel and transmission in gear.

3. Remove drive belt pulley (4 bolts).

4. Loosen and remove balancer retaining bolt.

5. Remove balancer from crankshaft with pulley puller. Install pulley puller to drive belt pulley bolt holes.

Install

1. Using engine oil, lubricate front seal surface of balancer.

2. Install balancer, engaging key on crankshaft with slot in balancer.

3. Tighten balancer retaining bolt to the proper torque specification.

Crankshaft Balancer Nut Torque Specification:

L,2L & 2L-T [50's & 60's Series]:
        1,400kg-cm, 101ft-lb, 137Nm

2L & 3L[80's series on]:
        1,700kg-cm, 123ft-lb, 167Nm

4. Install and inspect drive belt operation.

TIMING BELT COVER & BELT

** *Timing belts do have a life span, and the average life*

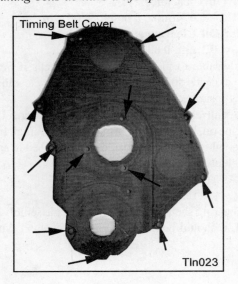

Tln023

of a timing belt should be 100,000 kilometres, 62,138mile for normal driving conditions.

Remove

1. Detach the battery cables and remove the battery shroud.

2. Empty the cooling system by disconnecting the lower radiator hose.

3. Detach the transmission oil cooler pipes from the radiator (auto).

4. Detach the upper radiator hose from the thermostat housing. Remove the radiator.

5. Detach belts from the fan, power steering, air conditioner etc.

6. Remove alternator.

a) Remove nuts from alternator adjuster bracket studs and remove engine harness earth wire connection and wiring harness retainer bracket.

b) Remove alternator, remove alternator support bolts, then remove support assembly.

7. Remove the fan/clutch from the water pump if fitted.

8. Remove the crankshaft damper bolt and washer and using a pulley remover, as described above.

9. Remove the timing belt cover 12 bolts, cover, gasket and exposed section of sump gasket.

10. Remove the timing belt idler pulley

11. Rotate the crankshaft so the crankshaft is at TDC/compression on number 1 cylinder. Check for alignment mark on camshaft gear in line with cylinder head.

12. Use an oil based crayon, place alignment marks the timing belt and cam shaft gear, injection pump gear and crankshaft gear. Also draw an arrow showing direction of rotation of timing belt, if the belt is to reinstalled on the engine.

13. Remove the tension spring.

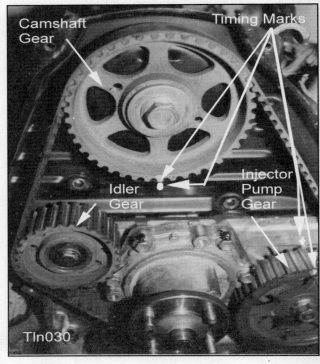

Tln030

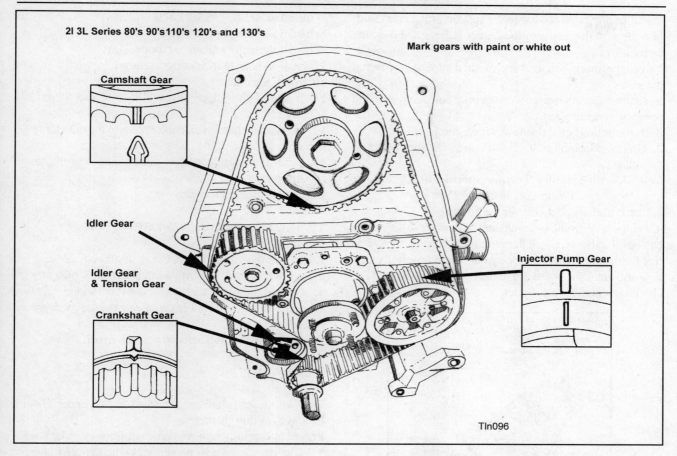

2l 3L Series 80's 90's 110's 120's and 130's

Mark gears with paint or white out

Camshaft Gear

Idler Gear

Idler Gear & Tension Gear

Crankshaft Gear

Injector Pump Gear

Tln096

14. Remove the timing pulley belt from the 3 pulleys and 2 idler pulleys.

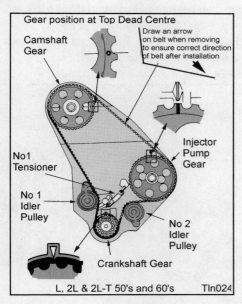

Gear position at Top Dead Centre

Camshaft Gear

Draw an arrow on belt when removing to ensure correct direction of belt after installation

Injector Pump Gear

No1 Tensioner

No 1 Idler Pulley

No 2 Idler Pulley

Crankshaft Gear

L, 2L & 2L-T 50's and 60's   Tln024

Inspect
** *Timing belts do have a life span, and the average life of a timing belt should be 100,000 kilometres, 62,138mile.*
1. Check the belt for deterioration.
a) Check for teeth that are badly worn or partly missing.

b) Check for small splits in the belt between the teeth.
c) Check for obvious wear or damage to one side of the belt. If the belt has damaged teeth check that the water pump and oil pump for excessive force to turn over.
If the belt is worn on one side check belt alignment or damaged idler pulleys.
2. Inspect that the idler pulleys will turn freely, if not replace.
3. Inspect the length of the tension spring for specification.
Free Length of Camshaft Belt Tension Spring
39.7 - 40.7 m, 1.563 - 1.602 in
Install
1. Install idler pulleys if removed, tighten idler pulley attaching bolts to specification.
Viewing from front of engine timing belt idler pulleys-
Left Idler Pulley: finger tight until belt is installed.
Right Idler Pulley: 400kg-cm, 29ft-lb, 39Nm
1. Install the timing belt to the original position aligning the timing marks made when removing the timing belt. Taking not that the belt is rotating the same direction as previously, check for direction arrow made when removing belt.
* New Timing Belt: Position the camshaft gear, injection pump gear and crankshaft gear into the correct position.
Camshaft gear mark is to aligned with the cylinder head and cylinder block joining line.
Injection pump gear alignment mark at the highest position.
Crankshaft gear at the highest position.

Install timing belt onto the lower section of the crankshaft gear, around the inside of the 2 idler pulleys and over the camshaft gear.

* Keep the timing belt tight and meshed into the grooves on the gears

Ensure the alignment marks on the injection pump gear and pump body are aligned.

Slide the timing belt onto the injection pump gear.

2. Tighten attaching bolts to left hand side idler pulley to specification.

Left Side Idler Pulley Torque Specification.
195kg-cm, 14ft-lb, 19Nm

3. Install the tension spring for the timing belt.

4. Temporally install the crankshaft pulley bolt so the engine can be turned over, check the timing belt runs correctly and that the timing marks on the camshaft gear, injection pump gear and crankshaft gear are in the correct position at TDC compression on No 1 cylinder.

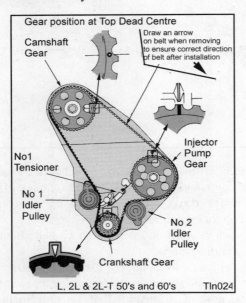

5. a) Install a new timing cover oil seal into the timing belt cover if new has not been installed. Tap oil seal home with a oil seal insertion tool or circular object same size as seal, do not damaged oil seal lips.

b) Install timing belt front cover and tighten the 12 bolts to specification.

Timing Belt Cover Bolts Specified Torque:
60kg-cm, 4.5ft-lb, 6Nm

6. Install the crankshaft pulley, tighten attaching bolt to specification.

Crankshaft Pulley Attaching Bolt:
L,2L & 2L-T[50's & 60's Series]:
1,400kg-cm, 101ft-lb, 137Nm
2L & 3L[80's Series on]:
1,700kg-cm, 123ft-lb, 167Nm

7. Reinstall the fan and clutch if one fitted

8. Install alternator.

a) Install mounting bracket bolts.
b) Install adjusting bracket bolt.
c) Install alternator and wiring loom.
9. Install all belts to their correct tension.
10. Install the radiator.
11. Reinstall the upper radiator hose to the thermostat housing.
12. Fit the transmission oil cooler pipes to the radiator (auto trans).
13. Refill the cooling system after connecting the lower radiator hose.
14. Connect the battery cables.

TIMING BELT COVER OIL SEAL
Replace
1. Remove the timing belt cover as described above.
2. Remove the old seal with a screw driver or punch.
3. Install the new seal with a seal installer (taking note that the seal is fitting as it should), lubricate the seal with grease before fitting.
4. Reinstall the timing belt cover as described above.

CAMSHAFT.
Remove
Remove the camshaft as described in "Cylinder Head - Remove" in this chapter.

Ensure to carefully remove camshaft from cylinder head.

* Avoid damaging bearing surfaces when removing camshaft.

Inspection
1. Check camshaft bearing journals and lobes for overheating, damage or wear (discoloration).
2. Measuring camshaft lobe lift. Use a micrometer to measure the widest point of the cam lobe.

Camshaft lobe height Intake and Exhaust:

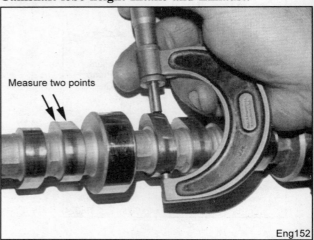

Eng152

Minimum Lift:
Intake Valve Lobe Minimum:

L & 2L [50's & 60's Series]	46.76mm, 1.8409in
2L-T[50's & 60's]	46.29mm, 1.8224in

2L [80's & 90's plus]	53.35mm, 2.1004in
3L [80's & 90's plus]	53.79mm, 2.1177in

Exhaust Valve Lobe Minimum:

L, 2L & 2L-T [50's & 60's Series]	47.25mm, 1.8602in
2L & 3L [80's & 90's plus]	54.49mm, 2.1453in

3. If camshaft lobe is not within specification, replace camshaft.

4. Inspect camshaft journal diameter with micrometer. Replace camshaft if journals are not as specified.

Camshaft Journal Diameter:

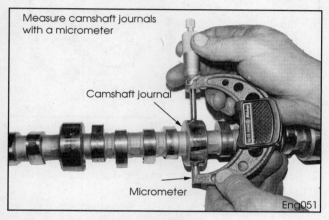

L, 2L & 2L-T [50's & 60's Series]
     34.969-34.985mm, 1.3767 - 1.3774in
Undersize by 0.125mm & 0.250mm bearings available
2L & 3L [80's & 90's plus]
No 1 Bearing   34.969-34.985mm, 1.3767 - 1.3774in
Other bearings 27.969-27.985mm, 1.1011 - 1.1018in

5. Position camshaft on 'V' blocks and check runout of centre camshaft journal.

Camshaft Centre Max. Runout: **0.10mm, 0.039in**

Install

1. Install the camshaft as described in "Cylinder Head - Assemble" in this chapter.

2. Check to see if camshaft will turn over.

3. If camshaft binds, remove camshaft, check bearings for high spots or incorrect installation. Remove any burrs if present. Inspect camshaft journal to bearing clearance.

FLYWHEEL/DRIVEPLATE

Remove

Before removal of flywheel/driveplate take note of the location of paint aligning marks on flywheel and pressure plate, before removing clutch pressure plate, the driveplate and torque converter also have paint aligning marks.

If not visible, scribe aligning marks on all parts.

1. To remove transmission refer to **MANUAL TRANSMISSION** or **AUTOMATIC TRANSMISSION** in this manual.

2. Vehicles with manual transmission:

Remove the clutch pressure plate and driven plate as per **CLUTCH** section in this manual.

3. Block flywheel driveplate from turning, using a screwdriver or suitable locking tool. Remove flywheel/driveplate crankshaft bolts and flywheel/driveplate.

Inspection.

The flywheel and flexplate are purposely out of balance and no attempt should be made to rebalance these as an individual unit.

1. Check flywheel/driveplate ring gear for badly worn, damaged or cracked teeth.

If needed, replace flywheel ring gear or driveplate, for details refer to **"ring gear"** section in this chapter.

Check starter motor pinion gear for damage, if ring gear teeth

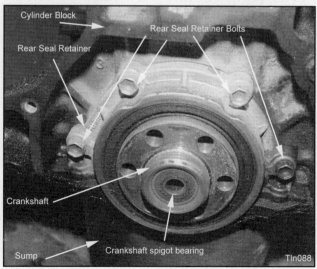

are damaged replace pinion gear, for details refer to **"Starting System chapter"**.

2. Inspect crankshaft and flywheel/driveplate matching surfaces for burrs. Using a fine file remove burrs if present.

Install

1. Install flywheel/driveplate to crankshaft, and tighten bolts to the correct specification.

[L, 2L & 2L-T 50's & 60's Series]
Flywheel Bolt (Manual Transmission) Specification:

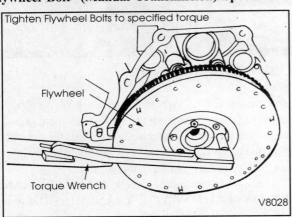

850kg-cm, 61ft-lb, 83m
Driveplate Bolt (Automatic Transmission) Spec:
750kg-cm, 54ft-lb, 74Nm
[2L & 3L 80's Series on]
Flywheel Bolt (Manual Transmission) Specification:
1,250kg-cm, 90ft-lb, 123m
Driveplate (Automatic Transmission) Bolt Spec:
1.000kg-cm, 72ft-lb, 98Nm

2. Mount a dial indicator on the rear of cylinder block for vehicles with automatic transmission. Inspect flexplate runout at the torque converter mounting bolt holes. Runout should not exceed the following specifications.

Flexplate Runout: **25 mm max.**

Try to correct by tapping high side with a mallet if runout exceeds specification. Replace driveplate if this condition can not be corrected.

3. Inspect starter motor operation.

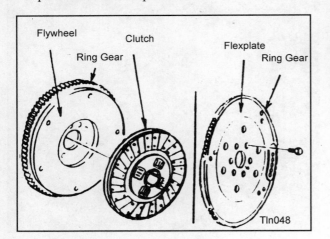

SPIGOT BEARING

Before removing flywheel or pressure plate, take note of the position of the paint aligning marks on flywheel and pressure plate. If marks are not visible, scribe aligning marks on both parts.

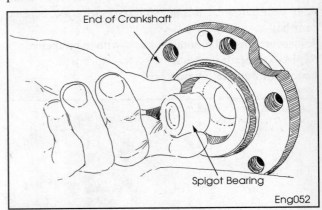

Replacement.

1. To remove transmission refer to **MANUAL TRANSMISSION** section in this manual for details.

2. To remove clutch pressure plate and driven plate refer to **CLUTCH** section in this manual.

3. To remove spigot bearing use a Slide hammer.

4. Use a piloted screwdriver to replace spigot bearing. Place new bearing on pilot of tool with radius in bore of bearing next to shoulder on tool. Drive bearing into crankshaft to the dimension as shown in the diagram. Use thin film of SAE 90 Gear Oil to lubricate the bearing.

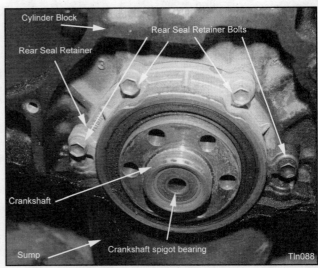

5. To install clutch assembly and transmission refer to **CLUTCH** and **MANUAL TRANSMISSION** sections in this manual.

ENGINE REBUILD.

ENGINE ASSEMBLY.
Remove
1. Disconnect battery leads

2. Remove bottom radiator hose from radiator to allow coolant to drain, and disconnect radiator hoses from engine.

3. Drain engine oil sump.

4. Using a felt tipped pen mark engine hood to hinge positions. Disconnect windshield washer hose. Remove hood hinge bolts and hood.

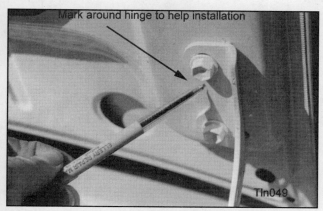

5. To remove cooling fan and radiator assembly refer to "Cooling systems" chapter section for details.

6. Disconnect heater supply and return hoses from engine heater pipe connections, including heater bypass pipe on the side of the block.

7. Disconnect breather hose from rocker cover.

8. Disconnect main wiring harness from engine and battery harness.

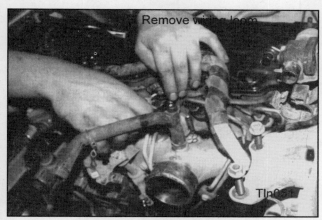

9. Unclip harness from oil sender unit and temperature sender unit.

10. To remove power steering pump (if applicable) refer to **Power Steering** section for details.

11. Disconnect air cleaner or "S" air intake tube.

12. Disconnect throttle cable from throttle linkage and mounting bracket.

13. Remove fuel feed and return lines from injectors.

14. Disconnect brake booster hose from engine vacuum connections.

15. Fully raise vehicle and place on safety stands.

16. To remove tail shaft refer to "Propeller shafts and universal joints" chapter for details. Place a suitable plug in end of transmission or transfer case.

17. Disconnect engine exhaust pipes from manifold assemblies.

18. Disconnect gear shift control from transmission refer to MANUAL TRANSMISSION or AUTOMATIC TRANSMISSION sections for details.

19. Disconnect clutch slave cylinder (for vehicles with manual transmission only) for details refer to CLUTCH section.

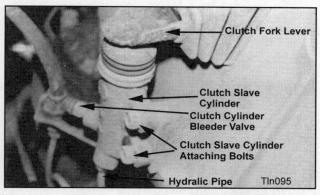

20. Disconnect speedo cable or wiring harness connector from speedometer speed sender at transmission.

Manual Transmission: Disconnect transmission harness from backup lamp switch.

Automatic Transmission: Disconnect transmission harness from solenoid.

21. Raise engine slightly to take weight off mounts by attaching an appropriate lifting hook and chain to engine lifting brackets if fitted. Otherwise care must be taken not to damage engine components with rope or chain while lifting engine.

22. Remove engine front mounting from mounting brackets.

23. Disconnect wiring harness connector from compressor clutch for vehicles with air conditioning.

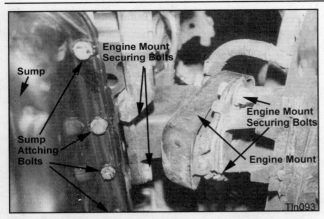

Tln093

24. Raise engine slightly and remove air compressor from engine mount bracket mounting bolts. Tie compressor back way from the engine.

25. Raise engine with front tilted upwards and a floor jack supporting rear of transmission assembly, make sure that engine exhaust manifolds, starter motor or transmission do not rest on steering gear.

* Do not allow engine to swing forward and damage air conditioning condenser (on vehicles with air conditioning condenser fitted at front) or optional transmission cooler.

26. Separate engine and transmission assemblies if necessary. Refer to MANUAL TRANSMISSION or AUTOMATIC TRANSMISSION for details.

Dismantle.

1. Mount engine assembly in an appropriate engine stand.

2. Remove the following parts:

a) Starter motor.

Str024

b) Drive belts to water pump, alternator etc.

c) Alternator and brackets.

3. Remove the following parts as previously described.

a) Intake manifold.

b) Exhaust manifold.

4. Remove the following parts as previously described or about to be described, in this chapter.

a) Rocker cover.

b) Crankshaft balancer.

c) Timing belt cover.

d) Timing belt, sprockets and shaft gears.

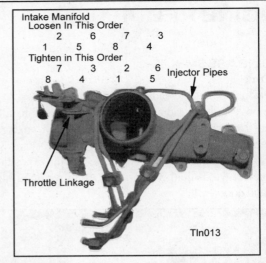

Tln013

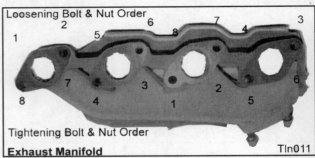

Tln011

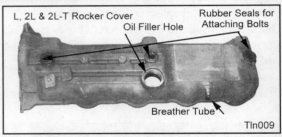

Tln009

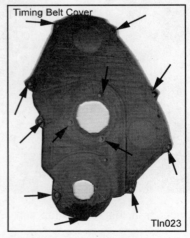

Tln023

e) Camshaft bearing caps.

f) Camshaft.

g) Cylinder head.

5. Remove the following parts as previously described or about to be described, in this chapter.

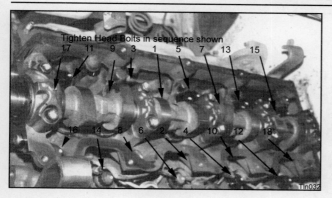

Tighten Head Bolts in sequence shown
17 11 9 3 1 5 7 13 15
16 14 8 6 2 4 10 12 18

TIn032

a) Oil filter.
b) Water pump.
c) Fuel Injection pump.
b) Engine sump.
c) Oil pump, suction pipe and screen,
d) Flywheel/driveplate
e) Main bearing caps
f) Crankshaft,
g) Piston and connecting rod assemblies.

Assembly.
Assembly techniques for each part are outlined in this section under their particular headings.
1. Make sure that all fasteners are tightened as specified in this section.
2. Use specified engine lubricant and coolant when refilling.
3. Inspect transmission fluid level, add lubricant as required.
4. Inspect for fuel, coolant, oil and exhaust leaks. Repair as required.
5. Check engine hood alignment.

OIL PAN (SUMP) & GASKET.

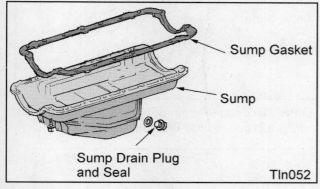

Sump Gasket

Sump

Sump Drain Plug
and Seal

TIn052

Remove
1. Drain oil from oil pan.
2. Remove the dip stick.
3. Remove cast brackets at the rear of the sump and either side.
4. Remove oil pan bolts, oil pan and seal, dispose of oil seal.
* Do not reuse the formed rubber oil pan seal.

Install
1. Clean all matching surfaces of oil pan and cylinder block

thoroughly.
2. Apply sealant to the oil pan surface groove and around the bolt holes.
3. Install new gasket onto oil pan, aligning oil pan bolt holes with the holes in gasket.
4. Install oil pan and seal to crankcase, and tighten as specified.
Oil Pan (Sump) Bolt Specification:
180kg-cm, 13ft-lb, 18Nm
5. Make sure oil pan drain plug is tightened as specified, use a new drain plug seal.
Oil Pan (Sump) Drain Plug Specification:
L,2L&2L-T [50's & 60's Series]
175kg-cm,13ft-lb, 17Nm
2L & 3L [80's Series on]   400kg-cm, 29ft-lb, 39Nm
6. Install brackets at rear of sump.
7. Replace dip stick.
8. Refill oil pan with the correct amount of engine oil as specified.
Lubricant Quantity Specification:
L,2L&2L-T [50's & 60's Series]
w/o new oil filter:
4.8 Litres, 5.1 US qts, 4.2 Imp qts
with new oil filter:
5.8 Litres, 6.1 US qts, 5.1 Imp qts
dry fill:
6.5 Litres, 6.9 US qts, 5.7 Imp qts
Europe - 2L & 3L [80's Series on]
w/o new oil filter:
5.0 Litres, 5.3 US qts, 4.4 Imp qts
with new oil filter:
5.9 Litres, 6.2 US qts, 5.2 Imp qts
dry fill:
6.4 Litres, 6.8 US qts, 5.6 Imp qts
Countries other than Europe - 2L & 3L [80's Series on]
w/o new oil filter:
5.0 Litres, 5.3 US qts, 4.4 Imp qts
with new oil filter:
6.0 Litres, 6.3 US qts, 5.3 Imp qts
dry fill:
6.9 Litres, 6.9 US qts, 5.7 Imp qts
Lubricant Quality:
Engine Oil Grade   API grade listed below
L, 2L & 3L: CC or CD
2L-T: CD
9. Start engine and inspect for oil leaks. Repair as required.
10. Stop engine and check oil level on dip stick.

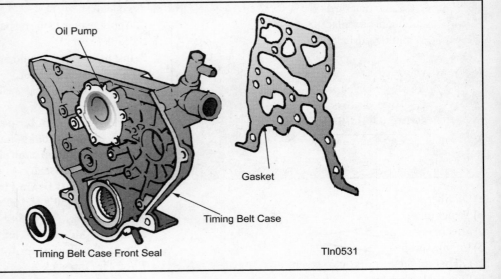

OIL PUMP

The oil pump is located at the rear of the timing belt case

Oil Pump

Gasket

Timing Belt Case

Timing Belt Case Front Seal

Tln0531

OIL PUMP

The oil pump is located at the rear of the timing belt case

Remove

1. Detach the battery cables and remove the battery shroud.

2. Empty the cooling system by disconnecting the lower radiator hose.

3. Detach the transmission oil cooler pipes from the radiator (auto).

4. Detach the upper radiator hose from the thermostat housing. Remove the radiator.

5. Detach belts from the fan, power steering, air conditioner etc.

6. Remove the fan/clutch from the water pump if fitted.

7. Remove the crankshaft balancer bolt, washer and pulley using a pulley remover, as described above.

8. a) Remove the timing belt cover bolts and timing belt cover.

b) Remove the timing belt, as previously described.

c) Remove the crankshaft gear, fuel injection pump gear and idler gears. (It is not necessary to remove the camshaft timing belt gear)

9. Remove the engine sump.

10. Remove the oil pump strainer, pipe, support bracket and gasket.

11. Remove the timing belt case (Oil pump)

a) Use a metal punch or felt pen to make alignment marks on the injection pump and the timing belt case.

b) Remove the 2 nuts attaching the injection pump to the timing belt case.

c) Remove the 5 bolts attaching the timing belt case to the engine cylinder block.

d) Remove the timing belt case from the engine cylinder block case, position the timing belt case on a bench taking care to protect the timing marker.

12. Remove the screws securing oil pump cover. Remove the pump cover and two rotors

13. Remove the relief valve plug, gasket, spring and valve

Inspect [L, 2L & 2L-T 50's & 60's Series]

Inspect the inside of the pump housing and the outer gear and inner rotor for damage or excessive wear.

Install the outer gear, crescent spacer and the inner rotor shaft assembly with the timing marks on the gear and rotor towards the pump cover. Inspect clearances of outer gear and rotor gear, replace if not within specification.

Inner gear tip to outer rotor tip specified clearance:
0.15-0.21mm, 0.0059-0.0083in   (0.30mm max)

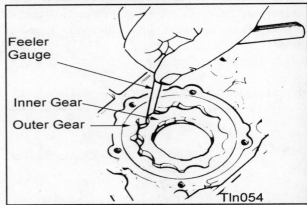

Feeler Gauge

Inner Gear

Outer Gear

Tln054

Outer Race to pump housing Specified Clearance:
0.15-0.21mm, 0.0059-0.0083in   (0.30mm max)

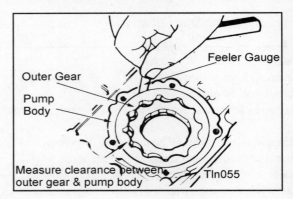

Feeler Gauge

Outer Gear

Pump Body

Measure clearance between outer gear & pump body

Tln055

The inner rotor and outer gear are serviced as an assembly. One part should not be replaced without replacing the other. Inspect the mating surface of the pump cover for wear. Replace the cover if the surface is worn, scored or grooved. Check that clearance between the pump cover and gear/rotor is within specification with a steel ruler.

Clearance of pump cover:
   0.03-0.09mm, 0.0012-0.0035in   (0.15mm max)

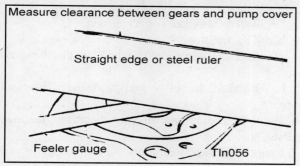

Oil all parts and install the oil pressure relief valve plunger, spring, and a nut, tighten to specification.

Oil Relief Valve Nut Specified Torque:
      210kg-cm, 27ft-lb, 37Nm

Inspect   [2L & 3L 80's Series on]
Inspect the inside of the pump housing and the outer gear and inner rotor for damage or excessive wear.

Install the outer gear and the inner rotor shaft assembly with the timing marks on the gear and rotor towards the pump cover. Inspect clearances of outer gear and rotor gear, replace if not within specification.

Inner gear tip to outer rotor tip specified clearance:

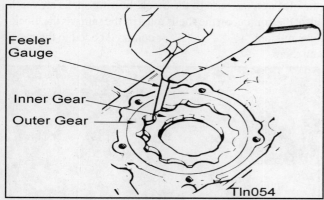

   0.11-0.24mm, 0.0043-0.0094in   (0.30mm max)
Outer race to pump housing clearance:
   0.144-0.219mm, 0.0057-0.0086in   (0.40mm max)
The inner rotor and outer gear are serviced as an assembly. One part should not be replaced without replacing the other. Inspect the mating surface of the pump cover for wear. Replace the cover if the surface is worn, scored or grooved. Check that clearance between the pump cover and gear/rotor is within specification with a steel ruler.

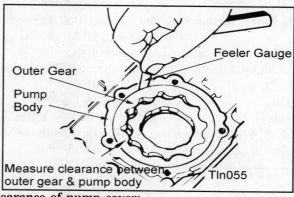

Clearance of pump cover:

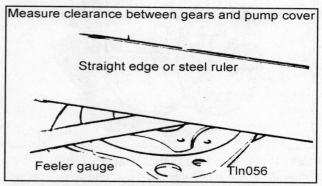

   0.03-0.09mm, 0.0012-0.0035in   (0.15mm max)
Oil all parts and install the oil pressure relief valve plunger, spring, and a nut, tighten to specification.
Oil Relief Valve Nut Specified Torque:
      375kg-cm, 27ft-lb, 37Nm
Install
1. Install the cover to the oil pump and tighten the cover screws.
2. Install the timing belt cover and oil pump, and a new gasket.
a) Align the alignment marks on the injection pump and the timing belt case.
b) Install the 2 nuts attaching the injection pump to the timing belt case.
Injection Pump to Timing Belt Casing Nut Torque:
      210kg-cm, 15ft-lb, 21Nm.
c) Install the 5 bolts attaching the timing belt case to the engine cylinder block, tighten the bolts to specification.
Timing Belt Cover / Oil Pump Attaching Bolt Specified Torque: **230kg-cm, 17ft-lb, 23Nm.**
3. Replace the oil pump strainer, pipe, support bracket and

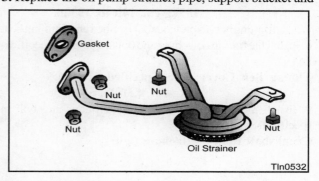

gasket.

Oil Pump Suction Pipe and Strainer Bolt Torque:
        120kg-cm, 9ft-lb, 12Nm.

4. Install the engine sump and tighten to specification.

Oil Sump Attaching Bolts & Nuts Specified Torque:
[L, 2L & 2L-T 50's & 60's Series]
 Bolts   **80kg-cm, 7ft-lb, 8Nm**
 Nuts   **175kg-cm, 13ft-lb, 17Nm**
[2L & 3L 80'sSeries on]: 180kg-cm, 13ft-lb, 18Nm

5. Install water pump tighten bolts to specification.

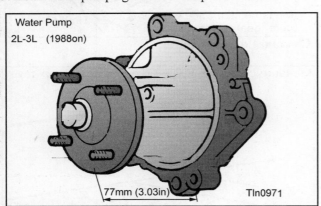

Water Pump
2L-3L (1988on)

77mm (3.03in)   TIn0971

Water Pump Attaching Bolts:230kg-cm, 17ft-lb, 23Nm.

6. Install the crankshaft gear, fuel injection pump gear and idler gears.

Fuel Injection Pump Gear Attaching Bolt

Injector Pump Pulley

Water Pump

TIn058

        650kg-cm, 47ft-lb, 64Nm.

Top Idler Gear Attaching Bolt
        340kg-cm, 25ft-lb, 33Nm.

Lower Idler Gear Attaching Bolts
        195kg-cm, 14ft-lb, 19Nm.

7. Install timing belt, as previously described under timing belt.

8. Install the timing belt cover and bolts, tighten to specification.

Timing Belt Cover Bolts Specified Torque:
        60kg-cm, 4.5ft-lb, 6Nm

9. Install the crankshaft pulley, tighten attaching bolt to specification.

Crankshaft Pulley Attaching Bolt:

L,2L & 2L-T[50's & 60's Series]:
        1,400kg-cm, 101ft-lb, 137Nm

2L & 3L[80's Series on]:
        1,700kg-cm, 123ft-lb, 167Nm

10. Reinstall the fan and clutch if one fitted

11. Install alternator.

(a) Install mounting bracket bolts.

(b) Install adjusting bracket bolt.

(c) Install alternator and wiring loom.

12. Install all belts to their correct tension.

13. Install the radiator.

14. Reinstall the upper radiator hose to the thermostat housing.

15. Fit the transmission oil cooler pipes to the radiator (auto trans).

16. Refill the cooling system after connecting the lower radiator hose.

17. Connect the battery cables.

MAIN BEARINGS.

Each crankshaft main bearing journal has 2 bearing halves or shells which are not the same and not interchangeable in the bearing cap or crankcase. The upper (crankcase) shell is grooved to supply oil to the connecting rod bearing, while the lower (bearing cap) shell is not grooved. The 2 bearing shells must not be interchanged. The No.3. bearing has thrust washers to take end thrust.

The main bearings are of the precision insert type and do not require reaming to size or utilise shims for adjustment.

Standard main bearing shells must be matched with the correct marked block. Identification marks are at the rear of the block on the base of the block, bearing shells are mark also, the number on the shells must be the same as the block, Nos marked "1", "2" or "3" or coloured coded to the mark numbers.

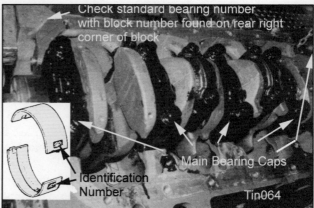

Check standard bearing number with block number found on rear right corner of block

Main Bearing Caps

Identification Number

Tin064

Main Bearing Standard Thickness:
Mark'1'colourBrown1.979-1.983m(0.0779-0.0781in)
Mark"2"colourBlack1.983-1.987m(0.0781-0.0782in)
Mark"3"colourBlue1.987-1.991m(0.0782-0.0784in)

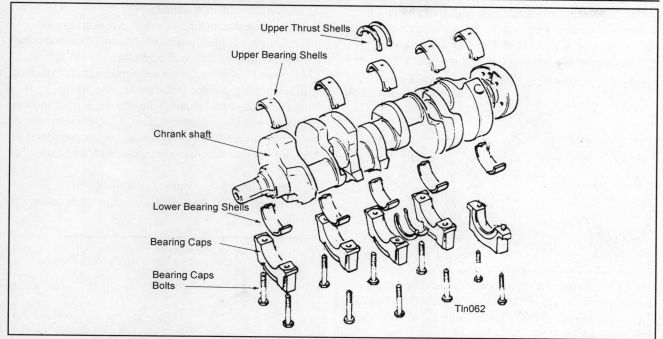

Standard size upper shells are used in the crankcase with 0.25mm undersized or standard size shells in the bearing caps, depending on bearing clearance.

When shells are placed in crankcase and bearing cap, the end extends slightly beyond the parting surfaces so that when cap bolts are tightened, the shells clamp tightly in place to ensure positive seating and to prevent turning.

The ends of the bearing shells must never be filed flush with parting surfaces of crankcase or bearing cap.

Inspection.

1. Disconnect battery earth lead.

2. Remove oil sump as described in OIL PAN (SUMP) AND SEAL section.

3. To remove oil pump, suction pipe and screen refer to OIL PUMP, SUCTION PIPE and SCREEN section for details.

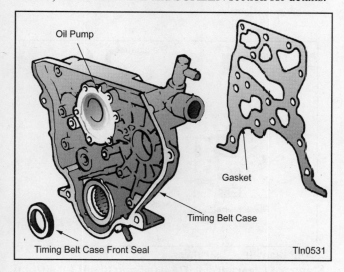

4. Remove main bearing cap bolts from bearing to be

inspected, and remove cap and lower bearing shell.

* Identify bearing caps with punch marks to ensure the same bearing caps are installed to the bearings, also ensure the bearing caps are installed the correct way.

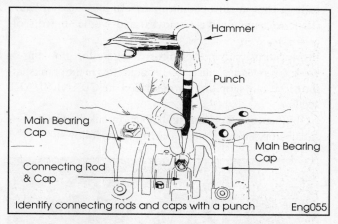

Identify connecting rods and caps with a punch   Eng055

* Tap rear main bearing cap to break cap to crankcase seal to remove. Install slide hammers into cap oil pan bolt holes and remove cap, if necessary.

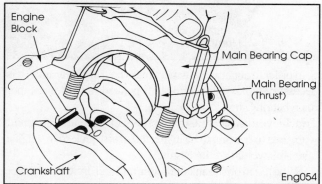

5. Check lower bearing shells and crankshaft journals. If the journal surface is ridged or heavily scored, replace crankshaft, refer to CRANKSHAFT section for details.

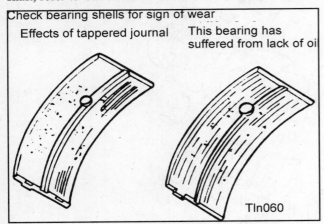

Check bearing shells for sign of wear

Effects of tappered journal — This bearing has suffered from lack of oi

TIn060

To ensure satisfactory engine operation, new bearing shells must be installed as described in MAIN BEARING section and if necessary CONNECTING ROD BEARINGS section.

Inspect inner surface of bearing shells for gouges, wear or embedded foreign material. If foreign material is found, determine its nature and source. Inspect outer surface of bearing shells for surface wear (indicates movement of shell or high spot in surrounding material), looseness, rotation (flattened tangs and wear grooves), and overheating (discoloration).

Inspect thrust surfaces of thrust washers for grooving or wear. Grooves are caused by irregularities in the crankshaft thrust surfaces or dirt as described in CRANKSHAFT section.

If condition of lower bearing shells and crankshaft journals is satisfactory, inspect bearing clearance as follows:

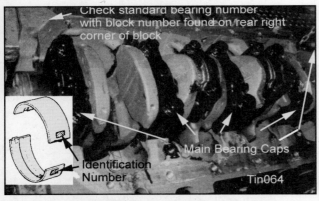

Check standard bearing number with block number found on rear right corner of block

Identification Number

Main Bearing Caps

Tin064

6. In order to accurately inspect main bearing clearance, it is necessary to have the crankshaft pushed toward the upper main bearing shells.

To achieve this, locate a small screw jack beneath crankshaft web, next to bearing to be inspected. Raise jack so that it just takes the weight of the engine.

7. Wipe oil from crankshaft journal and inner and outer surfaces of lower bearing shell.

Install bearing shell in original position in bearing cap.

8. Place a piece of plastigage across full width of crankshaft journal, parallel to crankshaft centreline.

* Make sure plastigage will not seat across oil hole in journal.

9. Install bearing cap and bolts into cylinder block.

* Install bearing caps by loosely installing cap bolts and then lightly tap bearing cap into position, in order to prevent the possibility of cylinder block and or main bearing cap damage.

* Do not pull the bearing cap into place with the bearing cap bolts.

10. Tighten bearing cap bolts as specified.

* Ensure that crankshaft does not rotate with plastigage installed.

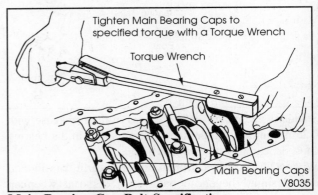

Tighten Main Bearing Caps to specified torque with a Torque Wrench

Torque Wrench

Main Bearing Caps

V8035

Main Bearing Cap Bolt Specification:
1,050kg-cm, 76ft-lb, 103Nm

11. Remove bearing cap bolts and cap. Look for flattened plastigage sticking to either crankshaft or bearing shell in bearing cap.

12. Check bearing clearance by comparing width of flattened plastigage at widest point with graduation on plastigage envelope. The number within the graduation on the envelope indicates the clearance.

Main bearing and crankshaft journal clearance should not exceed specification.

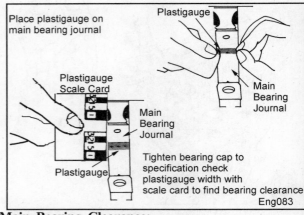

Place plastigauge on main bearing journal

Plastigauge

Plastigauge Scale Card

Main Bearing Journal

Main Bearing Journal

Plastigauge

Tighten bearing cap to specification check plastigauge width with scale card to find bearing clearance

Eng083

Main Bearing Clearance:
Standard Clearance: 0.034-0.065mm (0.0013-0.0026in)
Undersize 0.25&0.50mm:

0.033-0.079mm(0.0013-0.0031in)
Maximum Clearance: **0.10mm (0.0039in)**
* This method of checking main bearing clearance does not give any indication of crankshaft journal taper or out of round. To measure taper, out of round or undersized, the crankshaft must be removed from the cylinder block as described in CRANKSHAFT section.

13. Remove screw jack.

14. It is advisable to install new bearing shells if bearing clearance exceeds specification and recheck clearance as previously described.

* If lower bearing is standard size, install a 0.25 mm undersized shell and check clearance again.

Replace crankshaft as described in "Crankshaft" section if clearance is still not as specified.

Main Bearing Clearance:
Standard Clearance: 0.034-0.065mm (0.0013-0.0026in)
Undersize 0.25&0.50mm:
0.033-0.079mm(0.0013-0.0031in)
Maximum Clearance: **0.10mm (0.0039in)**

15. Make sure that main bearing cap bolt threads and crankcase threads are clean and dry. Apply some engine oil to the cap bolt threads.

* Before final installation of cap bolts, determine if bolts have stretched by comparing with new one. Replace bolt/s as required.

16. With main bearing caps installed (refer to earlier step) install and tighten cap bolts as specified.

* If the thrust bearing washer is disturbed or replaced, coat the surface using Molybdenum Disulphide Grease. It is also necessary to line up the thrust surfaces of the bearing shells before the cap bolts and tightened. To do this, move the crankshaft fore and aft the length of its travel several times (last movement forward) with the thrust bearing cap bolts finger tight.

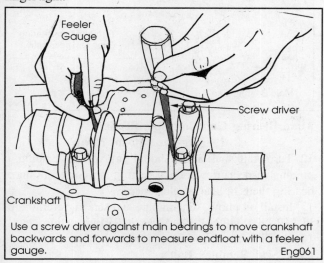

Use a screw driver against main bearings to move crankshaft backwards and forwards to measure endfloat with a feeler gauge.   Eng061

* If rear main bearing cap was removed, clean all sealant from cap and cylinder block matching surfaces. To reseal cylinder block and cap refer to CRANKSHAFT REAR MAIN BEARING OIL SEAL section this is important to stop possible future oil leaks.

Main Bearing Cap Bolt Specification:
1,050kg-cm, 76ft-lb, 103Nm

17. Push crankshaft forward and measure crankshaft end float between front of No.3 main bearing and crankshaft thrust faces using a feeler gauge.

Standard Clearance: 0.040-0.250mm (0.0016-0.0088in)
Maximum Clearance: **0.30mm (0.0118in)**

To replace No3. main bearing thrust washers refer to replacement procedures if clearance is excessive.

* Grooves in thrust washers face away from bearing.

Replacement.
The main bearing shells can be replaced with or without the crankshaft installed.

With Crankshaft Installed.

1. Remove oil pan (sump) from engine.

2. Remove one of the main bearing caps, after bearing shells have been replace, start to work on the next bearing.

3. Remove upper bearing shell as follows:

(a) Install a cotter pin or rivet in the oil hole of the crankshaft journal.

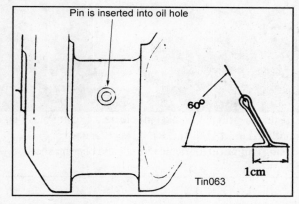

(b) Turn crankshaft anti-clockwise as viewed from front of engine. This will roll upper shell out of crankcase and remove cotter pin.

4. Clean crankshaft journal, crankcase bearing seat and bearing cap thoroughly.

5. Lubricate new selected upper bearing.

6. Insert un-notched end of shell between crankshaft journal and notched side of crankcase.

* Make sure that the correct bearing shell is fitted between the crankcase journal and crankcase.

* Standard main bearing shells must be matched with the correct marked block. Identification marks are at the rear of the block on the base of the block, bearing shells are mark also, the number on the shells must be the same as the block, Nos "1", "2" or "3" or coloured coded to the mark numbers.

Main Bearing Standard Thickness:

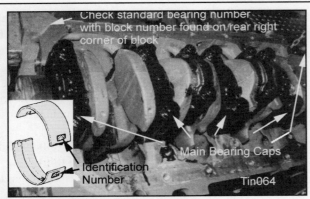

Mark "1"   Brown 1.979-1.983mm(0.0779-0.0781in)
Mark "2"   Black 1.983-1.987mm (0.0781-0.0782in)
Mark "3"   Blue 1.987-1.991mm (0.0782-0.0784in).
Bearing lower shells are not grooved and are either under-sized or standard size.

7. Turn bearing shell into place using crankshaft and cotter pin and then remove pin.

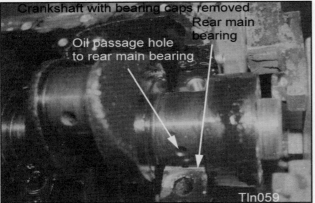

8. Inspect bearing to crankshaft clearance using plastigage as outlined in MAIN BEARING section above.

9. Using engine oil lubricate journal and bearing shells.

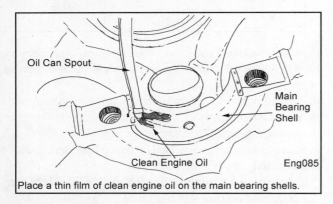

Place a thin film of clean engine oil on the main bearing shells.

* When replacing No.3 main bearing shells, coat thrust washer surfaces with Molybdenum Disulphide grease or equivalent.

10. Make sure that main bearing cap bolt threads and crankcase threads are clean and dry. Apply some engine oil to the cap bolt threads.

* Before final installation of cap bolts, determine if bolts have stretched by comparing with a new bolt. Replace bolts as needed.

11. Install bearing cap and tighten all bearing cap bolts to the

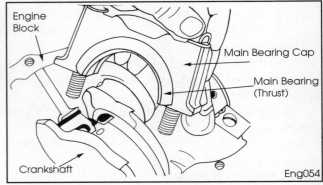

correct specification.

* Make sure that the bearing cap is installed into the crankcase in the correct manner.

* To eliminate the possibility of cylinder block or bearing cap damage, install bearing cap by installing cap bolts loosely and then lightly tap the bearing cap into position using a soft faced hammer. Do not pull the caps into place by using the bearing cap bolts.

* If it has been necessary to remove the rear main bearing cap, clean all sealant from bearing cap and crankcase. Install bearing cap and reseal, refer to CRANKSHAFT REAR MAIN BEARING OIL SEAL section this is important to stop possible future oil leaks.

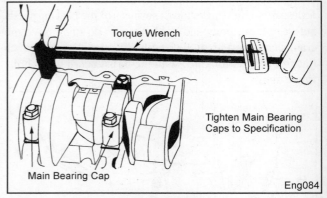

Main Bearing Cap Bolt Specification.
1,050kg-cm, 58ft-lb, 78Nm

12. Turn crankshaft and it should turn without binding. If binding, inspect orientation of bearing cap, correct fitting of bearing shells or bearing clearance.

13. Install oil pump, suction pipe and screen, refer to OIL PUMP, SUCTION PIPE AND SCREEN section.

14. Install rear seal retainer, tighten bolts to specification.
Rear Seal Retainer Bolts:
130kg-cm, 9ft-lb, 13Nm

15. Install engine end plate and flywheel/drive plate, tighten bolts to specification.

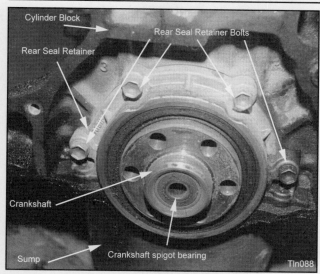

Cylinder Block
Rear Seal Retainer Bolts
Rear Seal Retainer
Crankshaft
Sump
Crankshaft spigot bearing
TIn088

Flywheel/Drive plate Bolt Specification:
[L, 2L & 2L-T 50's & 60's Series]
Flywheel Bolt (Manual Transmission) Specification:
        850kg-cm, 61ft-lb, 83m
Driveplate Bolt (Automatic Transmission) Spec:
        750kg-cm, 54ft-lb, 74Nm
[2L & 3L 80's & 90's Series]
Flywheel Bolt (Manual Transmission) Specification:
        1,250kg-cm, 90ft-lb, 123m
Driveplate (Automatic Transmission) Bolt Spec:
        1.000kg-cm, 72ft-lb, 98Nm

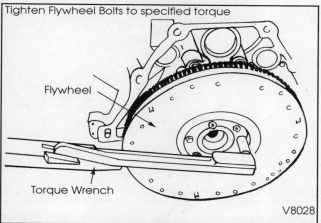

Tighten Flywheel Bolts to specified torque
Flywheel
Torque Wrench
V8028

16. Install oil pan, refer to Oil Pan (Sump) and Seal section.
17. Using the correct amount of engine oil refill the oil pan, refer to LUBRICATION section in this chapter for details.
18. Start engine and inspect for oil leaks, repair as needed. To inspect oil pressure refer CHECKING OIL PRESSURE section in this manual for details.

With Crankshaft Removed.
1. Remove crankshaft refer to CRANKSHAFT section.
2. Remove bearing shells from crankcase and bearing caps.
3. Remove rear main bearing oil seal.
4. Clean crankshaft journals, crankcase bearing seals and

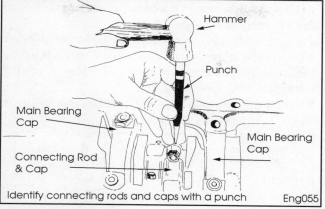

Hammer
Punch
Main Bearing Cap
Connecting Rod & Cap
Main Bearing Cap
Identify connecting rods and caps with a punch   Eng055

bearing caps thoroughly.
5. Install new bearing upper shells in crankcase, making sure notches in bearings line up with recesses in crankcase.
* Standard main bearing shells must be matched with the correct marked block. Identification marks are at the rear of the block on the base of the block, bearing shells are mark also, the number on the shells must be the same as the block, Nos "1", "2" or "3" or coloured coded to the mark numbers.

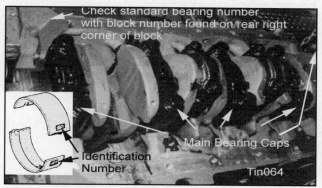

Check standard bearing number with block number found on rear right corner of block
Main Bearing Caps
Identification Number
TIn064

Main Bearing Standard Thickness:
Mark "1"   Brown 1.979-1.983mm(0.0779-0.0781in)
Mark "2"   Black 1.983-1.987mm (0.0781-0.0782in)
Mark "3"   Blue 1.987-1.991mm (0.0782-0.0784in)
* Make sure the bearing shells are fitted into the correct crankcase bearing seat.
All bearing upper shells are grooved.
Bearing lower shells are not grooved and are either 0.25 or 0.50mm undersized or standard size.

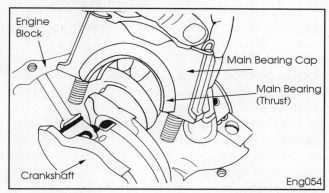

Engine Block
Main Bearing Cap
Main Bearing (Thrust)
Crankshaft
Eng054

6. Using Molybdenum Disulphide grease lubricate No.3 main bearing thrust washer surfaces.

7. Lay crankshaft in upper bearing shells, and install lower bearing shells in bearing caps, making sure the notches in the shells line up with the recesses in the caps and correct bearing is installed in the appropriate cap.

8. Measure bearing to crankshaft clearances as described in MAIN BEARINGS section.

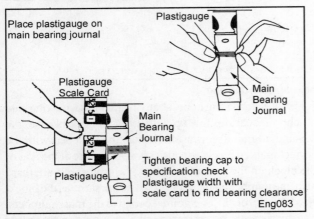

Place plastigauge on main bearing journal
Plastigauge
Plastigauge Scale Card
Main Bearing Journal
Main Bearing Journal
Plastigauge
Tighten bearing cap to specification check plastigauge width with scale card to find bearing clearance
Eng083

* Make sure that bearing cap is installed into the crankcase in the appropriate way.
* In order to prevent the possibility of cylinder block and or bearing cap damage, install bearing cap by installing cap bolts loosely, and then tapping into position using a soft faced hammer.

DO NOT USE THE CAP BOLTS TO PULL THE CAP INTO PLACE.

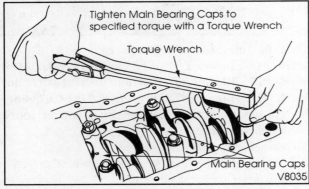

Tighten Main Bearing Caps to specified torque with a Torque Wrench
Torque Wrench
Main Bearing Caps
V8035

9. If clearances are satisfactory, continue assembly of crankshaft, refer to CRANKSHAFT section for installation details.

CONNECTING ROD BEARINGS

Each connecting rod bearing consists of 2 bearing halves or shells which are interchangeable in the rod and cap.

When the shells are in place, the ends extend slightly beyond the parting surfaces of the rod and cap. When the rod bolts are tightened, the shells are tightly clamped in place to ensure positive seating and to prevent rotation.

The connecting rod bearings are of the precision insert type

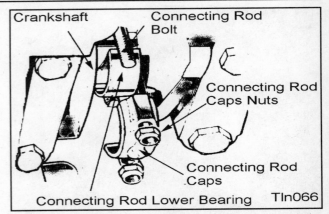

Crankshaft   Connecting Rod Bolt
Connecting Rod Caps Nuts
Connecting Rod Caps
Connecting Rod Lower Bearing   TIn066

and do not use shims for adjustment. The ends of the bearing shells must never be filed flush with parting surface of rod or cap.

Inspection and Replacement.
Connecting rod bearings can be replaced without removing the rod and piston assembly from the engine.

1. Disconnect battery earth lead and remove spark plugs.
2. To remove oil pan (Sump) refer to OIL PAN (SUMP) AND SEAL section for details.
3. To remove oil pump suction pipe and screen refer to OIL PUMP, SUCTION PIPE AND SCREEN section.
4. Using an etching marker or felt tipped pen, mark connecting rods and caps to indicate cylinder number and orientation of cap.

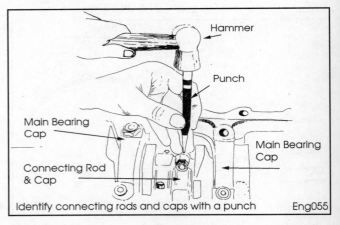

Hammer
Punch
Main Bearing Cap
Main Bearing Cap
Connecting Rod & Cap
Identify connecting rods and caps with a punch   Eng055

5. Remove connecting rod cap securing bolts and remove cap and lower bearing shell.
6. Push piston and connecting rod up cylinder bore, so that connecting rod is free from crankshaft journal. Remove bearing shell from connecting rod.
7. Clean crankshaft journal and measure for out of round or taper using a micrometer. Replace crankshaft, if not as specified in CRANKSHAFT section.

Crankshaft connecting rod Bearing Journal diameter
Standard Diameter:
L & 2L   52.988-53.000mm(2.0861-2.0866in)
2L-T & 3L   54.988-55.000mm(2.1649-2.1654in)
Under Size 0.25mm:

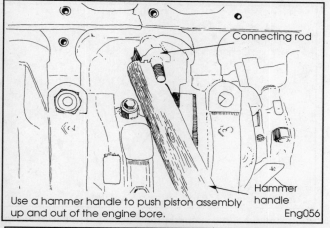

Use a hammer handle to push piston assembly up and out of the engine bore.

Eng056

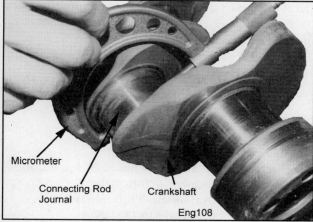

Micrometer

Connecting Rod Journal

Crankshaft

Eng108

L & 2L   52.745-52.755mm(2.0766-2.0770in)
2L-T & 3L   54.745-54.755mm(2.1553-2.1557in)

Under Size 0.50mm:
L & 2L   52.495-52.505mm(2.0667-2.0671in)
2L-T & 3L   54.495-54.505mm(2.1455-2.1459in)

Maximum Out of Round   .02mm (0.0008in)
Maximum Taper   .02mm (0.0008in)

8. Wipe oil from both inner and outer surfaces of bearing shells.

9. Inspect inner surface of bearing shells for gouges, wear or embedded foreign matter.

If foreign matter is found, determine its nature and source. Inspect outer surface of bearing shell for surface wear

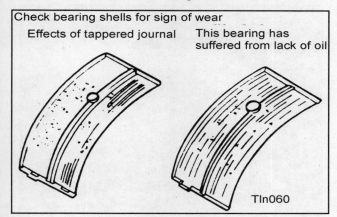

Check bearing shells for sign of wear

Effects of tappered journal   This bearing has suffered from lack of oil

TIn060

(indicates movement of shell or high spot in surrounding material), looseness or turning (flattened tangs and wear grooves), or overheating (discoloration).

The crankshaft may be bent or have tapered bearing journals if uneven side to side wear is found. If needed, remove crankshaft, refer to CRANKSHAFT section and inspect crankshaft for bend or journal taper.

* Bearing failure, other than normal wear, must be examined carefully.

10. Install bearing shells in original positions in connecting rod and cap if inspection reveals that crankshaft is OK.

11. Pull connecting rod down onto crankshaft so that upper bearing is seated against crankshaft journal.

12. Place a piece of plastigage across width of bearing journal, parallel to crankshaft centreline.

* Make sure plastigage is not placed across oil hole in journal.

13. Install connecting rod cap in original position as described in step 4. Tighten bolts as specified.

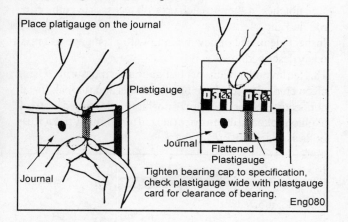

Place platigauge on the journal

Plastigauge

Journal

Journal   Flattened Plastigauge

Journal

Tighten bearing cap to specification, check plastigauge wide with plastgauge card for clearance of bearing.

Eng080

* Make sure that crankshaft does not rotate with plastigage installed.

Connecting Rod Cap Bolt Specification:
600kg-cm, 43ft-lb, 59Nm

14. Remove connecting rod cap bolts, and cap. Inspect for flattened plastigage sticking to either crankshaft or bearing shell in cap.

15. Determine bearing clearance by comparing width of flattened plastigage at widest point with graduation on plastigage envelope. The number within the graduation on the envelope indicates the clearance.

Clearance between connecting rod bearings and crankshaft should not exceed specification.

* Standard connecting rod bearing shells must be matched with the correct marked bearing cap. Identification marks on the connecting rod bearing cap, bearing shells are mark also, the number on the shells must be the same as the block, Nos "1", "2" or "3".

Connecting Rod Bearing Standard bearing thickness:
Mark "1"   1.478-1.482mm (0.0582-0.0583in)
Mark "2"   1.482-1.486mm (0.0583-0.0585in)
Mark "3"   1.486-1.490mm (0.0585-0.0587in)

* If a bearing is being fitted to an out of round journal, ensure to fit plastigage to the maximum diameter of the journal. If the bearing is fitted to the minimum diameter, and the journal is out of round 0.02mm, interference between the bearing journal and journal will result in rapid bearing failure.

Connecting Rod Bearing Clearance:
Standard Clearance: 0.036-0.064mm (0.0014-0.0025in)
Under Size 0.25mm:
L & 2L   0.023-0.073mm (0.0009-0.0029in)
2L-T & 3L   0.033-0.079mm (0.0013-0.0031in)
Maximum Clearance: 0.10mm (0.0039in)

16. Make sure that connecting rod cap bolt threads and connecting rod threads are clean and dry. Apply some engine oil to the cap bolt threads.

* Before final installation of cap bolts, determine if bolts have stretched by comparing with a new bolt. Replace bolt/s as needed.

17. Install bearing shells in connecting rod and cap making sure notches in shells match up with recesses in connecting rod and cap.

Inspect clearance of new bearing with plastigage as previously described.

18. Remove all remains of plastigage after measuring. Using clean engine oil lubricate bearing shells and journal. Install connecting rod cap in original position as described in step 4. Tighten bolts and then loosen one full turn. Finally tighten cap bolts as specified.

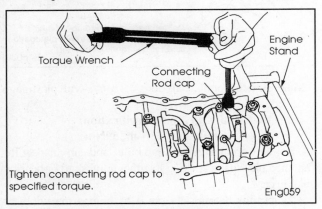

Tighten connecting rod cap to specified torque.

Eng059

Connecting Rod Cap Bolt Specification:
600kg-cm, 43ft-lb, 59Nm

19. With bearing shells installed and cap bolts tightened, it should be possible to move connecting rod backwards and forwards on crankshaft journal as allowed by end clearance. Also, the crankshaft should turn without binding.

Connecting Rod to crankshaft end clearance:
Standard Clearance: 0.080-0.300mm (0.0031-0.0118in)
Maximum Clearance: 0.35mm (0.0138in)

If connecting rod binds on crankshaft journal, loosen and retighten bearing cap bolts.

If rod still cannot be moved or crankshaft binds, inspect bearing cap to rod orientation, bearing clearance or connecting rod alignment.

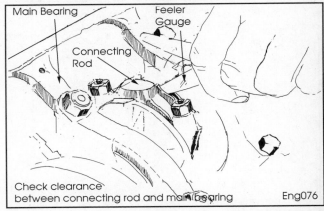

Check clearance between connecting rod and main bearing

Eng076

20. Install oil pump suction pipe and screen as described in OIL PUMP, SUCTION PIPE AND SCREEN section.

21. To install oil pan refer to OIL PAN (Sump) section in this manual for details.

22. Install rear seal retainer, tighten bolts to specification.

Rear Seal Retainer Bolts:
130kg-cm, 9ft-lb, 13Nm

23. Install engine end plate and flywheel/drive plate, tighten bolts to specification.

Flywheel/Drive plate Bolt Specification:
[L, 2L & 2L-T 50's & 60's Series]
Flywheel Bolt (Manual Transmission) Specification:
850kg-cm, 61ft-lb, 83m
Driveplate Bolt (Automatic Transmission) Spec:
750kg-cm, 54ft-lb, 74Nm
[2L & 3L 80's & 90's Series]
Flywheel Bolt (Manual Transmission) Specification:
1,250kg-cm, 90ft-lb, 123m
Driveplate (Automatic Transmission) Bolt Spec:
1.000kg-cm, 72ft-lb, 98Nm

24. Install spark plugs and tighten as specified.

Spark Plug Specification:
200kg-cm, 15ft-lb, 20Nm

25. Using the correct amount of engine oil, refill the oil pan, refer to LUBRICATION section for details.

26. Start engine and inspect for oil leaks, repair as needed, also inspect engine oil pressure as described in CHECKING OIL PRESSURE section.

Tin088

PISTON & CONNECTING ROD ASSEMBLY

Piston and connecting rod assemblies can be removed while the engine remains in the vehicle.

If the cylinder bore requires machining, remove the engine assembly as described in ENGINE ASSEMBLY section, remove piston and connecting rod, replace pistons and rings in oversize sets.

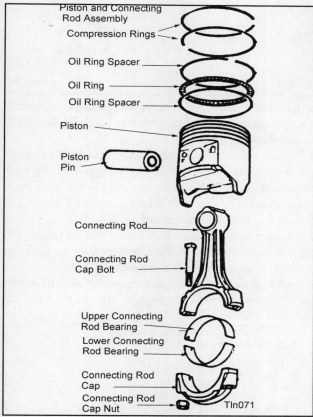

Tln071

Both piston and cylinder bore condition must be considered together when fitting new pistons. Production and service pistons have the same nominal weight and can be intermixed without affecting engine balance. If needed, used pistons may be fitted selectively to any cylinder of the engine, providing they are in good condition.

Piston pin assemblies and ring sets are available in oversize.

Remove

1. Disconnect battery earth lead.

2. Remove cylinder head as described in Cylinder Head

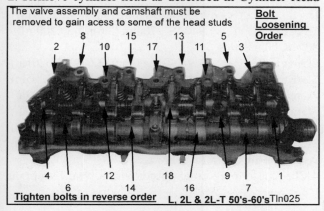

The valve assembly and camshaft must be removed to gain acess to some of the head studs

Bolt Loosening Order

Tighten bolts in reverse order   L, 2L & 2L-T 50's-60's Tln025

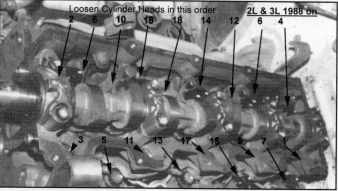

Loosen Cylinder Heads in this order   2L & 3L 1988 on

section.

3. To remove oil pan refer to OIL PAN (SUMP) section

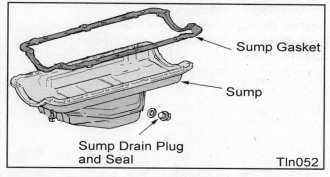

Sump Gasket

Sump

Sump Drain Plug and Seal   Tln052

4. Remove oil pump suction pipe and screen refer to OIL PUMP, SUCTION PIPE AND SCREEN section.

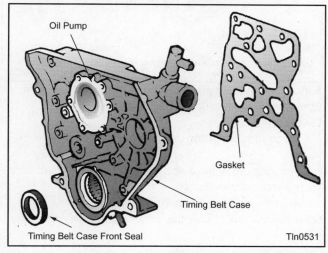

Oil Pump

Gasket

Timing Belt Case

Timing Belt Case Front Seal   Tln0531

5. Inspect cylinder bores above piston ring travel. If bores are worn so that a ridge or similar exists.

Turn crankshaft so that piston is at bottom of stroke and cover piston with a cloth to collect cuttings.

Remove the ridge with a ridge remover, this is to be done for each cylinder.

6. Using an etching marker or felt tipped pen, mark all connecting rods, caps and pistons to indicate cylinder identification.

7. Remove rod assemblies and piston as follows,

(a) With connecting rod crankshaft journal straight down

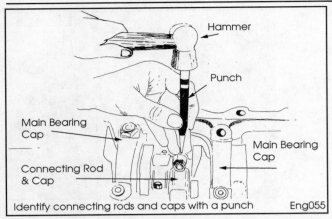

Identify connecting rods and caps with a punch   Eng055

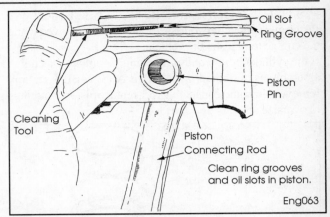

Clean ring grooves and oil slots in piston.   Eng063

(Bottom Dead Centre), remove connecting rod cap bolts and remove cap with bearing shell.

(b) Push piston and connecting rod from cylinder using a long guide. Remove guides and install cap and bolts to connecting rod.

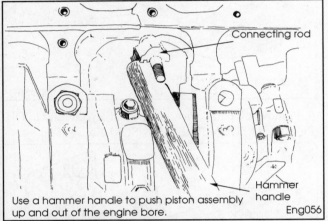

Use a hammer handle to push piston assembly up and out of the engine bore.   Eng056

8. Remove all other piston and connecting rod assemblies using the same procedure.

Dismantle.

1. Expand and slide piston rings off to remove and dispose of them.

* Worn rings may have sharp edges ensure to take care when removing piston rings.

2. Piston pin can now be removed as follows:

(a) Install remover guide into base, and put assembly in a press.

(b) Install mandrel, onto piston pin.

(c) Using care to locate piston on support and base, press piston pin out of connecting rod.

(d) Remove assembly from press. Remove pin from support and remove mandrel from piston and connecting rod.

Inspection.

1. Thoroughly clean carbon from piston heads and from ring grooves using a suitable tool and remove any gum or varnish from piston skirts using a suitable cleaning solvent.

2. Check cylinder walls for ridges, roughness or scoring which indicates excessive wear. Inspect cylinder bores for taper and out-of-round using an accurate cylinder gauge at top, middle and bottom of bore, both parallel and at right angles to centreline of engine. Refer to CYLINDER BLOCK section for details.

3. Examine piston skirt thoroughly for scored or rough surfaces, cracks in skirt or crown, chipping, broken ring lands or uneven wear which would cause rings to seat improperly or have excessive clearance in ring grooves. Pistons should be replaced if faulty or damaged.

Pistons are cam ground, which means that the diameter at right angles to the piston pin is greater than the diameter parallel to the piston pin. When a piston is checked for size, it must be done at points 90° to the piston bore. 80's & 90's Series pistons have an identification mark on the top of the piston "1", "2" or "3".

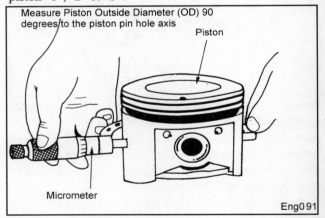

Eng091

Piston Size Standard:

50's & 60's Series

L	89.955-89.985mm (3.5415-3.5427in)
2L & 2L-T	91.940-91.970mm (3.6197-3.6209in)

80's & 90's Series

2L mark "1"	91.940-91.950mm (3.6197-3.6201in)
2L mark "2"	91.950-91.960mm (3.6201-3.6205in)
2L mark "3"	91.960-91.970mm (3.6205-3.6209in)
3L mark "1"	95.940-95.950mm (3.7772-3.7776in)
3L mark "2"	95.950-95.960mm (3.7776-3.7779in)
3L mark "3"	95.960-95.970mm (3.7779-3.7783in)

Available in 0.50mm oversize

4. Check piston pin bores and piston pins for wear. Piston pins

and piston pin bores must be free of scuffing or varnish when being measured. Use a micrometer to measure the piston pin, and a dial bore gauge or an inside micrometer to measure piston pin bore.

Piston and pin should be replaced if not as specified.

Piston Pin Clearance:
                    0.004-0.012mm (0.0002-0.0005in)
Maximum Limit   0.05mm (0.002in)

5. Remove bearing shells from connecting rod, install cap and bolts. Tighten bolts as specified.

Connecting Rod Cap Bolt Specification:
           600kg-cm, 43ft-lb, 59Nm

6. Place connecting rod assembly on a checking fixture and inspect rod for twist or bend.

Replace if twisted or bent, do not attempt to straighten rod. Inspect new connecting rods using the same procedure before using them.

Connecting Rod Alignment Max. Specification
    Bend   0.05mm per 100mm, 0.0020in per 4.0in
    Twist   0.15mm per 100mm, 0.0060in per 4.0in

7. Check outside of connecting rod bearing shells and internal diameter of connecting rod big end for wear indicating high spots in the rod big end.

8. Remove cap bolts and inspect bolts for stretching by comparing them with a new bolt, if stretched, replace.

Assembly and Installation.

1. Using engine oil, lubricate piston pin and piston pin bore.
2. Install piston pin on mandrel.
3. Assemble installer guide and piston support to base.
4. Using temperature indicating crayon, heat connecting rod to 60-70°C.

* Support rod as illustrated. The fire brick prevents excessive heat loss. If the small end is laid flat on the hotplate, heat flow is more even and rapid.

5. The colour of the heat crayon will turn black when the temperature is reached (60-70°C).
6. Using a heat proof glove, pick up connecting rod.
7. Quickly install piston and connecting rod over guide.
8. Quickly push piston pin into place with a mandrel, until piston pin bottoms.

* You may need an assistant to help, by holding the parts as the piston pin should be installed within 3-4 seconds once connecting rod has been removed. After 4 seconds, the pin will jam in the connecting rod, requiring the use of a hydraulic press.

9. To install piston rings refer to PISTON RINGS section.
10. Make sure connecting rod bearing shells, pistons, cylinder bores and crankshaft journals are totally clean, then, using clean engine oil, coat cylinder bores and all bearing surfaces.
11. Position the crankpin straight down before installation of a piston and rod assembly in its bore.
12. Remove cap, and with bearing upper shell seated in connecting rod, install the 'short' guide tool into inner bolt hole. Install 'long' guide tool into the other bolt hole.

Guides hold upper bearing shell in place and protects crankshaft journal from damage during installation of connecting rod and piston assembly.

13. Make sure piston ring gaps are separated as described in PISTON RINGS section.

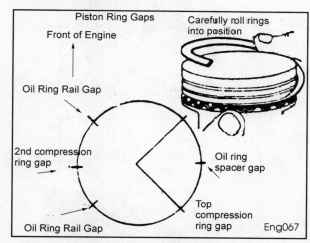

14. Using clean engine oil, lubricate piston and rings and cylinder bore. With a suitable ring compressor, compress

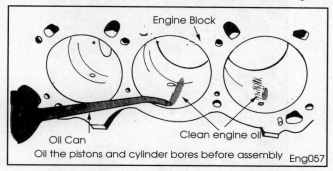

rings. Install each piston and connecting rod assembly into its cylinder bore.

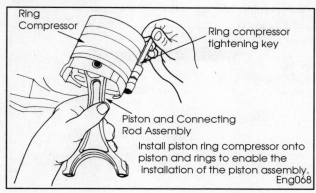

15. Lightly tap piston into its bore, using a hammer handle, while holding ring compressor firmly against cylinder block until all piston rings have entered bore.
16. Push piston down bore until connecting rod seats against crankshaft journal.
17. Remove connecting rod guides. Install bearing cap and

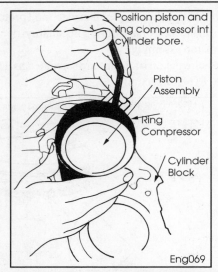

Position piston and ring compressor int cylinder bore.

Piston Assembly

Ring Compressor

Cylinder Block

Eng069

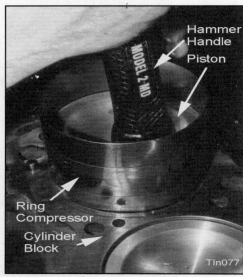

Hammer Handle

Piston

MODEL 2 M.D

Ring Compressor

Cylinder Block

Tln077

lower bearing shell assembly. Install cap bolts and tighten and then loosen one full turn. Then tighten again as specified.

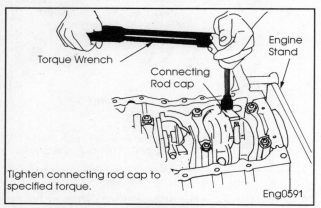

Torque Wrench

Connecting Rod cap

Engine Stand

Tighten connecting rod cap to specified torque.

Eng0591

Connecting Rod Cap Bolt Specification:
600kg-cm, 43ft-lb, 59Nm

18. Turn crankshaft to make sure crankshaft and connecting rod can move freely. If crankshaft binds, check bearing cap to rod orientation again and bearing clearance or connecting rod alignment.

19. Measure side clearance between crankshaft journal and connecting rod.

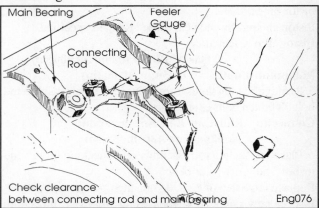

Main Bearing

Feeler Gauge

Connecting Rod

Check clearance between connecting rod and main bearing

Eng076

Connecting Rod to crankshaft end clearance:
Standard Clearance: 0.080-0.300mm (0.0031-0.0118in)
Maximum Clearance: 0.35mm (0.0138in)

If side clearance is not as specified, to check bearing clearance refer to CONNECTING ROD BEARING section, or connecting rod alignment.

20. Install remaining piston and connecting rod assemblies using the same procedure.

21. To install cylinder head refer to CYLINDER HEAD section, and to install oil pump, suction pipe and screen refer to OIL PUMP, SUCTION PIPE section.

22. To install oil pan refer to OIL PAN section in this manual.

23. Start engine and inspect for oil leaks, Repair as needed.

PISTON RINGS.

Install

* The pistons have three rings (two compression rings and one oil ring). The top ring is a molybdenum filled, balanced

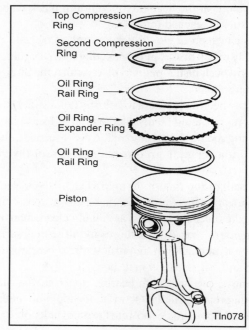

Top Compression Ring

Second Compression Ring

Oil Ring Rail Ring

Oil Ring Expander Ring

Oil Ring Rail Ring

Piston

Tln078

section, barrel lapped type. The second ring is an inverted torsional taper faced type. The oil ring is of three piece design, comprising two segments and a spacer.

1. Using a set of rings comparable in size to the piston being used install compression ring in relevant cylinder bore, then using the head of a piston, press ring down into the bore.

* Using a piston in this manner will place ring square with cylinder wall.

* Ensure not to distort the ring during this operation, or it may bind in the piston ring groove. Fit each ring separately to the cylinder in which it is going to be installed.

2. Using a feeler gauge, measure gap between ends of ring.

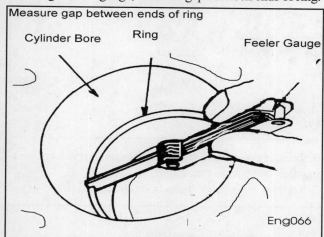

Measure gap between ends of ring

Cylinder Bore   Ring   Feeler Gauge

Eng066

Top Compression Ring End Gap Specification:
L   0.30-0.57mm, 0.0118-0.0224in
2L,2L-T & 3L   0.35-0.62mm, 0.0138-0.0244in
Maximum 1.30mm, 0.051in

Remove ring and try another, if the gap between the ends of a compression ring is below specification. The ring gap may be enlarged by filing.

Second Compression Ring End Gap Specification:
L   0.20-0.52mm, 0.0079-0.0205in
2L,2L-T & 3L   0.30-0.47mm, 0.0118-0.0185in
Maximum 1.07mm, 0.0421in

3. Inspect gap between ends of each oil control ring segment.

Oil Ring Steel Rail Gap Specification:
L   0.20-0.52mm, 0.0079-0.0205in
2L,2L-T & 3L   0.20-0.52mm, 0.0079-0.0205in
Maximum 1.12mm, 0.044in

4. Carefully remove all traces of carbon from ring grooves in piston and check grooves for any chips or burrs that might cause ring to bind when fitting. Use a ring gap cleaning tool or if you take care you can use a broken ring.

5. Slip outer surface of each compression ring in respective piston ring groove and roll ring entirely around groove to ensure that ring is free. Also measure ring to piston groove side clearance.

Piston Ring Side Clearance:
        0.025 - 0.070mm, 0.0010 - 0.0028n

Try another ring if it is too tight. If no ring can be found that

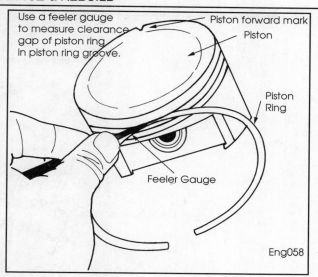

Use a feeler gauge to measure clearance gap of piston ring in piston ring groove.

Piston forward mark
Piston
Piston Ring
Feeler Gauge

Eng058

fits the specification, the ring may be ground to size using emery paper placed on a piece of glass.

If using a new piston, try another piston.

* High spots in the ring groove may be cleaned up with careful use of a fine file, do not try to cut the piston ring groove.

6. Install oil ring spacer in bottom piston ring groove.

* The ends of the spacer butt against each other.

7. Install one steel segment from top of piston downward into oil ring groove and install remaining steel segment from bottom of piston skirt upwards into the oil ring groove.

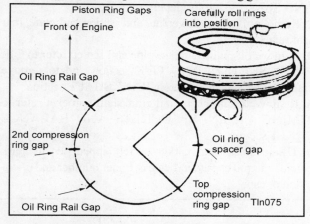

Piston Ring Gaps
Front of Engine
Carefully roll rings into position
Oil Ring Rail Gap
2nd compression ring gap
Oil ring spacer gap
Oil Ring Rail Gap
Top compression ring gap
Tln075

8. Install compression rings in first and second grooves of each piston.

* Make sure the correct compression ring are installed in the first and second grooves, and the correct way up.

9. Do a final test of ring fit in piston grooves. Separate ends as illustrated.

* Do not install piston with ring gaps in line, as this will allow compression leakage at this point.

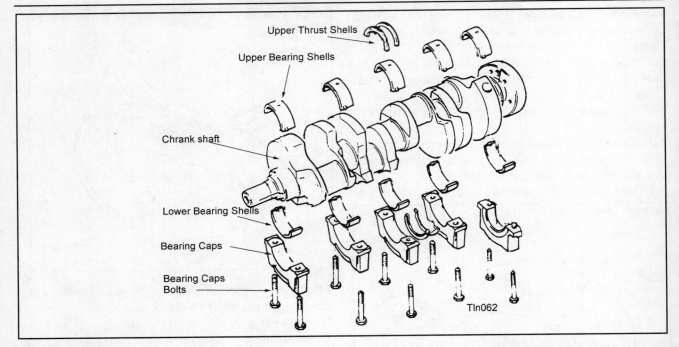

Upper Thrust Shells
Upper Bearing Shells
Chrank shaft
Lower Bearing Shells
Bearing Caps
Bearing Caps Bolts
TIn062

CRANKSHAFT.

Remove

* To check bearing clearance before removing crankshaft from crankcase refer to CONNECTING ROD BEARINGS and MAIN BEARING section for details.

1. When engine is removed from vehicle and mounted in a suitable stand, remove oil pan, refer to OIL PAN (SUMP) AND SEAL section for details.

2. Remove flywheel/driveplate and engine end plate, rear seal retainer.

3. Remove oil pump, suction pipe and screen refer to OIL PUMP, SUCTION AND PIPE section and to remove crankshaft balancer refer to CRANKSHAFT section.

4. Remove timing chain and crankshaft sprocket refer to TIMING CHAIN, SPROCKETS AND BALANCE SHAFT section.

5. Using an etching marker or felt tipped pen to mark connecting rod caps to indicate cylinder number and orientation of cap.

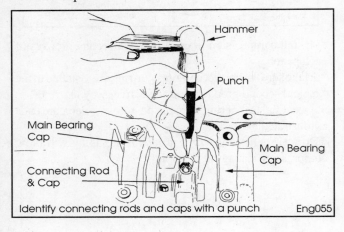

Hammer
Punch
Main Bearing Cap
Connecting Rod & Cap
Main Bearing Cap
Identify connecting rods and caps with a punch   Eng055

6. Remove connecting rod caps and bolts and push connecting rods away from crankshaft.

7. Remove main bearing cap bolts and caps.

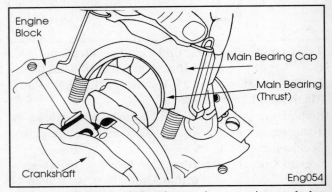

Engine Block
Main Bearing Cap
Main Bearing (Thrust)
Crankshaft   Eng054

* Remove the rear main bearing cap by removing cap bolts, and using a soft faced hammer tap the cap to break cap to crankcase seal. Install side hammers into cap oil pan bolt holes and remove cap.

8. Lift crankshaft from cylinder block.

9. Remove key from front end of crankshaft, if needed, using a suitable punch and hammer.

Inspection.

1. Using a suitable cleaning solvent, wash crankshaft and dry with compressed air.

2. Check crankshaft oil passages for obstructions.

3. Check all bearing journals and thrust surfaces for:

(a) Gouges

(b) Overheating (Discoloration)

(c) Cracks

(d) Grooving

(e) Chips

(f) Roughness

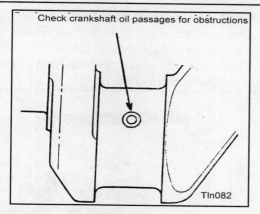
Check crankshaft oil passages for obstructions

TIn082

The crankshaft must be machined or replaced if it has any burned spots, cracks or sever gouging. Slight roughness may be removed using a fine polishing cloth soaked in clean engine oil. Burrs may also be removed using a fine oil stone.

4. Check connecting rod and main bearing shells for embedded foreign material and determine its source.

5. Using a micrometer measure bearing journals for taper, excessive wear or out-of-round.

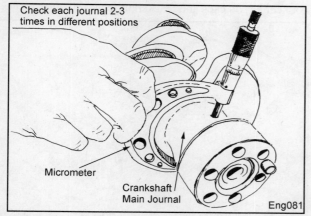
Check each journal 2-3 times in different positions

Micrometer

Crankshaft Main Journal

Eng081

Main Bearing Journal Diameter
Standard Size: **61.985-62.000mm (2.4403-2.4409in)**
Available in 0.25 & 0.50mm undersizer with 0.005mm tolerance
Ovality   **0.02mm, 0.0008in max.**
Out-Of-Round   **0.02mm, 0.0008in max.**

Crankshaft Connecting Rod bearing journal diameter
Standard Diameter:
L & 2L   52.988-53.000mm(2.0861-2.0866in)
2L-T & 3L   54.988-55.000mm(2.1649-2.1654in)
Under Size 0.25mm:
L & 2L   52.745-52.755mm(2.0766-2.0770in)
2L-T & 3L   54.745-54.755mm(2.1553-2.1557in)
Under Size 0.50mm:
L & 2L   52.495-52.505mm(2.0667-2.0671in)
2L-T & 3L   54.495-54.505mm(2.1455-2.1459in)
Maximum Out of Round   **.02mm (0.0008in)**
Maximum Taper   **.02mm (0.0008in)**

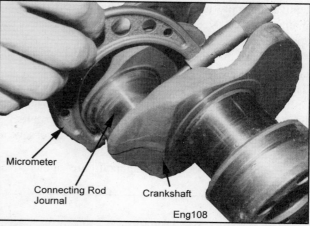
Micrometer

Connecting Rod Journal

Crankshaft

Eng108

6. Inspect crankshaft for run-out by supporting front and rear main bearing journals in 'V' blocks and checking journals with a dial gauge.

Crankshaft Runout Specification 0.1mm 0.0024in max.

7. Place a dial gauge indicator at crankshaft rear flange and inspect rear flange runout. During this inspection, make sure that crankshaft is thrust forward on 'V' blocks so that there is no possibility of crankshaft end float affecting dial gauge reading.

Crankshaft Rear Flange Runout: 0.05mm, 0.0020in.

8. If not as specified, replace crankshaft.

9. Ensure all traces of sealant are cleaned from rear main bearing cap and crankcase.

Installation.

1. To replace rear main bearing oil seal refer to CRANKSHAFT REAR MAIN BEARING OIL SEAL section.

Crankshaft with bearing caps removed

Rear main bearing

Oil passage hole to rear main bearing

TIn059

2. Inspect main bearing clearance, if needed, refer to MAIN BEARINGS section for details.

3. Using a clean engine oil lubricate all crankshaft journals and main bearing upper shells in crankcase.

4. Sit crankshaft in place in main bearing upper shells in crankcase. Ensure not to damage crank shaft thrust washers at No.3 main bearing. Also ensure not to contact connecting rod journals with connecting rod and install main bearing caps.

* Using a thin film of Loctite 515 Gasket Eliminator or

equivalent apply to rear main bearing cap to crankcase mating surface. Keep sealant out of bolt holes and use sparingly.

* Make sure that the bearing caps are installed onto the crankcase in the correct manner.
Tighten the bolts finger tight.

5. It will be necessary to line up thrust washers with No.3 bearing shells, before tightening main bearing cap bolts.
Move crankshaft fore and aft the length of its travel several times (last movement forward) to do this.

6. Ensure all main bearing cap bolts are tightened as specified.

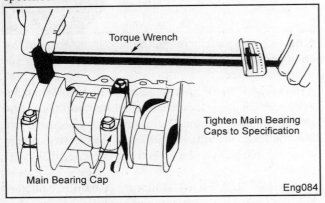

Torque Wrench

Tighten Main Bearing Caps to Specification

Main Bearing Cap

Eng084

Main Bearing Cap Bolt Specification
1,050kg-cm, 76ft-lb, 103Nm

7. Use a feeler gauge to measure crankshaft end float between front of No.3 main bearing thrust washer and crankshaft thrust faces, you will need to force crankshaft forward to do this.

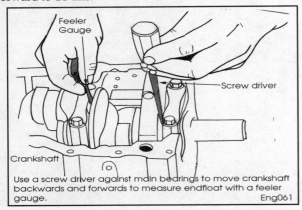

Feeler Gauge

Screw driver

Crankshaft

Use a screw driver against main bedrings to move crankshaft backwards and forwards to measure endfloat with a feeler gauge.

Eng061

Crankshaft End Float Specification   0.04-0.25 mm
Wear Limit   0.30mm

Replace No.3 main bearing thrust washers if clearance is excessive.

8. Using RTV1080 sealant or equivalent, inject into rear main bearing cap side grooves. Continue to inject sealant until you can see sealant at joint gaps.

9. Pull connecting rods up to crankshaft journals, using guide pin tools.

10. Inspect connecting rod bearing clearances, if needed,

refer to "Connecting rod bearing" section for details.

11. Lubricate crankshaft connecting rod journals and bearings, install connecting rod caps and bolts.

12. Tighten connecting rod cap bolts and then loosen one full turn. Tighten bolts as specified.

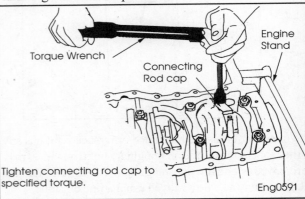

Torque Wrench

Engine Stand

Connecting Rod cap

Tighten connecting rod cap to specified torque.

Eng0591

Connecting Rod Cap Bolt Specification:
600kg-cm, 43ft-lb, 59Nm

13. Using a feeler gauge, measure clearance between connecting rod caps and crankshaft journal flanges.

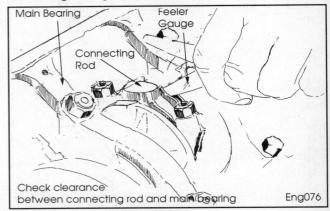

Main Bearing

Feeler Gauge

Connecting Rod

Check clearance between connecting rod and main bearing

Eng076

Connecting Rod Side Clearance:
Connecting Rod to crankshaft end clearance:
Standard Clearance: 0.080-0.300mm (0.0031-0.0118in)
Maximum Clearance: 0.35mm (0.0138in)

14. Turn crankshaft to make sure crankshaft and connecting rods have free movement. Inspect orientation of bearing caps, correct fitting of bearing caps (mains and connecting rods) or fitting of bearing shells or bearing clearance, if crankshaft binds.

15. Install key to front end of crankshaft if required.

16. Install flywheel/driveplate to crankshaft and tighten bolts as specified.

* The bolt holes are unevenly spaced so they can only be installed with the flywheel/driveplate in the correct position.

Flywheel/Drive plate Bolt Specification:
[L, 2L & 2L-T 50's & 60's Series]
Flywheel Bolt (Manual Transmission) Specification:
850kg-cm, 61ft-lb, 83m
Driveplate Bolt (Automatic Transmission) Spec:

750kg-cm, 54ft-lb, 74Nm
[2L & 3L 80's Series on]
Flywheel Bolt (Manual Transmission) Specification:
 1,250kg-cm, 90ft-lb, 123m
Driveplate (Automatic Transmission) Bolt Spec:
 1.000kg-cm, 72ft-lb, 98Nm

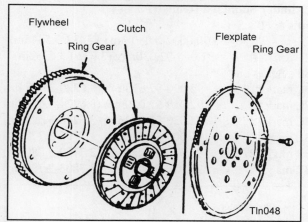

Tln048

17. To install crankshaft sprocket, timing chain, and front cover refer to "Timing chain, Sprockets & shaft gears "section for details and to install crankshaft balancer refer to Crankshaft balancer section.

18. Install spark plugs and tighten as specified.

Spark Plug Torque Specification
 200kg-cm, 15ft-lb, 20Nm

19. To install oil pump suction pipe and screen refer to "Oil pump suction pipe and screen" section and to install oil pan refer to "Oil pan (Sump) and gasket" section.

REAR MAIN OIL SEAL
Replace

1. Disconnect battery earth lead.

2. Remove transmission, as described under "Manual transmission" and "Automatic Transmission" in this manual.

3. Remove flywheel/driveplate, as described in "Flywheel/driveplate" in this manual.

4. Remove the end plate from the rear of the block.

Two Methods can be used:

 (1) With oil seal retainer assembled to block.

 (11) With oil seal retainer removed from block.

 (1) With oil seal retainer assembled to block.

a. Locate a piece of shim brass between seal lips and crankshaft. This is necessary so as to protect crankshaft seal surface.

b. Using a suitable lever, pry out seal, levering against shim brass strip and remove seal.

c. Check seal recess in cylinder block and rear bearing cap for nicks or burrs and correct as required.

d. Inspect crankshaft seal surface for nicks, burrs or damage. Repair or replace crankshaft as required.

e. Apply engine oil to new seal inner and outer surfaces.

** : Before continuing with step f, the crankshaft must be in

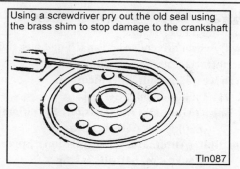

Using a screwdriver pry out the old seal using the brass shim to stop damage to the crankshaft

Tln087

the fully rearward position before installing the new seal. To achieve this, either pull on special tool or push on crankshaft balancer. Ensure that crankshaft is held in this position while installing seal.

f. Install the seal into the correct position, use a seal insertion tool to tap home the seal with a light hammer.

Should the seal be installed further than required, the oil return slot in the rear main bearing cap would be cut off and this would result in an overloading of the seals lip capability and cause oil leakage.

(11) With oil seal retainer removed from block.

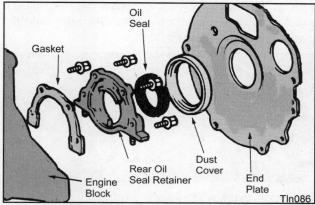

Tln086

a. Remove the oil seal retainer bolts and remove the oil seal retainer.

b. Remove old seal with a screw driver or punch.

c. Install new seal with a seal installer, ensure the seals lips are not pulled back or crooked.

5. Install end plate to rear of engine block.

Tln088

6. Clean flywheel/drive plate attaching bolt threads in rear of crankshaft using a thread tap.

Install new flywheel/driveplate and attaching bolts, tighten bolts to the correct torque specification.

Flywheel/Drive plate Bolt Specification:
[L, 2L & 2L-T 50's & 60's Series]
Flywheel Bolt (Manual Transmission) Specification:
    850kg-cm, 61ft-lb, 83m
Driveplate Bolt (Automatic Transmission) Spec:
    750kg-cm, 54ft-lb, 74Nm
[2L & 3L 80's Series on]
Flywheel Bolt (Manual Transmission) Specification:
    1,250kg-cm, 90ft-lb, 123m
Driveplate (Automatic Transmission) Bolt Spec:
    1.000kg-cm, 72ft-lb, 98Nm

7. Reinstall transmission, check engine and transmission lubricant levels.

8. Road-test vehicle and check for lubrication leaks.

CYLINDER BLOCK.
Inspection.

1. When engine is removed from vehicle and mounted in a suitable engine stand, remove all parts as outlined under the particular part heading in this section.

Clean all gasket surfaces
Tln089

2. Clean all cylinder block gasket surfaces.

3. Remove all coolant jacket welsh plugs.

4. Clean cylinder block thoroughly using a suitable cleaning solution. Flush with clean water or steam. Spray or wipe cylinder bores and machined surfaces using engine oil.

* Caustic cleaning solutions destroy all bearing and alloy materials. All bearing and alloy parts if not removed before cleaning must be replaced.

Do not use caustic solutions to clean bearing material or alloy parts.

5. Check all oil passages for obstructions.

6. Using a straight edge and feeler gauge, inspect cylinder block deck surface for flatness.

If any distortion or irregularity is less than specified, cylinder block surface may be machined.

Cylinder Block Deck Surfaces Flatness Specification
    Max 0.20mm, 0.0080in.

Replace cylinder block if irregularity or distortion is more than specified.

7. Check oil pan and timing chain cover area for burrs or damage. Minor damage may be cleaned up with a fine mill

file.

8. If needed, clean all threaded holes using a suitable threaded tap or drill out and install thread insert.

9. Measure cylinder bore walls for taper, excessive ridging, oversize and out-of-round.

Cylinder Standard Diameter:

50's & 60's Series

L	90.000-90.030mm (3.5433-3.5445in)
2L & 2L-T	92.000-92.030mm (3.6220-3.6232in)

80's Series on

2L mark "1"	92.000-92.010mm (3.6220-3.6224in)
2L mark "2"	92.010-92.020mm (3.6224-3.6228in)
2L mark "3"	92.020-92.030mm (3.6228-3.6232in)
3L mark "1"	96.000-96.010mm (3.7795-3.7799in)
3L mark "2"	96.010-96.020mm (3.7799-3.7803in)
3L mark "3"	96.020-96.030mm (3.7803-3.7807in)

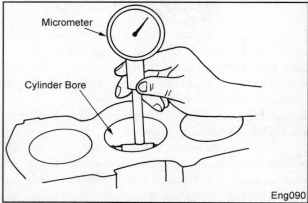
Micrometer
Cylinder Bore
Eng090

Limit rebore to   0.50mm oversize
Taper: .025 mm
Out-Of-Round: .025 mm

If bore is worn beyond limits, it may be rebored, honed and fitted with oversize pistons. The smallest available oversize piston should be selected, refer to CYLINDER RECONDITIONING AND PISTON FITTING section for details.

Cylinder Reconditioning and Piston Fitting.

It will be necessary to smooth bores to fit new pistons, if one or more cylinder bores are scored, rough or worn beyond limits.

It will not be necessary to rebore all cylinders to the same oversize order to maintain engine balance if few bores require correction, since all oversize service pistons are held to the same weight as standard size pistons.

Do not try to machine oversize pistons to fit cylinder bores, this will destroy the surface treatment and affect the weight. The smallest possible oversize service pistons should be used and the cylinder bores should be honed to size for proper clearances.

Measure all new pistons at right angles to the piston pin bore, as per diagram, before the honing or reboring operation is started.

© Copyright Ellery Publications www.ellery.com.au

"L" ENGINE MAINTENANCE & REBUILD

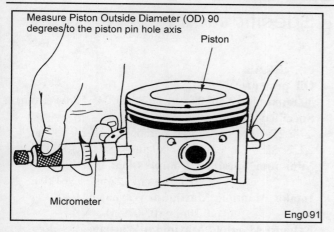

Measure Piston Outside Diameter (OD) 90 degrees to the piston pin hole axis

Piston

Micrometer

Eng091

Piston Size Standard:

50's & 60's Series

L	89.955-89.985mm (3.5415-3.5427in)
2L & 2L-T	91.940-91.970mm (3.6197-3.6209in)

80's Series on.

2L mark "1"	91.940-91.950mm (3.6197-3.6201in)
2L mark "2"	91.950-91.960mm (3.6201-3.6205in)
2L mark "3"	91.960-91.970mm (3.6205-3.6209in)
3L mark "1"	95.940-95.950mm (3.7772-3.7776in)
3L mark "2"	95.950-95.960mm (3.7776-3.7779in)
3L mark "3"	95.960-95.970mm (3.7779-3.7783in)

Available in 0.50mm oversize

Honing is recommended for truing bore if cylinder bore wear does not exceed specification. The bore should be trued up by boring and then hone finished, if wear or out-of-round exceeds specification.

All crankshaft bearing caps must be in place and tightened as specified when reboring cylinder bores, to prevent distortion of bores in final assembly.

Leave 0.025 mm on the diameter for final honing to give the specified clearance when taking the final cut.

Follow the Hone Manufacturers recommendations for the use of the hone and cleaning and lubrication during honing. Noting the following points.

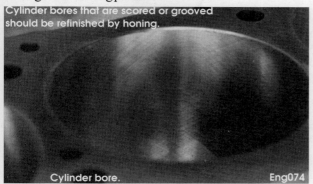

Cylinder bores that are scored or grooved should be refinished by honing.

Cylinder bore.

Eng074

Pass the hone through the entire length of the cylinder bore at the rate of approximately 60 cycles per minute when finished honing. This should produce the desired 45° cross hatch pattern on cylinder walls which will ensure minimum

oil consumption and maximum ring life.

Each piston must be fitted individually to the bore in which it will be installed and marked to ensure correct assembly during the final honing. After the final honing and before the piston is inspected for fit, each cylinder bore must be washed and dried thoroughly to remove all traces of abrasive and then allowed to cool. Apply clean engine oil to cylinder bores. The pistons and cylinder block must be at a common temperature before inspecting.

The glazed cylinder walls should be slightly dulled when new piston rings are installed without reboring cylinders, but without increasing the bore diameter, by means of the finest grade of stone in a cylinder hone.

Proceed as follows to inspect piston to cylinder bore.

1. Using a clean cloth wipe cylinder walls and pistons and apply clean engine oil to cylinder bores.
2. Measure the bore accurately using an inside micrometer.
3. Measure piston diameter and subtract piston diameter from cylinder bore diameter to determine piston-to-bore clearance.

Piston to Bore Clearance:

L	**0.035 - 0.055mm**	**0.0014 - 0.0022in**
2L, 2L-T & 3L	**0.050 - 0.070mm**	**0.0020 - 0.0028in**
Maximum	**0.14mm**	**0.0055in**

4. Mark each piston with cylinder number to which it will be fitted and proceed to hone cylinders and fit pistons.

**Handle the pistons with care and do not attempt to force them through the cylinder until cylinder has been honed to the correct size, as pistons can be damaged through careless handling.

Assemble parts as described under the correct heading in this section. If coolant and oil gallery plugs were removed when dismantling, install using specified sealant.

Problem Diagnosis.

Problems and Possible Causes.

Problems should be corrected, when proper diagnosis is made, by repair, adjustment or part replacement as needed. Refer to the correct section in this manual.

High Oil Loss

(1) Tighten bolts and/or replace gaskets and seals as required for external leaks.

(2) Check oil with car on a level surface and allow adequate drain down time to ensure a correct reading of dipstick.

(3) Severe usage such as towing or continuous high speed driving will normally cause oil consumption to increase.

(4) PCV system failure.

(5) Use recommended S.A.E viscosity for current temperatures. Refer to LUBRICATION Section for details on incorrect oil viscosity.

(6) Valve guides and/or valve stem seals worn, or seals omitted. Ream guides and install oversize service valves and/or new valve stem seals.

(7) Allow enough time for the piston rings to seat. Replace worn or broken rings as needed, if rings have been incorrectly installed, worn or broken, or not seated.

(8) Piston incorrectly installed or misfitted.

Gaskets.

(1) Incorrectly tightened fasteners or damaged/dirty threads.

(2) Worn or damaged gasket (cracking or porosity).

(3) Fluid pressure/level too high.

(4) Incorrect sealant used (when required)

Inspection of Seals.

(1) Damaged seal bore (burred, nicked, scratched)

(2) Worn or loose bearing which causes excessive seal wear.

(3) Worn or damaged seal or incorrect installation.

(4) Fluid pressure/level too high.

Oil Leak Investigation

Oil leaks are easily located and repaired by visually finding the leak and replacing or repairing the required parts.

(1) Determine whether the fluid is transmission lubricant, engine oil, power steering fluid etc.

(2) Run the car at normal operating temperature and park the car over a large sheet of paper. After a few minutes, you should be able to find the approximate location of the leak by drippings on the paper.

(3) Use a degreaser or steam to clean the area of the leak, drive the car for a few kilometres. Then visually inspect the suspected part for signs of an oil leak.

Black Light and Dye Method.

There are many dye and light kits available for finding leaks.

(a) Pour required amount of dye into leaking part.

(b) Operate the car under normal operating conditions as instructed in the kit.

(c) Shine the light in the suspected area. The dyed fluid will appear as a yellow path leading to the problem.

Low Oil Pressure

(1) Blocked oil filter.

(2) Incorrect oil viscosity for expected temperature, or oil diluted with moisture or unburned fuel mixtures.

(3) Excessive bearing clearance.

(4) If the oil level is low, fill to mark on dipstick.

(5) Oil pump dirty/worn, or oil pump suction pipe screen blocked, or hole in oil pump suction pipe.

(6) Incorrect or failing oil pressure sender.

Hydraulic Valve Lifters

The lifters are extremely simple in design and rarely need attention, readjustments are not required and servicing requires only that care and cleanliness be exercised whilst handling the parts. Using a piece of garden hose near the end of each intake and exhaust valve with the other end of the hose to the ear, is the easiest method for locating a noisy valve lifter. Using this method, the sound is localised, which makes it easier to find out which lifter is faulty. Or place a finger on the face of the valve spring retainer. If the lifter is not functioning correctly, a definite shock will be felt when the valve returns to its seat.

Specifications

GENERAL

Oil pressure:

3000 rpm plus: 2.5-6.0kg/cm 36-85psi, 245-588kPa(min)

Specified Compression:

L & 2L-T	30.0 kg/cm, 427pis, 2,942kPa.
2L & 3L	32.0 kg/cm, 455pis, 3,138kPa.

Minimum Specified Compression:

20.0 kg/cm, 284pis, 1,961kPa.

Intake Manifold Maximum Warpage:

0.20mm (0.0079in)

Exhaust Manifold Maximum Warpage:

0.20mm (0.0079in)

Turbocharger Shaft and Impeller Free Play:

0.13mm, 0.0051in

[L, 2L & 2L-T 50's & 60's Series]

Tappet (Valve) clearance. Cold engine.

Intake valve clearance:	0.27mm, 0.0106in
Exhaust valve clearance:	0.38mm, 0.0150in

Coolant

LN:

10.6 litres, 11.2 US qts, 9.3 Imp qts.

Piston Height Protrusion above Cylinder Block:

0.68 - 0.97mm, 0.0268 - 0.0382in

CYLINDER HEAD [2L & 3L 80's Series on]

Gaskets come in 3 option thickness and are identified by a stamped mark or a section of the gasket removed.

Piston Height Protrusion	Gasket Identification	Gasket Thickness
0.68-0.77mm	B	1.40-1.50mm
0.78-0.87mm	D	1.50-1.60mm
0.88-0.97mm	F	1.60-1.70mm

Valve Lifter Diameter Specification

40.892-40.902mm, 0.0023-0.0039in

Valve Lifter Bore Diameter specification.

40.960-40.980mm, 1.6126-1.6134in

Valve Lifter Oil Clearance Specification.

0.058-0.088imm, 0.0023-0.0035in - Max 0.10mm, 0.0157in

Coolant

LN:

2L	9.2 litres, 9.7 US qts, 8.1 Imp qts.
3L	9.0 litres, 9.5 US qts, 8.0 Imp qts.

Combustion Chamber Protrusion Specification:

0.01 - -.07mm, 0.0004 - 0.0028in

Maximum Clearance - Valve stem to Valve Guide:

[L, 2L & 2L-T 50's & 60's Series]

Intake - 0.021 - 0.057 mm Maximum 0.10mm

Exhaust - 0.040 - 0.076 mm Maximum 0.12mm

[2L & 3L 80's Series on]

Intake - 0.020 - 0.055 mm Maximum 0.08 mm

Exhaust - 0.035 - 0.070 mm Maximum 0.10 mm

[L, 2L & 2L-T 50's & 60's Series]

Ream bush out to specified diameter with an 8.5mm reamer.
[2L & 3L 80's Series on]
Ream bush out to specified diameter with an 8.0mm reamer.
Intake - 0.021 - 0.057 mm   Maximum 0.10mm
Exhaust - 0.040 - 0.076 mm Maximum 0.12mm
[2L & 3L 80's Series on]
Valve Guide Bush Inside Diameter:
[L, 2L & 2L-T 50's & 60's Series]
     8.51-8.53mm (0.3350-0.3358in)
[2L & 3L 80's Series on]
     8.010 - 8.030 mm
* Valve seat angles are 45⁰.
* Valve seat width:
Exhaust 1.2 - 1.6mm (0.047-0.063in)
Intake   1.2 - 1.6mm (0.047-0.063in)
Valve Springs
Maximum allowable variance in spring end length: 2.00 mm, while rotating spring on level desk.
[L, 2L & 2L-T 50's & 60's Series]
Valve Spring Free length: 47.98mm (1.8890in)
[2L & 3L 80's Series on]
Valve Spring Free length:
Blue Paint Identification Mark 49.14mm (1.9346in)
Yellow Paint Identification Mark 46.20mm (1.8189in)
Valve spring compressed height/load:
Also Valve Spring Install Height
Valve spring height:
 [L, 2L & 2L-T 50's & 60's Series]
Spring   Compressed height   39.3mm (1.547in)
          Compression pressure 29.2kg, 64.4lb, 286 N
 [2L & 3L 80's Series on]
Spring   Compressed height   30.7mm (1.457in)
          Compression pressure 32.0kg, 71.0lb, 315 N
Valves
[L, 2L & 2L-T 50's & 60's Series]
New Valve Length
Intake Valve: 122.95 mm (4.8405in)
Exhaust Valve: 122.75 mm (4.8327in)
Minimum Valve Length
Intake Valve: 122.45 mm (4.8209in)
Exhaust Valve: 122.25 mm (4.8130in)
[2L & 3L 80's Series on]
New Valve Length
Intake Valve: 103.29 - 103.69 mm (4.0665 - 4.0823in)
Exhaust Valve: 103.14 - 103.54 mm (4.0606 - 4.0764in)
Minimum Valve Length
Intake Valve: 102.79 mm (4.0468in)
Exhaust Valve: 102.64 mm (4.0409in)
Valve face angle: **44.5⁰.**
Minimum valve head margin thickness:
[L, 2L & 2L-T 50's & 60's Series]
Intake Valve: 0.9 mm (0.035in)
Exhaust Valve: 1.0 mm (0.039in)
[2L & 3L 80's Series on]

Intake Valve: 1.1 mm (0.043in)
Exhaust Valve: 1.2 mm (0.047in)
[L, 2L & 2L-T 50's & 60's Series]
Valve Spring Install Height
     39.3mm (1.547in)
Combustion Chamber Protrusion Specification:
     0.01 - -.07mm, 0.0004 - 0.0028in
Camshaft bearings
Specified Oil Clearance:
     0.022 - 0.074mm, 0.0009 - 0.0029in
Maximum Oil Clearance:
     0.1mm, 0.004in
Free Length of Camshaft Belt Tension Spring
     39.7 - 40.7 m, 1.563 - 1.602 in
Camshaft lobe height Intake and Exhaust:
Minimum Lift:
Intake Valve Lobe Minimum:
L & 2L [50's & 60's Series]   46.76mm, 1.8409in
2L-T[50's & 60's]   46.29mm, 1.8224in
2L [80's on]   53.35mm, 2.1004in
3L [80's on]   53.79mm, 2.1177in
Exhaust Valve Lobe Minimum:
L, 2L & 2L-T [50's & 60's Series] 47.25mm, 1.8602in
2L & 3L [80's on]   54.49mm, 2.1453in
Camshaft Journal Diameter:
L, 2L & 2L-T [50's & 60's Series]
          34.969-34.985mm, 1.3767 - 1.3774in
Undersize by 0.125mm & 0.250mm bearings available
2L & 3L [80's on]
No 1 Bearing   34.969-34.985mm, 1.3767 - 1.3774in
Other bearings 27.969-27.985mm, 1.1011 - 1.1018in
Camshaft Centre Max. Runout: 0.10mm, 0.039in
Lubricant Quantity Specification:
L,2L&2L-T [50's & 60's Series]
w/o new oil filter:
4.8 Litres, 5.1 US qts, 4.2 Imp qts
with new oil filter:
5.8 Litres, 6.1 US qts, 5.1 Imp qts
dry fill:
6.5 Litres, 6.9 US qts, 5.7 Imp qts
Europe - 2L & 3L [80's Series on]
w/o new oil filter:
5.0 Litres, 5.3 US qts, 4.4 Imp qts
with new oil filter:
5.9 Litres, 6.2 US qts, 5.2 Imp qts
dry fill:
6.4 Litres, 6.8 US qts, 5.6 Imp qts
Countries other than Europe - 2L & 3L [80's Series on]
w/o new oil filter:
5.0 Litres, 5.3 US qts, 4.4 Imp qts
with new oil filter:
6.0 Litres, 6.3 US qts, 5.3 Imp qts
dry fill:
6.9 Litres, 6.9 US qts, 5.7 Imp qts

Lubricant Quality:
Engine Oil Grade   API grade listed below
L, 2L & 3L: CC or CD
2L-T: CD

Oil Pump

L,2L & 2L-T 50's & 60's
Inner Gear Tip to Outer Rotor Tip Specified Clearance:
  0.15-0.21mm, 0.0059-0.0083in   (0.30mm max)
Crescent Spacer to Outer Race Specified Clearance:
  0.15-0.21mm, 0.0059-0.0083in   (0.30mm max)
Outer race to pump housing clearance:
  0.06-0.15mm, 0.0020-0.0059in   (0.20mm max)
Clearance of pump cover:
  0.03-0.09mm, 0.0012-0.0035in   (0.15mm max)
Oil Relief Valve Nut Specified Torque:
            210kg-cm, 27ft-lb, 37Nm

2L & 3L 80's Series on
Inner Gear Tip to Outer Rotor Tip Specified Clearance:
  0.11-0.24mm, 0.0043-0.0094in   (0.30mm max)
Outer race to pump housing clearance:
  0.144-0.219mm, 0.0057-0.0086in   (0.40mm max)
Clearance of pump cover:
  0.03-0.09mm, 0.0012-0.0035in   (0.15mm max)
Oil Relief Valve Nut Specified Torque:
            375kg-cm, 27ft-lb, 37Nm

Main Bearing Standard Thickness:
Mark "1" colour Brown 1.979-1.983mm (0.0779-0.0781in)
Mark "2" colour Black 1.983-1.987mm (0.0781-0.0782in)
Mark "3" colour Blue 1.987-1.991mm (0.0782-0.0784in)

Main Bearing Clearance:
Standard Clearance: 0.034-0.065mm (0.0013-0.0026in)
Undersize 0.25 & 0.50mm:
            0.033-0.079mm (0.0013-0.0031in)
Maximum Clearance: 0.10mm (0.0039in)

Thrust Bearing Clearance
Standard Clearance: 0.040-0.250mm (0.0016-0.0088in)
Maximum Clearance: 0.30mm (0.0118in)

Crankshaft Connecting Rod Bearing Journal Diameter

Standard Diameter:
L & 2L   52.988-53.000mm (2.0861-2.0866in)
2L-T & 3L   54.988-55.000mm (2.1649-2.1654in)

Under Size 0.25mm:
L & 2L   52.745-52.755mm (2.0766-2.0770in)
2L-T & 3L   54.745-54.755mm (2.1553-2.1557in)

Under Size 0.50mm:
L & 2L   52.495-52.505mm (2.0667-2.0671in)
2L-T & 3L   54.495-54.505mm (2.1455-2.1459in)

Maximum Out of Round   .02mm (0.0008in)
Maximum Taper   .02mm (0.0008in)

Connecting Rod Bearing Standard Bearing thicknes
Mark "1" 1.478-1.482mm (0.0582-0.0583in)
Mark "2" 1.482-1.486mm (0.0583-0.0585in)
Mark "3" 1.486-1.490mm (0.0585-0.0587in)

Connecting Rod to crankshaft end clearance:
Standard Clearance: 0.080-0.300mm (0.0031-0.0118in)
Maximum Clearance: 0.35mm (0.0138in)

Piston Size Standard:
50's & 60's Series
L   89.955-89.985mm (3.5415-3.5427in)
2L & 2L-T   91.940-91.970mm (3.6197-3.6209in)
80's Series on
2L mark "1"   91.940-91.950mm (3.6197-3.6201in)
2L mark "2"   91.950-91.960mm (3.6201-3.6205in)
2L mark "3"   91.960-91.970mm (3.6205-3.6209in)
3L mark "1"   95.940-95.950mm (3.7772-3.7776in)
3L mark "2"   95.950-95.960mm (3.7776-3.7779in)
3L mark "3"   95.960-95.970mm (3.7779-3.7783in)

Available in 0.50mm oversize

Piston Pin Clearance:
            0.004-0.012mm (0.0002-0.0005in)
Maximum Limit   0.05mm (0.002in)

Connecting Rod Alignment Max. Specification
    Bend   0.05mm per 100mm, 0.0020in per 4.0in
    Twist   0.15mm per 100mm, 0.0060in per 4.0in

Top Compression Ring End Gap Specification:
L   0.30-0.57mm, 0.0118-0.0224in
2L,2L-T & 3L   0.35-0.62mm, 0.0138-0.0244in
Maximum 1.30mm, 0.051in

Second Compression Ring End Gap Specification:
L   0.20-0.52mm, 0.0079-0.0205in
2L,2L-T & 3L   0.30-0.47mm, 0.0118-0.0185in
Maximum 1.07mm, 0.0421in

Oil Ring Steel Rail Gap Specification:
L   0.20-0.52mm, 0.0079-0.0205in
2L,2L-T & 3L   0.20-0.52mm, 0.0079-0.0205in
Maximum 1.12mm, 0.044in

Piston Ring Side Clearance:
            0.025 - 0.070mm, 0.0010 - 0.0028n

Main Bearing Journal Diameter
Standard Size: 61.985-62.000mm (2.4403-2.4409in)
Available in 0.25 & 0.50mm undersize with 0.005mm tolerance
Ovality   0.02mm, 0.0008in max.
Out-Of-Round   0.02mm, 0.0008in max.

Crankshaft Connecting Rod Bearing Journal Diameter

Standard Diameter:
L & 2L   52.988-53.000mm (2.0861-2.0866in)
2L-T & 3L   54.988-55.000mm (2.1649-2.1654in)

Under Size 0.25mm:
L & 2L   52.745-52.755mm (2.0766-2.0770in)
2L-T & 3L   54.745-54.755mm (2.1553-2.1557in)

Under Size 0.50mm:
L & 2L   52.495-52.505mm (2.0667-2.0671in)
2L-T & 3L   54.495-54.505mm (2.1455-2.1459in)

Maximum Out of Round   .02mm (0.0008in)
Maximum Taper   .02mm (0.0008in)

Crankshaft Runout Specification 0.1mm 0.0024in max.
Crankshaft Rear Flange Runout: 0.05mm, 0.0020in.
Crankshaft End Float Specification   **0.04-0.25 mm**
Wear Limit   0.30mm
Cylinder Standard Diameter:
50's & 60's Series
L   90.000-90.030mm (3.5433-3.5445in)
2L & 2L-T   92.000-92.030mm (3.6220-3.6232in)
80's Series on
2L mark "1"   92.000-92.010mm (3.6220-3.6224in)
2L mark "2"   92.010-92.020mm (3.6224-3.6228in)
2L mark "3"   92.020-92.030mm (3.6228-3.6232in)
3L mark "1"   96.000-96.010mm (3.7795-3.7799in)
3L mark "2"   96.010-96.020mm (3.7799-3.7803in)
3L mark "3"   96.020-96.030mm (3.7803-3.7807in)
Limit rebore to   0.50mm oversize
Taper   **.025 mm**
Out-Of-Round   **.025 mm**
Piston Size Standard:
50's & 60's Series
L   89.955-89.985mm (3.5415-3.5427in)
2L & 2L-T   91.940-91.970mm (3.6197-3.6209in)
80's Series on
2L mark "1"   91.940-91.950mm (3.6197-3.6201in)
2L mark "2"   91.950-91.960mm (3.6201-3.6205in)
2L mark "3"   91.960-91.970mm (3.6205-3.6209in)
3L mark "1"   95.940-95.950mm (3.7772-3.7776in)
3L mark "2"   95.950-95.960mm (3.7776-3.7779in)
3L mark "3"   95.960-95.970mm (3.7779-3.7783in)
Available in 0.50mm oversize
Piston to Bore Clearance:
L   0.035 - 0.055mm   0.0014 - 0.0022in
2L, 2L-T & 3L   0.050 - 0.070mm   0.0020 - 0.0028in
Maximum   0.14mm 0.0055in

TORQUE SPECIFICATIONS

Oil Pressure Sender Unit Torque:
55kg-cm, 4.8ft-lb, 5.4Nm.
Intake Manifold Bolts Torque:
240kg-cm, 17ft-lb, 24Nm
Injector Pipes Nut Specified Torque:
250kg-cm, 18ft-lb, 25Nm
Exhaust Manifold Bolts Torque:
L & 2L   400kg-cm, 29ft-lb, 39Nm
2L-T & 3L   530kg-cm, 38ft-lb, 52Nm
Exhaust Manifold Heat Shield Bolts Torque:
195kg-cm, 14ft-lb, 19Nm
Turbocharger Air Duct Intake Pipe Bolts Torque:
120kg-cm, 9ft-lb, 12Nm
Turbocharger to Exhaust Manifold Nuts Torque:
530kg-cm, 38ft-lb, 52Nm
Turbocharger to Exhaust Pipe Nuts Torque:
280kg-cm, 19ft-lb, 25Nm

Oil Pipe to Turbocharger Nuts Torque:
120kg-cm, 9ft-lb, 12Nm
Turbocharger Intake Pipe Flange Bolts Torque:
120kg-cm, 9ft-lb, 12Nm
Turbocharger Air Duct Intake Pipe Bolts Torque:
120kg-cm, 9ft-lb, 12Nm
Rocker Cover Bolts Torque:
60kg-cm, 4.5ft-lb, 6Nm
CYLINDER HEAD [L, 2L & 2L-T 50's & 60's Series]
Rocker Arm Assembly Bolts Specified Torque:
195kg-cm, 14ft-lb, 19Nm
Injector Torque Specification:
700kg-cm, 51ft-lb, 69Nm
Injector Pipe Torque Specification:
250kg-cm, 18ft-lb, 25Nm
Injector Leakage Pipe Torque Specification:
500kg-cm, 36ft-lb, 49Nm
Cylinder Head Bolt Torque:
1,200kg-cm, 87ft-lb, 118Nm
Rocker Arm and Shaft Assembly Bolt Specified Torque:
195kg-cm, 14ft-lb, 19Nm
Front Camshaft Oil Seal Retainer Plate Bolt Specified Torque: 185kg-cm, 13ft-lb, 18Nm
Camshaft Gear Attaching Bolt Specified Torque:
1000kg-cm, 72ft-lb, 98Nm
Timing Belt Cover Bolts Specified Torque:
60kg-cm, 4.5ft-lb, 6Nm
Crankshaft Pulley Attaching Bolt:
1400kg-cm, 101ft-lb, 137Nm
Rocker Cover Nuts Torque:
60kg-cm, 4.5ft-lb, 6Nm
Intake Manifold Nuts and Bolts Specified Torque:
240kg-cm, 17ft-lb, 24Nm
Coolant Outlet / Thermostat Housing Attaching Bolt
195kg-cm, 14ft-lb, 19Nm
Exhaust Manifold Bolts Torque:
L & 2L   400kg-cm, 29ft-lb, 39Nm
2L-T & 3L   530kg-cm, 38ft-lb, 52Nm
Exhaust Manifold Heat Shield Bolts Torque:
195kg-cm, 14ft-lb, 19Nm
Injector Pipe Torque Specification:
250kg-cm, 18ft-lb, 25Nm
Injector Leakage Pipe Torque Specification:
500kg-cm, 36ft-lb, 49Nm
CYLINDER HEAD [2L & 3L 80's Series on]
Cylinder Head Bolt Torque:
800kg-cm, 58ft-lb, 78Nm
Tighten a further 90^0 turn of each bolt in sequence
Tighten a further 90^0 turn of each bolt in sequence for the second time.

Camshaft Gear Attaching Bolt Specified Torque:
1000kg-cm, 72ft-lb, 98Nm

Timing Belt Cover Bolts Specified Torque:
60kg-cm, 4.5ft-lb, 6Nm
Crankshaft Pulley Attaching Bolt:
1700kg-cm, 123ft-lb, 167Nm
Rocker Cover Nuts Torque:
60kg-cm, 4.5ft-lb, 6Nm
Intake Manifold Nuts and Bolts Specified Torque:
240kg-cm, 17ft-lb, 24Nm
Coolant Outlet / Thermostat Housing Attaching Bolt
195kg-cm, 14ft-lb, 19Nm
Exhaust Manifold Bolts Torque:
530kg-cm, 38ft-lb, 52Nm
Exhaust Manifold Heat Shield Bolts Torque:
195kg-cm, 14ft-lb, 19Nm
Injector Pipe Torque Specification:
250kg-cm, 18ft-lb, 25Nm
Injector Leakage Pipe Torque Specification:
500kg-cm, 36ft-lb, 49Nm
Camshaft Bearing Caps Bolt Specified Torque:
195kg-cm, 14ft-lb, 19Nm
Front Camshaft Oil Seal Retainer Plate Bolt Specified Torque: 185kg-cm, 13ft-lb, 18Nm
[L, 2L & 2L-T 50's & 60's series]
Rocker Assembly Bolts Specification:
195kg-cm, 14ft-lb, 19Nm
[2L & 3L 80's Series on]
Bearing Cap Bolts Specification:
255kg-cm, 18ft-lb, 25Nm
Crankshaft Balancer Nut Torque Specification:
L,2L & 2L-T [50's & 60's Series]:
1,400kg-cm, 101ft-lb, 137Nm
2L & 3L[80's Series on]:
1,700kg-cm, 123ft-lb, 167Nm
Viewing from front of engine timing belt idler pulleys-
Left Idler Pulley: finger tight until belt is installed.
Right Idler Pulley: **400kg-cm, 29ft-lb, 39Nm**
Left Side Idler Pulley Torque Specification.
195kg-cm, 14ft-lb, 19Nm
Timing Belt Cover Bolts Specified Torque:
60kg-cm, 4.5ft-lb, 6Nm
Crankshaft Pulley Attaching Bolt:
L,2L & 2L-T[50's & 60's Series]:
1,400kg-cm, 101ft-lb, 137Nm
2L & 3L[80's Series on]:
1,700kg-cm, 123ft-lb, 167Nm
Injection Pump to Timing Belt Casing Nut Torque:
210kg-cm, 15ft-lb, 21Nm.
Timing Belt Cover / Oil Pump Attaching Bolt Specified Torque: 230kg-cm, 17ft-lb, 23Nm.
Oil Pump Suction Pipe and Strainer Bolt Torque:
120kg-cm, 9ft-lb, 12Nm.

Oil Sump Attaching Bolts & Nuts Specified Torque:
[L, 2L & 2L-T 50's & 60's Series]
Bolts 80kg-cm, 7ft-lb, 8Nm
Nuts 175kg-cm, 13ft-lb, 17Nm
[2L & 3L 80's series on]
180kg-cm, 13ft-lb, 18Nm
Water Pump Attaching Bolts
230kg-cm, 17ft-lb, 23Nm.
Oil Pan (Sump) Bolt Specification:
180kg-cm, 13ft-lb, 18Nm
Oil Pan (Sump) Drain Plug Specification:
L,2L&2L-T [50's & 60's Series] 175kg-cm, 13ft-lb, 17Nm
2L & 3L [80's series on] 400kg-cm, 29ft-lb, 39Nm
Injection Pump to Timing Belt Casing Nut Torque:
210kg-cm, 15ft-lb, 21Nm.
Fuel Injection Pump Gear Attaching Bolt
650kg-cm, 47ft-lb, 64Nm.
Top Idler Gear Attaching Bolt
340kg-cm, 25ft-lb, 33Nm.
Lower Idler Gear Attaching Bolts
195kg-cm, 14ft-lb, 19Nm.
Timing Belt Cover Bolts Specified Torque:
60kg-cm, 4.5ft-lb, 6Nm
Crankshaft Pulley Attaching Bolt:
L,2L & 2L-T[50's & 60's Series]:
1,400kg-cm, 101ft-lb, 137Nm
2L & 3L[80's Series on]:
1,700kg-cm, 123ft-lb, 167Nm
Main Bearing Cap Bolt Specification:
1,050kg-cm, 76ft-lb, 103Nm
Rear Seal Retainer Bolts:
130kg-cm, 9ft-lb, 13Nm
Flywheel/Drive plate Bolt Specification:
[L, 2L & 2L-T 50's & 60's Series]
Flywheel Bolt (Manual Transmission) Specification:
850kg-cm, 61ft-lb, 83Nm
Driveplate Bolt (Automatic Transmission) Spec:
750kg-cm, 54ft-lb, 74Nm
[2L & 3L 80's Series on]
Flywheel Bolt (Manual Transmission) Specification:
1,250kg-cm, 90ft-lb, 123Nm
Driveplate (Automatic Transmission) Bolt Spec:
1.000kg-cm, 72ft-lb, 98Nm
Connecting Rod Cap Bolt Specification:
600kg-cm, 43ft-lb, 59Nm
Main Bearing Cap Bolt Specification
1,050kg-cm, 76ft-lb, 103Nm

STARTING SYSTEM

General Information

When the ignition switch is turned to the START position, the solenoid pull-in and hold-in windings are energised and the solenoid plunger is drawn in. The plunger moves the engaging lever and fork which in turn moves the drive assembly towards the ring gear. The drive assembly rotates on the coarse thread of the drive shaft to facilitate engagement.

Should a pinion tooth come up against a ring gear tooth, the engaging lever compresses the spring on the drive assembly until the solenoid switch contacts close. The pinion is then turned and engages with the ring gear under spring force. Before the pinion is completely in mesh the contacts in the solenoid switch are closed by the action of the solenoid plunger, and the starter rotates and cranks the engine. When the starter rotates, the pull-in winding is de-energised by the isolation of its ground cranking. As the starting speed of the engine exceeds that of the starter, the pinion rotates freely and engine acceleration does not affect the starter.

LN Models use glow plugs to assist starting the engine.

NO LOAD TEST

* Check the armature is not seized before performing a NO LOAD TEST. Prise the pinion in a counter clockwise direction with a screwdriver. If the armature will not rotate freely, Do Not perform the No Load Test.

Clamp starter motor securely to test bench and make connections. Close the switch and compare the RPM, current, voltage readings with the following specifications.

Starter Motor Current Test

LN:	2.0kw	**120 AMPS (max.)**
	2.5kw	**180 AMPS (max)**
RN:		**90 AMPS (max)**
YN:		**90 AMPS (max)**
Terminal Voltage:		**12 Volts**

Check **Problem Solving & Diagnosis** if No Load test indicates that the starter motor is defective.

MAJOR MAINTENANCE

Remove

1. Detach battery earth cable at battery, raise front of vehicle, detach the electrical connectors from starter motor solenoid.
2. Loosen the starter motor mounting bolts, support starter motor, remove the mounting bolts. Move starter motor forwards, then withdraw rearwards from beneath vehicle.

L Series Starter Motor
Reduction Gear Starter
Attaching Bolt
Attaching Bolt
Str024

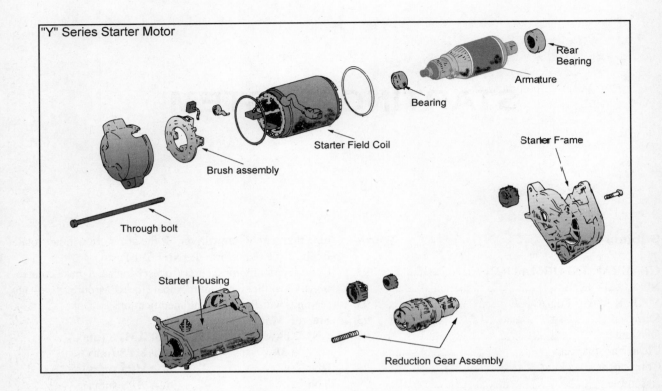

"Y" Series Starter Motor

Rear Bearing

Armature

Bearing

Starter Field Coil

Starter Frame

Brush assembly

Through bolt

Starter Housing

Reduction Gear Assembly

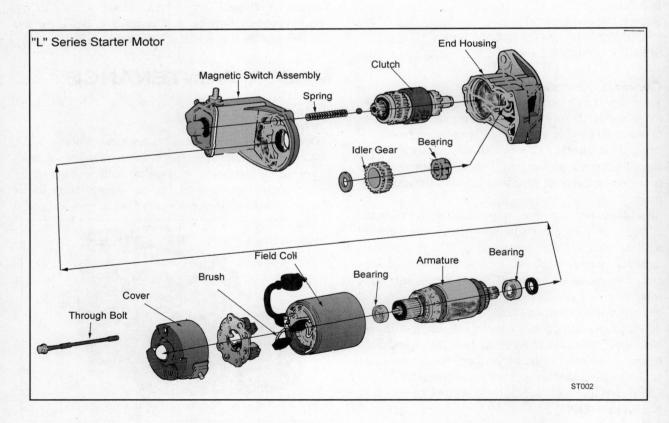

"L" Series Starter Motor

Magnetic Switch Assembly

Clutch

End Housing

Spring

Idler Gear

Bearing

Field Coil

Brush

Bearing

Armature

Bearing

Cover

Through Bolt

ST002

Dismantle

1. Remove nut and washer from the solenoid field coil terminal, then separate the lead from the terminal, remove the two solenoid retaining screws.

2. Match mark the commutator end cover and drive end housing to the field coil housing. Remove two through bolts securing commutator end cover and field coil housing to drive end housing, remove commutator end cover. LN, RN and YN models use reduction gears, so care must be taken that these gears and bearings can be identified for assembly.

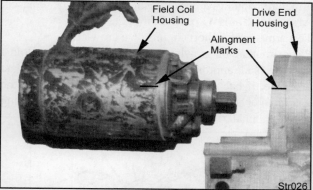

3. Remove two screws securing the commutator end cover bearing cap, separate the bearing cap. Remove seal from commutator end cover.

4. Remove 2 or 3 screws from drive end.

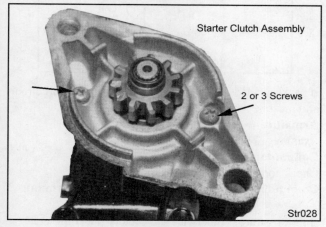

6. Expand and remove the spring clip using a pair of circlip pliers. Becareful not to scratch or damage the shaft. remove clutch assembly.

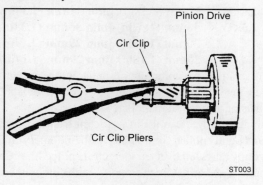

5. Remove spring and steel ball from the clutch shaft with the aid of a magnet.

5. Carefully bend back the brush spring retaining lugs on the positive brush holders (mounted on the insulating mica), remove springs and brushes. Remove the brush holder from commutator.

8. Remove any burrs from the grove on armature shaft using a fine file, remove stop ring and pinion assembly from armature shaft.

Cleaning and Inspection

With the starter motor completely disassembled, all components should be cleaned and inspected. Wash components except the armature and field coils in a suitable cleaning agent.

CAUTION: Do not clean armature or field coils with cleaning solvent as damage to the insulation could occur. Clean armature and field coils carefully using compressed air.

Component Checking
Field Coils

Connect a 12 volt powered D.C. test lamp or ohmmeter between field coil winding connection and a positive brush. The lamp will illuminate or the meter will show a reading to indicate continuity, if the field coil circuit is serviceable. Repeat on remaining positive brush.

2. Make sure brushes are not touching the field coil housing,

Short Circuit Test

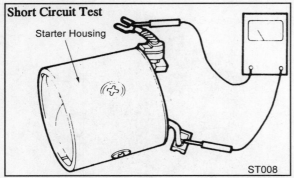

ST008

then connect a 240 volt powered test lamp or ohmmeter between field coil winding connection and field coil housing. The lamp will not illuminate or the ohmmeter will not shown a reading, if winding insulation is satisfactory.

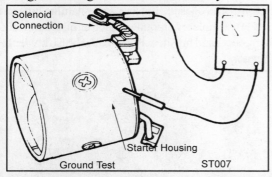

ST007

3. Visually inspect field coil windings for signs of insulation breakdown and/or burns.
4. Remove and replace defective field coil with an approved pole shoe screwdriver.

Armature Insulation Test

Connect a 240 volt powered test lamp or ohmmeter between the armature core and a commutator segment. If lamp illuminates, armature is grounded and should be replaced.

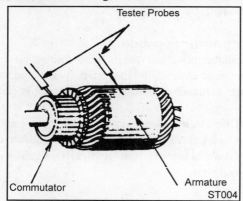

ST004

Repeat procedure on the remaining commutator segments.

Armature Continuity Test

Using an Ohmmeter (or 12 volt powered D.C. test lamp). Touch one probe onto a commutator segment, then touch the remaining probe to an adjacent segment, repeat procedure on each adjacent set of segments. If any adjacent set of segments indicates continuity (test lamp illuminant), the

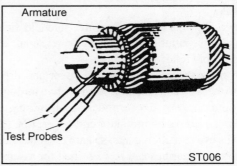

ST006

armature windings are shortened, armature to be replaced.

Armature Short Circuit Test

Test armature for short circuits on a growler.

Place armature on growler and switch on growler. Hold a hacksaw blade approx. 6mm above armature core and rotate armature. If hacksaw blade vibrates, undercut between the commutator segments (to a depth of approx. 0.7mm) using a suitable small file, then re-check armature.

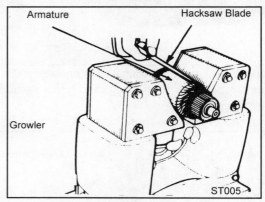

ST005

If hacksaw blade still vibrates, the armature is short circuit and must be replaced.

Armature to Commutator Leads

Examine, re-solder if required.

Commutator Surface

Check commutator for out-of-round.

Commutator Maximum Permissible out-of-round:
0.05mm

If the armature is otherwise satisfactory but commutator is worn, burnt, out-of-round, or has high insulation between the segments, the commutator should be machined.

Diameter of Commutator

LN:	**2.0kW**	**35mm (1.38in) [min 34mm (1.34in)]**
	2.5kW	**36mm (1.42in) [min 35mm (1.38in)]**
RN:		**30mm (1.18in) [min 29mm (1.14in)]**
YN:		**30mm (1.18in) [min 29mm (1.14in)]**

After machining the commutator, undercut the insulation, between the commuter segments to a depth of approx. 0.7mm using a suitable small file.

After undercutting, clean all dirt and debris from the segment slots, and lightly polish commutator with fine emery cloth to remove any burrs left by the undercutting procedure. Clean commutator and armature thoroughly with compressed air.

Brushes

Make sure that brushes slide smoothly in their respective holders, brush connections are good and brushes are clean and not chipped.

Brush Length

LN: 2.0kW   15.0mm (0.591in) [min 9.5mm (0.374in)]
    2.5kW 20.5mm (0.807in) [min 13mm (0.512in)]
RN: 1.0kW   13.5mm (1.38in) [min 8.5mm (0.335in)]
       1.4kW   15.5mm (0.61in) [min 10mm (0.394in)]
YN: 1.0kW   13.5mm (1.38in) [min 8.5mm (0.335in)]
       1.4kW   15.5mm (0.61in) [min 10mm (0.394in)]

If required replace brushes as follows:

Positive Brushes

Cut brush lead at field coil, dispose of brush and spring. Clean field coil terminal and any remaining section of the brush lead, 'Tin' the field coil terminal.

* Replacement brushes have ends of leads 'tinned'.
Hold the new brush lead in place on the field coil terminal, using a pair of pliers. Solder brush lead to field coil end.

* When soldering the new brush lead into place, don't allow the solder to run to far up the lead.

Negative Brushes

Cut brush lead at the brush holder terminal. Dispose of brush and spring. Clean the brush holder terminal, and any remaining section of the brush lead. Clean remaining brush lead on brush holder. 'Tin' brush holder terminal. Hold new brush lead in place on the brush holder terminal, using a pair of pliers. Solder brush lead to brush holder.

* When soldering the new brush lead into place, do not allow the solder to run to far up the lead.

Test brushes as described in the following information.

Brush Holder Assembly

Using an Ohmmeter, check insulation between the replaced brush holders and earth. If continuity exists, replace holder assembly. Check continuity between negative brushes and earth. If continuity does not exist, replace holder assembly. Check the condition of the positive brush spring tabs. Where tabs are weak, broken or if the tabs have been bent open more than twice before, replace brush holder assembly.

Brush

Lift coil spring away from brush top and slide brush out of brush holder.

Brush Spring

Str025

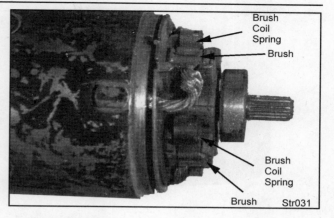

Brush Coil Spring
Brush
Brush Coil Spring
Brush   Str031

Drive Assembly Check

Examine pinion gear for burrs and worn or chipped teeth. Check operation of pinion, the pinion gear should rotate free and smooth in relation to the pinion housing when turned in a clockwise direction, but not rotate when turned in a counter clockwise direction.

Clutch Assembly

Str029

Bushes

Check fit of armature shaft in commutator end cover and drive end housing. If bushes are excessively worn, the starter motor is likely to operate inefficiently and/or the armature may foul on field coil poles.

To remove bushes, support the commutator end cover or drive end housing (as appropriate), carefully tap bush out using a suitable mandrel.

* If new bushes are to be installed, they must be soaked in clean engine oil for one hour prior to installation.

To install new bushes, press or tap into place with a suitable shouldered mandrel.

Do not ream bushes after they have been installed as self lubricating qualities of the bush will be diminished.

Solenoid

* a. The following tests require a 20 Ohm, 30 amp variable resistor, a voltmeter (0-20 volt scale) and a fully charged 12V battery.

  b. The tests are to be carried out quickly so that the results are not affected by increasing temperature.

  c. Test cables are required to be at least 10 gauge.

Connect a variable resistor in series with the battery positive terminal and the solenoid '50' terminal, then adjust the

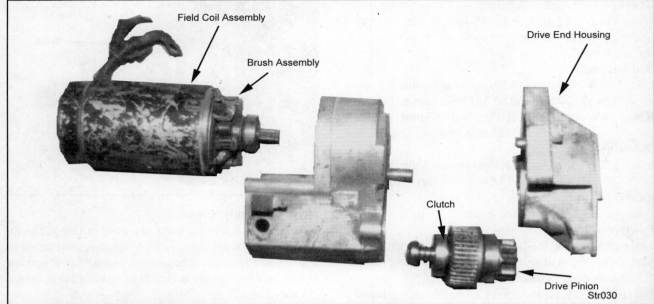

Field Coil Assembly

Brush Assembly

Drive End Housing

Clutch

Drive Pinion

Str030

maximum resistance. Connect a jumper lead from battery negative terminal to a good ground on the solenoid housing. Connect a jumper lead from solenoid field coil terminal to a good ground on solenoid housing. Connect the voltmeter positive lead to solenoid '50' terminal and negative lead to a good ground on solenoid housing.

Slowly adjust variable resistor until solenoid plunger 'pulls in' and note voltmeter reading. Quickly adjust variable resistor to minimum resistance. Full voltage is therefore applied to saturate the magnet core.

Immediately detach jumper lead from solenoid field coil terminal. Slowly adjust variable resistor until solenoid plunger springs out, and note voltmeter reading.

If solenoid does not operate within voltage limits, replace solenoid. Measurements at 20 DEG C.

Solenoid 'Pull In' Voltage Approx. 6 Volts or Less
Solenoid Plunger Spring Out Voltage   0.05-0.4 V Min

Assemble

1. Assembly is the reverse of the disassembly operation, noting the following. Lubricate drive end, pinion and commutator end bushes with clean engine oil. Lightly coat armature shaft bearing surfaces and helical splines, drive assembly internal splines and engaging clutch contact surfaces with Molybdenum Disulphide grease.

2. RN and YN models use reduction gears, so care must be taken that these gears and bearings are installed correctly.

3. Replace spring and steel ball into the clutch shaft with the aid of a magnet.

4. Install pinion and stop ring onto the armature shaft, then secure the spring clip in the groove, using a pair of circlip pliers. Secure armature in a soft jaw vice, turn drive assembly up to stop ring. Using multi-grips and a suitable insulator on the pinion gear teeth, continue to turn drive assembly until stop ring locks over spring clip. Adjust armature end play to

specification using shim/s between commutator end cover and circlip on armature shaft.

Armature Play Specification: 0.05-0.30mm.
If required, tighten field coil pole screws.

Pole Shoe Screws Torque Specification: 30-60 Nm.
With the starter motor assembled, a No Load Test should be conducted.

Failure of starter motor to perform according to the No Load specification may be due to tight or dirty bushes or high resistance connections. Rectify any faults found.

ELECTRICAL TESTS OF ASSEMBLED STARTER MOTOR ON TEST BENCH

The electrical test values depend upon the condition of the battery (capacity and charge). The testing period also plays an important part (heating of the starter and battery discharge). The starter performance is also influenced by the long cables on the test bench. Therefore, the test period should be as short as possible. The electrical values of a faulty starter will differ considerably from the specified test data, therefore, the battery must be in good condition and well charged.

Circuit Diagram

The electrical connections and the internal circuitry of the starter are given in the diagram.

Short Circuit

Clamp starter in test bench and connect in accordance with the wiring diagram.

The starter pinion and the ring gear of the test must have the same pitch; adjust backlash and out of mesh clearance.

Operate starter and apply test bench brake until pinion is almost to a standstill. Read current and voltage which must conform to specifications.

Load Test

If starter cranks engine slowly conduct this test and if it is

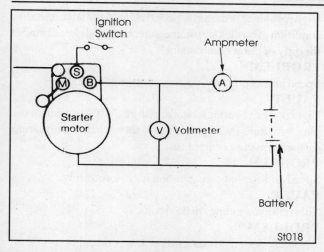

St018

required, compare starter current draw with specified current draw.

Clamp starter and connect as in short circuit test. Operate starter and apply brake until the specified current draw is recorded, read voltage and RPM.

No Load Test

So that the pinion and ring gear cannot engage, reposition the starter on the test bench. Connect as for previous tests.

Operate starter, read amperage, voltage and RPM.

No Load Specified Results:

2.0kW type less than 120A at 11.5volts
2.5kW type less than 180A at 11.5volts

SOLENOID SWITCH

The solenoid switch can be checked by connecting a 12 volt battery and a variable resistance to the pull-in and hold-in electrical circuits of the solenoid.

Increasing the voltage to 7.8 volts, the plunger moves into position at less than or around 7.8 volts.

Reduced the voltage to 0.5-0.4 volts this should cause the plunger to return to its original position.

STARTER RELAY TEST

Check for continuity or lack of continuity when check the relay terminals found on the left side of the engine bay.

Use an ohmmeter, digital will give the most accurate result,

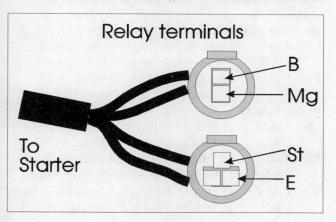

it may be possible to back probe the terminals.

Test Terminals: "E" to "St" there should be continuity.

Test Terminals: "B" to "Mg" there should be no continuity.

Connect battery current to terminals "E" and "St" then:

Test Terminals: "B" to "Mg" there should be continuity.

If above tests are NOT OK replace relay.

Installation

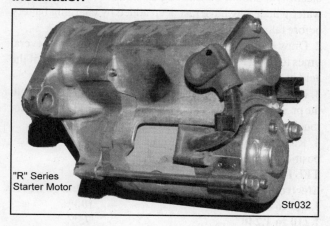

"R" Series Starter Motor

Str032

1. Place the starter assembly and start the starter retaining bolts, progressively tighten to specification.

Starter Motor Attaching Bolts: 19 - 24 lb. ft.

2. Reconnect the starter cable from battery and wiring to switch. Connect the battery earth cable.

Starter Motor To Block Bolts: 40-60Nm

Starter Motor Brace To Block: 12-16Nm

BATTERY INSPECTION

TESTING BATTERY ELECTROLYTE (ACID)

A hydrometer should be used to determine the specific gravity of battery electrolyte. The reading obtained indicates amount of unused sulphuric acid remaining in electrolyte and state of charge of battery.

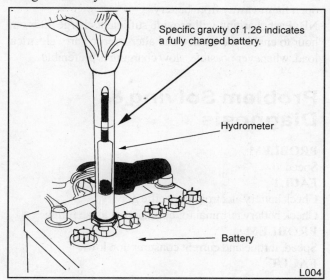

Specific gravity of 1.26 indicates a fully charged battery.

Hydrometer

Battery

L004

The reading obtained will vary in relation to the temperature of the electrolyte. As the temperature rises the density of the electrolyte decreases and the specific gravity falls. As the temperature falls the density increases and the specific gravity rises.

USING THE HYDROMETER

1. Liquid level of battery cell should be at normal height and electrolyte should be thoroughly mixed with any battery water which may have just been added by charging battery before taking hydrometer readings.

2. Draw electrolyte in and out of hydrometer barrel several times to bring temperature of hydrometer float to that of the acid in the cell.

3. Draw sufficient electrolyte into hydrometer barrel with the pressure bulb fully expanded to lift float so that it does not touch the sides, bottom or top of barrel.

4. Read the hydrometer with the hydrometer in a vertical position.

TEST RESULT INDICATIONS

Electrolyte specific gravity	Battery Charge Level.
1.240 to 1.260	**100%**
1.210 to 1.240	**75%**
1.180 to 1.210	**50%**
Below 1.130	**Completely discharged.**

A battery should be charged if the specific gravity is less than 1.210.

If there is more than 0.25 specific gravity variation between cells then a fault is most likely with the battery itself.

If battery charge is low and battery is serviceable, check alternator operation and all electrical connections.

BATTERY CHARGING

WARNING: When batteries are being charged explosive gas mixture forms beneath the cover of each cell.

* Do not smoke near batteries on charge or which have recently been charged.

* Do not break live circuit at terminals of batteries on charge. A spark will occur where the live circuity is broken. Keep all open flames away from battery.

NB: Fast charging will provide sufficient charge after one hour to enable the battery and alternator to carry electrical load, whenever possible, slow charging is preferable.

Problem Solving & Diagnosis

PROBLEM

Speed low.

FAULT

Check battery electrolyte specific gravity.
Check battery terminal for corrosion or loose fitting.

PROBLEM

Speed, torque and current consumption low.

FAULT

High resistance in motor. Check field to terminal connection, condition of bushes and their connections and check brushes for dirty or burnt commutator.

PROBLEM

Speed and torque low, current consumption high.

FAULT

Tight or worn bearings, bent armature shaft, insufficient end play, armature fouling pole shoe, short-circuited armature, earthed armature or field coil.

PROBLEM

Speed and current consumption high, torque low.

FAULT

Short circuit windings in field coils.

PROBLEM

Armature does not rotate, no current consumption.

FAULT

Open circuit armature, field coils or solenoid. If commutator is badly burned, there may be poor contact between brushes and commutator, owing to excessively worn or sticking brushes.

PROBLEM

Armature does not rotate, high current consumption.

FAULT

Earthed field winding or short-circuited solenoid. Armature physically prevented from rotating.

PROBLEM

Excessive arcing at commutator.

FAULT

Defective armature windings, sticking brushes or dirty commutator.

PROBLEM

Armature rotates but pinion does not mesh with ring gear.

FAULT

Pinion bearing fouled, burred, damaged ring gear or broken pinion teeth.

SPECIFICATIONS

Type	Four pole, four brush

Commutator:

Maximum permissible out of round	0.05mm
Depth of undercut	0.07mm

Diameter of Commutator

LN:	2.0kW	35mm (1.38in) [min 34mm (1.34in)]
	2.5kW	36mm (1.42in) [min 35mm (1.38in)]
RN:		30mm (1.18in) [min 29mm (1.14in)]
YN:		30mm (1.18in) [min 29mm (1.14in)]

Brush Length

LN:	2.0kW	15.0mm (0.591in) [min 9.5mm (0.374in)]
	2.5kW	20.5mm (0.807in) [min 13mm (0.512in)]
RN:	1.0kW	13.5mm (1.38in) [min 8.5mm (0.335in)]
	1.4kW	15.5mm (0.61in) [min 10mm (0.394in)]
YN:	1.0kW	13.5mm (1.38in) [min 8.5mm (0.335in)]
	1.4kW	15.5mm (0.61in) [min 10mm (0.394in)]

ALTERNATOR SYSTEM

GENERAL INFORMATION

When the engine is operating with the ignition switch turned on, a flow of electrical current passes through the rotor coil wiring which energises the rotating electro-magnet (the rotor). The spinning of the rotor causes the stator windings to cut the magnetic lines of force of the rotor, this creates an

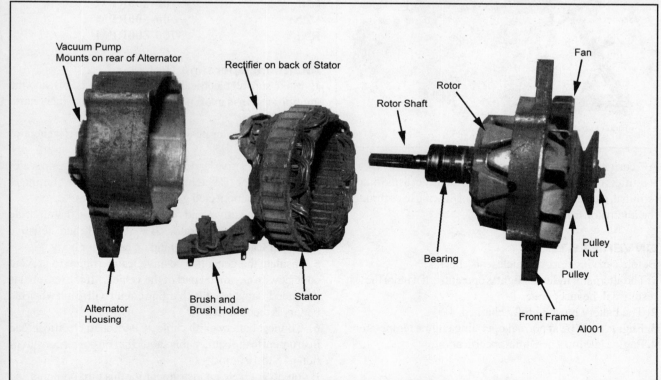

Vacuum Pump Mounts on rear of Alternator

Rectifier on back of Stator

Fan

Rotor

Rotor Shaft

Bearing

Pulley Nut

Pulley

Front Frame

Alternator Housing

Brush and Brush Holder

Stator

AI001

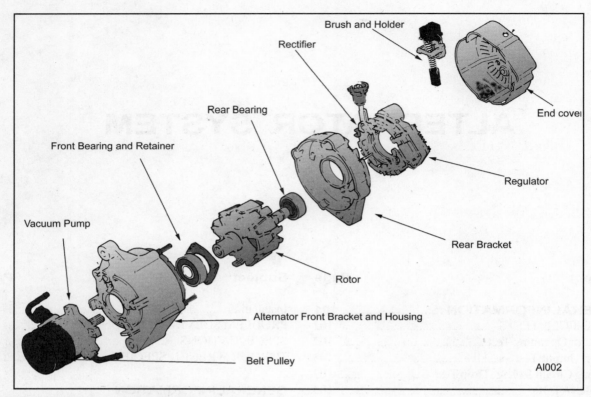

Brush and Holder

Rectifier

End cover

Rear Bearing

Front Bearing and Retainer

Regulator

Vacuum Pump

Rear Bracket

Rotor

Alternator Front Bracket and Housing

Belt Pulley

AI002

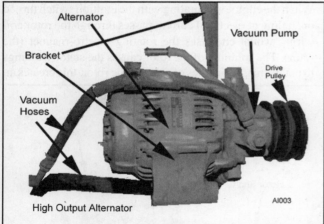

Alternator

Vacuum Pump

Bracket

Drive Pulley

Vacuum Hoses

High Output Alternator

AI003

AC current voltage in the stator windings.
Rectifiers convert the AC current to DC current at the output terminal, rectifiers also stop the current flowing back through the alternator from the battery.

ON VEHICLE TESTS
Before carrying out on vehicle tests check:
1. The alternator indicator light is operating, if it is not the test results will be inaccurate.
2. The battery must be fully charged.
3. Engine must be at normal operating engine temperature.
4. Engine idle must be within specification:

Check Tune-up chapter, but as a guide -

YN:	
Man Trans	650-800RPM
Auto Trans	750-850RPM
LN:	700-800RPM
VZN:	700-800RPM
RN:	700-800RPM

Alternator Operating Test
1. Make sure all electrical equipment is turned off, and the ignition system is in off position. Disconnect battery earth cable at battery.
2. Detach generator positive lead from the 'B+' generator terminal.
3. Connect positive lead of an ohmmeter (0-100 Amp scale) to the generator 'B+' terminal, and the negative ohmmeter lead to the disconnected generator positive lead.
4. Connect positive lead of a voltmeter (0-20 Volt scale minimum) to the generator 'B+' terminal, and negative voltmeter lead to a good ground on generator body.
5. Insulate the generator positive lead terminal to prevent contact with any metal part of the vehicle. If the terminal is grounded, damage to the charging circuit will result when the battery is reconnected.
6. Connect battery earth cable. Connect an electrical load instrument to the battery, this should have a power consumption of 8 to 10 amps.
If you do not have an instrument for this turn on lights and

other known power rated accessories to obtain power consumption of 8-10 amps.

7. Start engine and check generator output against rated output in the following chart.

Generator Rated Output

V = Model	Voltage Setting	RPM	Amps
RN 30's/40's	14.0-14.7	2000	30+
RN50's -110's	13.8-14.8	2000	30+
LN 50's/110's	13.8-14.8	2000	30+
YN50's /110's	13.8-14.8	2000	30+
VZN	13.8-15.0	2000	30+

* The power consumption described in point 6 above is used to achieve the desired voltage reading in this chart.

If generator doesn't provide rated output, it should be disassembled and inspected for faults.

When the Generator Output Check, is completed, to prevent excessive battery discharge occurring, the engine should be returned to idle speed and the loading device detached from battery terminals.

Detach the battery earth cable at battery, remove bolt and ohmmeters, then reconnect the generator positive lead (red wire) to the generator 'B+' terminal. Connect battery earth cable to the battery.

Current Output Test

1. Connect ohmmeter and voltmeter as described in 'OUTPUT CHECK', with the following alteration;

The positive voltmeter lead connected to the battery positive terminal, not the generator 'B+' terminal.

2. Connect a loading device (IE. an adjustable carbon pile) across the battery terminals, and regulate to maintain a current flow of 9.5 - 10.5 AMP.

3. Operate engine at approx. 2000 RPM, maintain this engine speed for 15 seconds and check the regulated voltage reading.

4. If regulated voltage reading is not 14.25-14.55 volts, replace voltage regulator.

5. Detach battery cable at battery. Remove the voltmeter and ohmmeter, then reconnect the generator positive lead to the generator 'B+' terminal. Connect battery earth cable.

Charging Circuit Voltage Drop Test

With normal connections made at generator, charging circuit can be checked for voltage drop as follows:

1. Connect positive lead of a low range voltmeter at the generator 'B+' terminal and the negative voltmeter lead to the battery positive terminal.

2. Start engine, switch on headlamps, then increase engine speed to approx. 2500 RPM and note voltmeter reading.

3. Stop engine and transfer voltmeter connections, negative lead to generator body and the positive lead to battery negative terminal. Start and operate the engine at approx.

2000 RPM and again note voltmeter reading.

4. If readings exceed 0.5 volts on positive side and 0.25 volts on negative side, there is a high resistance in charging circuit which must be traced and corrected. Stop engine, detach the voltmeter.

Maintenance

Removal

1. Detach battery earth cable at battery, loosen the generator attaching bolts. Remove wiring harness connector from generator terminal.

2. Pull back cap from generator 'B+' terminal, remove nut, washer and generator positive lead. Loosen generator brace bolt, and remove the generator retaining bolt.

3. Support generator, remove the bolts then remove the generator from vehicle.

Dismantle

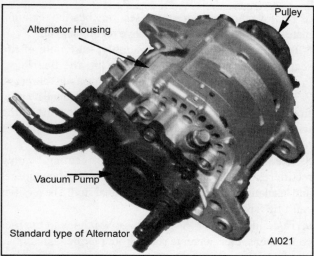

Standard type of Alternator — Pulley, Alternator Housing, Vacuum Pump — AI021

1. Remove the 3 bolts (small vacuum pump) 4 bolts (large pump) attaching the vacuum pump at the rear of the generator. YN have no vacuum pump.

2. Remove the brush holder cover (2 nuts).

(a) W/O IC Regulator. Disconnect the wire lead, remove nut and brush holder.

(b) W/ IC Regulator. Remove the screw and lead wire, pull out the brush holder and IC regulator from the holder, with the brush holder away from the generator remove screw and wire.

Remove the IC regulator from the brush holder.

3. Mark relative positions of end plate, stator and drive end plate, remove the retaining screws from slip ring end plate. Then withdraw the brush and voltage regulator assembly.

4. Remove (3-small vac pump) (4-large vac pump) through bolts and washers from the pulley end of generator. Separate the slip ring end plate and stator (as an assembly) from rotor and drive end plate.

5. Hold rotor in a soft jaw vice, and remove drive pulley

attaching nut and lock washer, withdraw the pulley assembly, fan and collar. Support drive end plate in a press and remove rotor.

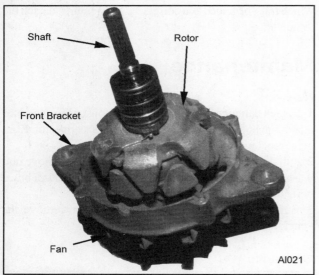

Al021

6. Remove three or four screws securing bearing retaining plate to drive end plate, then remove retaining plate.
* To make sure of correct assembly, take note of the sealing shield placing, when removing the bearings.
Press bearing out with drive end plate, using a suitable press.
7. Using a suitable puller tool, remove slip ring end bearing from rotor shaft, remove nut, wave, flat and insulating washers from the 'B+' terminal stud. Remove suppressor lead connection from rectifier terminal.
8. Remove three screws and washers securing bearing rectifier assembly to slip as an assembly, then remove spacer and insulating washer from 'B+' terminal stud. The rectifier can't be repaired
9. Tag and un-solder the four stator windings to rectifier connections, then separate stator from rectifier assembly.

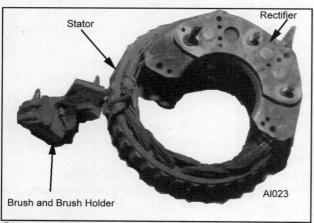

Al023

Clean and Inspect
With generator completely disassembled, clean and inspect all components. Wash the components, excluding stator, rotor, rectifier and regulator in a suitable cleaning agent. Don't clean stator or rotor windings with cleaning solvents as

damage to the insulation may result.

Component Checking
Rectifier Assembly
The rectifier can't be overhauled, and is serviced as an assembly only.
1. Using a powered D.C. test lamp (of less than 24 volts) or ohmmeter, touch probes to terminal thread and rectifier frame. Reverse probe connections and repeat test to check that current has passed in one direction only.
2. Repeat procedure with probes on negative side of rectifier.

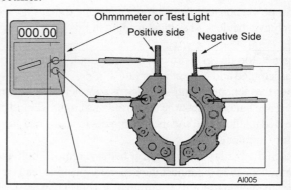

Al005

* The lamp or ohmmeter will show a short circuit if any one diode is grounded.
3. Replace the rectifier assembly if required.
Brush Gear
1. Measure length of brushes installed in the voltage regulator. Replace brushes if not at required specified length.
Specified brush exposed length is:
LN: 20mm (0.79in)- New Brush
      5.5mm (0.217in)- Service Minimum
RN 12.5mm (0.79in)- New Brush
      5.5mm (0.217in)- Service Minimum
YN: W/O IC Reg. 12.5mm (0.492in) - New Brush
    W/   16.5mm (0.65in) - New Brush
          5.5mm (0.217in) - Minimum

2. Inspect brushes for damage and replace if required, un-solder brush leads from regulator connections, carefully bend back the retaining lugs just enough to free the brush leads. Remove and dispose of the brushes and springs.
3. Place silicon tubing over brush leads, install new brush springs over brush leads, then install brushes into regulator and carefully solder leads to connections.
4. Bend the retaining tabs back into the original places and check that the brushes are free and move smoothly in and out of holder.
Rotor Insulation Test
Check insulation between slip rings and rotor core and shaft, using an ohmmeter or test light. If continuity exists, replace rotor.

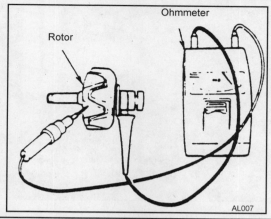

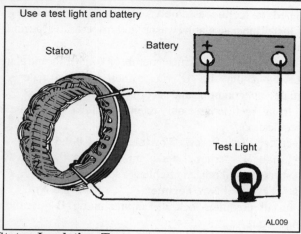

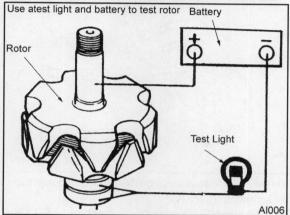

Rotor Open Circuit Test

Connect ohmmeter probes to slip rings and measure resistance of rotor windings. Replace the rotor if the resistance is not within the specification given in the following:

Rotor Winding Resistance @20 DEG C :

LN:	**W/O IC Reg.**	**3.9-4.1 Ohms**
	W/ IC Reg.	**2.8-3.0 Ohms**
RN:	**All ex 90A**	**3.9-4.1 Ohms**
	90A	**2.8-3.0 Ohms**
YN:	**W/O IC Reg.**	**3.9-4.1 Ohms**
	W/ IC Reg.	**2.8-3.0 Ohms**

Slip Rings

Check slip rings for wear or damage and polish with emery cloth until smooth or replace rotor as necessary.

Slip Ring Specifications:

RN & YN: Diameter   32.3-32.5mm (1.272-1.280in)
**   Min. Dia   32.1-(1.264in)**

Bearings

Examine the bearings for evidence of overheating, cracks or other damage. Check bearings for operation that is free and smooth. Check bearing bores in drive end slip ring end plates for wear. If bearing outer race is allowed to rotate in its bore, it will cause ovality of the bore and a lip will form in the bore. If the bearings are serviceable, pack bearings with grease. Replace damaged bearings if required.

Stator Insulation Test

Connect an ohmmeter or a test light to any stator lead and the stator frame. If there is current reading or the test light glows, this indicates earthed wiring, replace stator.

Stator Open Circuit Test

Connect ohmmeter to any two stator leads and note resistance, repeat the operation on remaining stator leads. Replace the stator if the resistance is not within the specification given in the following:

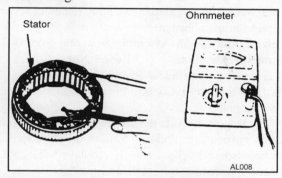

Stator Winding Resistance @ 20 DEG C :
Resistance   0.14 - 0.10 Ohms.

Assemble

1. Install front bearing in drive end plate. Check correct orientation of bearing (bearing sealing shield toward pulley). Install bearing retainer plate and screws to specified torque.

Bearing Retainer Plate Screws Torque Specification:
  2.1-3.0 Nm.

2. Install drive end plate assembly onto rotor shaft, install collar, cooling fan, pulley, lock washer and retaining nut. Secure rotor is a soft jaw vice, torque the retaining nut to specified torque.

Drive Pulley Retaining Nut Torque:

LN:	**900 kg-cm (65 ft-lb, 88 Nm)**
RN: All exp 90A	**600 kg-cm (45 ft-lb, 61 Nm)**
RN: 90A	**900 kg-cm (65 ft-lb, 88 Nm)**
YN:	**625 kg-cm (45 ft-lb, 61 Nm)**

3. Install slip ring end bearing (with sealing shield toward rotor) onto rotor shaft.

4. Solder four stator leads to original connector terminals (as

tagged) on rectifier assembly.

5. Install inner insulating washer and spacer to 'B+' terminal stud.

6. Install stator and rectifier assembly into slip ring end plate. Make sure that the 'O' ring in slip ring end plate is a satisfactory condition and is correctly located.

7. Install rectifier assembly retaining screws and torque to specification.

Rectifier Plate Screws Torque: **1.0-2.5 Nm.**

8. Install 'B+' terminal stud outer insulating, flat and wave washers. Install nut, and tighten to specified torque.

'B+' Terminal Nut Torque: **7.5-8.5 Nm.**

9. Install remaining lock washer and nut on 'B+' terminal finger tight.

10. Align the match marks, then install the stator and slip ring end plate assembly onto rotor and drive end plate assembly.

11. Install through bolts and washers, then tighten progressively to specified torque.

Through Bolt Torque Specification: **3.8-5.5 Nm.**

12. Install the voltage regulator and brush assembly to the slip ring end plate, making sure that the regulator engages with the spring connectors on the rectifier. Make sure the brushes are correctly located on slip rings.

13. Install regulator and brush assembly retaining screws, then torque to specification.

Regulator and Brush Assembly Securing Screws Torque Specification: **1.6-2.3 Nm.**

14. Replace the brush holder cover (2 nuts).

(a) W/O IC Regulator. Connect the wire lead, replace nut and brush holder.

(b) W/ IC Regulator. With the brush holder away from the generator replace screw and wire. Replace the screw and lead wire, push in the brush holder and IC regulator to the holder. Replace the IC regulator from the brush holder.

15. Remove the 3 bolts (small vacuum pump) 4 bolts (large pump) attaching the vacuum pump at the rear of the generator. YN have no vacuum pump.

16. Connect suppressor lead to '+' terminal, located at the rear of the generator.

Installation

1. Install the alternator bracket, then use the generator to achieve specified generator/water pump belt tension. Tighten the generator mounting bolts to specified torque.

Generator Upper Attaching Nut And Bolt Torque Specification: **34-44 Nm.**

Generator Attaching Bolt Torque Spec: **12-16 Nm.**

Generator/Water Pump Belt Deflection:

LN: New Belt	5-10mm	(0.20-0.39 in)
Used Belt	10-15mm	(0.39-0.59 in)
RN: New Belt	4-6mm	(0.16-0.24 in)
Used Belt	5-7mm	(0.20-0.28 in)
YN: New Belt	5-7mm	(0.20-0.28 in)
Used Belt	7-8mm	(0.28-0.31 in)

2. Install generator positive lead, washer and nut on 'B+'

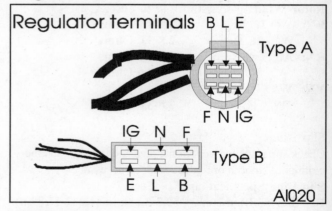

Alternator Belt Tension Adjusting Arm

Alternator Drive Belt

Alternator   Adjusting Nut   Vacuum Pump

AI024

Belt deflection of 9-11mm

TCo001

terminal. Tighten nut to specified torque, then refit cap over 'B+' terminal.

'B+' Terminal Nut Torque Specification: **5-12 Nm**

3. Connect wiring harness at the generator terminal block. Connect battery earth cable at battery.

Regulator L, 2L 2L-T 50's 60's upto 1988?

Regulator terminals   B L E

Type A

F N IG

IG   N   F

Type B

E   L   B

AI020

Adjustments

Voltage Regulator

To adjust regulator bend adjusting arm as indicated in illustration, to achieve specified voltage.

Specified Voltage: **13.8 - 14.8 volts**

Voltage Relay

To adjust voltage relay bend regulator adjusting arm as indicated in illustration, to achieve specified voltage.

Specified Voltage: **4.0 - 5.8 volts**

Testing

Use an ohmmeter on the terminals indicated to test regulator.

a. IG and F open points 0 ohms
b. IG and F shut points approx 100 ohms
c. L and E open points 0 ohms
d. L and E shut points approx 100 ohms
e. B and E open points Infinity ohms
f. B and E shut points approx 100 ohms
g. B and L open points Infinity ohms
h. B and L shut points approx 0 ohms
i. B and L open points approx 24 ohms

Problem Solving & Diagnosis

BATTERY WILL NOT CHARGE
* Battery cells not operating
* Battery terminals dirty or loose
* Battery acid level low
* Battery acid specific gravity specification of 1.230
* Loose or corroded connection in charging circuit
* Faulty generator
* Faulty voltage regulator

INDICATOR LIGHT DOES NOT GO ON
* Globe broken or blown
* Defective regulator
* Defective Wiring
* Open circuit in rotor winding

INDICATOR LIGHT STAYS ON
* Positive diode failure
* Defective voltage regulator
* Faulty alternator
* B + cable off or broken
* S cable off or broken
* Battery Overcharged

NOISY ALTERNATOR
* Worn bearings
* Loose alternator drive pulley
* Open or shorted diodes
* Open or shorted Stator winding
* Generator mounting brackets loose
* Worn or frayed drive belt

BATTERY OVERCHARGES
* Battery acid specific gravity not correct
* Shorted battery cell
* Faulty voltage regulator
* Short circuit in rotor winding

ALTERNATOR WILL NOT CHARGE
* Faulty regulator
* Brushes worn or sticking
* Brush springs broken or lost tension
* Faulty rectifiers
* Open circuit in stator wiring, charging circuit or field circuit
* Loose drive belt

SPECIFICATIONS

Earth polarity	Negative
Nominal voltage	12 V

Generator Rated Output

V = Model	Voltage Setting	RPM	Amps
RN 30's/40's	14.0-14.7	2000	30+
RN50's -110's	13.8-14.8	2000	30+
LN 50's/110's	13.8-14.8	2000	30+
YN50's /110's	13.8-14.8	2000	30+

Stator phases	3
Stator winding connections	Star
Number of poles	12

Specified brush exposed length is:
LN: 20mm (0.79in)- New Brush
    5.5mm (0.217in)- Service Minimum
RN: 12.5mm (0.79in)- New Brush
    5.5mm (0.217in)- Service Minimum
YN: W/O IC Reg. 12.5mm (0.492in)- New Brush
    W/ 16.5mm (0.65in)- New Brush
    5.5mm (0.217in)- Minimum

Rotor Winding Resistance @20 DEG C :
LN: W/O IC Reg.   3.9-4.1 Ohms
    W/ IC Reg.   2.8-3.0 Ohms
RN: All ex 90A   3.9-4.1 Ohms
    90A   2.8-3.0 Ohms
YN: W/O IC Reg.   3.9-4.1 Ohms
    W/ IC Reg.   2.8-3.0 Ohms

Stator Winding Resistance @ 20 DEG C :

Resistance	0.14 - 0.10 Ohms.
Voltage regulator setting	12mm (new)

TORQUE WRENCH SPECIFICATIONS   Nm

Through Bolt	3.8-5.5
Bearing Retainer Plate Screw	2.1-3.0
Regulator and Brush Assembly Securing Screw	1.6-2.3
'B+' Terminal Stud Nut	7.5-8.5
Battery Harness Terminal to B+Terminal Stud Nut	5-12
Rectifier Plate Retaining Screw	1.0-2.5
Capacitor Fixing Screw	2.9-4.1

Alternator

Upper Mounting Bolt	19-25
Lower Mounting Bolt	20-28

Drive Pulley Retaining Nut Torque:

LN:	900 kg-cm (65 ft-lb, 88 Nm)
RN: All exp 90A	600 kg-cm (45 ft-lb, 61 Nm)
RN: 90A	900 kg-cm (65 ft-lb, 88 Nm)
YN:	625 kg-cm (45 ft-lb, 61 Nm)

COOLING SYSTEM

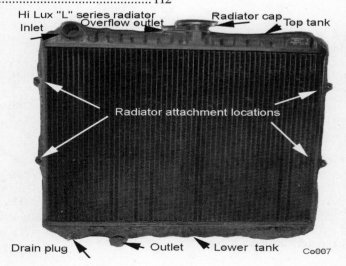

Hi Lux "L" series radiator
Inlet — Overflow outlet — Radiator cap — Top tank
Radiator attachment locations
Drain plug — Outlet — Lower tank — Co007

COOLING SYSTEM

The engine cooling system consists of a horizontal flow fin and tube type radiator with a pressure sealing cap, a coolant recovery bottle, a belt drive water pump, a thermostat and a belt driven fan.

Water is circulated by pump through cylinder block, head and then through top hose to top tank of radiator.

Water passing down through radiator is cooled by air flow through radiator fins.

Heated water is drawn from cylinder head to inlet manifold and heater unit.

*An effective concentration of recommend coolant/inhibitor must be maintained in the cooling system.

The radiator cap is a pressure sealing type. It incorporates two valves; a pressure release valve and a vacuum released valve, and has two functions:

1. To increase pressure in cooling system and thus raise boiling point of coolant.

2. In conjunction with the coolant recovery bottle, to maintain the coolant in radiator at maximum level.

The coolant recovery bottle is connected to radiator filler neck by a plastic tube. The system operates in the following manner.

As the coolant is heated it expands and pressure in the system increases. When pressure reaches a predetermined point pressure release valve in radiator cap opens and coolant is forced out of radiator and into recovery bottle.

As engine cools the coolant contracts thus creating a vacuum in radiator. The vacuum release valve in radiator cap opens and coolant is drawn back into radiator.

*Coolant recovery system will not operate if the cooling system has an air leak.

The water pump is a centrifugal type pump. It is mounted at the front of the motor and is belt driven by a pulley mounted to crankshaft.

The fan is mounted to the end of the water pump shaft.

The thermostat is a wax pellet type and incorporated in system to ensure quick engine warm up and to keep the engine at the optimum operating temperature.

A common misconception is that by removing the thermostat the engine will run cooler, this incorrect, as it can quite often increase the running temperature and induce overheating. The thermostat acts as a restrictor as well as stop coolant flow in a cold engine, if you remove the restriction of the coolant flow, fast flowing coolant does not have time to disperse the store heat from the engine therefore causing the engine to run hotter.

COOLANT

The alloy content of components makes it essential that an effective coolant additive is maintained in the cooling system. Coolant comes in two different colours Green and Red. Red has a reagent grade indicator dye built into it and as a result should any corrosive acids build up in the cooling

system from exhaust gas leaking past the head gasket the coolant will change from red to brilliant yellow. If the coolant does change colour it should be replaced.

As a general rule coolant manufactured by different companies should not be mixed even if the coolant is the same colour.

Glycol coolant has several properties other than antifreeze, it will help lubricate various valves in the cooling system, thermostat slides and water pump seal surfaces.

Glycol will also raise the boiling point of coolant.

GLYCOL BOILING POINT CHART

Kpa Pressure	PSI Pressure	33% Glycol	55% Glycol
0	0	04.5oC	108.5oC
25	3.7	110.5oC	114.0oC
50	7.4	116.5oC	119.5oC
75	11.0	121.0oC	125.0oC
100	14.7	125.0oC	129.0oC
150	22.1	132.5oC	136.0oC
200	26.4	139.0oC	142.5oC

GENERAL MAINTENANCE

Coolant Level Check

The coolant level is inspected by checking the coolant reservoir visually or by removing the radiator cap.

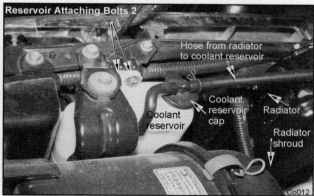

When the coolant is cold the coolant level should be at the FULL mark. Depending on the engine temperature the level will vary.

RADIATOR CAP PRESSURE TEST.

1. Remove cap from coolant supply tank.

2. Use water to clean cap seals and vacuum relief valve. Following manufacturer's directions, install cap on a pressure test unit.

3. Depress the plunger of test unit pump slowly until highest reading is achieved on gauge.

4. This reading should lie within the specification for the cap being tested. Repeat test several times.

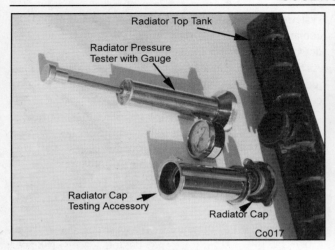

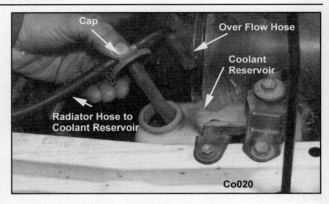

5. If gauge reading is not within specification replace cap.

ANTI-FREEZE SOLUTION.

It's recommended that anti-freeze be added to engine coolant if vehicles are to be operated in areas where the temperature may fall below 5°C.

DRAINING AND FILLING COOLING SYSTEM.
DRAIN.

WARNING: Under no circumstances must the coolant supply tank cap be completely removed prior to the pressure in the cooling system being relieved.

Remove supply tank cap and detach lower radiator hose from radiator or unscrew drain plug which is located in radiator lower tank.

REFILL.

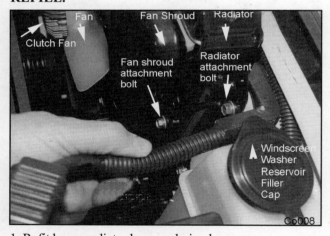

1. Refit lower radiator hose or drain plug.
2. Add the specified amount of corrosion inhibitor and/or anti-freeze to coolant supply tank.
3. Fill system with clean water to "ADD/MIN" mark on supply tank.
4. Install cap, or depress and turn it until fully locked.
5. Set heater control to "HOT".
6. Start engine and run it at 2000 rpm for 10 minutes to open thermostat and purge air from system.

7. Fill supply tank to "FULL/MAX" mark.
8. Replace cap.
Note: This entire procedure must be followed to ensure correct system performance.

DRIVE BELTS AND PULLEYS

Check tension of drive belt to make certain it's within specifications if it's noisy. Check for misaligned pulleys. If drive belt is worn or frayed, replace it using following procedures.

BELT ADJUSTMENT

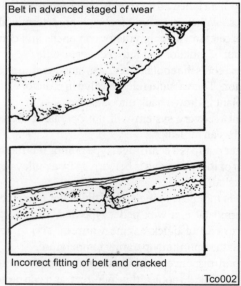

Drive belts should be properly adjusted at all times. A loose drive belt will cause incorrect operation of driven component(s). A belt that's too tight places severe strain on driven component bearings. Drive belts that are properly tensioned minimize noise and prolong the belt's service life. Any belt that's operated for a minimum of 10 minutes is considered a used belt, and when adjusted it must be adjusted to the reset tension shown in the specifications.

BELT TENSION.

Apply a thumb pressure of 100N (10kg) to the midpoint of the longest convenient span of belt, and noting the belt deflection

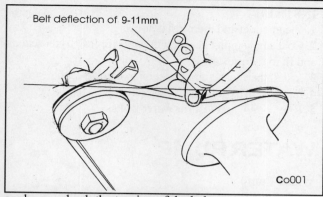

Belt deflection of 9-11mm

Co001

as shown, check the tension of the belt.

ALTERNATOR WATER PUMP.
NEW BELT DEFLECTION (mm) 7-8
USED BELT DEFLECTION (mm) 9-10
POWER STEERING PUMP
NEW BELT DEFLECTION (mm) 8-9
USED BELT DEFLECTION (mm) 10-11
AIRCONDITIONING
NEW BELT DEFLECTION (mm) 8-9
USED BELT DEFLECTION (mm) 10-11

Adjust at alternator or driven unit
1. Loosen alternator mounting bolts and adjusting arm pivot bolt.
2. Then turn adjusting nut on alternator upper mounting bolt to achieve correct tension.
3. Tighten mounting bolts and adjusting arm pivot bolt.

Adjust with adjusting idler pulley
1. Loosen lock nut on tensioner bolt.
2. Adjust tensioner bolt to obtain the correct tension of the belt.
3. Tighten lock nut on tensioner bolt of idler pulley.

BELT REPLACEMENT with IDLER PULLEY
1. Loosen the locknut on the idler pulley mounting stud and turning the stud, relieve the tension on the power steering pump belt.
2. Loosen the alternator mounting bolts and the adjusting arm pivot bolt.
3. To loosen the belt, turn the adjusting nut on the alternator upper mounting bolt.

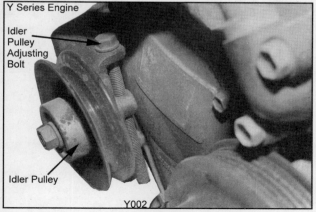

Y Series Engine

Idler Pulley Adjusting Bolt

Idler Pulley

Y002

4. Remove the belt.
5. Install fan belt on crankshaft, alternator and water pump pulleys.
6. As previously described, adjust belt. Install power steering pump belt.
7. Turn the idler pulley mounting stud to adjust to specified tension. Tighten the lock nut.

RADIATOR HOSE REPLACEMENT
Radiator hoses should be replaced whenever they become cracked, rotted or have a tendency to collapse.
1. Drain radiator.
2. Loosen the clamps at each end of hose to be removed.

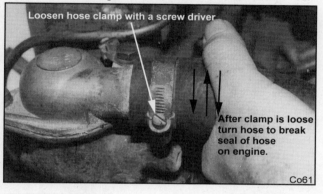

Loosen hose clamp with a screw driver

After clamp is loose turn hose to break seal of hose on engine.

Co61

3. Slide hose off radiator connection and the cylinder head water outlet or water pump connection.
4. Position clamps and hoses so they do not rub or contact any metal surface, otherwise they will soon deteriorate and fail.
5. Tighten clamps.
6. Fill coolant supply tank to the "FULL/MAX" mark.
7. Fill and bleed the cooling system as previously described.
NOTE: Install hose clamps as close as possible to the bead on inlet and outlet pipes.

THERMOSTAT
The thermostat is located in coolant outlet connector at front of cylinder head. Coolant flows to the water pump through the intake manifold, when thermostat is closed. When thermostat is open, coolant flows through coolant outlet (thermostat housing) to the radiator. For operating temperatures, refer to specifications.

Check a used thermostat before reinstalling it following the procedure under "Thermostat Test" in the preceding pages. Don't attempt to repair thermostat. It should be replaced if not operating properly.

REMOVE
1. Remove lower radiator hose and drain cooling system below level of coolant outlet housing.
2. Reinstall hose.
3. Remove coolant outlet housing retaining bolts and slide housing (with hose attached) to one side.
4. Remove thermostat and gasket.

THERMOSTAT TEST.

Test used thermostats before installing them in engine.

1. Remove thermostat and immerse it in boiling water.
2. Remove when open and place a .05 mm feeler gauge in throat of thermostat and allow thermostat to cool and clamp on feeler gauge.

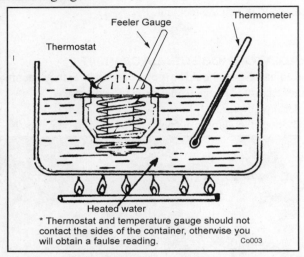

Feeler Gauge

Thermometer

Thermostat

* Thermostat and temperature gauge should not contact the sides of the container, otherwise you will obtain a faulse reading.

Heated water

Co003

3. Suspend thermometer into container of cool water and heat water.
4. When thermostat opens and drops off feeler gauge, note temperature.

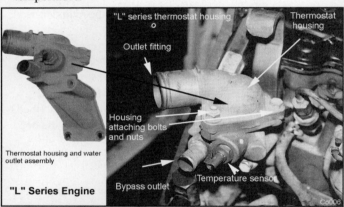

"L" series thermostat housing

Thermostat housing

Outlet fitting

Housing attaching bolts and nuts

Thermostat housing and water outlet assembly

Bypass outlet

Temperature sensor

"L" Series Engine

Co006

Intake manifold

Thermostat

20R, 21R & 22R Thermostat housing is located in the intake manifold.

Co005

INSTALL

1. Clean outlet and thermostat housing.
2. Coat a new outlet gasket with water proof gasket sealant and fit to thermostat.
3. Install thermostat and outlet on to thermostat housing.
4. Fill system as previously described.
5. Run engine and test for water leaks.

WATER PUMP

Water Pump

A centrifugal-type water pump is situated on the front of the cylinder block. A vane-type impeller provides coolant through centrifugal movement to the water pump outlet port.

Remove and discard a pump if it is found faulty, as it is of a sealed unit type which is unable to be repaired.

Remove

1. Disconnect the lower radiator hose from the radiator to empty the coolant and then detach the hose.
2. Take the fan and clutch assembly out. Detach the power steering pump and the fan drive belts.
3. Remove the water pump from the cylinder block.

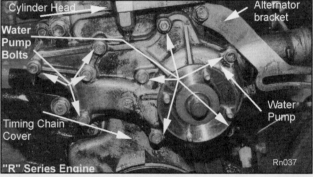

Cylinder Head

Alternator bracket

Water Pump Bolts

Water Pump

Timing Chain Cover

"R" Series Engine

Rn037

Y Series Engine Water Pump

Water Pump Bolts

Y001

4. Detach the drive belt pulley.
5. "L Series Engines remove the front timing belt cover as described in "Engine chapter".
6. Remove the water pump attaching bolts.
7. Remove water pump, it may be necessary to lever water pump away from the engine block.

Install

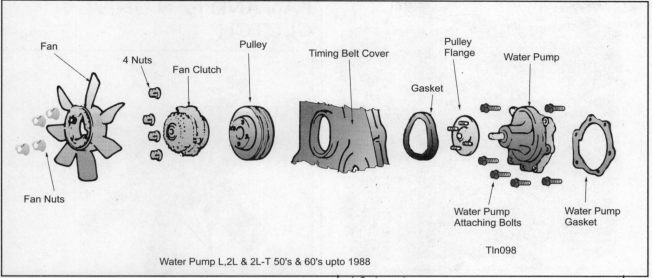

Fan
4 Nuts
Fan Clutch
Pulley
Timing Belt Cover
Pulley Flange
Gasket
Water Pump
Fan Nuts
Water Pump Attaching Bolts
Water Pump Gasket

Water Pump L,2L & 2L-T 50's & 60's upto 1988

TIn098

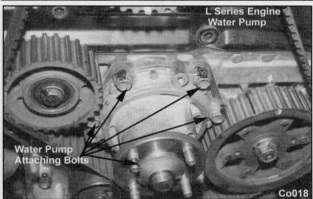

L Series Engine Water Pump

Water Pump Attaching Bolts

Co018

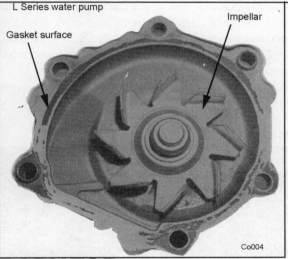

L Series water pump

Gasket surface
Impellar

Co004

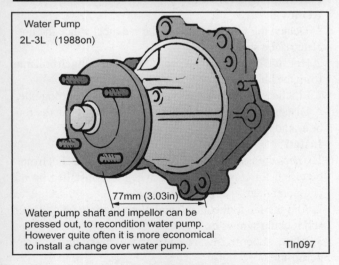

Water Pump
2L-3L   (1988on)

77mm (3.03in)

Water pump shaft and impellor can be pressed out, to recondition water pump. However quite often it is more economical to install a change over water pump.

TIn097

1. Clean the pump and cylinder block mating surfaces and place a new gasket coated with water resistant sealer.

2. Install the water pump on the cylinder block Install the bolts and tighten to specification.

3. Install the lower radiator hose and install the drive belt pulley.

4. Replace and tension the drive belts.

5. Install the fan and clutch assembly and the fan shroud, fill the cooling system.

RADIATOR

Removal

1. Detach the lower radiator hose to empty the cooling system. Detach the upper radiator hose.

2. Detach the coolant supply hose from the side of the radiator.

3. Detach the oil cooler lines at the radiator only on vehicles provided with automatic transmission.

4. Take the air cleaner intake duct out. Detach the battery cables. Loosen the battery clamp and detach the battery shroud.

5. Take the screws out that are securing the fan shroud to the top of the radiator, lift the shroud from the clips on the bottom of the radiator and lay it back over the fan.

6. Take the radiator support bolts out and gently lift the radiator from the vehicle.

Install

1. If required place an oil cooler line fittings to radiator (auto trans).

2. Locate the radiator in the vehicle and place the support bolts.

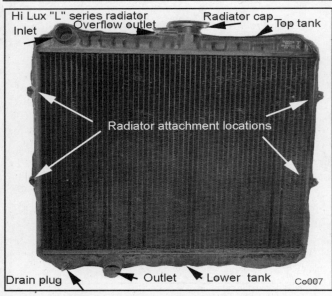

Hi Lux "L" series radiator
Overflow outlet
Inlet
Radiator cap
Top tank
Radiator attachment locations
Drain plug
Outlet
Lower tank
Co007

3. On the bottom of the radiator locate the shroud in the clips and put the two securing screws in at the top of the shroud.
4. Join the upper and lower hoses and the coolant supply hose.
5. Connect the battery cables.
6. Install the air cleaner duct, join the oil cooler lines (auto trans) and fill the cooling system.

COOLANT SUPPLY TANK

Reservoir Attaching Bolts 2
Hose from radiator to coolant reservoir
Coolant reservoir cap
Coolant reservoir
Radiator
Radiator shroud
Co012

Removal
1. Take the supply tank cap off and lower radiator hose and empty cooling system until no coolant is left in the supply tank.
2. Remove the bleed tube found on upper surface of supply tank.
3. Remove coolant supply tank from the vehicle.
4. Remove the coolant feed hose out that is fitted to the lower section of supply tank.

Install
1. Place the coolant feed hose onto supply tank and position the supply tank in the vehicle and secure coolant feed hose.
2. Connect the supply tank to vehicle. Connect the bleed tube to the top of the supply tank Fill the supply tank with coolant.

FAN AND FAN DRIVE CLUTCH

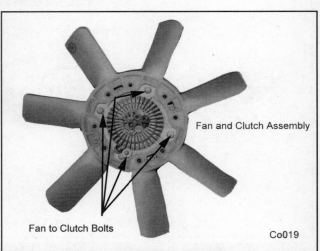

Fan and Clutch Assembly
Fan to Clutch Bolts
Co019

DESCRIPTION AND OPERATION
Fan and Fan Drive Clutch
The fan clutch enables the use of a powerful fan without paying the penalty of power loss or noise. The fan clutch produces maximum air flow through the radiator when required, and a minimum air flow when less than maximum cooling is essential. It can adjust between the maximum and the minimum air flows according to the conditions, and it narrows fan speed to a maximum rpm beyond a given input speed.

REMOVAL AND INSTALL
Fan and Fan Drive Clutch
Removal
1. Detach the fan shroud from the radiator. Place the hose clear of the shroud.
2. Hold the water pump hub and unscrew the clutch bolt nuts from the hub.
3. Lift the fan and clutch assembly from the vehicle together.
4. Disconnect the fan from the clutch by taking out the four bolts and nuts.

Install
1. Check the assembly for any fluid leakage. The clutch must be tested for correct operation when it is installed on the engine, if there is any sign of leakage.
2. Join the fan to the clutch and place the four socket head self locking screws in.
3. Apply 'Loctite 242' or equal to the thread on the water pump hub.
4. Join the fan/clutch assembly together with the fan shroud in the vehicle.
5. Place the clutch assembly on the water pump hub and secure to 40 Nm.
6. Replace the shroud to the radiator.
7. Put the air cleaner duct in and install the battery shroud, join the cables and secure the battery clamp.

PROBLEM SOLVING AND DIAGNOSIS

Quick Reference Diagnosis Chart

Engine Overheats

Loss of coolant.
Belt tension incorrect.
Radiator Fins obstructed.
Thermostat stuck closed, or otherwise defective.
Cooling system passage blocked by rust, scale or other foreign material.
Water pump inoperative.
Fan drive clutch defective.
Ignition initial timing incorrect.

Engine Fails to Reach Normal Operating Temperature or has Wrong Indicated Temperature.

Thermostat stuck open or of incorrect heat range.
Temperature sending unit defective (causing gauge to indicate low engine temperature).
Temperature gauge defective (not indicating true engine temperature) or incorrectly installed.

Loss of Coolant

Leaking radiator, or transmission oil cooler.
Leaking coolant supply tank.
Loose or damaged hose connections

Water leaking.

Cylinder head gasket defective.
Improper tightening of cylinder head bolts.
Cylinder block or head core plunge leaking.
Cracked or warped cylinder head or block.
Cracked intake manifold.
Supply tank pressure cap defective or of the wrong type.
Heater hose or engine hose with minor fault allowing water to leak.
Heater hose or engine hose not sealed correctly, or hose clamp not tight enough.

TESTING

Visual Inspection
Check for leakage at:
1. All hoses and hose connections.
2. Radiator seams and radiator core.
3. All engine core plugs and drain plugs.
4. Edges of cooling system gaskets.
5. Transmission oil cooler.
6. Vehicle heating system components.
7. Water pump.
8. Examine all dipstick for evidence of engine oil contaminated with coolant.
9. Check supply tank for evidence of oil coolant (leakage at transmission oil cooler).

Thermostat Test

Thermostat Removed
Detach the thermostat and place it in boiling water. Remove when open and place a 0.05 mm feeler gauge in the throat of the thermostat and allow the thermostat to cool and clamp on the feeler gauge.
Suspend a thermometer into a container of cool water and heat the water.
Suspend the thermostat by the feeler gauge into the container of warming water. When the thermostat opens and drops off the feeler gauge, note the temperature.

SPECIFICATIONS

Radiator bracket	**155kg-cm, 11 ft-lb, 15Nm**
Transmission oil cooler pipes	**55kg-cm, 11 ft-lb, 15Nm**
Water pump to cylinder block	**165kg-cm, 12 ft-lb, 16Nm**
Thermostat housing	**120kg-cm, 9 ft-lb, 12Nm**
Fan clutch to water pump	**155kg-cm, 11 ft-lb, 15Nm**
Fan to viscous clutch	**155kg-cm, 11 ft-lb, 15Nm**

Coolant Capacity:

1Y 1Y-C	7.3 litres, 7.7 US qts, 6.4 imp qts
2Y	7.0 litres, 7.4 US qts, 6.2 imp qts
3Y,4Y, 4Y-C & 4Y-E	7.4 litres, 7.8 US qts, 6.5 imp qts
12R	8.0 litres, 8.5 US qts, 7.0 imp qts
18R	9.0 litres, 9.5 US qts, 8.0 imp qts
20R	7.0 litres, 7.4 US qts, 6.2 imp qts
21R & 22R	8.4 litres, 8.9 US qts, 7.4 imp qts
L, 2L & 2L-T	10.6 litres, 11.2 US qts, 9.3 imp qts
3L	9.0 litres, 9.5 US qts, 8.0 imp qts

Thermostat starts to open:

1Y 1Y-C		80-84°C 176-183°F
2Y		80-84°C 176-183°F
3Y,4Y, 4Y-C & 4Y-E		80-84°C 176-183°F
12R	Low temp:	80-84°C 176-183°F
	High temp.	86-90°C 187-194°F
18R	Low temp:	80-84°C 176-183°F
	High temp.	86-90°C 187-194°F
20R	Low temp:	80-84°C 176-183°F
	High temp.	86-90°C 187-194°F
21R & 22R	Low temp:	80-84°C 176-183°F
	High temp.	86-90°C 187-194°F
L, 2L & 2L-T L		86-90°C 187-194°F
3L		86-90°C 187-194°F

DIESEL FUEL SYSTEM

Injector Pump on Vehicle   Dfu029

FUEL SYSTEM

GENERAL

The fuel system of the diesel engine is manufactured to extremely high precision to make it capable of maintaining adequate performance under high pressure. If by chance any minute particle of dirt or water should enter in the fuel, the longevity of the most important parts of the diesel engine, the injection pump and injection nozzles, could be extremely shortened. Thus, diesel fuel must be sufficiently filtered and cleaned, and for this purpose, a fuel strainer of high filtering performance is equipped on the engine. Of course, the fuel filled in the fuel tank must also be clean. The fuel in the fuel tank is drawn out by the fuel feed pump and passes through the pump filter located just in front of the feed pump. It then passes through the fuel pump and fuel filter and enters the injection pump for injection into the combustion chambers through the injectors.

Fuel that leaks past the injector passes out through the leakage pipe and returns to the feed pump inlet.

FUEL PUMP

The fuel feed pump is made up of the feed pump and priming pump. The feed pump is driven by the injection pump camshaft while the priming pump is operated by hand.

Sufficient fuel must always be kept in the injection pump fuel chamber, making it necessary to send the fuel to the injection pump under pressure since the pump element is not capable of supplying sufficient fuel at high speed. Therefore, the discharge pressure is regulated at from 1.8 to 2.2 kg/cm2 (25.6 to 31.1 psi) by the piston spring. The priming pump is used to bleed the fuel system for air removal.

The priming pump is operated by unlocking the knob at the top of the pump (by turning it counter clockwise) and then moving it up and down. After using the priming pump, the knob must be locked (by turning it clockwise). Failure to lock the knob might cause the feed pump to leak.

OPERATION

The feed pump is operated by the injection pump camshaft which imparts reciprocating motion to the piston, to such in and discharge the fuel under pressure.

When the camshaft is not pushing against the tappet roller, the piston is pressed on the push rod by the tension of a spring, to increase the volume of the pressure chamber. Thus, the inlet valve opens to draw in fuel.

The camshaft, on turning, allows the cam to push up the piston through the tappet roller and push rod. The rising of the piston compresses the fuel in the pressure chamber, causing the inlet valve to close and the outlet valve to open and discharge the fuel under pressure. A part of the discharge fuel enters the pressure chamber under the piston. If the fuel pressure below the piston is too great, the tension of the spring is then insufficient to lower the piston, therefore the pump ceases to function.

INJECTOR

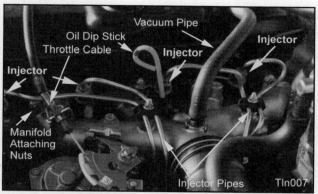

The fuel, pressure-fed by the injection pump, reaches the nozzle holder through an injection pipe, then through the small hole of the nozzle holder body and then through the ring groove of the distance piece. The fuel then flows into the pressure chamber after moving through the feed holes, the ring groove of the nozzle body and further feed holes.

When the oil pressure inside the pressure chamber reaches 110 kg/cm2 (due to the injection pump), the nozzle needle is lifted up so that the fuel is injected into the combustion chamber (being pressed by pressure spring through pressure pin).

When the pressure-feeding due to injection pump ends, the oil pressure inside the pressure chamber is lowered, which is due to the pumping-back action of the delivery valve, the nozzle needle closely sticks to the seat to stop the flow of fuel.

The fuel in the nozzle pressure chamber is under high pressure so that there is a minute amount of leakage of fuel between the nozzle body and needle. This leakage fuel lubricates the nozzle and needle sliding surfaces, and then passes out from the nozzle holder and flows through the leakage pipe to return to the fuel pump inlet side.

AUTOMATIC TIMER

The automatic advance angle adjustment of the automatic timer is performed as follows: As the RPM increases, the weight moves outward due to centrifical force. At this time, the weight curved surface, made according to required advanced angle, slides along the drive gear journal. Therefore, the drive gear and hub can relatively rotate up to the advance angle, causing the hub to increase the advance angle against the drive gear, as RPM increases.

Since the timer hub is connected to the injection pump spline shaft, injection timing is also quickened.

INJECTION PUMP

An injection pump is used continually to supply suitable fuel under any sort of operational conditions such as starting, idling, acceleration, high speed, economical running, and high load.

The injection pump comprises of an injection pump body,

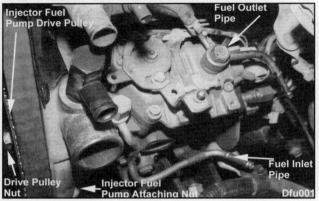

Injector Fuel Pump Drive Pulley — Fuel Outlet Pipe — Fuel Inlet Pipe — Drive Pulley Nut — Injector Fuel Pump Attaching Nut — Dfu001

pneumatic governor or mechanical governor fuel pump, and an automatic timer. The pump body has the same number of cylinders and plungers as the engine. The fuel control is set by a governor. The fuel pump is composed of a feed pump and priming pump. The air bleeding of the fuel line is performed by the priming pump before the engine will start.

The automatic timer is equipped with timer weights that serve to advance the injection period in accordance with the variations in engine speed, and functions independent of the engine load. This automatic timer is located inside the timing cover and driven by the engine idle gear. The timer is fitted on the injection pump on splines, and rotates at one-half the engine speed.

"L" SERIES INJECTION PUMP

Remove
1. **[2L-T]** Remove the boost compensator hose from the

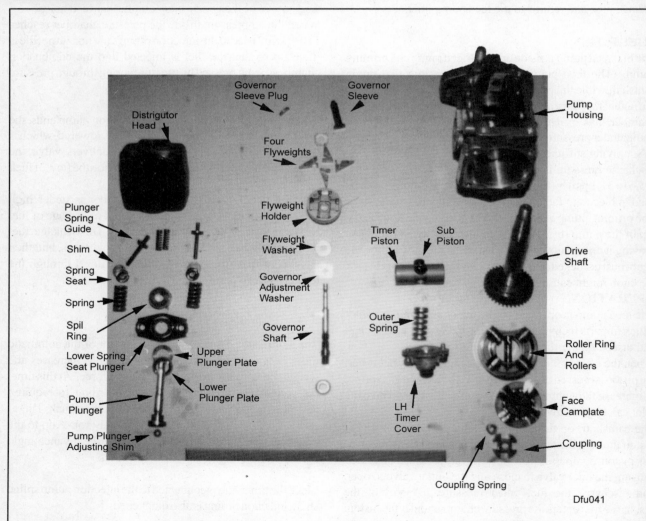

Dfu041

fuel pump.

2. Disconnect the fuel cut solenoid and pick-up sensor electrical connections.

3. Models with (ACSD). Remove the idle up lever attached by 3 bolts, remove the thermo wax by turning the cold starting lever 1/4 turn anti-clockwise insert a metal stop plate between the starting lever and thermo wax plunger. Remove the bolts and thermo wax and ring.

4. Disconnect all the inlet and outlet fuel hoses, they can be left connected to the fuel pipes.

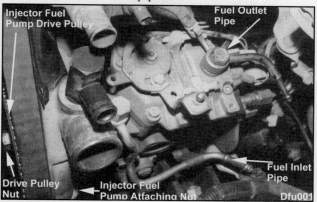

5. Remove accelerator connecting rod and on **[2L-T]** remove accelerator link.

6. Remove the four injection pipes from the engine, do not try to bend out of the way.

7. Remove fuel inlet pipe assembly including pipe, union nut, gaskets and inlet pipe.

8. Remove fuel outlet pipe assembly including pipe, union nut, gaskets and inlet pipe.

9. Remove the engine front cover, and timing belt as previously described in the engine chapter.

10. Remove injection pump drive pulley.

a. Hold pulley with a tool in pulley grooves, remove nut within a socket and handle.

b. Install a pulley puller to front of the pulley, use puller to

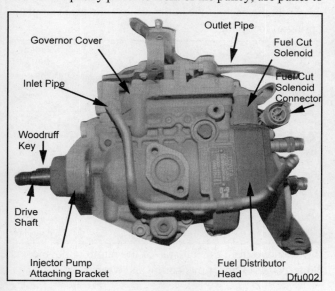

remove the pulley.

11. Remove injection pump.

(a) Use a felt pen or white out pen to mark the injection pump timing mark on the engine block.

(b) Remove the two nuts attaching the injection pump to the engine block.

(c) At the back of the injection pump remove the bracket and four bolts.

Dismantle Injection Pump

1. Install the injection pump into the pump bench frame.

2. Remove the woodruff key from the pump drive shaft if not already removed.

3. Remove the electrical fittings, fuel cut solenoid and pick-up sensor.

4. Remove the control levers on the top of fuel pump if necessary.

5. Remove the governor cover four bolts with an allen key. **(Manual Trans)** Take care and disconnect the spring which controls speed from the spring seat then remove governor cover with the following spring seat, damper spring and idle spring.

(Automatic Trans) Take care and remove the E-Clip, governor spring seat, damper spring and idle spring.

6. Remove the shaft lock nut for the governor, take note it needs to be turned clockwise. Rotate the governor shaft

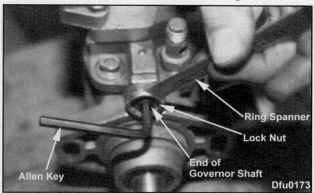

clockwise, then pull the shaft out from the front with these other components governor sleeve, No. 2 flyweight washer, four flyweights, flyweight holder, No. 1 flyweight washer, take care and remove the governor gear adjusting washer.

7. Use a socket and handle to unscrew the fuel distributor

Dfu034

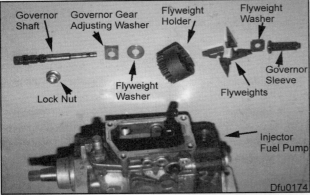

Dfu0174

Dfu036

head plug.

8. Use a socket and handle to unscrew four fuel delivery

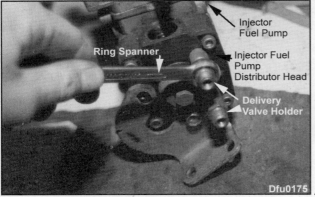

Dfu0175

valve holders, springs and seats. Then the four delivery valves with the gaskets.

* Do not touch the sliding surfaces of the delivery valve with your hand.

* Position the delivery valves, springs, spring seats and holders so they do not become mixed with each other, also the sliding surface of the delivery valves are not to be handled.

9. Remove distributor head four bolts with wire connector.

10. Remove and position the two lever support springs, two plunger spring guides, two plunger spring shims, two upper spring seats, two plunger springs, position these items so they do not become mixed with each other.

11. Use a pair tweezers to pull out spill ring, lower spring seat then the upper plunger plate and lower plunger plate. Also the adjusting shim.

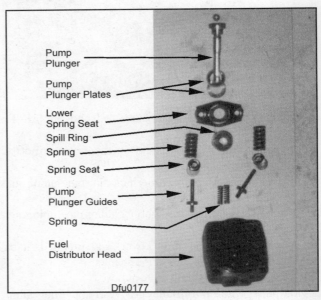

Dfu0177

12. Use a tube spanner to remove the two governor link support bolts then the gasket and governor link.

13. From the back of the pump remove the face camplate, spring and coupling.

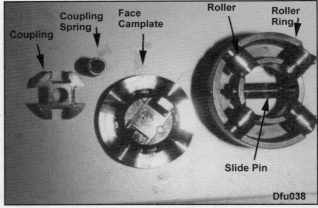

Dfu038

14. Remove from the left side of the pump remove cover bolts, cover, O ring, timer spring and washer.

15. Remove from the back of the pump using a pair of tweezers or pointy nose pliers the timer clip and stopper pin, you will need to push in on the slide pin.

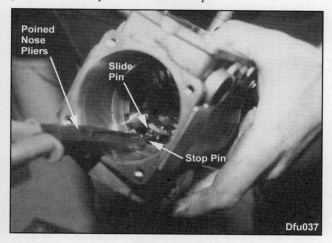

16. Push the drive shaft and roller ring from the front of the pump out the end section, remove the washer.

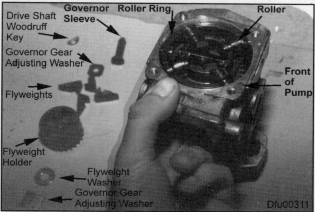

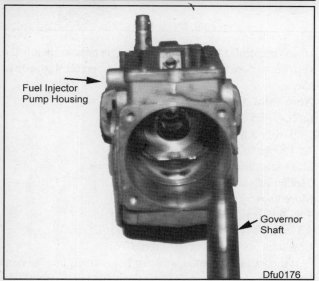

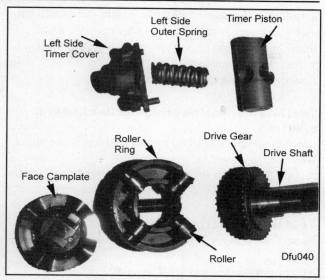

cover, it may be helpful to use a piece of wire in each of the screw holes to remove the cover.

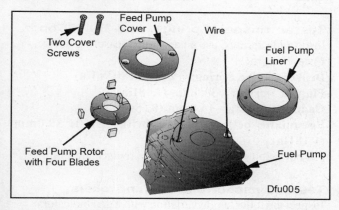

Remove the fuel feed pump rotor with the four blades and the pump liner, position these items so they do not become mixed with each other.

Inspection

Test and inspect pump plunger, spill ring and fuel distributor head.

Hold the spill ring (distributive head) on a 30^0 angle, lift the plunger, then let go the plunger allowing the plunger to slide down the spill ring (distributive head), do not push down.
If the above test do not function correctly replace the plunger and spill ring as an assembly.

Test and inspect delivery valves.

i. Hold the valve and seat assembly. Lift the valve, block the hole of the valve seat bottom with your finger, release the valve, the valve should go down reasonably quickly then stop when the relief ring blocks valve seat hole. If not replace the complete valve, do not try to repair the valve.

17. Remove from the right side of the pump remove cover bolts, cover, O ring, timer piston and sub piston.
18. Remove the two feed pump cover screws, then the

ii. Hold the valve seat. Block the hole of the valve seat bottom with your finger, install the valve and press it down with your finger, remove your finger, the valve should rise back up.
If any of the above test do not function correctly replace the valve and seat as an assembly.

Test and inspect the governor link ball and spill ring.

Install the governor link ball pin in the spill ring, it should move but not have looseness.
If the above test do not function correctly replace the governor link ball pin and spill ring as an assembly.

Test and inspect plunger springs.

Inspect the plunger springs for being square, use a metal square..
Maximum squareness: 2.0 mm (0.079 in.)
If not within correct specification replace the plunger spring.

Test and inspect Springs. 2L & 3L 1988 on

Inspect the springs, use an accurate measuring device.
Free Length:
Delivery Valve Spring: 24.4mm (0.961in)
Plunger Spring: 30.0mm (1.181in)
Coupling Spring: 16.6mm (0.654in)
Pneumatic bellows spring (with HAC): 30.0mm (1.181in)
If not within correct specification replace the spring.

Test and inspect roller ring and rollers.

Inspect the foller height variation with a dial indicator.
Roller height variation: 0.02 mm (0.0008 in.)
If not within correct variation specification replace the roller ring and rollers as an assembly.

Test and inspect fuel cut solenoid.

Cut Out Solenoid
Cut Out Solenoid Spring
Cut Out Solenoid Valve

Dfu035

Assemble the spring and valve to the solenoid valve body. Use vehicle battery power, connect the negative to the side of the solenoid, connect the positive to the solenoid terminal. The solenoid valve should be heard to close and open as the positive wire is connected to and removed from the solenoid.
If the above test do not function correctly replace the fuel cut solenoid.

Test and inspect pick-up sensor.

Use a digital ohmmeter, contact or back probe the resister wiring loom connector terminals, check the resistance between terminals for specification.
Resistance specification: 600 - 800 ohms
If not within correct specification replace the plunger spring.

Test and inspect plunger spring adjuster shim.

Assemble the distributor head by installing the two plunger spring guides, and two upper spring seats, then two plunger springs. Followed by lower spring seat, lower plunger plate, lower plunger plate, upper plunger plate, pump plunger, but not the plunger spring shims.

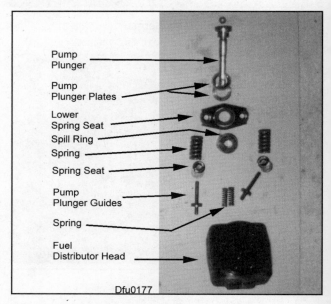

Pump Plunger
Pump Plunger Plates
Lower Spring Seat
Spill Ring
Spring
Spring Seat
Pump Plunger Guides
Spring
Fuel Distributor Head

Dfu0177

Use a vernier slide to measure the plunger position below the slip ring surface thereby determining the correct shim size to use.
New shim thickness:
L, 2L-T = 5.7 minus measured distance.
 2L   = 5.8 minus measured distance.
A: Plunger position measured:
Shim selection chart - mm (in.)

Measure clearance	Shim thickness
More than 5.3 (0.209)	0.5 (0.020)
4.8 - 4.9 (0.189 - 0.193)	1.0 (0.039)
4.3 - 4.5 (0.169 - 0.177)	1.5 (0.059)
Less than 3.9 (0.154)	2.0 (0.079)

* If the measurement is between listed sizes, use the next larger size. As an example if the thickness is 1.1 mm (0.043 in.) by calculation, use a 1.2 mm (0.047 in.) shim.
* Use two shims of the same thickness size.

Inspect the oil seal at the front of the pump.

Use a screw driver to pry out the oil seal, cover the front and rear surfaces of the new seal with MP grease, coat the outer circumference of the oil seal with liquid sealer.

Install the oil seal ,use a tube spanner to tap the seal home against the pump housing.

Assembly

1. Install the regulator valve with a new O-ring, use a torque wrench to tighten to specification.

Regulator Valve Torque: 90 kg-cm (78 in-lb, 8.8 Nm)

2. Install the feed pump to the pump body, install the pump liner, rotor and four blades. The liner and blades must be positioned correctly as well the blades must be free to move. Then install the pump cover, it must be aligned so the outlet hole lines up with the liner.

Pump Cover Bolts Torque: 25kg-cm (22in-lb, 2.5Nm)

3. The drive shaft is to be assembled, by installing the drive gear down the drive shaft to the end of the shaft. Two new joint rubbers should be installed to the back of the drive gear.

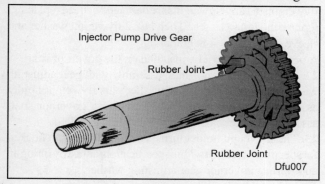

Injector Pump Drive Gear

Rubber Joint

Rubber Joint

Dfu007

4. Fit the woodruff key into the shaft, align the pump rotor with notch at the top, so the woodruff key will not fall out while installing the shaft. Install the drive shaft into the pump, when fully installed make sure the shaft turns freely.

5. Assembly and install the timer piston by coating some No. 50 Denso grease on the timer piston, then fit the sub-piston

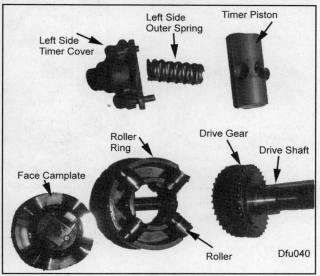

Left Side Timer Cover

Left Side Outer Spring

Timer Piston

Roller Ring

Drive Gear

Drive Shaft

Face Camplate

Roller

Dfu040

in the timer piston, install the piston assembly into the pump body.

6. Assembly roller ring assembly, fit the rollers and washers the flat surface of the washer is to be against the roller on top of the roller ring.

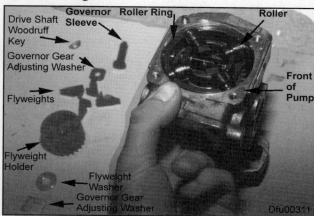

Drive Shaft Woodruff Key

Governor Sleeve

Roller Ring

Roller

Governor Gear Adjusting Washer

Flyweights

Front of Pump

Flyweight Holder

Flyweight Washer

Governor Gear Adjusting Washer

Dfu00311

Install the roller ring assembly and slide pin down into the pump body, then install the stopper pin and clip into the top of the roller ring.

Install right side covers to the pump body fit new "O" rings and two bolts then tighten each bolt.

7. Assemble the left side timing spring, cover assembly, Install the outer spring with adjusting washers to each side of the spring washer into the left side of the pump body, then the "O" ring and left side timing cover with two bolts.

2L & 3L 1988 on: Measure the preset length of the adjusting screw and lock nut from the timer cover.

2L & 3L 1988 on: Specified Length of adjusting screw:
7.5-8.0mm (0.295-0.315in)

8. Turn the pump so the fuel distributer end is facing up. Install the coupling and face camplate without the coupling spring, then fit the used (cleaned) adjusting shim, and pump plunger so the groove in the plunger lines up with the camplate pin.

9. Install the distributor head to the pump body with the bolts, tighten the bolts to specification.

Fuel Distributor Head Bolt Torque:
120 kg-cm (9 ft-lb, 12 N.m)

10. Use a vernier slide to measure the plunger position below the slip ring surface thereby determining the correct shim size to use.

Formula to be used:

Verner slide measurement plus installed shim size minus 3.3mm (0.130in) equals new shim to be used.

Example: Verner slide measurement 3.7mm plus installed shim size 2.2mm equals 5.9mm minus 3.3mm equals new shim to be used 2.6mm.

Install new shim recheck for specified clearance.

Plunger Clearance: 3.2-3.4mm(0.126-0.134in)

11. Remove the distributor head plus pump plunger and adjusting shim, then face camplate.

12. Turn the shaft so the key groove is at the top of the shaft, install the coupling spring, then reinstall the face camplate and the camplate pin facing upwards.

13. The governor link must now be installed, use new gaskets, tighten the two bolts to specification and check link is free to move.

L, 2L & 2L-T upto 1988:

Governor Link Bolt Torque:

115 kg-cm (8 ft-lb, 11 N.m)

2L & 3L 1988 on:

Governor Link Bolt: 140 kg-cm (10 ft-lb, 14 N.m)

14. Install the shim (determined in step No 10) onto the camplate.

15. Assemble the pump plunger, fit onto the plunger shaft the lower and upper plunger plates, the lower spring seat then the spill ring with the surface with the hole in it against the lower spring seat.

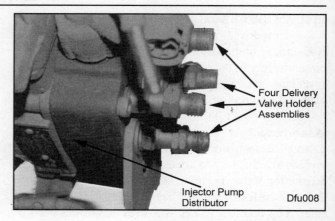

Four Delivery Valve Holder Assemblies

Injector Pump Distributor

Dfu008

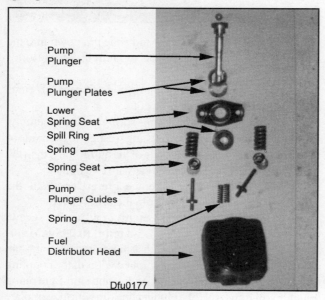

Pump Plunger

Pump Plunger Plates

Lower Spring Seat

Spill Ring

Spring

Spring Seat

Pump Plunger Guides

Spring

Fuel Distributor Head

Dfu0177

16. Assemble the fuel distributor head, these components should be coated with No50 Denso grease.

Place the fuel distributor head on a bench, fit plunger spring shim and seat to the two plunger guides, then install the two plunger guides to the fuel distributor head.

Install the two level support springs to the fuel distributor head.

Install a new "O" ring to the fuel distributor head.

17. Install the fuel distributor head to the fuel pump body, install the 4 bolts and tighten to specification, fit wire bracket.

Fuel Distributor Head Torque:

120 kg-cm (9 ft-lb, 12 Nm)

18. Install the four fuel pipe delivery valve holders to fuel distributor head with new gaskets, install the valve holder spring seats and springs onto the four fuel delivery valve holders. Use a torque wrench to tighten the four delivery valve holders to specification.

Fuel Delivery Valve Holders Specified Torque:

500 kg-cm (9 ft-lb, 49 N.m)

20. Install fuel distributor head plug with a new "O" ring. Use a torque wrench to tighten the fuel distributor head plug to specification.

Fuel Distributor Head Plug Specified Torque:

700 kg-cm (51 ft-lb, 69 N.m)

21. Assemble the governor shaft assembly, install the four flyweights, (if any flyweights are damaged or need replacing, replace the four as a set). Then No. 2 flyweight washer and sleeve on the flyweight holder.

A new "O" ring must be installed on the governor shaft.

22. Install the governor shaft assembly with gear adjusting washer and No. 1 flyweight washer plus flyweight holder assembly as a unit to the fuel pump turn governor shaft assembly counter clockwise as it is being installed.

23. The flyweight holder thrust clearance must be checked for specification, if not within specification, adjust by fitting an appropriate governor gear adjusting washer.

Flyweight Holder Thrust Specified Clearance:

0.15-0.35mm (0.005-0.0139in.)

24. Use vernier slide to measure the protrusion of the governor shaft, if not within specification, screw shaft in or out to specified protrusion, then fix with lock nut while securing with an allen key.

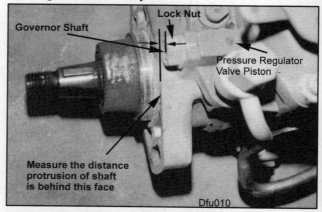

Governor Shaft

Lock Nut

Pressure Regulator Valve Piston

Measure the distance protrusion of shaft is behind this face

Dfu010

L, 2L & 2L-T upto 1988

Governor Shaft Protrusion Specification:

2.0 - 2.5 mm (0.079 - 0.098 in.)

2L & 3L 1988 on:

Governor Shaft Protrusion Specification:

0.5 - 2.0 mm (0.020 - 0.079 in.)

If the protrusion is not within specification, adjust by turning the governor shaft and tighten lock nut.

25. High Altitude Compensator (HAC) if fitted.

a. Slide connecting pin in governor cover.

b. Install control lever, fix with support pin.

c. Either side install gaskets and allen key bolts.

d. Pour a small amount (3-4cc) of engine oil into the governor bush hole.

e. Install bellow spring, push rod, shims, bellows, rubber caps and cover tighten 4 bolts.

f. Install lever control spring to the side then gasket and bolt.

26. The governor cover is to be installed with a new gasket.

[Manual /Transmission] Install damper spring and governor spring seat, then connect spring and seat with the control spring.

[Automatic /Transmission] Install the damper spring and governor spring seat, then connect spring seat with a C-clip. Install governor cover with four bolts and tighten to specification.

Governor Cover Bolts Torque:

85 kg-cm (74 in-lb, 8.3 N.m)

27. Install top control levers if dismantled from the top cover.

28. Install the two electrical units:

a. Install the fuel cut out solenoid valve and spring then screw in the fuel cut out solenoid with a new "O" ring, tighten solenoid. Fit on the wire connection and to the solenoid and

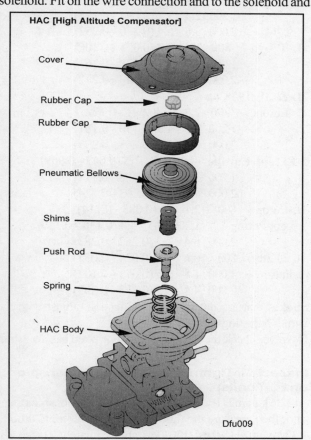

HAC [High Altitude Compensator]

Cover
Rubber Cap
Rubber Cap
Pneumatic Bellows
Shims
Push Rod
Spring
HAC Body

Dfu009

to bracket.

b. Screw in the pick-up sensor with a new gasket.

TESTS and ADJUSTMENTS

Air Tight Test.

(a) Fill a container that will hold the fuel pump, with diesel fuel.

(b) Install a bolt into the overflow port at thew top of the fuel pump.

(c) Connect a high pressure air hose to the fuel inlet pipe and submerge the injection pump into the container filled with diesel fuel.

(d) Test the fuel pump with .5 kg/cm2 (21 psi, 147 kPa) air pressure, check for air bubbles, if no air bubbles this will confirm there are no leaks.

(e) Test the fuel pump with 5.0 kg-cm 2 (71 psi, 490 kPa) air pressure, check for air bubbles, if no air bubbles this will confirm there are no leaks.

Pre-Test Check and Preparation.

Install fuel pump to a testing unit and fit recommended equipment.

Nozzle and nozzle holders testing specifications with a tested rpm accurate within 40rpm are as follows:

Test nozzle: DN12SD12 (NIPPONDENSO)

Test the test nozzle holder, if the nozzle holder is not up to specification replace it.

Test nozzle holder valve opening pressure:

145-155 kg/cm2   (2,062-2,205 psi, 14,220-15,200 kPa)

Mount the test unit as described by the manufacture. Mark on the key groove portion of the coupling.

The injection pump is to be connected to the testing unit, using high pressure pipes listed.

Outer diameter: 6.0 mm (0.236 in.)

Inner diameter: 2.0 mm (0.079 in.)

Length: 840 mm (33.07 in.)

Minimum bending radius: More than 25 mm (0.98 in.)

Always use the overflow screw installed on the pump to be adjusted.

Apply battery voltage (12 volts) power to the fuel cut solenoid, keeping in mind the safety aspect with fuel and sparks.

Fuel to the injection pump should be 0.2 kg-cm2 (2.8 psi, 20 kPa), with a fuel temperature of 40-45 degrees centigrade (104-113 degrees Fahrenheit).

Bleed the injection pipes.

Operate the injection pump for 5 minutes at 2,000 rpm.

Check for fuel leaks or abnormal noise.

Measure the volume of each injection cylinder with a measuring cylinder.

Before measuring the injection volume drain the cylinder to discard any fuel.

Pre-Setting of Full Load Injection Volume.

[2L-T] Apply 0.48 kg/cm2 (6.8 psi, 47 kPa) of pressure to the boost compensator.

Adjust the injection volume with the FULL LOAD SET SCREW.

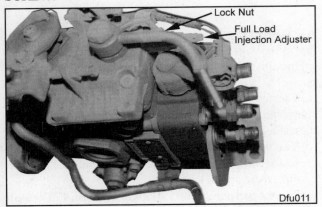

Dfu011

Pump rpm = 1,200

Number of measuring strokes = 200

Injection volume cc (cu.in)

L 7.54-7.86 (0.46-0.48)

2L upto 1988 9.34-9.66 (0.57-0.59)

2L-T 10.40-13.60 (0.63-0.83)

2L 1988 On-Except Hong Kong, Singapore, Malaysia
10.40-13.60 (0.63-0.83)

2L 1988 0n-Hong Kong, Singapore, Malaysia Only
9.62-9.94 (0.59-0.61)

3L 1988 On-Except Hong Kong, Singapore, Malaysia
10.96-11.28 (0.67-0.69)

3L 1988 0n-Hong Kong, Singapore, Malaysia Only
11.76-12.08 (0.72-0.74)

Injection volume will increase approximately 3 cc (0.2 cu.in.) with each half turn of the screw, if the screw has a spot welded lock nut, unscrew lock nut to break weld.

Pre-Set Load Sensing Timer. [Without HAC or with HAC (Switzerland)]

Adjust the protrusion of the governor shaft.

L, 2L and 2L-T upto 1988
Protrusion: 2.0 - 2.5 mm (0.079 - 0.098 in.)
2L & 3L 1988 on
Protrusion: 0.5 - 2.0 mm (0.020 - 0.079 in.)

Pump Inner Pressure.

Measure the pump inner pressure at each of the listed rpm:

	Inner Pressure kg/cm2 (psi, kPa)
400	2.2 - 2.8 (31 - 40, 216 - 275)
2,200	6.7 - 7.3 (95 - 104, 657 - 716)

Check pressure if low, try adjusting by lightly tapping the regulator valve piston as you take note of the pressure gauge.
Check pressure if high or if the regulator valve was tapped in too far, replace the regulator valve must be replaced.

Test, Check and Adjust Timer.

1. The timer cover is to be removed.

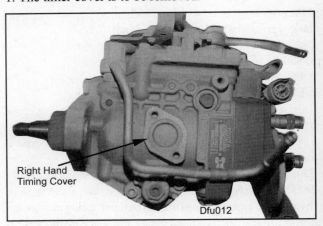

Dfu012

2. Timer measuring device part number 95095-10220 (NIPPONDENSO) is to be installed.

3. The timer measuring device is to be set at zero.

[2L-T] Apply 0.48 kg/cm2 (6.8 psi, 47 kPa) of pressure to the boost compensator.

4. Inspect piston stroke measurement for listed rpm below:

Item	Pump rpm	Piston stroke mm (in)
L, 2L & 2L-T upto 1988		
L	800	0.8 - 1.6 (0.031 - 0.063)
	1,200	2.4 - 3.2 (0.094 - 0.126)
	2,000	5.6 - 6.4 (0.220 - 0.252)
2L	800	0.8 - 1.6 (0.031 - 0.063)
	1,200	2.4 - 3.2 (0.094 - 0.126)
	2,000	5.6 - 6.4 (0.220 - 0.252)
2L-T	800	1.9 - 2.7 (0.075 - 0.106)
	1,000	3.3 - 4.1 (0.130 - 0.161)
	2,000	6.1 - 6.9 (0.240 - 0.272)
2L & 3L 1988 on		
2L Europe	800	2.3-3.1 (0.091 - 0.122)
	1,200	3.8 - 4.6 (0.150 - 0.181)
	2,000	6.8 - 7.6 (0.268 - 0.299)
2 Except Europe	800	0.7 - 1.5 (0.043 - 0.059)
	1,200	2.1 - 2.9 (0.128 - 0.177)
	2,000	4.9 - 5.7 (0.193 - 0.224)
3L Europe	800	2.1- 2.9 (0.083 - 0.114)
except Portugal	1,200	3.5 - 4.3 (0.138 - 0.169)
	2,000	6.4 - 7.2 (0.252 - 0.283)
3L all other	800	0.6 - 1.4 (0.024 - 0.055)
countries	1,000	1.8 - 2.6 (0.071 - 0.102)
	2,000	4.4 - 5.2 (0.173 - 0.205)

Strokes that are not within specification, adjust with the "timer adjusting screw" under cover.

However check the left side cover side plate has a washer.

Inspect Air Tightness of Boost Compensator on 2L-T units.

At 1.36 kg/cm2 (10.3psi, 133kPa) pressure to boost compensator then measure the time it takes for pressure to drop to 1.33 kg/cm2 (18.9 psi, 130 kPa), approximately 10 seconds.

Test, Check and Adjust Full Load Injection Volume.

The adjusting lever angle for the adjustment below should be as shown in the figure.

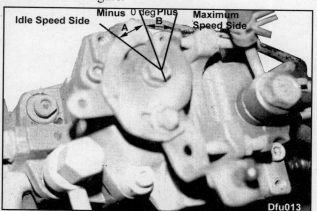

Dfu013

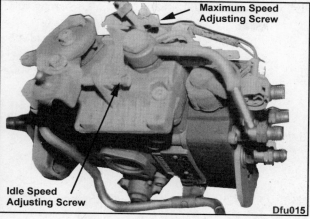

Dfu015

A = Maximum Speed Side   **B** = Idle Speed Side

Item   Adjusting lever angle
        A   B

Upto 1988

L   + 9.0-19.0 degrees - 14.0-24.0 degrees
2L   + 23.5-33.5 degrees- 12.5-22.5 degrees
2L-T + 23.5-33.5 degrees - 13.5-21.5 degrees
 # [2L-T] At 0.48 kg/cm2 (6.8 psi, 47 kPa) pressure to the boost compensator.

1988 on

2L 3L Man Tran: +23.5-33.5 degrees - 12.5-22.5 degrees
2L 3L Auto Tran: +23.5-33.5 degrees - 13.5-21.5 degrees

Measure the full load injection volume:

Pump at 1,200 rpm with the number of measuring strokes at 200.

Item Adjusting lever angle Injection Volume

Upto 1988

L   + 9.0 - 19.0 7.54 - 7.86 cc
2L   + 23.5 - 33.5 9.34 - 9.66 cc
2L-T + 23.5 - 33.5 10.40 - 10.36 cc

1988 on

2L Hong Kong, Singapore, Malaysia:
        + 23.5 - 33.5 10.42 - 10.74 cc

2L Except Hong Kong, Singapore, Malaysia:
        + 23.5 - 33.5 9.62 - 9.94 cc

3L Hong Kong, Singapore, Malaysia:
        + 23.5 - 33.5 10.96 - 11.28 cc

3L Except Hong Kong, Singapore, Malaysia:
        + 23.5 - 33.5 11.76 - 12.08 cc

Injection volume that are not within specification, adjust with the "full load test" on previous page.

Adjust Maximum Speed with the MAXIMUM SPEED ADJUSTING SCREW.

Measure 200 strokes

Engine	Lever Angle	RPM	InjVol	Result

Upto 1988

L	+ 9 - 19	2450	3.9-45	Adjust
		2250	5.7-6.9	Check
		2700	Less1.3	Check
2L*	23.5-33.5	2450	3.8-5.4	Adjust
		2250	6.8-8.0	Check
		2700	Less1.3	Check
2L	20.5-30.5	2250	3.8-5.4	Adjust
		2050	7.4-8.6	Check
		2500	Less1.3	Check
2L-T#	23.5-33.5	2450	3.8-5.4	Adjust
		2250	6.7-8.5	Check
		2700	Less1.3	Check

1988 0n

2L	23.5-33.5	2450	4.0-5.6	Adjust
		2250	7.66-9.26	
		2700	Less1.3	
2L**	23.5-33.5	2575	4.0-5.6	Adjust
		2250	8.0-9.6	
		2850	Less1.3	
2L***	23.5-33.5	2350	4.0-5.6	Adjust
		2150	6.9-8.9	
		2700	Less1.3	
3L	23.5-33.5	2300	4.6-6.2	Adjust
		2100	9.08-11.08	
		2550	Less1.3	

* 2L Singapore only
** Europe only
*** Hong Kong, Singapore & Malaysia
 # [2L-T] At 0.48 kg/cm2 (6.8 psi, 47 kPa) pressure

Test Injection Volume

Check injection volume cc for each pump rpm, measure 200 strokes.

Engine	Lever Angle	RPM	InjVol	Variation	Comment
L	9 - 19	100	8.2-12.	0.8	Starting vol.
		350	7.0-9.6	0.5	----
		500	6.3-7.3	0.5	----
		1200	7.5-7.8	0.4	Full load vol.
		2100	6.5-7.4	0.5	----

2L*	23.5 - 33.5	100	8.6-12.	0.8	Starting vol.
		500	7.2-8.2	0.5	----
		1200	9.3-9.6	0.4	Full load vol.
		2000	7.8-8.7	0.5	----
2L**	23.5 - 33.5	100	8.6-12.	0.8	Starting vol.
		500	7.2-8.2	0.5	----
		1200	9.34-9.66	0.4	Full load vol.
		2100	7.6-8.5	0.5	----
2L#*	9 - 19	100	8.6-12.4	0.8	Starting vol.
		500	7.2-8.2	0.5	----
		1200	9.34-9.66	0.4	Full load vol.
		2100	7.6-8.5	0.5	----
2L-T	23.5-33.5	100	10.2-13.6	0.8	Starting vol.
##		500	7.3-8.1	0.5	----
###		1200	9.34-9.66	0.4	Full load vol.
###		2100	10.0-11.2	0.5	----

* 50's & 60's Australia
** Man Trans except Australia
#* Auto Trans
[2L-T] At 0.48 kg/cm2 (6.8 psi, 47 kPa) pressure
[2L-T] At 0.04 kg/cm2 (0.57 psi, 3.9 kPa) pressure
Note: The 100 rpm should not be out of specification, if it is install a new governor sleeve ring.
Note: Lengthening the governor sleeve plug (head) 0.1 mm (0.004 in.) will decrease injection volume by 0.6 cc (0.04 cu.in.).
The variation limit should not exceed specification, if it does replace the delivery valve.

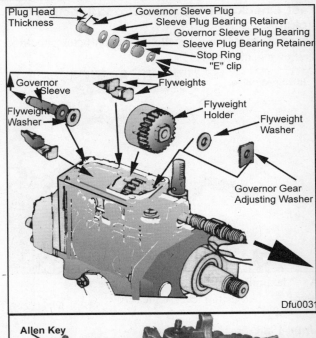

Dfu0031

Test, Measure and Adjust Full Load Minimum Injection Volume for 2L-T Engines.

Measure the injection volume at 1,200 rpm with 200 strokes. The injection volume should be 7.9-8.7 cc (0.48 - 0.53 cu.in.).
(b) Using an allen key, adjust the timer slide stopper.

Adjust Load Sensing Timer.

Adjust "governor shaft" to alter the starting and ending points of the load sensing timer.
* At 0.48 kg/cm2 (6.8 psi, 47 kPa) of pressure to the boost compensator for 2L-T engines.
Measure the injection volume of 200 strokes at the following rpm (adjusting lever in maximum speed position):
L - 1,200 rpm, **2L** - 1,200 rpm, **2L-T** - 1,750 rpm.
Adjust the adjusting lever from the maximum speed side to the idle speed side, fix the lever where the pump inner pressure starts to drop.
Measure the injection volume at the drop point, adjust by turning the governor shaft.
* The injection volume can be changed 3 cc (0.2 cu.in.) by turning the governor shaft half a turn.
Check the last injection point (volume) by slowly moving the adjusting lever from the maximum speed side to the idle speed side, and fix the lever where the pump inner pressure stops dropping, at **L** - 1,200 rpm, **2L** - 1,200 rpm, **2L-T** - 1,750

Dfu0171

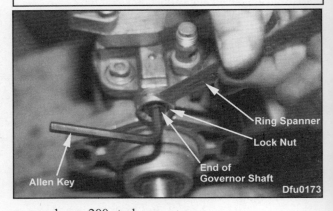

Dfu0173

rpm and over 200 strokes.
Injection volume:
L   2.6-3.0 cc (0.16 - 0.18 cu.in)
2L   6.2 - 6.6 cc (0.38 - 0.40 cu.in.)
2L-T 7.3 - 7.7 cc (0.45 - 0.47 cu.in.)
Inspect timer piston fluctuation when adjusting lever is moved from maximum speed side to idle speed side at **L** - 1,200 rpm, **2L** - 1,200 rpm, **2L-T** - 1,750 rpm and over 200 strokes.

Timer piston fluctuation:
L (w/0 HAC) 1.2-1.6 cc (0.047-0.063 cu.in)
2L (w/ HAC) 0.8-1.2 cc (0.031-0.047 cu.in)
2L-T 1.2-1.6 cc (0.047-0.063 cu.in)
Check the protrusion of the governor shaft it should be 1.0 - 2.0 mm (0.039 - 0.079 in.).

Adjust Idle Speed with the Idle Speed Adjusting Screw

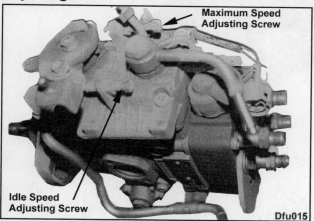

Maximum Speed Adjusting Screw

Idle Speed Adjusting Screw

Dfu015

Check injection volume cc for each pump rpm, measure 200 strokes.

Engine	Lever Angle	RPM	InjVol	Variat.Com
L	- 14.0 - 24.0	350	1.1-2.1	Adjust
		525	Less 0.3-	Check
2L Man T	- 12.5 - 22.5	350	1.3-2.30.34	Adjust
		525	Less 0.3-	Check
2L Auto T	- 13.5 - 21.5	375	1.66-2.66	Check
		400	1.3-2.3 0.34	Adjust
		475	0.6-1.2	Check
2L-T		375	1.76-2.76	Check
		400	1.4-2.4 0.34	Adjust
		525	0.6-1.2	Check
		650	less 0.4	Check

Adjust Fast Idle for 2L-T Engines.

The clearance between the adjusting lever and idle speed adjusting screw is to be measured. Fuel temperature 20 degrees centigrade (68 degrees Fahrenheit), clearance 6 mm (0.24 in.).

Post Adjustment Check.

Injection should stop if the fuel cut solenoid wiring connector is uncliped, at a pump revolution of 100 rpm. Check the idle adjusting lever movement.

Engine	Adjusting lever angle
L	30 - 36 degrees
2L A/T, 2L-T	41 - 51 degrees
2L M/T, 2L-T	43 - 49 degrees
2L & 3L 1988 on	43 - 49 degrees

Check Idle Lever Movement

Dfu018

Pump Installation

1. Align the injection pump timing marks on the fuel injection pump body and oil pump body. Install the two attaching nuts and tighten to specification.
Fuel Injection Pump Attaching Bolt Torque:
210 kg-cm (15 ft-lb, 21 N.m)
2. Install the pump bracket and four bolts. Tighten the four bolts to specification.
Fuel Pump Support Bracket Bolt Torque:
185 kg-cm (13 ft-lb, 18 N.m)
3. Install injection pump drive shaft woodruff key and pulley. Tighten to specification.
Injection Pump Drive Shaft Pulley Attaching Nut:
650kg.cm (47ft-lb, 64Nm)
4. Install timing belt as described in engine chapter.
5. Models with (ACSD). Install the thermo wax and new "O" ring and tighten bolts. Remove metal stop plate, turn lever slightly clockwise. Install the idle up lever and bolts.
6. Install fuel outlet pipe and bolt with 2 new gaskets. Tighten union bolt to specification.
Fuel Outlet Union Bolt Torque:
230 kg-cm (17 ft-lb, 23 N.m)
7. Install fuel outlet pipe and bolt with 2 new gaskets. Tighten union bolt to specification.
Fuel Outlet Union Bolt Torque:
230 kg-cm (17 ft-lb, 23 N.m)
8. Install the four injection pipes and tighten to specification.
Fuel Injector Pipe Torque:
250 kg-cm (18 ft-lb, 25 N.m)
9. [2L-T engines] Install accelerator link.
10. Install accelerator rod.
11. Install inlet and outlet fuel pipes and hoses.
12. Install fuel pump electrical units and wiring connectors, for fuel cut solenoid and pick-up sensor.
13. [2L-T engines] Install boost compensator hose and clamps.

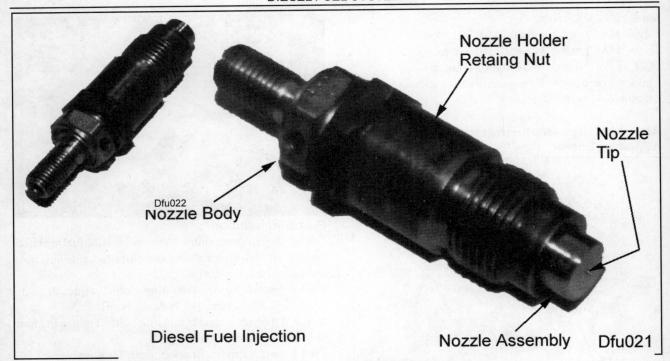

Nozzle Holder
Retaing Nut

Nozzle
Tip

Dfu022
Nozzle Body

Diesel Fuel Injection

Nozzle Assembly   Dfu021

INJECTORS L, 2L, 2L-T & 3L

Remove the Fuel Injectors

Note 2L & 3L 1988 on: Remove the glow plugs by removing the connector four bolts (fixed delay type) four nuts (other type) and connectors, remove the 2 insulators and connector per glow plug. Remove the glow plugs with a 12mm socket and handle.

1. Remove the injection pipe bracket bolts and brackets.

2. Loosen and remove the union nuts on the injection pipes between the fuel pump and nozzles, remove the pipes.

3. Remove nozzle leakage pipe nuts and gaskets, remove the leakage pipe.

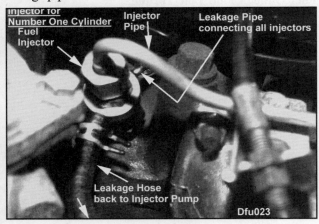

Injector for Number One Cylinder Fuel Injector

Injector Pipe

Leakage Pipe connecting all injectors

Leakage Hose back to Injector Pump

Dfu023

4. Use ring spanner to remove the nozzles, nozzle seats and gaskets. Keep the nozzles and nozzle parts in order.

INJECTOR TESTS

Injector Nozzle Pressure Test.

1. Install the injector into a commercial injector tester unit.

Caution: Do not place your finger over the nozzle injection hole.

2. Activate the tester handle a few times to discharge any carbon from the injection hole.

3. Pump the tester unit slowly, check the tester unit pressure gauge to see when the injector opens, by a drop on the pressure gauge. Check nozzle for specification if not within specification, disassemble the injector and replace the adjusting shim at the top of the pressure spring.

L, 2L & 2L-TUp to 1988:

Opening Pressure New Nozzle: 115 - 125 kg-cm2 (1,636 - 1,778 psi) (11,278 - 12,258 kPa)

Opening Pressure Reused Nozzle: 105 - 125 kg/cm2 (1,493 - 1,778 psi) (10,296 - 12, 258 kPa)

New Adjusted opening pressure:105 - 125 kg/cm2 (1,493 - 1,778 psi) (10,296 - 12,258 kPa)

2L and 3L 1988 on:

Opening Pressure New Nozzle: 151 - 159 kg-cm2 (2,148 - 2,261 psi) (14,808 - 15,593 kPa)

Opening Pressure Reused Nozzle: 145 - 155 kg/cm2

(2,062 - 2,205 psi) (14,220 - 15,200 kPa)

Opening Pressure Reused Nozzle: 145 - 155 kg/cm2 (2,062 - 2,205 psi) (14,220 - 15,200 kPa)

L, 2L & 2L-TUp to 1988: Use only one shim at a time, they alter in thickness by 0.05 mm (0.0020 in.) this will alter the pressure by about 6.4 kg/cm2 (91 psi, 628 kPa).

2L and 3L 1988 on: Use only one shim at a time, they alter in thickness by 0.025 mm (0.0010 in.) this will alter the pressure by about 3.5 kg/cm2 (50 psi, 343 kPa).

Test for injector leakage

Test for injector leakage with a pressure of about 10.0 - 20.0 kg/cm2 (142 - 284 psi, 981 - 1,961 kPa) below injector opening pressure, check for leakage from the injector hole or retaining nut for a period of 10 seconds. If the injector leaks, replace or recondition the injector.

Test for Injector Spray Pattern.

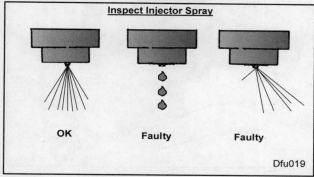

Inspect Injector Spray

OK   Faulty   Faulty

Dfu019

The injector nozzle should vibrate at pumping speeds of 15 - 60 times (old nozzle) or 30 - 60 times (new nozzle) per minute. The spray pattern is to checked while the nozzle is vibrating, if the pattern is not correct, replace or recondition the injector.

Disassemble

1. Disassemble fuel injector, by unscrewing the nozzle retaining nut. Take care not to drop any of the components.
2. Remove components these are adjusting shim, pressure spring, pressure pin, distance piece and the nozzle.

Inspection and Cleaning

Wash all components in diesel fuel and air dry, however do not touch any of the matching surfaces with your hands.
Clean off carbon deposits from the injector tip by scraping with something not abrasive such as a cleaned and fuel soaked wooden scraper.
The exterior of the injector can be cleaned with a nylon or brass brush.
Inspect the injector seat of the body and the injector needle tip for damage, burns or corrosion.
Hold the injector on an angle, pull the needle out about one third of its length, then release the needle, it should sink down into the body vent under its own weight. Repeat as you rotate the needle slightly each time, if the needle does not sink freely, replace the nozzle assembly.
If the injector is faulty in any way replace or recondition the injector.

Assemble

1. Assemble the injector body, the injector assembly, distance piece, pressure pin, pressure spring, adjusting shim and

injector holder retaining nut, finger tighten then tighten to specification.
L, 2L & 2L-TUp to 1988:
Injector Retaining Nut Torque:
     700 kg-cm (51 ft-lb, 69 N.m)
2L and 3L 1988 on:
Injector Retaining Nut Torque:
     375 kg-cm (27 ft-lb, 37 N.m)
Installation.
1. Install new injector gaskets on the injector seats in the cylinder head.
2. Install the injector and tighten to specification.
L, 2L & 2L-T Up to 1988:
Injector Torque Specification:
     700 kg-cm (51 ft-lb, 69 N.m)
2L and 3L 1988 on:
Injector Torque Specification:
     650 kg-cm (47 ft-lb, 64 N.m)
3. Install the leakage pipe, install injector leakage pipe gaskets and nuts, tighten to specification.
L, 2L & 2L-T Up to 1988:
Leakage Pipe Nuts Torque:

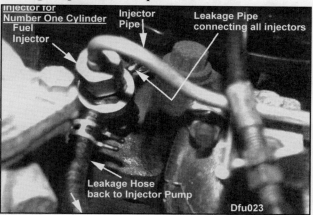

Injector for Number One Cylinder Fuel Injector   Injector Pipe   Leakage Pipe connecting all injectors

Leakage Hose back to Injector Pump

Dfu023

     500 kg-cm (36 ft-lb, 49 N.m)
2L and 3L 1988 on:
Leakage Pipe Nuts Torque:
     300 kg-cm (22 ft-lb, 29 N.m)
4. Install the injector pipes between the fuel pump and injectors and union nuts.
L, 2L & 2L-T Up to 1988:
Injection Pipe Union Nuts Torque:
     250 kg-cm (18 ft-lb, 25 N.m)
2L and 3L 1988 on:
Injection Pipe Union Nuts Torque:
     250 kg-cm (18 ft-lb, 25 N.m)
5. Install the injection pipe bracket brackets and bolts.
Note 2L & 3L 1988 on: Install the glow plugs by with a 12mm socket ad handle. Install the 2 insulators and connector per glow plug, removing the connector four bolts (fixed delay type) four nuts (other type) and connectors.
6. Start engine and inspect for fuel leaks.

FUEL FILTER

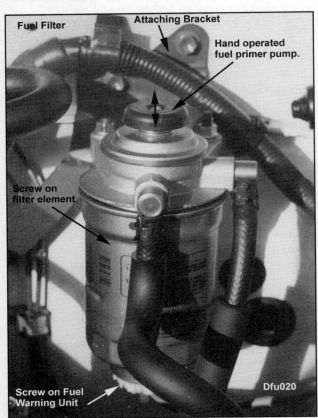

Fuel Filter
Attaching Bracket
Hand operated fuel primer pump.
Screw on filter element
Screw on Fuel Warning Unit
Dfu020

Replacement

1. Replace Fuel Filter. [Cartridge Type]

Replacement Filter
Dfu031

a. Use a filter grip handle and unscrew the filter, remove the fuel filter and "O" ring.

b. Install a new "O" ring that has been coated with fuel.

c. Install **the filter**, hand tighten until filter contacts the filter assembly, tighten an other 2/3 of a turn.

1. Replace Fuel Filter. [Power Element Type]

a. Unscrew the centre bolt, remove the bolt and the fuel filter bowl assembly.

b. Remove the upper body gasket from the fuel filter upper assembly.

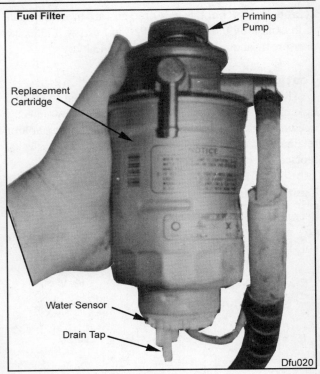

Fuel Filter
Priming Pump
Replacement Cartridge
Water Sensor
Drain Tap
Dfu020

c. Remove gaskets, element, spring plate and spring from the bowl.

d. Remove the "O" ring from the centre piece.

e. Cover a new "O" ring with fuel then install the "O" ring with the flat side toward the centre bolt head.

f. Install the spring, spring plate, a new rubber gasket, a new element and a new rubber gasket to filter bowl.

g. Coat a new upper body gasket with fuel, install the upper body gasket to the filter upper assembly.

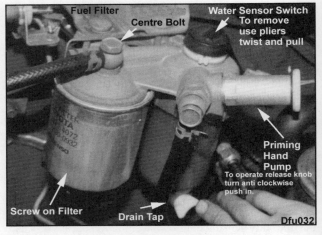

Fuel Filter
Centre Bolt
Water Sensor Switch To remove use pliers twist and pull
Priming Hand Pump To operate release knob turn anti clockwise push in.
Screw on Filter
Drain Tap
Dfu032

h. Install the fuel filter bowl and centre bolt.

2. Bleed fuel filter.

a. Connect bleeder tube to the fuel filter bleeder plug with the end draining into a container of fuel.

b. Unscrew the fuel filter bleeder plug just enough to allow fuel or air to be released from the filter assembly.

c. **[L, 2L & 2L-T : Upto 1988]** Turn the priming pump

handle counter clockwise to free it, pump the priming handle until there are no air bubbles emitted from the fuel filter bleeder plug.

c. **[2L & 3L : 1988 on]** Operate the fuel hand pump with your thumb on top of the fuel filter.

d. **[L, 2L & 2L-T : Upto 1988]** Return the priming pump handle by turning clockwise then tighten it. Remove the bleeder hose and tighten the fuel filter bleeder plug.

FUEL FILTER WARNING SWITCH

Top Fitting Model

Fuel Warning Switch
Turn (with multigrips) to remove.
Fuel Warning Switch Wiring
Hand Priming Pump
Turn anti clockwise to release primer pump knob. Dfu032

1. Disconnect the wiring loom connector.
2. Turn switch anticlockwise to unclip, it may be necessary to use multigrips, remove gasket.
3. Test switch by moving float up and down while an ohmmeter is connected to the wiring connector, compare with test specifications below. If the results are not as indicated below replace warning switch.
Test Result Specifications:
Float Up: Continuity between terminals.
Float Down: No continuity between terminals.
4. Install switch by fitting switch to top of filter unit, turn clockwise to clip lock, do not use multigrips.

Lower Fitting Model

1. Drain fuel filter by removing drain plug, place a container under unit to catch fuel.

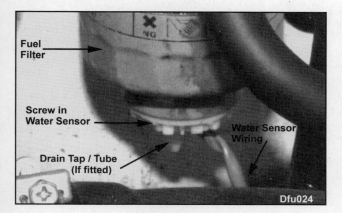

Fuel Filter
Screw in Water Sensor
Drain Tap / Tube (If fitted)
Water Sensor Wiring
Dfu024

2. Disconnect the wiring loom connector.
3. Turn switch anticlockwise to unclip, it may be necessary to use multigrips, remove gasket. Connect wiring connector.
4. Test switch by moving float up and down while an ohmmeter is connected to the wiring connector, compare with test specifications below. If the results are not as indicated below replace warning switch.
Test Result Specifications:
Float Up: Continuity between terminals.
Float Down: No continuity between terminals.
5. Install switch by fitting switch to top of filter unit, turn clockwise to clip lock, do not use multigrips. Connect wiring connector.
6. Install drain plug with new gasket.
7. Fill filter and check operation.

FUEL HEATER and VACUUM SWITCH
Remove

1. Disconnect fuel line hoses to heater unit and vacuum switch assembly, place a container under unit to catch fuel.
2. Disconnect wiring loom connectors.
3. Remove the attaching bolts, remove heater unit and vacuum switch assembly.
Test

Test heater unit by connecting an ohmmeter is connected to the wiring connector, compare with test specifications below. If the results are not as indicated below replace heater unit or vacuum switch.

[L, 2L & 2L-T: Upto 1988] Test Result Specifications:
Between Heater Connector Terminals: Resistance 0.73ohms +/- 0.29ohms @ 20⁰C (68⁰F)
Between Vacuum Connector Terminal and Vacuum Switch Body [with no vacuum]: No Continuity
Between Vacuum Connector Terminal and Vacuum Switch Body [with vacuum 140-260mmHg]: Continuity

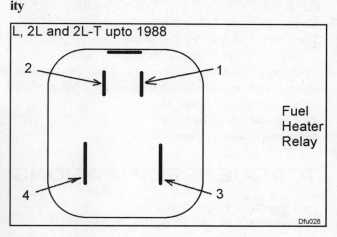

L, 2L and 2L-T upto 1988
2   1
4   3
Fuel Heater Relay
Dfu028

[2L & 3L: 1988 on] Test Result Specifications:
Between Heater Connector Terminals: Resistance 0.7ohms @ 20⁰C (68⁰F)

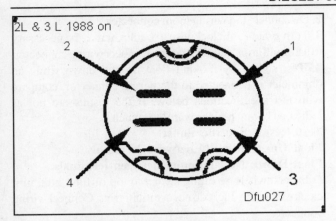

Between Vacuum Connector Terminals [with no vacuum]: No Continuity
Between Vacuum Connector Terminals [with vacuum 150-250mmHg]: Continuity

Install
1. Install heater unit and vacuum switch assembly. Install the attaching bolts and tighten.
2. Connect wiring loom connectors.
3. Connect fuel line hoses to heater unit and vacuum switch assembly.

FUEL HEATER RELAY
1. Relay is situated under bonnet in relay compartment.
Test relay by connecting an ohmmeter to the relay terminals, compare with test specifications below. If the results are not as indicated below replace relay.
[L, 2L & 2L-T : Upto 1988] Test Result Specifications:
Test Result Specifications:
Terminals 1 and 2: Continuity
Terminals 3 and 4: No Continuity
[2L & 3L : 1988 on] Test Result Specifications:
Terminals 1 and 3: Continuity
Terminals 2 and 4: No Continuity
2. Connect battery voltage to terminals 1 and 3.
Test relay by connecting an ohmmeter to the relay terminals, compare with test specifications below. If the results are not as indicated below replace relay.
Test Result Specifications:
Terminals 2 and 4: Continuity

TORQUE SPECIFICATIONS

Fuel Injection Pump Assembly
Fuel Injection Pump Attaching Bolt Torque:
    210 kg-cm (15 ft-lb, 21 N.m)
Fuel Pump Support Bracket Bolt Torque:
    185 kg-cm (13 ft-lb, 18 N.m)
Injection Pump Drive Shaft Pulley Attaching Nut:

650kg.cm (47ft-lb, 64Nm)
Fuel Outlet Union Bolt Torque:
    230 kg-cm (17 ft-lb, 23 N.m)
Fuel Outlet Union Bolt Torque:
    230 kg-cm (17 ft-lb, 23 N.m)
Fuel Injector Pipe Torque:
    250 kg-cm (18 ft-lb, 25 N.m)
Regulator Valve Torque: 90 kg-cm (78 in-lb, 8.8 Nm)
Fuel Distributor Head Bolt Torque:
    120 kg-cm (9 ft-lb, 12 N.m
Pump Cover Bolts Torque: 25kg-cm (22in-lb, 2.5Nm)
Fuel Delivery Valve Holders Specified Torque:
    500 kg-cm (9 ft-lb, 49 N.m)
Governor Cover Bolts Torque:
    85 kg-cm (74 in-lb, 8.3 N.m)
Governor Link Bolt Torque:
    115 kg-cm (8 ft-lb, 11 N.m)
2L & 3L 1988 on:
Governor Link Bolt: 140 kg-cm (10 ft-lb, 14 N.m)
Fuel Outlet Union Bolt Torque:
    230 kg-cm (17 ft-lb, 23 N.m)
Fuel Outlet Union Bolt Torque:
    230 kg-cm (17 ft-lb, 23 N.m)
Fuel Injector Pipe Torque:
    250 kg-cm (18 ft-lb, 25 N.m)
L, 2L & 2L-T Up to 1988:
Injection Pipe Union Nuts Torque:
    250 kg-cm (18 ft-lb, 25 N.m)
Injectors
L, 2L & 2L-T Up to 1988:
Injector Retaining Nut Torque:
    700 kg-cm (51 ft-lb, 69 N.m)
2L and 3L 1988 on:
Injector Retaining Nut Torque:
    375 kg-cm (27 ft-lb, 37 N.m)
Injector Torque Specification:
    650 kg-cm (47 ft-lb, 64 N.m)
L, 2L & 2L-T Up to 1988:
Leakage Pipe Nuts Torque:
    500 kg-cm (36 ft-lb, 49 N.m)
2L and 3L 1988 on:
Leakage Pipe Nuts Torque:
    300 kg-cm (22 ft-lb, 29 N.m)
L, 2L & 2L-T Up to 1988:
Injection Pipe Union Nuts Torque:
    250 kg-cm (18 ft-lb, 25 N.m)
2L and 3L 1988 on:
Injection Pipe Union Nuts Torque:
    250 kg-cm (18 ft-lb, 25 N.m)

TURBOCHARGER

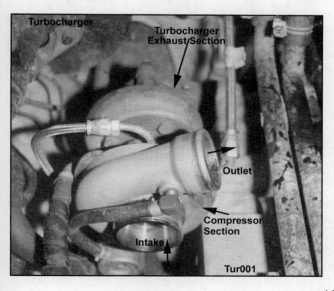

TURBOCHARGER

General Information

The engine should not be stopped immediately after pulling a trailer or high speed or uphill driving. Idle the engine 30-150 seconds, depending on the severity of the driving condition. Do not highly rev or acceleration immediately after starting a cold engine.

If for some reason the turbocharger is not operating correctly and it must be rebuilt or replaced, check for the cause of the fault or turbo break down. Initially check the engine oil level and quality, oil lines leading to turbocharger and conditions under which the vehicle was operating.

If removing the turbocharger, the intake and exhaust pots and oil inlet should be covered, to ensure dirt or foreign material does not entry the turbocharger.

When the turbocharger has been removed make sure the gaskets on the surface of the flange of the lubricating oil pipe and turbocharger oil flange are completely removed.

The turbocharger is quite fragile so when removing and installing a turbocharger, make sure you do not drop it or bang it against hard objects. Also do not hold or clamp the turbocharger by easily-deformed parts, such as the actuator or rod.

While installing a turbocharger, check for buildup of sludge particles in the oil pipes and, if necessary, replace the oil pipes. During installation of a turbocharger, place 20 cc (1.2 cu.in) of oil into the turbocharger oil inlet and rotate the impeller and shaft by hand to lubricate the bearing.

It quite important to replace bolts or nuts, with specified new ones.

After rebuilding or replacing the engine, stop the fuel supply while you turn over the engine for 30-40 seconds to lubricate the engine and turbocharger. Once the engine has been started idle for 60 seconds to allow further oil pressure buildup.

Inspect

\# Inspect the air intake assembly for broken or partially blocked air tubing between the air cleaner and turbocharger inlet and between the turbocharger outlet and cylinder head. If the air cleaner is blocked, clean or replace the element. Hoses that are collapsed or deformed must be repaired or replaced.

Air leakage from connections, check each connection and repair or replace components.

\# Inspect the exhaust system, inspect for leakage or blocked areas between the engine cylinder head and turbocharger inlet also between the turbocharger outlet and exhaust pipe.

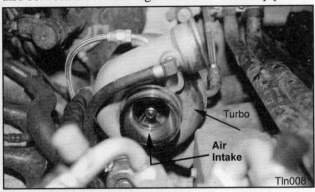

If foreign material is found it must be removed.

Any components found to be faulty must be replaced or repaired.

\# The turbocharger must function correctly, inspection and testing of the unit should be carried out.

The actuator and waste gate valve can be tested by using connecting a pressure gauge to the actuator hose, apply about 0.68 kg/cm^2 (9.7 psi, 67 kPa) of pressure to the actuator and check that the rod moves.

Do not apply greater than 0.8 kg/cm^2 (11.4 psi, 78 kPa) of pressure to the actuator, other wise the unit could be damaged.

\# The turbocharging pressure can be tested by connect a "T" union to the intake pipe pressure hose, install a pressure gauge to the "T" union.

This test is done when the engine is at operating temperature. Start the engine, transmission in neutral, accelerator the engine to a maximum speed of 2,200 - 2,400 rpm, check for specified pressure .

Turbocharging pressure:
0.39 - 0.53 kg/cm^2 (5.5 - 7.3 psi, 38 - 52 kPa)
If not as specified, inspect intake and exhaust systems for leakage. If there is no leakage, replace the turbocharger assembly.

If above specification, check actuator hose is not disconnected or cracked. If not, replace turbocharger.

Remove

1. Loosen the accelerator cable connections, place the cable to one side.
2. Remove all vacuum hoses from the intake ducting.
3. Remove the air intake ducting from the air cleaner to the turbocharger.
4. Remove the turbocharger heat shield attached by bolts.
5. Remove the turbocharger compressor elbow for the air intake.
6. Under the turbocharger remove the oil pipe, attached by flange and two bolts.
7. Remove the turbocharger by removing the four nuts attaching the turbocharger to the exhaust manifold.
8. Remove the turbine elbow from the turbocharger which is attached by four nuts.

Inspection of Turbocharger

The impeller needs to turn freely, check this by rotating the shaft nuts at either end of the shaft, if the shaft and impeller does not turn freely, the turbocharger needs to be replaced. Mount the turbocharger in a bracket, mount a dial gauge to check the impeller shaft end play, check for shaft end play movement, if not within specification, replace the turbocharger.

Impeller Shaft Axial play: 0.13 mm (0.0051 in) or less
Clean away all old gaskets, so there is a clean surface for installation.

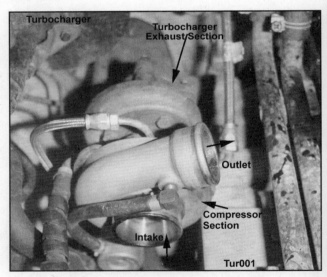

Installation

1. Install the turbine elbow to the turbocharger which is attached by four nuts, tighten nuts to specification.
Turbine Elbow to Turbocharger Torque: 260 kg-cm (19ft.lb, 25Nm)
2. Install the turbocharger to the exhaust manifold and oil pipe, by attaching the four nuts, install new gaskets. Tighten the four nuts to specification.

During installation of a turbocharger, place 20 cc (1.2

cu.in) of oil into the turbocharger oil inlet and rotate the impeller and shaft by hand to lubricate the bearing.

Turbocharger Attaching Bolts Torque:

530 kg.cm (38ft.lb, 52Nm)

3. Under the turbocharger attach the oil pipe, attached by flange and two bolts, install new gaskets. Tighten the two nuts to specification.

Turbocharger Oil Pipe Flange Nuts Torque:

195 kg.cm (14ft.lb, 19Nm)

4. Install the turbocharger compressor elbow for the air intake, attached by two bolts, install new gasket. Tighten the two nuts to specification.

Turbocharger Compressor Elbow Bolts Torque:

120 kg.cm (9ft.lb, 12Nm).

5. Install the turbocharger heat shield attached by bolts.

6. Install the air intake ducting from the air cleaner to the turbochargers.

Turbocharger Air Intake Clamp Bolts Torque:

120 kg.cm (9ft.lb, 12Nm).

7. Install all vacuum hoses to the intake ducting.

8. Install the accelerator cable and connections.

DIAGNOSIS

PROBLEM: No Power Excessive Fuel Consumption

Possible Cause: Air Intake System.

Inspect the air intake assembly for broken or partially blocked air tubing between the air cleaner and turbocharger inlet and between the turbocharger outlet and cylinder head. If the air cleaner is blocked, clean or replace the element. Hoses that are collapsed or deformed must be repaired or replaced.

Air leakage from connections, check each connection and repair or replace components.

Possible Cause: Exhaust System.

Inspect the exhaust system, inspect for leakage or blocked areas between the engine cylinder head and turbocharger inlet also between the turbocharger outlet and exhaust pipe. If foreign material is found it must be removed.

Any components found to be faulty must be replaced or repaired.

The turbocharger must function correctly, inspection and testing of the unit should be carried out.

The actuator and waste gate valve can be tested by using connecting a pressure gauge to the actuator hose, apply about 0.68 kg/cm^2 (9.7 psi, 67 kPa) of pressure to the actuator and check that the rod moves.

Do not apply greater than 0.8 kg/cm^2 (11.4 psi, 78 kPa) of pressure to the actuator, other wise the unit could be damaged.

The turbocharging pressure can be tested by connect a "T" union to the intake pipe pressure hose, install a pressure gauge to the "T" union.

This test is done when the engine is at operating temperature. Start the engine, transmission in neutral, accelerator the engine to a maximum speed of 2,200 - 2,400 rpm, check for specified pressure .

Turbocharging pressure:

0.39 - 0.53 kg/cm^2 (5.5 - 7.3 psi, 38 - 52 kPa)

If not as specified, inspect intake and exhaust systems for leakage. If there is no leakage, replace the turbocharger assembly.

If above specification, check actuator hose is not disconnected or cracked. If not, replace turbocharger.

PROBLEM: Turbocharger Noise Excessive

Possible Cause: Exhaust System.

Inspect exhaust system for broken flange or broken exhaust brackets.

Inspect heat shields for proper installation.

Inspect for broken exhaust pipes.

Inspect items listed under "No Power Excessive Fuel Consumption"

PROBLEM: Excessive Oil Consumption

Possible Cause: Turbocharger Seal.

Inspect for oil in the turbocharger, by removing the turbine elbow, if there are carbon deposit buildup on the turbine fins. If so the turbocharger will need to be replaced.

Inspect for excessive oil coming from the PCV system into the air intake.

Inspect for excessive turbocharger shaft axial end play as previously described.

Turbocharger Electrical Diagnosis
See page number 408.

SPECIFICATIONS

Impeller Shaft Axial play: 0.13 mm (0.0051 in) or less
Turbocharging pressure:

0.39 - 0.53 kg/cm^2 (5.5 - 7.3 psi, 38 - 52 kPa)
Turbine Elbow to Turbocharger Torque:

260 kg-cm (19ft.lb, 25Nm)
Turbocharger Attaching Bolts Torque:

530 kg.cm (38ft.lb, 52Nm)
Turbocharger Oil Pipe Flange Nuts Torque:

195 kg.cm (14ft.lb, 19Nm)
Turbocharger Compressor Elbow Bolts Torque:

120 kg.cm (9ft.lb, 12Nm).
Turbocharger Air Intake Clamp Bolts Torque:

120 kg.cm (9ft.lb, 12Nm).

CLUTCH

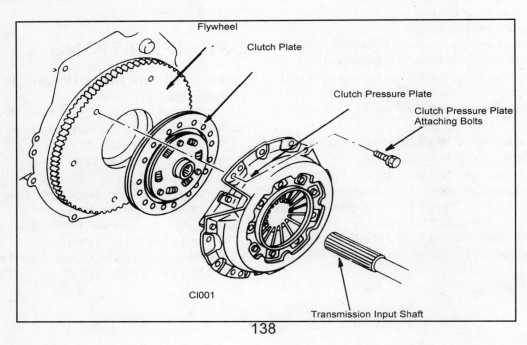

Flywheel
Clutch Plate
Clutch Pressure Plate
Clutch Pressure Plate Attaching Bolts
Transmission Input Shaft
CI001

CLUTCH

The clutch used is a hydraulically actuated single dry disc type. The hydraulic system consists of a master cylinder connected to the clutch pedal and a release cylinder mounted on the clutch bell housing which acts on the release bearing lever. There is no provision for pedal free play adjustment however it is important to maintain the pedal height adjustment.

The clutch plate and facing assembly has a conventional clutch facing riveted to each side of curved disc springs which provide axial cushioning during engagement. The disc springs are riveted to the circumference of the hub assembly, which incorporates coil springs and rubber dampers, for torsional cushioning, friction washers for torsional damping and an internal spline that mounts the assembly on the external splined transmission main drive gear clutch shaft. The pressure place is a diaphragm spring type. The diaphragm lever height is not adjustable and the unit is serviced only as an assembly.

The cover, pressure plate and diaphragm spring assembly is mounted over the clutch plate assembly and bolted to the flywheel. The pressure plate is held to the cover by tangential straps. The straps are attached to the pressure plate at one end and the clutch cover at the other. This holds the pressure plate concentrically, but allows it to move axially. Retraction of the pressure plate by means of retracting springs and release of the driven plate, is achieved when the diaphragm spring is operated.

MINOR MAINTENANCE

There are several items which affect good clutch operation, therefore it is necessary before performing any major clutch service, to make preliminary inspections to determine whether the trouble is actually in the clutch.

VISUAL INSPECTION

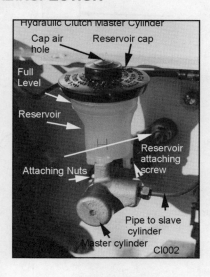

Hydraulic Clutch Master Cylinder

Cap air hole
Reservoir cap
Full Level
Reservoir
Attaching Nuts
Reservoir attaching screw
Pipe to slave cylinder
Master cylinder
CI002

1. Check condition of hydraulic lines and ensure that components are assembled correctly, taking note that the lines do not have sharp bends or are rubbing against other objects.
2. Check level of hydraulic reservoir.
3. Check clutch master cylinder for leaking seals.
4. Check clutch slave cylinder and lines for leaking seals and unions.
5. Check condition of clutch pedal bushes and shaft.
6. Check clutch pedal height and control rod adjustment, as outlined in this chapter.
7. Check condition of all engine and transmission mountings.

HYDRAULIC SYSTEM

Master Cylinder Inspection.
1. Check that the level of brake fluid is within the levels marked on the cylinder reservoir.
2. Refill with specified brake fluid.
Clutch fluid specified: Heavy duty brake fluid
3. Inspect to make sure the air vent in the reservoir cap is clear and air can be blown through it.

Bleed Hydraulic Clutch System.
1. Fit a tube onto the bleed valve located on the slave cylinder with the other end in a container half full of brake fluid.

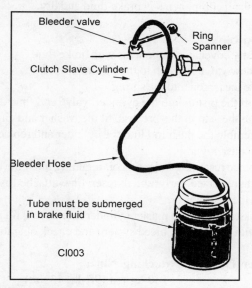

Bleeder valve
Ring Spanner
Clutch Slave Cylinder
Bleeder Hose
Tube must be submerged in brake fluid
CI003

2. With an assistant, push down on the clutch pedal several times, push down on the pedal while the bleed valve is loosened just enough to allow brake fluid (and air if present) to bleed out of the hose attached to the bleed valve.
3. Tighten the bleed valve before the clutch is allowed to return to its normal position.
4. Repeat steps 2 & 3 above until the system is free of air. This is detected by having a firm feeling clutch pedal when pushed down.
5. Check the level of the master cylinder reservoir brake fluid, top up to marked levels so as not to allow air to enter the

system.

6. Top up master cylinder with specified Brake fluid, do not use fluid bled out of clutch system.

Clutch fluid specified: Heavy duty brake fluid

CLUTCH MASTER CYLINDER

Remove

1. Remove the hydraulic brake lines from the master cylinder.
2. Detach the clutch pedal push rod from the clutch pedal.
3. Remove the two nuts attaching the master cylinder to the fire wall.
4. Remove the master cylinder from the fire wall.

Dismantle

1. Drain brake fluid from the master cylinder.
2. Remove the rubber protection cover and pushrod.
3. Remove the spring circlip and washer.
4. Remove the piston and spring from the cylinder.
5. Dismantle the piston and valve assembly. Remove rubber seals.
6. If necessary to remove reservoir, remove retaining pin and reservoir, early models reservoir is attached by a nut inside the reservoir.
7. Wash all components in brake fluid and dry.

Assemble

1. Lightly cover all components with brake fluid.
2. Fit new valve seals on to the piston.
3. Slide the piston into the spring.
4. Insert the piston into the cylinder, valve end first, do not damage the seal in this process, fit the washer and circlip.
5. Assemble the push rod into the cylinder and replace the rubber dust cover.
6. Replace reservoir and reservoir retaining pin if the reservoir was removed, early models reservoir is attached by a nut inside the reservoir.
7. Reassemble clutch master cylinder to fire wall, fill reservoir with brake fluid, bleed system and check operation of clutch.

Master Cylinder Attaching Nuts:
130 kg.cm (9ft-lb, 13Nm)

CLUTCH SLAVE CYLINDER

Remove

1. Remove the clutch fluid hose.
2. Remove the cylinder attaching bolts and remove cylinder, taking care of the clutch push rod.

Dismantle

1. Remove clutch push rod, rubber cover.
2. Slide out piston assembly and spring (some early models

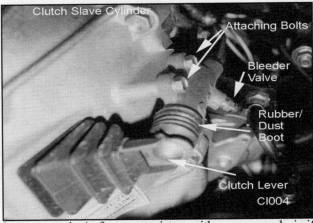

Clutch Slave Cylinder — Attaching Bolts — Bleeder Valve — Rubber/Dust Boot — Clutch Lever — CI004

have no spring), force out piston with compressed air if necessary.
3. Wash all parts in brake fluid and allow to drain.

Assemble

1. Fit a new seal (make sure the seal is fitted the correct way, concave side faces into the back of the cylinder), replace piston, rubber cover and clutch push rod.
2. Reassemble slave cylinder into position, fit clutch hydraulic hose.
3. Top up reservoir with fluid and bleed clutch system as previously described.

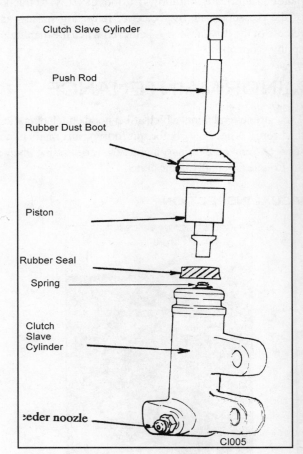

Clutch Slave Cylinder — Push Rod — Rubber Dust Boot — Piston — Rubber Seal — Spring — Clutch Slave Cylinder — Bleeder noozle — CI005

Install

1. Install the cylinder to housing and fit attaching bolts, taking care of the clutch push rod.

Slave Cylinder Attaching Bolts:
130 kg.cm (9ft-lb, 13Nm)

2. Install the clutch fluid hose.

CLUTCH PEDAL

Remove

1. Remove clutch pedal pivot bolt and pull clutch pedal down slightly and disconnect upper clevis of reservoir clutch control rod from clutch pedal.
2. Disconnect upper end of return spring from clutch pedal support and remove pedal.
3. Remove return spring from pedal. Remove bushes and spacer from pedal pivot bore.

Install

1. Lubricate all bearing surfaces with Molybdenum grease.
2. Install pedal bushes and spacer into pedal pivot bore.
3. Assemble clutch pedal return spring to clutch pedal.
4. Install pedal to clutch/brake pedal support and spring.
5. (a) Connect clutch control cable to top of clutch pedal.
(b) Install and torque clutch pedal pivot bolt.
Torque: 12 - 16 Nm.
6. Check clutch pedal adjustment as described in this Chapter.

CLUTCH PEDAL ADJUSTMENT

1. Check pedal height from the vehicle floor, not the carpet or floor padding.
2. If adjustment is necessary loosen adjuster lock nut near top of the pedal.

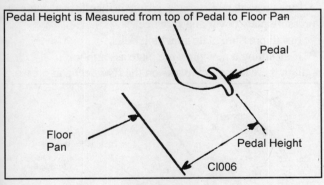

Pedal Height is Measured from top of Pedal to Floor Pan

Pedal

Floor
Pan

Pedal Height

CI006

Pedal Height :
Hi Lux

RN 30's & 40's (12R)	152 - 164mm (6.0 - 6.4in)
RN 30's & 40's (18 & 20R)	152 - 164mm (6.0 - 6.4in)
Series 50's & 60's	151.0mm
LN RN YN 80's,90's, 100's & 110	
Right Hand Drive	151.0mm (5.945in)
Left Hand Drive	157.5mm (6.201in)

3. Turn adjuster bolt to obtain correct adjustment, tighten adjuster lock nut.

MAJOR REPAIRS

The clutch pedal should not be operated fully after installation of a new clutch pressure plate throw-out bearing without first carrying out the appropriate clutch control adjustments, as damage may occur to the clutch diaphragm.

After installation of a new drive plate, flywheel or pressure plate, sudden engagement of the clutch with the engine running at an abnormal speed, or continual slipping of the clutch, may permanently injure driven plate facings and cause scoring of the flywheel and pressure plate. When these parts are new, they should be given moderate use for several days until they are burnished.

The transmission main drive gear clutch shaft spigot bearing should only require attention when the clutch is removed from the vehicle, at which time it should be inspected and lubricated with SAE 90 Gear Oil, or if necessary, replaced. The clutch throw-out bearing is lubricated during manufacture then sealed. Further lubrication is not necessary with the exception of the clutch fork contact surfaces and the inner recess of the throw-out bearing, which should be lubricated with grease.

CLUTCH ASSEMBLY

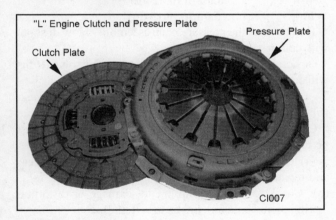

"L" Engine Clutch and Pressure Plate

Pressure Plate

Clutch Plate

CI007

Remove

1. Remove transmission and clutch bell housing assembly as outlined in this manual.
2. Disconnect the retaining spring from clutch fork and withdraw bearing and clutch fork from clutch housing by pulling toward front of vehicle.
(a) Remove clutch throw-out bearing.
(b) Pull clutch fork from ball stud and remove fork from clutch housing.
3. Mark flywheel and clutch pressure plate cover, this will correctly locate them when reinstalling (balance can be then maintained).
(a) Loosen and remove attaching bolts of clutch pressure

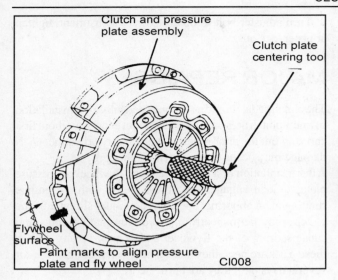

Clutch and pressure plate assembly

Clutch plate centering too

Flywheel surface

Paint marks to align pressure plate and fly wheel

CI008

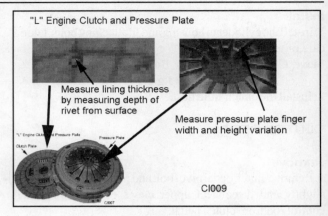

"L" Engine Clutch and Pressure Plate

Measure lining thickness by measuring depth of rivet from surface

Measure pressure plate finger width and height variation

CI009

plate cover (do this evenly to avoid pressure plate distortion).
(b) Remove clutch plate and pressure plate assemblies.

Inspection

1. With a soft cloth dampened with a cleaning solvent, wipe pressure plate and flywheel surfaces clean (DO NOT USE PETROLEUM BASED CLEANERS).
Check pressure plate diaphragm finger spring for depth and wear width.

Pressure Plate Finger Springs Depth & Wear Limits:
Depth   0.6mm (0.024in)
Width   5.0mm (0.197in)

* Do not wash the pressure plate assembly - blow dust out with compressed air.
* Do not soak the throw-out bearing in cleaning solvent (this will destroy the bearing lubricant).

2. (a) Check spigot bush of main drive gear shaft for wear.
(b) If necessary, replace the bush.
* Only remove the bush if, when inspected, you feel it must be replaced.

3. (a) Check clutch fork ball socket and ball stud for wear and replace if necessary.
(b) Check for retaining spring for damage or distortion (spring should hold fork tightly to ball stud).
(c) Check clutch fork for cracks or wear on fingers.

4. (a) Check throw-out bearing for roughness of operation of signs of wear and replace if necessary.
(b) Examine bearing hub bore for burrs - any burrs should be removed. (If burrs are found, inspect transmission main drive gear bearing retainer for scoring. If scoring is slight, remove, using fine emery cloth. Replace retainer if scoring is excessive.

5. Check flywheel and clutch pressure plate friction surfaces for burn marks, scoring or roughness.
- Slight roughness may be smoothed with fine emery cloth.
- Deep scoring of flywheel or pressure plate surfaces will require replacement of damaged component/s.

- Slight scoring of the flywheel surface may be removed by taking a slight cut across flywheel face in a lathe.
6. (a) Check driven plate of clutch for lining wear measure depth to rivet surface, broken hub springs or loose rivets.
Clutch Lining thickness to top of rivet: 0.3mm (0.012in)
(b) Examine clutch driven plate linings for oil or fluid contamination.
* If oil or fluid is found on the clutch linings, locate and correct the cause of the leak before proceeding with the clutch repairs.
* Check clutch hub for a free sliding fit on main drive gear clutch shaft splines.

Install

1. Lubricate spigot bush with a few drops of SAE 90 gear oil.
2. Assemble driven plate of clutch, together with cover and pressure plate assembly and insert a suitable clutch centring tool, through driven plate, into spigot bearing.
* Drive plate is installed with the long end of the splined hub facing forward and the damper springs inside the pressure plate.
3. Line up paint marks made during dismantle procedure on pressure plate cover and flywheel.
4. Install pressure plate attaching bolts.
* If installing a new pressure plate assembly:
- align the white paint marks on the flywheel and pressure

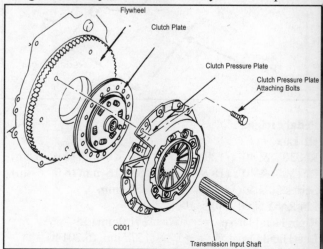

Flywheel

Clutch Plate

Clutch Pressure Plate

Clutch Pressure Plate Attaching Bolts

Transmission Input Shaft

CI001

Clutch assembled to flywheel

Flywheel

Clutch assembly

C1010

plate as close as possible.

- Tighten screws gradually and in rotation to avoid pressure plate distortion.
- Torque bolts and remove clutch centring tool.

Clutch Assembly bolts: 195kg-cm (14ft-lb, 19Nm)

5. Pack recess inside throw-out bearing and smear clutch fork groove area with grease.

6. (a) Lubricate ball stud and clutch fork pivot point with Molybdenum Disulphide grease.

(b) Assemble throw-out bearing to clutch fork.

(c) Install clutch fork (locating it on ball stud) and throw-out bearing assembly into clutch housing.

7. (a) Install clutch bell housing to rear of engine.

(b) Install and torque housing attaching screws.

Clutch Bell Housing to Engine: 380kg-cm(27ft-lb,37Nm)

9. Position clutch fork dust shield over clutch fork and snap into plate.

10. Install clutch slave cylinder if removed.

11. Start engine and check clutch operation.

PROBLEM DIAGNOSIS

Problem: Clutch fails to release (pedal pressured to floor - shift lever does not move freely in and out of reverse gear without gear clash)!

Possible Causes and Remedies:

* Improper pedal travel. Remedy - Adjust pedal height.
* Faulty driven plate. Remedy - Replace plate.
* Fork and bearing not assembled properly. Remedy - Install properly and (very lightly) lubricate fingers at release bearing.
* Driven plate hub binding on maindrive gear clutch shaft splines. Remedy - Repair or replace maindrive gear and/or drive plate assemblies.
* Driven plate warped or bent. Remedy - Replace driven plate.

* Insufficient brake fluid in master cylinder reservoir. Remedy - Top up reservoir to correct level.

Problem: **Slipping!**
Possible Causes and Remedies:
* Improper driver operation. Remedy - Observe correct operation.
* Oil soaked driven plate. Remedy - Install new plate and correct leak at its source.
* Worn facing or facing torn from driven plate. Remedy - replace plate.
* Warped pressure plate or flywheel. Remedy - Replace pressure plate or flywheel.
* Weak diaphragm spring. Remedy - Replace pressure plate.
* Driven plate not seated in. Remedy - Make 30 - 40 normal starts. (**Caution**: *Do not overheat!*)
* Driven plate overheated. Remedy - Allow to cool and re-check.

Problem: **Grabbing (chattering)!**
Possible Causes and Remedies:
* Oil on facing; burned or glazed facings. Remedy - Install new driven plate and correct leak at its source.
* Worn splines on maindrive gear clutch shaft splines. Remedy - Replace maindrive gear assembly.
* Loose engine mountings. Remedy - Tighten or replace mountings.
* Warped pressure plate or flywheel. Remedy - Replace pressure plate or flywheel.
* Burned or smeared resin on flywheel or pressure plate. Remedy - Sand off if superficial. Replace burned or heat-affected parts.

Problem: Rattling - transmission click!
Possible Causes and Remedies:
* Release fork loose. Remedy - Install properly.
* Oil in driven plate damper. Remedy - Replace driven plate and correct leak.
* Driven plate damper spring failure. Remedy - Replace driven plate.

Problem: **Noisy!**
Possible Causes and Remedies:
* Worn throw-out bearing. Remedy - Replace bearing.
* Fork shaft improperly installed. Remedy - Install properly and lubricate fork fingers at bearing.

Problem: **Pedal stays on floor!**
Possible Causes and Remedies:
* Binding throw-out bearing. Remedy - Lubricate and free up bearing.
* No brake fluid in master cylinder. Remedy - Top up reservoir and bleed system.

* Spring wear in pressure plate. Remedy - Replace pressure plate.

Problem: Hard pedal effort!
Possible Causes and Remedies:
* Bind in pedal. Remedy-Lubricate bushes and free up.
* Driven plate worn. Remedy - Replace driven plate.

SPECIFICATIONS

CLUTCH

Type	Single Plate - Diaphragm
Actuation	Hydraulic

Pressure Plate Finger Springs Depth & Wear Limits:

Depth	0.6mm (0.024in)
Width	5.0mm (0.197in)

Clutch Lining thickness to top of rivet: 0.3mm (0.012in)
Free Play at Pedal (Downwards)   5.0-10.0 mm

Pedal Height :
Hi Lux

RN 30's & 40's (12R)	152 - 164mm (6.0 - 6.4in)
RN 30's & 40's (18 & 20R)	152 - 164mm (6.0 - 6.4in)
Series 50's & 60's	151.0mm

LN RN YN 80's,90's, 100's & 110:

Right Hand Drive	151.0mm (5.945in)
Left Hand Drive	157.5mm (6.201in)

TORQUE SPEC'S

CLUTCH

Clutch Bell Housing to Engine: 380kg-cm(27ft-lb,37Nm)
Clutch Assembly to Flywheel bolts:
                                   195kg-cm (14ft-lb, 19Nm)
Master Cylinder Attaching Nuts: 130 kg.cm (9ft-lb, 13Nm)
Slave Cylinder Attaching bolts: 130 kg.cm (9ft-lb, 13Nm)
Clutch pedal pivot bolt: 12 - 16 Nm.

Memo

MANUAL TRANSMISSIONS

This chapter cover three different general types of manual transmissions, they were "G" types, "L" types and "W" types.

HiLux vehicles upto 1983 that is the 30's and 40's used L 40, L42 and L43 and W50 transmissions.

HiLux vehicles from 1983 to 1988 that is the 50's and 60's used G40, G52 and G54 plus L40 and L42 and W52 transmissions.

HiLux vehicles from 1988 on that is the 80's, 90's 100's and 110's used G40, G52 G54 and G58 plus L40 and and W56 transmissions.

"G" Type Transmission

Input Shaft

Front Bearing

Synchronizer Ring

Output Shaft

Fifth Gear Synchronizer

Counter Gear and Shaft

Reverse Idler Gear Shaft

Reverse Idler Gear

Fifth Gear

GRT026

"W" Type Transmission

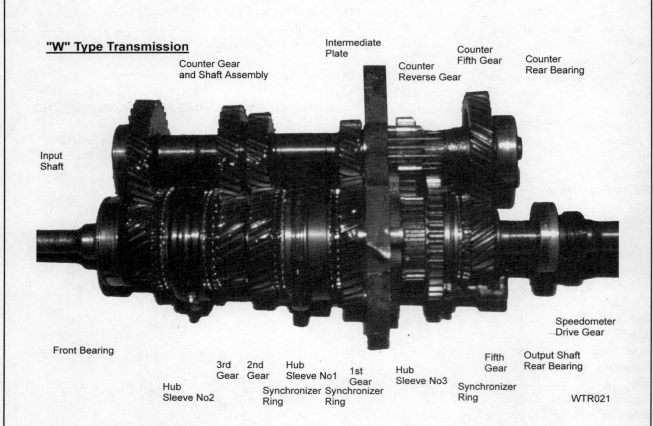

Counter Gear and Shaft Assembly

Intermediate Plate

Counter Reverse Gear

Counter Fifth Gear

Counter Rear Bearing

Input Shaft

Speedometer Drive Gear

Front Bearing

3rd Gear

2nd Gear

Hub Sleeve No1

1st Gear

Hub Sleeve No3

Fifth Gear

Output Shaft Rear Bearing

Hub Sleeve No2

Synchronizer Ring

Synchronizer Ring

Synchronizer Ring

WTR021

4/5 Speed Manual Transmission

G & W Series

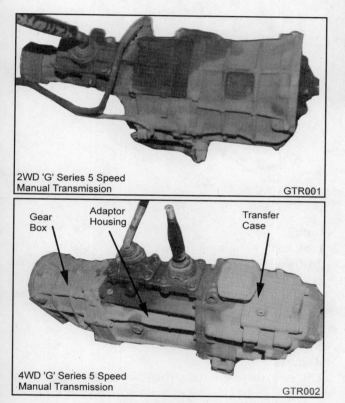

2WD 'G' Series 5 Speed Manual Transmission   GTR001

Gear Box   Adaptor Housing   Transfer Case

4WD 'G' Series 5 Speed Manual Transmission   GTR002

This transmission is a 5 speed manual utilising 5th gear as an overdrive. First through to fourth gears and reverse are meshed within the case. The 5th speed gear and synchronizes are located on the back of the case in the extension housing. The floor mounted shift lever operates a shift rail which advances from the extension housing turret to the shift cover. The 1st/2nd and 3rd/4th shift forks are mounted in the cover. The 5th speed synchronises and reverse sliding gear are shifted through an intermediate lever mounted on a pivot pin.

Maintenance

Checking and Replacing Transmission Oil

Position an oil catching tray under the transmission, make sure it has the capacity to hold the oil from the transmission, most of the transmission hold between 2 to 3 litres of transmission oil.

Remove the drain plug from the lower section of the transmission, if the vehicle has been recently driven take care as the oil could be hot enough to burn skin on contact.

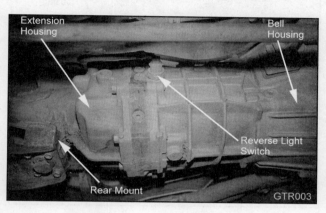

Extension Housing   Bell Housing   Reverse Light Switch   Rear Mount   GTR003

Replace the drain plug and tighten to specification.

Drain Plug torque: **250kg-cm, 18ft.lb, 27Nm**

Remove the filler plug approximately half way up the right side of the transmission, fill the transmission with the correct amount of specified oil.

Oil Specification and Capacity of Transmission:

G40, 52, 54:   API GL-4 SAE 75W90

4 Speed: 2.4 litres (2.5US qts, 2.1 Imp. qts)

5 Speed: 2.2 litres (2.3US qts, 1.9 Imp. qts)

W52:   API GL-4 SAE 75W90

2.6 litres (2.7US qts, 2.3 Imp. qts)

L40, 42:   API GL-4 SAE 90

1.9 litres (2.0US qts, 1.7 Imp. qts)

Check oil level by inserting your finger into the oil filler hole to check on oil level. The oil level should be at the same level as the filler plug, but so high that oil will run out when the plug is removed.

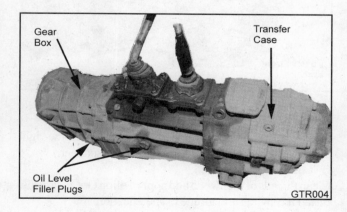

Gear Box   Transfer Case   Oil Level Filler Plugs   GTR004

Replace oil filler plug and tighten plug to specification.
Filler Plug torque: **250kg-cm, 18ft.lb, 27Nm**

Speedo Sender

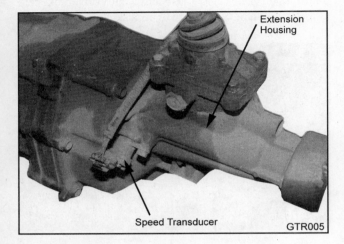

GTR005

Remove

Raise vehicle, remove bolt balt securing speedo driven gear and cable to extension housing then withdraw speedometer driven gear assembly and remove the 'O' ring seal.

Install

Install 'O' ring, install gear into extension housing and tighten retaining bolt to specification.
Speedometer Driven Gear Retaining Bolt: 11Nm

Reversing Light Switch

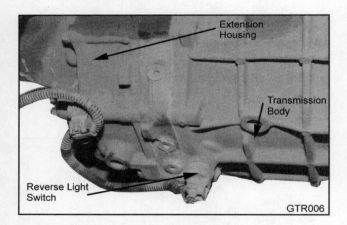

GTR006

Remove

Detach wiring plug and remove the switch from the right hand side of the case with a correct fitting spanner.

Install

Clean threads of the switch and apply Teflon tape to threads. Install the switch and torque to specification.
Reverse Light Switch specified torque:
                  250kg-cm, 18ft.lb, 27Nm

Extension Housing Seal (2WD)

1. Jack vehicle up and safely support vehicle to allow access to the transmission and drive / tail shaft..
2. (a) Remove drive / tail shaft as described in Tail / Drive Shaft and Universal Joints chapter in this manual.
(b) Place a drain tray beneath transmission extension.
(c) Remove bolts attaching brace assembly and remove brace.
3. Remove seal using seal remover.
4. (a) Inspect seal lip surface on slip yoke of propeller shaft for damage.
(b) Clean (or replace) as necessary.

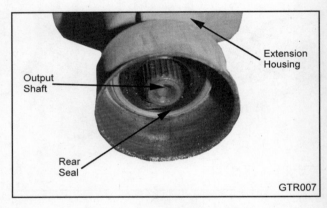

GTR007

Install

1.(a) Apply a little transmission lubricant to seal lip.
(b) Install seal into the extension with a seal insertion tool.
2. Replace tail / drive shaft.
3. Check transmission lubricant level as previously described in this Chapter.

Shift Lever and Boot Assembly
Remove

1. Remove the gearshift knob (unscrew) from the gear lever, then remove the four screws securing the boot retainer then pull back the boot to access shift lever.
2. Press down on the shift lever cap, then turn anti-clockwise and remove. Remove shift lever.

Install

1. Install the shift lever into place with the shift lever being coated with grease.
2. Then align the shift lever cap with the pin in the case cover, then press down the cap and twist clockwise.
3. Position the shift boot into place and tighten retaining screws.

Transmission
Remove

1. Remove the gearshift boot and lever. Raise vehicle.
2. Mark the drive shaft so that it may be installed in the same relative place. Detach the shaft at the universal joint and slide it off the transmission output shaft. Install a dust cover or

extension housing seal replacer into the extension housing to prevent lubricant leakage.

3. Detach the wiring to the reversing light switch and remove the speedometer driven gear and cable assemble, then remove the clutch release cylinder assembly.

4. Support the engine and transmission assembly with a transmission jack. Remove the insulator to mounting bracket bolts then remove the mounting bracket retaining bolts and bracket.

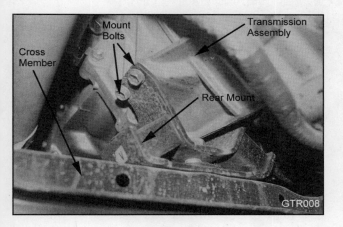

5. Detach muffler inlet pipe from exhuast maniflod.

6. Lower transmission jack until the rear of the engine rests against the bulkhead.

7. Remove the transmission to clutch housing bolts.

8. Move transmission rearward until the input shaft clears the flywheel housing then lower the jack and remove the transmission.

Install

1. Install transmission on the transmission jack, raise transmission and move it forward on the guide pins until the input shaft splines enter the clutch hub splines and the case is placed against the clutch housing.

2. Install the transmission to clutch housing bolts. Torque all bolts to specification.

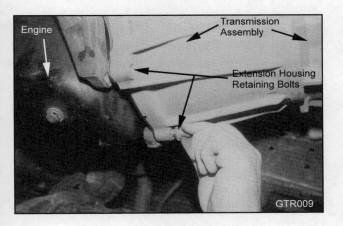

Transmission to Clutch Housing bolts:
Bolts (two at top and one below starter): 72 Nm
Bolts (four lower bolts - two each side): 37 Nm

3. Connect the wiring to the reversing light switch and the speedometer sending unit, raise transmission.

4. Install mounting bracket to transmission and tighten bolts. Remove the transmission jack and install the insulator to crossmember nut. Torque to specification.

Rear Mounting Bracket to Mounting: 61 Nm
Rear Mounting Bracket to Cross Member: 13 Nm
Install the exhuast pipe to the manifold. Torque bolts to specification.

Exhaust Pipe to Manifold Bolts: 62 Nm

5. Remove the dust cover or seal replacer from the extension housing and slide the drive shaft over the transmission output shaft. Align the index marks at the universal joint and connect the drive shaft as described in Tail / Drive shaft chapter.

6. Fill the transmission to the proper level with specified lubricant and torque filler plug.

Oil Specification and Capacity of Transmission:
G40, 52, 54:   API GL-4 SAE 75W90
4 Speed: 2.4 litres (2.5US qts, 2.1 Imp. qts)
5 Speed: 2.2 litres (2.3US qts, 1.9 Imp. qts)
W52:   API GL-4 SAE 75W90
               2.6 litres (2.7US qts, 2.3 Imp. qts)
L40, 42:   API GL-4 SAE 90
               1.9 litres (2.0US qts, 1.7 Imp. qts)
Drain Plug torque: 250kg-cm, 18ft.lb, 27Nm

7. Lower vehicle, install the gearshift lever and boot. Road test the vehicle for satisfactory transmission operation.

Major Repairs and Rebuild

4 & 5 SPEED TRANSMISSIONS [G40, G52 G54 and G58]

Dismantle

1. Place transmission on a clean bench to enable a complete pull down and rebuild. Using a long socket handle to remove drain plug located underneath the transmission case.

2. Place shift lever in neutral position and remove extension cover retaining bolts.

3. Using a suitable pry bar, break cover-to-extension housing seal by prying between housing and cover. Remove cover.

4. Remove shift lever and restrict pins.

5. Remove the restrict pins either side of the extension shift

turrent.

6. (2WD) Use a torx socket remove the screw in plug from the side of the rear extension, use a magnetic rod to remove the spring and steel ball.

7. (2WD) Remove the speedometer driven gear by removing the locking bolt. Use a screw driver to lever the speedo drive gear from the transmission, pull the unit out from the extension.

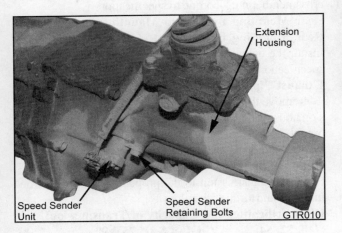

Extension Housing

Speed Sender Unit

Speed Sender Retaining Bolts

GTR010

8. (2WD) Remove the 8 extension housing retaining bolts then using a rubber hammer to tap and bar to lever and separate the extension housing from the intermediate plate leave the gasket on the intermediate plate.

9. (4WD) Use a torx socket remove the screw in plug from the side of the transfer adapter, use a magnetic rod to remove the spring and steel ball.

Torx Retaining Screws

Transmission Internal Assembly

GTR018

10. (4WD) Use socket drive remove the screw in plug from the back of the adapter housing.

Remove the gear shift shaft from the back of the adapter housing.

11. (4WD) Remove the 8 extension adapter housing retaining bolts then using a rubber hammer to tap and bar to lever and separate the adapter housing from the intermediate plate leave the gasket on the intermediate plate.

12. (2 WD) Remove the rear snap ring for the speedometer drive gear from the main shaft, then remove the speedometer

drive gear from the main shaft. Remove the lock ball and front snap ring.

13. (4WD) Use a puller to pull the sleeve off the output shaft.

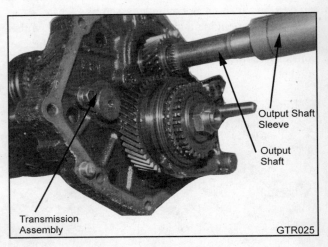

Output Shaft Sleeve

Output Shaft

Transmission Assembly

GTR025

14. Remove the bell housing from the intermediate plate.

15. Remove the front bearing retainer. Remove the two snap rings for the main drive gear bearing.

16. Remove the transmission front case from the intermediate plate.

Mount the intermediate plate into a bracket or a vice, to work on transmission. Do not clamp on intermediate plate, instead, install two bolts and nuts in lower section of intermediate plate, then clamp onto the bolts.

17. Remove the shifting forks attaching pins from the shifter shafts, using a punch and hammer, remove the "E" clip rings with pliers (4 speed, four plugs - 5 speed, two plugs).

18. Remove the torx screw in plugs (4 speed, three plugs - 5 speed, four plugs) from the centre plate remove the springs and balls by rolling assembly, to allow springs and balls to drop out, or use a magnetic rod.

19. Pull out the shift shafts rearwards and remove shift forks.

The inter lock pins from the intermediate plate will fall out, so place your hand at the intermediate plate to catch them, if they do not come out use a magnetic rod to remove them.

20. (5 speed) With a feeler gauge measure the thrust clearance between the back of the gear and the thrust washer for specification. If not within the specifications, replace the specific part when reassembling.

Fifth Gear Specified Thrust Clearance:

0.10-0.30mm   (0.0039-0.0118in)[max 0.30mm(0.0118in)]

21. (5 speed) Remove the 5th speed. Lock the fifth gear by double meshing, remove the lock nut by breaking staked section of the nut with a cold chisel and hammer. Use a gear pulley to remove gear spline, synchronizer ring, needle bearings, and 5th counter gear.

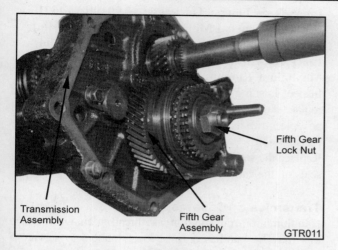

Transmission Assembly

Fifth Gear Lock Nut

Fifth Gear Assembly

GTR011

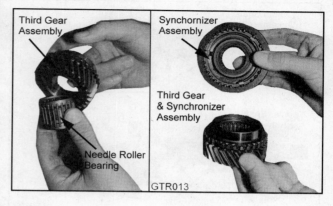

Third Gear Assembly

Synchornizer Assembly

Third Gear & Synchronizer Assembly

Needle Roller Bearing

GTR013

22. (4 speed) Remove the oil seperator. Lock the gears by double meshing, remove the lock nut by breaking staked section of the nut with a cold chisel and hammer. Remove the oil seperator.

23. (5 speed) Remove the spacer from behind the gear, use a magnetic rod to remove the steel ball.

24. Remove the 2 bolts attaching the reverse shift arm.

25. Remove the rear bearing retainer 4 bolts use a torx socket then remove the snap ring.

26. Seperate the input shaft from the output shaft, take note there are 14 needle roller bearings at this point.

27. Hold the intermediate plate and output shaft assembly, pull the output shaft assembly away from the intermediate plate, towards the front of the transmission. It may be necessary to tap the intermediate plate with a soft hammer to free the assembly.

28. Measure the endfloat of all the gears, if not within the specifications, replace the specific part when reassembling. Clearance of Gears Specification.

0.10-0.25mm   (0.0039-0.0098in)[max 0.25mm(0.0098in)]

29. (5 speed) Remove fifth gear ,bearing, first gear and bearings. Remove the rear snap ring from the fifth speed gear and bearing, then with a press remove the rear fifth speed gear and rear bearing, first gear and the inner race bearing and needle bearing.

30. (4 speed) Remove rear bearing, first gear and bearings. Remove the rear snap ring from the rear bearing, then with a press remove the rear bearing, first gear and the inner race bearing and needle bearing.

31. Remove the synchronizer ring assembly from the shaft.

32. Use a magnetic rod to remove the locking steel ball.

33. With a press remove the hub sleeve No1, synchronizer assembly, second gear and needle bearing.

34. Remove hub sleeve No2 assembly, syncro assembly, third gear and needle roller bearing. Remove the snap ring, then with a press remove the hub sleeve No2, synchronizer assembly and 3rd gear, remove the needle bearing.

Cleaning

Wash all parts except ball bearings, O-rings and seals in a suitable cleaning solvent. Brush or scrape all foreign matter from the parts, be careful not to damage any parts with the scraper. Do not clean, wash or soak transmission seals in cleaning solvents, all seals should be replaced with new seals. Dry all parts with compressed air.

Rotate ball bearings in a cleaning solvent until all lubricant is removed. Hold bearing assembly to prevent it from rotating and dry it with compressed air. Lubricate bearings with Multi-Purpose Grease and wrap them in a clean, lint-free cloth or paper until ready for use.

Inspect

Inspect transmission case for cracks, worn or damaged bearing bores, damaged bearing bores, damaged threads, or any other damage that could affect operation of the transmission. Inspect the front face of the case for small nicks or burrs that could cause misalignment of the transmission with the flywheel housing. Remove all small nicks or burrs with a fine file.

Replace any cover that is bent or distorted. Make sure that the vent hole in the case is open. Check the condition of the shift levers, forks, shift rails, and the lever and shafts. Inspect ball bearings. Refer to 'Ball Bearing Inspection'.

Replace roller bearings that are broken, worn or rough, and check their respective races.

Replace the counter shaft (cluster) gear if the teeth are chipped, broken or worn. Replace the counter shaft if it is bent, scored or worn. Replace the reverse idler gear or sliding gear if the teeth are chipped, worn or broken. Replace the idler gear shaft if bent, worn or scored.

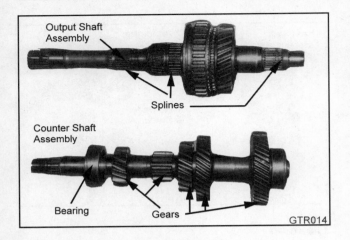

Output Shaft Assembly

Splines

Counter Shaft Assembly

Bearing

Gears

GTR014

Check oil clearance of gear and inner race or gear and shaft oil clearance. Use a dial indicator, check movement, if not within specification replace worn components.

1st Gear to Inner Race to Needle Bearing:
 0.009-0.032mm (0.00035-0.00126in)
 Max 0.032mm (0.00126in)
2nd & 3rd Gear to Shaft with Needle Brg Installed
 0.009-0.033mm (0.00035-0.00130in)
 Max 0.033mm (0.00130in)
Counter & 5th Gear to Shaft with Needle Brg Installed
 0.009-0.032mm (0.00035-0.00126in)
 Max 0.032mm (0.00126in)

Replace input shaft and gear if the splines are damaged or if the teeth are chipped, worn or broken. If the roller bearing surface in the bore is worn or rough, or if the cone surface is damaged, replace gear and gear rollers.

Replace all other gears that are chipped, broken or worn. Check the synchronized sleeves for free movement on their hubs. Make sure that the alignment marks (if present) are properly indexed.

Use a feeler gauge to inspect the clearance of the synchronizer ring back and gear spline end, if not with in specification replace worn components.

Synchronizer Ring Clearance:
Standard Clearance: 1.0-2.0mm (0.040-0.079in)
Minimum Clearance: 0.8mm (0.031in)

Inspect the synchronized blocking rings for widened index slots, rounded clutch teeth, and smooth internal surfaces (must have machined grooves). With the synchronized blocking ring on the cone, the distance between the face of the synchronized blocking ring and the clutch teeth on the gear must not be less than 0.5mm (0.020 inch).

Replace speedometer drive gear if teeth are stripped or damaged. Be sure to install the correct size replacement gear.

Replace the output shaft if there is any evidence of wear or if any splines are damaged.

Output Shaft Specifications:
Output Shaft Flange Thickness: 4.80mm (0.1890in)

Inner Race Flange Thickness: 3.99mm (0.1571in)
2nd Gear Journal Min Dia: 37.984mm (1.4954in)
3rd Gear Journal Min Dia: 34.984mm (1.3773in)
Inner Race Min Dia: 38.985mm (1.5348in)
Maximum Runout: 0.05mm (0.0020in)

Inspect bushing and seal in the extension housing, and replace if worn or damaged. The bushing and/or seal should be replaced after extension housing has been installed on the transmission.

Replace the seal in the input shaft bearing retainer, replace seals on the cam and shafts.

Transmission Case Inspection

If an aluminium transmission case thread is damaged, service kits may be purchased from local jobbers to service a damaged thread.

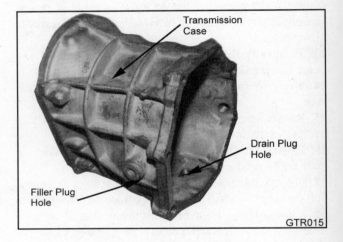

Transmission Case

Drain Plug Hole

Filler Plug Hole

GTR015

Drill out the damaged threads, using same drill size as the thread OD. Tap drilled hole. The tap is marked for the size of the thread being serviced. It cuts a thread large enough for the insert, and after the insert is installed to the original thread size.

Select coil inserting tool. Place insert on the tool and adjust the sleeve to the length of the insert against the face of the tapped hole. Turn the tool clockwise and wind the insert in one-half turn below the face.

Working through the insert, bend the insert tang straight up and down until it breaks off at the notch. Position extractor tool in the insert so that the blade rests against the top coil one-fourth to one-half turn away from the end of the coil. Exert downward pressure on the tool and turn it counter clockwise until the insert is removed.

With insert on tool adjust sleeve to the length of the insert being used. Press the insert against the face of the tapped hole. Turn the tool clockwise and wind the insert against the face of the tapped hole. Turn the tool clockwise and wind the insert into the hole until the insert is one-half turn below the face.

Assembly

1. Before reassembling lubricate all shafts, gears, bearing surfaces, baulk rings, cones and the oil seals with transmission fluid.

2. Assemble all the synchronized hub and sleeve assemblies.

3. Assemble the output shaft:

(a) Assemble the synchronizer ring onto 3rd gear, slide the needle bearing in the 3rd gear. Press this assembly with No2 hub sleeve onto the ouput shaft.

Synchronizer Ring — Third Gear

GTR016

(b) Install a snap ring that gives minimum play on the shaft.

(c) With a feeler gauge measure the thrust clearance for 3rd gear for specification.

Third Gear Specified Thrust Clearance:

0.10-0.25mm (0.0039-0.0098in)[max 0.25mm(0.0098in)]

(d) Assemble the synchronizer ring onto 2nd gear, slide the needle bearing in the 2nd gear. Press this assembly with No1 hub sleeve onto the ouput shaft.

(e) Install a locking steel ball in the shaft.

(f) Assemble the synchronizer ring onto 1st gear, slide the needle bearing and inner bearing race in the 1st gear. Slide this assembly with synchronizer ring slots aligned with the synchronizer keys onto the ouput shaft.

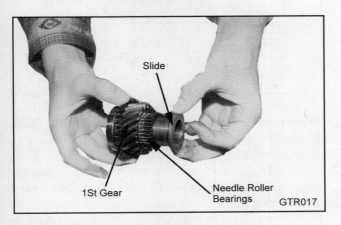

Slide

1St Gear — Needle Roller Bearings

GTR017

(g) Rotate the inner race so it will align with the locking ball.

(h) With a feeler gauge measure the thrust clearance for 2nd and 1st gears for specification.

Second and First Gears Specified Thrust Clearance:

0.10-0.25mm(0.0039-0.0098in)

[max 0.25mm(0.0098in)]

(i) **(5 speed)** Press 5th onto the ouput shaft . Install a snap ring that gives minimum play on the shaft.

(j) **(2 speed)** Use a pair of snap ring pliers to install the first snap ring for the speedometer drive gear, then install the lock ball and gear. Install the rear snap ring with a pair of snap ring pliers.

(k) **(4 Speed)** Install sleeve onto end of output shaft, tap home with a soft head hammer.

4. Assemble the centre plate.

(a) Install the output shaft assembly to the intermediate plate, tap home with a soft head hammer.

(b) Assemble input shaft by installing the 14 needle bearings, hold in position with multipurpose grease.

(c) Install the input shaft onto the out put shaft with the synchronizer keys and slots aligning with each other.

(d) Install the counter gear to the intermediate plate. As this is taking place fit the counter gear bearing, use rod or round hollow object tap home the bearing with a hammer.

(e) Install snap ring, this is a snug fit against the intermediate plate.

(f) Install the bearing retainer plate, install the four bolts with a torx bit, tighten to specification.

Bearing Retainer Plate Bolts Torque:

185kg.cm (13ft.lb, 18Nm.

5. Install reverse shift arn bracket, tighten bolts to specification.

Reverse Shift Arm Bracket Bolts Torque:

185kg.cm (13ft.lb, 18Nm.

6. (4 speed) Install the oil seperator. Install lock nut, lock the gears by double meshing, Tighten the lock nut to specification, stake the nut with a cold chisel and hammer.

Oil Seperator Lock Nut Torque:

1200 kg-cm (87lb.ft, 118 Nm)

7. (5 speed) (a) Install the spacerwhich is situated behind the fifth gear, also the steel ball.

(b) Assemble the synchronizer hub No3 and shufting keys onto 5th gear, install the springs under the keys.

(c) Install the 5th gear and hub No3 hub assembly needle bearing onto the shaft.

(d) Fit the synchronizer ring to the gear spline No5, align slits with keys, tap home with a hammer and drive, support counter gear with a weight when tapping with hammer.

(e) Install lock nut, lock the gears by double meshing, Tighten the lock nut to specification, stake the nut with a cold chisel and hammer.

Oil Seperator Lock Nut Torque:

1200 kg-cm (87lb.ft, 118 Nm)

8.(5 speed) With a feeler gauge measure the thrust clearance between the back of the gear and the thrust washer for specification. If not within the specifications, replace the specific part when reassembling.

Fifth Gear Specified Thrust Clearance:
   0.10-0.30mm (0.0039-0.0118in)
   [max 0.30mm(0.0118in)]

9. Fit the reverse shift arm onto the arm bracket.

10. Install the reverse idler gear onto the shaft, align the reverse shift arm shoe to the gear groove, then assemble to the intermediate plate. Then install the gear shaft stopper and nut. Tighten nut to specification.

Reverse Idler Gear Shaft Stopper Nut Torque:
   175kg-cm (13ft.lb, 17Nm)

11. (a)Install the shifting forks on to the gear hub grooves Nos 1 and 2.

(b) Install the shift shaft number 2 through fork Nos 1 and 2 then intermediate plate.

(c) Install a lock pin cover in grease onto a magnetic rod, slide this down through the intermediate plate, when the pin is in position in the shaft hole, free pin from magnetic rod with a screw driver.

12. (a)Install number 1 shifting shaft, install the interlock pin in the shaft.

(b) Install the shift shaft number 1 through fork Nos 1 then intermediate plate.

(c) Install a lock pin cover in grease onto a magnetic rod, slide this down through the intermediate plate, when the pin is in position in the shaft hole, free pin from magnetic rod with a screw driver.

13. (a)Install number 3 shifting shaft, [install the interlock pin in the shaft 5 speed].

(b) Install the shift shaft number 3 through fork Nos 3 on the reverse shaft arm, then through the intermediate plate.

14. (a) Install the reverse shift head into shaft (numder 5 shifting) fork.

(b) Install the shift shaft number 5 through the intermediate plate, then the reverse shaft head to shift shaft number 3.

15. (5 speed) (a) Install a lock pin cover in grease onto a magnetic rod, slide this through the reverse shift head hole, when the pin is in position in the shaft hole, free pin from magnetic rod with a screw driver.

(b) Move the hib sleeve No3 into the 5th speed position.

(c) Position shift fork No3 so it is located into hub sleeve No3, then shaft No4 to shift fork No4, then reverse shift arm.

(d) Install a lock pin cover in grease onto a magnetic rod, slide this down through the intermediate plate. Install shaft No4 into the intermediate plate. When the pin is in position in the shaft hole, free pin from magnetic rod with a screw driver.

16. Inpect operation of shifter forks by selecting 1st gear, the other shafts should not move.

17. If the selectors work correctly, install the slotted spring pins, 3 into the 3 shift forks 1 into the reverse shift arm and 1 into the reverse shift head, 5 in total.

18. Install the "E" ring clips 4 speed tranmissions have 4 clips, while 5 speed transmissions have 5 clips.

19. Install the locking balls, springs and torx srew in plugs to

the side of the intermediate plate. Tighten to specification.

Transmission Internal Assembly · Torx Retaining Screws

GTR018

Torx Screw InPlugs to Intermediate Plate:
   190 kg-cm (14lb.ft, 19Nm)

20. Install a new gasket to the front case surface of the intermediate plate.

21. Slide the front transmission case over the gear and shaft assemblies to the intermediate plate, it is necessary to align all the shaft ends with the case and the bearing outter race with the case. When it is all aligned tap the case home with a soft head hammer.

22. Install the teo snap rings to the front bearing.

23. Install front bearing retainer and 8 retaining bolts with sealer on each bolt. Tighten to specification.

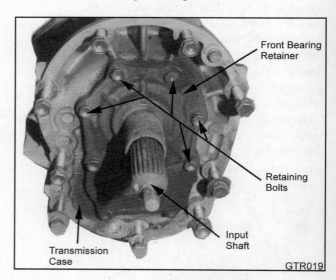

Front Bearing Retainer · Retaining Bolts · Input Shaft · Transmission Case

GTR019

Front Bearing Retainer Bolts:170kg-cm(12ft-lb, 17Nm)

24. Install a new gasket to the rear extension surface of the intermediate plate.

25. (2WD) (a)Slide the shift and select lever up into the rear extension, connect them to the fork shaft, then install the shift lever housing.

(b) Slide the rear extension over output shaft assembly to the intermediate plate, it is necessary to align shaft No5 with the hole in the rear extension. When it is all aligned tap the case home with a soft head hammer.

(c) Install rear extension housing retaining bolts. Tighten to specification.

Rear Extension Housing bolts: 380 kg-cm (27ft.lb, 37Nm)

(d) Install the shift lever housing bolt and lock washer, tighten to specification, then stack washer with hammer and chisle.

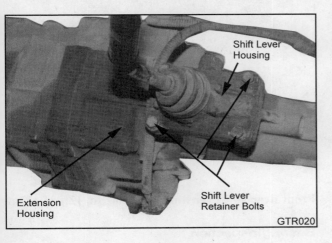

Shift Lever Housing

Extension Housing

Shift Lever Retainer Bolts

GTR020

Shift Lever Housing Bolt: 390 kg-cm (28ft.lb, 38Nm)
26. (4WD) (a) Slide the adapter housing over output shaft assembly to the intermediate plate. Install transfer adapter housing retaining bolts. Tighten to specification.

Adapter Housing bolts: 380 kg-cm (27ft.lb, 37Nm)
(b) Install the shaft lever housing to the transfer adapter housing, then connect the fork shafts, slide the shaft lever shaft into the adapter and shift lever housing.

(d) Install the shift lever housing bolt and lock washer, tighten to specification, then stack washer with hammer and chisle.

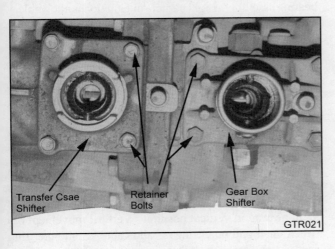

Transfer Csae Shifter

Retainer Bolts

Gear Box Shifter

GTR021

Shift Lever Housing Bolt: 390 kg-cm (28ft.lb, 38Nm)
27. Install the lock ball, spring and screw in torx plug with seal on the plug, tighten to specification.

Lock Ball Torx Plug Torque:190 kg-cm (14ft.lb, 19Nm)
28. Check transmission input and out put shafts rotate freely, and the gear shifter operates correctly.

29. Screw in and tighten the restrictor pins either side, tighten to specification.

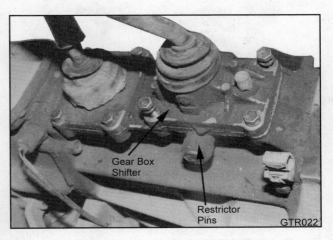

Gear Box Shifter

Restrictor Pins

GTR022

Restrictor Pins Torque: 190 kg-cm (14ft.lb, 19Nm)
30. Install clutch housing and housing retaining bolts. Tighten to specification.

Clutch Housing bolts: 380 kg-cm (27ft.lb, 37Nm}
31. Replace the shift lever retainer and new gasket, tighten to specification.

Shift Lever Retainer Bolts: 190 kg-cm (14ft.lb, 19Nm)
32. (2WD)Install speedo drive gear, install speedo drive gear and retaining clamp.Tighten bolt holding the retaining clamp.
33. Place some molybdenum disulphide lithium base grease on the clutch throw out bearing and clutch fork. Replace clutch fork and throw out bearing into place.
43. Install drain plug, tighten to specification.

Lubricant Drain Plug Torque Specs: 25 - 34 Nm.
44. Fill transmission to correct specifications.

Oil Capacity of Transmission:
G40, 52 and 54:
4 speed: 2.4 litres (2.5US qts, 2.1 Imp. qts)
5 speed: 2.2 litres (2.3US qts, 1.9 Imp. qts)
Specified Transmission Oil: API GL-4 SAE 75W90
Filler Plug specified torque: 25 - 34 Nm

Synchronises
Dismantle
* **The following operations apply to all synchronized assemblies. The gear synchronises are slightly different in design. Notation is made where procedural differences occur.**
1. Scribe alignment marks on the sleeve and hub for assembly reference before dismantling the synchronizes.
2. On 5th gear synchronizes only, remove insert retainer. With a screw driver, remove the two synchronized retaining springs. Remove the inserts.

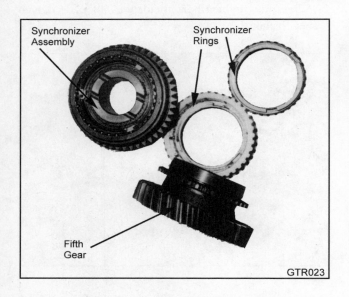

Synchronizer Assembly · Synchronizer Rings · Fifth Gear

GTR023

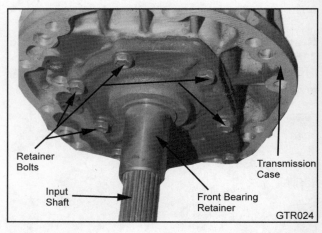

Retainer Bolts · Input Shaft · Front Bearing Retainer · Transmission Case

GTR024

Assembly

* When assembling a synchronized sleeve and hub, match alignment marks made during disassembly. The sleeve and hub are an extremely close fit and must be held square during assembly to prevent jamming. Do not force the sleeve onto the hub.

1. Assemble the inserts and synchronized retaining springs onto the sleeve and hub. The retaining springs engage the same insert but rotate in opposite directions.

2. On 5th gear synchronizes only, install the Reverse Block

3. On the 5th gear synchronizes only, install the detent ball and spring into the hub on the output shaft.

4. Assemble retaining springs, inserts and sleeve onto hub. Refer to diagram for placing of the retaining springs and inserts.

Input Shaft Bearing Cover.

Remove

1. Remove front bearing cover.

2. Remove cover and gasket.

Install

1. Install front bearing cover gasket to the front bearing cover.

2. Install front bearing cover and bolts, tighten to specification.

Front Bearing Cover Bolt: 170kg-cm, 12ft.lb, 17Nm

Bearing Inspection

Bearing Raceways

Inspect

Inner Raceway: While holding outer ring stationary, rotate inner ring at least three revolutions. Inspect the raceway of the inner ring from both sides for pits or spalling. A bearing assembly should be replaced when damaged. Light particle indentation is allowable.

Outer Ring Raceway: While holding inner ring stationary, rotate outer ring at least three revolutions. Inspect the raceway of the outer ring from both as with the raceway of the inner ring. If the raceway is spalled or pitted, replace the bearing assembly. Light particle indentation is allowable.

Bearing External Surfaces

The bearing must be replaced if damage is found in any of the following areas:

Radial cracks on front and rear faces of outer or inner rings. Cracks on outside diameter of outer ring (particularly around snap ring groove). Deformation or cracks in ball cage (particularly around rivets).

Spin Test

Lubricate bearing raceways with a slight amount of clean automatic transmission fluid turn the bearing back and forth slowly until the raceways and balls are coated.

With bearing in vertical position. Vertical movement between inner and outer rings is allowable. Spin outer ring several times by hand. If there is roughness or vibration, the bearing should be cleaned again and lubricated. Roughness could be foreign particles in the bearing. If bearing is still rough after cleaning and lubricating several times, it must be replaced.

Repeat the above with the bearing in the horizontal position.

4 & 5 SPEED TRANSMISSIONS [W50, W52 and W56]

Dismantle

1. Place transmission on a clean bench to enable a complete pull down and rebuild. Using a long socket handle to remove drain plug located underneath the transmission case.

2. Remove the reversing light switch, then remove speedometer driven gear by removing the locking bolt. Use a screw driver to lever the speedo drive gear from the transmission, pull the unit out from the extension.

3. Place shift lever in neutral position and remove extension cover retaining bolts.

4. Using a suitable pry bar, break cover-to-extension housing seal by prying between housing and cover. Remove cover.

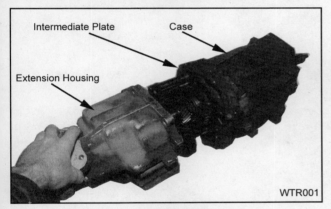

WTR001

5. Remove shift lever and restrict pins.

6. Remove the clutch release bearing, fork and the clutch housing from the transmission case.

8. Remove the front bearing retainer. Remove the two snap rings for the main drive gear bearing.

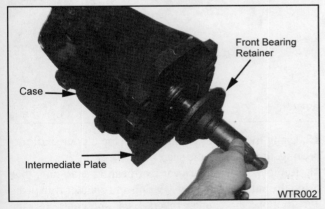

WTR002

9. Remove the transmission front case from the intermediate plate.

Mount the intermediate plate into a bracket or a vice, to work on transmission. Do not clamp on intermediate plate, instead, install two bolts and nuts in lower section of intermediate

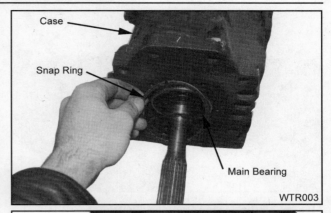

WTR003

WTR004

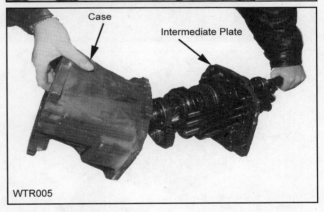

WTR005

plate, then clamp onto the bolts.

10. Remove the three plugs from the intermediate plate, then use a magnet to remove the three springs and balls.

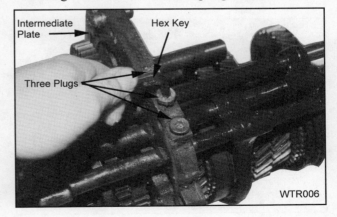

WTR006

157

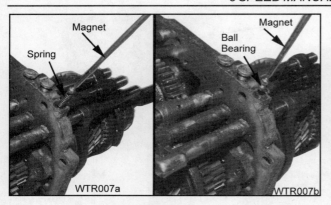

WTR007a

WTR007b

11. Remove the shifting forks attaching pins from the shifter shafts, using a punch and hammer, then remove the shift fork and No. 1 shaft.

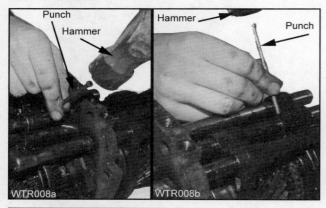

WTR008a

WTR008b

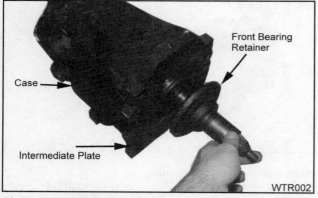

WTR002

12. Remove the No. 2 shaft, then remove the No. 3 shaft and

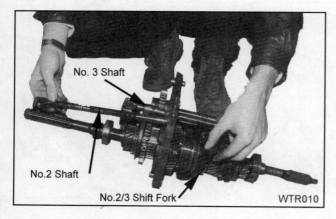

WTR010

No.2, 3 shift fork.

13. Remove the No.1 and No.2 interlock pins using a magnet

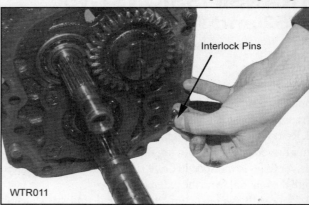

WTR011

14. Remove the rear snap ring for the speedometer drive gear from the main shaft, then remove the speedometer drive gear from the main shaft. Remove the lock ball and spacer.

WTR012

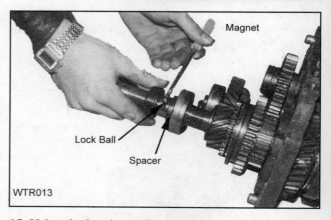

WTR013

15. Using the bearing puller remove the output shaft rear bearing, then remove the snap ring.

16. Remove the counter gear rear bearing snap ring, then using the puller remove the bearing and counter fifth gear.

17. Remove the counter reverse gear and centre bearing side race.

18. With a feeler gauge measure the thrust clearance between the back of the gear and the thrust washer for specification. If not within the specifications, replace the specific part when reassembling.

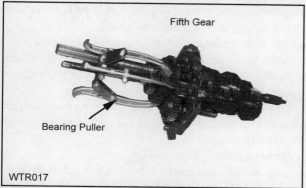

Fifth Gear

Bearing Puller

WTR017

Fifth Gear Specified Thrust Clearance:
0.10-0.25mm(0.0039-0.0098in)[max 0.30mm(0.0118in)]
19. Remove the retaining snap ring then remove the fifth gear assembly, and use a magnet to remove the locking ball.

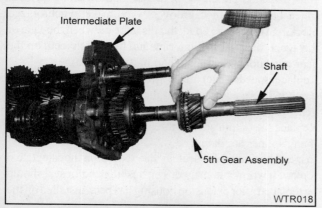

Intermediate Plate

Shaft

5th Gear Assembly

WTR018

Magnet

Locking Ball

WTR019

20. Remove the reverse gear from output shaft.

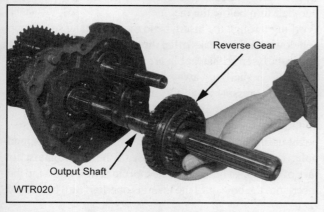

Reverse Gear

Output Shaft

WTR020

21. Remove the No. 3 assembly hub sleeve, then measure the reverse idler gear thrust clearance.
Reverse Idler Gear Thrust Clearance:
Standard   0.15-0.25 mm (0.0059 - 0.0098 in.)
Max   0.30 mm (0.0118 in.)
22. Remove the stopper for the reverse idler gear shaft, then remove the idler gear, shaft and spacer.

Reverse Idler Gear Shaft Stopper

Spanner

WTR014

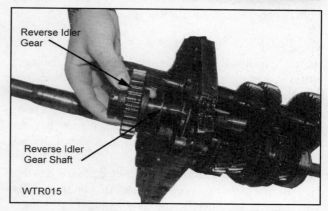

Reverse Idler Gear

Reverse Idler Gear Shaft

WTR015

23. Remove the centre bearing retainer and snap ring.

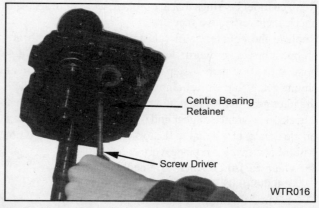

Centre Bearing Retainer

Screw Driver

WTR016

24. Hold the counter gear and pull while taping the intermediate plate with a soft face hammer to remove the output shaft, input shaft and counter gear as an assembly.
25. From the output shaft remove the input shaft, then measure the gear thrust clearance of each gear.
Gear Thrust Clearance:
Standard   0.15-0.25 mm (0.0059-0.0098 in.)

Max   0.30 mm (0.0118 in.)

26. Change the No.1 hub sleeve to the 2nd gear, then use a press to remove the centre bearing, 1st gear, needle roller bearing, inner race and the synchronizer ring.

27. Remove the locking ball, then use a press to remove the No. hub sleeve, 2nd gear and the synchronizer ring.

28. Remove the snap ring then press the No.2 hub sleeve, synchronizer ring and 3rd gear from shaft.

Cleaning

Wash all parts except ball bearings, O-rings and seals in a suitable cleaning solvent. Brush or scrape all foreign matter from the parts, be careful not to damage any parts with the scraper. Do not clean, wash or soak transmission seals in cleaning solvents, all seals should be replaced with new seals. Dry all parts with compressed air.

Rotate ball bearings in a cleaning solvent until all lubricant is removed. Hold bearing assembly to prevent it from rotating and dry it with compressed air. Lubricate bearings with Multi-Purpose Grease and wrap them in a clean, lint-free cloth or paper until ready for use.

Inspect

Inspect transmission case for cracks, worn or damaged bearing bores, damaged bearing bores, damaged threads, or any other damage that could affect operation of the transmission. Inspect the front face of the case for small nicks or burrs that could cause misalignment of the transmission with the flywheel housing. Remove all small nicks or burrs with a fine file.

Replace any cover that is bent or distorted. Make sure that the vent hole in the case is open. Check the condition of the shift levers, forks, shift rails, and the lever and shafts. Inspect ball bearings. Refer to 'Ball Bearing Inspection'.

Replace roller bearings that are broken, worn or rough, and check their respective races.

Replace the counter shaft (cluster) gear if the teeth are chipped, broken or worn. Replace the counter shaft if it is bent, scored or worn. Replace the reverse idler gear or sliding gear if the teeth are chipped, worn or broken. Replace the idler gear shaft if bent, worn or scored.

Check oil clearance of gear and inner race or gear and shaft oil clearance. Use a dial indicator, check movement, if not within specification replace worn components.

1st Gear to Inner Race to Needle Bearing:
    0.009-0.053 mm (0.0004-0.0021 in)
    Max 0.15mm (0.0059in)

2nd & 3rd Gear to Output Shaft:
    0.06-0.103 mm (0.0024-0.0041 in.)
    Max 0.20 mm (0.0079 in.)

5th Gear to Inner Race to Needle Bearing:
    0.009-0.051 mm (0.0004-0.0020 in)
    Max 0.15 mm (0.0059 in)

Replace input shaft and gear if the splines are damaged or if the teeth are chipped, worn or broken. If the roller bearing surface in the bore is worn or rough, or if the cone surface is damaged, replace gear and gear rollers.

Replace all other gears that are chipped, broken or worn. Check the synchronized sleeves for free movement on their hubs. Make sure that the alignment marks (if present) are properly indexed.

Use a feeler gauge to inspect the clearance of the synchronizer ring back and gear spline end, if not with in specification replace worn components.

Synchronizer Ring Clearance:

1st, 2nd & 5th   Standard:0.7-1.7mm(0.028-0.067in)
                Minimum: 0.5mm (0.02in)
3rd & 4th   Standard:1.0-2.0mm(0.039-0.079in)
            Minimum: 0.8mm (0.031in)

Inspect the synchronized blocking rings for widened index slots, rounded clutch teeth, and smooth internal surfaces (must have machined grooves). With the synchronized blocking ring on the cone, the distance between the face of the synchronized blocking ring and the clutch teeth on the gear must not be less than 0.5mm (0.020 inch).

Replace speedometer drive gear if teeth are stripped or damaged. Be sure to install the correct size replacement gear.

Replace the output shaft if there is any evidence of wear or if any splines are damaged.

Inspect bushing and seal in the extension housing, and replace if worn or damaged. The bushing and/or seal should be replaced after extension housing has been installed on the transmission.

Transmission Case Inspection

If an aluminium transmission case thread is damaged, service kits may be purchased from local jobbers to service a damaged thread.

Drill out the damaged threads, using same drill size as the thread OD. Tap drilled hole. The tap is marked for the size of the thread being serviced. It cuts a thread large enough for the insert, and after the insert is installed to the original thread size.

Select coil inserting tool. Place insert on the tool and adjust the sleeve to the length of the insert against the face of the tapped hole. Turn the tool clockwise and wind the insert in one-half turn below the face.

Working through the insert, bend the insert tang straight up and down until it breaks off at the notch. Position extractor tool in the insert so that the blade rests against the top coil one-fourth to one-half turn away from the end of the coil. Exert downward pressure on the tool and turn it counter clockwise until the insert is removed.

With insert on tool adjust sleeve to the length of the insert being used. Press the insert against the face of the tapped hole. Turn the tool clockwise and wind the insert against the face of the tapped hole. Turn the tool clockwise and wind the insert into the hole until the insert is one-half turn below the face.

160

Assembly

* Before reassembling lubricate all shafts, gears, bearing surfaces, baulk rings, cones and the oil seals with transmission fluid.

1. Install the clutch hubs No.1 and No.2 and the shifting keys into the hub sleeve, then install under the shifting keys install the key springs.

2. Install synchronizer ring to the gear aligning ring slots with key, then press the 3rd gear and No.2 hub sleve to the output shaft.

3. Install snap ring, then use a feeler guage, measure the 3rd gear thrust clearance.

Thrust Clearance:
Standard 0.15-0.25 mm (0.0059-0/0098 in.)
Max 0.30 mm (0.0118 in.)

4. Install synchronizer ring on second gear, aligning the ring slots with keys, then use a press to install the 2nd gear and No.1 hub sleeve to output shaft.

5. Install the locking ball in the shaft, then as an assembly install the 1st gear, synchronizer ring, needle roller bearing and bearing inner race to the output shaft, ensuring the stnchronizer ring slots align with keys, and align inner race with locking ball.

6. Using a press install the output shaft centre bearing , ensuring the outer race snap ring groove is toward the rear. Measure the 1st & 2nd gear thrust clearance.

Thrust clearance:
Standard 0.15-0.25 mm (0.0059-0.0098 in.)
Max 0.30 mm (0.0118 in.)

7. Install the output shaft assembly to the intermediate plate, buy pulling shaft through while gently taping intermediate plate.

8. Install bearing to input shaft then install the input shaft on the output shaft.

9. Install the counter gear, then install the counter centre bearing and side race and install snap ring.

10. Install centre bearing retainer and tighten to specifica-

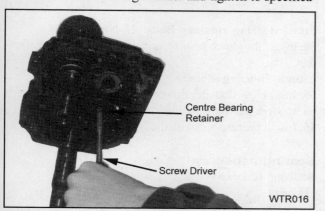

WTR016

tion.

Centre bearing retainer bolts: 13 Nm

11. To the idler shaft install the idler gear, ensuring the oil hole

is toward the rear, then insert the assembly ensuring the spacer tab fits into the notch on the intermediate plate and

Reverse Idler Gear Shaft Stopper — Spanner

WTR014

install the reverse idler shaft stopper.

12. Use a feeler guage to measure the reverse idler gear thrust clearance.

Reverse Idler Thrust Clearance:
Standard 0.15-0.25 mm (0.0059-0.0098 in.)
Max 0.30 mm (0.0118 in.)

13. Install No.3 clutch hub into reverse gearby installing the snap ring to the frooves of the hub and keys, then install the shifting key springs And install No.3 hub sleeve assembly.

14. Install locking ball then assemble the 5th gear, synchronizer

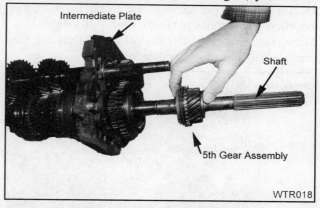

Intermediate Plate

Shaft

5th Gear Assembly

WTR018

ring, needle roller bearings and inner race.

15. Install the 5th gear assembly, ensuring the synchronizer ring slots align with shifting keys, then align the locking ball by turning inner race and install snap ring.

16. Measure the fifth gear thrust clearance.

Standard 0.10-0.25 mm (0.0039-0.0098 in.)
Max 0.30 mm (0.0118 in.)

17. Install counter reverse gear, then using the correct tool drive in the counter 5thg gear.

18. Using the correct tool drive counter rear bearing in, then install the snap ring.

19. Install the output shaft rear bearing snap ring, drive in rear bearing, then install speedometer spacer, locking ball and drive gear, secure with snap ring.

20. Install to the groove of No.3 hub sleeve the shift fork No.3, then through the intermediate plate install the No.3 fork shaft to shift fork.

Speedo Drive Gear

Snap Ring Pliers

WTR012

21. Install to the groove of No.2 hub sleeve the shift fork No.3, then install the No.4 fork shaft to shift fork.

22. Coat the interlock pin with greese then install interlock pin to intermediate plate and through the intermediate shaft install No.2 fork shaft to shift fork.

22. Coat the interlock pin with greese then install interlock pin to intermediate plate and shift fork No.2.

23. Into the groove of No. hub sleeve install the No.1 shift fork, then through the intermediate plate install No.1 fork shaft to No.1 shift fork.

24. Position the No.2 fork shaft to 3rd speed position, and ensure the No.1 and No.3 fork shafts do not move.

25. Align the fork pin hole with the hole in the shaft, then install the slotted spring pin so it is flush with the fork.

26. Into each hole install the balls and springs then install the three plugs tightening to specification.

Intermediate Plate

Hex Key

Three Plugs

WTR006

Plug Torque Specification: 25 Nm.

27. Remove the intermediate plate from the vise, align each of the shift fork shaft ends and outer race with case holes, then tap the case on and install the two snap rings.

28. To the intermediate plate install the extension gasket, then push the shift lever housing forward, with it turned anti-clockwise and push on the extension leaving a gap of 20-30 mm (0.79-1.18 in.) with the intermediate plate.

29. Slightly turn the extension housing clockwise and connect the select lever to shift fork shaft, then fully install extension and tighten bolts to specification.

Rear Extension Bolts: 46 Nm.

30. With the short springs on the left side install the springs and restrict pins, then install plugs with washers and tighten to specification.

Plug Torque Specification: 40 Nm.

31. Install the oil baffle and shift lever retainer tightening to Specification.

Retainer Specification: 18 Nm.

32. Firmly push the countershaft toward rear, then using a set of calipers, measure the space between the bearing and case surface.

Select the correct spacer, then install with the cover.

33. Install the front bearing retainer aligning the oil hole with the groove then tighten bolts to specification.

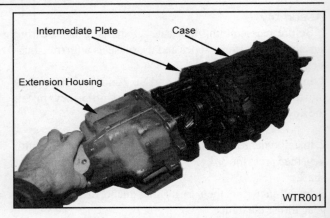

Intermediate Plate   Case

Extension Housing

WTR001

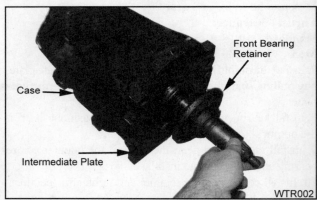

Front Bearing Retainer

Case

Intermediate Plate

WTR002

Front Bearing retainer Bolts: 12 Nm

34. Install the clutch housing and tighten bolts to specification.

Clutch Housing Bolts: 37 Nm.

35. Install speedometer driven gear, then install the clutch release fork into the boot and install into housing.

36. Install bearing hub with the two clips.

Bearing Inspection
Bearing Raceways
Inspect

Inner Raceway: While holding outer ring stationary, rotate inner ring at least three revolutions. Inspect the raceway of the inner ring from both sides for pits or spalling. A bearing assembly should be replaced when damaged. Light particle indentation is allowable.

Outer Ring Raceway: While holding inner ring stationary, rotate outer ring at least three revolutions. Inspect the raceway of the outer ring from both as with the raceway of the inner ring. If the raceway is spalled or pitted, replace the bearing assembly. Light particle indentation is allowable.

Bearing External Surfaces

The bearing must be replaced if damage is found in any of the following areas:
Radial cracks on front and rear faces of outer or inner rings. Cracks on outside diameter of outer ring (particularly around snap ring groove). Deformation or cracks in ball cage (particularly around rivets).

Spin Test

Lubricate bearing raceways with a slight amount of clean automatic transmission fluid turn the bearing back and forth slowly until the raceways and balls are coated.
With bearing in vertical position. Vertical movement between inner and outer rings is allowable. Spin outer ring several times by hand. If there is roughness or vibration, the bearing should be cleaned again and lubricated. Roughness could be foreign particles in the bearing. If bearing is still rough after cleaning and lubricating several times, it must be replaced.
Repeat the above with the bearing in the horizontal position.

PROBLEM SOLVING

PROBLEM
Transmission Noisy in Gear.
CAUSE
* Lubricate level low or wrong type.
ACTION
* Fill to bottom of filler plug hold with proper lubricant.
CAUSE
* Transmission to flywheel housing and flywheel housing to engine block bolts loose.
ACTION
* Tighten bolts to specification.
CAUSE
* Pilot bushing worn or damaged.
ACTION
*Remove transmission. If noise is howling during start-up, check pilot bushing. Check for loose flywheel and housing alignment. Service or replace as required.
CAUSE
* Improper transmission pilot engagement into flywheel housing.
ACTION
* Replace housing or input shaft bearing retainer as required. Refer to 'Clutch'.
CAUSE

* Worn or damaged internal components.
ACTION
* Disassemble transmission. Inspect input, output and counter shaft bearings, gear and gear teeth for wear and damage. Service or replace as required.

PROBLEM
Transmission Shifts Hard.
CAUSE
* Improper clutch release.
ACTION
*Refer to 'Clutch'.
CAUSE
* Internal shift mechanism binding.
ACTION
* Remove transmission and free up shift mechanism.
CAUSE
* Synchronizer sleeve to hub fit.
ACTION
* Remove and check for burrs or fit.
CAUSE
* Binding condition between input shaft and crank shaft pilot bearing.
ACTION
* Check alignment and service as required.
CAUSE
* Improper Fluid.
ACTION
* Drain and refill with specified fluid to bottom of filler plug hole.

PROBLEM
Transmission Will Not Shift into One Gear - All Other Gears OK.
CAUSE
* Floor shift, interference between shift handle and console of floor cut out.
ACTION
* Adjust console or cut out floorpan to eliminate interference.
CAUSE
* Restricted travel of internal shifter components.
ACTION
* Remove transmission. Inspect shift rail and fork system, synchronizer system and gear clutch teeth for restricted travel. Service and replace as required.

PROBLEM
Transmission is Locked in One Gear. It cannot be shifted Out of that Gear.
CAUSE
* Internal Shifter components worn or damaged.
ACTION
* Remove transmission. Inspect the problem gear or

gearshift rails and fork and synchronizer for wear or damage. Service or replace as required.

CAUSE * Selector arm finger broken.

ACTION * Remove transmission. Replace selector arm assembly.

CAUSE * Bent shifter forks at pads and selector slot.

ACTION * Service or replace as required.

PROBLEM

Transmission Will Not Shift Into Reverse (All Others OK).

CAUSE * Worn or damaged internal components.

ACTION * Remove transmission. Check for damaged reverse geartrain, misaligned reverse relay lever, shift rail and fork system.

Memo

TRANSMISSIONS G40, G52 G54 and G58 SPECIFICATIONS

OIL CLEARANCE:

1st Gear to Inner Race to Needle Bearing:
Standard:	0.009 - 0.032 mm
	(0.00035 - 0.00126 in)
Max:	0.032 mm (0.00126 in)

2nd & 3rd Gear to Shaft with Needle Brg Installed
Standard:	0.009 - 0.033 mm
	(0.00035 - 0.00130 in)
Max:	0.033 mm (0.00130 in)

Counter & 5th Gear to Shaft with Needle Brg Installed
Standard:	0.009 - 0.032 mm
	(0.00035 - 0.00126 in)
Max:	0.032 mm (0.00126 in)

SYNCHRONIZER RING CLEARANCE:
Standard:	1.0-2.0mm (0.040-0.079in)
Minimum:	0.8mm (0.031in)

OOUTPUT SHAFT SPECIFICATIONS:
Output Shaft Flange Thickness:	4.80mm
	(0.1890in)
Inner Race Flange Thickness:	3.99mm
	(0.1571in)
2nd Gear Journal Min Dia:	37.984mm
	(1.4954in)
3rd Gear Journal Min Dia:	34.984mm
	(1.3773in)
Inner Race Min Dia:	38.985mm
	(1.5348in)
Maximium Runout:	0.05mm
	(0.0020in)

THRUST CLEARANCES:
Third Gear	Standard:	0.10-0.25 mm
		(0.0039-0.0098in)
	Max:	0.25 mm
		(0.0098in)
Second & First Gears Standard:		0.10-0.25 mm
		(0.0039-0.0098in)
	Max :	0.25 mm
		(0.0098in)
Fifth Gear:	Standard:	0.10-0.30 mm
		(0.0039-0.0118in)
	Max:	0.30 mm
		(0.0118in)

TORQUE WRENCH SPECIFICATIONS

Bearing Retainer Plate Bolts Torque:	185kg.cm
	13ft.lb
	18Nm.
Reverse Shift Arm Bracket Bolts Torque:	185kg.cm
	13ft.lb
	18Nm.
Oil Seperator Lock Nut Torque:	1200kg.cm
	87lb.ft
	118 Nm
Oil Seperator Lock Nut Torque:	1200kg.cm
	87lb.ft
	118 Nm
Reverse Idler Gear Shaft Stopper Nut Torque:	175kg-cm
	13ft.lb
	17Nm
Reverse Idler Gear Shaft Stopper Nut Torque:	175kg-cm
	13ft.lb
	17Nm
Torx Screw InPlugs to Intermediate Plate:	190 kg-cm
	14lb.ft
	19Nm
Front Bearing Retainer Bolts:	170kg-cm
	12ft-lb
	17Nm
Rear Extension Housing bolts:	380 kg-cm
	27ft.lb
	37Nm
Shift Lever Housing Bolt:	390 kg-cm
	28ft.lb
	38Nm
Adapter Housing bolts:	380 kg-cm
	27ft.lb
	37Nm
Shift Lever Housing Bolt:	390 kg-cm
	28ft.lb
	38Nm
Lock Ball Torx Plug Torque:	190 kg-cm
	14ft.lb
	19Nm
Restrictor Pins Torque:	190 kg-cm
	14ft.lb
	19Nm
Clutch Housing bolts:	380 kg-cm
	27ft.lb
	37Nm
Shift Lever Retainer Bolts:	190 kg-cm
	14ft.lb
	19Nm
Lubricant Drain Plug Torque Specs:	25 - 34 Nm.

TRANSMISSION W56 SPECIFICATIONS

OIL CLEARANCE:

1st Gear to Inner Race to Needle Bearing:
Standard:	0.009-0.053 mm
	(0.0004-0.0021 in)
Max:	0.15mm (0.0059in)

2nd & 3rd Gear to Output Shaft:
Standard:	0.06-0.103 mm
	(0.0024-0.0041 in.)
Max:	0.20 mm (0.0079 in.)

5th Gear to Inner Race to Needle Bearing:
Standard:	0.009-0.051 mm
	(0.0004-0.0020 in)
Max:	0.15 mm (0.0059 in)

SYNCHRONIZER RING CLEARANCE:

1st, 2nd & 5th
Standard:	0.7-1.7mm
	(0.028-0.067in)
Minimum:	0.5mm (0.02in)

3rd & 4th
Standard:	1.0-2.0mm
	(0.039-0.079in)
Minimum:	0.8mm (0.031in)

THRUST CLEARANCES:

3rd Gear:
Standard:	0.15-0.25 mm
	(0.0059-0/0098 in.)
Max:	0.30 mm (0.0118 in.)

1st & 2nd gear:
Standard:	0.15-0.25 mm
	(0.0059-0.0098 in.)
Max:	0.30 mm (0.0118 in.)

Reverse Idler:
Standard:	0.15-0.25 mm
	(0.0059-0.0098 in.)
Max:	0.30 mm (0.0118 in.)

Fifth Gear:
Standard:	0.10-0.25 mm
	(0.0039-0.0098 in.)
Max:	0.30 mm (0.0118 in.)

TORQUE WRENCH SPECIFICATIONS

Bearing Retainer Plate Bolts Torque:	130kg.cm 9ft.lb 13Nm.
Front Bearing Retainer Bolts:	250kg-cm 18ft-lb 25Nm
Shift Lever Housing Bolt:	400 kg-cm 29ft.lb 39Nm
Shift Lever Retainer Bolt:	185 kg-cm 13ft.lb 18Nm
Restrictor Pins Torque:	410 kg-cm 30ft.lb 40Nm
Clutch Housing bolts:	375 kg-cm 27ft.lb 37Nm
Lubricant Drain Plug Torque Specs:	410 kg-cm 30 ft.lb. 40 Nm.
Shift Fork Bolt:	125kg.cm 19ft.lb 12Nm.
Straight Screw Plug:	250kg.cm 18ft.lb 25Nm.
Idler Shaft Stopper Bolt:	250kg.cm 18ft.lb 25Nm.
Rear Extension Bolts:	345 kg-cm 25 ft.lb. 34 Nm.

MANUAL TRANSMISSIONS

L40, 42 & 43   4 Speed

Gear and Shaft Assemblies

Ltr037

Cluster Gear and Washers

Ltr038

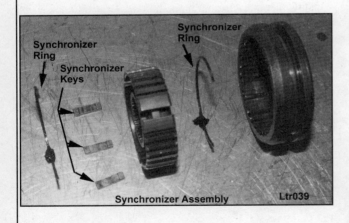

Synchronizer Ring

Synchronizer Ring

Synchronizer Keys

Synchronizer Assembly   Ltr039

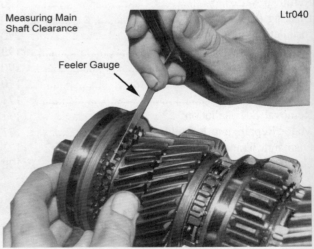

Measuring Main Shaft Clearance

Ltr040

Feeler Gauge

Manual Transmission

DESCRIPTION

The L40, L42 & L43 four speed synchronized manual transmission.

The four speed design incorporated both a floor shift and column shift transmission, the difference being in the shifter lever transmission side cover. The internal components of the synchronized four speed are the same for the column and floor shift. Some transmission cases incorporated the bell housing, where others were designed with a removable bell housing.

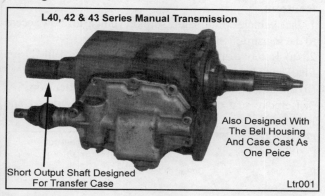

L40, 42 & 43 Series Manual Transmission

Also Designed With The Bell Housing And Case Cast As One Peice

Short Output Shaft Designed For Transfer Case

Ltr001

Maintenance

Checking and Replacing Transmission Oil

Position an oil catching tray under the transmission, make sure it has the capacity to hold the oil from the transmission (if oil level is at the full level the transmissions will hold 1.9 Litres.

Remove the drain plug which is on the lower left hand side of the casing, fitted with a copper washer. Housing.

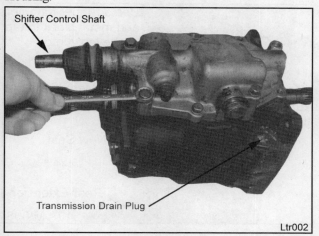

Shifter Control Shaft

Transmission Drain Plug

Ltr002

Replace the drain plug and tighten to specification.

Drain Plug torque specification: 25 - 34 Nm

Remove the filler plug approximately half way up the left side of the transmission, fill the transmission with the correct amount of specified oil.

Oil Capacity of Transmission: 1.9 Litres.

Specified Transmission Oil: SAE90, API GL-4

Check oil level by inserting your finger into the oil filler hole to check on oil level. The oil level should be at the same level as the filler plug, but not so high that oil will run out when the plug is removed.

Replace oil filler plug and tighten plug to specification.

Filler Plug specified torque: 25 - 34 Nm

Speedo Driven Gear and Oil Seal
Remove

1. Remove the clamp securing the speedometer cable to the rear extension by removing the retaining screw and lock washer.

2. Remove the speedometer cable from the rear extension by sliding out, then remove the gear from the cable fitting.

3. Remove the 'O' ring seal using a small flat blade screw driver.

Install

1. Install 'O' ring to the drive end fitting, then lubricate the "O" ring and gear in gear oil.

2. Install the driven gear to the cable fitting, then slide the speedometer cable fitting into the transmission rear extension.

3. Replace the lock washer and bolt to the clamp on the rear extension, then tighten bolt.

Speedo Drive Gear
Remove

1. Remove the clamp securing the speedometer cable to the rear extension by removing the retaining screw and lock washer.

2. Remove the speedometer cable from the rear extension by sliding out, then remove the gear from the cable fitting.

3. Remove the rear extension as described in Extension Housing section.

4. Remove gear:

(a) Remove rear circlip.

(b) Slide gear from shaft.

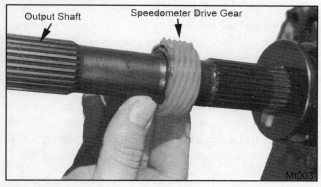

Output Shaft   Speedometer Drive Gear

Mt003

Install

1. Slide gear into shaft, then fit the rear circlip into position.

2. Replace the rear extension as described in the Extension Housing section.

3. Install the driven gear to the cable fitting, then slide the speedometer cable fitting into the transmission rear extension.

4. Replace the lock washer and bolt to the clamp on the rear extension, then tighten bolt.

Reversing Light Switch
Remove

1. Detach wiring plugs.

2. Remove the switch from the right hand side, in the back of the shifter cover with a spanner.

Install

Clean threads of the switch and apply Teflon tape to threads. Install the switch and torque to specification.

Reverse Light Switch torque: 10-14 lb.ft

Rear Extension Housing, Seal and Bushing.
Remove

1. Lift the vehicle and support on safety stands and position a drip tray under the transmission.

2. Remove the clamp securing the speedometer cable to the rear extension by removing the retaining screw and lock washer.

3. Remove the speedometer cable from the rear extension by sliding out, then remove the gear from the cable fitting.

4. Mark the drive shaft so that it may be installed in the same relative place. Detach the shaft at the universal joint and slide it off the transmission output shaft. Install a dust cover or extension housing seal replacer into the extension housing to prevent lubricant leakage.

5. Support the engine and transmission assembly with a transmission jack. Remove the rear mount to crossmember bolts.

6. Remove the bolts securing the mount to the transmission and remove the mount.

7. Remove the rear extension housing from the transmission case by removing the 5 retaining bolts.

Replace Bushing

1. From the transmission rear extension remove the old oil seal.

2. Heat the extension housing to 100°C, then remove the bushing using, rear extension bushing removal/replacer tool.

3. Heat the extension housing to 100°C, then replace the bushing using, rear extension bushing removal/replacer tool.

4. Replace the new seal into the rear extension with the use of the rear extension seal tool and hammer, after coating the outer edge of the seal with a sealing compound.

5. To initially lubricate the bushing, insert a small amount of gear oil into the extension.

Install

1. Fit a new gasket to the rear of the transmission, then install the rear extension.

2. Install the five attaching bolts and tighten to specification.

Rear extension retaining bolts torque: 22 - 32 lb.ft

3. Install speedometer cable unit and bolt.

4. Install the mount to the crossmember, then to the transmission. Torque the bolts to specification. Remove the transmission jack

Rear Mount to Transmission bolts: 14 - 22 Nm

Rear Mount to Crossmember bolts: 26 - 36 Nm

5. Slide the drive shaft into the transmission output shaft. Align the index marks at the universal joint and connect the drive shaft as described in Tail / Drive shaft chapter.

6. Road test the vehicle for satisfactory transmission operation.

Extension Housing Rear Seal
Remove

1. Jack vehicle up and safety support vehicle to allow access to the transmission and drive / tail shaft.

2. (a) Remove drive / tail shaft as described in Tail / Drive Shaft and Universal Joints chapter in this manual.

(b) Place a drain tray beneath transmission extension.

3. Remove seal using seal remover or screw driver and hammer.

Lever old seal out with screw driver

Screw Driver

Hammer

Seal

Bush

Mt006

4. (a) Inspect seal lip surface on slip yoke of propeller shaft for damage.

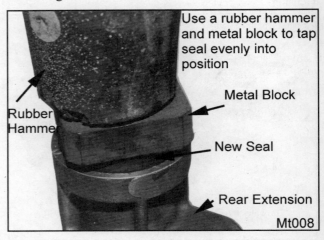

Use a rubber hammer and metal block to tap seal evenly into position

Rubber Hammer

Metal Block

New Seal

Rear Extension

Mt008

(b) Clean (or replace) as necessary.

Install

1. (a) Apply a little transmission lubricant to new seal lip.

(b) Install seal into the extension with a seal insertion tool and hammer, or block of wood.

2. Replace tail / drive shaft.

3. Check transmission lubricant level as previously described in this Chapter.

Transmission

Remove

1. Remove the negative battery terminal, then raise vehicle and place on safety stands.

2. (a) Disconnect the control rods from the shift levers (column shift transmissions).

(b) Remove the shift lever from transmission through the floor (floor shift transmissions).

3. Remove starter motor retaining bolts and motor and place out of the way (L40 & L43 only).

4. Disconnect clutch slave cylinder from the transmission case and clutch fork.

5. Disconnect the electrical connections for the reverse light switch.

6. Mark the drive shaft so that it may be installed in the same relative place. Detach the shaft at the universal joint and slide it off the transmission output shaft. Install a dust cover or extension housing seal replacer into the extension housing to prevent lubricant leakage.

7. Remove speedometer cable by unscrewing the outer case and withdrawing.

8. Detach engine pipe bracket from the transmission and the exhaust, then remove bracket.

9. Remove the flywheel cover (L42 only).

10. Support the engine and transmission assembly with a transmission jack. Remove the rear mount from the crossmember and transmission.

11. Lower transmission and engine, then raise the engine on its own until the transmission is hanging from the engine.

12. Remove the bolts securing the bell housing to the engine block.

13. Move transmission rearward until the input shaft clears the flywheel housing and remove the transmission.

Install

1. Move transmission rearward until the output shaft clears the centre crossmember, then lift and move the transmission towards flywheel until input shaft engages the clutch.

2. Install the bolts securing the bell housing to the engine block.

Clutch Housing to Block bolts:

L42	22 - 32 Nm
L40 & L43	37 - 57 Nm

3. Lower engine, then raise the transmission until the extension housing is lifted off the crossmember.

4. Replace the rear mount to the crossmember and transmis-

sion, tensioning the bolts.

Rear Mount to Crossmember bolts:	**26 - 36 Nm**
Rear Mount to Transmission bolts:	**14 - 22 Nm**

5. Replace the flywheel cover (L42 only).

6. Attach engine pipe bracket to the transmission and the exhaust, then tension bracket bolts.

Exhaust Pipe Bracket bolts:	**12 - 16 Nm**

7. Install speedometer cable, then screw the outer case into place.

8. Align the mark on the drive shaft when installing into place. Bolt the universal joint into place once the shaft is slid into the transmission.

9. Connect the electrical connections for the reverse light switch.

10. Connect clutch slave cylinder to the transmission case and clutch fork.

11. Replace starter motor retaining bolts and tension (L40 & L43 only).

12. (a) Connect the control rods to the shift levers (column shift transmissions).

(b) Replace the shift lever in the transmission through the floor (floor shift transmissions).

13. Fill transmission with recommended fluid, lower vehicle from the safety stands, and fit the negative battery terminal.

Oil Capacity of Transmission:	**1.9 Litres**
Specified Transmission Oil:	**SAE90, API GL-4**

Major Repairs and Rebuild

Dismantle Transmission

1. Place transmission on a clean bench to enable a complete pull down and rebuild.

2. Remove reverse light switch and speedo driven gear as previously described.

3. Remove the attaching bolts and washers securing the side cover, then remove cover.

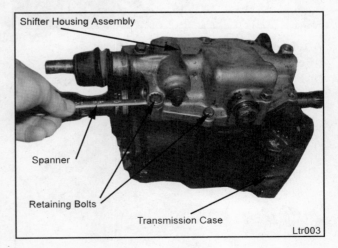

Shifter Housing Assembly
Spanner
Retaining Bolts
Transmission Case
Ltr003

4. Remove clutch release folk and bearing, and bell housing (L40 & L43 only).

5. Remove the rear extension housing from the transmission case by removing the 5 retaining bolts, then tap with rubber hammer.

6. Remove the front retainer by removing the four bolts securing the retainer to the casing.

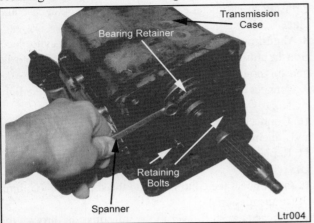

Ltr004

7. Take backlash measurements of each gear before disassembly.

* Record the readings for further reference.

8. From the front to the rear of the transmission case drive out the reverse idler gear shaft using a steel rod and hammer, lift gear from the casing.

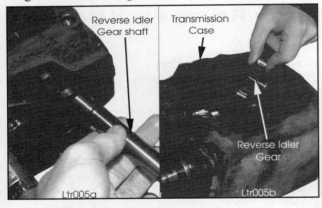

Ltr005a   Ltr005b

9. Take counter shaft thrust measurements.

* Record the readings for further reference.

10. From the front to the rear of the transmission drive out the counter gear shaft using a steel rod and hammer.

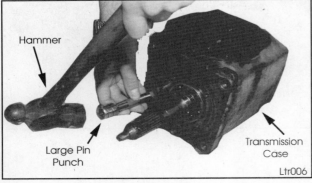

Ltr006

11. Position the counter gear to the side of the transmission case, remove the output shaft assembly from the transmission case by withdrawing carefully out the rear of the transmission case.

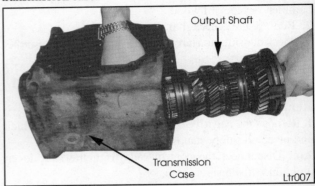

Ltr007

12. Becareful of the needle roller bearings as they may fall out of the gear, remove the clutch gear (input shaft), the synchronizing ring and the bearing assembly from the casing through the front.

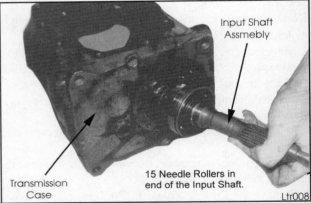

Ltr008

Note: There are 15 needle roller bearings.

13. Withdraw from the transmission case the counter shaft assembly and thrust washer.

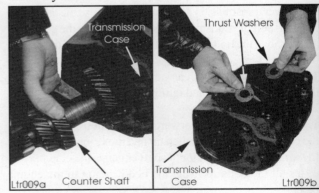

Ltr009a   Counter Shaft   Ltr009b

Dismantle Main shaft

* *During the disassembly of the main shaft, use a pair of snap ring pliers to remove all snap-springs.*

1. Remove speedometer drive gear:

If not removed on disassembly of transmission.

(a) Remove rear circlip using circlip pliers.

172

(b) Slide gear from shaft.

(c) Remove front circlip using circlip pliers.

2. From the output shaft remove the rear bearing locking circlip, press the rear bearing and first gear as an assembly from the shaft. The shaft assembly can also be hit onto a block of wood, this will free the bearing, then remove bearing from the shaft.

Ltr029

* Don't loose the locking ball bearing on removal.

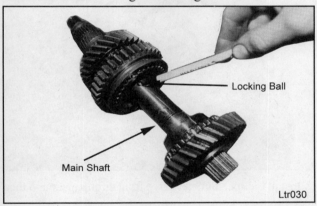

Ltr030

3. Also remove the 1st speed gear and synchronized ring.

4. Remove the No.1 clutch hub assembly from the output shaft, then the second gear synchronizer ring and gear.

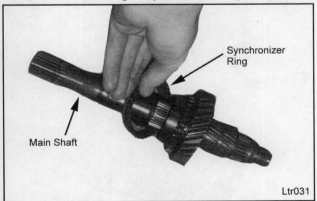

Ltr031

5. Using circlip pliers remove the clutch hub No. 2 assembly circlip.

6. Remove the No. 2 clutch hub assembly, then the third gear synchronizer ring and gear.

Ltr032

Inspection of Transmission Assembly

Cleaning

Wash all parts except bearings, O-rings and seals in a suitable cleaning solvent. Brush or scrape all foreign matter from the parts, be careful not to damage any parts with the scraper. Do not clean, wash or soak transmission seals in cleaning solvents, all seals should be replaced with new seals. Dry all parts with compressed air.

Rotate ball bearings in a cleaning solvent until all lubricant is removed. Hold bearing assembly to prevent it from rotating and dry it with compressed air. Lubricate bearings with Multi-Purpose Grease and wrap them in a clean, lint-free cloth or paper until ready for use.

Inspect

Inspect transmission case for cracks, worn or damaged bearing bores, damaged bearing bores, damaged threads, or any other damage that could affect operation of the transmission. Inspect the front face of the case for small nicks or burrs that could cause misalignment of the transmission with the flywheel housing. Remove all small nicks or burrs with a fine file.

Replace any side plate that is bent or distorted. Check the condition of the shift levers, forks, shift rails, and the lever and shafts. Inspect bearings.

Replace roller bearings that are broken, worn or rough, and check their respective races.

Replace input shaft and gear if the splines are damaged or if the teeth are chipped, worn or broken. If the roller bearing surface in the bore is worn or rough, or if the cone surface is damaged, replace gear and gear rollers.

Replace all other gears that are chipped, broken or worn. Check the synchronized sleeves for free movement on their hubs. Make sure that the alignment marks (if present) are properly indexed.

Replace speedometer drive gear if teeth are stripped or damaged. Be sure to install the correct size replacement gear.

Replace the output shaft if there is any evidence of wear or if any splines are damaged. Inspect bushing and seal in the extension housing, and replace if worn or damaged.

Assemble Main Shaft

* *During the assembly of the main shaft, use a pair of snap ring pliers to replace all snap-rings, also apply gear oil to bearings and sliding components.*

1. Slide the second gear and synchronizer ring onto the output shaft, then fit the No.1 clutch hub, ensuring that the keys on the hub are aligned with the slots in the ring of the second gear synchronizer.

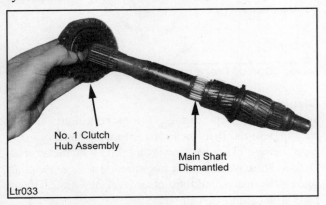

Ltr033

2. Replace lock ball into position, when bushing, bearings, first gear and synchronizer ring are assembled, slide the assembly on output shaft aligning the lock ball and the clutch hub shift keys with the first gear assembly.

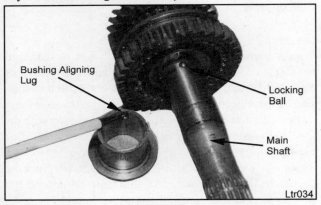

Ltr034

3. To the output shaft install the bearing and adaptor assembly, pressing it into position.

Ltr035

4. Install the thickest remaining lock ring behind the rear bearing on the output shaft, ensuring it is seated in the groove.

5. Onto the output shaft, assemble the 3rd gear and synchronizer ring, ensuring it is against the output shaft shoulder.

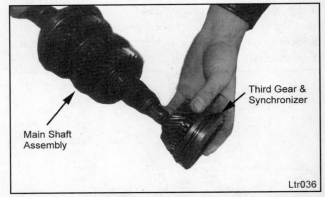

Ltr036

6. Onto the splines of the output shaft install the clutch hub No. 2 assembly, ensure the grooves in the synchronized ring are aligned with the hub keys. To the mainshaft, install the lock ring.

Mt023

7. Install the speedometer drive front circlip, gear and then rear circlip.

8. Measure all output shaft gear thrust clearances.

Thrust Clearance: **0.10 - 0.25 mm**

Ltr028

Input Shaft Front Bearing
Remove

174

* This procedure is only necessary if the bearing is to be replaced.

1. Secure the clutch gear shaft into a vice fitted with soft jaws to prevent damage.

2. Remove the bearing circlip with the use of circlip pliers.

3. Remove the assembly from the vice, then with the use of a press, remove the bearing from the shaft.

Note: Ensure the press plates are positioned between the bearing and clutch gear.

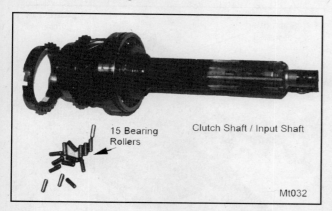

15 Bearing Rollers

Clutch Shaft / Input Shaft

Mt032

Install

1. Install new bearing:

(a) Position new bearing on the clutch shaft.

(b) Press bearing into place, use a sleeve that will rest on the inner bearing cone, to protect the bearing.

Note: Ensure the closed side of the bearing is facing towards the clutch gear.

2. Replace the circlip onto the shaft and ensure it is seated in its groove correctly.

Counter Shaft
Bearing Replacement

1. At either end of the countershaft, remove the roller bearing cages.

2. Each bearing cage contains the 16 roller bearings. Coat the new bearing cages with a smear of grease.

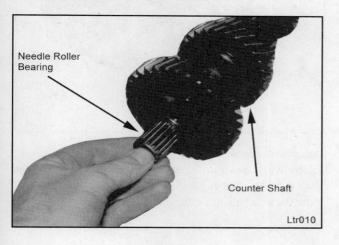

Needle Roller Bearing

Counter Shaft

Ltr010

3. Install the bearing cages into either end of the counter shaft, ensure that they are fully inserted.

4. Fit the thrust washers to either end of the counter shaft.

Transmission Assembly

1. Install the counter shaft into the casing, using counter shaft dummy to hold the thrust washers in place for easier assembly. Allow the counter shaft to drop to the bottom of the casing.

2. Align the flat section of the input shaft with the counter shaft, then fit the input shaft into position. Fit the synchronizer ring into place on the input shaft.

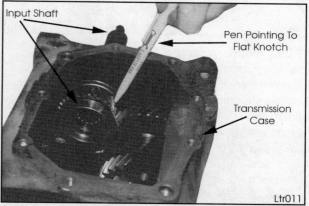

Input Shaft

Pen Pointing To Flat Knotch

Transmission Case

Ltr011

3. Slide the assembled out put shaft into the casing installing it in the back of the input shaft, align the retainer lug in the casing and push until retainer plate sits flush with the case.

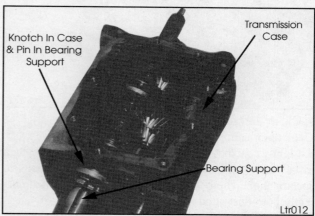

Knotch In Case & Pin In Bearing Support

Transmission Case

Bearing Support

Ltr012

4. Lift the counter shaft into position until the support shaft is able to be fitted. When fitting the support shaft install the key into the casing and counter shaft, driving it home.

175

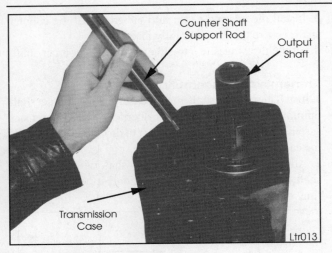

Counter Shaft Support Rod

Output Shaft

Transmission Case

Ltr013

5. Check the counter gear end play.

Counter gear end float: **0.10 - 0.20 mm**

6. Install the reverse gear into the transmission case, once it is in place slide the support shaft into place, ensuring the key is fitted.

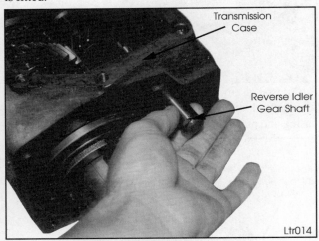

Transmission Case

Reverse Idler Gear Shaft

Ltr014

7. Check the backlash in each gear.

Gear backlash: **0.10 - 0.20 mm**

8. Lightly coat the retainer securing bolts with silastic, then install the front bearing retainer and tighten the bolts to specification. The bearing retainer must be installed correctly, note illustration.

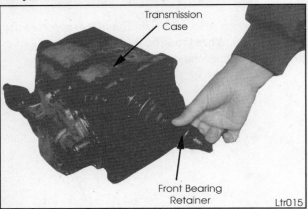

Transmission Case

Front Bearing Retainer

Ltr015

Front Bearing Retainer bolts torque: 5 - 6 lb.ft

9. Fit a new gasket to the rear of the transmission.

10. Assemble the rear extension, install the five attaching bolts and tighten to specification.

Rear Extension retaining bolts torque spec: 22 - 32 lb.ft

11. Ensure the transmission is selected in neutral, then install a new side cover gasket, cover and retaining bolts, tighten to specification.

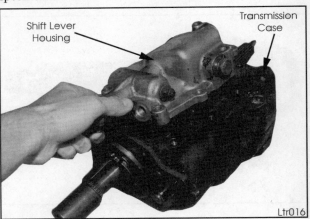

Shift Lever Housing

Transmission Case

Ltr016

Side Cover retaining bolt specification: 11 - 15 lb.ft

12. Replace reverse light switch as described previously.

Transmission Side Cover
Remove

1. Raise the vehicle on a hoist or support on safety stands.

2. Remove the gear control rods.

3. Drain the oil from the transmission by removing the drain plug from the casing. Once oil has drained, replace and tighten.

4. Remove the side cover by removing the retaining bolts.

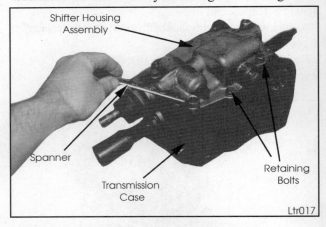

Shifter Housing Assembly

Spanner

Transmission Case

Retaining Bolts

Ltr017

Dismantle (floor shift)

1. Remove roll pin from the third/forth shift fork, then slide the shaft from the housing and remove the shift fork. Do not loose the lock ball and spring.

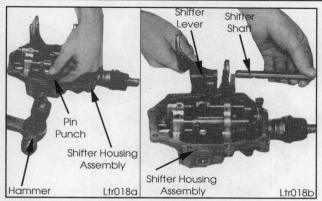

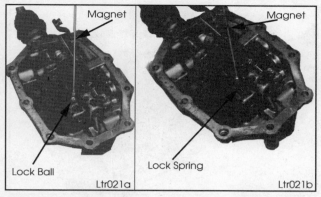

2. Remove the interlock pin, lock ball and spring.
3. Remove roll pin from the first/second shift fork, then slide the shaft from the housing and remove the shift fork. Do not loose the lock ball and spring.

8. Remove the reverse shift arm and pivot from the casing.
9. Remove the reverse restrict ball holder, spring and locking ball from the housing.

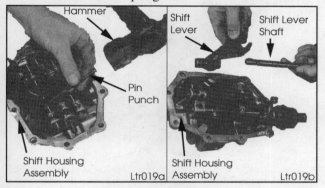

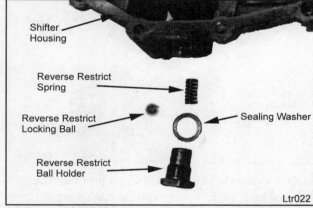

4. Remove the interlock pin, lock ball and spring.
5. Remove the nut, washers and seal from the reverse shift arm pivot.

10. Loosen the shift and select lever retainer bolt, then slide the shift lever shaft from the housing and remove the shift lever and select lever.

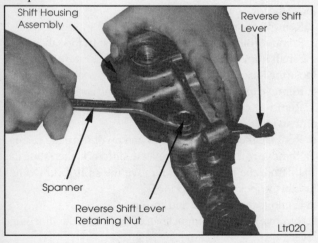

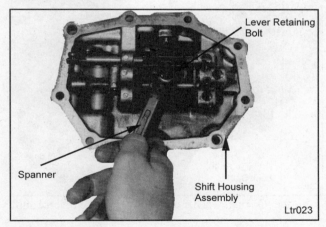

6. Remove roll pin from the reverse shift fork, then slide the shaft from the housing and remove the shift fork. Do not loose the lock ball and spring.
7. Remove the lock ball and spring.

11. Before reassembling inspect all parts for wear or damage, and if necessary replace.

Assembly (floor shift)
1. Fit the shift lever shaft into the casing, as it is slid into place install shift & select lever into the case over the end of the shaft, securing it in place with the locking bolt.
2. Install the lock ball, spring and reverse restrict ball holder into the case. Then the reverse shift arm & pivot can be fitted into the housing.

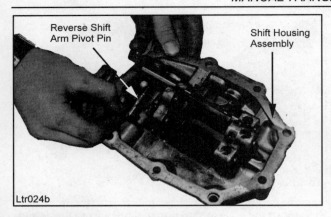

Reverse Shift Arm Pivot Pin

Shift Housing Assembly

Ltr024b

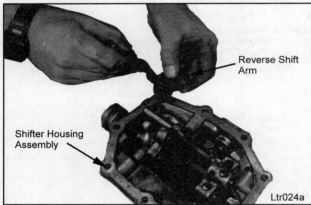

Reverse Shift Arm

Shifter Housing Assembly

Ltr024a

3. Install reverse shift lock ball and spring, then install the shift shaft and lever, fit the roll pin into place to secure the lever to the shaft.

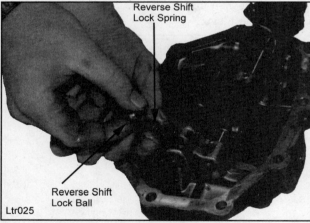

Reverse Shift Lock Spring

Reverse Shift Lock Ball

Ltr025

4. Fit the 'O' ring, washer and lock nut to the reverse shift arm pivot.

5. Install first/second shift shaft and reverse shift shaft interlock pin, then the first/second shift shaft spring and lock ball.

6. Fit the first/second shift lever and shaft into the casing, then the roll pin is to be fitted to lock it into place.

7. Install the third/fourth shift shaft interlock pin, then the third/fourth shift shaft spring and lock ball, then fit the third/fourth shift lever and shaft into the casing, then the roll pin is to be fitted to lock it into place.

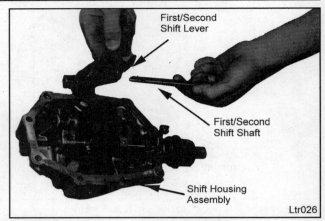

First/Second Shift Lever

First/Second Shift Shaft

Shift Housing Assembly

Ltr026

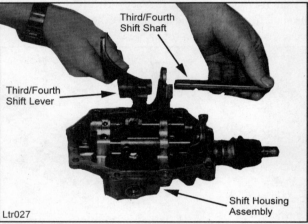

Third/Fourth Shift Shaft

Third/Fourth Shift Lever

Shift Housing Assembly

Ltr027

Dismantle (column shift)

1. Remove roll pin from the third forth shift fork, then slide the shaft from the housing and remove the shift fork. Do not loose the lock ball and spring.

2. Remove the interlock pin, lock ball and spring.

3. Remove roll pin from the first/second shift fork, then slide the shaft from the housing and remove the shift fork. Do not loose the lock ball and spring.

4. Remove the interlock pin, lock ball and spring.

5. Remove the nut, washers and seal from the reverse shift arm pivot.

6. Remove the reverse shift arm and pivot from the casing.

7. Remove roll pin from the reverse shift fork, then slide the shaft from the housing and remove the shift fork. Do not loosen the lock ball and spring.

8. Remove the lock ball and spring.

9. Remove the select output lever & shaft, then the shift outer lever.

10. Remove the shift lever shaft & sliding shaft lever, then withdraw the lock ball and spring.

11. Before reassembling inspect all parts for wear or damage, and if necessary replace.

Assembly (column shift)

1. Install the lock ball and spring, then the sliding shaft lever, shift lever shaft and the shift outer lever.

2. Install the select outer lever and shaft into the casing.

178

3. Install reverse shift lock ball and spring, then the shift shaft and lever, fit the roll pin into place to secure the lever to the shaft.

4. Then the reverse shift arm & pivot can be fitted into the housing.

5. Fit the 'O' ring, washer and lock nut to the reverse shift arm pivot.

6. Install first/second shift shaft and reverse shift shaft interlock pin, then the first/second shift shaft spring and lock ball.

7. Fit the first second shift lever and shaft into the casing, then the roll pin is to be fitted to lock it into place.

8. Install the third/fourth shift shaft interlock pin, then the third/fourth shift shaft spring and lock ball, then fit the third/fourth shift lever and shaft into the casing, then the roll pin is to be fitted to lock it into place.

Install

1. Fit a new cover gasket to the transmission case and ensure the shift levers are in the correct centre position.

2. Ensure the shift forks are aligned with the clutch sliding sleeves when installing the side cover plate.

3. Install the retaining bolts for the side cover and tighten to specification.

Side Cover retaining bolt specification: 11 - 15 lb.ft

4. Reconnect the gear shift rods.

5. Replace the transmission filler plug, refill transmission to appropriate level and lower vehicle.

PROBLEM SOLVING

PROBLEM

Transmission Noisy in Gear.

CAUSE

* Lubricate level low or wrong type.

ACTION

* Fill to bottom of filler plug hole with proper lubricant.

CAUSE

* Transmission to flywheel housing and flywheel housing to engine block bolts loose.

ACTION

* Tighten bolts to specification.

CAUSE

* Pilot bushing worn or damaged.

ACTION

* Remove transmission. If noise is howling during start-up, check pilot bushing. Check for loose flywheel and housing alignment. Service or replace as required.

CAUSE

* Improper transmission pilot engagement into flywheel housing.

ACTION

* Replace housing or input shaft bearing retainer as required.

Refer to 'Clutch'.

CAUSE

* Worn or damaged internal components.

ACTION

* Disassemble transmission. Inspect input, output and counter shaft bearings, gear and gear teeth for wear and damage. Service or replace as required.

PROBLEM

Transmission Shifts Hard.

CAUSE

* Improper clutch release.

ACTION

Refer to 'Clutch'.

CAUSE

* Internal shift mechanism binding.

ACTION

* Remove transmission and free up shift mechanism.

CAUSE

* Synchronize sleeve to hub fit.

ACTION

* Remove and check for burrs or fit.

CAUSE

* Binding condition between input shaft and crank shaft pilot bearing.

ACTION

* Check alignment and service as required.

CAUSE

* Improper Fluid.

ACTION

* Drain and refill with correct fluid to bottom of filler plug hole.

PROBLEM

Transmission Will Not Shift into One Gear - All Other Gears OK.

CAUSE

* Floor shift, interference between shift handle and console or floor cut out.

ACTION

* Adjust console or cut out floorpan to eliminate interference.

CAUSE

* Restricted travel of internal shifter components.

ACTION

* Remove transmission. Inspect shift rail and fork system, synchronized system and gear clutch teeth for restricted travel. Service and replace as required.

PROBLEM

* Transmission is Locked in One Gear. It cannot be shifted Out of that Gear.

CAUSE

* Internal Shifter components worn or damaged.

ACTION

* Remove transmission. Inspect the problem gear or gearshift rails and fork and synchronized for wear or damage. Service or replace as required.

CAUSE

* Selector arm finger broken.

ACTION

* Remove transmission. Replace selector arm assembly.

CAUSE

* Bent shifter forks at pads and selector slot.

ACTION

* Service or replace as required.

PROBLEM

Transmission Will Not Shift Into Reverse (All Others OK).

CAUSE

* Worn or damaged internal components.

ACTION

* Remove transmission. Check for damaged reverse geartrain, misaligned reverse relay lever, shift rail and fork system.

SPECIFICATIONS

TRANSMISSION

Types: - 4-Speed Manual
Lubricant: SAE90, API GL-4
Capacity: 1.9 Litres

Clearances

Thrust Clearance:	0.10 - 0.25 mm
Counter gear end float:	0.10 - 0.20 mm
Gear backlash:	0.10 - 0.20 mm

Torque Specifications

Drain Plug torque specification:			
	600kg-cm	43ft-lb	59 Nm
Filler Plug specified torque:			
	600kg-cm	43ft-lb	59 Nm
Reverse Light Switch torque:			
	55kg-cm	4.8ft-lb	5.4 Nm
Rear extension retaining bolts torque:			
	375kg-cm	27ft-lb	37 Nm
Rear Mount to Transmission bolts:			
	260kg-cm	19ft-lb	25 Nm
Rear Mount to Crossmember bolts:			
	620kg-cm	45ft-lb	61 Nm
Clutch Housing to Block bolts:			
L42	600kg-cm	43ft-lb	59 Nm
L40 & L43	730kg-cm	53ft-lb	72 Nm
Exhaust Pipe Bracket bolts:			
	380kg-cm	27ft-lb	37 Nm
Front Bearing Retainer bolts torque:			
	75kg-cm	6.5ft-lb	7.4 Nm
Side Cover retaining bolts torque:			
	kg-cm	ft-lb	Nm
Reverse Restrict Ball Holder bolts torque:			
	410kg-cm	30ft-lb	40 Nm
Starter Motor bolts torque:			
	400kg-cm	29ft-lb	31Nm

Memo

AUTOMATIC TRANSMISSION A340H

A42D, A43D, A42DL, A43DL, A44DL & A43DE 191

AUTOMATIC - A340H - TRANSMISSIONS

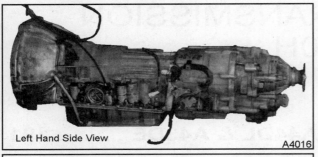

Left Hand Side View

A4016

Right Hand Side View

A4017

MAINTENANCE & ADJUSTMENT

TRANSMISSION FLUID

Note: Fluid check under "Problem Solving and Diagnosis".
1. Check fluid level.
* The vehicle must have been driven so that the engine and transmission are at normal operating temperature (fluid temperature: 70 - 80°C or 158 - 176°F).
(a) Park the vehicle on a level surface.
(b) With the engine idling, shift the selector into each gear from the "P" range to the "L" range and return to the "P" range again.
(c) Pull out the transmission dipstick and wipe it clean.
(d) Push it back fully into the filler tube.
(e) Pull it out and check that the fluid level is in the HOT range. If low, add fluid.
Fluid type specification: ATF DEXRON^R II
* Do not overfill.
2. Check Fluid Condition. If the fluid smells burnt or is black, replace it.
3. Replace Fluid.
(a) Remove the drain plug and drain the fluid.
(b) Reinstall the drain plug securely.
Drain plug specified torque: 205 kg-cm (15 ft-lb, 20 N·m)
(c) Pour ATF through the filler tube.
Specified Fluid: ATF DEXTRON^R II
(d) With the engine idling, shift the selector into each gear from the "P" range to the "L" range and return to the "P" range again.

(e) With the engine idling, check the fluid level. Add fluid up to the "COOL" level on the dipstick.
(f) Check the fluid level with the normal fluid temperature (70 - 80°C or 158 - 176°F) and add as necessary.
* Do not overfill
Drain and refill capacity:
4.5 lts (4.8 US qts, 4.0 Imp.qts)
Dry fill capacity:
10.3 lts (10.9 US qts, 9.1 Imp.qts)

ADJUSTMENT OF THROTTLE CABLE

1. Press down accelerator pedal and check that throttle valve opens fully.
Adjust the accelerator link if the throttle valve does not open fully.
2. Check and Adjust Throttle Cable.
(a) Check that the throttle cable is installed correctly and not bending.
(b) When the throttle valve is fully closed, adjust the cable so that the distance between the end of the cable housing and the cable stopper is correct.
Throttle Cable End Distance: 0.8 - 1.5 mm (0.031 - 0.059in)
If not within specification, loosen the adjusting nut and adjust by moving the adjusting cam. Then re-check the adjustment.

ADJUSTMENT OF SHIFT LINKAGE.

1. Loosen the nut on the connecting rod.
2. (a) Pull the transmission lever fully back.
(b) Move the transmission lever 2 notches to the "neutral" position.
(c) Place the shift lever at "neutral".
3. (a) Hold the lever towards "reverse" position, tighten the connecting linkage rod nut.
(b) Road test vehicle, checking gear changes.

Adjustment of Neutral Start Switch

Check that the engine does not start in any of the forward or reverse positions, if so adjust the neutral start switch.
1. Loosen the neutral start switch attaching bolt.
2. Position the shift lever into "N" or "P".
3. Adjust neutral start switch.

Switch Attaching Bolt

Neutral Start Switch

Shifter Shaft

A4019

a) Disconnect the neutral start switch wiring connector. Test the terminals of the switch with an ohmmeter.

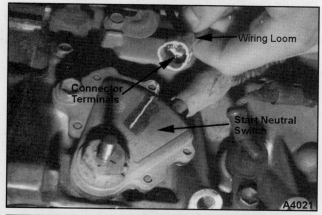

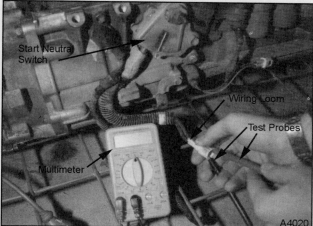

(b) Adjust the switch so that there is continuity between terminals shown. Reconnect the neutral start switch wiring loom connector.

4. Tighten neutral start switch bolt to specification.

Neutral Start Switch bolts torque:

130kg-cm (9ft-lb, 13Nm)

REPAIRS

MAINTENANCE NOTES

While maintaining the transmission, all parts should be cleaned and inspected. Individual units should be reassembled before disassembly of other units to avoid confusion and interchanging of parts.

1. Thoroughly clean the exterior before disassembly of the unit.

2. Disassembly and assembly must be made on a clean work bench. Cleanliness is of the utmost importance. The bench tools, and parts must be kept clean at all times.

3. Before installing screws into aluminium parts, dip screws into transmission fluid to prevent galling aluminium threads and to prevent screws from seizing.

4. To prevent thread stripping, always use a torque wrench when installing screws.

5. If threads in aluminium parts are stripped or damaged the part can be made serviceable by the use of suitable thread inserts.

6. Protective tools must be used when assembling seals to prevent damage. The slightest flaw in the sealing surface of the seal can cause an oil leak.

7. Aluminium castings and valve are very susceptible to nicks, burns, burrs, etc., and should be handled with care.

8. Internal snap rings should be expanded and external snap rings compressed if they are to be re-used. This will ensure proper seating when reinstalled.

9. "O" rings, gaskets and oil seals that are removed should not be re-used.

10. Teflon oil seal rings should not be removed unless damaged.

11. During assembly of each unit, all internal moving parts must be lubricated with transmission fluid.

OIL COOLER PIPES

If replacement of transmission steel tubing cooler pipes is required, only use double wrapped and brazed steel tubing meeting transmission manufacturers specifications or equivalent. Under no condition use copper or aluminium tubing to replace steel tubing. These materials do not have satisfactory fatigue durability to withstand normal car vibrations.

Steel tubing should be flared using the double flare method.

CLEAN AND INSPECT

After complete disassembly of a unit, wash all metal parts in a clean solvent and dry with compressed air. Blow oil passages out and check to make sure they are not obstructed. Small passages should be checked with tag wire. All parts should be inspected to determine which parts are to be replaced.

Pay particular attention to the following:

1. Inspect linkage and pivot points for excessive wear.

2. Bearing and thrust surfaces of all parts should be checked for excessive wear and scoring.

3. Check for broken score seal rings, damaged ring lands and damaged threads.

4. Inspect seal and `O' rings.

5. Mating surfaces of castings should be checked for burrs. Irregularities may be removed by lapping the surface with emery paper. The emery paper is laid on a flat surface, such as a piece of plate glass.

6. Castings should be checked for cracks and sand holes.

* Do not use solvents on neoprene seals, composition faced clutch plates or thrust washers as damage to parts may occur.

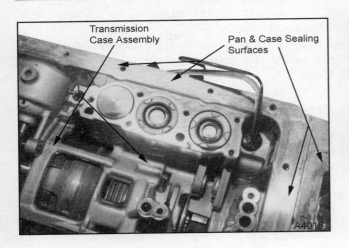

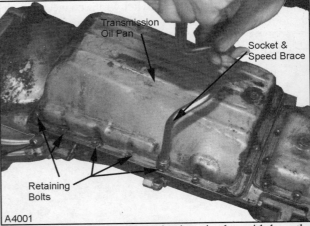

(b) The transmission may need to be raised to withdraw the oil pan from the vehicle.

5. Withdraw the eleven strainer retaining bolts, strainer and gasket from the vehicle, then repeat the process for the strainer case, five bolts.

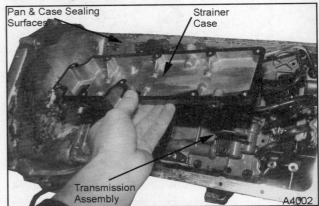

6. If solenoids are to be changed disconnect the wiring, remove the retaining bolt and withdraw the solenoid from the valve body.

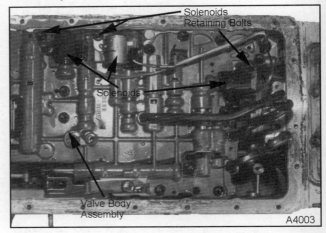

7. Lever the oil pipes at either end to release from the valve body and casing and then withdraw from the case.

8. To withdraw the valve body follow the procedure below:

(a) Release the throttle cable from the cam assembly.

Manual Shift Test

1.(a) With the solenoid wiring loom disconnected check the manual drive operation, refer to the following table for shift and gear positions.

Transmission Shift Position	Gear Position
D range	O/D
2 range	3rd
L range	1st
R range	Reverse
P range	Pawl Lock
Transfer Shift Position	Gear Position
H2 Position	high gear 2WD
H4 Position	high gear 4WD
L2 Position	high gear 4WD

(b) Ensure to shift through all positions when road testing, if any differences occure the problem is in the transmission and not electrical.

2. Join the loom again and remove the codes by detatching the negative battery terminal.

3. Road test to ensure there no codes existing in the memory still.

OIL PAN / SUMP & VALVE BODY ASSEMBLY

Remove

1. Place vehicle on safety stands.

2. Drop the front stablizer bar and front propeller shaft from the vehicle.

3. Place an oil collection tray underneath the transmission.

4.(a) Release the oil pan/sump retaining bolts, then use tool No. 09032-00100 to seperate the oil pan/sump from the casing.

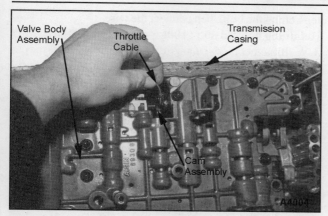

(b) Release and withdraw the retaining bolts from the valve body.

(c) Lower the valve body slightly and withdraw the C_0 accumulator piston spring.

(d) Continuing to lower the valve body withdraw the check ball assembly from the casing, then the valve body also.

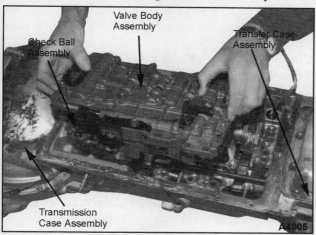

Install

1. Lift the valve body into position, fitting the check ball assembly and C_0 accumulator spring into place.

2. Ensure the manual control valve lever and manual valve are aligned.

3. Fit most of the bolts loosely to the valve body, then tension to the correct tension, also attach the throttle cable to cam

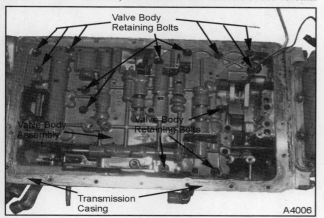

assembly.

Torque Valve Body Bolts: 100kg-cm (7ft-lb, 10Nm)

4. Fit solenoids in position, secure and tension retaining bolts, then connect the wiring loom.

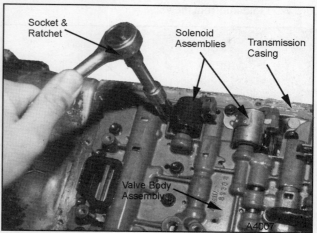

Solenoid Retaining Bolts : 100kg-cm (7ft-lb, 10Nm)

5. Fit the oil pipes to ther transmission and valve body, tap they with a rubber wallet until seated firm.

6. Fit and retain the oil strainer case to valve body, then strainer to strainer case, tighten bolts to specification.

Oil Strainer Case Bolts : 100kg-cm (7ft-lb, 10Nm)
Oil Strainer Bolts : 70kg-cm (61in-lb, 6.9Nm)

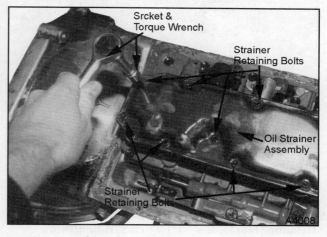

7. Place magnets in oil pan/sump and refit with a new gasket using gasket sealer, then tension the retaining bolts.

Torque Transmission Oil Sump : 75kg-cm (65in-lb, 7.4Nm)

8. Fill transmission with correct specified fluid.

9. Remove from safety stands and road test vehicle.

TRANSFER VALVE BODY
Remove

1. Drain transmission into tray, by removing the transfer drain plug from the oil pan.

2. Support and slightly lift the transmission, then release and withdraw the rear cross member from the vehicle and transmission.

3. Loosen and withdraw the oil pan retaining bolts, then using tool No. 09032-00100 seperate and withdraw the oil pan from transfer case.

4. Detatch the solenoid wire, if necessary detatch and withdraw the solenoid from the valve body.

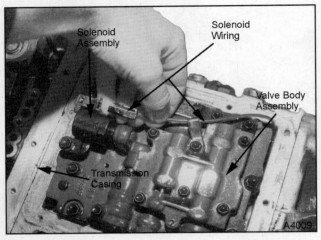

5. Loosen and withdraw the valve body retaining bolts, then lower the valve body from the transfer case.

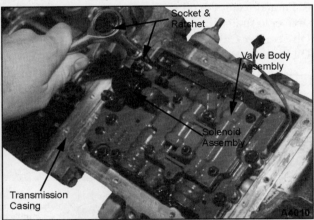

Install

1. Raise the valve body into place ensuring the manual valve lever lines up with the manual valve, then fit and tension valve body retaining bolts.

Retaining bolt tension : 100kg-cm (7ft-lb, 10Nm)

2. If the solenoid was removed, refit and secure it into place,

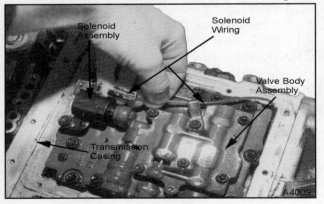

tensioning the bolt, then connect the wire.

Retaining bolt tension : 100kg-cm (7ft-lb, 10Nm)

3. With magnets and sealant fitted to the oil pan, place the pan into position on the transfer case, then refit and tension the retaining bolts.

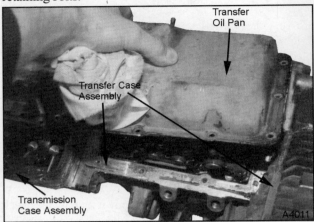

4. Fit the crossmember assembly to the transfer case and chasis tensioning the retaining bolts, also check the drain plug.

Chasis bolt tension : 970kg-cm (70ft-lb, 95Nm)
Transfer bolt tension : 130kg-cm (9ft-lb, 13Nm)
Pan drain plug : 205kg-cm (15ft-lb, 20Nm)

5. Fill the transmission and road test the vehicle.

REPLACE THROTTLE (Kickdown) CABLE:
Dismantle

1. From the linkage detatch the throttle cable, then release the clamp from the throttle cable.

2. Release the drain plug from the oil pan and drain, then drop the front stabilizer bar and tail shaft from the vehicle.

3. Loosen and withdraw pan retaining bolts, then using tool No. 09032-00100, brake the seal between the pan and case, lower pan.

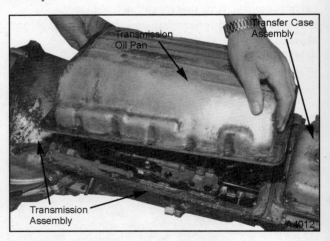

4. Detach the solenoid wire, then unclip the throttle cable from the valve body cam assembly.

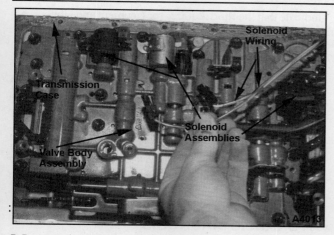

5. Loosen the throttle cable retainer bolt, then withdraw the cable assembly from the transmission case.

Assemble

1. Fit the cable assembly into place in the transmission case and retain with the securing bolt.

2. Atatch the throttle cable to the valve body cam assembly and reconnect the solenoid wire.

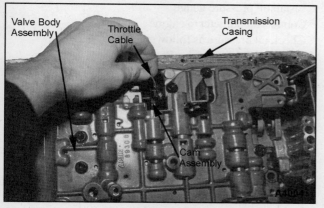

3. Replace transmission oil pan with a new gasket, tension all the pan bolt to correct torque spec's.

Torque Transmission Oil Sump: 75kg-cm (65in-lb, 7.4Nm)

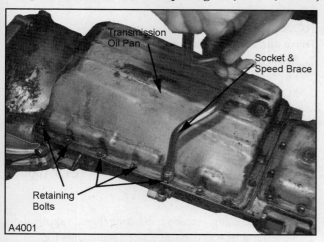

A4001

4. To fit a stopper to a new cable, follow previously described procedure.

5. Fit the front tail shaft and stabilizer bar to the vehicle, then retain the cable with the clamp and connect to the throttle linkage.

6. Fill the transmission with fluid and check the level until it is correct.

Trans fluid : ATF DEXTRON II

7. Adjust the throttle cable as previously described.

8. The vehicle will now need road testing.

PARKING LOCK PAWL

Disassemble

1. Withdraw the transfer valve body from the transmission case as previously decribed in this chapter.

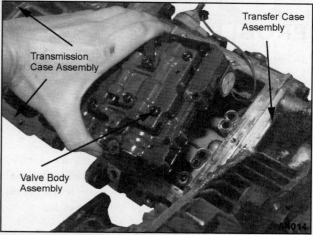

2. Release the retaining bracket bolts and withdraw the bolts and bracket, then withdraw the parking lock pawl assembly.

Assemble

1. Fit the parking lock pawl assembly into the transmission case.

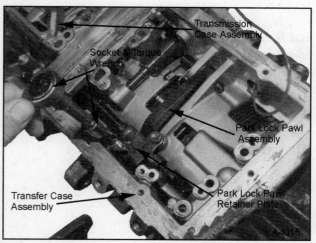

2. Fit the retaining bracket to the case, then bolts, check that the parking lock pawl works properly and tension retaining bolts.

Parking Lock Pawl Retain bolt: 70kg-cm (61in.-lb, 6.9Nm)

3. Fit the valve body as previously described in this chapter.

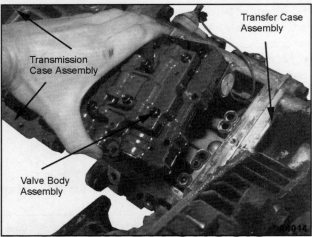

Transfer Case Assembly

Transmission Case Assembly

Valve Body Assembly

PROBLEM DIAGNOSIS

General Notes

Problems occurring with the automatic transmission can be caused by either the engine or the automatic transmission itself. These two areas should be distinctly isolated before proceeding with diagnosis.

Problem diagnosis should begin with the simplest operation, working up in order of difficulty, but initially determine whether the trouble lies within the engine or transmission. Proceed with the inspection in the following order:

PRELIMINARY CHECK:

(a) Check the fluid level.
(b) Check the throttle cable mark.
(c) Check the shift linkage.
(d) Check the neutral start switch.
(e) Check the idling speed.

IDLE SPEED

Idle speed with transmission in neutral.

50's-60's Series

3Y Engine with P.S.:	850 RPM
3Y Engine without P.S.:	750 RPM
2L Engine:	800 RPM

90's-110's Series

22R Engine:	750 RPM
2L Engine:	800 RPM

OIL PRESSURE CHECK

Fluid Check

Transmission fluid changes colour and smell very early in life, these indicators should not necessarily be relied on to diagnose either transmission internal condition nor fluid deterioration.

The chart on the next page shows that a dark brown fluid colour, coupled with a delayed shift pattern, may only indicate that the fluid requires replacement and alone, is not a definite indication of a potential transmission failure.

The fluid level should only be checked when the transmission reaches operating temperature (82-93 degrees Celsius). Transmission fluid colour when new and unused, is red. A red dye is added so that it can be distinguished from other oils and lubricants. The red dye is not an indicator of fluid quality and is not permanent. As the vehicle is driven, the transmission fluid will begin to look darker in colour. The colour will then appear light brown. A DARK brown colour with a distinctively burnt odour MAY indicate fluid deterioration and a need for the fluid to be changed.

HYDRAULIC DIAGNOSIS

Oil Pressure Check Information
Preliminary Check Procedure
* Check transmission oil level and condition
* Check and adjust Kickdown Cable
* Check outside manual linkage and correct
* Check engine tune
* Install oil pressure gauge
* Connect tachometer to engine
* Check oil pressure as follows:

Minimum Kickdown Line Pressure Check

Set the Kickdown cable to specification; and with the brakes applied, take the line pressure readings in the ranges and at the engine r.p.m.'s indicated in the chart below.

Full Kickdown Line Pressure Check

Full Kickdown line pressure readings are obtained by tying or holding the Kickdown cable to the full extent of it's travel; and with the brakes applied, take the line pressure readings in the ranges and at the engine r.p.m.'s indicated in the chart shown later.

** **NOTICE** - Total running time for this combination not to exceed 2 mins.

** **CAUTION** - Brakes must be applied at all times.

ROAD TEST
Drive and Reverse Engagement Shift Check.
1. Start engine.
2. Depress brake pedal.
3. Move gear selector:
    a. `P' (Park) to `R' (Reverse)
    b. `R' (Reverse) to `N' (Neutral) to `D' (Drive).
    c. Gear selections should be immediate and not harsh.

Upshifts and Torque Converter Clutch (TCC) Application

With gear selector in `D' :-
1. Accelerate using a steady increasing throttle application.
2. Note the shift speed point gear engagements for:
    a. 2nd gear
    b. 3rd gear

c. Overdrive

3. Note the speed shift point for the Torque Converter Clutch (TCC) application. This should occur while in 3rd gear.

IMPORTANT

The TCC will not engage if engine coolant temperature is below 45 degrees Celsius or road speed is to low.

Part Throttle Downshift

At a speed of 70-90 km/h, quickly depress the accelerator to half open position and observe:

a. TCC releases.

b. Transmission downshafts to 2nd gear immediately.

Full Throttle (Detente) Downshift

Operate the vehicle at 70-90km/h in `D', then quickly depress to wide open throttle position and observe:

a. TCC releases.

b. Transmission downshifts to 2nd gear immediately.

Manual Downshift

1. Operate the vehicle at 70-90km/h in `D' , then release the accelerator pedal (closed throttle position) and simultaneously move the gear selector to `D' (Drive), and observe:

a. TCC release occurs at zero throttle.

b. Transmission downshifts to 2nd gear immediately.

c. Engine should slow vehicle.

2. Operate the vehicle at 70-80 km/h in `D' .

Release the accelerator pedal and simultaneously move the gear selector `2' (second) gear position, and observe:

a. TCC release occurs at zero throttle.

b. Transmission downshifts to 2nd gear immediately.

c. Engine should slow vehicle.

3. Move gear selector to `D' and accelerate to 40km/h. Release the accelerator pedal (closed throttle position) and simultaneously move the gear selector to `1' (first) gear and observe:

a. Transmission downshifts to 1st gear immediately.

b. Engine should slow vehicle.

Shifting Speeds
Transfer Shift Position 'H2' or 'H4'
Throttle Valve Open Fully   [--] Closed Fully

Manual		Shift	Throttle	Km/h, MPH
D	(N)	1-2	KD	41-45, 25-28
D	(N)	2-3	KD	80-86, 50,53
D	(N)	3-O/D	KD	115-121, 71-75
[D	(N)	3-O/D	KD	34-38, 21-24]
[D	(N)	O/D-3	KD	20-24, 12-15]
D	(N)	O/D-3	KD	110-116, 68-72
D	(N)	3-2	KD	72-76, 45-47
D	(N)	2-1	KD	38-41, 24-25
Range		Shift	Throttle	Km/h, MPH
D	(P)	1-2	KD	45-49, 28-30
D	(P)	2-3	KD	88-95, 55-59
D	(P)	3-O/D	KD	137-143, 85-89
[D	(P)	3-O/D	KD	48-51, 30-32]
[D	(P)	O/D-3	KD	20-24, 12-15]

D	(P)	O/D-3	KD	132-138, 82-86
D	(P)	3-2	KD	81-88, 50-55
D	(P)	2-1	KD	40-41, 25-25
Range		Shift	Throttle	Km/h, MPH
2	(N, P)	1-2	KD	41-45, 25-28
2	(N, P)	2-3	KD	99-105, 62-65
2	(N, P)	3-O/D	KD	----------------
2	(N, P)	O/D-3	KD	----------------
2	(N, P)	3-2	KD	93-99, 58-62
2	(N, P)	2-1	KD	38-41, 24-25
Range		Shift	Throttle	Km/h, MPH
L	(N, P)	1-2	KD	----------------
L	(N, P)	2-3	KD	----------------
L	(N, P)	O/D-3	KD	----------------
L	(N, P)	O/D-3	KD	---------------
L	(N, P)	3-2	KD	79-86, 49-53
L	(N, P)	2-1	KD	45-49, 28-30

Transfer Shift Position 'H2' or 'H4'
Throttle Valve Open   5%

Range		Shift	Lock-up	Km/h, MPH
D	(N)	O/D	ON	53-57, 33-35
D	(N)	O/D	OFF	50-54, 31-34
D	(P)	O/D	ON	64-68, 40-42
D	(P)	O/D	OFF	59-62, 37-39

Line Pressure Charts
Line Pressure   kg/cm² (kPa, PSI)

Gear	Idle
D	3.7-4.2 (53-61, 363-422)
Rev	5.1-6.1 (73-87, 500-598)
Gear	Stall
D	9.3-11.8 (1321-168, 912-1,157)
Rev	13.0-16.5 (185-235, 1,275-1,618)

SPECIFICATIONS

Fluid type specification: ATF DEXRON[R] II

Drain and refill capacity:

4.5 lts (4.8 US qts, 4.0 Imp.qts)

Dry fill capacity:

10.3 lts (10.9 US qts, 9.1 Imp.qts)

Throttle Cable End Distance:0.8 - 1.5 mm (0.031 - 0.059in)

TORQUE SPECIFICATIONS

Drain plug: 205 kg-cm (15 ft-lb,20 N·m)

Neutral Start Switch bolts:130kg-cm (9ft-lb, 13Nm)

Torque Valve Body Bolts: 100kg-cm (7ft-lb, 10Nm)

Solenoid Retaining Bolts : 100kg-cm (7ft-lb, 10Nm)

Oil Strainer Case Bolts : 100kg-cm (7ft-lb, 10Nm)

Oil Strainer Bolts : 70kg-cm (61in-lb, 6.9Nm)

Torque Transmission Oil Sump : 75kg-cm (65in-lb, 7.4Nm)

Chasis bolt tension : 970kg-cm (70ft-lb, 95Nm)

Transfer bolt tension : 130kg-cm (9ft-lb, 13Nm)

Parking Lock Pawl Retaining bolt:70kg-cm(61in.-lb,6.9Nm)

SOLENOID OPERATION

Solenoid Operation and Gear Position Malfunction Referance Chart

Operation Normal

D range No. 1	No. 2	Gear	2 range No. 1	No. 2	Gear	L range No. 1	No. 2	Gear
ON	OFF	1st	ON	OFF	1st	ON	OFF	1st
ON	ON	2nd	ON	ON	2nd	ON	ON	2nd
OFF	ON	3rd	OFF	ON	3rd	-----	-----	-----
OFF	OFF	O/D	-----	-----	-----	-----	-----	-----

Solenoid No. 1 F ailty   (Solenoid not working ***)

D range No. 1	No. 2	Gear	2 range No. 1	No. 2	Gear	L range No. 1	No. 2	Gear
***	ON	3rd	***	ON	3rd	***	OFF	1st
***	ON	3rd	***	ON	3rd	***	ON	2nd
***	ON	3rd	***	ON	3rd	-----	-----	-----
***	OFF	O/D	-----	-----	-----	-----	-----	-----

Solenoid No. 2 Failty   (Solenoid not working ***)

D range No. 1	No. 2	Gear	2 range No. 1	No. 2	Gear	L range No. 1	No. 2	Gear
ON	***	1st	ON	***	1st	ON	***	1st
OFF	***	O/D	OFF	***	3rd	ON	***	1st
OFF	***	O/D	OFF	***	3rd	-----	-----	-----
OFF	***	O/D	-----	-----	-----	-----	-----	-----

Solenoid Both Failty   (Solenoid not working ***)

D range No. 1	No. 2	Gear	2 range No. 1	No. 2	Gear	L range No. 1	No. 2	Gear
***	***	O/D	***	***	3rd	***	***	1st
***	***	O/D	***	***	3rd	***	***	1st
***	***	O/D	***	***	3rd	-----	-----	-----
***	***	O/D	-----	-----	-----	-----	-----	-----

Transmission Operation Chart

Range	Gear	S No.1	S No.2	C_0	C_1	C_2	B_0	B_1	B_2	B_3(IP)	B_3(OP)	F_0	F_1	F_2
P	Parking	ON	OFF	*	-	-	-	-	-	-	-	-	-	-
R	Reverce	ON	OFF	*	-	*	-	-	-	*	*	*	-	-
N	Neutral	ON	OFF	*	-	-	-	-	-	-	-	-	-	-
D	1st	ON	OFF	*	*	-	-	-	-	-	-	*	-	*
D	2nd	ON	ON	*	*	-	-	-	*	-	-	*	*	-
D	3rd	OFF	ON	*	*	*	-	-	*	-	-	*	-	-
D	O/D	OFF	OFF	-	*	*	*	-	*	-	-	-	-	-
2	1st	ON	OFF	*	*	-	-	-	-	-	-	*	-	*
2	2nd	ON	ON	*	*	-	-	*	*	-	-	*	*	-
2	3rd	OFF	ON	*	*	*	-	-	*	-	-	*	-	-
L	1st	ON	OFF	*	*	-	-	-	-	*	*	*	-	*
L	2nd*	ON	ON	*	*	-	-	*	*	-	-	*	*	-

* Down shift only no up shift   (IP) Inner piston   (OP) Outer Piston

Transfer Operation Chart

Gear Position	Solenoid No. 4	C_3	C_4	B_4
H2	OFF	*	-	-
H4	OFF	*	*	-
L4	ON	-	*	*

AUTOMATIC TRANSMISSIONS

A42D, A43D, A42DL, A43DL, A44DL & A43DE

AUTOMATIC - A42D, A43D, A42DL, A43DL, A44DL, A43DE - TRANSMISSIONS

MAINTENANCE & ADJUSTMENT

Transmission Fluid

Note: Fluid check under "Problem Solving and Diagnosis".
1. Check fluid level.
* The vehicle must have been driven so that the engine and transmission are at normal operating temperature (fluid temperature: 50 - 80°C or 122 - 176°F).
(a) Park the vehicle on a level surface.
(b) With the engine idling, shift the selector into each gear from the "P" range to the "L" range and return to the "P" range again.
(c) Pull out the transmission dipstick and wipe it clean.
(d) Push it back fully into the filler tube.
(e) Pull it out and check that the fluid level is in the HOT range. If low, add fluid.
Fluid type specification: ATF DEXRON^R II
* Do not overfill.
2. Check Fluid Condition. If the fluid smells burnt or is black, replace it.
3. Replace Fluid.
(a) Remove the drain plug and drain the fluid.
(b) Reinstall the drain plug securely.
Drain plug specified torque: 205 kg-cm (15 ft-lb, 20 N·m)
(c) Pour ATF through the filler tube.
Specified Fluid: ATF DEXTRON^R II
(d) With the engine idling, shift the selector into each gear from the "P" range to the "L" range and return to the "P" range again.
(e) With the engine idling, check the fluid level. Add fluid up to the "COOL" level on the dipstick.
(f) Check the fluid level with the normal fluid temperature (50 - 80°C or 122 - 176°F) and add as necessary.
* Do not overfill
Drain and refill capacity:
2.4 lts (2.5 US qts, 2.1 Imp.qts)
Dry fill capacity:
6.5 lts (6.9 US qts, 5.7 Imp.qts)

Adjustment of Throttle Cable

1. Press down accelerator pedal and check that throttle valve opens fully.
* 50's & 60's series remove air cleaner
Adjust the accelerator link if the throttle valve does not open fully.

2. Check and Adjust Throttle Cable.
(a) Check that the throttle cable is installed correctly and not bending.
(b) When the throttle valve is fully closed, adjust the cable so that the distance between the end of the cable housing and the cable stopper is correct.
Throttle Cable Housing End Clearance Distance:
0 - 1.0 mm (0 - 0.04 in) 50's and 60's models
0.8 - 1.5 mm (0.031 - 0.059in) 80's to 130's models
If not within specification, loosen the adjusting nut and adjust by moving the adjusting cam. Then re-check the adjustment.

Adjustment of Shift Linkage

Adjust Floor Shift Linkage.
1. Loosen the nut on the connecting rod.
2. (a) Pull the transmission lever fully back.
(b) Move the transmission lever 2 notches to the "neutral" position.
(c) Place the shift lever at "neutral".
3. (a) Hold the lever towards "reverse" position, tighten the connecting linkage rod nut.
(b) Road test vehicle, checking gear changes.

Adjustment of Neutral Start Switch

Check that the engine does not start in any of the forward or reverse positions, if so adjust the neutral start switch.
1. Loosen the neutral start switch attaching bolt.
2. Position the shift lever into "N" or "P".
3. Adjust neutral start switch.
(a) Disconnect the neutral start switch wiring connector. Test the terminals of the switch with an ohmmeter.
(b) Adjust the switch so that there is continuity between terminals shown. Reconnect the neutral start switch wiring loom connector.
4. Tighten neutral start switch bolt to specification.
Neutral Start Switch bolts torque:

55kg-cm (48in-lb, 5.4Nm)

MINOR REPAIRS

MAINTENANCE NOTES

While maintaining the transmission, all parts should be cleaned and inspected. Individual units should be reassembled before disassembly of other units to avoid confusion and interchanging of parts.
1. Thoroughly clean the exterior before disassembly of the unit.
2. Disassembly and assembly must be made on a clean work bench. Cleanliness is of the utmost importance. The bench tools, and parts must be kept clean at all times.
3. Before installing screws into aluminium parts, dip screws into transmission fluid to prevent galling aluminium threads

192

and to prevent screws from seizing.

4. To prevent thread stripping, always use a torque wrench when installing screws.

5. If threads in aluminium parts are stripped or damaged the part can be made serviceable by the use of suitable thread inserts.

6. Protective tools must be used when assembling seals to prevent damage. The slightest flaw in the sealing surface of the seal can cause an oil leak.

7. Aluminium castings and valve are very susceptible to nicks, burns, burrs, etc., and should be handled with care.

8. Internal snap rings should be expanded and external snap rings compressed if they are to be re-used. This will ensure proper seating when reinstalled.

9. "O" rings, gaskets and oil seals that are removed should not be re-used.

10. Teflon oil seal rings should not be removed unless damaged.

11. During assembly of each unit, all internal moving parts must be lubricated with transmission fluid.

OIL COOLER PIPES

If replacement of transmission steel tubing cooler pipes is required, only use double wrapped and brazed steel tubing meeting transmission manufacturers specifications or equivalent. Under no condition use copper or aluminium tubing to replace steel tubing. These materials do not have satisfactory fatigue durability to withstand normal car vibrations. Steel tubing should be flared using the double flare method.

CLEAN AND INSPECT

After complete disassembly of a unit, wash all metal parts in a clean solvent and dry with compressed air. Blow oil passages out and check to make sure they are not obstructed. Small passages should be checked with tag wire. All parts should be inspected to determine which parts are to be replaced.

Pay particular attention to the following:

1. Inspect linkage and pivot points for excessive wear.

2. Bearing and thrust surfaces of all parts should be checked for excessive wear and scoring.

3. Check for broken score seal rings, damaged ring lands and damaged threads.

4. Inspect seal and `O' rings.

5. Mating surfaces of castings should be checked for burrs. Irregularities may be removed by lapping the surface with emery paper. The emery paper is laid on a flat surface, such as a piece of plate glass.

6. Castings should be checked for cracks and sand holes.

* Do not use solvents on neoprene seals, composition faced clutch plates or thrust washers as damage to parts may occur.

OIL PAN / SUMP & VALVE BODY ASSEMBLY

Remove

1. Place vehicle on safety stands.

2. Place an oil collection tray underneath the transmission.

3. Remove the oil pan/sump and gasket.

4. Remove the two fluid pipes (taking care because they will contain trans fluid), four pipes for A43DE transmission. These pipes are pushed into the valve body and servo's, it may be

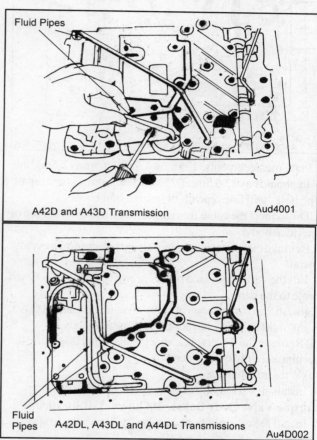

A42D and A43D Transmission   Aud4001

A42DL, A43DL and A44DL Transmissions   Au4D002

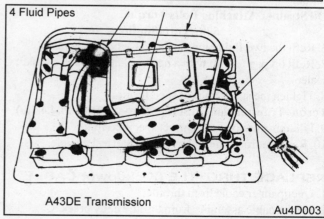

A43DE Transmission   Au4D003

necessary to prise them out with a screw driver.

* Do not damage the pipes.

5. Remove the oil strainer and gasket, five bolts.

6. Remove 17 bolts (15 bolts A43DE) of the valve body, securing the valve body assembly slide in a plate as described below, this will keep the accumulator in position while the valve body is removed.

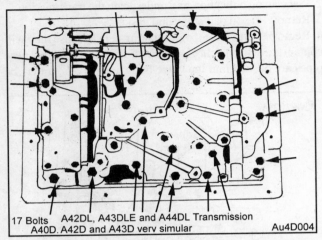

17 Bolts   A42DL, A43DLE and A44DL Transmission
A40D. A42D and A43D verv simular   Au4D004

* Plate measurements: 115mm(4.5in) x 65mm(2.5in), this plate should have 2 6.5mm(.25in) holes 68mm(2.68in) apart. The holes will line up with two sump bolt holes.

7. Disconnect the cable from the downshift cam at the top of the valve body.

8. Remove the valve body assembly by pulling down evenly.

Install

1. Lift the valve body into position, engaging the kick down cable to the cam.

2. Install the manual control valve lever to the manual valve.

3. Fit most of the bolts loosely to the valve body.

(a) Remove the 2 bolts attaching the plate that is holding the accumulator piston in place.

(b) Withdraw the plate.

4. Install all valve body bolts to specification.

Torque Valve Body Bolts: 100kg-cm (7ft-lb, 10Nm)

5. Install the oil strainer and gasket, tighten bolts to specification.

Oil Strainer Attaching Bolts Torque:

55kg-cm (48in-lb,5.4Nm)

6. Refit the two fluid pipes to the valve body assembly.

7. Refit oil pan / sump with a new gasket do not use gasket sealer.

8. Tighten the sump bolts to specification.

Torque Transmission Oil Sump: 45kg-cm (39in-lb, 4.4Nm)

9. Fill transmission with correct specified fluid.

10. Remove from safety stands and road test vehicle.

REPLACE THROTTLE (Kickdown) CABLE:

1. Unclip inner cable from throttle.

2. Unclip cable assembly from throttle body bracket.

3. Place an oil collection tray under the transmission and remove the oil pan (sump) from bottom of transmission.

4. Remove valve body as previously described.

5. Disconnect the downshift inner cable from the downshift

valve cam.

6. Remove the outer cable from transmission, push out with a socket or similar.

 Unclip and remove outer cable from the transmission.

7. Install outer cable and fit to transmission, push in fit.

8. Connect the inner cable to the downshift valve cam.

9. Install valve body as previously described.

Torque Valve Body Bolts: 100kg-cm (7ft-lb, 10Nm)

Oil Strainer Attaching Bolts Torque:

55kg-cm (48in-lb,5.4Nm)

10. Replace transmission oil pan with a new gasket and fill transmission with fluid.

Torque Transmission Oil Sump: 45kg-cm (39in-lb, 4.4Nm)

9. Reconnect the downshift cable to the throttle linkage.

10. Ensure cable is routed correctly. Reset cable as described above.

SPEEDOMETER GEAR UNIT

Remove

1. Raise rear of vehicle and place on safety stands. Place drip tray beneath speedo gear.

2. Remove the snap ring retaining the speedometer drive gear.

3. Withdraw fitting assembly including driven gear from case extension.

4. Remove the oil seal with a thin blade or small screw driver.

Install

1. Inspect fitting assembly `O' ring oil seal and replace it if unsatisfactory.

2. Install the assembly including driven gear into case, fit the snap ring.

3. Lower vehicle test run vehicle.

GOVERNOR

Remove

1. Raise rear of vehicle and place on safety stands.

2. Remove the speedo drive gear, as above.

3. Remove the snap clip attaching the governor.

4. Prise away the lock plate tag from the bolt on the side of the governor.

5. Remove the bolt and lock plate.

6. Remove the governor.

Install

1. Install the governor on the shaft.

2. Install the bolt and lock plate, bend over lock plate.

3. Replace the snap clip attaching the governor.

4. Replace the speedo drive gear, as above.

5. Lower vehicle test run vehicle.

REMOVE & INSTALL TRANSMISSION

Remove

1. Disconnect the earth cable from the battery, disconnect the downshift cable from the throttle linkage.

2. Remove the upper starter motor attaching bolt.

3. Place vehicle on safety stands.

4. Place drip tray beneath rear of transmission.

5. Drain the fluid from transmission, retighten the sump drain plug.

6. Remove the tail shaft and install a plug or seal into the extension housing to stop oil from leaking out.

7. Remove the shifter linkage to the transmission.

8. Remove the 4 converter cover attaching bolts at the lower side of the converter housing, remove the cover.

9. Disconnect the speedo drive cable.

10. Remove the exhaust clamp and filler tube and oil cooler tubes.

11. Disconnect the change linkage rod.

12. Remove the neutral start switch wiring connector.

13. Remove the starter motor.

14. Raise the transmission slightly.

(a) Remove transmission housing rear mounting to crossmember bolts.

(b) Support engine sump with a block of wood between the crossmember and engine sump.

15. Prise out the hole covers at the rear of the engine, this will allow access to the 6 converter bolts.

16. Remove the bolts attaching the converter to the flywheel it may be an advantage to insert guide pins as each converter bolt is removed.

17. Remove the support brackets at either side of the transmission.

18. Remove the bolts attaching the converter housing to the engine.

19. With the jack underneath the transmission secure the transmission to the jack if possible.

20. Lever back and lower the transmission and converter assembly and remove from the car with care.

Install

1. Fill converter with specified fluid if the converter has been drained.

Converter Fluid spec: **Automatic Trans Dexron 11**
Converter Fluid Capacity:
2.0 litres (2.1US qts, 1.8Imp qts)

2. Install the converter to the transmission, check that runout is within specification.

Converter Runout specification: 0.30mm (0.0118in)

3. (a) Place the transmission on a mobile jack and secure the transmission.

(b) Measure converter to bell housing clearance.

50's - 60's series: **20mm (0.79in)**
80's - 13's series:
R engine 22.4mm (0.882in)
L engine 29.4mm (1.157in)

3. Move the transmission under the car, lift and slide forward the transmission up to the rear of the engine. Install the bolts attaching the converter housing to the engine, torque to specification. Remove the wooden block between the engine sump and engine crossmember.

Converter housing to Engine attaching bolts:
650kg-cm (47ft-lb,64Nm)

4. Install the crossmember and rear mounting, lower transmission and torque mounting bolts to specification.

Rear Engine mounting attaching bolts:
425kg-cm(31ft-lb, 42Nm)
Transmission Mounting bolts;
250kg-cm(18ft-lb, 25Nm)

5. Fit the 6 flywheel to converter bolts and torque to specification.

Flywheel to Converter bolts: 185kg-cm(13ft-lb, 18Nm)

6. Replace the support brackets at either side of the transmission.

Supporting Bracket Attaching bolts:
380kg-cm(27ft-lb, 37Nm)

7. Remove the mobile jack.

8. Fit the converter housing cover and torque to specification.

Converter housing cover bolts:
185kg-cm(13ft-lb, 18Nm)

9. Connect the fluid cooler tubes to specification, fit the filler tube and exhaust bracket.

Fluid Cooler Tubes spec: 350kg-cm(25ft-lb, 34Nm)

10. Install the neutral start wiring connector.

11. Connect the change linkage rod to the transmission manual control lever.

12. Install speedo drive gear cable to the transmission.

13. Install the starter motor and torque bolts to specification.

Starter Motor bolts: 16-20Nm

14. Install the tail shaft, torque bolts to specification.

Tail shaft bolts (universal joint / pinion flange):
750kg-cm(54ft-lb, 74Nm)
Tail shaft centre bearing mounting bolts:
370kg-cm(27ft-lb, 36Nm)

15. Remove vehicle from safety stands.

16. Fill transmission with correct amount of specified automatic transmission fluid.

Dry fill capacity:
6.5 lts (6.9 US qts, 5.7 Imp.qts)

17. Install and adjust kickdown cable.

18. Adjust gear selector linkages.

19. Reconnect the earth cable to the battery.

20. Road test vehicle.

MAJOR REBUILD

Transmission Disassemble

1. Remove transmission assembly form the vehicle as previously described in this chapter.

2. Remove the following components from the transmission assembly.

- Shift handle

- Throttle cable & wiring loom clamp
- Neutral safety switch
- Solenoid & kick down switch
- Speedo output gear
- (A43DE) Speed sensor

3. Withdraw oil pump retaining bolts, then using special tool to pull pump from the housing and lift clear of the casing, being careful of pump rear bearings.

Tool No. 09610-20012

Race & Bearings = A43D, A42DL, A43DL, A44DL, A43DE

Race = A40D, A42D

4. Loosen & remove extension housing retaining bolts, then withdraw the extension housing.

5. Undo torque converter housing bolts and withdraw the housing from the transmission assembly.

6. Release the speedo drive gear from the output shaft.

7.(a) Loosen the governor body locking bolt & remove, then leaver the retaining clip to allow the governor to be removed from the output shaft, the filter can then be released & removed.

Models - A40D, A42D, A43D, A42DL, A43DL, A44DL

(b) Snap ring can be released from the output shaft, then the sensor rotor is able to be leavered fron the output shaft.

Model - A43DE

8. Withdraw all oil pan retaining bolts, then lift transmission from the oil pan turning the assembly upside down onto a clean work bench.

9. Using a screwdriver leaver both ends of the fluid tubes from the transmission, take note of the positioning of the, refer to the different diagrams for transmission types following.

A40D Transmission

A42D, A43D Transmissions

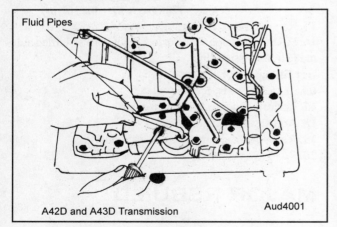

A42D and A43D Transmission   Aud4001

A42DL, A43DL, A44DL Transmissions

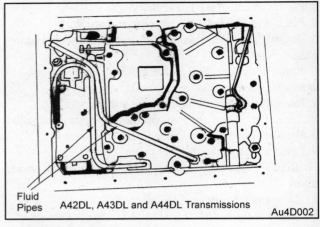

Fluid Pipes   A42DL, A43DL and A44DL Transmissions   Au4D002

A43DE Transmission

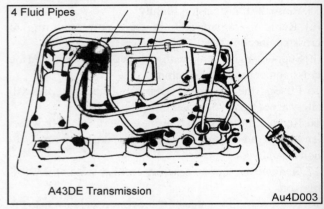

4 Fluid Pipes

A43DE Transmission   Au4D003

10. Disconnect the wiring loom from the solenoids.

A43DE Transmission

11. Withdraw the oil filter from the valve body.

12. Loosen the valve body retaining bolts, the lift the valve body, then disconnect the throttle cable from the valve body & place the valve body to one side.

The valve body retaining bolt locations for the different model transmissions is shown in the following diagrams.

A40D Transmission, A42D, A43D Transmissions, A42DL, A43DL, A44DL Transmissions all simular

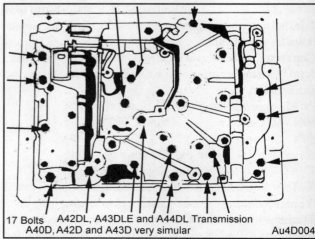

17 Bolts   A42DL, A43DLE and A44DL Transmission
A40D, A42D and A43D very simular   Au4D004

196

A43DE Transmission 15 Bolts.

13. Release throttle cable plastic retainer clips and withdraw the throttle cable assembly.

14. The parking lock rod is able to be removed from the casing, then the park pawl assembly is able to be withdrawn from the casing.

15. To dismantle the cross shaft & manual lever, lever collar across from the roll pin then drive it from the shaft with pin punch and hammer, the shaft and manual lever can then be withdrawn from the casing.

16. Apply compressed air (14psi) to the ports shown in the diagram, this will push the accumulator pistons from the case, then place pistons and springs in order on clean work bench.

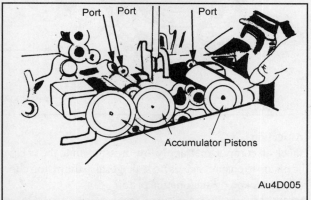

Au4D005

17.(a) Place transmission on a stand with the front pointing up, then check the casing to clutch drum clearance using special tool and record.

Tool No. 09350-20013

(b) The overdrive clutch assembly can be lifted from the housing, then the overdrive case assembly can be lifted clear as well, placing both sections on a clean work bench.

18. Case flange to front drum gap can also be recorded, follow the same procedure as in the previous step part A.

19. Withdrawing the front clutch, being careful of the bearings and races, located either side of the assembly.

20. Lift the rear clutch assembly from the transmission casing, then the retaining bolts for the centre support can be unscrewed from the casing, to enable the centre support and sun gear to be lifted from the casing.

21.(a) With screwdrive unclip and withdraw the retaining ring for the reaction plate, then holding the intermediate shaft raise the rear assembly from the transmission case

(b) The rear bearing, races and brake apply tube may need to be withdrawn from the casing if not removed with the rear assembly.

Transmission Sub-assemblies
Disassemble & Assemble

Transmission Case & Rear Brake Piston
Disassemble

1.(a) Use the special tool to compress the assembly and allow

the retaining circlip to be removed, once withdrawn from the case, loosen the compressing tool slowly to ensure that the return springs don't jump out of there position.

(b) When fully released the spring retainer and springs are then able to be withdrawn from the case.

2.(a) Grasp the outer piston using pointy nose pliers and withdraw it from the case, then the reaction sleeve can be hooked from underneath and removed.

(b) The inner piston is now able to be withdrawn using the same procedure, then carefully pry the 'O' rings from the components.

Inspection

Check the case for damaged threads, wear , and other inporfections. Change the manual shift seal by prying out with a screwdriver and installing the new one using tool No. 09350-20013.

Assembly

1.(a) With the new 'O' ring seals fitted fit the outer piston to the reaction sleeve, then the inner piston, ensure they are firmly fitted together.

(b) The piston and reaction sleeve assembly can then be positioned into the case being careful not to damage the seals.

2. With the special tool base in position place the return springs into position with the retainer on top, compress the assembly with the tool until the retaining clip is able to be fitted in place, then release the assembly.

Governor Body
Disassemble

1. With finger inside the output shaft journal and on top of the weight push together to reduce the spring pressure to enable the E-ring to be removed,

2. Lift the weight from the governor valve shaft then drop the rest of the valve assembly out through the governor body journal. Disconnect the retaining clip from the governor body.

Inspection

Check all components for any signs of damage or wear, also insure that the springs have not been broken or damaged. The lock plate will need to be replaced upon assembly.

Assembly

1. Fit the retaining clip to the governor body, then assemble the shaft, secondary weight and springs.

2. Drop the governor valve into the governor body through the journal, then the shaft assembly can be fitted in the same way. Place the weight over the shaft appling pressure to enable the E-clip to be fitted to the shaft.

Oil Pump
Disassemble

1. Carefully remove the sealing rings from the pump cover, then place the pump assembly onto the torque convertor to provide a stable working platform.

2. Undo and withdraw the pump cover retaining bolts, then lift the covver from the pump. Lift the 'O' ring from the pump aseembly and disguard.

3. Ensure that the pump gears are able to be identified as the top and bottom for assembly purposes, then lift the pump from the torque convertor and lift the pump gears from the housing.

Inspection

The components must be checked for wear and damage as well as checking the clearances.

Gear side clearance.

With streight edge placed across the pump the clearance between it and the gears is able to be checked using feeler gauges.

Standard side clearance = 0.02 - 0.05 mm

Maximumside clearance = 0.1mm

Driven gear to body clearance.

The feeler gauges are fitted between the body and driven gear with the gears moved hard to the oppisite side of the housing.

Standard body clearance = 0.07 - 0.15mm

Maximum body clearance = 0.3mm

Gear teeth tip clearance.

The clearance is measured between the gear teeth tips and the half moon shape of the pump body.

Standard tip clearance = 0.11 - 0.14mm

Maximum tip clearance = 0.3mm

The pump cover front seal will need to be inspected and it is advisable to replace it, be prying it out with a screw driver and installing it using tool No. 09350-20013

Assembly

1. With the gears in the upward position, place them into the pump housing, then the housing is able to be placed onto the torque converter.

2.(a) The pump cover is able to be fitted onto the housing lightly, then tool No. 09350-20013 is fitted to align the housing and cover.

(b) All cover retaining bolts are to be tensioned to 7.5Nm (65in.-lb, 75 kg-cm), once all tensions are reached the aligning tool is able to be withdrawn from the assembly.

3. Seals and 'O' ring can be fitted to the pump assembly, then check the gear rotation is able to be inspected for smooth operation.

Front Clutch

Disassemble

1. Races and thrust bearings are able to be withdrawn from the assembly, place on clean work bench in order to ensure correct installation on assembly.

2. Release the snap ring from the drum, then the front and rear drums can be withdrawn, the extension housing is able to be use as a work stand if needed.

3. Clutch plate or discs, races and thrust bearings can be withdrawn from the assembly, then a thinner snap ring and the plates and discs retained underneith.

4. Fit the tool No. 09350-20013 and apply pressure to the piston return spring, until snap ring is able to be removed using a screw driver. Release the pressure and remove the tool.

5. Withdraw the spring retainer and return springs, then the front clutch and over drive case will need placing together to allow the piston to be pushed out using compress air or pliers, also remove pistons 'O' ring seal.

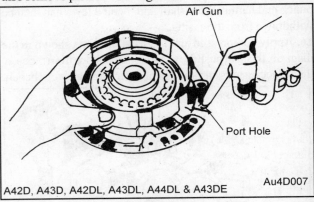

A42D, A43D, A42DL, A43DL, A44DL & A43DE   Au4D007

Inspection

Check all components, apply low pressure air to the valve in the piston to ensure there is no leakage, also the piston check ball is checked by shaking the piston.

Assembly

1. With new 'O' ring seal fitted to the piston it can the be fitted into the clutch drum, spring seat side up, then fit the return springs and retainer.

2. Fit tool No. 09350-20013 to compress the springs, and fit the snap ring to retain the assembly.

3. With low pressure blow trans fluid from discs and plates, then place discs and plates in assembly leaving thin snap ring out at this stage, assembly fitted to over drive case.

Three Discs - plate, disc, plate, disc, plate, disc, plate.

Four Discs - Plate, disc, plate, disc, plate, disc, plate, disc.

4. Fit rear clutch hub and snap ring then using dial gauge on clutch pack apply compressed air into overdrive case and read the pack movement reading.

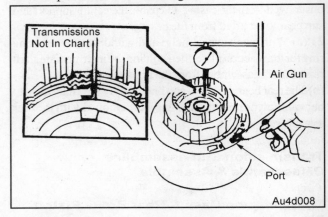

Au4d008

Standard Piston Stroke:

Disc No.	Stroke mm	Comments
3	1.18-2.34	
4	1.32-2.66	
4	1.40-2.48	A43DE(MA)
5	1.43-2.93	
5	1.40-2.48	A43DE(MS,MX)

5. Withdraw the snap ring, rear clutch hub and plate or disc, then fit the thin snap, disc or plate, races and thrust bearing.

6. Fit the front clutch hub into the assembly until located in the disc teeth, then fit the rear hub and snap ring, the remaining races and thrust bearings are to be fitted on assembly.

Center Support
Disassemble

1. Using circlip pliers withdraw the snap ring off the sun gear shaft, then withdraw the shaft from the center support and place to one side.

2. To withdraw the clutch pack from the front of the center support release the snap ring and lift out of the assembly, placing on bench in order for easy assembly.

3. With tool No. 09350-20013 installed and pressure applied release the return spring retainer snap ring, then withdraw the tool, spring retainer and springs from the assembly.

4. Applying low air pressure to the center support oil hole, pop the No 1 brake piston from the assembly, pointy nose pliers may be needed also if piston will not move, then carefully detatch inner and outer 'O' ring oil seals.

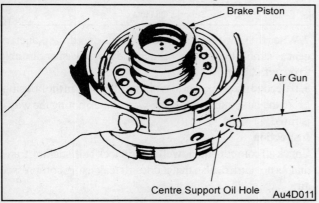

Brake Piston

Air Gun

Centre Support Oil Hole   Au4D011

5. With the assembly fliped over withdraw the clutch pack from the rear of the center support release the snap ring and lift out of the assembly, placing on bench in order for easy assembly.

6. With tool No. 09350-20013 installed and pressure applied release the return spring retainer snap ring, then withdraw the tool, spring retainer and springs from the assembly.

Twelve Springs - A42D, A43D (YH), A42DL, A44DL (LH).

Twenty Springs - A43D, A42DL (GX71), A43DL, A44DL (YH), A43DE.

7. Applying low air pressure to the center support oil hole, pop the No 2 brake piston from the assembly, pointy nose

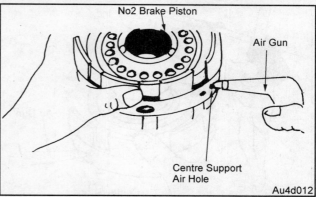

No2 Brake Piston

Air Gun

Centre Support Air Hole   Au4d012

pliers may be needed also if piston will not move, then carefully detatch inner and outer 'O' ring oil seals.

8. Withdraw the one-way clutch from the sun gear shaft.

9. Withdraw the oil seal, two from the planetary sun gear shaft and three from the center support assembly.

Inspection

Check all components for signs of damage, wear, etc. If fitting new discs they will need to be soaked for at two hour in trans fluid before assembly, old discs will need to be kept moist.

1. Check the one way clutch, clockwise it should turn freely, in the antyclockwise direction it should lock.

2. To replace the one-way clutch remove the retainer from one side by bending back the tabs and levering it off with a screw driver.

3. Withdraw the clutch assembly, then fit the new clutch assembly.

4. Fit the retainer back onto the assembly, bending the tabs back into position.

Assembly

1. Fit seals that were removed in step 9 of disassembly procedure, then fit the one-way clutch assembly over the sun gear shaft into position.

2. With new 'O' ring seal fitted to the No 1 brake piston, carefully slide the piston into the assembly, not damaging the seal, then place the twelve return springs and retainer plate into position.

3. Fit tool No. 09350-20013, applying pressure until return spring retaining snap ring can be fitted, then remove the tool and repeat the procedure for the No 2 brake piston.

No 2 brake piston return springs :

Twelve Springs - A42D, A43D (YH), A42DL, A44DL (LH).

Twenty Springs - A43D, A42DL (GX71), A43DL, A44DL (YH),   A43DE.

4. Fit the No 1 brake piston clutch pack into position

Clutch Pack Order :

  One Disc = plate, disc, flange.

  Two Discs = plate, disc, plate, disc, flange.

5. Fit the snap ring into place in the center support, then with dial indicator on clutch pack, apply low air pressure to the oil hole to get reading of piston stroke.

Standard Stroke :

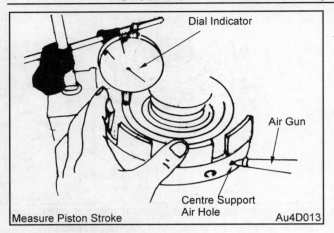

Measure Piston Stroke | Au4D013

Disc No	Stroke mm
1	0.58-1.30mm
2	0.80-1.73mm

6. Flip the assembly over and fit the No 2 brake piston clutch pack into position

Clutch Pack Order :

Two Discs = plate, disc, plate, disc, flange.

Three Discs = plate, disc, plate, disc, plate, disc, flange.

7. Fit the snap ring into place in the center support, then with dial indicator on clutch pack, apply low air pressure to the oil hole to get reading of piston stroke.

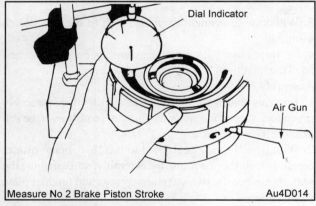

Measure No 2 Brake Piston Stroke | Au4D014

Standard Stroke :

Disc No	Stroke mm
2	0.78-1.72mm
3	1.01-2.25mm

8. Fit the center support assembly and sun gear together ensuring No 2 brake disc flukes align with the brake hub., then fit the snap ring into place.

Overdrive Input Shaft And Clutch

Disassemble

1. Withdraw the races and thrust bearings from the assembly, planetary gear side thrust washer may need to be levered from the assemble.

Race = A43D, A42DL, A43DL, A44DL, A43DE.

Race and Bearing = A42D

2.(a) Release the snap ring retaining the over drive brake hub

to the planetary gear, then withdraw the overdrive brake hub. (A42D)

(b) Slide the input shaft from the overdrive clutch assembly, then slide the race and bearing from the input shaft assembly. (A43D, A42DL, A43DL, A44DL, A43DE)

3. Release the snap ring from the overdrive clutch assembly, then the hub is able to be removed. (A43D, A42DL, A43DL, A44DL, A43DE)

4. Release the second snap ring, then the flange and clutch pack can be withdrawn from the assembly.

5. Using tool No. 09350-20013 to releave piston return spring pressure, release the retaining snap ring, withdraw the tool, spring retainer and return springs.

6. To pop piston from the overdrive clutch, fit it to the oil pump and then apply low pressure air, if piston does not move use pointy nose pliers, then the piston 'O' ring seal is able to be disguarded.

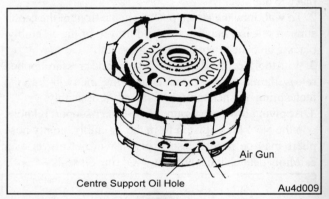

Centre Support Oil Hole | Air Gun | Au4d009

7. When the snap ring is released from the overdrive planetary gear assembly the one-way clutch and thrust washers are able to be withdrawn.

8. If needed use a magnet to withdraw the plug in the housing. From the outer race lift the one-way clutch, noting the way it is fitted.

Inspection

Check all components as well as the check ball, shaking to see that its not jamed, also that it doesn't leak using compressed air.

Assembly

1. Fit the four plug into place.

2. Slide bearing and thrust washer over planetary gear shaft into place in the planetary gear assembly. (A43D, A42DL, A43DL, A44DL, A43DE)

3. Fit the one-way clutch into the outer race with the cage spring towards the front of the assembly, then fit the one-way clutch into the planetary assembly with a thrust washer on either side, then position the snap ring and lock into place.

4. The clutch piston have a new 'O' ring seal fitted then the piston can be placed into the overdrive clutch drum, also fit the piston return springs and spring retainer, then using tool No. 09350-20013 to apply pressure to springs and retainer so the snap ring can be fitted.

5. With low pressure blow trans fluid from discs and plates, then place discs and plates in the assembly, leaving thin snap ring out at this stage, assembly fitted to overdrive clutch drum.

One Discs - plate, disc, flange.

Two Discs - plate, disc, plate, disc, flange.

6. Fit overdrive clutch hub and snap ring then using dial gauge on clutch pack apply compressed air into overdrive case and read the pack movement reading.

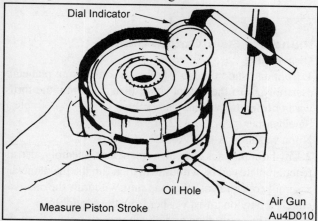

Dial Indicator

Oil Hole

Air Gun
Au4D010

Measure Piston Stroke

Standard Piston Stroke:

Disc No.	Stroke mm	comments
1	1.47-2.28	
2	1.56-2.53	

7. Withdraw the snap ring and overdrive clutch hub, then fit the thin snap ring.

8. Fit the overdrive hub and snap ring into position, then slide the planetary assembly and overdrive clutch assembly together ensuring the hub and discs mesh together. (A43D, A42DL, A43DL, A44DL, A43DE)

9. Slide the planetary assembly and overdrive clutch assembly together ensuring the hub and discs mesh together, then the outer snap ring can be fitted to retain the assembly as one. (A42D)

10. The remaining thrust bearing, thrust washer and race together untill assembly, the one-way clutch can be checked by rotating the input shaft either direction.

Antyclockwise = lockup

Clockwise = Free spinning

Rear Clutch
Disassemble

1. Release the clutch plate retaining snap ring and remove the clutch pack keeping them all in order, then fit tool No. 09350-20013 to releave piston return spring pressure, release the retaining snap ring, withdraw the tool, spring retainer and return springs.

2. To pop piston from the rear clutch, fit the clutch assembly to center support and use air pressure to release the piston, other wise pliers may be needed.

3.(a) Disguard 'O' ring seals from the piston. (A43D[5M,

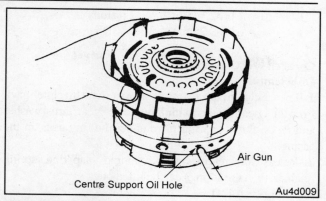

Centre Support Oil Hole

Air Gun

Au4d009

5M-E, 22R] A42DL, A44DL)

(b) Disguard 'O' ring seals from both inner and outer pistons. (A42D, A43D[L, 2L, 2Y, 3Y] A42DL, A44DL)

Inspection

Check all components, apply low pressure air to the valve in the piston to ensure there is no leakage, also the piston check ball is checked by shaking the piston.

Assembly

1.(a) Fit new 'O' ring seals to the piston, the place the piston into the rear clutch assembly. (A43D[5M, 5M-E, 22R] A42DL, A44DL)

(b) Fit new 'O' ring seals to the piston, the place the inner piston into the rear clutch assembly, then the outer piston. (A42D, A43D[L, 2L, 2Y, 3Y] A42DL, A44DL)

2. Place the piston return springs and retainer, then fit tool No. 092-350-20013 to apply pressure to the springs enough to fit the retaining snap ring, onced fitted withdraw the tool.

3. Place the discs, plates and flange into the rear clutch assembly, then fit the retaining snap ring into position.

Three discs = plate, disc, plate, disc, plate, disc, flange

Two discs = plate, disc, plate, plate, disc, flange

4. Place rear clutch assembly into center support, then with dial indicator on clutch pack, apply low air pressure to thecenter support to get reading of piston stroke.

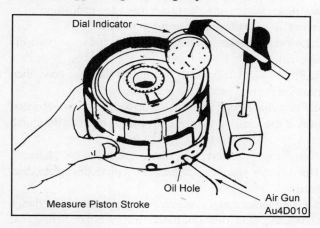

Dial Indicator

Oil Hole

Air Gun
Au4D010

Measure Piston Stroke

Standard Stroke :

Disc No	Stroke mm	Comments
2	0.93-1.82mm	
3	0.91-1.99mm	1 piston

201

| 3 | 1.06-2.14mm | 2 pistons |
| 3 | 0.90-1.75mm | A43DE |

Overdrive Case And Brake
Disassemble
1. Release clutch pack retaining snap ring and lift clutch pack from the assembly, then withdraw the ring gear, thrust washer and races, thrust bearing from under the ring gear, in the casing.

2. Release the return spring retaining snap ring, spring retainer, then the springs can be lifted out.

16 springs = A42D

12 springs = A43D, A42DL, A43DL, A44DL, A43DE

3. Pop piston from the casing by applying low air pressure to the casing hole indicated in the diagram, then disguard the two oil seals on the overdrive case and the 'O' ring seals on the brake piston.

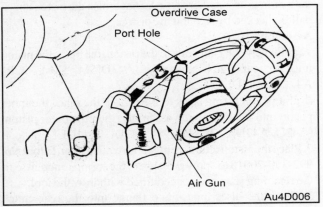

Overdrive Case

Port Hole

Air Gun

Au4D006

Inspection
Check all components for signs of damage, wear, etc. If fitting new discs they will need to be soaked for at two hour in trans fluid before assembly, old discs will need to be kept moist.

Assembly
1. Before assembly fit new 'O' ring seals to the piston and oil seal rings to the casing, then place the piston in position in the casing, also fit the return springs into place.

2. Lower return spring retainer into place and secure with the snap ring.

3. Fit the races and thrust bearing to the ring gear, then position the ring gear in the overdrive case.

4. Place clutch pack into the overdrive case in correct order, then fit the securing snap ring in position to retain the clutch pack.

Two discs = cushion plate, plate, disc, plate, disc, flange

Three discs = cushion plate, plate, disc, plate, disc, plate, disc, flange

5. Using feeler gauges measure the gap between the flange and the snap ring, this is the brake clearance, then fit ring gear washer into place.

Standard Clearance :

Disc No	Stroke mm	Comments
2	0.16-1.50mm	A42D
3	0.26-1.83mm	A42D
2	0.56-1.92mm	
3	0.65-2.21mm	
3	0.40-1.38mm	A43DE

Planetary Gear Output Shaft
Disassemble
1. Split and slide the No 3 brake pack and front planetary assembly from the output shaft, then withdraw the thrust washer from the planetary assembly.

Steel washer = A42D, A42DL, A44DL

Nilon washer = A43D, A43DL, A43DE

2. Lift the brake pack clear of the planetary assembly, also the reaction plate can be withdrawn, then flip the the planetary assembly over, release the snap ring, withdraw the one-way clutch and nylon thrust washer from the assembly.

3. Slide the apply tube and clutch pressure plate from the output assembly, then pull the front planetary ring gear and release the circlip, which will release the ring gear.

4. Withdraw the intermediate shaft away from the output shaft, then from output shaft lift the races and thrust bearings clear, also disguard the oil seals from the shaft.

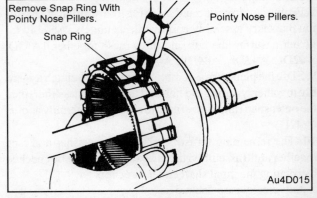

Remove Snap Ring With Pointy Nose Pillers.

Pointy Nose Pillers.

Snap Ring

Au4D015

5. Lift the thrust washer from the intermediate shaft, then the rear pinion gears, followed by the race and thrust bearing.

Steel washer = A42D, A42DL, A44DL

Nilon washer = A43D, A43DL, A43DE

6. Flip the intermediate shaft over so that the rear planetry gear retaining ring can be released and withdrawn, followed by the thrust bearing race.

Inspection
Check all components for signs of damage, wear, etc. If fitting new discs they will need to be soaked for at two hour in trans fluid before assembly, old discs will need to be kept moist.

Assembly
1. Place the planetary ring gear and thrust bearing race to the

intermediate shaft, then secure into place using the retaining ring.

2. Flip the assembly over, lower the thrust bearing and race over the shaft into position, then fit the pinion gear assembly and thrust washer in the same manner.

Steel washer = A42D, A42DL, A44DL

Nilon washer = A43D, A43DL, A43DE

3. Fit the oil seals to the output shaft, and place the output shaft assembly into the extension housing as a stand or something suitable, then fit the thrust bearing and race into place.

4. Lower the intermediate shaft into the output shaft assembly, then the planetary carrier assembly orer the intermediate shaft, aligning the locking lugs.

5. Place the front planetary ring gear into position and engage the snap ring to retain it in place.

6. Fit the nylon thrust washer into the planetary pinion carrier, then the one way clutch can be fitted with the spring cage towards the front.

7. To test the one-way clutch place the reaction plate on the planetary, then turn the assembly either way, once chesked withdraw the reaction plate.

Antyclockwise = free spinning

Clockwise = lockup

8. To the front of the planetary carrier fit the thrust, then slide the assembly over the intermediate shaft into position.

Steel washer = A42D, A42DL, A44DL

Nilon washer = A43D, A43DL, A43DE

9. Place the pressure plate over the intarmediate shaft and lower into place, then repeat this process for the No 3 brake clutch pack, ensuring in correct order.

Clutch pack order = disc, plate, disc, plate, disc, plate, disc, plate, disc.

10. The remaining parts are to be used during assembly of transmission.

Valve Body
(A42D, A43D, A42DL, A43DL, A44DL)
Disassemble (Seperating Valve Body)

1. Withdraw the retaining dolt for the detent spring, the lift detent spring from valve body, also slide the manual valve out of valve body, then detatch small cover.

2. On the upper side of the valve body withdraw the 10 bolts

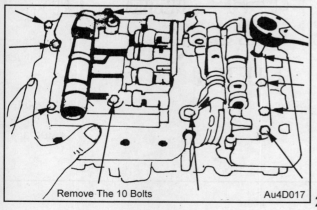

Remove The 10 Bolts   Au4D017

retaining the upper valve body to the lower, then flip and withdraw the bolts retaining the lower to the upper.

Lower side retaining bolts :

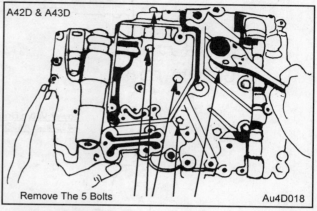

A42D & A43D

Remove The 5 Bolts   Au4D018

A42D, A43D = 5 bolts

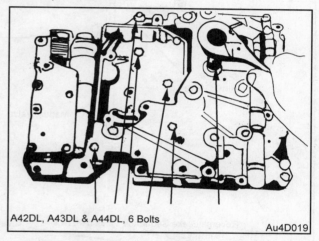

A42DL, A43DL & A44DL, 6 Bolts   Au4D019

A42DL, A43DL, A44DL = 6 bolts

3. Holding the center plate to the lower valve body lift it clear from the two upper sections, careful not to loose any balls or ckeck valves.

Disassemble (Lower Valve Body)

1. Lift the center plate and gaskets from the lower valve body, then withdraw oil cooler by-pass valve and spring, also the check balls, and damping check valve spring.

2. Flip over the valve body and loosen the lower cover bolts, then withdraw the bolts, lower body cover, plate and gaskets.

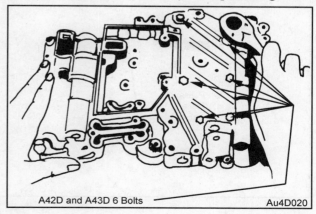

A42D and A43D 6 Bolts   Au4D020

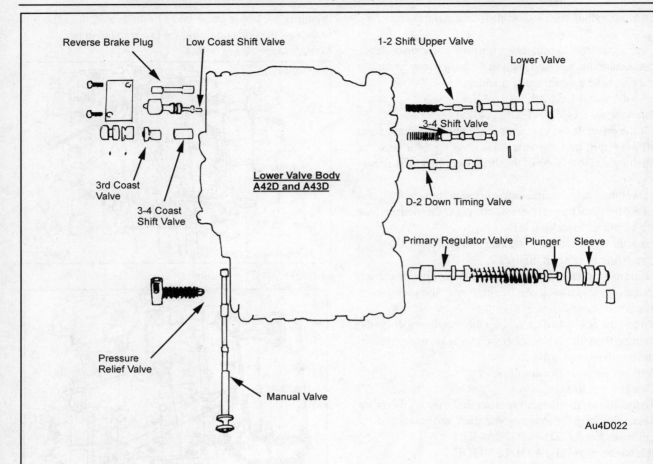

Reverse Brake Plug
Low Coast Shift Valve
1-2 Shift Upper Valve
Lower Valve
3-4 Shift Valve
3rd Coast Valve
3-4 Coast Shift Valve
**Lower Valve Body
A42D and A43D**
D-2 Down Timing Valve
Primary Regulator Valve
Plunger
Sleeve
Pressure Relief Valve
Manual Valve

Au4D022

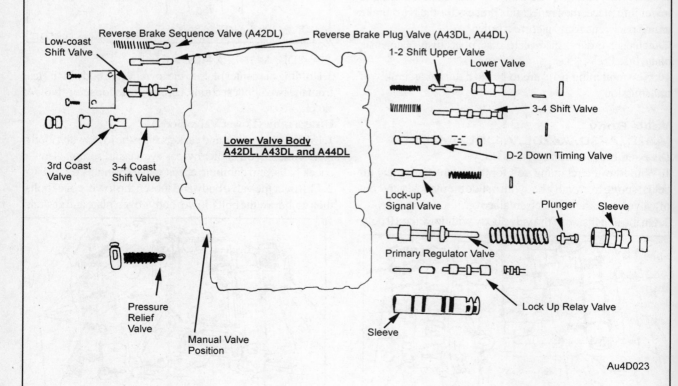

Reverse Brake Sequence Valve (A42DL)
Reverse Brake Plug Valve (A43DL, A44DL)
Low-coast Shift Valve
1-2 Shift Upper Valve
Lower Valve
3-4 Shift Valve
3rd Coast Valve
3-4 Coast Shift Valve
**Lower Valve Body
A42DL, A43DL and A44DL**
D-2 Down Timing Valve
Lock-up Signal Valve
Plunger
Sleeve
Primary Regulator Valve
Lock Up Relay Valve
Pressure Relief Valve
Manual Valve Position
Sleeve

Au4D023

204

A42D, A43D = 6 bolts

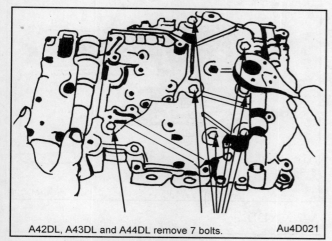

A42DL, A43DL and A44DL remove 7 bolts.　　　Au4D021

A42DL, A43DL, A44DL = 7 bolts

3. Carefully withdraw the check valve balls, not loosing them.

No. of balls = 　3 balls - w/o kick-down switcth
　　　　　　　　4 balls - w/ kick-down switch

4. To withdraw pressure releif spring and ball, disengage the spring retainer from the releif assembly.

5.(a) Loosen the lock-up relay valve cover bolts, then withdraw the bolts, cover, gasket, plug retainer, plug, and the valve assembly. (A42D, A43D, A44DL)

(b) Release the lock-up signal valve retaining pin, then the plug, spring and valve will slide from the valve body. (A42DL, A43DL, A44DL)

6. Withdraw the primary regulator valve spring retainer, then slide the valve components from the valve body keeping them in order for assembly procedure.

7. Release the 3-4 shift valve retainer pin, to allow the valve and spring to slide from the valve body, then repeat this process for the 1-2 shift valve, keep them in order for easier assembly.

8. Withdraw the D-2 down timing valve retaining pin, then slide the plug and valve from the valve body.

9.(a) Detatch the cover plate to allow the low-coast shift valve to be withdrawn from the valve body.

(b) Slide the reverse brake plug from the valve body. (A42D, A43D, A43DL, A44DL)

(c) Slide the reverse brake sequence valve and spring from the valvel body. (A42DL)

10. Withdraw the third coast valve and 3-4 control valve retainer pins, then slide the plugs and valves from the valve body.

Inspection

Inspect the valve springs for any form of damage and measure springs to confferm they are the connect height.

Spring	- Height mm (in.)	- Trans
Primary regulator	- 61.20 (2.4094)	- A43D(MS), A43DL, A44DL
valve	- 62.89 (2.4760)	- A42D(YR)
	- 73.32 (2.8866)	- A42D(LX, LS), A43D(YH)
1-2 shift valve	- 34.62 (1.3630)	-
3-4 shift valve	- 33.65 (1.3246)	- A43D, A43DL, A44DL(LX)
	- 35.18 (1.3850)	- A42D(YR, 2Y), A42DL, A44DL(YH)
	- 36.28 (1.4283)	- A42D(YR, 2Y-C)
Oil cooler by-pass Valve	- 33.32 (1.3118)	-
Pressure releif valve	- 32.14 (1.2654)	-
Damping check ball	- 20.00 (0.7874)	-
Lock-up relay valve	- 18.50 (0.7283)	- A42DL, A43DL
Lock-up signal valve	- 45.56 (1.7937)	- A42DL, A43DL
	- 37.38 (1.4717)	- A44DL
Reverse brake sequence valve	- 37.55 (1.4783)	- A42D(CT, CA), A42DL

Assemble (Lower Valve Body)

1.(a) Insert the reverse brake plug into the valve boby. (A42D, A43D, A43DL, A44DL)

(b) Insert reverse brake sequence valve and spring into the valve body. (A42DL)

2. Insert the low coast shift valve into the valve body, then the 3-4 coast shift valve and third coast valve, followed by the plugs and the retaining pins.

3. Fit the cover plate and bolts, and tension the bolts to tension.

4. Insert the lock-up signal valve, spring and plug, and retain the assembly with the locating pin.(A42DL, A43DL, A44DL)

5. Slide the D-2 down timing valve and plug into the valve body, then fit the retainer.

6. Place the 1-2 shift spring, valves (upper and lower) and plug in the valve body securing with the retainer, then fit the 3-4 shift spring, valve and plug and secure with locating pin.

7. Fit the primary regulator valve and spring into the valve body, making sure that it sits flush when fitted, then fit the regulator valve plunge to the sleeve, fit the sleeve to the valve body and secure with retainer.

8. Assemble the lock-up relay valve and insert the assembly into the valve body, then fit retaining pin, also the cover plate and gasket. (A42DL, A43DL)

9. Fit the pressure releif ball and spring into position, and install the retainer, then check all retainers and locating pin are in correct position.
A42D, A43D
A42DL, A43DL, A44DL

10. Fit all check ball to the valve body assembly, then fit the lower body cover to retain the balls in position and tension bolts.

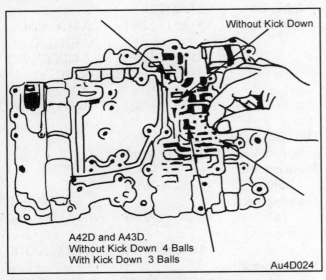

A42D and A43D.
Without Kick Down 4 Balls
With Kick Down 3 Balls

Au4D024

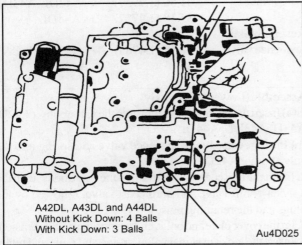

A42DL, A43DL and A44DL
Without Kick Down: 4 Balls
With Kick Down: 3 Balls

Au4D025

Check balls = 4 balls w/o kick-down switch
= 3 balls w/ kick-down switch
Cover gasket order =
gasket, plate, gasket, cover plate
A42D, A43D (6 bolts)
A42DL, A43DL, A44DL (7 bolts)

11. Fit the ckeck balls, large ball with the spring for damping,then the oil cooler by-pass valve and spring.

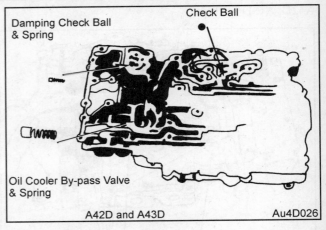

Damping Check Ball & Spring

Check Ball

Oil Cooler By-pass Valve & Spring

A42D and A43D

Au4D026

A42D, A43D

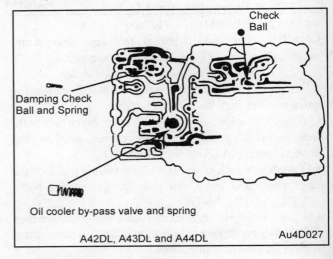

Check Ball

Damping Check Ball and Spring

Oil cooler by-pass valve and spring

A42DL, A43DL and A44DL

Au4D027

A42DL, A43DL, A44DL

12. Fit the gasket to the lower valve body and the body plate, then secure in position with a couple of bolts to apply pressure on the ckeck valve.

Disassemble (Upper Front Valve Body)

1. Withdraw the check ball and cut-back plug retainer, then withdraw the cut-back plug and valve.

2. Withdraw one bolt from the secondary regulator valve and pivot the cover on the remaining bolt until the valve and spring is able to be withdrawn, then withdraw remaining bolt and cover.

3. With the throttle valve held in, withdraw the throttle cam bolt and throttle cam, then withdraw the down shift plug and spring.

4. Withdraw the throttle valve and spring.

Inspection

Inspect the valve springs for any form of damage and measure springs to conferm they are the connect height.

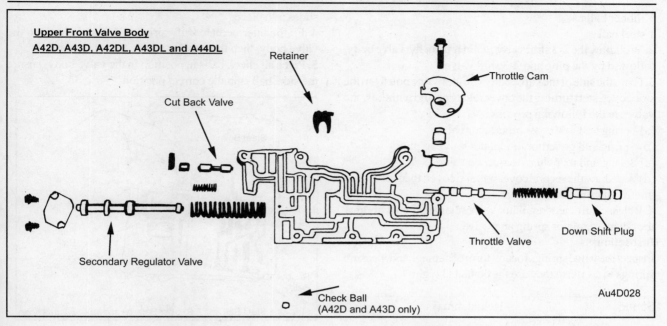

Upper Front Valve Body
A42D, A43D, A42DL, A43DL and A44DL

Retainer

Throttle Cam

Cut Back Valve

Secondary Regulator Valve

Throttle Valve

Down Shift Plug

Check Ball
(A42D and A43D only)

Au4D028

Spring	- Height mm (in.)	
Secondary regulator valve	- 71.27 (2.8059)	
Down shift plug	- 39.71 (1.5634)	RA
	- 43.00 (1.5643)	RX
Throttle valve	- 21.94 (0.8638)	

Assemble (Upper Front Valve Body)
1. Place the throttle valve into the valve body, ensuring it is properly seated, then fit the retainer, also fit the spring on the throttle valve shaft.
2. Fit the down shift spring and plug in valve body, holding it down in the bore so the throttle cam can also be fitted easily, then tension the mounting bolt and release the down shift plug.
Bolt tension = 7.4Nm (65in.-lb, 75kg-cm)
3. Fit the cover to the valve body with one bolt and slide the secondary regulator valve into the valve body, then push down and slide the cover over the end of the valve.
4. Fit the second cover bolt and tension both bolts to correct torque, then the ckeck ball can be fitted.
Bolt Tension = 5.4Nm (48in.-lb, 55kg-cm)
Disassemble (Upper Rear Valve Body)
1. Withdraw the check balls from the valve body, then the intermediate shift valve retainer can be withdrawn, followed by the plug, intermediate shift valve and spring.

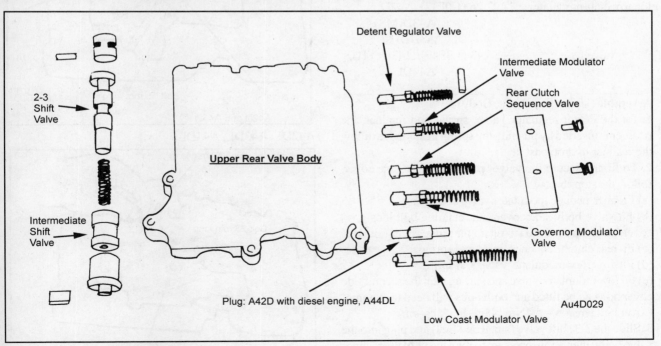

2-3 Shift Valve

Intermediate Shift Valve

Detent Regulator Valve

Intermediate Modulator Valve

Rear Clutch Sequence Valve

Upper Rear Valve Body

Governor Modulator Valve

Plug: A42D with diesel engine, A44DL

Low Coast Modulator Valve

Au4D029

3 rubber balls

1 steel ball

2. Withdraw the 2-3 shift valve retainer from the valve body, followed by the plug and 2-3 shift valve.

3. From the side of the valve body withdraw one bolt from the side cover, start turning the cover releasing and withdraw the valves in the following process :

(a) Spring and low coast modulator valve.

(b) Spring and governor modulator valve or plug.

(c) Spring and rear clutch sequence valve.

(d) Withdraw the second cover bolt and cover, then spring and intermediate modulator valve.

4. Release the detent regulator valve retainer, then withdraw the detent regulator spring and valve.

Inspection

Inspect the valve springs for any form of damage and measure springs to conferm they are the connect height.

Spring	- Height mm (in.)
Low-coast modulator valve	- 42.35 (1.6673)
Rear clutch sequence valve	- 37.55 (1.4783)
Governor modulator Valve	- 36.07 (1.4201)
2-3 shift valve	- 35.10 (1.3819)
Detent regulator valve	- 26.44 (1.0409) A42D(LX, LS), A44DL
	- 29.93 (1.1783) A43D(MS), A42DL, A43DL
	- 32.08 (1.2630) A42D(YR), A44DL(YH), A42DL(YH)
Intermediate modulator	- 27.26 (1.0732) A42D, A43D(MS) A42DL, A43DL
valve	- 35.43 (1.3949) A43D(YH), A44DL

Assemble (Upper Rear Valve Body)

1. Fit the detent regulator valve, spring and retainer, the retainer is inserted by pushing the spring in enough to allow the retainer to drop past it.

2. To fit and secure the valves retained by the side cover, follow the steps below.

(a) Fit intermediate modulator valve and spring.

(b) Fit valve body side cover and retaining bolt loosly, so cover is able to be turned to retain the valves being fitted..

(c) Fit rear clutch sequence valve and spring.

(d) Fit governor modulator valve and spring.

(e) Fit low modulator valve and spring, then the second side cover bolt can be fitted and both bolts will need tensioning. Cover bolt tension = 5.4Nm (48in.-lb, 55kg-cm)

3. Slide the 2-3 shift valve (small end first) and plug into the valve body, then apply pressure to the plug until the retainer slides into place.

4. Fit the intermediate shift spring, valve and plug into the valve body, then the retainer can be fitted to secure.

5. Place all check balls in position in the valve body, ensure the steel ball is in the correct position.

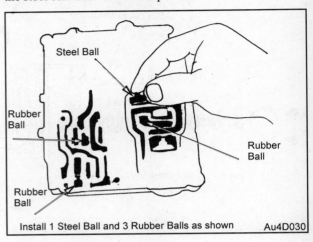

Install 1 Steel Ball and 3 Rubber Balls as shown   Au4D030

3 rubber balls

1 steel ball

Assemble (Complete Valve Body)

1. On the upper rear valve body position a new gasket, then the lower valve body is able to be placed on top and the securing bolts fitted.

A42D, A43D

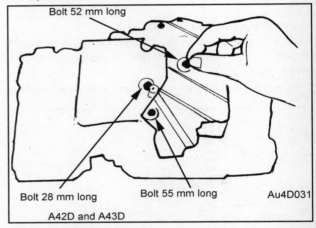

A42D and A43D   Au4D031

A42DL, A43DL, A44DL

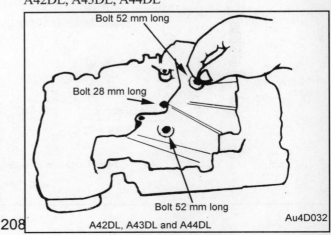

A42DL, A43DL and A44DL   Au4D032

2. Flip the assembly over and fit the remaining retaining bolts to upper valve body, then withdraw the temporary retaining bolts holding the plate to the lower valve body.

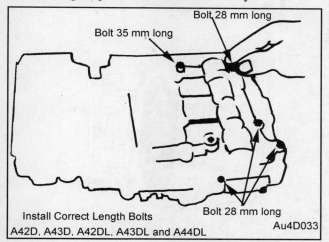

Install Correct Length Bolts
A42D, A43D, A42DL, A43DL and A44DL   Au4D033

3.(a) Place the lower valve body assembly on top of the front upper valve body.

(b) Fit the retaining bolts, installing the small cover plate at the same time. (A42D, A43D, = 4 bolts)

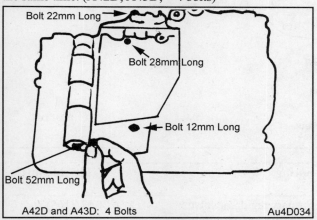

A42D and A43D: 4 Bolts   Au4D034

(c) Fit the retaining bolts. (A42DL, A43DL, A44DL, = 3 bolts)

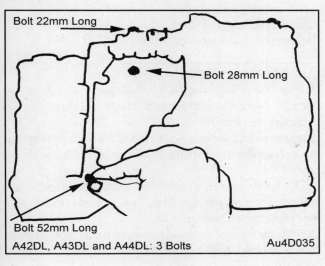

A42DL, A43DL and A44DL: 3 Bolts   Au4D035

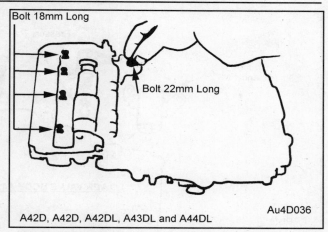

A42D, A42D, A42DL, A43DL and A44DL   Au4D036

4. Flip the assembly over and fit the remaining retaining bolts in the top of the assembly, then tension all upper and lower assembly bolts.

Bolt tension = 5.4Nm (48in.-lb, 55kg-cm)

5. Fit the manual valve into the valve body, then fit and secure the detent spring, tension the bolt.

Bolt tension = 5.4Nm (48in.-lb, 55kg-cm)

Valve Body (A43DE)

Disassemble (Seperating)

1. Withdraw the detent spring and slide the manual valve from the valve body, then withdraw the nine upper valve body retaining bolts.

2. Flip the assembly over, then withdraw the seven lower valve body retaining bolts and lift the lower assembly (with center plate) clear of the upper assemblies.

3. Careful not to loose any of the retainers, pins and steel balls.

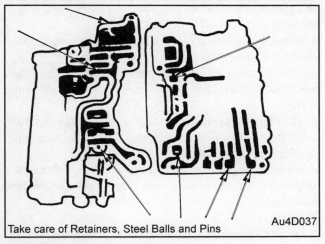

Take care of Retainers, Steel Balls and Pins   Au4D037

Disassemble (Lower Valve Body)

1. Carefully lift the center plate and both gaskets from the lower valve body, then withdraw the cooler by-pass check, damping ball and two springs from valve body.

2. Flip assembly and withdraw the cover plates from the assembly, then the pressure releif valve retainer, bolt spring and steel ball.

3. Withdraw the No. 3 solenoid, also the No. 1 & 2 solenoid

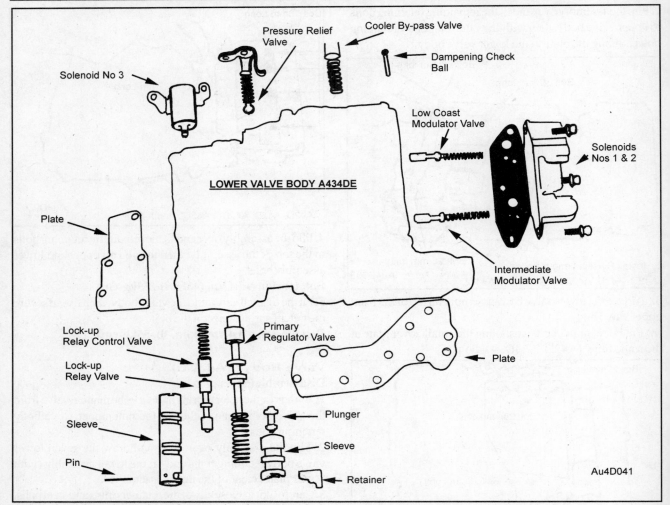

and gasket, then the springs from under the No. 1 & 2 solenoid.

4. Withdraw the low coast modulator valve and intermediate modulator valve from the valve body.

5. Release the lock-up relay valve retaining pin , then withdraw the lock-up relay sleeve, valve, control valve and spring.

6.(a) Before releasing the primary regulator valve retainer, mark the position of the retainer on the sleeve, then apply pressure to release retainer.

(b) Release the pressure of the spring and then withdraw the sleeve, plunger, spring and primary regulator valve from the valve body.

Inspection

Inspect the valve springs for any form of damage and measure springs to conferm they are the connect height.

Spring	- Height mm (in.)
Primary regulator valve	- 56.30 (2.2165)
Oil cooler by-pass Valve	- 33.32 (1.3118)
Pressure releif valve	- 32.14 (1.2654)
Damping check ball	- 20.00 (0.7874)
Lock-up relay control valve	- 34.60 (1.3622)
Low coast modulator valve	- 42.35 (1.6673)
Intermediate modulator valve	- 35.43 (1.3949)

Assemble (Lower Valve Body)

1. Install the primary regulator valve bigger end first, spring, then the sleeve with plunger fitted inside, and align mark for retainer when fitting.

2.(a) Fit the lock-up relay valve inside the sleeve, the spring in the control valve, then the control valve inside the sleeve aswell.

(b) Slide the complete assembly in the valve body and secure with the retaining pin, then fit the No. 3 solenoid to the valve body and tighten retaining bolt.

3. Slide the intermediate and low-coast modulator valves in the valve body, then springs on top and No. 1 & 2 solenoids to retain them in place, tension bolt.

Retaining bolt tension = 10Nm (7ft-lb, 100kg-cm)

4. Position the pressure releif ball and spring in the valve body, then fit the retainer and bolt, tension to torque.

Retaining bolt tension = 5.4Nm (48in.-lb, 55kg-cm)

5. Place the two cover in position and tighten the retaining bolts, then check the retainers and pins are still in position.

6. Fit the cooler by-pass check valve, damping ball and springs, then position gasket and center plate on lower valve body, retain with two small bolts.

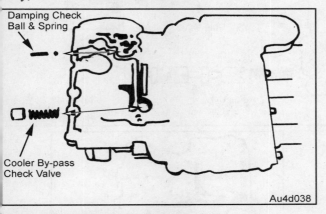

Spring	- Height mm (in.)
Secondary regulator valve	- 71.27 (2.8059)
Cut-back valve	- 23.00 (0.9055)
Throttle valve	- 19.24 (0.7575)
Down-shift plug	- 39.55 (1.5571)

Assemble (Upper Front Valve Body)

1.(a) Slide the throttle valve to bottom of the bore and fit the retainer, then fit the adjusting rings and spring over the end of the throtle valve shaft.

(b) With the down shift spring fitted in the plug slide into valve body as an assembly, applying pressure until the retainer pin will drop into place.

2. With the throttle cam assembled, put in place and and fit the retaining bolt.

Retaining bolt tension = 7.4Nm (65in.-lb, 75kg-cm)

3.(a) Fit cover plate with one bolt to the valve body and slide the secondary regulator spring and valve into the valve body.

(b)Apply pressure to the valve and slide the cover plate over the valve, then fit the second bolt and tension.

Retaining bolt tension = 5.4Nm (48in.-lb, 55kg-cm)

4. Slide the spring and cut-back valve into the valve body, small end first, then fit the plug and retaining pin,

5. Ensure that the pins are in place correctly.

Disassemble (Upper Front Valve Body)

1. Release throttle valve and cut-back retainers, then slide the cut-back valve and spring from the valve body.

2. Withdraw one retaining bolt from the secondary regulator valve cover plate and slide the plate from the end of the valve, then withdraw the valve and spring.

3. Loosen the throttle cam retaining bolt, then withdraw the bolt and throttle cam assembly from the valve body.

4.(a) Apply pressure to the down shift plug and release the retaining pin, then withdraw the down shift plug, sleeve, spring, throttle valve and spring.

(b) Remove the adjusting rings taking note of how many there are fitted.

Inspection

Inspect the valve springs for any form of damage and measure springs to conferm they are the connect height.

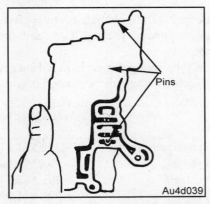

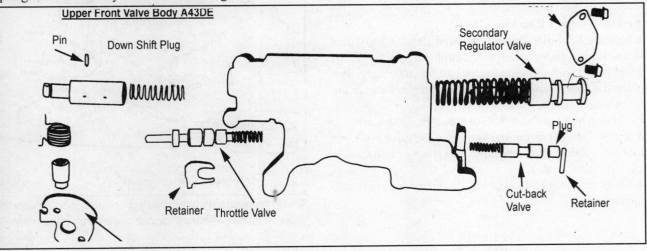

Upper Front Valve Body A43DE

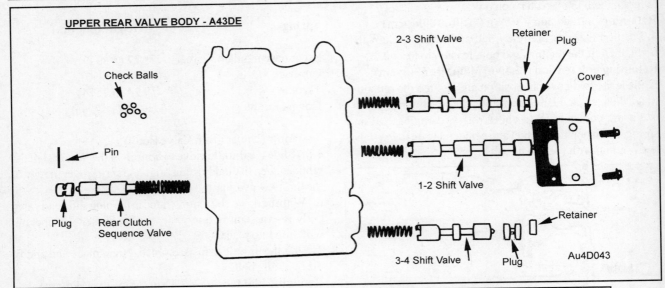

UPPER REAR VALVE BODY - A43DE

Au4D043

Disassemble (Upper Rear Valve Body)

1. Withdraw the check balls and the rear clutch sequence valve retaining pin, then slide the plug, valve and spring from the valve body.

2. Apply pressure to the 3-4 shift plug to release the retainer, then withdraw the plug, valve and spring from the valve body.

3. Loosen and withdraw the 1-2 shift valve cover from the valve body, then slide the valve and spring from the valve body.

4. Release the 2-3 shift valve retainer by applying pressure to the plug then withdraw the plug, valve and spring.

Inspection

Inspect the valve springs for any form of damage and measure springs to confirm they are the connect height.

Spring	- Height mm (in.)
Rear clutch sequence valve	- 37.55 (1.4783)
1-2 shift valve	- 29.15 (1.1476)
2-3 shift valve	- 29.15 (1.1476)
3-4 shift valve	- 29.15 (1.5571)

Assemble (Upper Rear Valve Body)

1. Slide the 2-3 shift spring and valve into the valve body, then secure using retainer coated with petroleum jelly.

2. Fit the 1-2 shift spring and valve into the valve body, then place the cover plate, gasket and retaining bolts over the valve, tension bolts.

Retaining bolt tension = 5.4Nm (48in.-lb, 55kg-cm)

3. Fit the 3-4 shift spring and valve into the valve body and insert the retaining pin, then repeat this procedure on the rear clutch sequence valve.

4. Fit the six check ball and ensure the retainers are correctly in place.

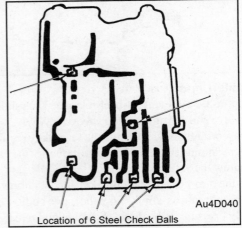

Location of 6 Steel Check Balls

Au4D040

Assemble (Complete Valve Body)

1. With new gasket in position on the upper rear valve body, fit the lower valve body on top and fit the retaining bolts securing the two together.

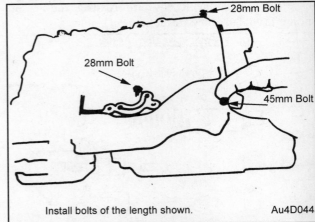

Install bolts of the length shown.

Au4D044

2. Flip the assembly over and fit the retaining bolts from the other side, then withdraw the center plate retaining bolts.

212

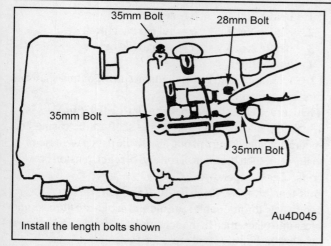

Install the length bolts shown   Au4D045

3. Fit the lower valve body on top of the front upper valve body, fit the retaining bolts, then flip the assembly and fit the

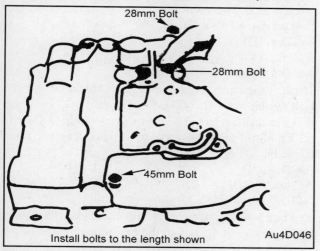

Install bolts to the length shown   Au4D046

retaining bolts on the opersite side.

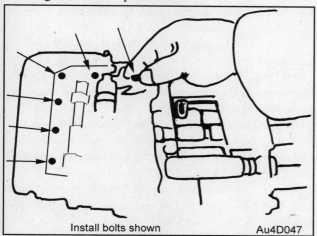

Install bolts shown   Au4D047

4. Using tension wrench torque the upper and lower assembly retaining bolts to specified tension, then fit manual valve and detent spring to lower valve body.

Transmission - Assemble

1. With the transmission standing upright, place the bearing and thrust washer (cup down) into the casing, followed by the apply tube, locking it into the lug slot in the outer rear brake piston. See diagram

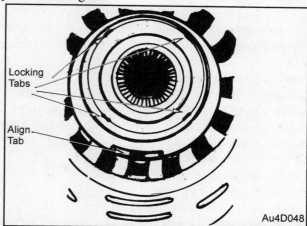

Au4D048

2. Fit the output shaft assembly in the casing, then check the clearance between the ledge below the snap ring groove and the clutch pack, when clearance is correct fit the reaction plate (notched section towards valve body) and snap ring retainer.

Disc No.	Cleanance mm (in.)
4	0.56-2.29 (0.0220-0.0902)
5	0.61-2.64 (0.0240-0.1039)

3. Lower the center support into the case lining up the bolt hole, fit the retaining bolts and tighten, then position the rear clutch in the case and check that the end of the sun gear shaft is level with the splined center of the clutch.

4. Fit the bearing race in the case over the rear clutch, then to the front clutch assembly fit the thrust bearing and race, and slide the assembly into the case, ensuring the clutch and hub mesh together.

5. Measure the case lip to front clutch clearance using tool No. 09350-20013, then fit tool No. 09350-20013 to the case as well as the thrust bearing to the front clutch.

Clearance = measured value - SST width
= 2mm (0.08in.)

6. To the overdrive case fit the thrust washer using petroleum jelly to retain, then place the overdrive case in position on the

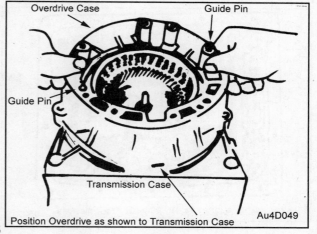

Position Overdrive as shown to Transmission Case   Au4D049

transmission case with the guide pins aligned correctly.

7. Fit the overdriver planetary carrier thrust washer into place using petroleum jelly to retain and insert the assembly into the case, then check the case to clutch assembly clearance.

Clearance = measured value - SST width
= 3.5mm (0.138in.)

8. Fit the sealing 'O' ring to the overdrinve case and slide the converter housing into place, then fit and tension the retaining bolts.

Retaining bolt torque :
Bolts No. 1 = 34Nm (25ft-lb, 345kg-cm)(10mm bolts)
Bolts No. 2 = 57Nm (42ft-lb, 580kg-cm)(12mm bolts)

9.(a) Place the thrust washer over the input shaft and seat it on the overdrive clutch.

A42D (race & bearing)   Other (race)

(b) Place the thrust washer in place on the oil pump body retaining with petroleum jelly.

A42D (race)   Other (bearing & race)

10. Lower the oil pump down into the casing over the input shaft, the retaining bolts will need to have seal packing applied to them as being fitted, withdraw aligning tools and fit last two bolts, tension to specs.

Bolt tension = 21Nm (16ft-lb, 215kg-cm)

11. Tension the center support bolts to correct torque, then using low pressure air check the piston operations, see list below.

Bolts tension = 25Nm (19ft-lb, 260kg-cm)

Piston test passages :

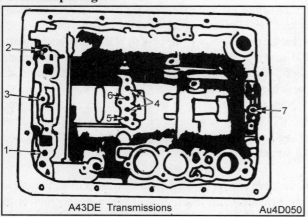

A43DE Transmissions   Au4D050

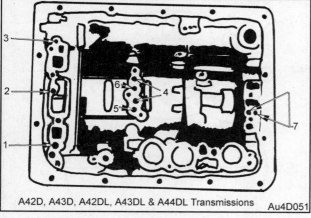

A42D, A43D, A42DL, A43DL & A44DL Transmissions   Au4D051

1 = brake No. 1   5 = rear clutch
2 = brake No. 2   6 = overdrive clutch
3 = brake No. 3   7 = overdrive brake
4 = front clutch

12. Check input shaft has movement and the output shaft has thrust movement.

Thrust movement = 0.3-0.9mm (0.012-0.035in.)

13. Fit the manual valve lever and shaft to the casing and secure together using roll pin, also fit the park pawl assembly to the case, then the control rod and bracket, tension bracket bolts, check it operation.

Bolt tension = 7.4Nm (65in-lb, 75kg-cm)

14. Fit new throttle cable seal and slid cable into the case and press into place, then fit the accumulator pistons and springs, then lower the valve body into the transmission case.

15. Clip the throttle cable onto the cam and ensure the lower spring is installed onto the piston, then fit the valve body retaining bolts and torque.

Bolt tension = 10Nm (7ft-lb, 100kg-cm)
A42D, A43D
A42DL, A43DL, A44DL
A43DE

16.(a) Fit the detent spring and oil strainer to the valve body.

Bolt tension = 5.4Nm (48in.-lb, 55kg-cm)

(b) Connect the solenoid wiring to all solenoids. (A43DE)

(c) Fit all oil tubes in place, ensure that they are fitted correctly.

A42D, A43D
A42DL, A43DL, A44DL
A43DE

17. Place new pan gasket on transmission case, with magnet in the oil pan fit the pan to the transmission, then fit the retaining bolts and tension to correct torque, also fit and tension drain plug..

Pan bolt tension = 4.4Nm (39in.-lb, 45kg-cm)
Pan magnet = 1 piece , A42D, A43D
         = 2 piece , A42DL, A43DL, A44DL, A43DE
Drain plug tension = 17Nm (13ft-lb, 175kg-cm)

18.(a) Fit the governor line strainer and plate, then slide the governor over the output shaft untill it locks into place, then fit the lock plate and bolt.

Lock plate bolt tension = 3.9Nm (35in.-lb, 40kg-cm)

(b) Fitting the speedo drive gear by sliding first circlip, lock ball, drive gear and second circlip into place over the shaft. (A42D, A43D, A42DL, A43DL, A44DL)

19. Fit the large snap ring, woodruff key, sensor rotor, lock ball speedo drive gear and second snap ring over the output shaft and into position. (A43DE)

20. Slide the rear extension housing over the output shaft, then fit and tension the retaining bolts.

Bolt tension = 34Nm (25ft-lb, 345kg-cm)

21. Fit the following components in the order listed:
(a) speedo 'O' ring seal and driven gear assembly
(b) speed sensor assembly

(c) Neutral start safety switch and shift handle

(d) Solenoid switch and kickdown switch

22. To adjust the neutral start safety switch use an ohmmeter on terminals, push the handle right back then forward two notches adjust the swith until there is a constant reading between terminals, lock the switch in place.

PROBLEM DIAGNOSIS

General Notes
Problems occurring with the automatic transmission can be caused by either the engine or the automatic transmission itself. These two areas should be distinctly isolated before proceeding with diagnosis.

Problem diagnosis should begin with the simplest operation, working up in order of difficulty, but initially determine whether the trouble lies within the engine or transmission. Proceed with the inspection in the following order:

PRELIMINARY CHECK:
(a) Check the fluid level.

(b) Check the throttle cable mark.

(c) Check the shift linkage.

(d) Check the neutral start switch.

(e) Check the idling speed.

IDLE SPEED
Idle speed with transmission in neutral.

50's-60's Series

3Y Engine with P.S.:	850 RPM
3Y Engine without P.S.:	750 RPM
2L Engine:	800 RPM

80's-130's Series

22R Engine:	750 RPM
2L Engine:	800 RPM

Oil Pressure Check

FLUID CHECK
Transmission fluid changes colour and smell very early in life, these indicators should not necessarily be relied on to diagnose either transmission internal condition nor fluid deterioration.

The chart on the next page shows that a dark brown fluid colour, coupled with a delayed shift pattern, may only indicate that the fluid requires replacement and alone, is not a definite indication of a potential transmission failure.

The fluid level should only be checked when the transmission reaches normal operating temperature (82-93 degrees Celsius).

Transmission fluid colour when new and unused, is red. A red dye is added so that it can be distinguished from other oils and lubricants. The red dye is not an indicator of fluid quality and is not permanent. As the vehicle is driven, the transmission fluid will begin to look darker in colour. The colour will then appear light brown. A DARK brown colour with a distinctively burnt odour MAY indicate fluid deterioration and a need for the fluid to be changed.

Details of transmission oil pressure check procedures refer to `Oil pressure check information' chart at the start of this chapter.

HYDRAULIC DIAGNOSIS

OIL PRESSURE CHECK INFORMATION
Preliminary Check Procedure

* Check transmission oil level and condition
* Check and adjust Kickdown Cable
* Check outside manual linkage and correct
* Check engine tune
* Install oil pressure gauge
* Connect tachometer to engine
* Check oil pressure as follows:

Minimum Kickdown Line Pressure Check

Set the Kickdown cable to specification; and with the brakes applied, take the line pressure readings in the ranges and at the engine r.p.m.'s indicated in the chart below.

Full Kickdown Line Pressure Check

Full Kickdown line pressure readings are obtained by tying or holding the Kickdown cable to the full extent of it's travel; and with the brakes applied, take the line pressure readings in the ranges and at the engine r.p.m.'s indicated in the chart shown later.

** NOTICE - Total running time for this combination not to exceed 2 mins.

** CAUTION - Brakes must be applied at all times.

ROAD TEST
Drive and Reverse Engagement Shift Check.

1. Start engine.
2. Depress brake pedal.
3. Move gear selector:
   a. `P' (Park) to `R' (Reverse)
   b. `R' (Reverse) to `N' (Neutral) to `D' (Drive).
   c. Gear selections should be immediate and not harsh.

Upshifts and Torque Converter Clutch (TCC) Application

With gear selector in `D' :-

1. Accelerate using a steady increasing throttle application.
2. Note the shift speed point gear engagements for:
   a. 2nd gear
   b. 3rd gear
   c. Overdrive
3. Note the speed shift point for the Torque Converter Clutch (TCC) application. This should occur while in 3rd gear.

IMPORTANT

The TCC will not engage if engine coolant temperature is below 45 degrees Celsius or road speed is to low.

Part Throttle Downshift

At a speed of 70-90 km/h, quickly depress the accelerator to half open position and observe:

    a. TCC releases.

    b. Transmission downshafts to 2nd gear immediately.

Full Throttle (Detente) Downshift

Operate the vehicle at 70-90km/h in `D', then quickly depress to wide open throttle position and observe:

    a. TCC releases.

    b. Transmission downshifts to 2nd gear immediately.

Manual Downshift

1. Operate the vehicle at 70-90km/h in `D', then release the accelerator pedal (closed throttle position) and simultaneously move the gear selector to `D' (Drive), and observe:

    a. TCC release occurs at zero throttle.

    b. Transmission downshifts to 2nd gear immediately.

    c. Engine should slow vehicle.

2. Operate the vehicle at 70-80 km/h in `D'.

Release the accelerator pedal and simultaneously move the gear selector `2' (second) gear position, and observe:

    a. TCC release occurs at zero throttle.

    b. Transmission downshifts to 2nd gear immediately.

    c. Engine should slow vehicle.

3. Move gear selector to `D' and accelerate to 40km/h. Release the accelerator pedal (closed throttle position) and simultaneously move the gear selector to `1' (first) gear and observe:

    a. Transmission downshifts to 1st gear immediately.

    b. Engine should slow vehicle.

Shifting Speeds 50's - 60's Series

3Y Engine Diff Ratio 4.556

Manual	Shift	Throttle	Km/h, MPH
D	1-2	KD	44-53, 27-33
D	2-3	KD	80-90, 50,56
D	O/D-3	KD	---------
D	3-2	KD	76-86, 47-53
D	2-1	KD	35-44, 22-27

3Y Engine Diff Ratio 4.30

Manual	Shift	Throttle	Km/h, MPH
D	1-2	KD	46-56, 29-35
D	2-3	KD	85-95, 53-59
D	O/D-3	KD	---------
D	3-2	KD	81-91, 50-57
D	2-1	KD	36-47, 22-29

2L Engine Diff Ratio 4.875

Manual	Shift	Throttle	Km/h, MPH
D	1-2	KD	33-45, 21-27
D	2-3	KD	63-74, 39-46
D	O/D-3	KD	88-105, 55-65
D	3-2	KD	58-69, 36-43
D	2-1	KD	26-36, 16-22

Shifting Speeds 80's - 13's Series

22R Engine

Manual	Shift	Throttle	Km/h, MPH
D	1-2	KD	49-63, 30-39
D	2-3	KD	91-107, 57-66
D	O/D-3	KD	--------
D	3-2	KD	83-98, 52-61
D	2-1	KD	34-47, 21-29

2L Engine Australia

Manual	Shift	Throttle	Km/h, MPH
D	1-2	KD	33-42, 21-26
D	2-3	KD	62-71, 39-44
D	O/D-3	KD	88-102, 55-63
D	3-2	KD	57-67, 35-42
D	2-1	KD	26-35, 16-21

2L Engine Excluding Australia Tyre size 14in Comm

Manual	Shift	Throttle	Km/h, MPH
D	1-2	KD	39-50, 25-31
D	2-3	KD	73-84, 45-62
D	O/D-3	KD	103-120, 64-75
D	3-2	KD	68-79, 42-49
D	2-1	KD	31-42, 19-26

2L Engine Excluding Australia Tyre size 14in Radial

Manual	Shift	Throttle	Km/h, MPH
D	1-2	KD	36-45, 22-28
D	2-3	KD	67-77, 42-48
D	O/D-3	KD	94-109, 58-68
D	3-2	KD	61-71, 38-44
D	2-1	KD	28-38, 17-24

Line Pressure Charts 50's - 60's Series

3Y Engine
Line Pressure
kPa Pressure, PSI

Gear	Idle	Stall
D	343-431, 50-63	941-1079, 137-156
Rev	490-628, 71-91	1344-1667, 195-242

2L Engine
Line Pressure
kPa Pressure, PSI

Gear	Idle	Stall
D	343-431, 50-63	1098-1294, 159-188
Rev	451-657, 65-95	1471-1863, 213-270

Line Pressure Charts 90's - 110's Series
22R Engine
Line Pressure
kPa Pressure, PSI

Gear	Idle	Stall
D	353-402, 51-58	1030-1196, 149-174
Rev	500-569, 73-83	1422-1785, 206-259

2L Engine
Line Pressure
kPa Pressure, PSI

Gear	Idle	Stall
D	343-431, 50-63	1098-1294, 159-188
Rev	451-657, 65-95	1471-1863, 213-270

SPECIFICATIONS

Dry fill capacity:
6.5 lts (6.9 US qts, 5.7 Imp.qts)
Fluid type specification: ATF DEXRON^R II
Throttle Cable Housing End Clearance Distance:
0 - 1.0 mm (0 - 0.04 in) 50's and 60's models
0.8 - 1.5 mm (0.031 - 0.059in) 80's to 130's models

Converter Fluid spec: Automatic Trans Dexron 11
Converter Fluid Capacity:
                    2.0 litres (2.1US qts, 1.8Imp qts)
2. Install the converter to the transmission, check that runout
is within specification.
Converter Runout specification: 0.30mm (0.0118in)
Converter to bell housing clearance.
50's - 60's series: 20mm (0.79in)
80's - 13's series:
          R engine 22.4mm (0.882in)
          L engine 29.4mm (1.157in)

TORQUE SPECIFICATIONS

Drain plug specified torque: 205 kg-cm (15 ft-lb,20 N·m)
Neutral Start Switch bolts torque:
                    55kg-cm (48in-lb, 5.4Nm)
Valve Body Bolts: 100kg-cm (7ft-lb, 10Nm)
Oil Strainer Attaching Bolts Torque:
                    55kg-cm (48in-lb,5.4Nm)
Transmission Oil Sump: 45kg-cm (39in-lb, 4.4Nm)
Converter housing to Engine attaching bolts:
                    650kg-cm (47ft-lb,64Nm)
Rear Engine mounting attaching bolts:
                    425kg-cm(31ft-lb,42Nm)
Transmission Mounting bolts;
                    250kg-cm(18ft-lb,25Nm)
Flywheel to Converter bolts: 185kg-cm(13ft-lb, 18Nm)
Supporting Bracket Attaching bolts:
                    380kg-cm(27ft-lb,37Nm)
Converter housing cover bolts:
                    185kg-cm(13ft-lb, 18Nm)
Fluid Cooler Tubes spec: 350kg-cm(25ft-lb,34Nm)
Starter Motor bolts: 16-20Nm
Tail shaft bolts (universal joint / pinion flange):
                    750kg-cm(54ft-lb,74Nm)
Tail shaft centre bearing mounting bolts:
                    370kg-cm(27ft-lb,36Nm)

Memo

TRANSFER

Description

TRANSFER

Transfer case is situated behind the transmission on 4WD vehicles, and provides power to the front wheels when the vehicle is placed into 4WD.

Vehicles that are 30's, 40's, 50's, 60's and some later models use a counter gear reduction type transfer.

Most of the vehicles that are 80's to 130's series use a planetary gear reduction type transfer, with either manual or electronic shift.

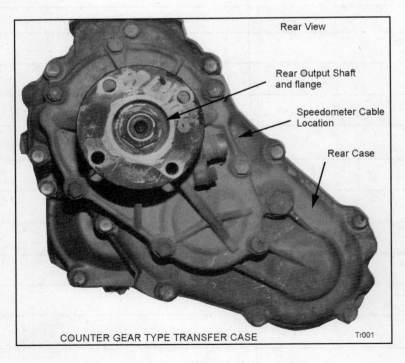

Rear View

Rear Output Shaft and flange

Speedometer Cable Location

Rear Case

COUNTER GEAR TYPE TRANSFER CASE   Tr001

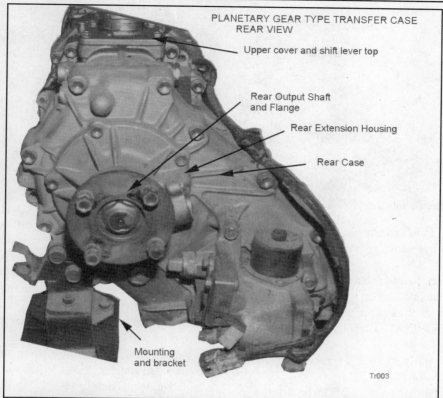

PLANETARY GEAR TYPE TRANSFER CASE
REAR VIEW

Upper cover and shift lever top

Rear Output Shaft
and Flange

Rear Extension Housing

Rear Case

Mounting
and bracket

Tr003

Replacement Front & Rear Output Shaft Oil Seal

1. Place vehicle on safety stands.
2. Drain gear oil from transfer case.
3. Remove front and rear propeller shafts as described in tail/propeller shaft chapter.
4. Remove companion flange retaining nut and companion flange.
5. Remove the front output shaft oil seal with a seal remover, or screw driver.
6. Install new front oil seal, use a round special tool seat seal in correct position.
7. Remove the rear extension housing.
8. Remove the front and rear seal of the rear extension seals with a seal remover or screw driver.
9. Install new front and rear oil seals to rear extension

housing, use a round special tool to seat seals in correct position.
10. Install rear extension housing and tighten bolts to specification.

Rear Extension Housing Nut Torque:
400 kg-cm 29 ft-lb, 39 Nm

11. Install companion flange and lock nut, tighten to specification.

Front Companion Flange Retaining Nut Torque:
1,250 kg-cm 90 ft-lb, 123 Nm

12. Stake the companion flange lock nut.
13. Install front and rear propeller shafts, tighten nuts to specification.

Propeller Shaft to Flange Retaining Nut Torque:
750 kg-cm 54 ft-lb, 74 Nm

14. Fill transfer with oil.

Oil Grade: API GL-4 \ GL-5
Oil Viscosity: SAE 75W-90
Capacity: Counter Gear Type:
1.6 lts (1.7 US qts, 1.4 Imp.qts)
Capacity: Planetary Gear Type:
1.1 lts (1.2 US qts, 1.0 Imp.qts)

TRANSFER CASE
Remove

1. Remove fan shroud from radiator, otherwise it may be damaged during the removal of the transmission.
2. Vehicles with floor mounted gear shifter lever, remove the gear shifter lever by pushing on the cap and turning anticlock-

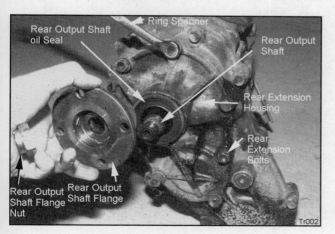

Rear Output Shaft oil Seal

Ring Spanner

Rear Output Shaft

Rear Extension Housing

Rear Extension Bolts

Rear Output Shaft Flange Nut

Rear Output Shaft Flange

Tr002

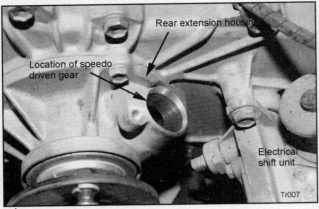

Tr007

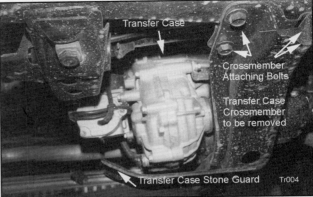

Tr004

wise.

3. Vehicles with floor mounted transfer shift lever, remove the transfer shift lever by removing spring clip, then lift lever out.

4. Disconnect battery earth lead and raise vehicle (front and rear) and support on safety stands.

5. Remove propeller shaft as described in PROPELLER SHAFT AND UNIVERSAL JOINTS Chapter in this Manual.

6. Vehicles with column gear shift lever, remove shifter linkages from transmission.

7. Disconnect wiring harness connector from back-up lamp switch.

8. (a) Disconnect Speedo cable connector from the left side of the transmission.

(b) Disconnect any electrical plugs to transmission or transfer case, as the transmission may be electrical shift.

(c) Position cable and connector away from transmission.

(d) Remove breather hose from transfer case.

9. Place a suitable drain tray under the transmission and transfer case, remove drain plugs and allow transmission and transfer fluid to drain out.

10. (a) Remove the clutch slave cylinder attaching bracket and fluid pipe. Gently position the fluid pipe and slave cylinder to one side.

(b) *Hi Lux RN*: Remove the starter motor and position the starter to one side.

11. Disconnect engine front exhaust pipe from engine, it may be necessary to remove the exhaust manifold.

12. Place a lifting jack beneath engine and support weight of engine.

13. Place a lifting jack beneath transmission and support weight of transmission.

14. Remove rear engine mounting bracket bolts and washers.

(a) Four bolts attaching the mount.

(b) Lift transmission to allow the four bolts attaching the mounting bracket to be removed.

(e) Remove the mount from the transmission.

(d) Remove the crossmember which supports the transmission and transfer case.

15. *Vehicles other than Hi Lux RN:* (RN - Starter motor has

been removed) Lower transmission and engine slightly to allow starter motor to be removed, position starter to one side.

16. Remove transmission case attaching bolts to engine, lower and withdraw transmission / transfer case assembly.

* Keep the transmission assembly supported so that it will not tilt in relation to the engine, until the maindrive gear splines are clear of the clutch plate.

* If the transmission is allowed to hang on the splines, the clutch plate will be damaged.

17. Separate the transfer case from the transmission by removing the attaching bolts. When separating the transfer case, lift and pull back.

Dismantle Transfer (Counter Gear Type)

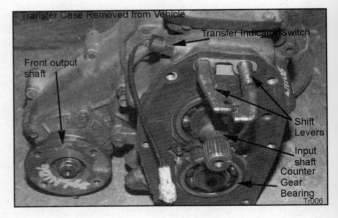

Tr006

1. Remove diaphragm cylinder (electrical shift type).

2. Remove transfer front drive shift lever (mechanical shift type).

(a) Remove the transfer front drive shift lever.

(b) Remove the dust boot.

3. Remove 4WD indicator switch.

4. Remove L4 position switch (electrical shift type).

5. Remove the shift lever plugs with an Allen Key, springs and locking balls.

[**Mechanical Shift Type**] Remove the plugs and roll transfer on to side and allow springs and ball to fall out, or use a magnetic finger to remove the springs and locking balls.

[**Electrical Shift Type**] Remove the plugs and roll transfer on to side and allow springs and ball to fall out, or use a

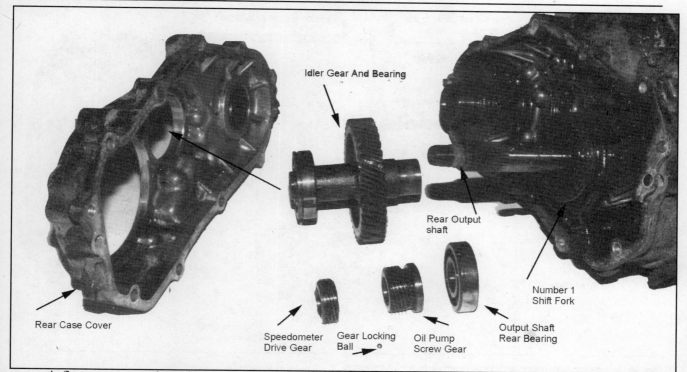

Idler Gear And Bearing

Rear Output shaft

Number 1 Shift Fork

Rear Case Cover

Speedometer Drive Gear

Gear Locking Ball

Oil Pump Screw Gear

Output Shaft Rear Bearing

magnetic finger to remove the springs and locking balls.

6. Remove speedometer driven gear, if still fitted.

7. Remove front and rear companion flanges with nuts.

8. Remove the rear extension housing attached by 7 bolts.

9. Remove the speedo drive gear and locking ball.

10. Remove the oil pump screw and relative bearing.

11. Split the rear case from the main case by removing the 10 bolts, if rear case will not separate tap with a soft hammer or use a large screw driver.

12. Remove the two oil pipes from inside the transfer case, pull out with pliers.

13. Remove the front output shaft.

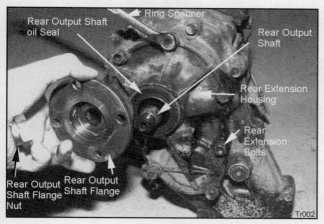

Rear Output Shaft oil Seal

Ring Spanner

Rear Output Shaft

Rear Extension Housing

Rear Extension Bolts

Rear Output Shaft Flange Nut

Rear Output Shaft Flange

Tr002

(a) Remove the front output shaft bearing retainer plate, attached by 4 bolts.

(b) Remove the spring clip, locking the shaft in position.

(c) Tap shaft out with a hammer and block of wood.

14. Remove shift fork shaft.

(a) Drive out the slotted spring pin with a pin punch and hammer.

(b) Remove the shift fork shaft from the shift fork.

15. Remove the drive gear and clutch with a gear puller, remove roller bearing, spacer and lock ball.

16. Remove the front wheel drive shifting fork shaft and lock pin.

17. Remove the high low speed drive shifting fork shaft and

Front output shaft and bearing assembly

Front Output Shaft

Location of front output shaft bearing retainer

Front output shaft bearing clip

Tr011

Hammer

Punch

Front shifting fork

Oil pipe (pull out)

Punch out pin from front shifting fork

Front input shaft

Tr012

221

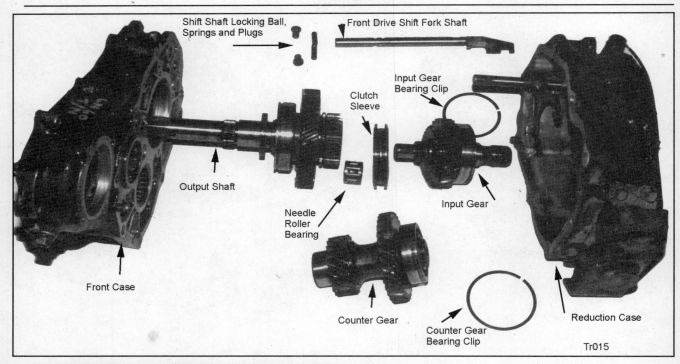

Shift Shaft Locking Ball, Springs and Plugs

Front Drive Shift Fork Shaft

Input Gear Bearing Clip

Clutch Sleeve

Output Shaft

Needle Roller Bearing

Input Gear

Front Case

Counter Gear

Counter Gear Bearing Clip

Reduction Case

Tr015

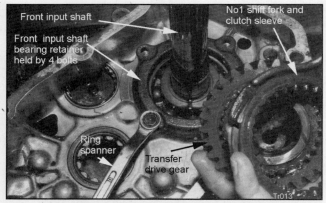

Front input shaft

No1 shift fork and clutch sleeve

Front input shaft bearing retainer held by 4 bolts

Ring spanner

Transfer drive gear

Tr013

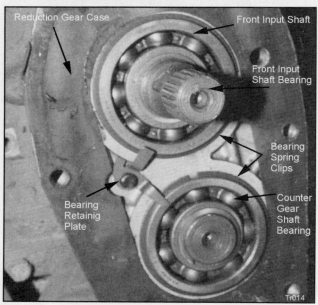

Reduction Gear Case

Front Input Shaft

Front Input Shaft Bearing

Bearing Spring Clips

Counter Gear Shaft Bearing

Bearing Retainig Plate

Tr014

lock pin.

18. Split the front case from the main case by removing the 4 bolts, if front case will not separate tap with a soft hammer or use a large screw driver.

19. Pull off by hand the shift fork and clutch with bearing from the front input shaft.

20. Remove gears from the reduction case. Remove the spring clips from the gears, tap the gears out with a piece of wood and hammer.

Assemble Transfer (Counter Gear Type)

1. Install gears to the reduction case. Tap the gears in with a piece of wood and hammer, install the spring clips to the gears bearings.

2. Place the shift fork and clutch with bearing to the front input shaft.

3. Replace the front output shaft.

(a) Install the shaft and seat into position with a hammer and block of wood.

(b) Replace the locking spring clip into position.

(c) Replace the inside front output shaft bearing retainer plate, and 4 bolts, tighten to specification.

Front Output Shaft Bearing Retainer Plate Bolt Torque 185 kg-cm 13 ft-lb, 18 Nm

4. Assemble the front case to the main case and the 4 bolts, 3 bolts are 47mm long and one is 49mm long, use a new gasket, tighten to specification.

Front Case to Main Case Bolt Torque Specification: 400 kg-cm 29 ft-lb, 39 Nm

5. Replace the front wheel drive gear and bearing retainer.

(a) Replace the front wheel drive gear, tap into position, fit spring clip.

222

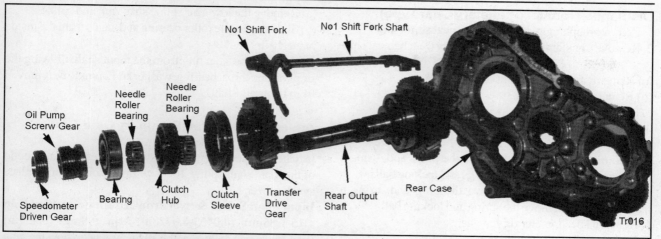

No1 Shift Fork • No1 Shift Fork Shaft • Oil Pump Screrw Gear • Needle Roller Bearing • Needle Roller Bearing • Speedometer Driven Gear • Bearing • Clutch Hub • Clutch Sleeve • Transfer Drive Gear • Rear Output Shaft • Rear Case

Tr016

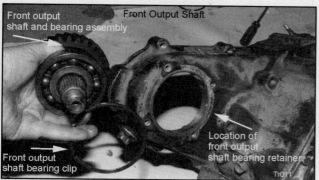

Front output shaft and bearing assembly • Front Output Shaft • Front output shaft bearing clip • Location of front output shaft bearing retainer

Tr011

(b) Replace the front output shaft bearing retainer plate, fit a new gasket and tighten 4 bolts, tighten to specification.

Front Wheel Drive Shaft Retainer Bolt Torque:
185 kg-cm 13 ft-lb, 18 Nm

6. Replace the high low speed drive shifting fork shaft and lock pin, tap pin in with hammer.

7. Replace the front wheel drive shifting fork shaft, cut out sections away from transfer case, and lock pin.

8. At the base of the case replace the locking ball spring and plug on either side, apply sealant to plugs, tighten plugs to specification.

Transfer Case Lower Plugs Torque specification:
120 kg-cm 9 ft-lb, 12 Nm

9. Replace front input shaft, gear, shift fork.

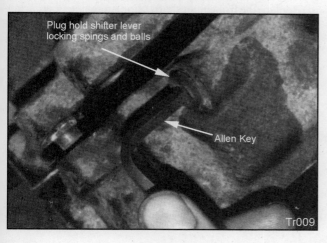

Plug hold shifter lever locking spings and balls • Allen Key

Tr009

(a) Replace shaft, fit locking spring clip.

(b) Replace metal ball and spacer.

(c) Replace needle roller bearing, lower gear with clutch hub and shift fork to front input shaft.

(d) Align pin hole in fork and fork shaft, install pin, tap in with a hammer.

10. Replace the two oil pipes to the inside of the transfer case, pipe side openings to the top of case.

11. Assemble rear cover of transfer.

(a) Tap the idler gear into position in the rear cover.

(b) Lock idler gear into position with a spring clip.

(c) Install the rear cove to the case, use a new gasket, tighten the 10 bolts to specified torque.

Rear Cover Attaching Bolt Specified Torque:
400 kg-cm 29 ft-lb, 39 Nm

12. Replace the oil pump screw and relative bearing.

13. Replace the locking ball and speedo drive gear.

14. Install the rear extension housing, new gasket and 7 bolts, tighten to specification.

Rear Extension Attaching Bolt Specified Torque:
400 kg-cm 29 ft-lb, 39 Nm

15. Replace front and rear companion flanges with nuts, stake nuts.

Companion Flange Retaining Nut Torque:
1,250 kg-cm 90 ft-lb, 123 Nm

16. Replace the transfer bottom cover and new gasket.

17. Replace speedometer driven gear.

Speedometer Driven Gear Retaining Nut Torque:
115 kg-cm 8 ft-lb, 11 Nm

18. Replace L4 position switch (electrical shift type).

19. Install 4WD indicator switch.

4WD Indicator Switch Nut Torque:
350 kg-cm 25 ft-lb, 34 Nm

20. Install transfer front drive shift lever (mechanical shift type).

(a) Replace the transfer front drive shift lever.

(b) Replace the dust boot.

21. Remove diaphragm cylinder (electrical shift type).

Dismantle Transfer (Planetary Gear Type)

1. Remove diaphragm cylinder (electrical shift type).
2. Remove transfer front drive shift lever (mechanical shift type).
(a) Remove the transfer front drive shift lever.
(b) Remove the dust boot.
3. Remove 4WD indicator switch.
4. Remove L4 position switch (electrical shift type).
5. Remove the 2 plugs, 2 springs and 2 locking balls.
[Mechanical Shift Type] Remove the plugs and, using a magnetic finger, remove the springs and locking balls.
[Electrical Shift Type] Remove the plug and, using a magnetic finger, remove the spring and locking ball.
6. Remove speedometer driven gear.
7. Remove the transfer top cover.
8. Remove front and rear companion flanges with nuts.
9. Remove the rear extension housing attached by 5 bolts.
10. Remove the speedo drive gear and locking ball.
11. Split the rear case from the main case by removing the 12 bolts, if rear case will not separate tap with a soft hammer or use a large screw driver.
12. Remove the front fork and shaft.
(a) Remove the two shift shaft stoppers, by removing the pin in each stopper, then remove stopper.
(b) Punch out the 2 spring pins holding the shifting fork to the fork shaft. The pin in the front fork shaft also releases the shaft, so as the punch is remove the shaft will spring out.
(c) Remove the shifting fork shaft lock pin from the case.
(d) Remove the other shift fork and shaft.
14. Remove the rear output shaft.
(a) Remove the rear output shaft bearing spring clip on the outside of the rear case.
(b) Grip the rear output shaft and pull firmly, it may be necessary to tap the rear case to loosen the shaft.
(c) Inside the rear case pull the shaft away from the rear case and remove the drive chain from the sprocket.
15. Remove oil pump and strainer.
(a) Remove the 3 bolts attaching the separator plate and oil strainer.
(b) Remove the 3 bolts attaching the oil pump to the transfer case.
(c) Lift the oil pump drive gear from the transfer case.
16. Remove the front input shaft.
(a) Remove the front input shaft bearing retainer and 7 bolts.
(b) Remove the front input shaft bearing spring clip on the outside of the transfer case.
(c) Remove the synchronized ring from inside the planetary gear.
(d) From inside the case grip the planetary gear and pull the planetary gear and input shaft away from the case.
17. From inside the case remove the planetary ring gear snap ring, on the outside of the case remove the plug, spring and locking pin, lift the planetary ring gear away from the case.
18. Dismantle the planetary gear.

(a) Remove the low gear spline snap ring and spline.
(b) Slide the needle roller bearing and cages from the inside input shaft.
(c) Remove the snap ring from the input shaft allowing the stop washer, thrust bearing, washer and 2 pins to be removed from the input shaft.

Assemble Transfer (Planetary Gear Type)

1. Assemble the planetary gear.
(a) Check gap between back of synchronizer ring and the end of the input shaft spline. If not within specification, replace synchronizer.
Input Shaft Spline & Synchronized Ring Specified Gap 1.15-1.85mm (0.0453-0.0728in) Min. 0.8mm (0.031in)
(b) Check gap between the planetary gear housing and planetary pinion gears. If not within specification, replace planetary gear assembly.
Planetary Gear Housing and Planetary Pinion Gear Specified Gap
0.11-0.86mm (0.0043-0.0339in) Min. 0.8mm (0.031in)
(c) Fit the thrust bearing, bearing race and input shaft, into the planetary gear.
(c) Install the input shaft into the planetary gear, then 2 pins, washer, thrust bearing, stop washer to the input shaft.
(d) Lock into position with a snap ring which will give the shaft a clearance of 0.05-0.15mm free play.
(e) Slide the needle roller bearing and cages into the inside input shaft.
(f) Install the low gear spline and snap ring to the spline.
2. Fit the planetary ring gear into the case, it may help to heat case with an electric heater, secure into place with the snap ring. On the outside of the case install locking pin, spring and tighten plug.
3. Replace the front input shaft.
(a) Lift the planetary gear and input shaft into position and slide in through ring gear.
(b) Replace the front input shaft bearing spring clip on the outside of the transfer case.
(c) Replace the synchronized ring to the inside of the planetary gear.
(d) Replace the front input shaft bearing retainer, new gasket and 7 bolts, tighten to specification.
Front Input Shaft Bearing Retainer Plate Bolt Torque
115 kg-cm 8 ft-lb, 11 Nm
4. Install oil pump and strainer.
(a) Fit the oil pump drive gear into the transfer case.
(b) Replace the oil pump into the transfer case and 3 attaching bolts, tighten to specification.
Oil Pump Bolt Torque
115 kg-cm 8 ft-lb, 11 Nm
(c) Install the separator plate and oil strainer, tighten the 3 bolts to specification.
Separator Plate and Oil Strainer Bolt Torque
185 kg-cm 13 ft-lb, 18 Nm

TRANSFER

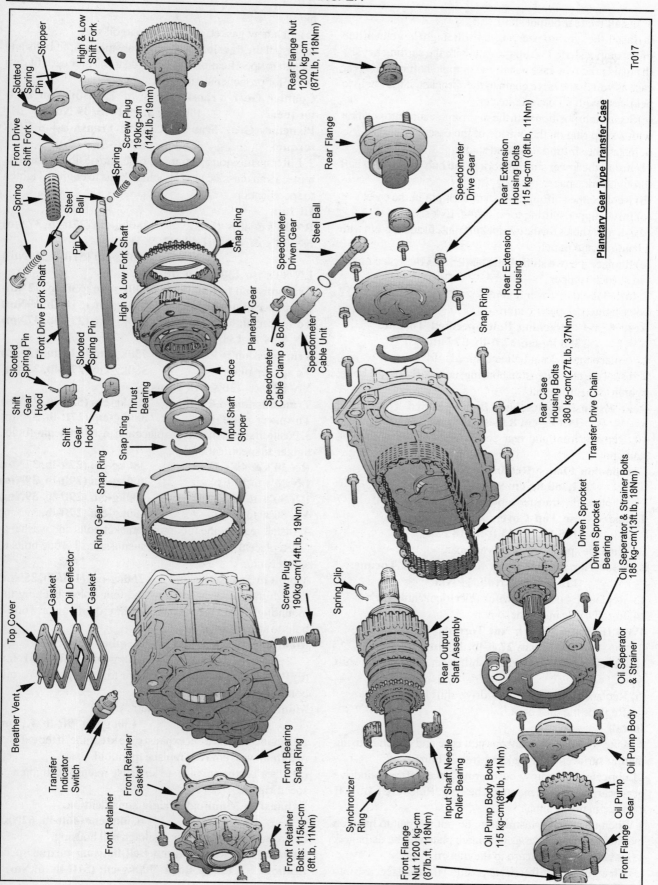

Stopper

Slotted Spring Pin

High & Low Shift Fork

Front Drive Shift Fork

Spring

Spring

Screw Plug 190kg-cm (14ft.lb, 19nm)

Steel Ball

Spring

Pin

High & Low Fork Shaft

Snap Ring

Slooted Spring Pin

Front Drive Fork Shaft

Slooted Spring Pin

Shift Gear Hood

Shift Gear Hood

Thrust Bearing

Race

Snap Ring

Snap Ring

Input Shaft Stoper

Speedometer Cable Clamp & Bolt

Speedometer Driven Gear

Steel Ball

Speedometer Cable Unit

Planetary Gear

Ring Gear

Screw Plug 190kg-cm(14ft.lb, 19Nm)

Spring Clip

Rear Flange Nut 1200 kg-cm (87ft.lb, 118Nm)

Tr017

Rear Flange

Speedometer Drive Gear

Rear Extension Housing Bolts 115 kg-cm (8ft.lb, 11Nm)

Rear Extension Housing

Snap Ring

Rear Case Housing Bolts 380 kg-cm(27ft.lb, 37Nm)

Transfer Drive Chain

Planetary Gear Type Transfer Case

Driven Sprocket

Driven Sprocket Bearing

Oil Seperator & Strainer Bolts 185 kg-cm(13ft.lb, 18Nm)

Oil Seperator & Strainer

Oil Pump Body

Oil Pump Body

Oil Pump Gear

Front Flange

Top Cover

Gasket

Oil Deflector

Gasket

Breather Vent

Transfer Indicator Switch

Front Retainer

Front Retainer Gasket

Front Bearing Snap Ring

Front Retainer Bolts: 115kg-cm (8ft.lb, 11Nm)

Synchronizer Ring

Rear Output Shaft Assembly

Input Shaft Needle Roller Bearing

Front Flange Nut 1200 kg-cm (87lb.ft, 118Nm)

Oil Pump Body Bolts 115 kg-cm(8ft.lb, 11Nm)

225

5. Install the rear output shaft.

(a) Install the synchronizer ring, on to the high/low clutch hub of the output shaft, line up the ring with the shifting keys.

(b) Inside the rear case install the output shaft into the rear case as you fit the drive chain to the sprocket, it may help to heat case with an electric heater.

(c) Secure into position with the snap ring, secure into position with a snap ring on the outside of the case.

6. Install the shifting forks and shafts.

(a) Install the lower shifting fork to the hub, slide fork shaft through fork, spacer.

(b) Replace the shifting fork shaft lock pin in the case.

(c) Install upper shifting fork, spring, fork shaft.

(d) Align the holes for the two locking pins, fit and drive in with a hammer and punch.

(e) Replace the two shift shaft stoppers, fix by replacing the pin in each stopper.

7. Install the rear cover and new gasket to the case and 12 bolts, tighten to specification.

Rear Cover Attaching Bolt Specified Torque:
380 kg-cm 27 ft-lb, 37 Nm

8. Replace the locking ball and speedo drive gear.

9. Install the rear extension housing, new gasket and 5 bolts, tighten to specification.

Rear Extension Attaching Bolt Specified Torque:
115 kg-cm 8 ft-lb, 11 Nm

10. Replace front and rear companion flanges with nuts, stake nuts.

Companion Flange Retaining Nut Torque:
1,250 kg-cm 90 ft-lb, 123 Nm

11. Replace the transfer top cover and new gasket.

Transfer Case Top Cover bolt Torque:
185 kg-cm 13 ft-lb, 18 Nm

12. Replace speedometer driven gear.

Speedometer Driven Gear Retaining Nut Torque:
115 kg-cm 8 ft-lb, 11 Nm

13. Replace L4 position switch (electrical shift type).

14. Install 4WD indicator switch.

4WD Indicator Switch Nut Torque:
380 kg-cm 27 ft-lb, 37 Nm

15. Install transfer front drive shift lever (mechanical shift type).

(a) Replace the transfer front drive shift lever.

(b) Replace the dust boot.

Install

* Make sure that the transmission case and clutch housing mating surfaces are clean and free of burrs.

* Lubricate clutch throw-out bearing surface of the maindrive gear bearing retainer and spigot bearing. Refer to **CLUTCH** Chapter in this Manual.

* When installing transmission, do not allow it to hang on maindrive gear splines as the clutch plate will be damaged.

1. Install the transfer case to the transmission

(a) Change the 2 shift forks to position the transfer case into high 4.

(b) Fit a new gasket, apply grease to oil seal.

(c) Install the transfer case to the transmission, fit bolts and tighten to specification. (Counter gear transfer case fit dust cover for propeller shaft)

Counter Gear Transfer Case to Transmission Bolts torque: **400 kg-cm 29 ft-lb, 39 Nm**
Planetary Gear Transfer Case to Transmission Bolts torque: **380 kg-cm 27 ft-lb, 37 Nm**

2. Lift transmission and transfer case into position on a jack, replace transmission case attaching bolts to engine. Tighten to specification.

Hi Lux

RN 30's & 40's (L42)	**380kg-cm (27ft-lb, 37Nm)**
RN 30's & 40's (L40, 42 & W50)	**700kg-cm (51ft-lb, 69Nm)**
LN 80's to 130's (All trans)	
Transmission to Engine	**730kg-cm (53ft-lb, 72Nm)**
To spacer plate (higher)	**700kg-cm (51ft-lb, 69Nm)**
To spacer plate (lower)	**380kg-cm (27ft-lb, 37Nm)**
RN 80's to 130's (All trans)	
Transmission to Engine	**730kg-cm (53ft-lb, 72Nm)**
To spacer plate	**380kg-cm (27ft-lb, 37Nm)**
YN 80's to 130's (All trans)	
Transmission to Engine	**730kg-cm (53ft-lb, 72Nm)**
To spacer plate	**380kg-cm (27ft-lb, 37Nm)**

3. Position starter motor into place and install attaching bolts, tighten to specification.

RN 30's & 40's (L42)	**380kg-cm (27ft-lb, 37Nm)**
LN 80's to 130's	**400kg-cm (29ft-lb, 39Nm)**
RN 80's to 130's	**400kg-cm (29ft-lb, 39Nm)**
YN 80's to 130's	**400kg-cm (29ft-lb, 39Nm)**

4. Install rear engine mounting bracket bolts and washers.

(a) Replace the mount to the transmission. Torque bolts to specification.

Mount to Transmission : **260kg-cm (19ft-lb, 25Nm)**

(b) Lift transmission to allow the four bolts attaching the mounting bracket to be installed to the crossmember. Torque bolts to specification.

Mounting bracket to Crossmember: **620kg-cm (45ft-lb, 61Nm)**

(c) Four bolts attaching the mount to the bracket. Torque bolts to specification.

Mount to Mounting Bracket: **130kg-cm (9ft-lb, 13Nm)**

5. Connect engine front exhaust pipe to engine, if the exhaust manifold was removed replace manifold.

(a) Install exhaust pipe to exhaust manifold, tighten to specification.

Exhaust to Manifold torque specification: **630kg-cm (46ft-lb, 62Nm)**

(b) Install exhaust bracket to clutch bell housing.

Exhaust Bracket to clutch Bell housing torque specification: **Large Bolts 700kg-cm (51ft-lb, 69Nm)**

TRANSFER - PLANETARY GEAR TYPE

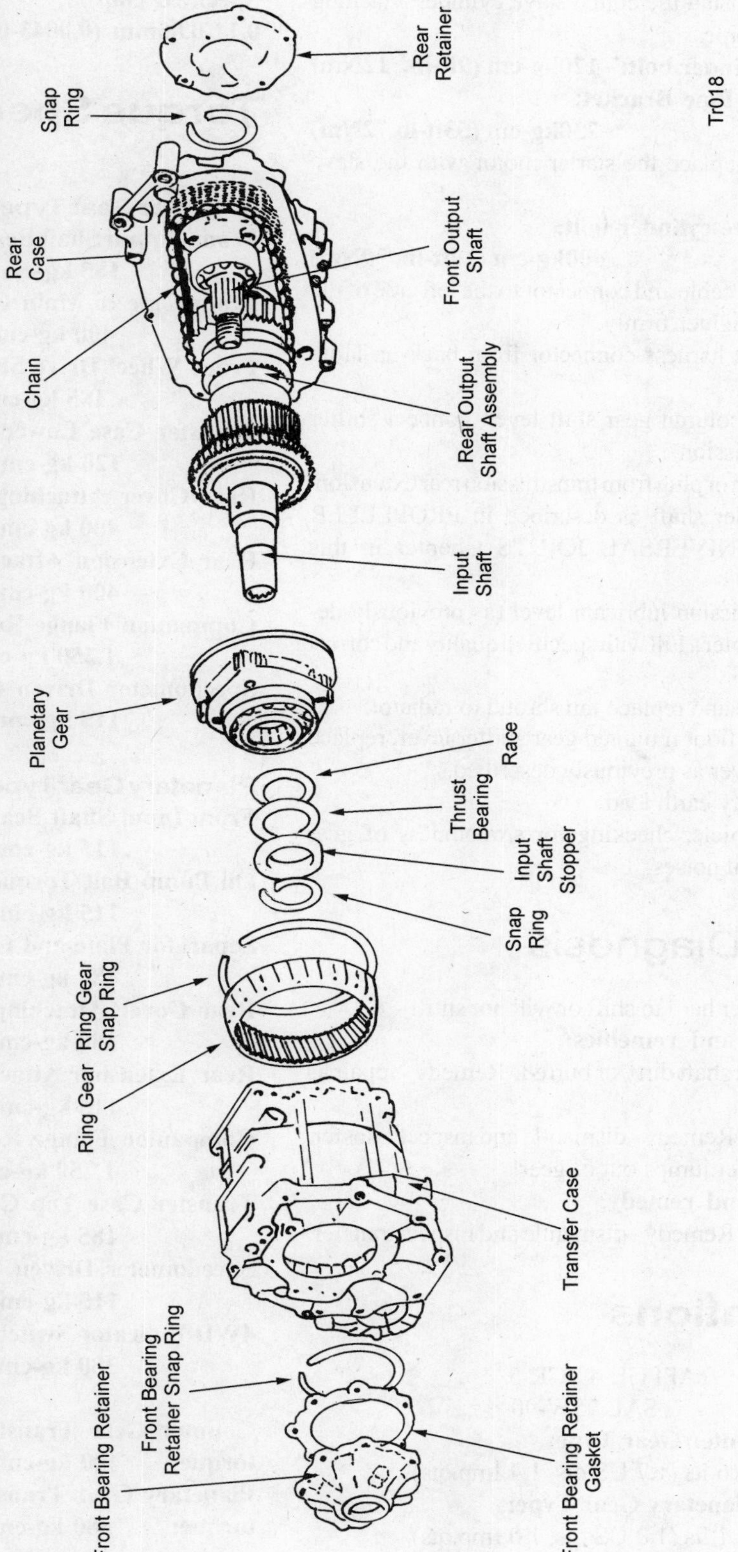

Rear Retainer

Snap Ring

Rear Case

Chain

Front Output Shaft

Rear Output Shaft Assembly

Input Shaft

Planetary Gear

Race

Thrust Bearing

Input Shaft Stopper

Snap Ring

Ring Gear Snap Ring

Ring Gear

Transfer Case

Front Bearing Retainer

Front Bearing Retainer Snap Ring

Front Bearing Retainer Gasket

Tr018

Small Bolts   380kg-cm (27ft-lb, 37Nm)

6. (a) Gently position the fluid pipe and slave cylinder into the correct position. Install the clutch slave cylinder attaching bracket and fluid pipe.

Clutch Slave Cylinder bolt: 120kg-cm (9ft-lb, 12Nm)
LN & RN Fluid Pipe Bracket:
                        730kg-cm (53ft-lb,72Nm)

(b) *Hi Lux RN*: Replace the starter motor with the slave cylinder.

RN Starter / slave cylinder bolt:
                        400kg-cm (29ft-lb, 39Nm)

6. Connect speedo cable and connector to the left side of the transmission, and tighten firmly.

7. Connect wiring harness connector from back-up lamp switch.

8. Vehicles with column gear shift lever, connect shifter linkages to transmission.

9. (a) Remove cloth or plug from transmission rear extension.
(b) Install propeller shaft as described in PROPELLER SHAFT AND UNIVERSAL JOINTS Chapter in this Manual.

10. Check transmission lubricant level (as previously described in this Chapter). Fill with specified quality and correct amount of oil.

11. Lower vehicle and replace fan shroud to radiator.

12. Vehicles with floor mounted gear shifter lever, replace the gear shifter lever as previously described.

13. Connect battery earth lead.

14. Road test vehicle, checking for smoothness of gear changes or unusual noises.

Problem Diagnosis

Problem: Transfer hard to shift or will not shift!
Possible causes and remedies:
* Splines on input shaft dirty or burred. Remedy - repair as necessary.
* Transfer faulty. Remedy - dismantle and inspect transfer.
Problem: Transfer jumps out of gear!
Possible cause and remedy:
* Transfer faulty. Remedy - dismantle and inspect transfer.

Specifications

Oil Grade: API GL-4 \ GL-5
Oil Viscosity: SAE 75W-90
Capacity: Counter Gear Type:
          1.6 lts (1.7 US qts, 1.4 Imp.qts)
Capacity: Planetary Gear Type:
          1.1 lts (1.2 US qts, 1.0 Imp.qts)

Planetary Gear Type
Input Shaft Spline & Synchronizer Ring Specified Gap

1.15-1.85mm (0.0453-0.0728in) Min. 0.8mm (0.031in)
Planetary Gear Housing and Planetary Pinion Gear Specified Gap
0.11-0.86mm (0.0043-0.0339in) Min. 0.8mm (0.031in)

Torque Specifications

(Counter Gear Type)
Front Output Shaft Bearing Retainer Plate Bolt Torque
          185 kg-cm 13 ft-lb, 18 Nm
Front Case to Main Case Bolt Torque Specification:
          400 kg-cm 29 ft-lb, 39 Nm
Front Wheel Drive Shaft Retainer Bolt Torque:
          185 kg-cm 13 ft-lb, 18 Nm
Transfer Case Lower Plugs Torque specification:
          120 kg-cm 9 ft-lb, 12 Nm
Rear Cover Attaching Bolt Specified Torque:
          400 kg-cm 29 ft-lb, 39 Nm
Rear Extension Attaching Bolt Specified Torque:
          400 kg-cm 29 ft-lb, 39 Nm
Companion Flange Retaining Nut Torque:
          1,250 kg-cm 90 ft-lb, 123 Nm
Speedometer Driven Gear Retaining Nut Torque:
          115 kg-cm 8 ft-lb, 11 Nm

Planetary Gear Type
Front Input Shaft Bearing Retainer Plate Bolt Torque
          115 kg-cm 8 ft-lb, 11 Nm
Oil Pump Bolt Torque
          115 kg-cm 8 ft-lb, 11 Nm
Separator Plate and Oil Strainer Bolt Torque
          185 kg-cm 13 ft-lb, 18 Nm
Rear Cover Attaching Bolt Specified Torque:
          380 kg-cm 27 ft-lb, 37 Nm
Rear Extension Attaching Bolt Specified Torque:
          115 kg-cm 8 ft-lb, 11 Nm
Companion Flange Retaining Nut Torque:
          1,250 kg-cm 90 ft-lb, 123 Nm
Transfer Case Top Cover bolt Torque:
          185 kg-cm 13 ft-lb, 18 Nm
Speedometer Driven Gear Retaining Nut Torque:
          115 kg-cm 8 ft-lb, 11 Nm
4WD Indicator Switch Nut Torque:
          380 kg-cm 27 ft-lb, 37 Nm

Counter Gear Transfer Case to Transmission Bolts torque: 400 kg-cm 29 ft-lb, 39 Nm
Planetary Gear Transfer Case to Transmission Bolts torque: 380 kg-cm 27 ft-lb, 37 Nm

Transmission to Engine
Hi Lux
RN 30's & 40's (L42)   380kg-cm (27ft-lb, 37Nm)
RN 30's & 40's (L40, 42 & W50)
                        700kg-cm (51ft-lb, 69Nm)
LN 80's to 130's (All trans)
Transmission to Engine   730kg-cm (53ft-lb, 72Nm)
To spacer plate (higher)   700kg-cm (51ft-lb, 69Nm)
To spacer plate (lower)   380kg-cm (27ft-lb, 37Nm)
RN 80's to 130's (All trans)
Transmission to Engine   730kg-cm (53ft-lb, 72Nm)
To spacer plate   380kg-cm (27ft-lb, 37Nm)
YN 80's to 130's (All trans)
Transmission to Engine   730kg-cm (53ft-lb, 72Nm)
To spacer plate   380kg-cm (27ft-lb, 37Nm)
RN 30's & 40's (L42)   380kg-cm (27ft-lb, 37Nm)
LN 80's to 130's   400kg-cm (29ft-lb, 9Nm)

RN 80's to 130's   400kg-cm (29ft-lb, 39Nm)
YN 80's to 130's   400kg-cm (29ft-lb, 39Nm)
Mount to Transmission :   260kg-cm (19ft-lb, 25Nm)
Mounting bracket to Crossmember:
                        620kg-cm (45ft-lb, 61Nm)
Mount to Mounting Bracket:
                        130kg-cm (9ft-lb, 13Nm)
Exhaust to Manifold torque specification:
                        630kg-cm (46ft-lb, 62Nm)
Exhaust Bracket to clutch Bell housing torque specification: Large Bolts 700kg-cm (51ft-lb, 69Nm)
                    Small Bolts 380kg-cm (27ft-lb, 37Nm)
Clutch Slave Cylinder bolt: 120kg-cm (9ft-lb, 12Nm)
LN & RN Fluid Pipe Bracket:
                        730kg-cm (53ft-lb, 72Nm)
RN Starter / slave cylinder bolt:
                        400kg-cm (29ft-lb, 39Nm)

Memo

TAIL /DRIVE SHAFT AND UNIVERSAL JOINTS

DRIVE / TAIL SHAFT

Remove

1. Raise rear of vehicle and support rear axle assembly on safety stands.

2. Remove bolts and nuts holding propeller shaft rear universal joint flange to pinion flange. Disengage rear universal joint flange from pinion flange.

* Paint or scribe a mark on both flanges so that they may be installed in their original positions.

3. *2 Wheel Drive:* Remove propeller shaft by pulling it toward the rear of vehicle to disengage front universal joint from transmission.

* Take care to protect the outer diameter of the front yoke of the drive shaft. Nicks or abrasions will damage the sleeve section of the drive shaft during assembly.

4. *4 Wheel Drive:* (a) Remove cover from front of drive shaft at transfer case. 4 bolts for "Counter Gear" transfer case and 3 bolts for "Planetary Gear" transfer case.

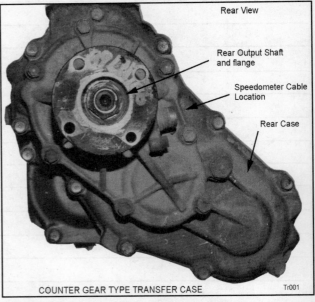

Rear View

Rear Output Shaft and flange

Speedometer Cable Location

Rear Case

COUNTER GEAR TYPE TRANSFER CASE   Tr001

(b) Some Drive shafts have a centre bearing. Scribe alignment marks on the crossmember, showing the position of the centre bearing bracket, this will help during installation of the drive shaft. Remove the two bearing attaching bracket bolts to lower the centre bearing.

(c) Remove bolts and nuts holding propeller shaft front universal joint flange to transfer flange. Disengage front universal joint flange from transfer flange.

* Paint or scribe a mark on both flanges so that they may be installed in their original positions.

5. Front drive shaft.

(a) Raise front of vehicle and support front axle assembly on

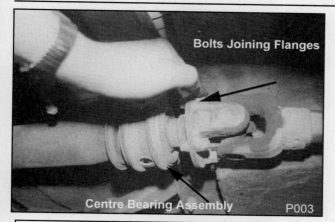

Bolts Joining Flanges

Centre Bearing Assembly

P003

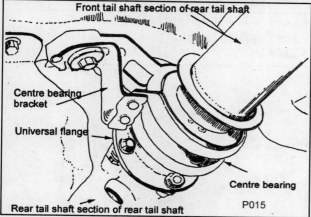

Front tail shaft section of rear tail shaft

Centre bearing bracket

Universal flange

Centre bearing

Rear tail shaft section of rear tail shaft

P015

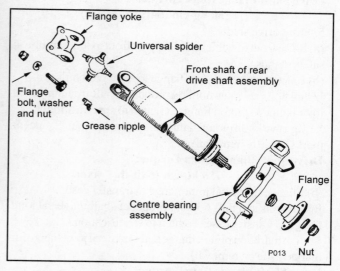

Flange yoke

Universal spider

Front shaft of rear drive shaft assembly

Flange bolt, washer and nut

Grease nipple

Centre bearing assembly

Flange

P013   Nut

safety stands.

(b) Remove bolts and nuts holding propeller shaft front universal joint flange to pinion flange.

* Paint or scribe a mark on both flanges so that they may be installed in their original positions.

(c) Remove bolts and nuts holding front propeller shaft rear universal joint flange to transfer case.

* Paint or scribe a mark on both flanges so that they may be installed in their original positions.

(d) Remove propeller shaft by pulling it toward the front of vehicle to disengage front universal joint from transfer case.

Installation

1. Remove any foreign matter that may have adhered to the universal joint yoke and lubricate with transmission lubricants. Guide propeller shaft yoke into other section of drive shaft.

2. Before attaching propeller shaft rear universal joint flange to pinion flange, align marks on pinion flange and rear universal joint flange (or marks made on removal).

3. Care must be taken to use new genuine bolts and nuts. Torque drive shaft rear universal joint flange to pinion flange bolts. Tighten to specification.

Drive Shaft Flange Bolts Torque:
750 kg-cm (54ft-lb, 74Nm)

4. *4 Wheel Drive:* (a) Some drive shafts have a centre bearing, for these models support the drive shaft while the two bearing attaching bracket bolts are fitted. Align the bearing support

brackets to the marks made while removing the centre bearing. Tighten to specification.

* Align marks on pinion flange and universal joint flange (or marks made on removal).

Drive Shaft Centre Bearing Bracket Bolts Torque:
370 kg-cm (27ft-lb, 36Nm)

(b) Replace the cover from the front of drive shaft at transfer case. 4 bolts for "Counter Gear" transfer case and 3 bolts for "Planetary Gear" transfer case.

(c) Engage front universal joint flange to transfer flange. Install bolts and nuts holding propeller shaft front universal joint flange to transfer flange. Tighten to specification.

* Align marks on pinion flange and universal joint flange (or marks made on removal).

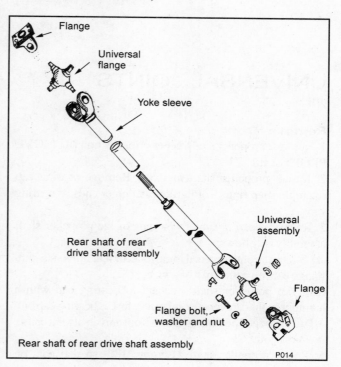

Flange

Universal flange

Yoke sleeve

Rear shaft of rear drive shaft assembly

Universal assembly

Flange

Flange bolt, washer and nut

Rear shaft of rear drive shaft assembly

P014

Drive Shaft Flange Bolts Torque:
750 kg-cm (54ft-lb, 74Nm)

5. Front drive shaft.

(a) Raise front of vehicle and support front axle assembly on safety stands.

(b) Engage universal joint flange to front pinion flange. Install bolts and nuts holding propeller shaft front universal joint flange to pinion flange. Tighten to specification.

* Align marks on pinion flange and universal joint flange (or marks made on removal).

Drive Shaft Flange Bolts Torque:
750 kg-cm (54ft-lb, 74Nm)

(b) Engage universal joint flange to transfer case. Install bolts and nuts holding propeller shaft universal joint flange to transfer case. Tighten to specification.

* Align marks on pinion flange and universal joint flange (or marks made on removal).

Drive Shaft Flange Bolts Torque:
750 kg-cm (54ft-lb, 74Nm)

Inspection On Vehicle:

1. Raise vehicle and support front (4WD) and rear axle assembly on safety stands.

2. Measure propeller shaft runout at several points by rotating final drive flange by hand.

Runout maximum: **0.8mm (0.031in)**

Off Vehicle:

1. Remove propeller shaft as described above.

2. Place propeller shaft on "V" blocks, measure runout with micrometer gauge.

3. Measure propeller shaft runout at several points by rotating final drive flange by hand.

Runout maximum: **0.8mm (0.031in)**

UNIVERSAL JOINTS

Remove

1. Remove propeller shaft as per prior Section [REMOVE PROPELLER SHAFT].

2. Mount propeller shaft in vice. Remove bearing cap retaining snap rings from grooves at inner ends of bearing caps.

3. Remove bearing caps from ends of the propeller shaft assembly as follows:

(a) Support front universal joint yoke, or rear universal joint flange ears on open jaws of a vice.

(b) Tap propeller shaft adjacent to bearing cap with a hammer so that universal joint spider forces bearing cap out.

4. Pull dislodged bearing cap from front universal joint or rear universal joint.

5. Rotate propeller shaft assembly 180° so that ears on

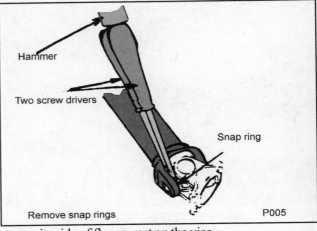

Remove snap rings   P005

opposite side of flange, rest on the vice.

6. Remove 2nd bearing cap from propeller shaft as per Steps 3 and 4.

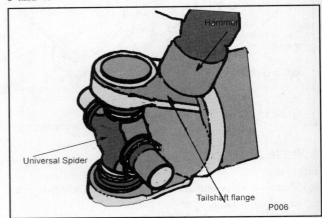

P006

7. Separate flange from universal joint spider.

8. Remove bearing caps from yoke or flange by resting exposed ends of spider on the vice, and removing bearing caps as previously described.

9. Remove the spider from the yoke or flange.

(a) Thoroughly clean yoke or flange and propeller shaft universal joint bearing cap bores.

(b) Check bearing cap bores and remove any burrs.

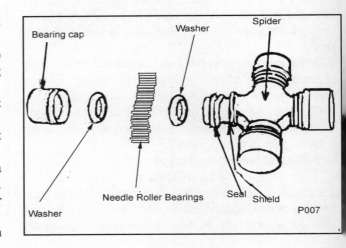

P007

232

Install

Before installing universal joint, note the following:

* Cleanliness is of prime importance to ensure maximum universal joint life.

* Do not allow any needle rollers to become dislodged. Install bearing caps in the upright position.

* Universal joint assemblies are prepacked with lubricant and do not require any further lubrication.

* Take care not to damage bearing cap seals during installation. Gently ease bearing caps into their bores during assembly.

1. Remove bearing caps from spider.

2. Position spider in yoke or flange. Hold spider to one side in yoke or flange and position a bearing cap on the end of spider.

3. While holding spider in bearing cap, push by hand then use a "G" clamp to push bearing cap into yoke or flange until bearing cap snap ring groove is fully visible. Install snap ring into groove.

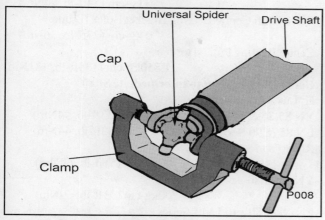

4. Turn yoke or flange around and install opposite bearing cap by positioning spider into bearing cap to prevent needle rollers from being dislodged.

5. (a) To fully install 2nd bearing cap, position yoke or flange in vice with 2 of the old universal joint bearing caps. Squeeze

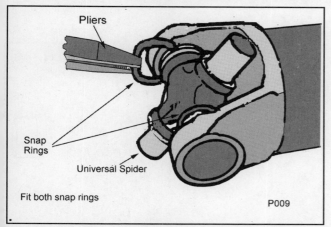

Fit both snap rings

new bearing caps into position using the vice jaws or G clamp.

* Ensure that the 2 old bearing caps are positioned centrally

on the new bearing caps, and not up against the edge of the flange or yoke.

(b) Install 2nd snap ring.

6. Install spider and yoke or flange assembly to propeller shaft. Install remaining bearing caps and snap rings as previously described.

7. Tap propeller shaft, yoke and flange ears with a hammer and ensure that all bearing cap snap rings are seated correctly in bearing cap grooves and that universal joints are free to move in all directions.

8. Install propeller shaft as per prior Section [INSTALLATION - PROPELLER SHAFT].

CENTRE BEARING

Remove

1. Remove propeller shaft as per prior Section [REMOVE

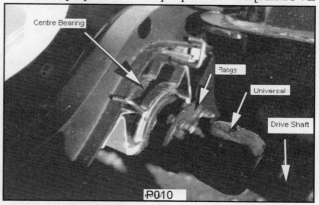

PROPELLER SHAFT].

2. Mount propeller shaft in vice.

* Paint or scribe a mark on flanges so that they may be installed in their original positions.

3. Remove bolts and nuts holding propeller shaft universal joint flange to front drive shaft flange. Disengage universal joint flange.

4. Remove the nut supporting the centre bearing while stopping the flange from turning. The nut thread may be punch marked to lock on.

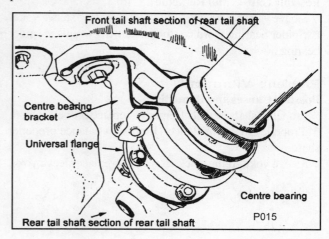

233

5. Separate the bearing from the intermediate shaft, it may need to be pulled off within a bearing puller.

Install

1. Grease the spline with multi purpose grease, fit bearing to spline, pull bearing onto spline with nut at special bearing torque.

Centre Bearing Pull on torque
1,850kg-cm (135ft-lb, 181Nm)

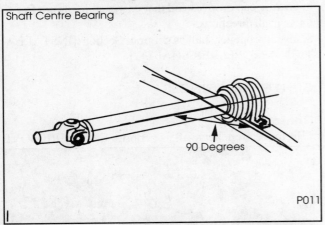

Shaft Centre Bearing

90 Degrees

P011

Tighten the nut to specification. Punch mark the nut thread to lock on.

Centre Bearing Nut to Intermediate Shaft:

Hi Lux and 4 Runner:

YN 85,86 & 90 Series   450kg-cm (33ft-lb, 44Nm)

LN 85 & 90 Series   450kg-cm (33ft-lb, 44Nm)

RN 80' to 130's Series
700kg-cm (51ft-lb, 69Nm)

YN other 80's to 130's Series
700kg-cm (51ft-lb, 69Nm)

LN other 80's to 130's Series
700kg-cm (51ft-lb, 69Nm)

PROBLEM DIAGNOSIS

Problem: Noise!
Possible Causes and Remedies:

* Sleeve yoke spline worn. Remedy - replace sleeve yoke.
* Spider bearing worn or stuck. Remedy - replace spider bearing.

Problem: Vibration!
Possible Causes and Remedies:

* Propeller shaft runout. Remedy - replace propeller shaft.
* Propeller shaft imbalance. Remedy - balance propeller shaft.
* Sleeve yoke spline stuck. Remedy - replace sleeve yoke.

SPECIFICATIONS

Maximum runout of Propeller Shaft
Runout maximum: 0.8mm (0.031in)
This is best measured accurately on a suitable propeller shaft jig, where the propeller shaft assembly is correctly supported through its entire length. However if a shaft jig is not available use "V" blocks in preference to checking on vehicle.

Lubricant
Front and Rear Universal Joints   Lithium soap grease

TORQUE WRENCH SPECS

Drive Shaft Flange Bolts Torque:
750 kg-cm (54ft-lb, 74Nm)
Drive Shaft Centre Bearing Bracket Bolts Torque:
370 kg-cm (27ft-lb, 36Nm)
Centre Bearing Pull on torque
1,850kg-cm (135ft-lb, 181Nm)
Centre Bearing Nut to Intermediate Shaft:
Hi Lux and 4 Runner:
YN 85,86 & 90 Series   450kg-cm (33ft-lb, 44Nm)
LN 85 & 90 Series   450kg-cm (33ft-lb, 44Nm)
RN 80's to 130's Series
700kg-cm (51ft-lb, 69Nm)
YN other 80's to 130's Series
700kg-cm (51ft-lb, 69Nm)
LN other 80's to 130's Series
700kg-cm (51ft-lb, 69Nm)

REAR AXLE & DIFFERENTIALS

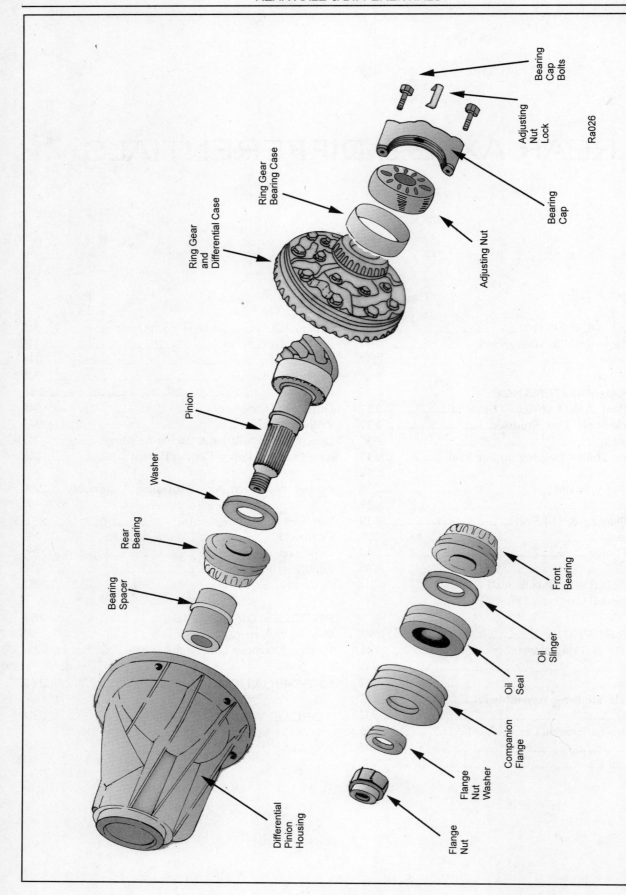

Bearing Cap Bolts

Adjusting Nut Lock

Ra026

Bearing Cap

Adjusting Nut

Ring Gear Bearing Case

Ring Gear and Differential Case

Pinion

Washer

Rear Bearing

Bearing Spacer

Differential Pinion Housing

Front Bearing

Oil Slinger

Oil Seal

Companion Flange

Flange Nut Washer

Flange Nut

REAR AXLE

GENERAL DESCRIPTION & MAINTENANCE

Maintenance
Rear Axle Breather.
The breather valve should be checked regularly to ensure that the cover rotates freely and that the exhaust is not restricted or blocked by mud.

Rear Axle Drain Plug.
The drain plug is located in the centre at the base of the differential housing.

Axle Bearing.
The axle bearings are lubricated by the oil in the rear axle assembly and therefore require no periodic maintenance. Differential Carrier Assemblies.

Check for lubricant leaks at every maintenance service. If there is evidence of leakage, correct leak and add lubricant as necessary.

Every 20,000 kms or 12 months, check to ensure that the lubricant level is to the bottom of the filler plug hole when the rear axle is COLD.

Four Wheel Drive & Limited Slip Differential Cautions
* If servicing a vehicle fitted with four wheel drive or limited slip differentials, never run the engine with the transmission in gear and one wheel raised. The driving force to the other wheels on the ground may cause the vehicle to move.

* Wheel balancers that are designed to use on the vehicle are not recommended. One rear wheel will drive if in contact with the ground when the opposite wheel is raised.

This type of balancer may be used by removing the wheel opposite to the one being balanced with the vehicle raised, refit wheel nuts, reversed, to retain brake disc. Ensure that safety stands are used to support the vehicle.

Lubrication
The lubricant level should be checked every 20,000 kms or 12 months when the unit is cold. Refer to checking rear axle lubricant level section in this Chapter. At this temperature, the lubricant should be level with the bottom of the filler plug. If necessary, top up level with API GL-5 Hypoid gear oil 80W-90 lubricant. Do not use other types of lubricant in the differential.

The Limited Slip Differential use only LSD oil only.

* If an incorrect lubricant is accidentally used at any time, then the rear axle should be drained and flushed out with Hypoid gear oil 80W-90 GL5 lubricant. Then refilled with the specified lubricant.

GENERAL MAINTENANCE

CHECK REAR AXLE LUBRICANT LEVEL
1. Ensure vehicle is level.
2. Clean area around filler plug.
3. Remove filler plug at the rear of the differential housing.
4. The lubricant level is to be maintained at the bottom edge of the filler plug hole. Top up the differential with specified lubricant.

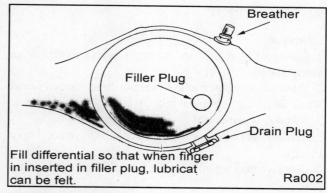

Breather

Filler Plug

Drain Plug

Fill differential so that when finger in inserted in filler plug, lubricat can be felt.

Ra002

Specified Lubricant:
API GL-5 Hypoid gear oil 80W-90
5. Inspect filler plug for damage. If OK, refit in axle housing cover. If damaged, replace plug.

REAR AXLE SHAFT HUB STUDS

Replacement
1. Remove axle shaft assembly as described in Rear axle shaft, bearing and/or seal section in this chapter.
2. Drive or press hub studs from axle shaft flange.
3. Drive or press new hub studs into axle shaft flange, with support around stud.
4. Install axle shaft as described in Rear axle shaft, bearing and/or seal section in this chapter.

REAR AXLE SHAFT - BEARING AND/OR SEAL
* To check for a failed bearing, conduct a road test.

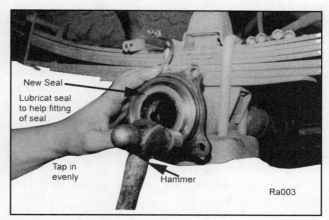

New Seal

Lubricat seal to help fitting of seal

Tap in evenly

Hammer

Ra003

* If failure of the bearing is not obvious after removal of shaft from vehicle, the bearing should be washed.
* Clean all the oil and dirt from inside the bearing. Re-oil with a light engine oil, then rotate the outer race with an oscillating motion while exerting a radial hand pressure.
* Check for any rough or gritty feeling. Examine the outer race track, rollers, cage and rib ring for any damage or wear. Refer to **"Problem Diagnosis"** Section in this Chapter for identification of bearing failures.

Check bearing for end float as outlined in the following "remove" instructions.

Remove

1. Raise rear of vehicle and support rear axle assembly on safety stands.
2. Mark relationship of wheel to brake drum. Remove road wheel attaching nuts and remove wheel.
3. Remove brake drum.
4. Remove brake hose which is attached to the wheel brake cylinder.
5. Remove parking brake cable from linkage and backing plate.
6. Before removing axle assembly, measure bearing end float by mounting a dial indicator so that the stylus is on the end of the axle shaft. If end float exceeds specification,

Slide axle from Axle Housing   Ra004

bearing should be replaced.
* Bearings should be settled by oscillating the shaft while pressing in each direction on the axle flange while measuring end float.

Axle bearing end float specification (axle shaft installed):

New bearing:	**0.76 mm**
Used bearing:	**0.04 - 0.48 mm**

7. Remove 4 flange nuts on backing plate.
8. Remove rear axle, seal, bearing assembly and backing plate from housing, first of all remove snap ring, use rear axle adaptor, together with slide hammer to remove axle.
* To assist in assembly, the retaining ring on the tapered roller bearing is cemented to the bearing cup. In some cases this ring may break away during bearing removal operations, leaving the bearing cup in the housing.
* To remove bearing cup, use slide hammer together with bearing cup remover.

Bearing Replacement

1. Press rear axle from backing plate, taking care of the oil seal. Remove bearing retaining snap ring.

If Bearing has Collapsed and bearing seized onto axle

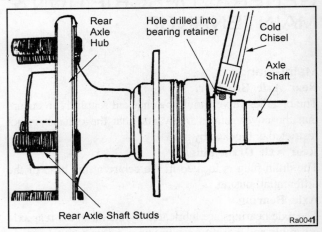
Rear Axle Shaft Studs   Ra004

shaft.
2. *Remove bearing inner retainer, drill a 6 mm hole into retainer at right angles to axle shaft. Do not drill all way through retainer as drill will damage axle shaft.*
3. *After drilling retainer, support it in a vice. Then carefully split retainer with a chisel across drilled hole as shown below.*
4. Pull out inner oil seal from axle housing.
5. Pull bearing from backing plate housing with a bearing puller.
6. Clean axle shaft (ensure that there is no damage on bearing seating surface or seal surface).
7. If old bearing is to be used, thoroughly clean bearing. Lubricate it with light engine oil, then check for wear or roughness as previously described.
8. Install bearing with radius on inner cone towards shoulder on axle shaft.

If the old bearing is to be reinstalled, and the cup has pulled away from the other race during removal, make sure that the cup and mating faces on the bearing are thoroughly clean and free of hard adhesive cement before assembly.
9. Press new or cleaned old bearing into backing plate housing. Install new oil seal. Install seal so that lip of the seal is towards the axle bearing.
* Ensure that the correct type of seal is fitted.
* Before installation of the seal, pack between the seal lips with Lithium No. 2 Grease.
10. Fit axle shaft through bearing and backing plate housing.
* Care must be taken to ensure that the bearing and retainer are guided on squarely during installation. Apply sufficient load to ensure the proper seating of all components.
11. Lubricate bearing with recommended axle lubricant.
* Check that the bearing has a minimum of 0.25 mm end float and is free to rotate without binding.

Installation

1. Assembly the backing plate and bearing housing on to the axle shaft, press the backing plate and bearing housing onto the shaft.

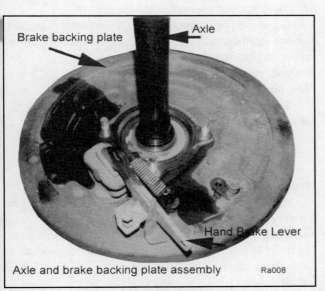

Axle and brake backing plate assembly   Ra008

2. Install spring clip to retain bearing into place.

3. Install axle shaft assembly, taking care to engage the splines of the axle shaft with differential side gears. Push shaft assembly, but do not tap end of axle shaft. Until the shaft assembly is fully 'home' in axle housing.

* Place a thin coat of grease around flange, as this will held to keep axle water proof, especially if driving through water above axle depth.

Place a coating of grease around flange to help keep the joint water proof   Ra006

* On vehicles with Limited Slip Differential, do not rotate the axle shaft until the opposite side axle shaft is installed.

* Rotation of one axle shaft without the other shaft installed will result in misalignment of the cone and the side gear splines and prevent entry of the second shaft.

4. Install and torque 4 axle bearing housing plate nuts, drawing in oil seal at the same time.

Torque: 700 kg.cm, (51ft-lb, 69Nm).

5. Measure bearing end float by mounting a dial indicator so that the stylus is on the end of the axle shaft. If end float exceeds specification, bearing should be replaced.

* Bearings should be settled by oscillating the shaft while pressing in each direction on the axle flange while measuring end float.

Axle bearing end float specification (axle shaft installed):

New bearing:	**0.76 mm**
Used bearing:	**0.04 - 0.48 mm**

6. Install brake hose and bleed brakes.

7. Install parking brake cable.

8. Install brake drum and road wheel, tighten wheel nuts to specified torque.

Torque: 1,150 kg.cm, (83ft-lb, 113Nm).

9. Check lubricant level of differential.

PINION BEARING and or OIL SEAL
Replacement

1. Raise rear of vehicle and support rear axle assembly on safety stands.

2. Disconnect tail shaft from pinion flange.

3. Lightly centre-punch alignment marks on the pinion flange nut, pinion flange and pinion end so as to help in assembly.

4. Using a special tool, holding pinion flange and remove flange retaining nut.

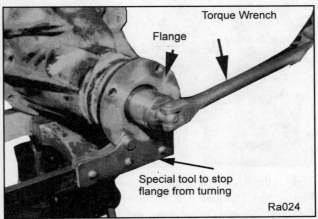

Ra024

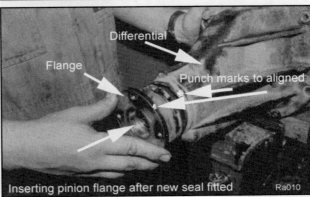

Inserting pinion flange after new seal fitted   Ra010

5. Withdraw pinion flange using special tool with nut and screw. Place a drain tray beneath differential carrier housing.

6. Prise pinion oil seal from carrier bore using a universal seal removing tool.

7. Remove the bearing with a special bearing puller.

8. Remove the bearing spacer.

9. Install a NEW bearing spacer.

10. Replace bearing or fit new bearing if required, lubricate the bearing with differential oil.

11. Lubricate new pinion oil seal lips with rear axle lubricant. Lightly coat outside of seal shell with a non-hardening gasket cement.

12. Start oil seal in differential carrier housing and drive seal squarely into position using special tool. Seal fits flush to 0.25 mm below the carrier housing surface.

13. Ensure that pinion shaft is free from burrs and that flange oil seal surface is free from damage.

14. Coat splines and seal surface of pinion flange with differential gear lubricant, and install flange on pinion shaft splines. ENSURE THAT CENTRE-PUNCH MARKS ALIGN.

15. Install flange retaining nut and tighten nut until centre-punch marks align, then tighten nut carefully to a position nor more than 5° past aligned setting.

Hold the flange with a special tool.

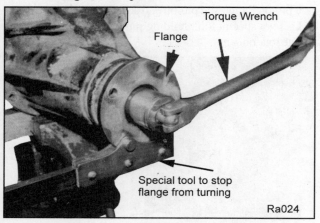

Ra024

Tighten the flange nut to specification.

Flange Nut Torque: 2,000 kg.cm, (145ft-lb, 196Nm).

Caution: *Should the retaining nut be over-tightened and the pre-load exceeded, it will be necessary to remove the pinion from the housing and install a 0.75 mm shim*

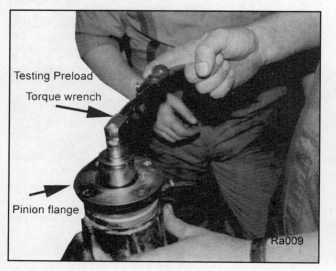

Ra009

between the spacer and the front pinion bearing. Under no circumstances must the retaining nut be backed off to decrease the pre-load setting. The collapsible spacer may only be reused once.

16. Check preload pressure of the pinion.

Use a sensitive torque wrench applied to the pinion flange nut, lightly tighten the nut to check the backlash between the drive pinion and the ring gear.

Preload starting.

New oil seal & bearing preload:

   19-26 kg.cm, (16.5-22.6 in-lb, 1.9-2.5Nm).

Old oil seal & bearing preload:

   9-13 kg.cm, (7.8-11.3 in-lb, 0.9-1.3Nm).

If the preload tension is higher than specification, the bearing spacer must be replaced.

If the preload tension is lower than specification, tighten the flange nut while holding the flange, a little at a time until the correct preload is obtained.

Do not tighten the flange nut any further than 2,000 kg.cm, (145ft-lb, 196Nm) to obtain the specified preload torque.

Do not back off the flange nut to obtain the specified preload torque.

17. Reconnect tail shaft rear universal joint flange to pinion flange. Refer to TAIL/DRIVE SHAFT AND UNIVERSAL JOINTS Chapter in this Manual.

18. Check lubricant level and top up if as necessary.

PINION FLANGE

Due to production tolerances in the length of the pinion flange, it is essential that the following method be used when installing a new pinion flange and/or pinion nut.

Remove

1. Raise rear of vehicle and support rear axle assembly on safety stands.

2. Disconnect tail shaft from pinion flange.

3. Test preload tension and record figures, preload example. Example preload:

9-13 kg.cm, (7.8-11.3 in-lb, 0.9-1.3Nm).

4. Lightly centre-punch alignment marks on the pinion flange nut, pinion flange and pinion end so as to help in assembly.

5. Using a special tool, holding pinion flange and remove flange retaining nut.

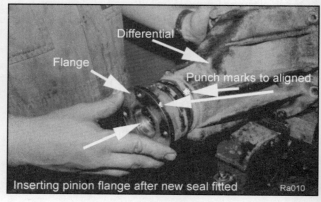

Inserting pinion flange after new seal fitted   Ra010

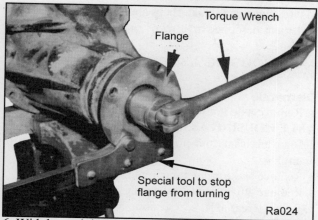

Torque Wrench

Flange

Special tool to stop
flange from turning

Ra024

6. Withdraw pinion flange using special tool with nut and screw. Place a drain tray beneath differential carrier housing.

7. Replacement [Using Old Oil Seal]

(a) Ensure that pinion shaft thread is free from burrs, then coat splines of pinion flange with rear axle lubricant and install flange on pinion shaft splines.

Install pinion flange and nut.

* The new flange is an interference fit on the pinion shaft splines, and should be pulled into plate by tightening the retaining nut. DO NOT, UNDER ANY CIRCUMSTANCES, USE FORCE OR HAMMER DURING INSTALLATION ONTO THE PINION SHAFT.

Caution: Should the retaining nut be over-tightened and the pre-load exceeded, it will be necessary to remove the pinion from the housing and install a new spacer behind front pinion bearing. Under no circumstances must the retaining nut be backed off to decrease the pre-load reading.

(b) If original pinion oil seal has not been disturbed, and is not being replaced by a new seal, tighten nut gradually until end play on pinion shaft is reduced to approximately 0.50 mm. Continue tightening nut while alternately turning pinion to seat bearings until pre-load figure previously recorded (see Step 3) is reached. Then increase this original pre-load reading by .11 to 34 Nm. FURTHER ROTATE THE PINION AN EXTRA 30 - 40 TURNS AND RECHECK THE PRE-LOAD TO ENSURE THAT NO CHANGE HAS OCCURRED.

8. Replacement (Using New Oil Seal)

(a) Prise pinion oil seal from carrier bore using a suitable removing tool.

(b) With rear axle lubricant, lubricate new pinion oil seal.

(c) Using special tool, start new oil seal in differential carrier housing and drive seal squarely into position.

(d) Ensure that pinion shaft thread is free from burrs, then coat splines of pinion flange with rear axle lubricant and install flange on pinion shaft splines.

* The new pinion flange is an interference fit on the pinion shaft splines and should be pulled into place by tightening the retaining nut. Do not use force or hammer the new flange

on to the pinion shaft.

(c) Continue tightening retaining nut until end play on the pinion shaft is reduced to approximately 0.50 mm.

(d) Check new oil seal and differential pre-load as previously outlined in Steps 3 above. Record reading for assembly reference.

Caution: Should the retaining nut be over-tightened and the pre-load exceeded, it will be necessary to remove the pinion from the housing and install a new spacer behind front pinion bearing. Under no circumstances must the retaining nut be backed off to decrease the pre-load reading.

(e) Continue tightening retaining nut while alternately turning pinion assembly to seat bearings until total pre-load figure obtained in Step 15 (above) is achieved. Then increase this pre-load reading by .11 to .34 Nm. Further rotate pinion an extra 30 - 40 turns and recheck pre-load to ensure that no change has occurred.

9. Preload starting.

New oil seal & bearing preload:
    19-26 kg.cm, (16.5-22.6 in-lb, 1.9-2.5Nm).

Old oil seal & bearing preload:
    9-13 kg.cm, (7.8-11.3 in-lb, 0.9-1.3Nm).

10. Reconnect tail shaft rear universal joint flange to pinion flange. Tighten bolts to specification.

Torque specification: 1,150 kg.cm, (83ft-lb, 113Nm).

11. Check axle lubricant level.

MAJOR REPAIRS

AXLE HOUSING ASSEMBLY
Remove

1. Using a floor jack under centre of the axle, jack up vehicle. Then place safety stands under the rear body jacking points.

2. Mark relationship of wheels to axle flanges. Remove road wheel attaching nuts and remove wheels.

3. Remove brake drum.

4. Remove parking brake cable from linkage and backing plate.

5. Remove tail shaft.

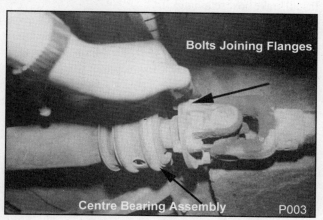

Bolts Joining Flanges

Centre Bearing Assembly

P003

6. Install a brake hose clamp on brake hose, then disconnect brake hose at union where the hose is connected to the axle housing. Remove brake hose retaining clip.

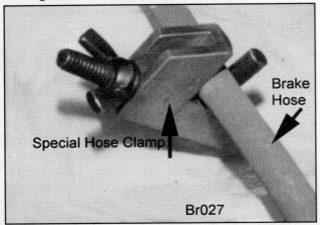

7. Support only lightly rear axle housing under centre with a floor jack.
8. Disconnect rear shock absorbers at lower mounting points.
9. Remove rear suspension "U" bolt nuts, "U" bolts, (and rubber spring bumper on 4WD models) and spring seat.
10. Lower differential housing on jack and remove assembly from underneath vehicle, it may be necessary lift rear exhaust pipe while manoeuvring axle assembly out from vehicle.

Installation
1. With differential assembly on a floor jack and the help of an assistant manoeuvre the differential assembly under the vehicle and into the correct position with the rear springs.
2. Replace rear suspension spring seat, "U" bolts (and rubber spring bumper on 4WD models) and nuts and tighten nuts to specification.
Torque: 1,250 kg.cm, (90ft-lb, 123Nm).
3. Reconnect rear shock absorbers at lower mounting points and tighten bolt to specification.
2WD: Torque: 260 kg.cm, (19ft-lb, 25Nm).
4WD: Torque: 650 kg.cm, (47ft-lb, 64Nm).
4. Disconnect brake pipe at underbody rear connection. Install brake hose retaining clip.
5. Replace tail shaft as described in propeller shaft chapter, tighten propeller to differential flange bolts to specification.
Torque: 750 kg-cm (54ft-lb, 74Nm)
6. Replace parking brake cable to linkage and backing plate.
7. Replace brake drum.
8. Replace road wheel taking note of mark made during removal for position of wheel to brake drum, and attaching nuts tighten to specification.
Torque: 1,150 kg.cm, (83ft-lb, 113Nm).
9. Remove safety stands from under the rear body jacking points.
10. Check and fill rear axle differential to correct level with specified lubricant.

11. Re-adjust park brake shoes and bleed brake hydraulic system, as described in "Brake" chapter.

AXLE HOUSING ASSEMBLY

Dismantle
1. Remove axle housing assembly as per **REMOVE OF AXLE HOUSING ASSEMBLY** Section in this Chapter.
2. Drain lubricant from differential carrier by removing rear drain plug.
3. Remove brake drum, if not removed.
4. Remove 4 flange nuts on backing plate.
5. Remove rear axle, seal, bearing assembly and backing plate from housing, first of all remove snap ring, use rear axle adaptor, together with slide hammer to remove axle.
6. Remove axle shaft.

Slide axle from Axle Housing   Ra004

7. Remove the nuts attaching the differ differential carrier to the differential housing assembly.
8. Using a soft hammer, separate two differential case halves by driving against thrust block.
* Do not use a screwdriver to prise apart the differential case halves.

Take care when lifting differential from or to housing

9. Before dismantling differential case assembly and drive pinion from differential case, the following inspection procedures should be adopted. These inspections can help find the cause of rear axle noise and determine corrections needed.
(a) Inspect the moving parts for chipped or scuffed surfaces.
(b) Check the torque of the ring gear bolts, differential carrier bearing cap bolts and the pinion flange nut.

* Ring gear bolts have a left-hand thread.

(c) Rotate the differential case through several turns whilst having a dial indicator set up (against the back face of the ring gear) to measure ring gear runout.

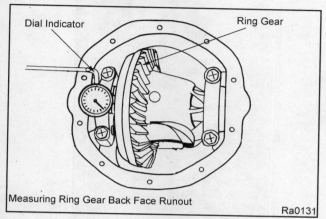

Measuring Ring Gear Back Face Runout

Ra0131

Ring gear rear face run-out: 0.10 mm(0.0039in) max.

(d) Leave the dial indicator set up as in (c). Push the ring gear hard one way, then hard the opposite way to measure side play. There should be no side play present. Check to ensure that there is no pinion end play.

(e) Set up the dial indicator to measure ring gear backlash at three equally spaced positions at the highest point).

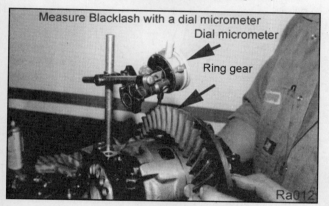

Ra012

Backlash: 0.13-0.18 mm (0.0051-0.0071in)

(f) Measure preload with a torque wrench.

Backlash preload:

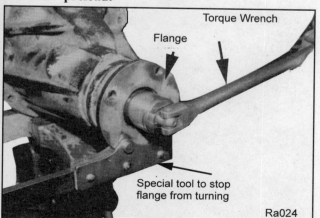

Ra024

9-13 kg.cm, (7.8-11.3 in-lb, 0.9-1.3Nm).

(g) If no obvious faults are found, check the gear tooth contact pattern.

10. Mark one of bearing caps and adjacent side of axle housing with a daub of paint. This will aid in the correct assembly of bearing caps.

11. Remove bearing adjusting nuts, bearing cap bolts and remove caps bearing outer races.

Ra014

* Place left and right bearing cups with bearing caps so that they may be reinstalled in their original location. Place shim with appropriate cups.

Ra013

12. Remove differential case from the differential carrier.

13. Use a bearing puller and remove the side bearings from the differential case.

14. Place the carrier in a vice and remove the ring gear bolts, use a soft hammer and brass drift to separate the ring gear from the carrier.

15. Install special tool (tool to hold differential flange from turning) to the pinion flange and remove pinion flange nut.

16. Remove pinion flange, may need a puller.

17. Pry pinion oil seal out of carrier bore using a suitable tool or screw driver.

18. Remove pinion by tapping on front end with a soft faced hammer.

19. Remove pinion front bearing from carrier bore. Discard pinion bearing spacer.

243

Differential Housing

Bearing

Differential

Ring gear

Inspect all components

Ra017

Press

Pinion shaft

Bearing

Bearing clamp

Ra015

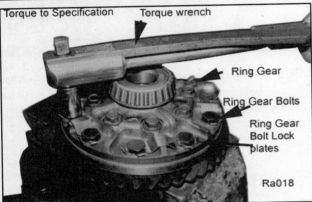

Torque to Specification   Torque wrench

Ring Gear

Ring Gear Bolts

Ring Gear Bolt Lock plates

Ra018

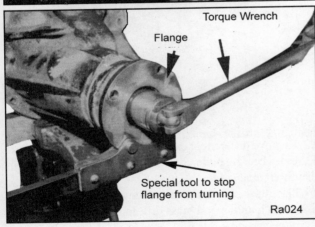

Torque Wrench

Flange

Special tool to stop flange from turning

Ra024

21. If the pinion bearing cups are to be replaced, remove them from the carrier casting by tapping out with a brass drift and

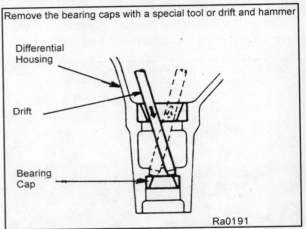

Remove the bearing caps with a special tool or drift and hammer

Differential Housing

Drift

Bearing Cap

Ra0191

hammer or with a special tool, (which with the aid of a nut and

Tap bearing case in with a soft drift and hammer

Bearing case

Soft drift

Ra023

20. If pinion bearings are to be replaced, remove bearing cups using bearing clamp and press pinion from bearing.

threaded shaft will force the bearing cups from the carrier casting).

Differential Case - Dismantle

1. Before dismantling differential case, inspect differential side bearings for any signs of damage.

* Both side bearings and their cups are matched pairs. If either bearing is to be replaced, its matching cup must also be replaced.

2. If necessary, use a bearing puller to remove side bearings from differential case. Discard side bearings once they are removed.

3. Grip the differential case in a vice with soft jaws.

4. Remove ring gear attaching bolts.

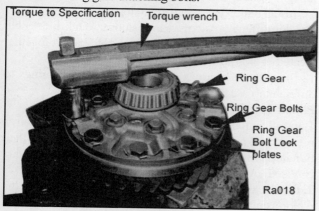

5. Remove differential case from vice.

6. Using a soft faced hammer, remove ring gear from differential case by hitting down on ring gear. Support ring gear during this operation so that it does not strike bench top as it comes free of case.

* Do not use a screwdriver to pry between ring gear and case.

7. Drive out differential pinion shaft retaining pin from differential case using a suitable size pin punch and hammer.

8. Remount the differential case in vice with soft jaws. Using a brass drift and hammer, drive out pinion shaft from differential case cover.

9. Lift out pinion gears, thrust washers from differential case. Remove differential side gears and thrust washers from differential case halves.

* Keep the gears with their respective thrust washers in pairs so that they may be reinstalled in their original position.

Inspection

* All components should be thoroughly cleaned and dried, then inspected.

Differential Case

Check case for general soundness and pay particular attention to the following points:

1. If differential case side bearings have been removed, check case journals for damage and that bearing seating surfaces are free from dirt and burrs.

2. The ring gear spigot and mounting face should be clean and free from dirt and burrs.

3. The mating surfaces for differential case halves should be clean and free from burrs.

4. The thrust surfaces for differential side gears and pinions should be examined for excessive wear.

5. The differential side gear journal bores should be clean and free from scoring.

6. The case bores for differential pinion gear shafts should be checked for "out of roundness".

Differential Side Gears and Pinion Gears

1. Examine all gear teeth for cracks and hard contact marks.

2. The differential side gear splines should be checked for excessive wear. Wear on splines can contribute to excessive driveline backlash.

3. Check differential side gear journals and back faces for scoring.

4. Check fit of differential side gears in differential carrier.

5. Inspect differential pinion bores and thrust surfaces for scoring. Also check differential pinion gear shaft is not bent and that surfaces where pinions run are not worn or scored.

6. Check thrust washers, they should be free from cracks, nicks and burrs. Excessive wear of thrust washers or pinion gear thrust surfaces can also contribute to excessive driveline backlash.

Ring Gear and Pinion

1. Inspect gear teeth for scoring or damage. Scoring of gear teeth is usually caused by excessive shock loading, use of incorrect lubricant or insufficient "run in" before towing a heavy load. Scored gears must be replaced.

2. The ring gear bore and back face should be clean and free from burrs.

3. The rear bearing seating surface on the pinion should be clean and free from burrs.

4. Inspect pinion splines and flange splines for evidence of wear.

5. Inspect thread and bearing journals of pinion.

Bearings

Identification of bearing failures are described in Problem Diagnosis.

1. Bearing cups should have an even wear pattern and must be free from flaking or pitting. Ensure that seating surfaces are clean and free from burrs or raised metal.

2. The bearing assemblies should feel smooth when turned in their cups.

3. The assembly should be free from loose particles.

4. No cracks should be present in roller cages, and bores should show no evidence of flaking or pitting.

Differential Carrier

1. Check casting all over for general soundness.

2. The bore for pinion oil seal should be free from burrs.

Inspect case for cracks or signs of wear

Ra016

3. Inspect rear cover face and bolt holes for damage.

Assembly
Differential Case

1. Lubricate all differential gears, bearings, thrust washers, differential pinion gear shaft and ring gear with rear axle lubricant before assembly.

2. Place ring gear into position (check location marks made during "Remove") on differential case cap and install ring gear attaching bolts.

* For ease of assembly, it may be necessary to heat the ring gear on a hot plate until it is hot to touch, prior to installing onto the differential case cap.

* On no account must a flame be used to heat the ring gear. Also, use left-hand threaded guide pins to pilot the ring gear over the differential case spigot.

3. Tighten ring gear attaching bolts evenly until gear face is flush with differential case spigot. Torque bolts.

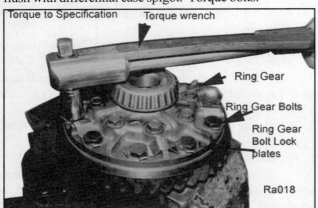

Torque to Specification   Torque wrench

Ring Gear

Ring Gear Bolts

Ring Gear Bolt Lock plates

Ra018

Ring Gear Bolt torque: 985 kg-cm, 71ft-lb, 97Nm.

4. Bend nut locking plates so the nuts can work loose.

5. Position differential side gears with their thrust washers into differential case halves.

6. Using a soft faced hammer, install pinion gear shaft into differential case, just enough to allow a pinion gear thrust washer to sit on the end of each shaft.

* Ensure that the retaining pin holes in the differential case and pinion gear shaft is aligned.

7. Install one of the pinion gear thrust washers over inside end of the shaft.

8. Position appropriate pinion gear next to thrust washer and knock short shaft in until it comes through centre of the gear.

9. Install pinion gear thrust washer and gear to cross shaft. Knock shaft through gear.

10. Install remaining pinion gear and thrust washer. Knock shaft through pinion gear, ensuring that thrust washer aligns with shaft. Knock shaft into differential case until retaining pin hole in shaft aligns with hole in differential case.

11. Install pinion gear shaft retaining pins.

Holding differential side gear in position through differential case cover bore. Push 2 differential case halves together located on protruding retaining pins.

12. Install side bearings by pressing on side bearings to differential case journals.

Pinion Installation

1. Install pinion rear bearing cup using special tool, such as press or two plates and shaft with both ends threaded, then turn nuts to seat bearing cup into position. Ensure that cup is seated squarely in bore.

2. Press rear bearing inner race against the shoulder of the pinion using special tool.

* To avoid possible damage to the pinion gear teeth when pressing the bearing on, ensure that the press plates are perfectly flat, free of burrs and foreign matter prior to installing the bearing cone.

* Locate bearing inner race squarely on the pinion and press only on inner race surface.

* Lubricate the bearing with rear axle lubricant.

3. Place the pinion in the carrier.

4. Lubricate pinion front bearing with rear axle lubricant, and assemble collapsible pinion bearing spacer and front bearing onto pinion whilst supporting pinion head.

5. Position pinion in close to correct position, check tooth

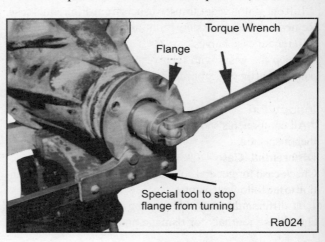

Torque Wrench

Flange

Special tool to stop flange from turning

Ra024

pattern. Install spacer, oil slinger and oil seal. Lubricate pinion oil seal lips with rear axle lubricant.

6. Install pinion flange and the original pinion flange retaining nut. Using a special tool (large clamp) to hold pinion flange, tighten retaining nut until pinion front bearing starts on pinion shaft.

Flange Nut Torque: 2,000 kg.cm, (145ft-lb, 196Nm).

7. Carry out a preliminary preload adjustment to the specified torque.

New oil seal & bearing preload:
**   19-26 kg.cm, (16.5-22.6 in-lb, 1.9-2.5Nm).**
Old oil seal & bearing preload:
**   9-13 kg.cm, (7.8-11.3 in-lb, 0.9-1.3Nm).**

Installation of Differential Case & Back Lash Setting.

1. Install differential case / ring gear assembly into the differential carrier. Install the correct bearing races and adjusting nuts.

Adjusting nut and bearing cap

Paint marks

Adjusting nut

Ra013

2. Install the correct bearing caps (check for identification marks made during "Remove").

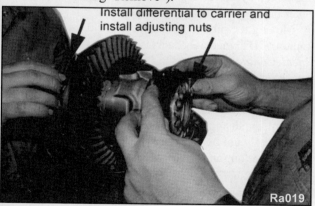

Install differential to carrier and install adjusting nuts

Ra019

Differential Case Side Bearing Preload

3. Tighten to bearing cap bolts to specification.
Differential Case Bearing Cap bolts torque:
**   1,250 kg.cm, (90ft-lb, 123Nm).**

4. Loosen differential case bearing cap bolts to figure tightness.

5. Tighten adjusting nut on ring gear side. Use a special tool

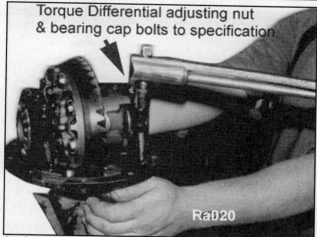

Torque Differential adjusting nut & bearing cap bolts to specification

Ra020

(tool to grip side adjusting nut) tighten side bearing nut until there is a backlash of 0.2mm (0.008in).

6. Tighten the adjusting nut on pinion side. Use a special tool (tool to grip side adjusting nut) tighten side bearing nut while turning the ring gear. When the adjusting nut is tight loosen the pinion side nut.

7. Install a dial gauge on the ring gear side adjusting nut, set gauge to zero.

8. Tighten pinion side adjusting nut until gauge needle starts to move. Tighten the pinion a further 1 to 1.5 notches. Remove dial gauge from differential carrier.

9. Tighten to bearing cap bolts to specification.
Differential Case Bearing Cap bolts torque:
**   1,250 kg.cm, (90ft-lb, 123Nm).**

Differential Ring Gear Back Lash Setting.

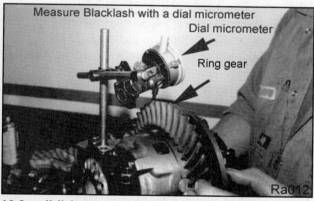

Measure Blacklash with a dial micrometer
Dial micrometer

Ring gear

Ra012

10. Install dial gauge to differential carrier to check back lash.

11. Check back lash for specification. Check readings at 4 equally spaced positions around ring gear.

* Position the dial indicator so that the indicator stylus is perpendicular to the ring gear tooth and in line with gear rotation.

Back Lash specification:
**   0.13-0.18mm (0.0051-0.0071in)**

12. If back lash is not within specification adjust by turning the side adjusting nuts an equal amount until the back lash is within specification (by turning each of the side adjusting nuts an equal amount Differential Case Bearing Preload will not

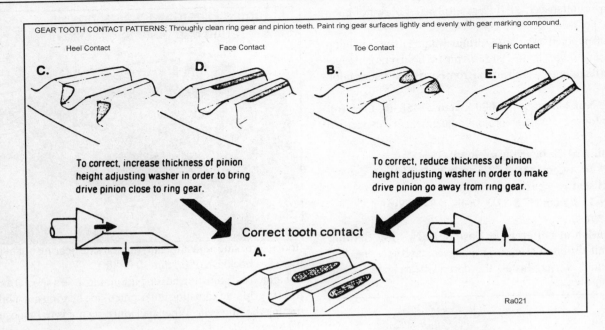

GEAR TOOTH CONTACT PATTERNS; Throughly clean ring gear and pinion teeth. Paint ring gear surfaces lightly and evenly with gear marking compound.

be effected).

\# If backlash is excessive, tighten side adjusting nut on pinion side of ring gear and loosen side adjusting nut on the ring gear side by the same amount.

\# If backlash is insufficient, loosen side adjusting nut on pinion side of ring gear and tighten side adjusting nut on ring gear side by same amount.

13. Tighten to bearing cap bolts to specification.

Differential Case Bearing Cap bolts torque
1,250 kg.cm, (90ft-lb, 123Nm).

14. Re-check back lash for specification. Check readings at 4 equally spaced positions around ring gear.

* Position the dial indicator so that the indicator stylus is perpendicular to the ring gear tooth and in line with gear rotation.

Back Lash specification: 0.13-0.18mm (0.0051-0.0071in)

15. Check and adjust pinion preload to specification.

New oil seal & bearing preload:
19-26 kg.cm, (16.5-22.6 in-lb, 1.9-2.5Nm).

Old oil seal & bearing preload:
9-13 kg.cm, (7.8-11.3 in-lb, 0.9-1.3Nm).

Ring Gear and Pinion Contact Pattern

1. Thoroughly clean ring gear and pinion teeth.

2. Paint ring gear teeth lightly and evenly with gear marking compound of a suitable consistency to produce a contact pattern.

3. Inspect contact pattern produced by above procedure.

* The large end of the tooth is called the 'HEEL' and the small end the 'TOE'.

* The top of the tooth which is above the pitch line is called the 'FACE' while the area below the pitch line is called the 'FLANK'.

* The clearance between the pinion and ring gear teeth is

referred to as 'BACKLASH'.

The figure illustrates correct and incorrect contact patterns.

i) Contact pattern 'A' provides the ideal marking for quietness and long life.

ii) If the pattern shows a toe contact 'B', it indicates not enough backlash. If the pattern shows a flank contact 'E', it indicates that the pinion is in too far. To correct, move the ring gear away from the pinion by increasing the size of the shim on the pinion shaft before the collapsable spacer.

iii) If the pattern shows a heel contact 'C', it indicates too much backlash. To correct a pattern such as 'D', it will be necessary to adjust. To correct, move the ring gear towards the pinion by decreasing the size of the shim on the pinion shaft before the collapsable spacer.

* Moving the pinion 'IN' reduces backlash and moving pinion 'OUT' increases backlash.

Ideal Contact:

Drive Side:

* A central toe contact marking, lengthwise in position and slightly low contact in the profile position.

* Total length approximately 5/8 of the gear face width.

* There should be clearance of about 1 mm between the contact marking and the toe and along the top face angle line.

Ideal Tooth Contact Pattern

Coast Side:

* A centrally located marking, lengthwise in position and slightly high in the profile position.
* Total length approximately 5/8 of the gear face width.
* There should be clearance between the contact and the face angle line of the gear.

Acceptable Heel Contacts:

Drive Side:

* A central face contact marking, lengthwise in position, is shown in figure. This represents the limit of acceptability of the contact marking towards the heel.
* Marking should fade out at least 5 mm before heel end.
* A central profile marking position is shown and is acceptable, although low contact marking is preferred.

Coast Side:

* The centre of the contact marking is located at 5/8 of the face width from the toe and it does not approach the heel end by less than 5 mm.
* A high contact marking, as shown in figure, is preferred for coast side contacts which tend to be toward the heel.
* A central profile marking position is acceptable, providing the pinion face angle edge lines do not appear low on the gear.

Acceptable Toe Contacts:

Drive Side:

* The contact markings begin almost at the toe end face and extend in length by approximately half the face width.
* A slightly low contact marking is shown in figure. This is preferable although a centrally located profile position is acceptable.

Coast Side:

* The contact marking being almost at the toe end face and may appear pointed as shown in figure. A square end is equally acceptable.
* The total length of the contact marking is approximately 1/2 of the face width.
* A high profile marking position is desirable, although a central profile is acceptable.

4. (a) After satisfactory contact pattern is produced, clean ring gear and pinion gear teeth and pour a liberal quantity of rear axle lubricant onto gears and bearings.

(b) Turn gears to work lubricant into all surfaces.

5. Check preload pressure of the pinion.

Use a sensitive torque wrench applied to the pinion flange nut, lightly tighten the nut to check the backlash between the drive pinion and the ring gear.

Preload starting.

New oil seal & bearing preload:
   19-26 kg.cm, (16.5-22.6 in-lb, 1.9-2.5Nm).

Old oil seal & bearing preload:
    9-13 kg.cm, (7.8-11.3 in-lb, 0.9-1.3Nm).

If the preload tension is higher than specification, the bearing spacer must be replaced.

If the preload tension is lower than specification, tighten the flange nut while holding the flange, a little at a time until the

correct preload is obtained.

Assemble Rear Axle Housing Assembly

Take care when lifting differential from or to housing

Ra011

1. Assemble the carrier to the differential housing assembly.

2. Replace the nuts attaching the differential carrier to the differential housing assembly. Tighten to specification.

Differential Carrier attaching nut torque:
    250 kg.cm, (18ft-lb, 25Nm).

3. Install axle shaft assembly, taking care to engage the splines of the axle shaft with differential side gears. Push shaft assembly, but do not tap end of axle shaft. Until the shaft assembly is fully 'home' in axle housing.

4. Install and torque 4 axle bearing housing plate nuts,

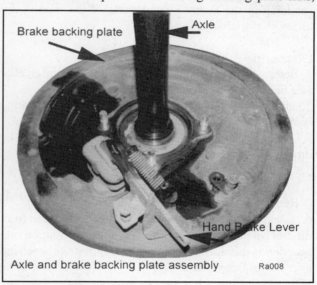

Brake backing plate — Axle

Hand Brake Lever

Axle and brake backing plate assembly — Ra008

drawing in oil seal at the same time.

Torque: 700 kg.cm, (51ft-lb, 69Nm).

5. Replace brake drum

6. Check and fill rear axle differential to correct level with specified lubricant.

7. Re-adjust park brake shoes and bleed brake hydraulic system.

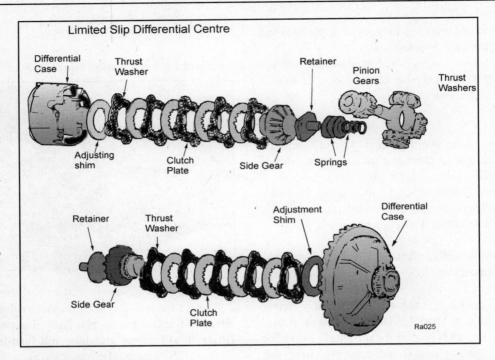

Limited Slip Differential Centre

Limited Slip Differential

The overhaul procedures, ring gear and pinion positioning and tooth markings for the limited slip differential are the same as for the standard type of rear axle assembly, except for the servicing of the internal components of the limited slip differential assembly.

Dismantle

1. Before dismantling differential case, inspect differential side bearings for any signs of damage.
* Side bearings and their cups are matched. If either bearing is to be replaced, its matching cup must also be replaced.
2. Use a bearing puller and remove the side bearings from the differential case.
3. Grip differential case in a vice with soft jaws.
4. Remove ring gear attaching bolts.
5. Remove differential case from vice.
6. Using a soft faced hammer, remove ring gear from differential case by hitting down on ring gear. Support ring gear during this operation so that it does not strike bench top as it comes free of case.
*Do not use a screwdriver to pry between ring gear & case.
7. Place differential case in a vice equipped with soft jaws.
8. Mark left and right side of differential case, so when installing the two sections can be assembled back to the same position.
9. Loosen and remove differential case cover bolts evenly. Lift off differential case cover.
10. *Left side:*
Remove side gear and 5 thrust washers and 4 clutch plates.
Right side:
Spring for left side retainer plus two springs.

Spider and the pinion gear. Spring for right side retainer. Remove side gear and 5 thrust washers and 4 clutch plates.
* Keep the pinion gears with their respective thrust washers in sets so that they may be installed in their original position.

Inspection

All components should be thoroughly cleaned and dried, then inspected. Check the case for general soundness and pay particular attention to the following points:
1. If differential case side bearings have been removed, check case journals for damage and that seating surfaces are free form dirt and burrs.
2. The mating surfaces for differential case halves should be clean and free from burrs.
3. The thrust washer surfaces should be examined for excessive wear and should not have any metal surface. Check for specified thickness of thrust washers.
Thrust Washer specified thickness: 1.74mm (0.0685in)
4. Clutch plate surface must be examined for excessive wear.
5. Inspect the length of the springs with a micrometer.
Specified Spring Limits:
       Spring: 31.3mm (1.232in)
6. Inspect gear teeth for scoring or damage. Scoring of the gear teeth is usually caused by excessive shock loading, use of the incorrect lubricant. Scored gears must be replaced.
7. Bearing cups should have an even wear pattern and be free from flaking or pitting. Ensure the seating surfaces are clean and free from burrs or raised metal.
Shim Selection.
1. Measure the depth of the left and right side cases for shim selection.
(a) Right side measure depth from top of case.
(b) Left side measure depth from lower section of chamfer.
2. Assemble side gear, clutch plates and thrust washers,

clamp down to 10kg (22lb) and measure each assembly (left and right).

3. (a) Deduct the measurement of the right assembly from the measured depth of the right case as in 1.(a) for shim thickness.

(b) Deduct the measurement of the left assembly from the measured depth of the left case as in 1.(b) for shim thickness.

Assembly

1. Lubricate all gears, bearings, thrust washers and clutch plates with LSD rear axle lubricant before assembly.

2. Install respective shim (shim selected from above if necessary) clutch plates thrust washers and side gear into left and right cases.

3. Assembly the right side pinion gears, washers to the spider. Install the assembled right spider to the right case.

4. Install the right retainer plate and pin.

5. Check right case assembled pinion back lash, use a dial meter

6. Assembly the left side pinion gears, washers to the spider. Install the assembled left spider to the left case.

7. Install the left retainer plate and pin.

8. Check left case assembled pinion back lash with a dial meter

9. Assemble left and right cases to each other, aligning them at the alignment marks made during dismantle. Install attaching bolts and tighten to specification.

Differential Case Attaching bolts:
480 kg.cm, (35ft-lb, 47Nm).

PROBLEM DIAGNOSIS

GENERAL PROBLEMS

* Very often, rear axles are considered noisy, when in reality, the noise is emanating from some other source, such as tyres, front wheel bearings, rear wheel bearings, transmission rear bearing (manual transmission), engine noises, muffler roar, automatic transmission or power steering pump.

* All rear axles have some slight humming noise. This will vary with the type of body construction, load and tyre pressure.

* Noise which emanates from any one of these can quite easily be confused with a rear axle noise and unless a series of elimination tests are carried out to definitely confirm the real source of the noise, rear axle assemblies may be (and often are) dismantled unnecessarily.

* Although not infallible, the following diagnosis guide will assist in locating and defining the different characteristics of the components which could be responsible for a noise.

Road Test

* Ensure that the axle lubricant is correct.

* Drive at low speed until thoroughly familiar with vehicle noises, by which time the rear axle should have warmed up. Accelerate gradually from the lowest practical speed in top gear to 100 km/h, noting any noises and the speeds at which they occur. Release the accelerator and without using the brakes, allow the vehicle to lose speed.

* Next, allow the vehicle to coast to rest from 100 km/h with the transmission in neutral position. Any noises common to earlier tests may be eliminated as rear axle gear noise, as the rear axle is not under load under these conditions.

* Engine noise is gauged by gradually accelerating the engine with the vehicle at rest.

PROBLEM DIAGNOSIS - DIFFERENTIAL AND REAR AXLE BEARING

* Consider the following factors when diagnosing bearing condition:

1. General condition of all parts during dismantling and inspection.

2. Note the type of failure.

3. Determine the cause.

4. Make all repairs following recommended procedures.

Problem: Abrasive roller wear!
Possible Cause:
* Pattern on races and rollers caused by fine abrasive.
Remedy:
* Clean all parts and housings.
* Check seals and bearings and replace if leaking, rough or noisy.

Problem: Galling!
Possible Cause:
* Metal smears on roller ends due to overheating lubricant failure or overload.
Remedy:
* Replace bearing, check seals and check for proper lubrication.

Problem: Bent cage!
Possible Cause:
* Cage damage due to improper handling or tool use.
Remedy:
* Replace bearing.

Problem: Abrasive step wear!
Possible Cause:
* Pattern on roller ends caused by fine abrasives.
Remedies:
* Clean all parts and housing.
* Check seals and bearings and replace if leaking, rough or noisy.

Problem: Etching!
Possible Cause:
* Bearing surfaces appear grey (or greyish black) in colour with related etching away of material usually at roller spacing.
Remedy:
* Replace bearings, check seals and check for proper lubrication.

Problem: Indentations!
Possible Cause:
* Surface depressions on race and rollers caused by hard particles of foreign materials.

Remedies:
* Clean all parts and housing and check seals
* Replace bearings if rough or noisy.

Problem: Cage wear!

Possible Cause:
* Wear around outside diameter of cage and roller pockets caused by abrasive materials and inefficient lubrication.

Remedies:
* Replace bearings, check seals
* Check for proper lubrication.

Problem: Misalignment!

Possible Cause:
* Outer race misalignment due to foreign object.

Remedies:
* Clean related parts and replace bearing.
* Make sure races are properly seated.

Problem: Cracked inner race!

Possible Cause:
* Race cracked due to improper fit, cocking, or poor bearing seats.

Remedy:
* Replace bearing and correct bearing seat.

Problem: Fatigue spalling!

Possible Cause:
* Flaking of surface metal resulting from fatigue.

Remedy:
* Replace bearing and clean all related parts.

Problem: Discolouring!

Possible Cause:
* Surface indentations in raceway caused by rollers either under impact loading or vibration while the bearing is not rotating.

Remedy:
* Replace bearing if rough or noisy.

Problem: Frottage!

Possible Cause:
* Corrosion set up by relative movement of parts with no lubrication.

Remedies:
* Replace bearing, clean related parts.
* Check seals and check for proper lubrication.

Problem: Stain discoloration!

Possible Cause:
* Discoloration can range from light brown to black caused by incorrect lubrication or moisture.

Remedies:
* Re-use bearing if stains can be removed by light polishing or if no evidence of over heating is observed.
* Check seals and related parts for damage.

SPECIFICATIONS

Rear Axle Type   Semi Floating
Housing Type   Unitized Carrier Construction

Lubricant
Type   API GL-5 Hypoid gear oil 80W-90
LSD   Approved LSD differential Oil

Standard & L.S.D. Axles
Gear Type   Hypoid

Differential Gears
Type   Straight Bevel

Axle Shaft
Type   Semi Floating
Bearing Type   Tapered Roller

Axle End Float
Axle bearing end float specification (axle shaft installed):
New bearing: 0.76 mm
Used bearing: 0.04 - 0.48 mm

Differential Pinion Gear
Bearing Type   Adjustable Tapered Roller
Bearing Adjustment   Collapsible Spacer
Preload starting.
New oil seal & bearing preload:
          19-26 kg.cm, (16.5-22.6 in-lb, 1.9-2.5Nm).
Old oil seal & bearing preload:
          9-13 kg.cm, (7.8-11.3 in-lb, 0.9-1.3Nm).

Differential Side Bearings
Type   Tapered Roller
Adjustment   Shims
Preload starting.
New oil seal & bearing preload:
          19-26 kg.cm, (16.5-22.6 in-lb, 1.9-2.5Nm).
Old oil seal & bearing preload:
          9-13 kg.cm, (7.8-11.3 in-lb, 0.9-1.3Nm).

Differential Ring Gear
Backlash   0.10 - 0.18mm [at the tightest point]
Ring gear rear face run-out: 0.10 mm(0.0039in) max.
Ring Gear Backlash: 0.13-0.18 mm (0.0051-0.0071in)

Run out specifications
Case Assembly [w/o ring gear attached]   0.5 mm (max)
Ring Gear Rear Face [when assembled onto case assembly]   0.13 mm (max)

TORQUE SPECIFICATION

Road Wheel Nuts torque 1,150 kg.cm, (83ft-lb, 113Nm).
Flange Nut Torque: 2,000 kg.cm, (145ft-lb, 196Nm).
Tail Shaft universal to flange torque:
          1,150 kg.cm, (83ft-lb, 113Nm).
U Bolt nut Torque: 1,250 kg.cm, (90ft-lb, 123Nm).
Rear Shock Absorber Lower Mounting Bolt:
2WD: Torque: 260 kg.cm, (19ft-lb, 25Nm).
4WD: Torque: 650 kg.cm, (47ft-lb, 64Nm).
Ring Gear Bolt torque: 985 kg-cm, 71ft-lb, 97Nm.
Differential case bearing cap bolts:
          1,250kg.cm, (90ft-lb, 123Nm)
Differential Carrier attaching nut torque:
          250 kg.cm, (18ft-lb, 25Nm).

STEERING

STEERING COLUMN

STEERING WHEEL

Remove

1. Disconnect battery earth cable.
2. Pull or prise snap fit centre from steering wheel.
3. Remove steering wheel to steering shaft retaining nut.

Push on Horn Button

Plastic Clips

Steering Wheel
Attaching Nut

Str033

4. To aid installation of steering wheel to its original position, scribe an aligning mark on steering wheel centre section and steering shaft.
5. Using a suitable puller or carefully hit the under side of the steering wheel firmly with your hand or arm, remove steering wheel.

Install

1. Install steering wheel to steering shaft, aligning marks made on removal.
2. Install and torque steering wheel retaining nut.

Steering Wheel Attaching Nut:
350kg-cm, 25ft-lb, 34Nm

3. Refit centre bar to steering wheel.
4. Reconnect battery earth lead and check electrical components that have their switch located on the side of the steering column.

TILT ASSEMBLY on TILT STEERING COLUMN up to 1988

1. With steering column cover removed, remove the spring and cable at the top of the assembly.
2. From under the tilt assembly detach the centre shaft universal, use some paint for alignment of the shaft when assembling.
3. Remove steering shaft tube from bracket.
4. Turn the ignition key to ACC, while you insert a thin rod or wire into the lock housing to push in the locking tab, pull out the ignition lock assembly barrel.
5. Remove the cir-clip holding the top shaft into the top of the

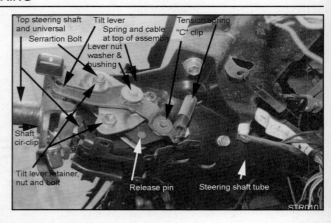

Top steering shaft and universal
Serrartion Bolt
Tilt lever
Spring and cable at top of assembly
Lever nut washer & bushing
Tension spring
"C" clip
Shaft cir-clip
Tilt lever retainer, nut and bolt
Release pin
Steering shaft tube
STR010

tilt assembly. Remove the shaft.
6. Remove the spring attached to the tilt lever and "C" clip and bushing.
7. Remove the lever nut, washer and bushing attaching the tilt lever.
8. Remove the tilt lever retainer and one nut and one bolt attaching the retainer.
9. Remove the tilt release pin.
10. Remove the serration bolt, remove the tilt pawl.
11. Remove the tilt support, by removing the various bolts, washers and spacers.

Install

1. Install the tilt support, with the various bolts, washers and spacers.
2. Install the 2 pawls, attaching nut and bolt to the steering column, and install the serration bolt.
3. Install the tilt release pin.
4. Replace the tilt lever retainer and one nut and one bolt attaching the retainer.
5. Replace the lever nut, washer and bushing attaching the tilt lever.
6. Install the "C" clip and bushing to the tilt lever and spring.
7. Insert the top steering shaft into the top of the tilt assembly and cir-clip holding the top steering shaft.
8. Turn the ignition key to ACC, while push in the ignition lock assembly barrel, push in until the barrel locks into position.
9. Install steering shaft tube to bracket and 2 bolts, apply locktite to bolt thread, tighten bolts to specification.

Steering Shaft Tube Bolt Specified Torque:
185kg-cm, 13ft-lb, 18Nm.

10. From under the tilt assembly connect the centre shaft universal, use the paint alignment marks when assembling. Tighten bolts to specification.

Steering Shaft Universal Bolt Specified Torque:
260kg-cm, 19ft-lb, 26Nm

11. Replace the spring and cable at the top of the assembly.
12. Install steering column cover and test operation of the steering column.

TILT ASSEMBLY on TILT STEERING COLUMN 1988 on

Remove

1. With steering column cover removed, remove the shear bolts by drilling a hole into the centre of the stud and removing the bolt with a bolt remover.

2. Remove the bolt at the top of the column holding the compressed spring and 2 bushes. Remove the tension spring at the top also.

3. Remove the two springs, one from either side of steering column.

4. Remove the two sets of "C" clip, nut and tilt lever retainer, one either side of steering column.

5. Remove the two pawl stoppers, one either side of steering column.

6. Remove the 2 pawl attaching nut and bolt, and 2 pawls, one either side of steering column.

7. Remove the tilt assembly attaching screw, remove the assembly, (tilt lever, sub lever and lever locking bolt).

Install

1. Install the assembly, (tilt lever, sub lever and lever locking bolt). Install the tilt assembly attaching screw.

2. Install the 2 pawls, attaching nut and bolt to the steering column. Tighten to finger tightness only.

3. Install the two pawl stoppers, one either side of steering column. Engage with the pawl stoppers with the pawls either side. Tighten the pawl attaching bolt and nut to specification.

Tilt Steering Pawl Attaching Bolt and Nut:
60kg-cm, 5ft-lb, 6Nm

4. Remove the two tilt lever retainers plus "C" clip and nut, one either side of steering column.

Tilt Steering retainer levers Nuts:
150kg-cm, 11ft-lb, 15Nm

5. Install the bolt at the top of the column with the compressed spring and 2 bushes.

Tilt Steering Top Bolt and Spring:
80kg-cm, 7ft-lb, 8Nm

6. Replace the two springs, one to either side of steering column.

7. Lift steering column to support under dash, install the two bracket bolts and tighten until the bolt head brakes off.

8. Install steering column cover and test operation of the steering column.

IGNITION SWITCH and STEERING LOCK

Remove

1. Disconnect battery earth lead.

2. Remove steering column lower cover to column and upper cover attaching screws, and remove covers.

3. Disconnect wiring harness

50's & 60's Series

4. Remove the bolts attaching the lock assembly to the steering column support.

5. Insert a wire or pin in hole on side of barrel housing to push

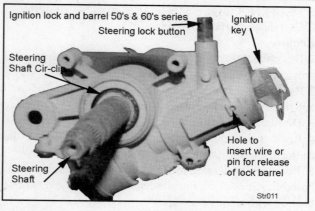

Str011

in tab holding the barrel in position.

6. Remove lock barrel and slide lock assembly from shaft.

80's Series on

4. Remove the support shear bolts by drilling a hole into the centre of the stud and removing the bolt with a bolt remover.

5. Remove the steering lock / ignition key assembly shear bolts by drilling a hole into the centre of the stud and removing the bolt with a bolt remover.

6. Remove the steering lock / ignition key.

Inspection

1. Turn key to ensure the lock rod operates OK, if not replace lock barrel and rod.

Lock Barrel Replace

2. To remove lock barrel. Insert wire or small pin into lock barrel locking hole, turn ignition key to ACC position and pull out lock barrel and key.

3. Insert new key into new lock barrel and turn to ACC position, push firmly into the barrel housing.

Install

1. Replace the steering lock / ignition key assembly only if necessary, as described above.

2. 50's & 60's series: Slide lock assembly over shaft, install lock barrel, install bolts holding lock assembly to steering column support.

80's series on: Fit the steering lock to the steering column, install the two shear head bolts and tighten until the bolt head brakes off.

3. Connect wiring harness.

4. Lift steering column to support under dash, install the two bracket shear head bolts and tighten until the bolt head brakes off.

5. Install steering column cover.

6. Install steering wheel, tighten nut to specification and test operation of the steering column.

Steering Wheel Attaching Nut:
350kg-cm, 25ft-lb, 34Nm

STEERING COLUMN TUBE and STEERING COLUMN TUBE BEARINGS

Remove

1. Disconnect battery earth lead and remove steering wheel as previously described.

2. Remove lower cover attaching screws on steering column and remove upper and lower cover.

3. Disconnect wiring harness.

4. Remove the support shear bolts by drilling a hole into the centre of the stud and removing the bolt with a bolt remover.

5. Remove the steering lock / ignition key assembly shear bolts by drilling a hole into the centre of the stud and remove the bolt with a bolt remover.

Retaining Spring Clip

50's & 60's Series   Str020

6. Remove the retaining spring clip at the top of the shaft, lift column tube from steering column shaft.

7. Remove steering column tube bushing at the lower end of the tube by pushing in the bushing lock-in tab releasing the bushing. Pull bushing out of tube.

8. **Non Tilt Steering Column:** If the top bearing is worn the steering column tube must be replaced.

Tilt Steering Column: Check the push in top bearing, if worn replace the bearing.

Install

1. Fit new bushing (if necessary) to the lower end of steering column tube, lock into position.

2. Check lower tube bearing as above.

3. Slide the steering column tube over shaft, and fit retaining spring clip.

Tilt Steering Column

Fit bushing, thrust collar and spring onto top of shaft before sliding the steering column tube over shaft, and fit retaining spring clip.

4. Fit the steering lock to the steering column, install the two shear head bolts and tighten until the bolt head brakes off.

5. Connect wiring harness.

6. Lift steering column to support under dash, install the two bracket shear head bolts and tighten until the bolt head brakes off.

7. Install steering column cover.

8. Install steering wheel, tighten nut to specification and test operation of the steering column.

Steering Wheel Attaching Nut:
          350kg-cm, 25ft-lb, 34Nm

STEERING SHAFTS

Remove

Some models may be need the dash lower panel and heater duct removed.

1. Disconnect battery earth lead and remove steering wheel as previously described.

2. Remove lower cover attaching screws on steering column and remove upper and lower cover.

3. Disconnect wiring harness.

4. Remove the support shear bolts by drilling a hole into the centre of the stud and removing the bolt with a bolt remover.

5. Remove the steering lock / ignition key assembly shear bolts by drilling a hole into the centre of the stud and remove the bolt with a bolt remover.

6. Remove the retaining spring clip at the top of the shaft, lift column tube from steering column shaft.

[Non Tilt Steering Column]

7. Remove the top shaft universal clamping bolt, slide the top shaft from the intermediate shaft.

8. Remove the steering column floor plate 2 attaching bolts at the base of the steering column tube, remove the bracket.

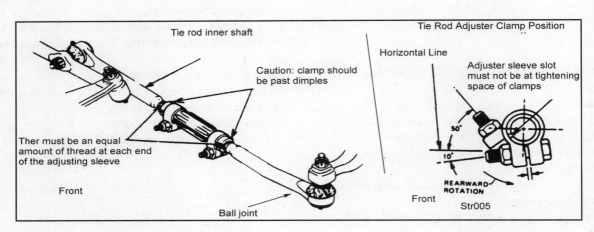

Tie rod inner shaft

Caution: clamp should be past dimples

Ther must be an equal amount of thread at each end of the adjusting sleeve

Front

Ball joint

Tie Rod Adjuster Clamp Position

Horizontal Line

Adjuster sleeve slot must not be at tightening space of clamps

50°

10°

REARWARD ROTATION

Front   Str005

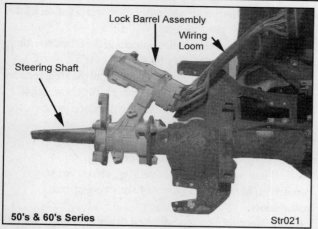

Steering Shaft

Lock Barrel Assembly

Wiring Loom

50's & 60's Series   Str021

9. Remove the steering column floor plate attaching bolts to the floor pan.

10. Near the steering box remove the flexible coupling clamping bolt, slide the intermediate shaft and coupling from the steering box shaft.

[Tilt Steering Column]

7. Remove the coupling clamp bolt at the lower end of the main steering shaft.

8. Pull the main shaft out from the lower steering column tube.

Middle East: From the lower column tube remove the collar retaining spring clip and shaft stopper, collar from the main shaft.

Other Countries: Remove the bush from the lower column tube.

Install

[Tilt Steering Column]

1 (a). **Middle East Countries:** Install lower busing collar, shaft stopper to the lower column tube. Install collar retaining clip.

Other Countries: Fit bush to the lower column tube.

(b). Install the main shaft into the lower column tube and coupling.

(c). Install the coupling clamp bolt at the lower end of the main steering shaft, tighten to specification.

Steering Shaft Coupling Bolt torque:

    360kg-cm, 26ft-lb, 35Nm

[Non Tilt Steering Column]

1 (a). Slide the intermediate shaft and coupling onto the steering box shaft. Near the steering box install the flexible coupling clamping bolt.

Steering Shaft Coupling Bolt torque:

    360kg-cm, 26ft-lb, 35Nm

(b). Install the steering column floor plate and attaching bolts to the floor pan. Tighten the bolts to specification.

Floor Plate Bolts Torque:

    80kg-cm, 7ft-lb, 7.8Nm

(c). Install the bracket to the steering column floor plate and 2 attaching bolts at the base of the steering column tube. Tighten bolts to specification.

Floor Bracket Bolts Torque:

    80kg-cm, 7ft-lb, 7.8Nm

(d). Slide the top shaft to the intermediate shaft. Align universal clamp with shaft, install clamp bolt and tighten to specification.

Universal Clamping Bolt Torque:

    360kg-cm, 26ft-lb, 35Nm

2. Fit new bushing (if necessary) to the lower end of steering column tube, lock into position.

3. Check lower tube bearing as above.

4. Slide the steering column tube over shaft, and fit retaining spring clip.

Tilt Steering Column

Fit bushing, thrust collar and spring onto top of shaft before sliding the steering column tube over shaft, and fit retaining spring clip.

5. Fit the steering lock to the steering column, install the two shear head bolts and tighten until the bolt head brakes off.

6. Connect wiring harness.

7. Lift steering column to support under dash, install the two bracket shear head bolts and tighten until the bolt head brakes off.

8. Install steering column cover.

9. Install steering wheel, tighten nut to specification and test operation of the steering column.

Steering Wheel Attaching Nut:

    350kg-cm, 25ft-lb, 34Nm

10. Install the heater duct if removed, install lower dash panel and screw.

ADJUST STEERING WHEEL FREE PLAY.

1. Check steering wheel free play for specified freeplay, if not within specification adjust as described below.

Steering Wheel Free Play Maximum at edge of Steering Wheel: **30mm (1.18in)**

2. Turn steering wheel so that the front wheels are straight ahead.

3. Hold the adjusting screw in position while you loosen the adjusting screw locknut situated in the centre of the steering gear housing cover.

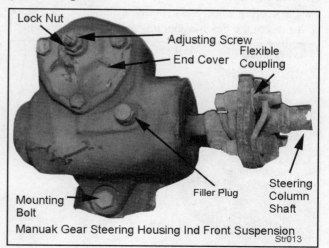

Lock Nut

Adjusting Screw

End Cover

Flexible Coupling

Filler Plug

Steering Column Shaft

Mounting Bolt

Manuak Gear Steering Housing Ind Front Suspension   Str013

4. Adjust the free play by turning the adjusting screw.
Clockwise decreases steering wheel free play.
Counter clockwise increases steering wheel free play.
5. Hold the adjusting screw in position while you tighten the adjusting screw locknut.
6. Check the action of the steering system.

STEERING GEAR OIL LEVEL

Check the level of the oil by removing the filler plug, dip a clean dip stick to measure the level from the top of the filler plug hole.
If not at specified level top up with specified steering gear oil.
Two Wheel Drive:

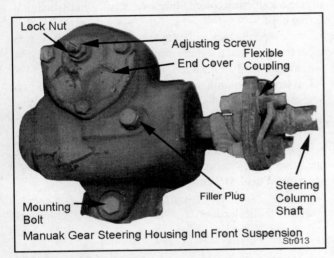

Manuak Gear Steering Housing Ind Front Suspension
Str013

18-28mm (0.71 - 1.10in)
Four Wheel Drive [Ind. Susp.]:
14-17mm (0.55 - .67in)
Four Wheel Drive [Leaf Spring Front Susp.]:
12-17mm (0.47 - .67in)
Specified Steering Gear Oil: **API GL-4, SAE 90**

STEERING COUPLING

Remove
1. Position the front wheels are pointing straight ahead, check that the steering wheel is also pointing straight ahead. Mark both sides of the flexible coupling and flexible coupling to

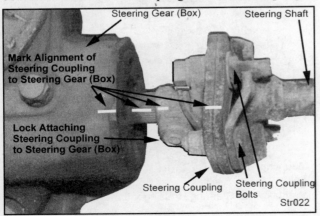

Str022

shaft, this will help with assembly, also the position of the input shaft to the steering gear.
2. Remove the nut and lock plate attaching the fabric coupling to the input shaft of the steering gear.
3. The fabric coupling must be turned so that the steel section of the coupling attached to the steering box is horizontal.
4. Remove the bolts and nuts attaching the steering box to the side rail.
5. Remove the coupling clamp bolt.
6. With a puller remove the fabric coupling.
Note: When removing the coupling strain must not be transferred to the components of the steering box.
Installation
1. Ensure steering gear is positioned straight ahead, marks on pinion (input shaft) and housing made during removal are aligned. Ensure steering wheel is positioned straight ahead.
2. Install the fabric coupling onto the input shaft making sure the markings on the coupling line up with the input shaft.
3. Install the steering box onto the side rail and tighten the bolts to specification.
Manual Steering Gear [Not Power Steering] to Side Frame Bolt Torque:
Two Wheel Drive:
      1,250kg-cm, 90ft-lb, 123Nm
Four Wheel Drive [Ind. Susp.]:
      1,450kg-cm, 130ft-lb, 177Nm
Four Wheel Drive [Leaf Spring Front Susp.]:
      575kg-cm, 42ft-lb, 56Nm
Power Steering Gear to Side Rail Bolt Torque:
Two Wheel Drive:
      1,200kg-cm, 87ft-lb, 118Nm
Four Wheel Drive [Ind. Susp.]:
      1,450kg-cm, 130ft-lb, 177Nm
Four Wheel Drive [Leaf Spring Front Susp.]:
      575kg-cm, 42ft-lb, 56Nm
4. Install and tighten the flexible coupling clamping bolt to the input steering gear shaft to specification.
Steering Shaft Coupling Bolt torque:
      360kg-cm, 26ft-lb, 35Nm
5. Tighten the fabric coupling attaching nuts and bend locking plate into place.
Fabric Coupling To Steering Shaft Nuts:
      260kg-cm, 19ft-lb, 25Nm

POWER STEERING SERVICE

CHECK FLUID LEVEL
1. Unscrew reservoir cap and check fluid level on dipstick with fluid at operating temperature.
2. Top up fluid level as necessary with specified fluid (DEXRON IID automatic transmission fluid) to 'H' (hot

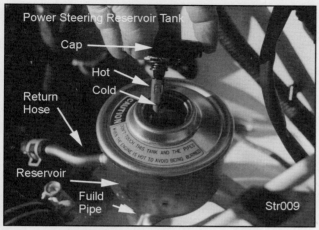

Power Steering Reservoir Tank
Cap
Hot
Cold
Return
Hose
Reservoir
Fuild
Pipe
Str009

full) mark on the dipstick.

Specified Power Steering Fluid: **Dexron 11**

* If the reservoir is dry, it will be necessary to bleed the system. [Refer to BLEED HYDRAULIC SYSTEM Section of this Chapter.]

3. Once completed, check system for leaks.

* If there is evidence of fluid leakage around the top of the reservoir, remove the cap and check the cap breather holes for blockage.

POWER STEERING PUMP BELT ADJUSTMENT

Idler pulley
adjusting bolt

Idler pulley

Tu010

Belt Tension
Check drive belt tension as follows:
1. Inspect drive belt condition.
2. Check belt for correct tension by pushing down on top of belt with 10kg (22lb) force and measure the belt deflection.

Drive Belt Deflection:
Hi Lux:
YN Series
New belt: 5-7mm (0.20-0.28in)
Used belt: 7-9mm (0.28-0.35in)
LN Series
New belt: 7-9mm (0.28-0.35in)
Used belt: 9-12mm (0.35-0.47in)
RN Series
New belt: 5-7mm (0.20-0.28in)

Used belt: 7-10mm (0.28-0.39in)
* *A drive belt is considered used after 10 minutes of use.*

To adjust the Drive Belt Tension:
1. Loosen power steering pump mounting bracket pivot and adjusting bolts.
2. Adjust pump position to achieve specified drive belt tension.
* Do not move pump by prying against reservoir or by pulling on pump filler neck.
3. Torque pump mounting bracket pivot and adjusting bolts.
Pump Mounting Bracket Pivot Bolt Torque:
Hi Lux

YN	400kg-cm, 29ft-lb, 39Nm
LN	625kg-cm, 45ft-lb, 61Nm
RN	375kg-cm, 27ft-lb, 37Nm

BLEED HYDRAULIC SYSTEM
During bleeding, it is important that the front wheels are clear of the ground and that the steering is not held forcibly against the steering stops.
1. Raise front of vehicle and place on safety stands.
2. With engine not running, turn steering wheel from lock to lock several times and add fluid to reservoir to maintain fluid level. Repeat until level remains constant.
3. Start engine and allow to idle. Turn steering wheel from lock to lock several times, contacting steering stops.
* System is bled when no air bubbles are visible in reservoir and level remains constant.
4. Lower vehicle to ground, turn steering wheel to straight ahead position and turn ignition 'OFF'.

IDLE RPM VALVE
E.F.I. vehicles have a fluid activated valve. This valve is activated by the fluid pressure when the steering wheel is turned, the valve increase air flow to the throttle body, there by increasing idle RPM when the steering wheel is turn while the engine is idling.

CHECK HYDRAULIC SYSTEM
The following procedures outline methods to identify and isolate power steering hydraulic circuit difficulties. This test is divided into 2 parts.
Test 1 provides a means of determining whether the power steering system hydraulic parts are faulty. If test 1 results in readings indicating faulty hydraulic operation, test 2 will identify the faulty part. Before performing hydraulic circuit test, carefully check drive belt tension, condition of driving pulley and fluid level.
Engine must be at normal operating temperature. Inflate front tyres to correct pressure. All tests are made with engine idling.
To perform the 2 pressure checks, it is necessary to connect a pressure gauge and valve (tap) assembly in the hydraulic

line between the pump and steering gear as follows:

1. Raise front of vehicle and support on safety stands.
2. Place a drain tray beneath steering gear valve housing.
3. Loosen and remove high pressure hydraulic line from steering gear valve housing.
4. Install pressure gauge and valve (tap), (valve on steering gear side of pressure gauge) assembly into the high pressure port of the valve housing and onto the disconnected high pressure line.
6. Refill system with fluid to the correct level as previously described. Ensure that there is not any leaks at hose and gauge connections.

Test 1 - Hydraulic Circuit Open
1. With valve open, start engine and with steering LIGHTLY on full lock, check connections for leakage.
2. Insert thermometer into reservoir filler and move steering from lock to lock until fluid reaches 60^0-70^0C.
3. Turn steering to full lock momentarily; if pressure is below specification, a faulty hydraulic circuit is indicated.

Specified Pressure
2WD: 75kg/cm², (1,067psi, 7,355kPa)
4WD: 65kg/cm², (924psi, 6,374kPa)

Test 2 - Hydraulic Circuit Closed
1. Slowly turn valve to closed position; note pressure and quickly re-open valve to avoid pump damage.
2. If pressure was less than specified, pump may be considered faulty.

Specified Pressure
2WD: 75kg/cm², (1,067psi, 7,355kPa)
4WD: 65kg/cm², (924psi, 6,374kPa)

3. If pressure was between more than specified, steering gear, external hoses or connections may be faulty.

* If pump proves faulty, retest after overhaul to check repairs and condition of steering gear.

* At the completion of tests, remove pressure gauge, hoses and connectors.

* The chart near the end of this chapter is an alternative procedure for checking power steering pump pressures.

POWER STEERING PUMP
Remove
1. Loosen power steering pump mounting bracket pivot and adjusting bolts and remove belt from pump pulley as previously described.
2. Place a drain tray beneath pump assembly.
3. E.F.I. Models: Remove the Idle RPM Valve hoses.
4. (a) Disconnect hoses at pump and secure hose ends in raised position to prevent oil loss.
 (b) Cap or tape hose ends and pump fittings to prevent entry of foreign matter.
5. (a) Y Series. Remove the reservoir tank.
 (b) R & L Series. Remove reservoir hose.
6. Remove bolts securing pump to mounting bracket and remove pump.

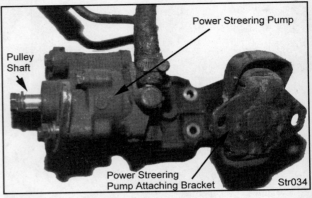

Str034

Install
1. Install pump on mounting bracket and torque pump mounting bolts.

Pump Mounting Bracket Bolt Torque:
Y Series
                    400kg-cm, 29ft-lb, 39Nm
L Series
                    625kg-cm, 45ft-lb, 61Nm
R Series
                    375kg-cm, 27ft-lb, 37Nm

2. Reconnect hoses to pump and tighten. Torque high pressure hose flare nut to specification.

Pump Fluid Hoses and Union Bolt Torque:
Y Series
                    450kg-cm, 33ft-lb, 44Nm
L Series
                    450kg-cm, 33ft-lb, 44Nm
R Series
                    475kg-cm, 34ft-lb, 47Nm

3. (a)Y Series. Replace the reservoir tank.
(b) R & L Series. Replace reservoir hose.
4. E.F.I. Models: Replace the Idle RPM Valve hoses.
5. Fill reservoir with fluid and turn pulley anti-clockwise (as view from front) until air bubbles cease to appear.
6. Install drive belt and adjust as previously described.
7. Bleed hydraulic system as previously described.

Dismantle
1. Remove drive belt pulley nut and pulley.
2. E.F.I. models remove Idle RPM Valve.
3. Clamp pump, in vice with soft jaws. Do not use excessive force or pump will distort.
4. L & R Series. Remove inlet fitting and associated O-ring. Y Series: Remove reservoir O-ring from pump housing.
5. Remove out let pressure union. Take care as spring loaded flow control valve will force outlet fitting from pump housing.
6. Remove four front housing bolts. Mark the front housing and pump body, so the front housing will be assembled correctly.
7. Remove front housing plate. (A slight rocking motion or light tapping with a soft-faced hammer will free plate if it should stick.)

8. Remove cam ring from body.

9. Remove vanes from rotor, then rotor from shaft.

10. (a) Remove dowel pins.

(b) Pry shaft seal from pump housing with a screwdriver and discard seal. Take care not to damage housing bore.

(c) Remove spring clip from shaft.

11. Remove shaft from pump housing by tapping on shaft with soft-faced hammer. Hold hand over pump body as end plate is spring-loaded and may spring out.

12. (a) Remove end plate and spring from housing, by tapping on back of pump with soft-faced hammer, if end plate is not loose.

(b) Remove end plate spring.

Clean and Inspect

Clean all metal parts in solvent, air dry and inspect:

1. Flow control valve must slide freely in housing bore. If sticking is observed, check for dirt and burrs.

2. Check cap screw in end of flow control valve for looseness: if loose, tighten (being careful not to damage machined surfaces).

3. Be sure that end plate surface is flat and parallel with pump ring. Check for cracks and scoring.

* A high polish is always present on rotor, pressure plate and thrust plate as a result of normal wear. Do not confuse this with scoring.

4. Ensure vanes move freely in rotor slots.

5. If the flow control plunger is suspected of being faulty, install a new component. This part is serviced as a unit only and is factory calibrated.

6. Check drive shaft for worn splines, breaks, bush material pick-up, etc.

7. Using a piece of wire, probe through shaft seal relief hole to check for blockage.

8. Always replace all seals and O-rings when pump is dismantled.

9. Check reservoir, bolts, casting, etc., for burrs and other faults which would impair proper operation.

Assembly

1. Install shaft into pump housing. Light tapping with a soft-faced hammer will seat shaft and rotor into place. Fit new spring clip to lock into position.

2. Lubricate new seal with DEXRON IID automatic transmission fluid, install in pump housing seat in with seal seat tool and light hammer.

3. (a) Install dowel pins in pump housing.

(b) Install new O ring.

(c) Install cam ring with the fluid passages aligned.

5. Install rotor, which must be free on shaft splines, with countersunk side towards the front.

Check that the rotor and cam ring are a matched pair that is both inscribed with the same identification mark. i.e. 1, 2, 3, 4, or no mark.

6. Install vanes into rotor slots.

7. Install the end plate to the pump assembly, align the fluid passages with the cam ring and end plate.

8. Place the spring on the end plate then fit the rear pump housing over the pump assembly

9. Install 4 bolts attaching the front housing to the pump body and gradually tighten to specification.

Steering Pump Body Bolts:

470kg-cm, 34ft-lb, 46Nm

10 (a). Install the flow control valve O ring and seat, install spring clip.

(b) Fit new O rings to flow control valve, install flow control valve spring and valve.

Check that the flow control valve and pump body are a matched pair that is both inscribed with the same identification mark. i.e. A, B, C, D, E, or F.

(c) Install new O ring to the outlet union and tighten to specification.

Pump Outlet Union torque:

700kg-cm, 50ft-lb, 70Nm

11. *L & R Series*. Replace inlet fitting and new O-ring.

Y Series: Fit new reservoir O-ring to pump housing.

12. E.F.I. models replace Idle RPM Valve.

13. Replace drive belt pulley and pulley nut, tighten to specification.

Steering Pump Pulley Nut Torque:

440kg-cm, 32ft-lb, 43Nm

STEERING MECHANISM

TIE ROD BALL JOINT
Replacement

Tie rod ball joints are serviced as an assembly and must be replaced when excessive up or down movement is evident, or if any lost motion or end play exists at the ball end of the stud.

1. Remove split pin and nut from tie rod ball stud.

2. Tighten centre bolt with special tool to force stud from taper in steering arm.

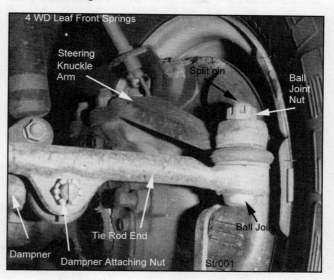

4 WD Leaf Front Springs — Steering Knuckle Arm — Split pin — Ball Joint Nut — Tie Rod End — Dampner — Dampner Attaching Nut — Ball Joint — Str001

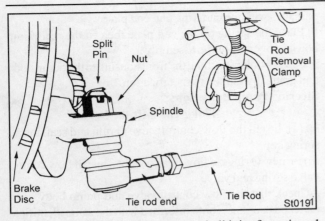

3. Loosen tie rod lock nut. Unscrew ball joint from tie rod, counting the number of turns to wind ball joint from tie rod.

4. Install new ball joint onto tie rod and wind on the same number of turns as in Step 3.

5. Install ball joint to steering arm. Install and torque castellated nut.

Tie Rod Ball Joint Specified Torque:
          930kg-cm, 67ft-lb, 91Nm

* Ensure that the nylon spacer is positioned on the tie rod ball joint stud before installing into steering arm.

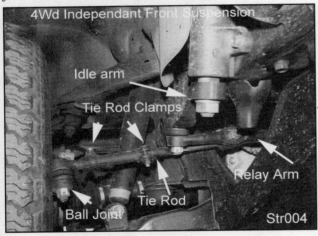

6. Install new split pin and check front wheel toe-in as described in this manual.

DRAG LINK
Remove

1. Remove the split pin from the end which you wish to dismantle.

2. Use a screw driver, screw plug and ball seat from the drag link or loosen the plug enough to allow the ball stud to be loose.

3. Pull the drag link from the ball stud.

Install

1. Loosen off the plug and ball stud seat to allow the ball stud to be fitted to the drag link.

2. Install the drag link to the ball stud, push the ball stud into the drag link opening.

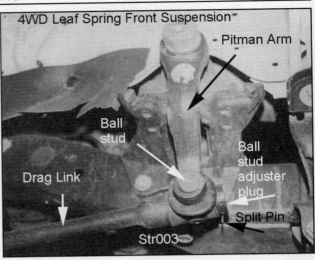

3. (a) Screw the plug and ball stud seat tightly with a screw driver.

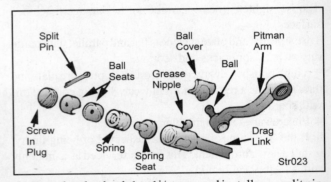

(b) Turn the plug back 1 to $1\frac{1}{2}$ turns and install new split pin.

PITMAN ARM
Remove

1. Paint a mark across the pitman arm and the steering gear output shaft to help during installation.

2. Remove the steering gear (box) output shaft and nut.

3. Use a puller to help remove the pitman arm from the steering gear.

4. Remove the pitman arm from the drag link as described above.

Install

1. Install pitman arm to steering gear output shaft.

\# Ensure that the alignment marks on the steering gear output shaft and pitman arm are aligned and in the correct position.

2. Install washer and nut, tighten nut to specified torque.

Pitman Arm to Steering Gear Output Shaft Nut Torque:
Two Wheel Drive:
          1,250kg-cm, 90ft-lb, 125Nm
Four Wheel Drive [Ind. Susp.]:
          1,800kg-cm, 130ft-lb, 177Nm
Four Wheel Drive [Leaf Spring Front Susp.]:
          1,750kg-cm, 127ft-lb, 172Nm

3. Install pitman arm to the drag link as described above.

262

KNUCKLE ARM
Remove

1. Remove drag link from knuckle arm as described above.

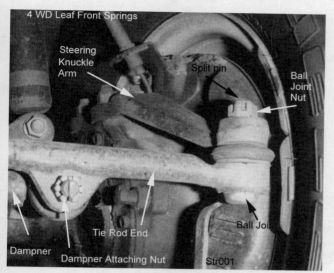

2. Remove tie rod from knuckle arm as described above.

3. Remove the knuckle arm attaching bolts, remove the steering knuckle arm from the steering knuckle.

Install

1. Install the steering knuckle arm and back dust cover to the steering knuckle, tighten 4 bolts to specification.

Steering Knuckle Arm & Back Dust Cover Bolt Torque: 1,100 kg-cm, 80ft-lb 108Nm

2. Install split pins to knuckle arm attaching bolts.
3. Install tie rod end to knuckle arm as previously described.
4. Install drag link to knuckle arm as previously described.

STEERING DAMPER
Remove

1. Remove split pin and nut from steering damper ball stud.
2. Tighten centre bolt with special tool to force stud from taper in tie rod.
3. Remove the nut, washer and rubber bush from the steering damper. (Some models remove a bolt.)
4. Remove steering damper from vehicle.

Install

1. Install steering damper to vehicle, fit new rubber bushes if required, washers and nut, tighten to specification. (Some models install bolt through a rubber bush).

Steering Damper Attaching Nut Specified Torque: 130 kg-cm, 9ft-lb 13Nm

Steering Damper Attaching Bolt Specified Torque: 260 kg-cm, 18t-lb 25Nm

2. Install ball joint to tie rod. Install and torque castellated nut.

Steering Damper Ball joint Specified Torque: 600kg-cm, 43ft-lb, 59Nm

3. Install new split pin

MANUAL STEERING GEAR [Manual Steering Box]

Before removing the steering gear have the front wheels pointing straight ahead and keep the steering wheel in the central position.

Remove

1. At the steering gear, mark both sides of the flexible coupling [universal] and flexible coupling [universal] to steering wheel shaft, this will help with assembly, also the position of the input shaft to the steering gear.

2. Flexible Coupling: (a) Remove the nut and lock plate attaching the fabric coupling to the input shaft of the steering gear.

(b) The fabric coupling must be turned so that the steel section of the coupling attached to the steering box is horizontal.

Universal Joint: (a) Remove both clamp bolts of the universal that is the steering column side and the steering gear side.

(b) With the aid of screw driver slide the universal joint up the steering wheel shaft, as push the shaft back enough to allow the universal to be free of the steering gear input shaft.

3. Remove the nut holding the pitman arm to the steering gear output shaft.

4. (a) Paint a mark across the pitman arm and the steering gear output shaft to help during installation.

(b) Use a puller to help remove the pitman arm from the steering gear.

(c) Swing the pitman arm to one side, this will give access to the steering gear.

5. Remove the bolts and nuts attaching the steering gear to the side rail.

6. [Flexible coupling] (a). Remove the coupling clamp bolt.

(b). With a puller remove the fabric coupling.

Note: When removing the coupling strain must not be transferred to the components of the steering box.

Install

Ensure that the alignment marks on the steering shaft, steering shaft joint flexible coupling or universal joint, steering gear and pitman arm are aligned and in the correct position while installing components.

1. Install the steering gear to the vehicle side frame, before installing the attaching bolts, temporary install the steering shaft joint flexible coupling or universal joint to the input shaft of the steering gear.

Ensure that the alignment marks on the steering shaft and steering shaft joint flexible coupling or universal joint are aligned and in the correct position.

2. After the steering shaft flexible coupling or universal joint has been temporary installed to the steering gear input shaft, tighten the steering gear attaching bolts to specification.

Manual Steering Gear [Not Power Steering] to Side Frame Bolt Torque:

Two Wheel Drive: 1,250kg-cm, 90ft-lb, 123Nm

Four Wheel Drive [Ind. Susp.]: 1,450kg-cm, 130ft-lb, 177Nm

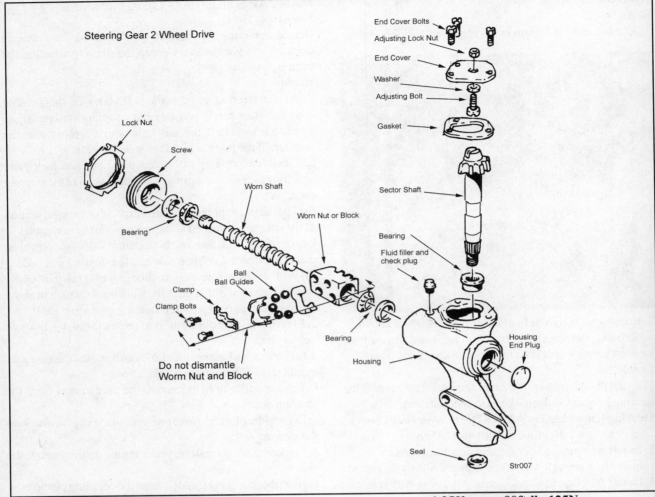

Steering Gear 2 Wheel Drive

End Cover Bolts
Adjusting Lock Nut
End Cover
Washer
Adjusting Bolt
Gasket
Sector Shaft
Bearing
Fluid filler and check plug
Housing End Plug
Housing
Seal

Lock Nut
Screw
Worn Shaft
Worn Nut or Block
Bearing
Ball
Ball Guides
Clamp
Clamp Bolts
Do not dismantle Worn Nut and Block
Bearing

Str007

Four Wheel Drive [Leaf Spring Front Susp.]:
575kg-cm, 42ft-lb, 56Nm

3. *Flexible Coupling:* (a) Install and tighten the flexible coupling clamping bolt to the input steering gear shaft to specification.

Steering Shaft Coupling Bolt torque:
360kg-cm, 26ft-lb, 35Nm

(b) Tighten the fabric coupling attaching nuts and bend locking plate into place.

Fabric coupling to steering shaft nuts:
260kg-cm, 19ft-lb, 25Nm

Universal Joint: Slide the universal joint into the correct position on the steering gear input shaft, while ensuring the universal joint is correctly located on the steering shaft. Install the clamping bolts and tighten to specification.

Steering Shaft Universal Joint Bolt torque:
360kg-cm, 26ft-lb, 35Nm

4. Install pitman arm to steering gear output shaft.
#Ensure that the alignment marks on the steering gear output shaft and pitman arm are aligned and in the correct position. Install washer and nut, tighten nut to specified torque.

Pitman Arm to Steering Gear Output Shaft Nut Torque:
Two Wheel Drive:

1,250kg-cm, 90ft-lb, 125Nm
Four Wheel Drive [Ind. Susp.]:
1,800kg-cm, 130ft-lb, 177Nm
Four Wheel Drive [Leaf Spring Front Susp.]:
1,750kg-cm, 127ft-lb, 172Nm

Dismantle
Refer to figure for identification of components.
1. Clean all dirt and foreign matter from exterior of steering

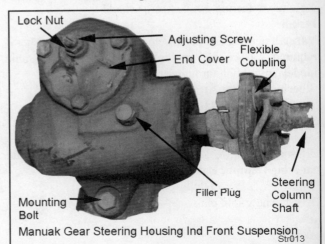

Lock Nut
Adjusting Screw
End Cover
Flexible Coupling
Mounting Bolt
Filler Plug
Steering Column Shaft
Manuak Gear Steering Housing Ind Front Suspension
Str013

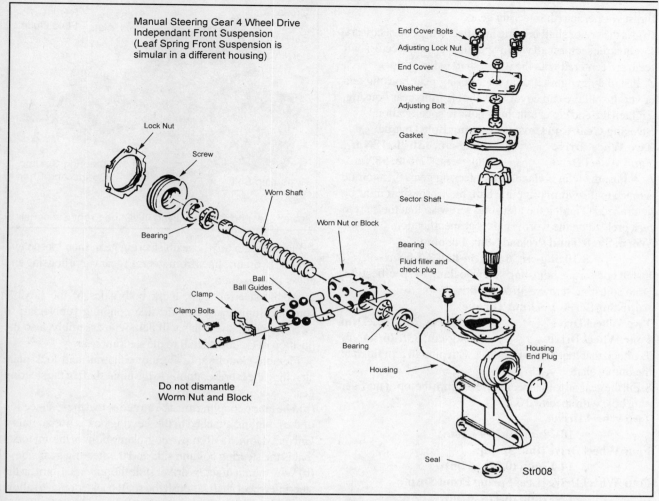

Manual Steering Gear 4 Wheel Drive
Independant Front Suspension
(Leaf Spring Front Suspension is
simular in a different housing)

End Cover Bolts
Adjusting Lock Nut
End Cover
Washer
Adjusting Bolt
Gasket
Sector Shaft
Bearing
Fluid filler and
check plug
Housing
End Plug
Housing
Bearing
Seal
Str008

Lock Nut
Screw
Worn Shaft
Bearing
Worn Nut or Block
Ball
Ball Guides
Clamp
Clamp Bolts
Bearing

Do not dismantle
Worm Nut and Block

gear assembly.

2. Press Pitman arm from steering gear if still fitted.

3. Mount steering gear housing in a vice with soft jaws.

4. (a) Place a drain tray beneath steering gear, then remove the top cover bolts.

(b) Loosen the adjusting screw lock nut it also helps if the adjusting screw is loosened one full turn.

5. (a) Turn the input shaft one eighth of a turn towards the right lock off centre.

(b) Carefully remove the top cover (as there will still be oil in the gear) from the end of the sector shaft.

(c) Pull the sector (input) shaft assembly from the top opening of the housing.

6. Place the steering gear in the vice so that the worn (output) shaft can be accessible.

7. Remove the bearing lock nut and adjusting screw on the end of the worm shaft. Taking care of teflon seals at all times.

8. Pull out the oil seal, worm shaft oil seal, worm shaft bearing and worm shaft, from the steering gear.

Clean and Inspection

Wash all components and inspect for cracks, corrosion around seal areas, scour marks and bearings and shaft damage.

Do-not dismantle the ball nut block from the worm shaft. Damaged bearings should be pressed from the worm shaft or steering gear housing and press in new bearing.

If shafts are damaged replace with new shaft.

Check the sector (input) shaft adjusting screw thrust washer, with the adjusting screw installed to the sector shaft, measure the clearance between the adjusting screw head and the sector shaft. This clearance measurement is the thickness of thrust washer required.

Assemble

Cover all components with multi purpose grease before assembly.

1. Install the worm shaft, bearings and oil seal into the steering gear.

2. (a) Install the bearing adjusting screw, and tighten gradually until the preload on the worn (output) shaft is at specified level.

(b) Hold adjusting screw and tighten lock nut to specification.
**Worm (Output) shaft Adjusting Screw Locknut Torque:
1,110kg-cm, 80ft-lb, 109Nm**

3. Move the worm shaft ball nut block into the centre of the worm shaft.

4. (a) Install the sector (input) with bearings, adjusting screw,

thrust washer into the steering gear.

(b) As the sector shaft is being installed, it may be necessary to adjust the sector shaft with a screw driver so the sector shaft teeth are centered with the worm shaft ball nut block.

5. Install a new gasket onto the steering gear housing end cover. Install the end cover onto the steering gear housing. Tighten the end cover attaching bolts to specification.

Steering Gear End Cover Attaching Bolt Torque:

Two Wheel Drive	**185kg-cm, 13ft-lb, 18Nm**
Four Wheel Drive	**100kg-cm, 72ft-lb, 98Nm**

6. Adjust the total preload of the steering gear. Fit a torque wrench to the worm (output) shaft, the worm shaft must be centralized. Tighten the adjusting screw so that the start to turn preload on the worm shaft is at specification.

Worm Shaft Total Preload Start Turning:

8-10.5kg-cm, 6.9-9.1in-lb 0.8-1.0Nm

Install and torque adjusting screw locknut to specification. Hold adjusting screw with screw driver.

Adjusting Screw Locknut Torque:

Two Wheel Drive	**275kg-cm, 20ft-lb, 27Nm**
Four Wheel Drive	**450kg-cm, 33ft-lb, 44Nm**

7. Check that there is no backlash with pitman arm fitted to the output shaft.

8. Fill the gear oil to the specified level from the top of the filler plug hole with specified oil.

Two Wheel Drive:

18-28mm (0.71 - 1.10in)

Four Wheel Drive [Ind. Susp.]:

14-17mm (0.55 - .67in)

Four Wheel Drive [Leaf Spring Front Susp.]:

12-17mm (0.47 - .67in)

Specified Steering Gear Oil: API GL-4, SAE 90

9. Install filler plug and tighten to specification.

Filler Plug Torque:

200kg-cm, 15ft-lb, 20Nm

POWER STEERING GEAR [Power Steering Box]

Before removing the steering gear have the front wheels pointing straight ahead and keep the steering wheel in the central position.

Remove

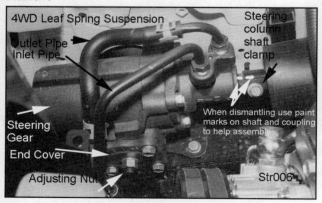

Str006

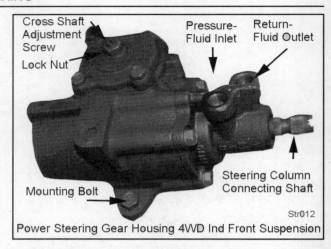

Power Steering Gear Housing 4WD Ind Front Suspension

1. Place a drain tray beneath steering gear, then loosen and remove hydraulic lines from steering gear valve housing and allow fluid to drain.

2. At the steering gear, mark both sides of the flexible coupling [universal] and flexible coupling [universal] to steering wheel shaft, this will help with assembly, also the position of the input shaft to the steering gear.

3. Flexible Coupling: (a) Remove the nut and lock plate attaching the fabric coupling to the input shaft of the steering gear.

(b) The fabric coupling must be turned so that the steel section of the coupling attached to the steering box is horizontal.

Universal Joint: (a) Remove both clamp bolts of the universal that is the steering column side and the steering gear side.

(b) With the aid of screw driver slide the universal joint up the steering wheel shaft, as push the shaft back enough to allow the universal to be free of the steering gear input shaft.

4. Remove the nut holding the pitman arm to the steering gear output shaft.

5. (a) Paint a mark across the pitman arm and the steering gear

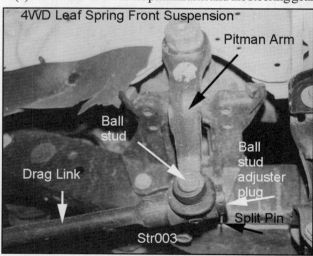

Str003

output shaft to help during installation.

(b) Use a puller to help remove the pitman arm from the steering gear.

(c) Swing the pitman arm to one side, this will give access to the steering gear.

6. Remove the bolts and nuts attaching the steering gear to the side rail.

7. [Flexible coupling] (a). Remove the coupling clamp bolt. (b). With a puller remove the fabric coupling.

Note: When removing the coupling strain must not be transferred to the components of the steering box.

Install

Ensure that the alignment marks on the steering shaft, steering shaft joint flexible coupling or universal joint, steering gear and pitman arm are aligned and in the correct position while installing components.

1. Install the steering gear to the vehicle side frame, before installing the attaching bolts, temporary install the steering shaft joint flexible coupling or universal joint to the input shaft of the steering gear.

Ensure that the alignment marks on the steering shaft and steering shaft joint flexible coupling or universal joint are aligned and in the correct position.

2. After the steering shaft flexible coupling or universal joint has been temporary installed to the steering gear input shaft, tighten the steering gear attaching bolts to specification.

Power Steering Gear to Side Frame Bolt Torque:
Two Wheel Drive:
1,200kg-cm, 87ft-lb, 118Nm
Four Wheel Drive [Ind. Susp.]:
1,450kg-cm, 130ft-lb, 177Nm
Four Wheel Drive [Leaf Spring Front Susp.]:
575kg-cm, 42ft-lb, 56Nm

3. *Flexible Coupling:* (a) Install and tighten the flexible coupling clamping bolt to the input steering gear shaft to specification.

Steering Shaft Coupling Bolt torque:
360kg-cm, 26ft-lb, 35Nm

(b) Tighten the fabric coupling attaching nuts and bend locking plate into place.

Fabric coupling to steering shaft nuts:
260kg-cm, 19ft-lb, 25Nm

Universal Joint: Slide the universal joint into the correct position on the steering gear input shaft, while ensuring the universal joint is correctly located on the steering shaft. Install the clamping bolts and tighten to specification.

Steering Shaft Universal Joint Bolt torque:
360kg-cm, 26ft-lb, 35Nm

4. Install power hydraulic lines to steering gear housing, tighten flange nuts to specification.

Hydraulic Line Flange Nut Torque:
450kg-cm, 33ft-lb, 44Nm

5. Install pitman arm to steering gear output shaft.

Ensure that the alignment marks on the steering gear output shaft and pitman arm are aligned and in the correct position. Install washer and nut, tighten nut to specified torque.

Pitman Arm to Steering Gear Output Shaft Nut Torque:

Two Wheel Drive:
1,800kg-cm, 130ft-lb, 177Nm
Four Wheel Drive [Ind. Susp.]:
1,800kg-cm, 130ft-lb, 177Nm
Four Wheel Drive [Leaf Spring Front Susp.]:
1,750kg-cm, 127ft-lb, 172Nm

6. (a) Unscrew reservoir cap and check fluid level on dipstick with fluid at operating temperature.

(b) Top up fluid level as necessary with specified fluid (DEXRON IID automatic transmission fluid) to 'H' (hot full) mark on the dipstick.

Specified Power Steering Fluid: Dexron 11D

* If the reservoir is dry, it will be necessary to bleed the system. [Refer to BLEED HYDRAULIC SYSTEM Section of this Chapter.]

(c) Once completed, check system for leaks.

Dismantle

Refer to figure for identification of components.

1. Clean all dirt and foreign matter from exterior of steering gear assembly.

2. Press Pitman arm from steering gear if still fitted.

3. Mount steering gear housing in a vice with soft jaws.

4. (a) Place a drain tray beneath steering gear, then remove the top cover bolts.

(b) Loosen the adjusting screw lock nut it also helps if the adjusting screw is loosened one full turn.

5. (a) Turn the input shaft one eighth of a turn towards the right lock off centre.

(b) Carefully remove the top cover (as there will still be oil in the gear) from the end of the sector shaft.

(c) Pull the cross (input) shaft assembly from the top opening of the housing, it may need a tap with a soft hammer.

6. *Two Wheel Drive:* Remove plunger nut, O ring, spring, plunger guide and plunger from the steering gear housing.

7. Place the steering gear in the vice so that the worm (output) shaft can be accessed.

7. Remove the worm (output) gear valve body assembly attaching bolts. Turn the worm shaft clockwise as you hold the power piston from moving. Remove the worm gear valve and power piston assembly. Taking care of teflon seals at all times.

8. Pull out the O ring oil seal and worm shaft teflon seal from the steering gear.

Clean and Inspection

Wash all components and inspect for cracks, corrosion around seal areas, scour marks and bearings and shaft damage.

Damaged bearings should be pressed from the worm shaft or steering gear housing and press in new bearing. Note some bearings are held into place with a spring clip.

If shafts are damaged replace with new shaft.

Check the sector (input) shaft adjusting screw thrust washer, with the adjusting screw installed to the sector shaft, measure the clearance between the adjusting screw head and the sector shaft. This clearance measurement is the thickness of thrust washer required.

Assemble

1. *Two Wheel Drive:* Install plunger, plunger guide, spring, new O ring and plunger nut. Tighten plunger nut to specification.

Plunger Nut torque Specification:
205kg-cm, 15ft-lb, 20Nm

2. Fit a new teflon seal to base of gear housing for the worm shaft and valve body, the seal will need to squeezed by hand so it has a small diameter to be installed. Then seated correctly.

3. Fit a new oil seal into position.

4. (a) Fit a new teflon oil seal if necessary to worm valve body, if fitted the seal should be compressed for 7-8 minutes with a ring compressor before installing the worm valve shaft assembly.

(b) Install new O rings to the valve body and gear housing.

(c) Install worm shaft and valve body assembly, taking care of the teflon seals in step No 2. & 4. (a).

(d) Install the valve attaching bolts and tighten to specified torque.

Worm Shaft / Valve Body Attaching Bolts Torque:
470kg-cm, 34ft-lb, 46Nm

5. Check the preload on the worm (output) shaft is at specified level. Hold the piston nut block with finger to stop moving.

Worm Shaft Preload during assembly:
3-5.5kg-cm, 2.6-4.8in-lb 0.3-0.5Nm

6. Move the worm shaft piston nut block into the centre of the worm shaft.

7. (a) Install the adjusting screw, shim and end cover to the cross shaft, have the adjusting screw loosened off.

(b) Install a new O ring to the end cover.

(c) Install the cross (input) shaft with bearings, adjusting screw, into the steering gear.

(d) As the cross shaft is being installed, it may be necessary to adjust the cross shaft with a screw driver so the cross shaft teeth are centered with the worm shaft piston nut block.

(e) Install the end cover bolts and tighten the end cover attaching bolts to specification.

Cross Shaft End Cover Attaching Bolt Torque:

Two Wheel Drive	**470kg-cm, 34ft-lb, 46Nm**
Four Wheel Drive	**470kg-cm, 34ft-lb, 46Nm**

8. Turn the worm shaft from lock to lock so as to find centre, mark with paint worm shaft and housing at centre positions

9. (a) Install adjusting screw washer and nut loosely.

(b) Adjust the adjusting screw so the preload on the worm (output) shaft is 5.5kg-cm, 4.8in-lb .5Nm above the measured preload in step No. 5 this should give you a total preload between specification listed below. The worm shaft must be centralized. Tighten the adjusting screw so that the start to turn preload on the worm shaft is at specification.

Worm Shaft Total Preload Start Turnings:
8-10.5kg-cm, 6.5-9.1in-lb 0.6-1.0Nm

Install and torque adjusting screw locknut to specification. Hold adjusting screw with screw driver.

Adjusting Screw Locknut Torque:

Two Wheel Drive	**470kg-cm, 34ft-lb, 46Nm**
Four Wheel Drive	**470kg-cm, 34ft-lb, 46Nm**

7. Check that there is no backlash with pitman arm fitted to the output shaft.

SPECIFICATIONS

Specified Power Steering Fluid: Dexron 11D
Steering Wheel Free Play Maximum at edge of Steering Wheel: 30mm (1.18in)
Specified Pressure
2WD: 75kg/cm², (1,067psi, 7,355kPa)
4WD: 65kg/cm², (924psi, 6,374kPa)
Drive Belt Deflection:
YN Series
New belt: 5-7mm (0.20-0.28in)
Used belt: 7-9mm (0.28-0.35in)
LN Series
New belt: 7-9mm (0.28-0.35in)
Used belt: 9-12mm (0.35-0.47in)
RN Series
New belt: 5-7mm (0.20-0.28in)
Used belt: 7-10mm (0.28-0.39in)
* *A drive belt is considered used after 10 minutes of use.*
Worm Shaft Total Preload Start Turnings:
8-10.5kg-cm, 6.9-9.1in-lb 0.8-1.0Nm

TORQUE SPEC'S

Steering Wheel Attaching Nut: 350kg-cm, 25ft-lb, 34Nm
Tilt Steering Pawl Attaching Bolt and Nut:
60kg-cm, 5ft-lb, 6Nm
Tilt Steering retainer levers Nuts: 150kg-cm, 11ft-lb, 15Nm
Tilt Steering Top Bolt and Spring: 80kg-cm, 7ft-lb, 8Nm
Steering Shaft Coupling Bolt torque:
360kg-cm, 26ft-lb, 35Nm
Floor Plate Bolts Torque: 80kg-cm, 7ft-lb, 7.8Nm
Floor Bracket Bolts Torque: 80kg-cm, 7ft-lb, 7.8Nm
Universal Clamping Bolt Torque: 360kg-cm, 26ft-lb, 35Nm
Manual Steering Gear [Not Power Steering] to Side Frame Bolt Torque:
Two Wheel Drive: 1,250kg-cm, 90ft-lb, 123Nm
Four Wheel Drive [Ind. Susp.]:1,450kg-cm, 130ft-lb, 177Nm
Four Wheel Drive [Leaf Spring Front Susp.]:
575kg-cm, 42ft-lb, 56Nm
Power Steering Gear to Side Rail Bolt Torque:
Two Wheel Drive: 1,200kg-cm, 87ft-lb, 118Nm
Four Wheel Drive [Ind. Susp.]: 1,450kg-cm, 130ft-lb, 177Nm

STEERING

Four Wheel Drive [Leaf Spring Front Susp.]:
575kg-cm, 42ft-lb, 56Nm
Steering Shaft Coupling Bolt torque:
360kg-cm, 26ft-lb, 35Nm
Fabric Coupling To Steering Shaft Nuts:
260kg-cm, 19ft-lb, 25Nm
Pump Mounting Bracket Bolt Torque:
Y Series   400kg-cm, 29ft-lb, 39Nm
L Series   625kg-cm, 45ft-lb, 61Nm
R Series   375kg-cm, 27ft-lb, 37Nm
Pump Fluid Hoses and Union Bolt Torque:
Y Series   450kg-cm, 33ft-lb, 44Nm
L Series   450kg-cm, 33ft-lb, 44Nm
R Series   475kg-cm, 34ft-lb, 47Nm
Steering Pump Body Bolts: 470kg-cm, 34ft-lb, 46Nm
Pump Outlet Union torque: 700kg-cm, 50ft-lb, 70Nm
Steering Pump Pulley Nut Torque:
440kg-cm, 32ft-lb, 43Nm
Tie Rod Ball Joint Specified Torque:
930kg-cm, 67ft-lb, 91Nm
Manual Steering Gear [Not Power] to Side Frame Bolt Torque:
Two Wheel Drive: 1,250kg-cm, 90ft-lb, 123Nm
Four Wheel Drive [Ind. Susp.]: 1,450kg-cm, 130ft-lb, 177Nm
Four Wheel Drive [Leaf Spring Front Susp.]:
575kg-cm, 42ft-lb, 56Nm
Steering Shaft Universal Joint Bolt torque:
360kg-cm, 26ft-lb, 35Nm
Pitman Arm to Steering Gear Output Shaft Nut Torque:
Two Wheel Drive: 1,250kg-cm, 90ft-lb, 125Nm
Four Wheel Drive [Ind. Susp.]:
1,800kg-cm, 130ft-lb, 177Nm
Four Wheel Drive [Leaf Spring Front Susp.]:
1,750kg-cm, 127ft-lb, 172Nm
Worm (Output) shaft Adjusting Screw Locknut Torque:
1,110kg-cm, 80ft-lb, 109Nm
Steering Gear End Cover Attaching Bolt Torque:
Two Wheel Drive   185kg-cm, 13ft-lb, 18Nm
Four Wheel Drive   100kg-cm, 72ft-lb, 98Nm
Adjusting Screw Locknut Torque:
Two Wheel Drive   275kg-cm, 20ft-lb, 27Nm
Four Wheel Drive   450kg-cm, 33ft-lb, 44Nm

Two Wheel Drive: 8-28mm (0.71 - 1.10in)
Four Wheel Drive [Ind. Susp.]: 14-17mm (0.55 - .67in)
Four Wheel Drive [Leaf Spring Ft Susp.]:
12-17mm (0.47 - .67in)
Specified Steering Gear Oil: API GL-4, SAE 90
Filler Plug Torque: 200kg-cm, 15ft-lb, 20Nm
Power Steering Gear to Side Frame Bolt Torque:
Two Wheel Drive: 1,200kg-cm, 87ft-lb, 118Nm
Four Wheel Drive [Ind. Susp.]:
1,450kg-cm, 130ft-lb, 177Nm

Four Wheel Drive [Leaf Spring Front Susp.]:
575kg-cm, 42ft-lb, 56Nm
Steering Shaft Coupling Bolt torque:
360kg-cm, 26ft-lb, 35Nm
Fabric coupling to steering shaft nuts:
260kg-cm, 19ft-lb, 25Nm
Steering Shaft Universal Joint Bolt torque:
360kg-cm, 26ft-lb, 35Nm
Hydraulic Line Flange Nut Torque:
450kg-cm, 33ft-lb, 44Nm
Pitman Arm to Steering Gear Output Shaft Nut Torque:
Two Wheel Drive: 1,800kg-cm, 130ft-lb, 177Nm
Four Wheel Drive [Ind. Susp.]:
1,800kg-cm, 130ft-lb, 177Nm
Four Wheel Drive [Leaf Spring Front Susp.]:
1,750kg-cm, 127ft-lb, 172Nm
Specified Power Steering Fluid: Dexron 11D
Plunger Nut torque Specification:
205kg-cm, 15ft-lb, 20Nm
Worm Shaft / Valve Body Attaching Bolts Torque:
470kg-cm, 34ft-lb, 46Nm
Cross Shaft End Cover Attaching Bolt Torque:
Two Wheel Drive   470kg-cm, 34ft-lb, 46Nm
Four Wheel Drive   470kg-cm, 34ft-lb, 46Nm
Worm Shaft Total Preload Start Turnings:
8-10.5kg-cm, 6.5-9.1in-lb 0.6-1.0Nm
Adjusting Screw Locknut Torque:
Two Wheel Drive   470kg-cm, 34ft-lb, 46Nm
Four Wheel Drive   470kg-cm, 34ft-lb, 46Nm
Steering Knuckle Arm & Back Dust Cover Bolt Torque:
1,100 kg-cm, 80ft-lb 108Nm
Steering Damper Attaching Nut Specified Torque:
130 kg-cm, 9ft-lb 13Nm
Steering Damper Attaching Bolt Specified Torque:
260 kg-cm, 18t-lb 25Nm
Steering Damper Ball joint Specified Torque:
600kg-cm, 43ft-lb, 59Nm

269

FRONT SUSPENSION

FRONT SUSPENSION

The front suspension chapter covers two wheel drive vehicles, four wheel drive with leaf springs and four wheel drive with independent front suspension.

WHEEL ALIGNMENT

DESCRIPTION

Front wheel alignment is the mechanics of adjusting all interrelated factors that affect steering; namely, caster, camber and toe-in.

Caster

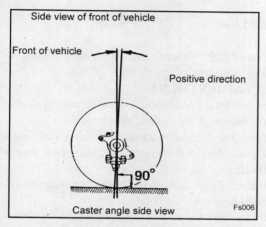

Caster angle side view   Fs006

This refers to the tilting of the steering axis either forward or backward from the vertical (when viewed from the side of the vehicle). A backward tilt is said to be positive (+) and a forward tilt is said to be negative (-).

Camber

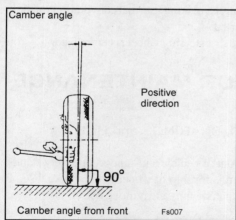

Camber angle from front   Fs007

When the wheels tilt outward at the top, the camber is said to be positive (+). When the wheels tilt inward at the top, camber is said to be negative (-).

Toe-In

This refers to the turning in of the wheels. The actual amount of toe-in is normally only a few millimetres. The purpose of a toe specification is to ensure parallel rolling of the wheels. Excessive toe-in or toe-out may increase tyre wear. A slight

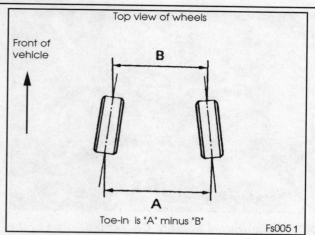

Toe-in is "A" minus "B"   Fs005 1

amount of positive toe-in, measured statically with the vehicle at rest, is required to offset the small deflections due to rolling resistance and brake applications which tend to turn the wheels outward.

WHEEL ALIGNMENT ADJUSTMENT
Visual Inspection

It is necessary that before any attempt is made to check camber, caster or toe-in, carry out the following preliminary checks :

1. Check tyre and tyre mountings. Always check camber and toe-in at the mean run-out position on the tyre or rim.
2. Check and adjust tyre pressures to recommended values.
3. Front wheel bearings should be correctly adjusted.
4. Lower control arm ball joints and inner bushes should be checked for wear.
5. Check steering gear mounting bolts for tightness and tie rod ball joints for wear.
6. The vehicle should be at curb weight, fuel tank full (without driver, passengers or luggage, etc.).
7. Check for improperly operating front or rear shock absorbers.
8. Check for loose or missing stabilizer bar and other attachments.

CASTER ADJUSTMENT
Hi Lux 30's & 40's

2WD: Caster is adjusted by adjusting the strut from the lower arm nuts at the chassis.

Caster: $^1/_2$ Ton 1^0 +/-30': $^3/_4$ & 1 Ton 30' +/- 40'

Positive Caster: Loosen the rear nut of the strut and tighten the front nut.

Negative Caster: Loosen the front nut of the strut and tighten the rear nut.

Caster Bush nut specification   69-108 ft-lb

4WD: No adjustment except for replacing worn parts.

Specified Caster $3^030'$ +/- 40'

Hi-Lux (50's & 60's ind sus) 80's, 90's 100's & 110's

2WD: Caster is adjusted by adjusting the thickness of the shims in the upper arm

Specified Caster: Depends on tyres $0^035'$ +/- 45'

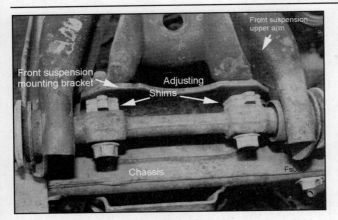

4WD w-/ Ind. Sus. :Caster and Camber is adjusted by the position of the adjusting front and rear cams. Loosen the cam nuts and adjust cam.

Specified Caster: $2^0 30^/$ +/- $45^/$

4WD Leaf Sus.: No adjustment except for replacing worm parts.

Specified Caster : $1^0 30^/$ +/- $45^/$

Maximum difference between caster of front wheels should not be greater than $1/_2 0$*, preferably* $1/_4 0$

CAMBER ADJUSTMENT

Hi Lux   **30's & 40's**

2WD: Caster is adjusted adding or removing shims on the front suspension.

Caster: $1/_2$**Ton** 1^0+/-$30^/$: $3/_4$ **& 1 Ton** 1^0+/-$30^/$

4WD: No adjustment except for replacing worm parts.

Specified Camber 1^0 +/- $40^/$

Specified King Pin Angle 9^0 $30^/$+/- $40^/$

Hi-Lux and $ Runner   **80's, 90's, 100's, 11's, 12's & 130's**

2WD: Camber is adjusted by adjusting the thickness of the shims in the upper arm

Specified Camber: **Depends on tyres** $0^0 45^/$ +/- $45^/$

4WD w-/ Ind. Sus. :Caster and Camber is adjusted by the position of the adjusting front and rear cams. Loosen the cam nuts and adjust cam.

1. Hold the head of the cam bolt (attaching bolt for lower arm), loosen the nut.
2. Place frictionless pads or trolley under front wheels.
3. Rotate the cam to adjust the desired camber.
4. Hold cam bolt head, torque nut to specification.

Cam bolt nut specification:

     2000kg-cm (145ft.lb, 196Nm)

Specified Camber: $45^/$ +/- $45^/$

4WD Leaf Sus.: No adjustment except for replacing worm parts.

Specified Camber 1^0 +/- $45^/$

Maximum difference between camber of front wheels should not be greater than $1/_2 0$, preferably $1/_4 0$

TOE IN ADJUSTMENT

Toe-in, the inward pointing of both front wheels, is checked with the wheels in the straight ahead position.

Adjustment is achieved by winding the tie rods in or out of the tie rod ends, thus increasing or decreasing their length and thereby altering the toe-in setting.

1. Set steering gear and wheels in straight ahead position.
2. Loosen lock nut at end of each tie rod.
3. Turn each tie rod as required until the correct toe-in is obtained.
* During toe-in adjustment, ensure that steering wheel is held in the straight ahead position.
4. Tighten lock nuts, ensuring that tie rods ends are in alignment with their ball studs, then tighten outer bellows clips securely, making sure that convolutions of the boots are not distorted.
5. Ensure that steering wheel is centralized.

MINOR MAINTENANCE

WHEEL BEARINGS and HUB

Remove

1. Lift front of vehicle and support on safety stands.
2. Mark relationship of wheel to hub/brake disc. Remove wheel attaching nuts and remove wheel.

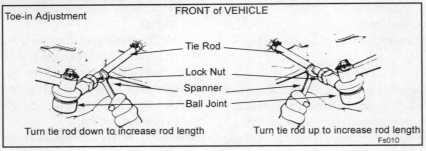

Toe-in Adjustment   FRONT of VEHICLE

Tie Rod
Lock Nut
Spanner
Ball Joint

Turn tie rod down to increase rod length   Turn tie rod up to increase rod length

Fs010

3. [Disc Brakes] Remove brake calliper anchor plate retaining bolts and washers, lift calliper assembly from hub/brake disc. Remove torque plate. Suspend calliper on wire or hook to avoid strain on brake hose.

4. 2WD: Remove front wheel bearing cover, then remove split pin and spindle nut.

4WD: Remove free wheeling hub as described later on.

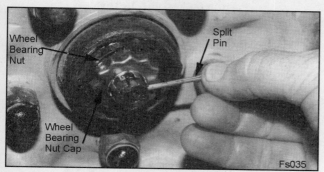

Remove nut lock washer and axle nut.

5. [Drum Brakes] Remove the brake drum, making sure outer

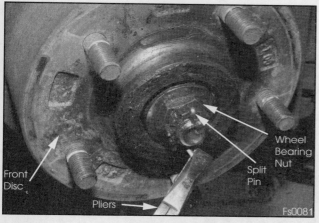

bearing does not fall from hub. Keep dust or mud from falling into or around the bearing.

6. [Disc Brakes] Remove hub/brake disc from knuckle, making sure outer bearing does not fall from hub. Keep dust or mud from falling into or around the bearing.

7. Remove the wheel bearing washer and wheel bearing, if

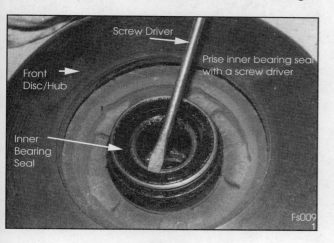

there is some resistance with the bearing, hold the hub in both hands and slightly wobble, while gently removing the hub.

8. Remove the bearing seal from inside bearing.

9. Remove the inside bearing.

10. If necessary remove the bearing cups from the hub by tapping around the bearing cup with a brass drift and hammer.

Inspect and Clean

1. Bearing cups should have an even wear pattern and must be free from flaking or pitting. Ensure that seating surfaces are clean and free from burrs or raised metal.

2. The bearing assembly should feel smooth when turned in the cup.

3. The assembly should be free from loose particles.

4. Clean bearings and outer races in a suitable cleaning solvent. Air dry all components with clean, dry compressed air.

Caution: *Do not allow bearings to spin when drying with compressed air; turn them slowly by hand. A spinning bearing will damage the race and needles.*

5. After the bearing has been washed and air dried the bearing should spin freely with no abrasive type noises.

6. Check bearing outer races for looseness in brake disc/hub.

7. Check to ensure that inner cones of the bearings are free to

revolve on the steering knuckle.

8. Check wheel studs to ensure threads are not damaged, and that bolts are pressed firmly into brake disc/hub.

9. Examine brake disc/drum for scores or damage. If either condition exists, the brake disc/drum should be machined.

To Replace Bearing Outer Cups

1. Drive out cup using a suitable brass drift, tapping lightly around circumference of cup.

2. Press a new cup into hub or brake drum, making sure that cup is not cocked and that it fully seats against shoulder in hub.

Pack Bearings

* New bearings may already be prepacked with grease.

1. Fill the palm of one hand with bearing grease.

Bearing Grease specified: **ESA MIC 75B**

2. Take the bearing in the other hand and force the bearing (largest diameter side) into the grease and the palm of your

Pack the bearing with grease until the grease is forced out past the bearing rollers.
Push the grease into the bearing by forcing the the bearing down into the grease in your hand.

Grease forced out of the bearing

Grease

Fs033
Fs033

hand, this will pack the grease into the bearing cage and around the rollers.

3. Continue to pack the bearing with grease, turning the complete bearing assembly between each packing action.

4. The bearing is completely packed when grease is forced out from around the rollers and cage, for the full diameter of the bearing.

Install

1. The bearings should be packed with wheel bearing grease conforming to specification. Apply 5g to inner bearing and 3g to outer bearing.

Front Bearing Lubrication Type: ESA MIC 75B

* Do not pack the wheel bearing cover or the brake disc/hub, between the inner and outer bearing assemblies, as excessive lubrication results in lubricant working out onto the brake pads.

2. Install a new inner wheel bearing seal, inner and outer bearings. Lips of seal should be lubricated with wheel bearing grease to specification before installation of the bearing.

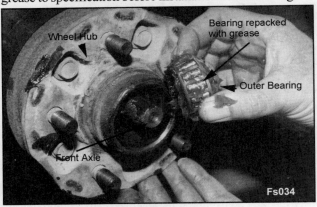

Wheel Hub

Bearing repacked with grease

Outer Bearing

Front Axle

Fs034

3. [Drum Brakes] Replace the brake drum, making sure outer bearing does not fall from hub. Keep dust or mud from falling into or around the bearing.

4. [Disc Brakes] Replace hub/brake disc to knuckle, making sure outer bearing does not fall from hub.

5. Install wheel bearing nut. Before installing split pin or nut lock washer, adjust wheel bearings as outlined under **FRONT WHEEL BEARING ADJUSTMENT** Section in this Chapter.

6. 2WD: Replace bearing nut split pin and front wheel

bearing cover.

4WD: Replace nut lock washer and nut. Replace free wheeling hub as described later on.

7. [Disc Brakes] Replace calliper assembly to hub/brake disc. Replace torque plate. Replace brake calliper anchor plate retaining bolts and washers.

Disc Brake Calliper Anchor Bolts:
1,100 kg-cm, 80ft-lb 108Nm

8. Install Road Wheel and tighten nuts to specification.

Wheel Nut Torque: 1,150 kg.cm, (83ft-lb, 113Nm)

* When installing the wheel, align the marks made prior to removal.

9. Remove jack stands and lower vehicle.

FRONT WHEEL BEARING ADJUSTMENT

1. Jack up front of vehicle and support on safety stands.

2. Mark relationship of wheel to hub. Remove wheel attaching nuts and remove wheel.

3. [Disc Brakes] Remove brake calliper anchor plate retaining bolts and washers, lift calliper assembly from hub/brake disc. Suspend calliper on wire or hook to avoid strain on the hose.

4. 2WD: Remove front wheel bearing cover, then remove split pin and spindle nut.

4WD: Remove free wheeling hub as described later on. Remove nut lock washer and axle nut.

5. Hand spin hub/brake disc and snug up spindle nut to fully seat bearings.

6. Tighten spindle nut to 30 Nm and then back off nut.

7. Hand spin hub/brake disc and, while spinning, tighten

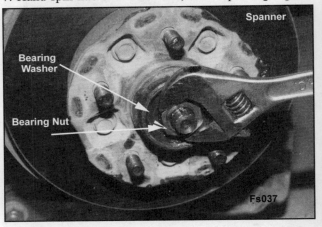

Spanner

Bearing Washer

Bearing Nut

Fs037

spindle nut to 30 Nm.

8. Back off nut, 90°.

9. 2WD: Replace spindle nut, install split pin and lock securely. Refit front wheel bearing cover.

4WD: Replace spindle nut, install lock washer. Replace free wheeling hub.

10. [Disc Brakes] Reinstall brake calliper and road wheel.

Torque the calliper attaching bolts to the correct torque

274

specification.

Brake Calliper torque bolts:
1,100kg-cm (80ft-lb, 108Nm)

* When installing the wheel, align the marks made prior to removal.

11. Remove jack stands and lower vehicle.

12. Torque road wheel attaching nuts to correct torque specification.

Wheel Nut Torque: 1,150 kg.cm, (83ft-lb, 113Nm)

FREE WHEELING HUB - 4 WD
Remove

1. Turn the free wheeling hub so that the hub is in the free position.

2. Remove the 6 cover attaching bolts, remove the cover.

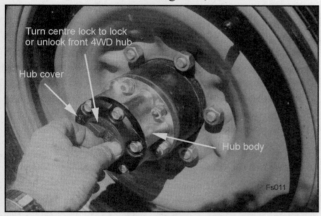

3. [Leaf Spring Type] Use pointy nose pliers, remove the spring ring clip.

[Ind. Sus.] Remove bolt and washer.

4. Remove the free wheeling hub attaching nuts and washers. Remove the cone washers by tapping on the free wheel hub attaching bolts with a soft hammer (plastic head hammer).

5. Remove the free wheeling hub.

Dismantle

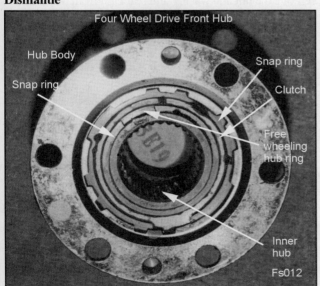

1. Remove the inner hub from the hub body. At the rear of the hub use a small screw driver to remove the spring clip, slide the inner hub from the hub body.

2. Remove the inner hub snap clip, free wheeling hub ring and spacer.

3. Dismantle cover by pushing in the clutch and spring, turn the clutch clockwise and release. Remove cover centre by removing spring clip.

Assemble

Wash all components with solvent, air dry, apply multi purpose grease to clutch and inner hub components.

1. Assemble inner hub, spacer, free wheeling hub ring and spring clip as an assembly.

2. Assemble hub cover by fitting new seal to centre section, also fit spring and steel ball, slide centre section into hub body, fit spring clip to lock into position.

3. Install hub clutch and tension spring, push tension spring into clutch groove, install (tension) spring end against a large tab. Fit the follower pawl on the tension spring.

4. Install the clutch spring to the clutch, narrowest spring end to the clutch.

5. Install the clutch and spring to the cover, align the follower pawl and to the cover centre cam. Push clutch in and turn anticlockwise to lock into position.

6. Install inner hub into hub body, secure by fitting spring clip.

7. Turn hub cover centre to free position, fit align clutch to suit, fit cover to hub body and check that the inner hub turns freely, if hub turns freely remove cover for installation.

Install

1. Fit free wheeling hub to axle hub, use a new gasket. Install the con washers to bolts, nuts and tighten to specification.

Free Wheeling Hub Nuts:
315 kg-cm, 23ft-lb 31Nm

2. [Leaf Spring Type] Use pointy nose pliers, replace the centre spring ring clip.

[Ind. Sus.] Replace centre bolt and washer, tighten to specification.

Free Wheeling Hub Centre Nut:
185 kg-cm, 13ft-lb 18Nm

3. Install a new gasket and cover to free wheeling hub.

4. Turn hub cover centre to free position, fit align clutch to suit, fit cover to hub body, install bolts and tighten to specification.

Free Wheeling Hub Cover bolts torque:
100 kg-cm, 7ft-lb 10Nm

STABILIZER BAR
Remove

1. Raise front of vehicle and support on safety stands.

2. Position a ring spanner or socket on upper and lower nuts of stabilizer bar stud. Remove nut securing stabilizer bar spacer studs on each end of stabilizer bar. Remove lower washers and bushes.

3. Remove bolts securing support bracket to each side

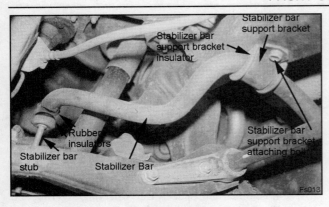

member and remove stabilizer bar. Remove support brackets and insulators from stabilizer bar.

Install

1. Assemble two insulators and support brackets to stabilizer bar and bolt brackets to side members.

* The slot in each insulator should face the side member (cut the insulator on the flat surface if necessary.

2. Install stabilizer bar to spacer studs with bushes and washers installed in the correct order. Torque attaching nuts on stabilizer bar studs.

* When tightening the spacer stud attaching nuts, ensure that the spacer stud is stopped from rotating.

Stabilizer Bar Nuts torque:
2WD   **100 kg-cm, 7ft-lb 10Nm**
4WD   **260 kg-cm, 19ft-lb 25Nm**

3. Torque insulator support bracket to side member attaching bolts.

Stabilizer Bar Support Bracket bolt torque:
2WD   **185 kg-cm, 13ft-lb 18Nm**
4WD   **300 kg-cm, 22ft-lb 29Nm**

4. Remove safety stands and lower vehicle.

MAJOR REPAIRS - 2WD

SUSPENSION LOWER ARM

Remove

1. Raise front of vehicle and support on safety stands.

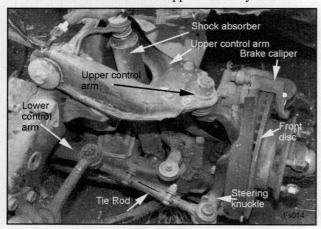

2. Mark relationship of wheel to hub/brake disc. Remove road wheel attaching nuts and remove wheel.

3. Position a ring spanner or socket on upper and lower nuts of stabilizer bar stud. Remove nut securing stabilizer bar spacer studs on each end of stabilizer bar. Remove lower washers and bushes.

4. Remove the upper and lower nuts of the shock absorber, remove the shock absorber.

5. Remove the three bolts attaching the ball joint to the lower suspension arm.

6. Remove torsion bar (as described in this chapter).

(a) Measure length of thread exposed from adjusting nut to help with installation. Loosen nut.

(b) Remove the two bolts and nuts supporting the torsion bar arm to the lower suspension arm.

(c) Remove the torsion bar from the lower suspension arm.

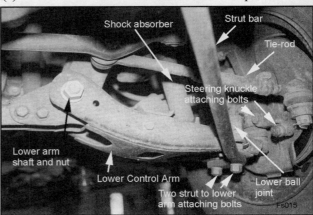

7. Remove the two strut to lower arm bolts.

8. Remove the lower ball joint by removing the three attaching bolts and top nut to the ball joint. Using a suitable bar, prise ball joint out of steering knuckle.

9. Remove the nut and bolt attaching the lower suspension arm to the vehicle frame. Hold the bolt head stationary and remove the nut and washer and rear cam from the bolt.

10. Remove the cam bolt and lower arm.

Install

1. Install the torque arm to the lower suspension arm. Install the lower suspension arm shaft with the torsion arm in the correct position.

Do not tighten at this stage.

2. Install the lower arm to the under body and fit the bolt, washer and nut.

Do not tighten at this stage.

3. Install ball joint to the lower suspension arm, tighten the bolts to specification.

Ball Joint to Lower Suspension Arm bolts torque:
        1,300 kg-cm, 95ft-lb 127Nm

4. Install steering tie rod end ball joint stud to steering knuckle and Torque castellated attaching nut.

Tie Rod end Ball Joint nut torque:
        920 kg-cm, 67ft-lb 90Nm

Install new split pin.

* Ensure that the nylon spacer is positioned on the tie rod ball joint stud and that it is in good condition before fitting to steering knuckle. Replace spacer if damaged.

5. Install stabilizer bar spacer stud, seat, bush, washer and nut to arm housing. Torque nut.

* When torques the spacer stud attaching nut, ensure that the spacer stud is held from rotating.

Stabilizer Bar to Lower Suspension Arm nut torque:
130 kg-cm, 9ft-lb 13Nm

6. Install shock absorber to lower arm and top bracket. Tighten nut and bolts to specification.

Shock Absorber Lower Arm bolt torque:
185 kg-cm, 13ft-lb 18Nm

Shock Absorber Upper Bracket nut torque:
250 kg-cm, 18ft-lb 25Nm

7. Install the strut to the lower arm.

Strut to Lower Arm bolt torque:
970 kg-cm, 70ft-lb 95Nm

8. Finish installing the torsion bar spring assembly.
(a) Take note of right and left tension bar springs.
(b) Grease the spline on the torsion bar to help installation and function.
(c) Insert the bar spring aligning the spline with the anchor arm with the torsion bar spring.
(d) Install the torque arm, taking care to align the spline of the bar spring.
(e) Fit the torque arm side, fit anchor arm to adjusting bolt and nuts to finger tightness. Tighten torque arm nuts to specification.

Torque Arm nuts torque:
500 kg-cm, 35ft-lb 50Nm

(f) Fit adjusting nut to thread to the measured distance [6. (a)] of the exposed thread.

* *If distance not known, after lower suspension arm is installed bounce vehicle and adjust to specified road height.*
(g) Fit and tighten lock nut to specification.

Adjusting Lock Nut torque:
850 kg-cm, 60ft-lb 83Nm

9. Install road wheel, tighten nuts to specification. Remove vehicle from safety stands.

Road Wheel Nuts torque: kg-cm, ft-lb Nm

10. Bounce vehicle several times and torque nut at lower suspension arm to vehicle frame.

Lower Suspension Arm to Frame Nut Torque:
2.300 kg-cm, 166ft-lb 226Nm

11. Check caster, camber and toe-in.

UPPER SUSPENSION ARM
Remove
1. Raise front of vehicle and support on safety stands.
2. Mark relationship of wheel to hub/brake disc. Remove road wheel attaching nuts and remove wheel.
3. Place a jack under the lower arm, raise jack so as the jack

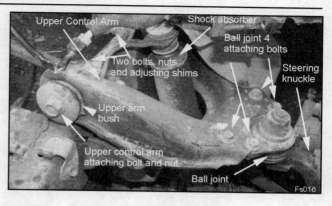

will take the weight of the suspension unit.

4. Remove the four ball joint nuts that attach the ball joint to the upper suspension arm.

5. Remove the two nuts and bolt plus shims from inside of the upper suspension arm.

* Record the shims and location of the shims to help when installing upper suspension arm.

6. Remove the upper suspension arm attaching nut and bolt.
7. Remove upper suspension arm.

Install
1. Install upper control arm to frame and slide in attaching bolt, fit nut to figure tightness.
2. Install the two nuts and bolt plus shims to the inside of the upper suspension arm. Tighten to specification.
* Fit the camber shims in the same location as when removed.

Upper Suspension Arm Inside Attaching Nuts:
980 kg-cm, 70ft-lb 95Nm

3. Position the ball joint to the upper control arm, and install the 4 bolts and nuts. Tighten to specification.

Ball Joint Attaching Bolts and Nuts:
320 kg-cm, 23ft-lb 31Nm

4. Install road wheel, tighten nuts to specification. Remove vehicle from safety stands.

Wheel Nut Torque: 1,150 kg.cm, (83ft-lb, 113Nm)

10. Bounce vehicle several times and torque nut at upper suspension arm to vehicle frame.

Upper Suspension Arm to Frame Nut Torque:
1,280 kg-cm, 93ft-lb 126Nm

11. Check caster, camber and toe-in.

STEERING KNUCKLE
Remove
1. Lift front of vehicle and support on safety stands.
2. Mark relationship of wheel to hub/brake disc. Remove wheel attaching nuts and remove wheel.
3. [Disc Brakes] Remove brake calliper anchor plate retaining bolts and washers, lift calliper assembly from hub/brake disc. Remove torque plate. Suspend calliper on wire or hook to avoid strain on brake hose.
4. Remove front wheel bearing cover, then remove split pin and spindle nut.
5. [Drum Brakes] Remove the brake drum, making sure outer

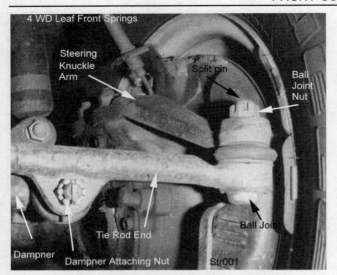

4 WD Leaf Front Springs
Steering Knuckle Arm
Split pin
Ball Joint Nut
Dampner
Tie Rod End
Dampner Attaching Nut
Ball Joint
Str001

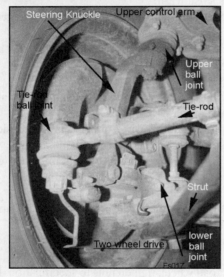

Steering Knuckle
Upper control arm
Upper ball joint
Tie-rod ball joint
Tie-rod
Strut
Two wheel drive
lower ball joint
Fs017

bearing does not fall from hub. Keep dust or mud from falling into or around the bearing.

6. [Disc Brakes] Remove hub/brake disc from knuckle, making sure outer bearing does not fall from hub. Keep dust or mud from falling into or around the bearing.

7. Remove the four bolts attaching the back dust plate.

8. Remove the steering knuckle arm from the steering knuckle.

9. Place a jack under the lower arm, raise jack so as the jack will take the weight of the suspension unit.

10. Remove split pin from upper ball joint stud and remove castellated nut.

11. Use a ball joint remover to remove ball joint from top of steering knuckle.

12. Remove split pin from lower ball joint stud and remove castellated nut.

13. Use a ball joint remover to remove ball joint from bottom of steering knuckle.

14. Remove the steering knuckle from the vehicle.

Install

1. Place a jack under the lower arm, raise jack so as the jack will take the weight of the suspension unit.

2. Position the steering knuckle between the upper and lower suspension arm ball joints

3. Fit the steering knuckle to the top ball joint, fit retaining nut.

4. Lift the steering knuckle with the upper suspension arm so that the steering knuckle will fit onto the lower suspension ball joint, fit retaining nut.

5. Tighten the upper and lower ball joints to specification.

Upper Suspension Arm Ball Joint Nut torque:
1,100 kg-cm, 80ft-lb 108Nm

Install split pin to ball joint.

Lower Suspension Arm Ball Joint Nut torque:
1,450 kg-cm, 105ft-lb 142Nm

Install split pin to ball joint.

6. Install the steering knuckle arm and back dust cover to the steering knuckle, tighten 4 bolts to specification.

Steering Knuckle Arm & Back Dust Cover Bolt Torque:
1,100 kg-cm, 80ft-lb 108Nm

Install split pins to bolts.

7. [Drum Brakes] Replace the brake drum, making sure outer bearing does not fall from hub. Keep dust or mud from falling into or around the bearing.

8. Install wheel bearing nut. Before installing split pin or nut lock washer, adjust wheel bearings as outlined under **FRONT WHEEL BEARING ADJUSTMENT** Section in this Chapter.

9. Replace bearing nut split pin and front wheel bearing cover.

10. [Disc Brakes] Replace calliper assembly to hub/brake disc. Replace torque plate. Replace brake calliper anchor plate retaining bolts and washers.

Disc Brake Calliper Anchor Bolts:
1,100 kg-cm, 80ft-lb 108Nm

11. Install Road Wheel and tighten nuts to specification.

Wheel Nut Torque: 1,150 kg.cm, (83ft-lb, 113Nm)

* When installing the wheel, align the marks made prior to removal.

12. Remove jack stands and lower vehicle.

TORSION BARS
Remove

1. Raise front of vehicle and support on safety stands.

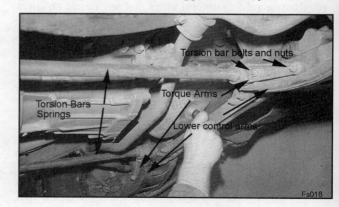

Torsion bar bolts and nuts
Torque Arms
Torsion Bars Springs
Lower control arms
Fs018

2. Mark relationship of wheel to hub/brake disc. Remove road wheel attaching nuts and remove wheel.

3. Measure length of thread exposed from torsion bar adjusting nut and bolt to help with installation. Loosen nut.

4. Remove the two bolts and nuts supporting the torsion bar arm to the lower suspension arm.

5. Remove the torsion bar springs and anchor plate from the lower suspension arm.

Install

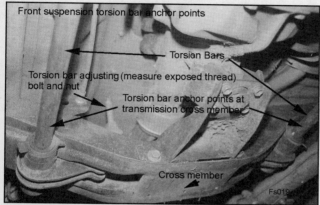

Front suspension torsion bar anchor points

Torsion Bars

Torsion bar adjusting (measure exposed thread) bolt and nut

Torsion bar anchor points at transmission cross member

Cross member

Fs019

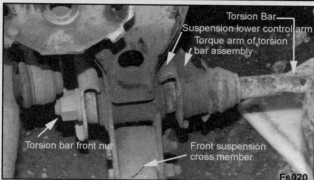

Torsion Bar
Suspension lower control arm
Torque arm of torsion bar assembly

Torsion bar front nut

Front suspension cross member

Fs020

1. Install the torsion bar spring assembly.

(a) Take note of right and left tension bar springs.

(b) Grease the spline on the torsion bar to help installation and function.

(c) Insert the bar spring aligning the spline with the anchor arm with the torsion bar spring.

2. Install the torque arm, taking care to align the spline of the bar spring.

3. Fit the torque arm side, fit anchor arm to adjusting bolt and nuts to figure tightness. Tighten torque arm nuts to specification.

Torque Arm Nuts Torque;
500 kg-cm, 35ft-lb 50Nm

4. Fit adjusting nut to thread to the measured distance [3.] of the exposed thread.

* *If distance not known, after lower suspension arm is installed bounce vehicle and adjust to specified road height.*

5. Fit and tighten lock nut to specification.

Adjusting Lock Nut Torque:
850 kg-cm, 60ft-lb 83Nm

6. Install road wheel, tighten nuts to specification. Remove

vehicle from safety stands.

Wheel Nut Torque: 1,150 kg.cm, (83ft-lb, 113Nm)

7. Bounce vehicle several times and torque nut at lower suspension arm to vehicle frame.

Lower Suspension Arm to Frame Nut Torque:
2.300 kg-cm, 166ft-lb 226Nm

8. Check caster, camber and toe-in.

REPLACE LOWER SUSPENSION ARM BUSH
Replacement

1. Remove lower suspension arm as described in this Chapter.

2. Cut off bush against the arm and press bush from rear side of suspension arm.

3. Install new bush, with the aid of a press.

* The bush can be installed with soapy water to assist assembly. DO NOT LUBRICATE.

* Install control arm as described in this Chapter.

REPLACE UPPER SUSPENSION ARM BUSH
Replacement of "rubber push in" Bushes

1. Remove upper suspension arm as described in this Chapter.

2. Remove bolt, nut and washer if fitted, press bushes from suspension arm.

3. Install new bushes, with the aid of a press.

4. Install bolt, nut and washer as removed.

* The bush can be installed with soapy water to assist assembly. DO NOT LUBRICATE.

* Install control arm as described in this Chapter.

Replacement of "screw in" Bushes

1. Remove upper suspension arm as described in this Chapter.

2. Screw the old bushes from the upper arm.

3. Cover the new bush threads with grease.

4. Screw the new bushes into the upper arm evenly from each side until they become tight, then torque to specification, making sure the pivot bolt will freely turn..

Screw-in Bush to Upper Suspension Arm Torque:
2,300 kg-cm, 170ft-lb 230Nm

STRUT BAR
Remove

1. Raise front of vehicle and support on safety stands.

2. Mark relationship of 2nd nut to thread on the adjustable end of strut bar, use a dab of paint on nut and thread.

* *If new bushes are not being fitted, it may not be necessary to alter the position of this nut, the mark is just a precautionary move.*

3. Remove the 1st nut, washer and rubber bush.

4. Remove the two bolts attaching the strut arm to the lower suspension bar.

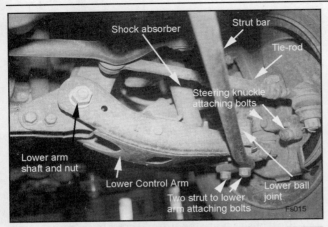

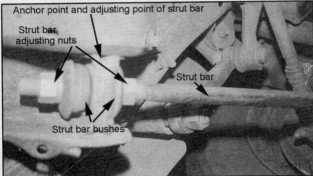

2. Mark relationship of wheel to hub/brake disc. Remove road wheel attaching nuts and remove wheel.

3. Position a ring spanner or socket on upper and lower nuts

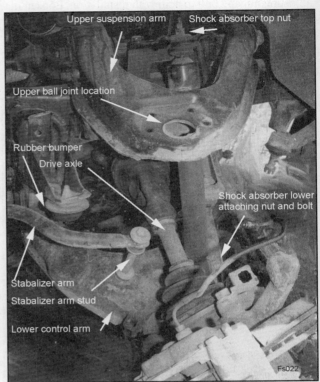

5. Carefully pull the strut back from the front anchor point.

6. If replacing new bushes, remove the existing bushes from strut bar.

Install

1. If fitting new bushes. Install a washer and new bush to strut bar.

2. Fit strut bar through front anchor point.

3. Install the strut bar to the lower suspension arm, install the two bolts attaching the strut bar. Tighten to specification.

Strut Bar to Lower Suspension Arm Bolt Torque:
970 kg-cm, 70ft-lb 95Nm

4. Install rubber bush, washer and nut to front of strut bar, tighten to approximately 600kg.cm.

5. Remove vehicle from safety stands. Bounce vehicle several times and torque nut at lower suspension arm to vehicle frame.

Lower Suspension Arm to Frame Nut Torque:
1,250 kg-cm, 90ft-lb 123Nm

6. Check caster, camber and toe-in.

MAJOR REPAIRS - 4WD [Ind. Sus.]

SUSPENSION LOWER ARM & SHOCK ABSORBER

Remove

1. Raise front of vehicle and support on safety stands.

of stabilizer bar stud. Remove nut securing stabilizer bar spacer studs on each end of stabilizer bar. Remove lower washers and bushes.

4. Remove the upper nuts and lower bolt & nut of the shock absorber, remove the shock absorber.

5. Remove the split pin and nut from the ball joint to the lower suspension arm. Use a puller to remove the ball joint from the lower suspension arm.

6. The location of the lower suspension arm cams should be

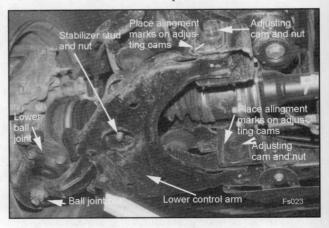

marked at bracket of the lower arm attached to the underbody.

7. Hold the bolt head stationary and remove the nut and rear cam from each of the cam bolts.

8. Remove the cam bolts and lower arm.

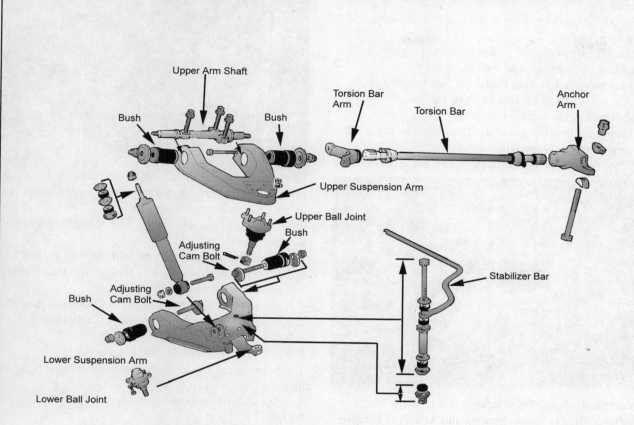

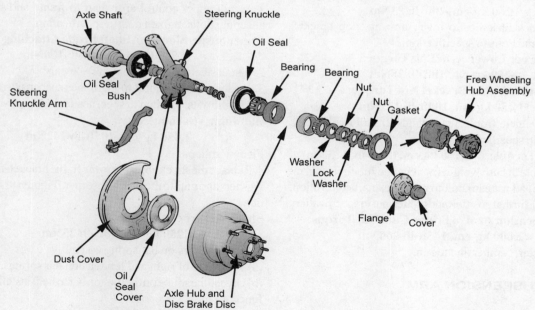

FRONT SUSPENSION and AXLE ASSEMBLY for INDEPENDANT FRONT SUSPENSION.

Fs040

Install

1. Install the lower arm to the under body and fit the cam bolts, rear cam, and nut.

2. Install ball joint stud in the front steering knuckle, fit retaining nut, torque install split pin.

Lower Suspension Arm Ball Joint Nut torque:
        1,450 kg-cm, 105ft-lb 142Nm

Install split pin to ball joint.

3. Install stabilizer bar spacer stud, seat, bush, washer and nut to arm housing. Torque nut.

* When torques the spacer stud attaching nut, ensure that the

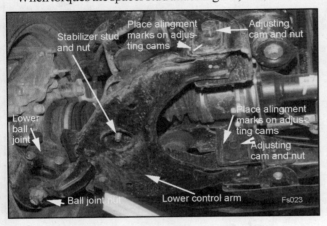

spacer stud is held from rotating.

Stabilizer Bar to Lower Suspension Arm Nut Torque:
        260 kg-cm, 20ft-lb 25Nm

4. Install shock absorber to lower arm and top bracket. Tighten nut and bolts to specification.

Shock Absorber Lower Arm Bolt Torque:
        250 kg-cm, 18ft-lb 25Nm

Shock Absorber Upper Bracket Nut Torque:
        1,450 kg-cm, 100ft-lb 137Nm

5. Remove vehicle from safety stands. Install road wheel, tighten nuts to specification.

Wheel Nut Torque: 1,150 kg.cm, (83ft-lb, 113Nm)

6. With vehicle at curb weight (no luggage full fuel tank, on level surface) adjust cam bolt to previous marked position. Hold bolt head in that position and tighten nut to specification.

Lower Suspension Arm to Frame Cam Nut Torque:
        2.000 kg-cm, 145ft-lb 200Nm

7. Check caster, camber and toe-in.

UPPER SUSPENSION ARM
Remove

1. Raise front of vehicle and support on safety stands.

2. Mark relationship of wheel to hub/brake disc. Remove road wheel attaching nuts and remove wheel.

3. Place a jack under the lower arm, raise jack so as the jack will take the weight of the suspension unit.

4. Remove torsion bar spring (as described in this chapter).

(a) Place paint dabs, as match marks on torsion bar spring, anchor arm and torque arm.

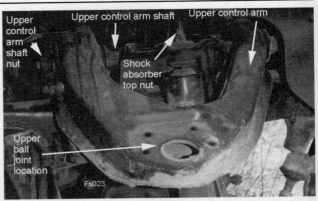

(b) Measure length of thread exposed from adjusting nut to help with installation. Loosen nut.

(c) Remove the torsion bar spring anchor arm from the upper suspension arm.

4. Remove the ball joint split pin and nut from the ball joint to the upper suspension arm. Use a ball joint puller to remove ball joint from upper suspension arm.

5. Remove the upper nuts, washers and bushes of the shock absorber, remove the shock absorber from the frame bracket only.

6. Remove steering centre shaft if necessary.

7. Remove the 3 upper suspension arm attaching bolts and nuts.

8. Remove upper suspension arm.

Install

1. Install upper control arm shaft to frame and slide in 3 attaching bolts, tighten nuts to specification.

Upper Suspension Arm Shaft Inside Attaching Nuts:
        1,810 kg-cm, 130ft-lb 180Nm

2. Install steering centre shaft if necessary.

3. Position the ball joint to the upper suspension arm, and install the nuts. Tighten to specification.

Ball Joint Attaching Nut:
        1,450 kg-cm, 105ft-lb 142Nm

Fit new split pin

4. Replace the shock absorber to the frame bracket, fit bushes, washers and nuts to the shock absorber. Tighten to specification.

Shock Absorber Top Nut:
        250 kg-cm, 18ft-lb 25Nm

5. Instal the torsion bar spring assembly.

(a) Take note of right and left tension bar springs.

(b) Grease the spline on the torsion bar to help installation and function.

(c) Insert the bar spring aligning the spline with the torque arm with the torsion bar spring.

(d) Install the anchor arm, taking care to align the spline of the bar spring.

(e) Fit adjusting nut to thread to the measured distance [4.(b)] of the exposed thread.

* *If distance not known, after lower suspension arm is installed bounce vehicle and adjust to specified road height.*

(f) Fit and tighten lock nut to specification.

Adjusting Lock Nut torque:

850 kg-cm, 60ft-lb 83Nm

6. Install road wheel, tighten nuts to specification. Remove vehicle from safety stands.

Road Wheel Nuts torque:

1,150 kg-cm, 83ft-lb 113Nm

7. Check caster, camber and toe-in.

STEERING KNUCKLE
Remove

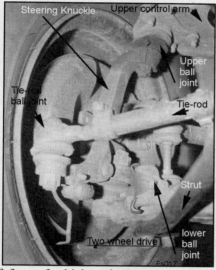

1. Lift front of vehicle and support on safety stands.

2. Mark relationship of wheel to hub/brake disc. Remove wheel attaching nuts and remove wheel.

3. [Disc Brakes] Remove brake calliper anchor plate retaining bolts and washers, lift calliper assembly from hub/brake disc. Remove torque plate. Suspend calliper on wire or hook to avoid strain on brake hose.

4. Remove front wheel bearing cover, then remove split pin and spindle nut.

5. [Drum Brakes] Remove the brake drum, making sure outer bearing does not fall from hub. Keep dust or mud from falling into or around the bearing.

6. [Disc Brakes] Remove hub/brake disc from knuckle, making sure outer bearing does not fall from hub. Keep dust or mud from falling into or around the bearing.

7. Remove the four bolts attaching the back dust plate.

8. Remove the tie rod ball joint nuts and tire rod from the axle/spindle arm.

9. Remove the steering knuckle arm from the steering knuckle.

10. Position a ring spanner or socket on upper and lower nuts of stabilizer bar stud. Remove nut securing stabilizer bar spacer studs. Remove lower washers and bushes.

11. Remove the lower bolt & nut of the shock absorber, move the shock absorber up from the lower suspension arm.

12. Check steering knuckle bushing thrust clearance.

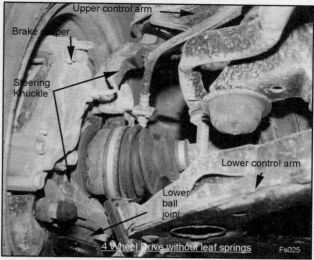

(a) Screw in a shaft with thread or a long bolt into the end of the axle drive shaft.

(b) Apply a pulling force of 9-10kg, 22lb or 98Nm to the long bolt.

(c) Measure the clearance between the axle shaft spacer and bush.

(d) If clearance is not within specification, replace steering knuckle bushes.

Axle Drive Shaft Spacer to Bush Maximum Clearance:

1.0 mm or 0.039 in

13. Remove the axle drive shaft spring clip and spacer.

14. Place a jack under the lower arm, raise jack so as the jack will take the weight of the suspension unit.

15. Remove split pin from upper ball joint stud and remove castellated nut.

16. Use a ball joint remover to remove ball joint from top of steering knuckle.

17. Remove the lower suspension arm ball joint 4 attaching bolts, remove the lower suspension arm / ball joint away from the steering knuckle.

18. Lower the jack to drop the lower suspension arm and remove the steering knuckle from the vehicle.

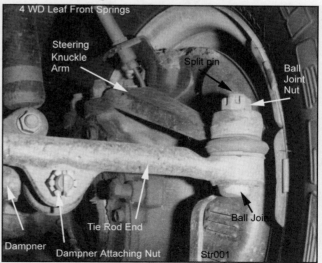

Install

1. Place a jack under the lower arm, raise jack so as the jack will take the weight of the suspension unit.
2. Coat the axle drive shaft end with molybdenum base grease. Slide steering knuckle on axle drive shaft.
3. Position the steering knuckle between the upper and lower suspension arms.
4. Fit the steering knuckle to the top ball joint, fit retaining nut.
5. Lift the steering knuckle with the upper suspension arm so that the steering knuckle will fit onto the lower suspension arm / ball joint, install 4 bolts and nuts.
6. Tighten the upper and lower ball joints to specification.

Upper Suspension Arm Ball Joint Nut torque:
1,450 kg-cm, 105ft-lb 142Nm

Install split pin to ball joint.

Lower Suspension Arm / Ball Joint Bolt & Nut torque:
590 kg-cm, 43ft-lb 58Nm

7. Install spacer and spring clip to axle drive shaft, and check spacer to bush clearance.
(a) Screw in a shaft with thread or a long bolt into the end of the axle drive shaft.
(b) Apply a pulling force of 9-10kg, 22lb or 98Nm to the long bolt.
(c) Measure the clearance between the axle shaft spacer and bush.
(d) If clearance is not within specification, replace steering knuckle bushes.

Axle Drive Shaft Spacer to Bush Maximum Clearance:
1.0 mm or 0.039 in

8. Install stabilizer bar spacer stud, seat, bush, washer and nut to arm housing. Torque nut.
* When torques the spacer stud attaching nut, ensure that the spacer stud is held from rotating.

Stabilizer Bar to Lower Suspension Arm Nut Torque:
260 kg-cm, 20ft-lb 25Nm

9. Install shock absorber to lower arm. Tighten nut and bolt to specification.

Shock Absorber Lower Arm Bolt Torque:
250 kg-cm, 18ft-lb 25Nm

10. Install the steering knuckle arm to the steering knuckle, tighten 2 bolts to specification.

Steering Knuckle Arm & Back Dust Cover Bolt Torque:
1,870 kg-cm, 135ft-lb 183Nm

11. Fit the connecting spindle arm to the tie rod joint, tighten to specification, install cotter pin.

Tie Rod Ball Joint Specification:
260 kg-cm, 20ft-lb 25Nm

12. Install back dust cover to the steering knuckle, tighten bolts to specification.

Steering Knuckle Arm & Back Dust Cover Bolt Torque:
185 kg-cm, 13ft-lb 18Nm

13. [Drum Brakes] Replace the brake drum, making sure outer bearing does not fall from hub. Keep dust or mud from falling into or around the bearing.

14. [Drum Brakes] Install wheel bearing nut. Before installing split pin or nut lock washer, adjust wheel bearings as outlined under **FRONT WHEEL BEARING ADJUSTMENT** Section in this Chapter.
15. Replace bearing nut split pin and front wheel bearing cover.
16. [Disc Brakes] Replace calliper assembly to hub/brake disc. Replace torque plate. Replace brake calliper anchor plate retaining bolts and washers.

Disc Brake Calliper Anchor Bolts:
1,100 kg-cm, 80ft-lb 108Nm

17. Install Road Wheel and tighten nuts to specification.

Road Wheel Nut Torque:
1,150 kg-cm, 83ft-lb 113Nm

* When installing the wheel, align the marks made prior to removal.
18. Remove jack stands and lower vehicle.

STEERING KNUCKLE BUSHES
Remove
1. Remove steering knuckle as previously described.
2. Pull out the outer bush with a puller or sliding hammer.
3. Remove seal at back of steering knuckle.
4. Pull inner seal out from steering knuckle or drive seal out with a drift and hammer.
Install
1. Insert the inner seal into steering knuckle, use seal insertion tool and hammer to carefully drive seal home. Coat back of seal with lithium base grease, then insert dust seal.
2. Insert outer seal into steering knuckle, use seal insertion tool and hammer to carefully drive seal home.
3. Install steering knuckle as previously described.

REPLACE LOWER SUSPENSION ARM BUSH
Replacement
1. Remove lower suspension arm as described in this Chapter.
2. Press bush from outside of suspension arm.
3. Install new bush, with the aid of a press.
* The bush can be installed with soapy water to assist assembly. DO NOT LUBRICATE.
4. Install lower suspension arm as described in this Chapter.

REPLACE UPPER SUSPENSION ARM BUSH
Replacement
1. Remove upper suspension arm as described in this Chapter.
2. Remove the nut of the front bush, pull off front rubber bush and washer from outside of suspension arm.
3. Remove the rear seal by pushing it outwards.
4. Install new rear bush, with the aid of a press.
5. Install new front bush, with the aid of a press.

* The bush can be installed with soapy water to assist assembly. DO NOT LUBRICATE.

6. Install upper suspension arm as described in this Chapter.

MAJOR MAINTENANCE 4WD [Leaf Spring Sus.]

STEERING KNUCKLE
Remove

1. Lift front of vehicle and support on safety stands.

2. Mark relationship of wheel to hub/brake disc. Remove wheel attaching nuts and remove wheel.

3. Remove the tie rod ball joint nut and tire rod from the axle/ spindle arm or steering drag link if applicable.

4. Remove free wheeling hub.

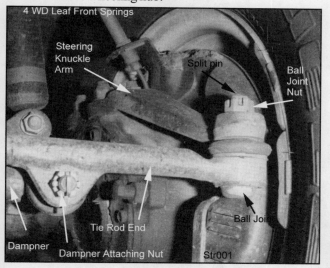

4 WD Leaf Front Springs — Steering Knuckle Arm, Split pin, Ball Joint Nut, Ball Joint, Tie Rod End, Dampner Attaching Nut, Dampner. Str001

5. Remove axle hub.

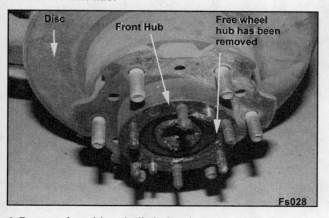

Disc, Front Hub, Free wheel hub has been removed. Fs028

6. Remove knuckle spindle bolts, dust cover and seal.

7. Separate the knuckle spindle and steering knuckle by using a brass drift and hammer.

8. Turn the axle drive shaft so that one of the flat areas aligns with the flat section of the steering knuckle, pull the axle drive shaft down and out.

9. Place axle drive shaft into a vice, grip the inner shaft with the vice. Use a brass drift and hammer hit the outer shaft away from the inner shaft.

10. Remove the oil seal retainer.

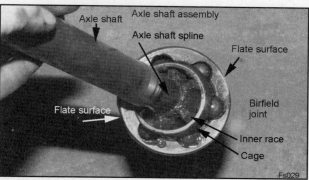

Axle shaft, Axle shaft assembly, Axle shaft spline, Flate surface, Birfield joint, Inner race, Cage, Flate surface. Fs029

11. Remove the steering knuckle arm nuts from the steering knuckle.

12. Tap on bolts to remove the coned washers

13. Install a spreader into the steering knuckle, use this to force out the steering knuckle arm and shims. Identify components to help during assembly.

14. Install a spreader into the steering knuckle to force out the bearing cap and shims. Identify components to help during assembly.

15. Remove bearings from steering knuckle. Identify components to help during assembly.

16. Remove steering knuckle housing from steering knuckle.

Upper bearing (rollers and cage), Oil seal, Bearing race. Fs026

Adjust Steering Knuckle

1. Remove drive shaft oil seal at the back of the steering knuckle.

2. Mount a special tool into back of steering knuckle in place of oil seal (special tool to have a centre point which can mark the special tool - bolt - in point 3).

3. Mount a special tool into the steering knuckle. (Special tool is a shaft that will fit down through the upper and lower bearings of the steering knuckle, this shaft should be a bolt, washers, spacers & arm the length of the steering knuckle or similar) (spacers need to be Toyota parts to obtain correct thickness).

4. Tighten nut on bolt (3. - special tool) until a load of 3-6 kg is necessary to turn special tool arm.

FRONT SUSPENSION and AXLE ASSEMBLY
FOUR WHEEL DRIVE LEAF SUSPENSION

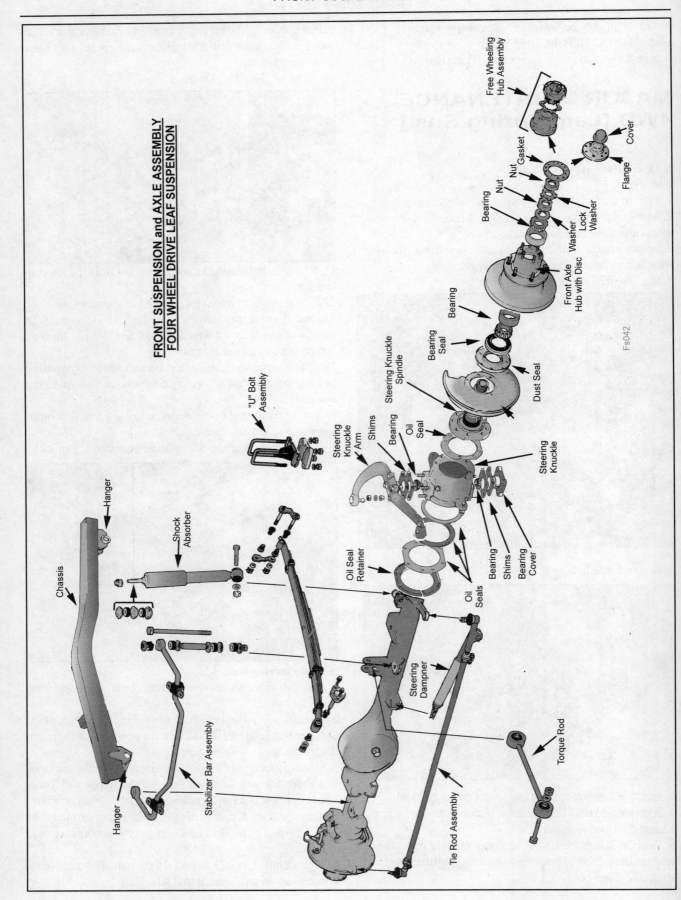

Free Wheeling Hub Assembly

Nut Gasket

Nut

Bearing

Nut

Washer
Lock
Washer
Washer

Flange

Cover

Front Axle Hub with Disc

Bearing

Bearing Seal

Steering Knuckle Spindle

Dust Seal

Oil Seal

Bearing

Shims

Steering Knuckle Arm

Steering Knuckle

"U" Bolt Assembly

Bearing
Shims
Bearing Cover

Oil Seal Retainer

Oil Seals

Shock Absorber

Hanger

Chassis

Steering Dampner

Hanger

Stabilizer Bar Assembly

Tie Rod Assembly

Torque Rod

Fs042

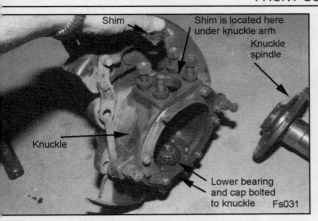

Fs031

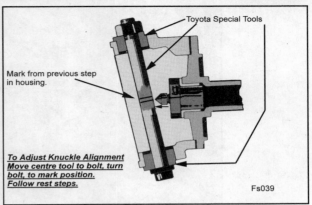

To Adjust Knuckle Alignment
Move centre tool to bolt, turn
bolt, to mark position.
Follow rest steps.

Fs039

5. Measure the difference between X & Y in diagrams to help calculate shim thickness "Z".
6. Coat the centre of bolt with marking paint or chalk, move

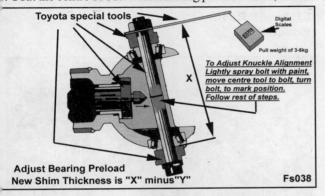

Adjust Bearing Preload
New Shim Thickness is "X" minus"Y"   Fs038

oil seal special tool until it will just mark the centre bolt as it is turned.
7. Mount the special tools from 2. and 3. onto the steering knuckle housing as shown.
8. Move oil seal special tool until it will just mark the centre bolt as it is turned. Measure the difference between the two marks "R". The thickness "S" of knuckle lower bearing shim is "R" minus 3mm. The thickness of knuckle higher bearing

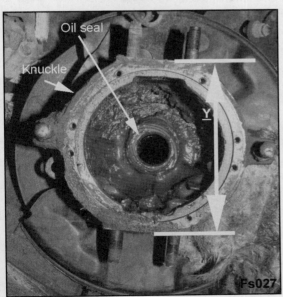

Fs027

shim is the "Z" minus "S".

Assemble

Wash all components with cleaning solvent and allow to air dry. Pack bearing with grease before assembly. Inner drive shaft should have a light coating of multi purpose grease.

1. Install new oil seal into back of steering knuckle.
2. Assemble bearings from steering knuckle housing. Components should have been identified during dismantle.
3. Install the steering knuckle arm, housing and steering knuckle. Use special tool as used during dismantle to press bearing cups
(a) Install the steering knuckle arm over upper shims, tap the steering knuckle arm to seat the bearing inner race.
(b) Install the bearing cap over lower shims, tap the bearing cap into seat the bearing inner race.
(c) Remove special tool from the steering knuckle.
(d) Install washers (coned) to the knuckle arm bolts, nuts and tighten to specification.
(e) Install washers to the bearing cap bolts, nuts and tighten to specification.

Steering Knuckle Lower Bearing Cap Nuts Torque:
975 kg-cm, 70ft-lb 95Nm

4. Apply pressure to the steering knuckle arm so it will start to turn, to check preload pressure is within specification.

Steering Knuckle Arm Preload Pressure Specification:
3.0 - 6.0kg, 6.5-13.2lb, 29-59N

5. Fit the connecting steering knuckle arm to the tie rod joint, tighten to specification, install cotter pin.

Tie Rod Ball Joint Specification:
25-30Nm

OR

Install drag link to steering knuckle arm, fit screw in plug 1.25 turns in the end of drag link, fit split pin.

6. Install the inner and outer drive shaft axle.
(a) Fit a new spring clip to inner shaft, slide the inner shaft into the outer shaft make sure the inner spring clip is compressed and looks into place. Check that they will not separate and are held to gather by spring clip.
(b) Fit new oil seal.

7. Position the axle drive shaft so that one of the flat areas aligns with the flat section of the steering knuckle, push the axle drive shaft up and into the steering knuckle.

Front steering knuckle and axle components
(note more than one assemblies components are shown). Fs030

8. Cover inside steering knuckle housing and drive shaft axle with molybdenum base grease.

9. Install knuckle spindle with new gasket, seal and dust cover steering knuckle, tighten bolts to specification.

Steering Spindle Attaching bolt Torque:

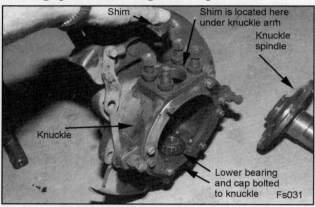

475 kg-cm, 34ft-lb 47Nm

10. Install axle hub as previously described.
Adjust wheel bearing as previously described.

11. Install free wheeling hub as previously described.

Free Wheeling Hub Nuts:

315 kg-cm, 23ft-lb 31Nm

Free Wheeling Hub Cover bolts torque:

100 kg-cm, 7ft-lb 10Nm

12. [Disc Brakes] Reinstall brake calliper. Torque the calliper attaching bolts to the correct torque specification.

Brake Calliper torque bolts:

1,100kg-cm(80ft-lb, 108Nm)

13 Install road wheel

* When installing the wheel, align the marks made prior to removal.

14. Remove jack stands and lower vehicle.

15. Torque road wheel attaching nuts to correct torque specification.

Wheel Nut Torque: 1,150 kg.cm, (83ft-lb, 113Nm)

LEAF SPRINGS
Remove

1. Using a floor jack under centre of the axle, jack up rear of vehicle. Then place safety stands under the rear body jacking points.

2. Mark relationship of wheels to axle flanges. Remove road wheel attaching nuts and remove wheels.

3. Disconnect brake pipe at underbody connection. Remove brake hose retaining clip, only if the differential is going to be removed from the vehicle.

4. Remove the tie rod ball joint nut and tire rod from the axle/spindle arm or steering drag link if applicable.

5. Remove stabilizer arm from axle housing.

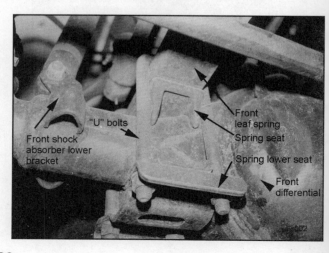

288

6. Remove torque rod attaching bolt at differential housing end.

7. Support axle housing (only lightly) under centre with a floor jack.

8. Disconnect shock absorbers at lower mounting points.

9. Remove suspension "U" bolt nuts, "U" bolts, upper and lower spring seat.

10. Lower differential housing on jack and remove assembly from underneath vehicle.

11. Remove the front hanger nut and remove hanger bolt.

12. Remove the rear shackle nut and remove the shackle bolt.

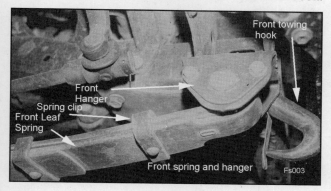

Remove spring assembly from vehicle.

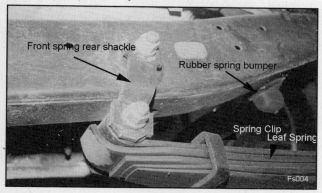

Dismantle
1. Bend leaf clip away from spring leaves.
2. Remove centre bolt.

Assemble
1. Assembly spring leaves incorrect order, clamp in a vice.
2. Install centre spring bolt and tighten to specification.

Spring Centre Bolt Torque:
450kg-cm, 33ft-lb, 44Nm

3. Bend spring leaf clamps into position.

Installation
1. Position spring under vehicle into correct position. Replace the front hanger bolt and nut. Tighten to finger tightness only.

2. Replace the rear shackle bolt and nut. Tighten to finger tightness only.

3. With differential assembly on a floor jack and the help of an assistant manoeuvre the differential assembly into position with the springs.

4. Replace front suspension spring seat, "U" bolts and rubber

spring bumper and nuts and tighten nuts to specification.

Front Suspension "U" Bolt Torque:
1,250 kg.cm, (90ft-lb, 123Nm).

5. Reconnect front shock absorbers at lower mounting points and tighten bolt to specification.

Front Shock Absorber Lower Bolt torque:
970 kg.cm, (70ft-lb, 95Nm).

6. Install stabilizer bar spacer stud, seat, bush, washer and nut to arm housing. Torque nut.

* When torqueing the spacer stud attaching nut, ensure that the spacer stud is held from rotating.

Stabilizer Bar to Lower Suspension Arm Nut Torque:
260 kg-cm, 20ft-lb 25Nm

7. Install torque rod, washer and nut to differential housing. Torque nut.

Torque Rod Bolt Specified Torque:
1,900 kg-cm, 137ft-lb 186Nm

8. Connect brake pipe at underbody rear connection. Install brake hose retaining clip.

9. Replace parking brake cable to linkage and backing plate.

10. Replace road wheel taking note of mark made during removal for position of wheel to brake drum, and attaching nuts tighten to specification.

Torque Road Wheel Nuts: 1,150 kgcm, (83ft-lb, 113Nm)

11. Remove safety stands from under the front body jacking points.

12. Tighten front spring hanger and shackle bolts to specified torque.

Hanger Bolt and Nut Torque:
930 kg.cm, (67ft-lb, 90Nm).

Shackle Bolt and Nut Torque:
930 kg.cm, (67ft-lb, 90Nm).

13. Re-adjust park brake shoes and bleed brake hydraulic system.

SHOCK ABSORBERS

Remove

1. Using a floor jack under centre of the axle, jack up rear of vehicle. Then place safety stands under the rear body jacking points.

2. Remove the lower bolt attaching the shock absorber to differential housing.

3. Remove the nut, washers and rubber bushes from the top mounting bracket for the shock absorber.

Install

1. Connect the shock absorber the top mounting bracket, ensure that the washers and rubber bushes are fitted in the correct order. Tighten nut to specified torque.

Shock Absorber Top Nut Torque:
260kg-cm, 19ft-lb, 25Nm

2. Install the shock absorber to the mounting bracket on the differential housing. Fit the lower mounting bolt and tighten to specification.

Lower Shock Absorber Bolt Torque:

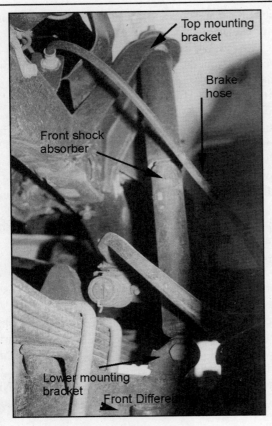

970kg-cm, 70ft-lb, 96Nm

3. Remove jack stands and lower vehicle.

TORQUE ROD
Remove
1. Using a floor jack under centre of the axle, jack up rear of vehicle. Then place safety stands under the rear body jacking points.
2. Remove the bolt attaching the torque rod to differential housing.
3. Remove the bolt attaching the torque rod to the vehicle frame. Remove the torque rod.
4. If bushes need to be replaced use a press to remove bushes.
Install
1. If bushes have been removed use a press to install new bushes.
2. Connect the torque rod to the vehicle frame mounting bracket. Tighten nut to specified torque.

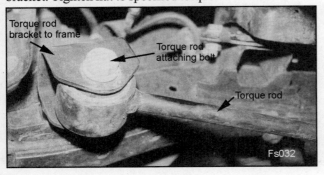

Torque Rod Bolt Specified Torque:
  1,900 kg-cm, 137ft-lb 186Nm
3. Install the torque rod to the mounting bracket on the differential housing. Fit the mounting bolt and tighten to specification.
Torque Rod Bolt Specified Torque:
  1,900 kg-cm, 137ft-lb 186Nm
4. Remove jack stands and lower vehicle.

PROBLEM DIAGNOSIS

Testing Shock Absorbers!
Test shock absorber action as follows:
* This test procedure is not for gas pressurised shock absorbers.
1. Clamp shock absorber by its bottom mount in a vice.
2. Slowly pump shock absorber up and down the full stroke at least six times before checking it resistance.
3. Pump shock absorber by hand at various rates of speed and observe resistance.
* When extending the shock absorber, the resistance should be marginally greater than when collapsing the unit. The resistance should be consistent throughout both strokes and there should be no 'slack' spots.
* 'Slack' spots indicate either loss of oil (which is usually visible on the outside- or valve not seating).
4. It is normal to detect a hissing noise (orifice swish). The following conditions are considered abnormal and reason for replacement:
(a) A skip or lag at reversal near mid-stroke.
(b) A seize (except at either extreme end of travel).
(c) A noise such as a grunt or squeal after completing one full stroke in both directions.
(d) A clicking noise at fast reversal.
(e) Fluid leakage.

General
When diagnosing suspected front suspension problems, it should be remembered that steering, wheels and tyres all have an effect on front end performance. Refer to **STEERING** and **WHEELS AND TYRES** Chapters.
Strut Diagnosis
* Test by quickly pushing up and down on the bumper bar at the front corner of the vehicle.
* Inspect the struts for excessive fluid leakage.

Problem: Hard or heavy steering!
Possible Causes and Remedies:
* Low or uneven tyre pressures.
* Steering gear or connections too tight or misaligned.
* Insufficient lubricant in steering gear.
* Excessive caster.
* Lower control arms or tension rods bent. Remedy - Check

290

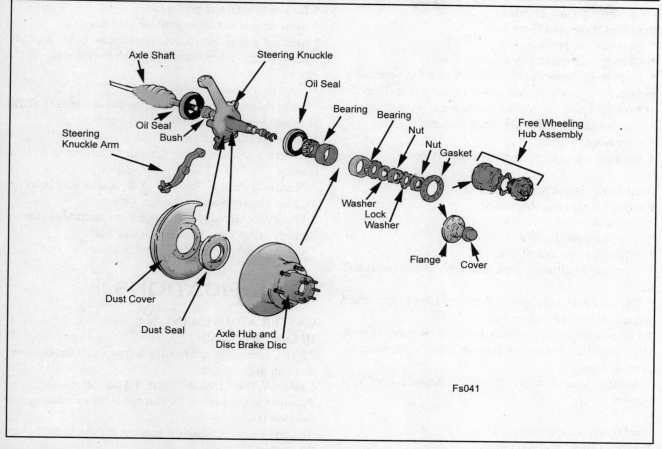

Fs041

front wheel alignment, check alignment or control arms and tension rods.
* Excessive toe-in. Remedy - Check and adjust toe-in.

Problem: Excessive play or looseness in steering!
Possible Causes and Remedies:
* Steering gear or connections loose or worn. Remedy - Adjust steering gear or install new components as necessary.
* Control arm ball joint loose or worn.
* Front wheel bearings incorrectly adjusted or worn. Remedy - Adjust bearings or replace as necessary.
* Loose attachment of front suspension assembly to frame. Remedy - Check and tighten front suspension attaching nuts.

Problem: Erratic steering on application of brakes!
Possible Causes and Remedies:
* Low or uneven tyre pressures.
* Excessive front brake disc runout. Remedy - Machine front brake discs.
* Oil soaked front brake pads. Remedy - Replace brake pads, check and correct cause of oil leakage.
* Insufficient or uneven caster. Remedy - Check front wheel alignment and adjust as necessary.
* Steering knuckle bent. Remedy-Replace strut housing

* Excessive play in steering gear. Remedy - Adjust steering gear or replace worn components as necessary.

Problem: Vehicle pulls to one side!
Possible Causes and Remedies:
* Lower or uneven tyre pressures.
* Rear wheels not tracking with front wheels. Remedy - Check alignment of rear wheels with front wheels and correct faults as necessary.
* Oil soaked front brake pads. Remedy - Replace brake pads, check and correct cause of oil leakage.
* Toe-in incorrect.
* Incorrect or uneven caster or camber. Remedy - Check wheel alignment and adjust as necessary.
* Rear axle assembly shifted. Remedy - Check attaching bolts for looseness and control arm bushes for wear.
* Steering knuckle bent. Remedy - Replace front strut housing.

Problem: Front or rear wheel tramp!
Possible Causes and Remedies:
* Wheels and tyres out of balance.
* Front struts or rear shock absorbers operating incorrectly or unevenly, leaking fluid or inoperative. Remedy - Check operation and replace components as necessary.

Problem: Road shocks!
Possible Causes and Remedies:
* Incorrect tyre pressures.
* Steering gear incorrectly adjusted.
* Front shock absorbers or rear shock absorbers operating incorrectly or unevenly, leaking fluid or inoperative. Remedy - Check operation and replace components as necessary.
* Compression or rebound rubbers missing.
* Unbalanced wheels.
* Incorrect wheel alignment. Remedy - Adjust.

Problem: Scuffed tyres!
Possible Causes and Remedies:
* Toe-in incorrect.
* Tyres improperly inflated.
* Wheels or tyres out-of-true.
* Control arm ball joints worn. Remedy - Replace worn ball joints.
* Uneven caster and camber. Remedy - Check front wheel alignment, adjust as necessary.
* Lower control arms or tension rods bent. Remedy - Check alignment of control arms and tension rods. Replace components as necessary.
* Steering knuckle bent. Remedy - Replace front strut housing.

Problem: Cupped tyres!
Possible Causes and Remedies:
* Tyres improperly inflated.
* Wheels and tyres out of balance.
* Dragging brakes. Remedy - Check for seizing of brake callipers.
* Control arm ball joints worn, or incorrectly adjusted or worn wheel bearings. Remedy - Replace ball joints or bearings, adjust as required.
* Uneven caster. Remedy - Check wheel alignment and adjust as necessary.
* Steering knuckle bent. Remedy - Replace front strut housing.

Problem: Front wheel shimmy!
Possible Causes and Remedies:
* Low or uneven tyre pressures.
* Steering connections incorrectly adjusted or worn.
* Control arm ball joints or front wheel bearings loose or worn.
* Wheels and tyres out of balance.
* Wheels or tyres out-of-true.
* Incorrect or uneven caster or toe-in incorrect.
* Steering knuckle bent. Remedy - Replace front strut housing.

Problem: Vehicle wanders!
Possible Causes and Remedies:

* Low or uneven tyre pressures.
* Steering gear or connections loose or worn.
* Steering gear or connections adjusted too tight. Remedy - Test steering system for binding with front wheels off the ground.
* Control arm ball joints worn.
* Wheels toe-in too much to toe-out in straight ahead position. Remedy - Adjust toe-in to specification.
* Incorrect or uneven caster.
* Steering knuckle bent. Remedy - Replace front strut housing.
* Rear axle shifted. Remedy - Check attaching bolts for looseness and control arm bushes for wear.
* Loose attachment of front suspension assembly to frame. Remedy - Check and tighten attaching nuts.
* Incorrect front wheel bearing adjustment.

SPECIFICATIONS

CASTER ADJUSTMENT
Hi Lux 30's & 40's
2WD: Caster is adjusted by adjusting the strut from the lower arm nuts at the chassis.
Caster: $\frac{1}{2}$ Ton 1^0 +/-30': $\frac{3}{4}$ & 1 Ton 30' +/- 40'
Positive Caster: Loosen the rear nut of the strut and tighten the front nut.
Negative Caster: Loosen the front nut of the strut and tighten the rear nut.
Caster Bush nut specification 69-108 ft-lb
4WD: No adjustment except for replacing worm parts
Specified Caster $3^030'$ +/- 40'

Hi Lux 50's & 60's
2WD: Caster is adjusted by adjusting the thickness of the shims in the upper arm
Inspeciation Specified Caster $0^040'$ +/- 45'
Left right error 30'
Adjusting Specified Caster $0^040'$ +/- 30'
Left right error 30'
4WD: No adjustment except for replacing worm parts
Specified Caster : $1^030'$ +/- 45'

Hi-Lux and 4 Runner 80's, 90's, 100's, 11's, 12's & 130's
2WD: Caster is adjusted by adjusting the thickness of the shims in the upper arm
Specified Caster: Depends on tyres $0^035'$ +/- 45'
4WD w-/ Ind. Sus. :Caster and Camber is adjusted by the position of the adjusting front and rear cams. Loosen the cam nuts and adjust cam.
Specified Caster: $2^030'$ +/- 45'
4WD Leaf Sus.: No adjustment except for replacing worm parts.
Specified Caster $1^030'$ +/- 45'

Maximum difference between caster of front wheels should not be greater than $1/_2 0$, preferably $1/_4 0$

CAMBER ADJUSTMENT

Hi Lux   30's & 40's

2WD: Caster is adjusted adding or removing shims on the front suspension.

Caster: $1/_2$ Ton 1^0 +/-30$'$: $3/_4$ & 1 Ton 1^0 +/-30$'$
4WD: No adjustment except for replacing worm parts.
Specified Camber 1^0 +/- 40$'$
Specified King Pin Angle 9^0 30$'$ +/- 40$'$

Hi-Lux and 4 Runner   50's & 60's

2WD: Camber is adjusted by adjusting the thickness of the shims in the upper arm.
Inspeciation Specified Camber $0^0 30'$ +/- 45$'$
Left right error 30$'$
Adjusting Specified Caster $0^0 30'$ +/- 30$'$
Left right error 30$'$
4WD: No adjustment except for replacing worm parts.
Specified Camber 1^0 +/- 45$'$
Specified King Pin Angle 9^0 30$'$ +/- 45$'$

Hi-Lux and 4 Runner 80's, 90's, 100's, 11's 12's & 130's

2WD: Camber is adjusted by adjusting the thickness of the shims in the upper arm
Specified Camber: Depends on tyres $0^0 45'$ +/- 45$'$
4WD w-/ Ind. Sus. :Caster and Camber is adjusted by the position of the adjusting front and rear cams. Loosen the cam nuts and adjust cam.
1. Hold the head of the cam bolt (attaching bolt for lower arm), loosen the nut.
2. Place frictionless pads or trolley under front wheels.
3. Rotate the cam to adjust the desired camber.
4. Hold cam bolt head, torque nut to specification.
Cam bolt nut specification:
        2000kg-cm(145ft.lb, 196Nm)
Specified Camber: 45$'$ +/- 45$'$
4WD Leaf Sus.: No adjustment except for replacing worm parts.
Specified Camber: 1^0 +/- 45$'$

Maximum difference between camber of front wheels should not be greater than $1/_2 0$, preferably $1/_4 0$

TOE - IN ADJUSTMENT
30's and 40's models
Toe-in Unloaded 5mm +/- 1mm Loaded 2mm +/-1mm
50's and 60's models 2WD (standard height)
Bias tyre   6mm +/- 4mm if adjusted 6+/- 1mm
Radial tyre   3mm +/- 4mm if adjusted 3+/- 1mm
50's and 60's models 4WD
Bias tyre   4mm +/- 4mm if adjusted 4+/- 1mm

Radial tyre   1mm +/- 4mm if adjusted 1+/- 1mm
80's to 130's models 4WD (IFS) (standard height - Front 58.5mm (2.3in) between the centre of front side adjusting cam bolt and centre of drive shaft - Rear 61.0mm (2.4in) bewteen the centre of rear axle shaft and centre of rear leaf spring)
        1mm +/- 2mm if adjusted 1+/- 1mm
80's to 130's models 4WD (Leaf Spring FS)
Radial Tyre   1mm +/- 2mm if adjusted 1+/- 1mm
Bias Tyre   4mm +/- 2mm if adjusted 4+/- 1mm

TORQUE SPECIFICATIONS

Disc Brake Calliper Anchor Bolts:
                1,100 kg-cm, 80ft-lb 108Nm
Wheel Nut Torque: 1,150 kg.cm, (83ft-lb, 113Nm)
Free Wheeling Hub Nuts:
                315 kg-cm, 23ft-lb 31Nm
Free Wheeling Hub Centre Nut:
                185 kg-cm, 13ft-lb 18Nm
 Free Wheeling Hub Cover bolts torque:
                100 kg-cm, 7ft-lb 10Nm
Stabilizer Bar Nuts torque:
2WD   100 kg-cm, 7ft-lb 10Nm
4WD   260 kg-cm, 19ft-lb 25Nm
Stabilizer Bar Support Bracket bolt torque:
2WD   185 kg-cm, 13ft-lb 18Nm
4WD   300 kg-cm, 22ft-lb 29Nm
Ball Joint to Lower Suspension Arm bolts torque:
                1,300 kg-cm, 95ft-lb 127Nm
Tie Rod end Ball Joint nut torque:
                920 kg-cm, 67ft-lb 90Nm

2 Wheel Drive
Ball Joint to Lower Suspension Arm bolts torque:
                1,300 kg-cm, 95ft-lb 127Nm
Tie Rod end Ball Joint nut torque:
                920 kg-cm, 67ft-lb 90Nm
Stabilizer Bar to Lower Suspension Arm nut torque:
                130 kg-cm, 9ft-lb 13Nm
Shock Absorber Lower Arm bolt torque:
                185 kg-cm, 13ft-lb 18Nm
Shock Absorber Upper Bracket nut torque:
                250 kg-cm, 18ft-lb 25Nm
Strut to Lower Arm bolt torque:
                970 kg-cm, 70ft-lb 95Nm
Torque Arm nuts torque:
                500 kg-cm, 35ft-lb 50Nm
Adjusting Lock Nut torque:
                850 kg-cm, 60ft-lb 83Nm
Lower Suspension Arm to Frame Nut Torque:
                2.300 kg-cm, 166ft-lb 226Nm

FRONT SUSPENSION

Upper Suspension Arm Inside Attaching Nuts:
   980 kg-cm, 70ft-lb 95Nm
Ball Joint Attaching Bolts and Nuts:
   320 kg-cm, 23ft-lb 31Nm
Upper Suspension Arm to Frame Nut Torque:
   1,280 kg-cm, 93ft-lb 126Nm
Upper Suspension Arm Ball Joint Nut torque:
   1,100 kg-cm, 80ft-lb 108Nm
Lower Suspension Arm Ball Joint Nut torque:
   1,450 kg-cm, 105ft-lb 142Nm
Steering Knuckle Arm & Back Dust Cover Bolt Torque:
   1,100 kg-cm, 80ft-lb 108Nm
Disc Brake Calliper Anchor Bolts:
   1,100 kg-cm, 80ft-lb 108Nm
Torque Arm Nuts Torque;
   500 kg-cm, 35ft-lb 50Nm
Adjusting Lock Nut Torque:
   850 kg-cm, 60ft-lb 83Nm
Lower Suspension Arm to Frame Nut Torque:
   2.300 kg-cm, 166ft-lb 226Nm
Screw-in Bush to Upper Suspension Arm Torque:
   2,300 kg-cm, 170ft-lb 230Nm
Strut Bar to Lower Suspension Arm Bolt Torque:
   970 kg-cm, 70ft-lb 95Nm
Lower Suspension Arm to Frame Nut Torque:
   1,250 kg-cm, 90ft-lb 123Nm

4 Wheel Drive [Ind. Sus.]
Lower Suspension Arm Ball Joint Nut torque:
   1,450 kg-cm, 105ft-lb 142Nm
Stabilizer Bar to Lower Suspension Arm Nut Torque:
   260 kg-cm, 20ft-lb 25Nm
Shock Absorber Lower Arm Bolt Torque:
   250 kg-cm, 18ft-lb 25Nm
Shock Absorber Upper Bracket Nut Torque:
   1,450 kg-cm, 100ft-lb 137Nm
Lower Suspension Arm to Frame Cam Nut Torque:
   2.000 kg-cm, 145ft-lb 200Nm
Upper Suspension Arm Inside Attaching Nuts:
   1,810 kg-cm, 130ft-lb 180Nm
Ball Joint Attaching Nut:
   1,450 kg-cm, 105ft-lb 142Nm
Adjusting Lock Nut torque:
   850 kg-cm, 60ft-lb 83Nm
Axle Drive Shaft Spacer to Bush Maximum Clearance:
   1.0 mm or 0.039 in
Upper Suspension Arm Ball Joint Nut torque:
   1,450 kg-cm, 105ft-lb 142Nm
Lower Suspension Arm / Ball Joint Bolt & Nut torque:
   590 kg-cm, 43ft-lb 58Nm
Stabilizer Bar to Lower Suspension Arm Nut Torque:
   260 kg-cm, 20ft-lb 25Nm
Shock Absorber Lower Arm Bolt Torque:
   250 kg-cm, 18ft-lb 25Nm

Steering Knuckle Arm & Back Dust Cover Bolt Torque:
   1,870 kg-cm, 135ft-lb 183Nm
Tie Rod Ball Joint Specification:
   260 kg-cm, 20ft-lb 25Nm
Steering Knuckle Arm & Back Dust Cover Bolt Torque:
   185 kg-cm, 13ft-lb 18Nm
Disc Brake Calliper Anchor Bolts:
   1,100 kg-cm, 80ft-lb 108Nm

4 Wheel Drive [Spring Leaf Sus.]
Steering Knuckle Arm Nuts Torque:
   975 kg-cm, 70ft-lb 95Nm
Steering Knuckle Arm Preload Pressure Specification:
   3.0 - 6.0kg, 6.5-13.2lb, 29-59N
Tie Rod Ball Joint Specification:
   25-30Nm
Steering Spindle Attaching bolt Torque:
   475 kg-cm, 34ft-lb 47Nm
Free Wheeling Hub Nuts:
   315 kg-cm, 23ft-lb 31Nm
Free Wheeling Hub Cover bolts torque:
   100 kg-cm, 7ft-lb 10Nm
Brake Calliper torque bolts:
   1,100kg-cm(80ft-lb, 108Nm)
Road Wheel Nut Torque:

LEAF SPRING TORQUE:
Spring Centre Bolt Torque:
   450kg-cm, 33ft-lb, 44Nm
Front Suspension "U" Bolt Torque:
   1,250 kg.cm, (90ft-lb, 123Nm).
Front Shock Absorber Lower Bolt torque:
   970 kg.cm, (70ft-lb, 95Nm).
Stabilizer Bar to Lower Suspension Arm Nut Torque:
   260 kg-cm, 20ft-lb 25Nm
Shock Absorber Top Nut Torque:
   260kg-cm, 19ft-lb, 25Nm
Torque Rod Bolt Specified Torque:
   1,900 kg-cm, 137ft-lb 186Nm
Hanger Bolt and Nut Torque:
   930 kg.cm, (67ft-lb, 90Nm).
Shackle Bolt and Nut Torque:
   930 kg.cm, (67ft-lb, 90Nm).
Torque Rod Bolt Specified Torque:
   1,900 kg-cm, 137ft-lb 186Nm

REAR SUSPENSION

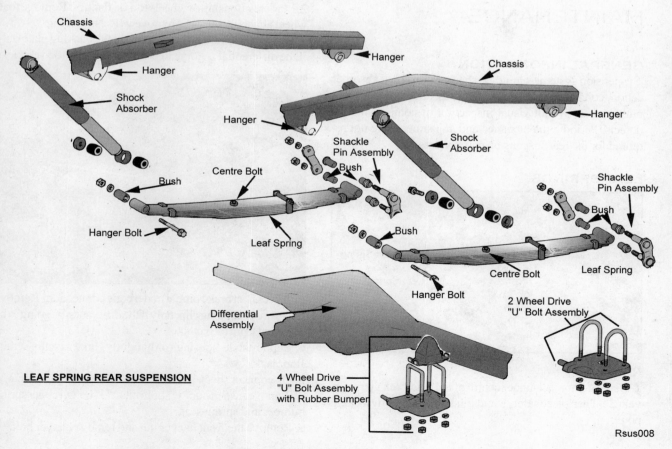

LEAF SPRING REAR SUSPENSION

Rsus008

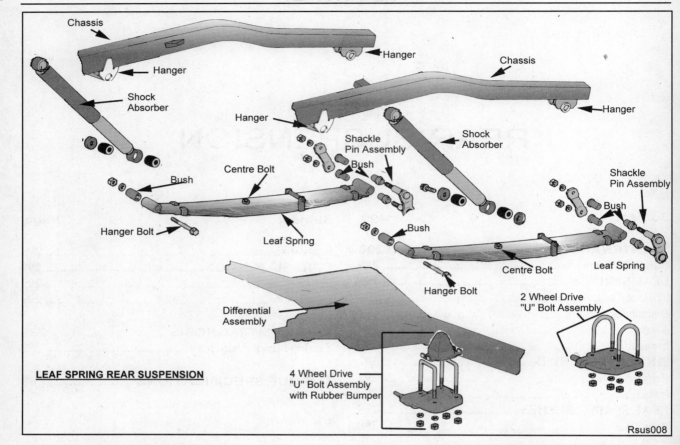

LEAF SPRING REAR SUSPENSION

Rsus008

MAINTENANCE

GENERAL INFORMATION

Suspension systems should be checked for shock absorber action, condition of suspension bushes, attaching bolts and nuts, and an overall visual inspection of components for defects. Periodic maintenance and adjustments are not required for the rear suspension components.

LEAF SPRINGS

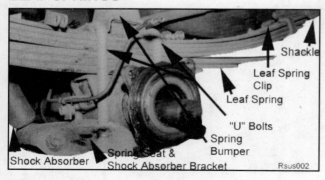

Rsus002

Remove

1. Using a floor jack under centre of the axle, jack up rear of vehicle. Then place safety stands under the rear body jacking points.

2. Mark relationship of wheels to axle flanges. Remove road wheel attaching nuts and remove wheels.

3. Disconnect the hand brake cable at the backing plate only if the differential is going to be removed from the vehicle.

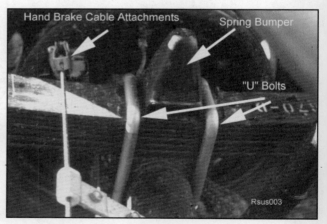

Rsus003

4. Disconnect brake pipe at underbody connection. Remove brake hose retaining clip, only if the differential is going to be removed from the vehicle..

5. Support axle housing (only lightly) under centre with a floor jack.

6. Disconnect shock absorbers at lower mounting points.

7. Remove suspension "U" bolt nuts, "U" bolts, rubber spring bumper and spring seat.

9. Remove the front hanger nut and remove hanger bolt.

296

10. Remove the rear shackle nut and remove the shackle bolt. Remove spring assembly from vehicle.

Dismantle

1. Bend leaf clip away from spring leaves.

2. Remove centre bolt.

Assemble

1. Assembly spring leaves incorrect order, clamp in a vice.

2. Install centre spring bolt and tighten to specification.

Spring Centre Bolt Torque:

    450kg-cm, 33ft-lb, 44Nm

3. Bend spring leaf clips into position.

Installation

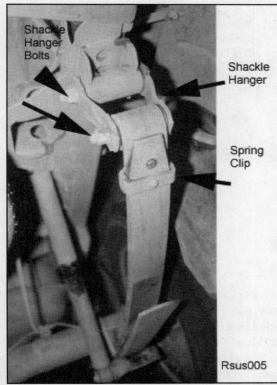

1. Position spring under vehicle into correct position. Replace the front hanger bolt and nut. Tighten to finger tightness only.

2. Replace the rear hanger pin and or rear hanger pin bolts and nuts. Tighten to finger tightness only.

3. With differential assembly on a floor jack and the help of

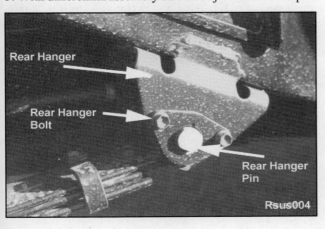

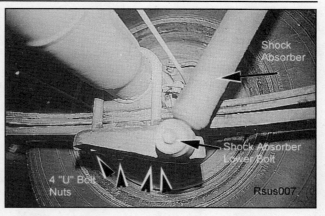

an assistant manoeuvre the differential assembly into position with the springs.

4. Replace suspension spring seat, "U" bolts and rubber spring bumper and nuts and tighten nuts to specification.

Suspension "U" Bolt Torque:

    1,250 kg.cm, (90ft-lb, 123Nm).

5. Reconnect shock absorbers at lower mounting points and tighten bolt to specification.

Rear Shock Absorber Lower Bolt (Leaf Sus) Torque:

Two Wheel Drive   260 kg.cm, (19ft-lb, 25Nm).

Four Wheel Drive   650 kg.cm, (47ft-lb, 64Nm).

6. Connect brake pipe at underbody rear connection. Install brake hose retaining clip (if removed).

7. Replace parking brake cable to linkage and backing plate, (if removed).

8. Replace road wheel taking note of mark made during removal for position of wheel to brake drum, and attaching nuts tighten to specification.

Road Wheel Nuts Torque:

    1,150 kg.cm, (83ft-lb, 113Nm).

9. Remove safety stands from under the front body jacking points.

10. Tighten front spring hanger and shackle bolts to specified torque.

Spring Hanger Bolt and Nut Torque:

Rubber Bush Type   930 kg.cm, (67ft-lb, 90Nm).

Pressed-in Bush Type   1,600 kg.cm, (116ft-lb, 157Nm).

Shackle Bolt and Nut Torque:

    930 kg.cm, (67ft-lb, 90Nm).

11. Re-adjust park brake shoes and bleed brake hydraulic system (if systems where disconnected).

SHOCK ABSORBERS

Remove

1. Using a floor jack under centre of the axle, jack up rear of vehicle. Then place safety stands under the rear body jacking points.

2. Remove the lower bolt attaching the shock absorber to differential housing.

3. Remove the nut, washers and rubber bushes from the top mounting bracket for the shock absorber.

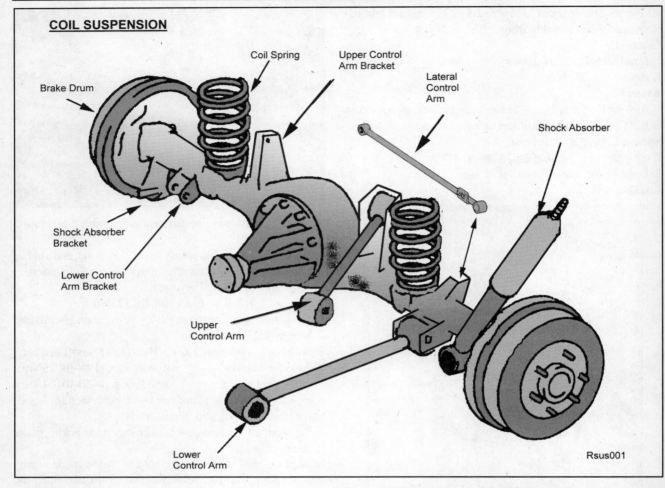

COIL SUSPENSION

Coil Spring

Upper Control Arm Bracket

Lateral Control Arm

Brake Drum

Shock Absorber

Shock Absorber Bracket

Lower Control Arm Bracket

Upper Control Arm

Lower Control Arm

Rsus001

Install
1. Connect the shock absorber the top mounting bracket,

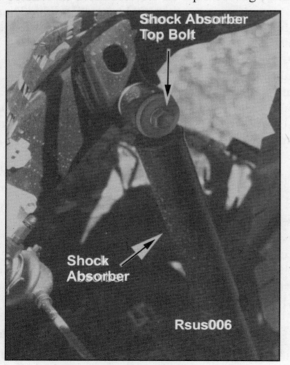

Shock Absorber Top Bolt

Shock Absorber

Rsus006

ensure that the washers and rubber bushes are fitted in the correct order. Tighten nut to specified torque.

Shock Absorber Top Nut Torque:

Two Wheel Drive   **260kg-cm, 19ft-lb, 25Nm**

Four Wheel Drive   **650kg-cm, 47ft-lb, 64Nm**

2. Install the shock absorber to the mounting bracket on the differential housing. Fit the lower mounting bolt and tighten to specification.

Lower Shock Absorber Bolt Torque:

Shock Absorber Top Nut Torque:

Two Wheel Drive   **260kg-cm, 19ft-lb, 25Nm**

Four Wheel Drive   **650kg-cm, 47ft-lb, 64Nm**

3. Remove jack stands and lower vehicle.

LEAF SPRING BUSHES
Remove
1. Raise vehicle and support on safety stands under rear jacking points.
2. Remove the leaf spring assembly as described above.
3. Remove the front bush if necessary in a press or press out with a special tool.
4. Remove shackle and rubber bushes, a press may be necessary.

Installation
1. Press new bushes into the spring if replacing the bushes.
2. If rubber bushes install bushes into spring eye, soak bushes in soapy hot water if necessary.
3. Install new bushes into shackle hanger, soak bushes in soapy hot water if necessary.
4. Install spring assembly as previously described.
5. Remove safety stands and lower vehicle.

Coil Suspension
Remove
1. Using a floor jack under centre of the axle, jack up rear of vehicle. Then place safety stands under the rear body jacking points.
2. Mark relationship of wheels to axle flanges. Remove road wheel attaching nuts and remove wheels.
3. Disconnect the hand brake cable at the backing plate only if the differential is going to be removed from the vehicle.
4. Disconnect brake pipe at underbody connection. Remove brake hose retaining clip, only if the differential is going to be removed from the vehicle.
5. Support axle housing (only lightly) under centre with a floor jack.
6. Disconnect shock absorbers at lower mounting points.
7. Remove the axle housing, bolt and nut from both upper control arms.
8. Remove the axle housing connecting bolt and nut to the lateral control rod.
9. Lower the axle housing, checking the brake hoses, if pulled tight, disconnect the brake hoses.
10. Remove the coil springs and insulators.

Installation
1. Assembly the coil springs with insulator and install to the axle housing spring base.
2. Jack up the axle housing, taking care the springs are fitting into the lower and upper spring seats, raise the axle housing enough to connect control arms etc.
3. Connect both the upper control arms and install bolt and nut tighten to specification.

Axle Housing to Upper Control Rods Bolt and Nut Torque: 880kg.cm, 64ft.lb, 86Nm
4. Connect the axle housing connecting bolt and nut to the lateral control rod, and tighten to specification.

Axle Housing to Lateral Control Rods Bolt and Nut Torque: 880kg.cm, 64ft.lb, 86Nm
5. Reconnect shock absorbers at lower mounting points and tighten bolt to specification.

Rear Shock Absorber Lower Bolt torque:
Two Wheel Drive   260 kg.cm, (19ft-lb, 25Nm).
Four Wheel Drive   650 kg.cm, (47ft-lb, 64Nm).
6. Reconnect the suspension stabilizer bar from the rear axle. Tighten bolts to specification.

**Axle Housing to Stabilizer Bar Bolt Torque:
130kg.cm, 9ft.lb, 13Nm**

7. Connect brake pipe at underbody rear connection. Install brake hose retaining clip (if removed).
8. Replace parking brake cable to linkage and backing plate (if removed).
9. Replace road wheel taking note of mark made during removal for position of wheel to brake drum, and attaching nuts tighten to specification.
Wheel Nut Torque: 1,150 kg.cm, (83ft-lb, 113Nm).
10. Remove safety stands from under the front body jacking points.
11. Re-adjust park brake shoes and bleed brake hydraulic system (if systems where disconnected).

PROBLEM DIAGNOSIS

Testing Shock Absorbers!
* This test procedure is not for gas pressurised shock absorbers.
1. Clamp shock absorber by its bottom mount in a vice.
2. Slowly pump shock absorber up and down the full stroke at least six times before checking its resistance.
3. Pump shock absorber by hand at various rates of speed and observe resistance.
* When extending the shock absorber, the resistance should be marginally greater than when collapsing the unit. The resistance should be consistent throughout both strokes and there should be no 'slack' spots.
* 'Slack' spots indicate either loss of oil or valve not seating.
4. It is normal to detect a hissing noise (orifice swish).
Replace shock absorber if listed conditions occur:
(a) A skip or lag at reversal near mid-stroke.
(b) A seize (except at either extreme end of travel).
(c) A noise such as a grunt or squeal after completing one full stroke in both directions.
(d) A clicking noise at fast reversal.
(e) Fluid leakage.

Torque Specifications

LEAL SPRING SUSPENSION
Spring Centre Bolt Torque:
        450kg-cm, 33ft-lb, 44Nm
Suspension "U" Bolt Torque:
        1,250 kg.cm, (90ft-lb, 123Nm).
Rear Shock Absorber Lower Bolt (Leaf Sus) Torque:
Two Wheel Drive   260 kg.cm, (19ft-lb, 25Nm).
Four Wheel Drive   650 kg.cm, (47ft-lb, 64Nm).
Road Wheel Nuts Torque:
        1,150 kg.cm, (83ft-lb, 113Nm).
Spring Hanger Bolt and Nut Torque:
Rubber Bush Type   930 kg.cm, (67ft-lb, 90Nm).

Pressed-in Bush Type   1,600 kg.cm, (116ft-lb, 157Nm).
Shackle Bolt and Nut Torque:
                930 kg.cm, (67ft-lb, 90Nm).
Shock Absorber Top Nut Torque:
Two Wheel Drive   260kg-cm, 19ft-lb, 25Nm
Four Wheel Drive   650kg-cm, 47ft-lb, 64Nm
Lower Shock Absorber Bolt Torque:
Shock Absorber Top Nut Torque:
Two Wheel Drive   260kg-cm, 19ft-lb, 25Nm
Four Wheel Drive   650kg-cm, 47ft-lb, 64Nm

Coil Suspension
Axle Housing to Upper Control Rods Bolt and Nut Torque:
                880kg.cm, 64ft.lb, 86Nm
Axle Housing to Lateral Control Rods Bolt and Nut Torque:
                880kg.cm, 64ft.lb, 86Nm
Rear Shock Absorber Lower Bolt torque:
Two Wheel Drive   260 kg.cm, (19ft-lb, 25Nm).
Four Wheel Drive   650 kg.cm, (47ft-lb, 64Nm).
Axle Housing to Stabilizer Bar Bolt Torque:
                130kg.cm, 9ft.lb, 13Nm
Wheel Nut Torque: 1,150 kg.cm, (83ft-lb, 113Nm).

Memo

BRAKES

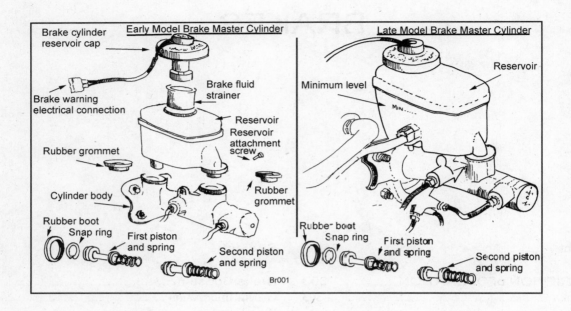

Early Model Brake Master Cylinder

Brake cylinder reservoir cap

Brake warning electrical connection

Rubber grommet

Cylinder body

Rubber boot
Snap ring
First piston and spring

Brake fluid strainer

Reservoir
Reservoir attachment screw

Rubber grommet

Second piston and spring

Br001

Late Model Brake Master Cylinder

Reservoir

Minimum level

Rubber boot
Snap ring
First piston and spring

Second piston and spring

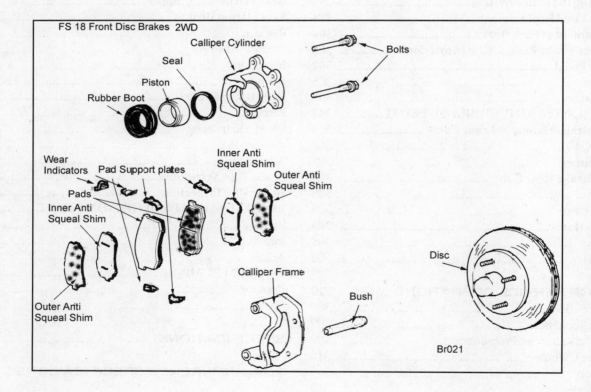

FS 18 Front Disc Brakes 2WD

Calliper Cylinder

Seal

Piston

Rubber Boot

Bolts

Wear Indicators

Pads

Pad Support plates

Inner Anti Squeal Shim

Inner Anti Squeal Shim

Outer Anti Squeal Shim

Outer Anti Squeal Shim

Calliper Frame

Bush

Disc

Br021

302

DESCRIPTION OF OPERATION
Disc Brake

When the brake pedal is applied, brake fluid is displaced into the calliper bore moving the piston outwards. This action forces the inner pad assembly against the disc. The resultant reaction forces the calliper body and outboard pad assembly inwards against the disc. Braking torque is transferred from the outer and inner brake pads to the mounting plate.

The piston seal retracts the piston a small amount allowing the pads to clear the disc, when the brake pedal is released.

Each master cylinder has the bore size cast into the master cylinder body on the upper front edge.

The components of callipers are illustrated. All callipers are similar in operation, even though some have extra pistons or anti rattler-plates fitted.

The anchor plate is rigidly fixed to the steering knuckle whilst the housing slides within the anchor plate by means of two guide pins bolted to the housing. Rubber boots are fitted to the guide pins to keep out dirt and foreign matter.

ROUTINE MAINTENANCE
CHECKING BRAKE LINES, HOSES AND LININGS

Raise the rear of vehicle, position on safety stands and remove rear wheels. Inspect braking disc, linings and calliper. Check all brake tube connection for possible leaks and flexible hoses for deterioration. Install new flexible hoses if required.

NB: Ensure hose is not twisted more than 15° after final fitment.

If a brake pad lining has worn to the minimum specification, replace both inboard and outboard pads. It is necessary that both rear wheel sets be replaced whenever a respective brake pad is worn beyond specifications or damaged.

The brake fluid used is hydroscopic and absorbs moisture from the air through the brake hoses, etc. The boiling resistance of the fluid decreases as the moisture content increases and so the possibility of a vapour lock under heavy braking conditions increases with the age of the fluid. Therefore, for maximum brake effectiveness, a 2 yearly change of brake fluid is mandatory.

* Approved and Toyota recommended brake fluid should be used.

* Brake fluid is extremely damaging to paint. If fluid should accidentally touch a painted surface, immediately wash from paint and clean painted surface.

BRAKE SHOE LINING WEAR

If a visual inspection doesn't adequately determine condition of lining, a physical check will be necessary. Visual inspection is possible on most later model drum brakes by removing the inspection hole rubber on the backing plate, then inspecting the thickness of the lining.

To check amount of lining wear, remove the brake drum. Three thickness measurements with a micrometer should be taken across the centre of each pad or brake shoe, one reading at each end and one in the centre.

BLEEDING THE BRAKE SYSTEM

While working on the brake system, pockets of air may be trapped in the LHF brake pipe, the front brake hoses and in the master cylinder and various other parts of the brake

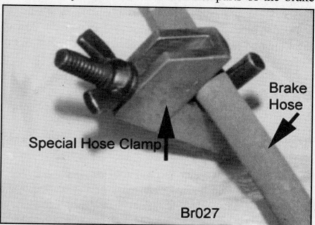

Special Hose Clamp

Brake Hose

Br027

system.

A quick method of locating air pockets is to clamp the brake hoses near the pipe end. This must be done using a specially designed clamp that will not damage the brake hoses.

* Do not use 'G' clamps under any circumstances. When approved clamps are used, extreme care must be taken to ensure they are removed before the vehicle is driven on the road.

The front chamber of the master cylinder can be bled by loosening the pipe to the LHF brake at the master cylinder and allowing brake fluid to drip from the connection for approximately 1 minute. Do not operate the brake pedal or apply pressure to the master cylinder during this operation.

Remove air from other components of the brake system as follows:

1. Remove master cylinder cap and fit pressure bleed cap.
2. Connect cap to pressure bleed pump and pressurise system to no more than 345 kPa.

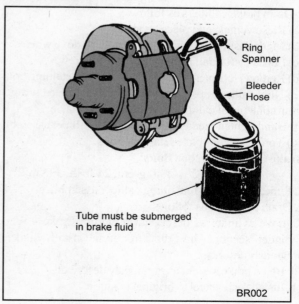

Ring Spanner

Bleeder Hose

Tube must be submerged in brake fluid

BR002

3. Open brake bleeder of line to be bled and pump brake pedal one stroke/second for approximately 10 strokes, then close bleeder. During this operation the pressure bleeder to the master cylinder should not be turned off. It is essential that this volume and rate of flow is maintained to ensure air trapped in pipes is carried out of the system with the flow of the fluid and not allowed to retreat between strokes of the brake pedal.

BRAKE FLUID REPLACEMENT

1. Thoroughly clean master cylinder especially around wheel brake line connections.
2. Disconnect wheel brake lines from master cylinder and remove reservoir cap.
3. Allow master cylinder to drain until empty.
4. Fill master cylinder reservoir with new specified brake fluid, do not allow master cylinder to below half full.

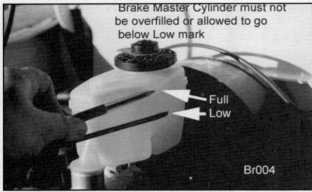

Brake Master Cylinder must not be overfilled or allowed to go below Low mark

Full
Low

Br004

5. Allow fluid to flow from open connection ports until fluid is free of air. Collect discharged fluid in suitable container then discard. Do not allow fluid to contact paint work.
6. Reconnect wheel brake lines to master cylinder and torque flare nut.

Brake Line Flare Nut Torque:
155kg-cm, 11 ft-lb, 15Nm

7. Drain brake callipers as follows:
 (a) Raise vehicle and place on stands.
 (b) Mark position of wheels to hub and remove wheels.
 (c) Loosen left-hand front calliper bleed screw.
 (d) Remove left-hand calliper anchor plate retaining bolts.
 (e) Hold calliper upside down and remove bleed screw to drain contents of calliper into suitable receptacle.
 (f) Hand tighten bleed screw and install calliper assembly.
 (g) Torque anchor plate retaining bolts.

Brake Calliper Anchor Bolts:
400kg-cm, 24 ft-lb, 39Nm

8. Repeat Step 7 for remaining calliper assemblies.
9. Drain cylinders as follows:
Remove cylinder as described in "Drum Brake - Wheel Cylinder" section. Allow fluid to drain and install cylinder as previously described.
10. Bleed brake system as previously described.
11. Install road wheel to original position.

ADJUSTMENT OF PARK BRAKE

1. Support rear of vehicle on jack stands.
2. Operate park brake lever with moderate effort twice, then release. Pull lever out from fully released position.
3. Check the number of clicks the brake lever has travelled with a force of 20kg, 44lb or 200Nm.

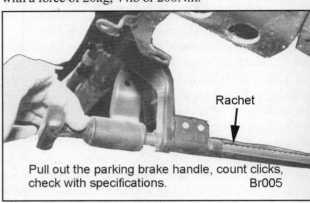

Rachet

Pull out the parking brake handle, count clicks, check with specifications.   Br005

Park Brake Lever Clicks at 20kg, 44lb or 200Nm.
Hi Lux 30's & 40's

All Countries	10-16 clicks

Hi Lux & 4 Runner 50's & 60's Series
All Countries other than Australia & New Zealand

2WD	10-16 clicks
4WD	7-15 clicks

Australia & New Zealand

2WD	6-9 clicks
4WD	4-8 clicks

Hi Lux & 4 Runner 80's Series on (1988 on)
All countries other than Australia 1-2 ton vehicles:

2WD	11-17 clicks

Australia 1-2 ton vehicles:

2WD	12-18 clicks

All Countries

4WD:	11-17 clicks

4. If necessary, adjust park brake relay rod to achieve the above specification. Tighten relay rod lock nut.

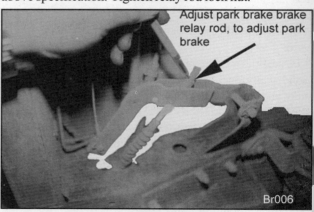

Adjust park brake brake relay rod, to adjust park brake

Br006

5. Release park brake and check that rear wheels rotate freely. Lower vehicle.

* If park brake cannot be adjusted satisfactorily by means of

the relay rod, it is necessary to replace the rear brakes. If brake cannot be adjusted by this method check Park Brake Shoe-Adjust.

REPLACE BRAKE PADS & DISC INSPECTION

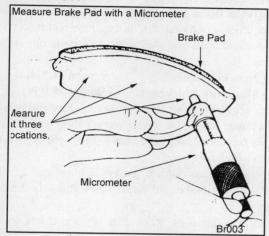

Measure Brake Pad with a Micrometer

Brake Pad

Measure it three locations.

Micrometer

Br003

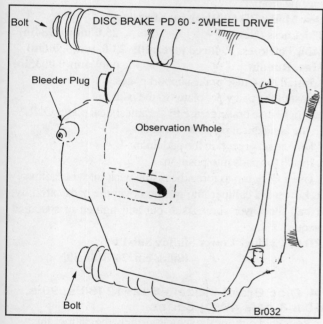

Bolt

DISC BRAKE PD 60 - 2WHEEL DRIVE

Bleeder Plug

Observation Whole

Bolt

Br032

This procedure refers to front brake pads on disc brakes.

1. Remove master cylinder cap. Loosen front left wheel brake line connection at master cylinder and allow fluid to bleed down into a container until master cylinder reservoir is approximately 1/3 full. Retighten the connection and refit master cylinder cap.

* Do not remove the brake line or empty the reservoir or it will be necessary to bleed the system.
* Discard the fluid removed.
* Removal of fluid from the reservoir is necessary to prevent reservoir overflow when calliper piston is pushed back in its bore during pad replacement.
* Brake fluid is extremely damaging to paint work.

2. Raise front of vehicle and place on jack stands.
3. Mark relationship of wheel to hub. Remove wheel.

4. Disc Brake Model - K [30's & 40's Series]

a. Check thickness by looking through the pad inspection hole. Measure used disc pad wear, replace if not within specification.

Lining Minimum Thickness: 1.0 mm(0.039in)

b. To replace the pads - Remove the top and lower bolt of the calliper, this will allow you to remove the anti rattle spring, anti squeal shim, support plate and guide plate.

c. Remove the 2 pads.

d. Measure used disc pad wear, replace if not within specification. As in No.a.

e. Inspect condition of brake disc, replace if not within specification.

Disc Model - K - 30's & 40's Series Wear specifications
Thickness (New):   20.0 mm(0.787in)
Min. Thickness Refaced (overall): 19.0 mm(0.75in)
Max. Runout: 0.15 mm(0.006in)

f. Install the pads into position.

g. Install the anti squeal shims and anti squeal spring.

h. Use a G clamp to force the piston back into the calliper.

i. Lower the calliper into position over the pads carefully, install the upper and lower guide plate, support spring and pad support plate. Install retaining bolts and tighten to specification.

Pad Support Plate bolt:

500kg-cm, 30 ft-lb, 50Nm

4. Disc Brake Model - S16 [30's & 40's Series]

a. Check thickness by looking through the pad inspection hole. Measure used disc pad wear, replace if not within specification.

Lining Minimum Thickness: 1.0 mm(0.039in)

b. To replace the pads - Remove the clip on the vehicle outside of the calliper, this will allow you to move the 2 pins.

c. Remove the anti rattle spring.

d. Remove the 2 pads and anti squeal shims.

e. Measure used disc pad wear, replace if not within specification.

Lining Minimum Thickness: 1.0 mm(0.039in)

f. Using a steel bar or screw driver, force the piston back from the disc.

g. Inspect condition of brake disc, replace if not within specification.

Disc Model S 16 Wear specifications
Thickness (New):   12.5 mm(0.49in)
Min. Thickness Refaced (overall): 11.5 mm(0.45in)
Max. Runout: 0.15 mm(0.0059in)

h. Install the 2 anti squeal shims, apply brake grease to anti squeal shims only, and new pads.

i. Install the anti rattle spring.

j. Install the 2 pins and pin clip.

4. Disc Brake Model - S12+8 [30's, 40's, 4WD] [50's & 60's 4WD] Series

a. Check thickness by looking through the pad inspection hole. Measure used disc pad wear, replace if not within specification.

Lining Minimum Thickness: **1.0 mm(0.039in)**

b. To replace the pads. Remove the clip on the vehicle inside of the calliper, this will allow you to move the 2 pins.

c. Remove the anti rattle spring.

d. Remove the 2 pads.

e. Measure used disc pad wear, replace if not within specification.

Lining New Thickness: **9.5mm (0.374in)**

f. Using a steel bar or screw driver, force the piston (2 pistons one at a time) back from the disc.

g. Inspect condition of brake disc, replace if not within specification.

Disc Model S 12+8 Wear specifications

Thickness (New):   **12.5 mm(0.497in)**
Min. Thickness Refaced (overall): **11.5 mm(0.45in)**
Max. Runout: **0.15 mm(0.0059in)**

h. Install the new pads.

i. Install the anti rattle spring.

j. Install the 2 pins and pin clip.

4. Disc Brake Model FS 17 [50's & 60's 2WD] Series

a. Check thickness by looking through the pad inspection hole. Measure used disc pad wear, replace if not within specification.

Lining New Thickness: **10.0mm(0.393in)**
Lining Minimum Thickness: **1.0 mm(0.039in)**

b. To replace the pads - remove the lower sliding sub pin with a ring spanner, loosen the top sliding sub pin.

c. Lift the brake calliper up, tie back with a piece of wire, do not stretch the brake hose.

d. Remove the 2 brake pads, anti squeal shim and 4 brake pad support plates.

e. Inspect condition of brake disc, replace if not within specification.

Disc Model FS 17 Wear specifications

Thickness (New):   **22.0 mm(0.866in)**
Min. Thickness Refaced (overall): **21.0 mm(0.827in)**
Max. Runout: **0.15 mm(0.0059in)**

f. Install the 4 disc brake support plates.

g. Apply disc brake grease to the anti squeal plates ONLY, fit the anti squeal plate to the pads.

* Do not get grease on the pad lining.

h. Install the pads into position.

i. Use a G clamp to force the piston back into the calliper.

j. Lower the calliper into position over the pads carefully,

install the lower sliding sub pin and tighten to specified torque.

FS 17 Calliper Lower Sliding Sub Pin:
   850kg-cm, 84 ft-lb, 93Nm

4. Disc Brake Model PD 60 [50's 60's 2WD][80's 90's 10's &11's 2WD] Series

a. Check thickness by looking through the pad inspection hole. Measure used disc pad wear, replace if not within specification.

Lining New Thickness: **9.5mm (0.374in)**
Lining Minimum Thickness: **1.0 mm(0.039in)**

b. To replace the pads - remove the lower sliding sub pin with a ring spanner, loosen the top sliding sub pin.

c. Lift the brake calliper up, tie back with a piece of wire, do not stretch the brake hose.

d. Remove the 2 anti squeal springs, 2 brake pads, 2 anti squeal shims, 2 brake pad wear plates and 4 brake pad support plates.

e. Inspect condition of brake disc, replace if not within specification.

Disc Model PD 60 Wear specifications

Thickness (New):   **25.0 mm(0.984in)**
Min. Thickness Refaced (overall): **23.0 mm(0.906in)**
Max. Runout: **0.09 mm(0.0035in)**

f. Install the 4 disc brake support plates.

g. Install the pad wear plates to the pads.

h. Apply disc brake grease to the anti squeal plates ONLY, fit the anti squeal plates to the pads.

* Do not get grease on the pad lining.

i. Install the pads into position.

j. Use a G clamp to force the piston back into the calliper.

k. Lower the calliper into position over the pads carefully, install the lower sliding sub pin and tighten to specified torque.

PD 60 Calliper Lower Sliding Sub Pin:
   400kg-cm, 24 ft-lb, 39Nm

4. Disc Brake Model - S12+12 [80's, 90's, 10's & 11's 4WD] Series

a. Remove the clip on the vehicle inside of the calliper, this will allow you to move the 2 pins.

b. Remove the anti rattle spring.

c. Remove the 2 pads and anti squeal shims.

d. Measure used disc pad wear, replace if not within specification.

Lining New Thickness: **9.5mm (0.374in)**
Lining Minimum Thickness: **1.0 mm(0.039in)**

e. Using a steel bar or screw driver, force the piston (2 pistons one at a time) back from the disc.

f. Inspect condition of brake disc, replace if not within specification.

Disc Model S 12+12 Wear specifications

Thickness (New):   **20.0 mm(0.787in)**

Min. Thickness Refaced (overall):	**18.0 mm(0.709in)**
Max. Runout: Ind. Front Susp.	**0.09 mm(0.0035in)**
Max. Runout: Leaf Spring Susp.	**0.15 mm(0.0059in)**

f. Install the 4 anti squeal shims and new pads.

g. Install the anti rattle spring.

h. Install the 2 pins and pin clip.

4. Disc Brake Model FS 18 [80's, 90's 10's & 11's 2WD] Series

a. Check thickness by looking through the pad inspection hole. Measure used disc pad wear, replace if not within specification.

Lining New Thickness:	**10.0mm(0.393in)**
Lining Minimum Thickness:	**1.0 mm(0.039in)**

b. To replace the pads - remove the lower sliding sub pin with a ring spanner, loosen the top sliding sub pin.

c. Lift the brake calliper up, tie back with a piece of wire, do not stretch the brake hose.

d. Remove the 2 brake pads, 4 anti squeal shims, 2 brake pad plates and 4 brake pad support plates.

e. Inspect condition of brake disc, replace if not within specification.

Disc Model FS 18 Wear specifications

Thickness (New):	**22.0 mm(0.866in)**
Min. Thickness Refaced (overall):	**20.0 mm(0.787in)**
Max. Runout:	**0.09 mm(0.0035in)**

f. Install the 4 disc brake support plates.

g. Install the pad wear plates to the pads.

h. Apply disc brake grease to the anti squeal plates ONLY, fit the anti squeal plates to the pads.

* Do not get grease on the pad lining.

i. Install the pads into position.

j. Use a G clamp to force the piston back into the calliper.

k. Lower the calliper into position over the pads carefully, install the lower sliding sub pin and tighten to specified torque.

FS 18 Calliper Lower Sliding Sub Pin:

400kg-cm, 24 ft-lb, 39Nm

5. Fill master cylinder to correct level with fresh, specified brake fluid.

6. Depress brake pedal several times to bring pad assemblies into position against disc.

7. Refill master cylinder if necessary.

8. Install wheels and lower vehicle. Tighten road wheel nuts.

BRAKE PEDAL

Remove

1. Remove spring, push rod retaining clip, push rod and washers from brake pedal.

2. Remove brake light switch wiring connection and switch.

3. Remove nut securing pedal support shaft to pedal support.

4. Carefully withdraw shaft from pedal support.

* Shaft is snug fit in support and may need to be tapped at threaded end with soft hammer.

* Do not lose washers and other components. Automatic vehicles are fitted with a longer spacer in lieu of the clutch pedal, return spring and washer.

5. Withdraw brake pedal and return spring assembly.

Install

1. Lubricate bearing surfaces with Molybdenum Disulphide grease.

2. Hold brake pedal and return spring in position and insert pedal support shaft through pedal support.

3. Push shaft further through pedal support and progressively install components.

4. Install and torque shaft retaining washer and nut. Prevent shaft from turning when tightening by means of flats at unthreaded end of shaft.

Brake Pedal Shaft

Torque:	**12 - 16 Nm.**

5. Install brake push rod, washers and retaining clip on brake pedal.

6. Adjust stop switch as follows:

Stop Switch - Adjust brake pedal switch pad to switch body with pedal in rest position. Tighten lock nut at correct location.

7. Adjust brake pedal to achieve correct floor clearance as described below.

INSPECT and ADJUST BRAKE PEDAL

1. Measure the distance from the metal plate covering to the top of the pedal rubber, if not within specification adjust.

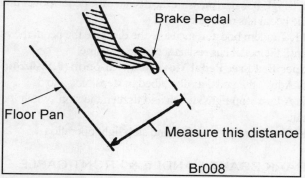

Br008

Hi Lux 30's & 40's Series

2WD

All Countries	162.0mm(6.4in) - 172.0mm(6.8in)

4WD

All Countries	162.0mm(6.4in) - 172.0mm(6.8in)

Hi Lux and 4 Runner 50's & 60's Series

2WD

All Countries	151.0mm(5.94in) - 156.0mm(6.14in)

4WD

All Countries	151.0mm(5.94in) - 156.0mm(6.14in)

Hi Lux and 4 Runner 80's, 90's, 100's, 11's, 12's and 13's Series
2WD
Australia and Other Countries

Regular Cab	147.5mm(5.81in) - 152.5mm(6.00in)
Double Cab	148.0mm(5.83in) - 153.0mm(6.02in)
Xtra Cab	148.0mm(5.83in) - 153.0mm(6.02in)

All Countries except Australia

Regular Cab	151.0mm(5.94in) - 156.0mm(6.14in)
Double Cab	151.0mm(5.94in) - 156.0mm(6.14in)
Xtra Cab	148.0mm(5.83in) - 153.0mm(6.02in)

4WD
Australia and Other Countries

Regular Cab	147.0mm(5.79in) - 152.0mm(5.98in)
Double Cab	147.0mm(5.79in) - 152.0mm(5.98in)
Xtra Cab and 4 Runner	
	145.0mm(5.71in) - 150.0mm(5.91in)

2. Adjust by loosening off stop switch nut.

3. Loosen the lock nut of the brake pedal push rod.

4. Adjust the push rod to give the correct specified clearance of the brake pedal to the floor as described above.

5. Tighten the lock nut of the pedal push rod.

6. Check pedal free play, if not as specified adjust.

a. Start engine, idle for 1 minute, turn off engine.

b. By hand, press brake down very slowly to measure free play.

1. Single booster, measure the distance the pedal moves until the pedal has resistance.

11. Tandem booster, measure the distance the pedal moves until the pedal has resistance a second time.

Specified Free Pedal Movement: 3-6mm (0.12-0.24in)

c. Adjust the pedal as described in steps Nos 2 to 5.

7. Adjust stop light switch and tighten the stop switch lock nut.

8. Check brake operation and stop light operation.

PARK BRAKE HANDLE & FRONT CABLE
Remove

1. Remove nuts securing yoke to relay rod and remove yoke.

2. Detach the inner cable from the control assembly, lift up the

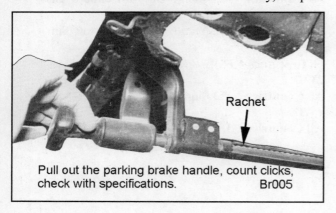

Pull out the parking brake handle, count clicks, check with specifications.   Br005

spring loaded retainer and remove handle.

3. Remove clip securing front cable to relay rod.

4. Remove mounting bolts and lift park brake lever upwards.

5. Disconnect electrical connector from park brake switch, if fitted.

Installation

1. Fit the handle into the assembly, connect the cable to the control assembly.

2. Install the cable pulley and handbrake warning light switch.

3. Refit the inner cable to the relay lever and fit spring.

4. Lubricate inside surface of yoke with Molybdenum Disulphide grease before installing cable in yoke.

5. Adjust park brake relay rod as previously described.

PARK BRAKE REAR CABLE
Remove

1. Raise vehicle and place on jack stands.

2. Loosen relay rod adjustment and remove cable from yoke.

3. Pull outer cable rearward out of front retaining clips and slip inner cable between clips and floor.

4. Pry open remaining clips sufficiently to unfasten cable.

5. Disconnect park brake cable from actuating lever and remove from backing plate support.

6. Remove rear brake drum and disconnect return spring from actuating lever.

7. Disconnect the parking brake cable from the actuating lever.

Installation

1. Lubricate inside surface of relay rod yoke with Molybdenum Disulphide grease before installing inner cable in yoke.

2. Connect park brake cable to actuating lever and to the backing plate support.

3. Connect return spring to actuating lever.

4. Install brake drum.

5. Fit the cable into the retaining clips of the floor and chassis.

6. Adjust park brake relay rod as previously described.

7. Ensure cable assembly is properly secured by retaining clips.

8. Lower vehicle from jack stands and test hand brake.

BRAKE HOSES
Remove

1. Raise vehicle and place on jack stands.

2. Mark position of wheel relative to hub and remove road wheel.

3. Thoroughly clean connections at each end of brake hose.

4. Disconnect brake pipe from hose and plug pipe.

5. Unfasten retainer from hose and withdraw hose from bracket if one is fitted.

6. Unfasten hose and grommet from bracket on suspension tower.

7. Unbolt and remove brake hose from calliper or drum.

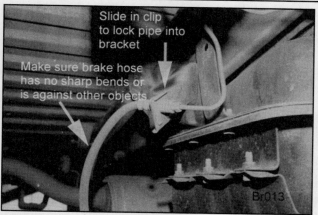

Install

1. Ensure brake hose and calliper mating surfaces are clean and free from burrs.

2. Reconnect brake tube/hose to drum/calliper and torque nut to specified torque.

Brake Hose or Tube Flange Nut Torque:
                  155kg-cm, 11 ft-lb, 15Nm

3. Clip hose and grommet into bracket if present.

4. Fit hose correctly into wheel arch bracket and install retainer.

5. Remove plug from brake pipe and reconnect to hose.

6. Check that hose is not twisted.

7. Bleed brake as previously described.

8. Install wheel and lower vehicle.

9. Tighten wheel nuts.

MAJOR SERVICE OPERATION

BRAKE PAD WEAR

If a visual inspection doesn't adequately determine condition of lining, a physical check will be necessary. To check amount of lining wear, remove brake pad assemblies ("Brake Pads"). Three thickness measurements with a micrometer should be taken across the centre of each pad, one reading at each end and one in the centre.

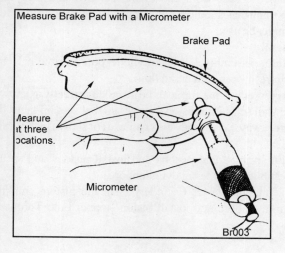

BRAKE ROUGHNESS

The most common cause of brake roughness (or chatter) with disc brake is excessive disc face run-out. This is easily checked with a dial indicator. If measurement is out of specification, disc must be re-surfaced or replaced.

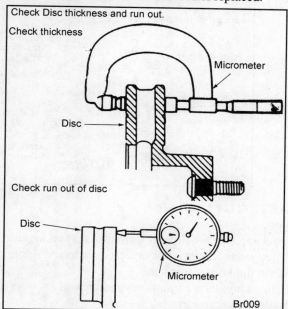

Other less prevalent causes of roughness can be the use of some type of non-standard lining material and extreme abrasion of the disc faces. Vehicles which stand unused for periods of time in areas of high humidity or salt air may incur rust on the disc which could cause a temporary brake surge and roughness. Normally, however, this condition should correct itself after a short period of usage. If rust is severe enough, roughness will not clear up and the disc must be resurfaced or replaced.

DISC BRAKE SERVICE PRECAUTIONS

- Grease and any foreign material must be kept off calliper assembly and surfaces of braking disc during service procedures. The braking disc and calliper should be handled, avoiding deformation of the disc and scratching or nicking of the pad linings.

- If inspection reveals square sectioned calliper piston seal is worn or damaged, it should be replaced immediately.

- During removal and installation of a wheel and tyre assembly, use care not to strike the calliper.

- Before vehicle is moved after any brake service work, obtain a firm brake pedal by using correct bleeding procedures.

- Dragging the brakes (common result of left foot application on vehicles with automatic transmission) should be avoided during vehicle operation.

- As brake pad lining wears, reservoir level will go down. If fluid has been added between relines, then reservoir overflow may occur when piston is pushed back into new lining position. Overflow can be avoided by removing a small amount of fluid from reservoir.

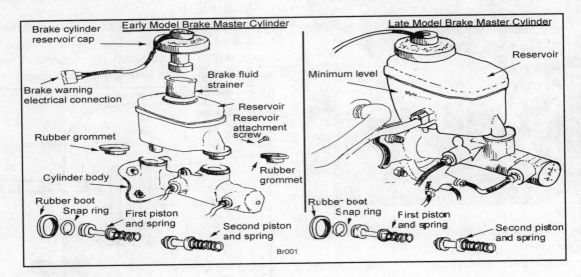

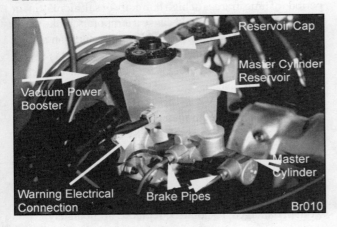

MASTER CYLINDER

Remove

1. Disconnect electrical connector from brake warning switch.
2. Disconnect brake lines from master cylinder and plug lines.
3. Drain fluid into a container.
4. Remove nuts securing master cylinder to brake booster and remove master cylinder.

* Do not disturb brake booster push rod. Do not depress brake pedal with master cylinder removed or reaction disc may become dislodged in booster.

Dismantle

1. Clean the outside of the master cylinder.
2. Remove reservoir cap and seal. Pour out and discard any fluid in reservoir.
3. Unscrew and remove nut and washer located inside plastic reservoir, later models remove reservoir attaching screw from outside the reservoir.
4. Remove reservoir and reservoir seals.
5. [Tandem Brake Master Cylinders] Push pistons in with a rod and remove the piston stopper bolt.
6. Remove rubber boot of the master cylinder bore.
7. Using suitable pliers, remove circlip from master cylinder body. Take care to ensure that piston does not spring out of bore when removing circlip.
8. Remove piston and spring for tandem master cylinders remove two pistons and two springs. If the second piston does not come out readily, tap the cylinder down into your hand which should move piston to the end of the bore.

Clean and Inspect

1. Wash master cylinder body, reservoir and cap in clean methylated spirits.
2. Wash all internal parts in brake fluid.
3. Check all recesses, openings and passages to ensure they are open and free of foreign matter.
4. Place all parts on a clean surface.
5. Inspect the master cylinder bore for signs of etching, pitting, scoring or rust. If in poor condition, replace the cylinder.
6. When replacing cups, plastic retainers may be removed by cutting with a sharp knife or razor blade, ensuring that piston is not damaged in anyway.

* Because of the special rubber compounds used for seals and cups, use a genuine kit which includes new rubber components. Ensure all sections of the cylinder are repaired.

* The operating pressures of the proportioning valve are stamped on the front end of the cylinder and it is most important that, should a cylinder need replacing, an identical cylinder be used.

Assembly

* Before assembly, lubricate cylinder bore and internal parts with fresh, specified brake fluid.

* It is essential that cup seals be installed correctly as shown.

1. Install seals into piston grooves so that seal lip faces the correct way. i.e. the way they came off or shown in the brake kit.
2. Fit springs onto pistons and install pistons and spring assemblies into master cylinder bore.
3. [Tandem Master Cylinder] Push the pistons into the bottom of bore and install piston stopper bolt. Torque to

310

specification.
Piston Stopper Bolt Specified Torque:
            100kg-cm, 7 ft-lb, 10Nm
4. Depress piston and install circlip.
5. Install rubber boot to master cylinder.
6. Install reservoir, washer and mounting nut or external attaching screw. Torque to specification.
Reservoir Internal Mounting Nut Torque:
            250kg-cm, 18 ft-lb, 250Nm
Reservoir External Mounting Screw Torque:
            100kg-cm, 7 ft-lb, 10Nm
7. Install cap seal and cap.

Install
1. Install master cylinder assembly on brake booster taking care not to disturb brake booster push rod. Torque master cylinder nuts.
Master Cylinder Attaching Nuts
            130kg-cm, 9 ft-lb, 13Nm
2. Unplug brake lines and master cylinder and securely reconnect brake lines to master cylinder. Tighten to specification.
Brake Hose or Tube Flange Nut Torque:
            155kg-cm, 11 ft-lb, 15Nm
3. Reconnect electrical connector to brake warning switch.
4. Fill the master cylinder with fresh, recommended brake fluid and bleed brake system as previously described.

BRAKE BOOSTER
GENERAL INFORMATION
The Brake Booster is fitted between the brake pedal and brake master cylinder and supplements the driver's pedal effort. It derives power from permanent use of vacuum and controlled application of atmospheric pressure.
The booster consists of a vacuum chamber divided by a diaphragm to the brake pedal to control the application and release, and a push rod to apply the developed force to the brake cylinder which is bolted to the front of the booster.
In the case of engine failure and consequent loss of engine vacuum, two application of brakes are possible by using vacuum retained in the power unit. In case of complete vacuum loss, brakes can be applied in the conventional manner, although more effort is required due to loss of power assistance.
Removal
1. Remove vacuum hose from brake booster body.
2. Remove master cylinder as previously described.
Do not depress brake pedal with master cylinder removed or reaction disc may become dislodged in booster.
3. Remove push rod retaining clip, push rod and washers from brake pedal.
4. Remove brake booster assembly retaining nuts from inside the vehicle firewall.
5. Withdraw booster from engine compartment.
Installation

1. Install booster to firewall in the engine compartment, install the attaching nuts from inside the vehicle and tighten to specification.
Booster Attaching Nuts:
            130kg-cm, 9 ft-lb, 13Nm
2. Lubricate brake pedal and push rod component bearing surfaces with Molybdenum Disulphide grease.
3. Install brake booster hose ensure brake booster hose is routed correctly.
4. Install master cylinder assembly on brake booster as previously described taking care not to disturb brake booster push rod. Torque master cylinder nuts.
Master Cylinder Attaching Nuts
            130kg-cm, 9 ft-lb, 13Nm

BRAKE DRUMS & CALLIPERS
When servicing wheel brake parts, do not create dust by grinding or sanding brake linings, or by cleaning wheel brake parts with a dry brush or with compressed air. Many wheel brake parts contain asbestos fibres which can become airborne if dust is created during servicing. Breathing dust containing asbestos fibres is to be avoided at all costs. Wash down components that could be contaminated with these fibres using a water based solution that can be purchased. This will help stop airborne fibres.

FRONT DRUM BRAKES
Remove
1. Raise front of vehicle and place on jack stands.
2. Remove wheel and thoroughly clean around brake hose to pipe connection.
3. Disconnect brake pipe from brake hose and plug pipe.
4. Unfasten brake hose retainer and withdraw brake hose from shield bracket. Plug brake hose.
5. Remove the drum from the axle, if the drum will not come off, pry the rubber covers from the backing plate. Insert a narrow screwdriver through the hole in the backing plate, and push the adjusting lever in away from the adjusting screw. While holding the adjusting lever away from the adjusting screw, back off the adjusting screw with the brake adjusting tool.
6. With drum off, take note of the colour and the location of springs. Install a clamp over the ends of the brake cylinder or cylinders. Remove the secondary shoe to anchor spring with a screw driver or similar. With the same tool remove the primary shoe to anchor spring. Remove shoe and hold-down springs.
Remove brake shoes, adjusting screws, socket and automatic adjustment parts.
8. Remove the brake cylinders.
9. Remove the brake cylinder pistons, it may be necessary to use compressed air into the brake pipe inlet hole and force the piston out of the brake cylinder.

Clean and Inspect

1. Clean all metal parts thoroughly with methylated spirits. Clean rubber parts with brake fluid only. Use clean, dry compressed air to dry parts.

2. Examine bore and piston carefully for signs of damage, abrasion, scuffing or corrosion replace if necessary. If the bore is unserviceable, a new housing must be fitted. Light scuffing in the bore or on the piston can be removed with 600 grade wet and dry paper soaked in brake fluid.

3. Blow through port in bleed screw with compressed air.

4. Inspect the brake shoe lining, if broken away from shoe or not within specified thickness replace the lining / lining and shoe.

Brake Shoe Lining Minimum Thickness:
1.0mm (0.039in)

5. Inspect drum for corrosion or gouge marks, machine drum if necessary to obtain a good surface.

Install

1. Lubricate cylinder bore and piston with specified brake fluid.

2. Install the rubber seal to the piston.

3. Install piston into cylinder.

4. Install rubber boot onto the cylinder and into grove in brake cylinder. Ensure boot flange is squarely and firmly seated in groove.

5. Install brake cylinder to back plate tighten bolts to specification.

Brake Cylinder Bolts Torque
185kg-cm, 13 ft-lb, 18Nm

6. Install brake fluid hose to the cylinder and tighten to specification.

Brake Hose Specified Torque:
155kg-cm, 11 ft-lb, 15Nm

7. At the points where the brake shoes contact the backing plate apply a light coating of high temperature grease.

8. Install the adjusting nuts to the wheel cylinders. The adjusting nuts and screw must be fitted to the correct brake side of the vehicle, to ensure this the adjusting nuts are colour coded.

Yellow adjusting nuts are fitted to the right side front wheel. These have a right hand thread.

White adjusting nuts are fitted to the left side front wheel. These have a left hand thread.

9. Position the brake shoes on the backing plate and secure the shoes with the hold down springs. Ensure the shoes are correctly located into the end of the adjusting nuts.

10. Install the return springs to the brake shoes.

11. Turn the adjusting screw into the adjusting pivot nut to the limit of the threads and then back off half a turn. Apply high-temperature grease to the threads and socket end of the adjusting screw. Turn the adjusting screws in to enable the brake drum to be fitted.

12. Fit the brake drum, do not damage the brake lining while fitting the brake drum.

13. Adjust brakes as described below.

14. Bleed the brake system as described in this manual.

15. Fit the wheel onto the wheel studs, tighten the nuts.

ADJUSTMENT

* Always adjust both front brakes at the same time.

1. Raise front of vehicle and place on jack stands.

2. Remove wheel and thoroughly clean around the brake adjustment rubber plugs.

3. Remove the adjusting hole cover from the backing plate.

4. Working from the backing plate side, turn the adjusting screw upward to expand the shoes.

5. Expand the shoes until a drag is felt when the drum is rotated

6. Replace the adjusting hole cover from the backing plate.

7. Install wheel and wheel nuts , tighten the nuts.

8. Test drive vehicle.

REAR DRUM BRAKES

* 2 WD and 4 WD vehicles have different designed rear brake, however the principles are the same.

Remove

1. Raise rear of vehicle and place on jack stands.

2. Remove wheel and thoroughly clean around brake hose to pipe connection.

3. Slacken off park brake cable adjustment at relay rod.

4. Disconnect brake pipe from brake wheel cylinder and plug pipe.

5. Remove the drum from the axle, if the drum will not come off, pry the rubber cover from the backing plate. Insert a narrow screwdriver through the hole in the backing plate, and push the adjusting lever in away (down) from the adjusting screw. While holding the adjusting lever away from the adjusting screw, back off the adjusting screw with the brake adjusting tool.

6. With drum off, take note of the colour and the location of

springs. Remove the top spring from the brake shoes. Remove the lower spring from the brakes shoes.

7. Install a clamp over the ends of the brake cylinder.

8. Remove the secondary shoe to anchor spring with a screw driver or similar. With the same tool remove the primary shoe to anchor spring and unhook the cable eye from the anchor pin. Remove and shoe hold-down springs.

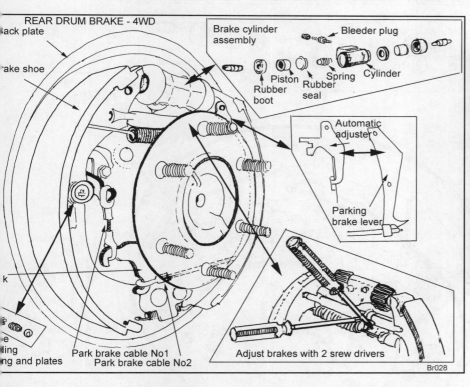

REAR DRUM BRAKE - 4WD
Back plate
Brake shoe
Brake cylinder assembly
Bleeder plug
Piston
Rubber boot
Rubber seal
Spring
Cylinder
Automatic adjuster
Parking brake lever
Park brake cable No1
Park brake cable No2
Adjust brakes with 2 srew drivers
Br028

Brake Shoe & Lining
Parking Brake Bellcrank
Parking Brake Cable
Br015

9. Remove brake shoes, adjusting screw, socket and automatic adjustment parts.

10. Remove the parking brake lever and clip. Disconnect the parking brake cable from the park brake lever.

11. 4WD models for 80's, 90's 10's & 11's series remove the

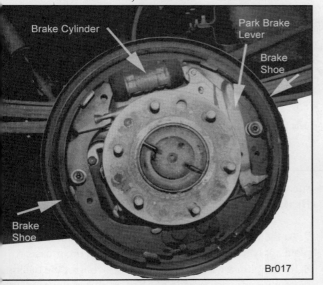

Brake Cylinder
Park Brake Lever
Brake Shoe
Brake Shoe
Br017

parking brake bell crank, clip and spring.

12. Remove the brake cylinder.

13. Remove the brake cylinder pistons, it may be necessary to use compressed air into the brake pipe inlet hole and force the pistons out of the brake cylinder.

Clean and Inspect

1. Clean all metal parts thoroughly with methylated spirits. Clean rubber parts with brake fluid only. Use clean, dry compressed air to dry parts.

2. Examine bore and piston carefully for signs of damage, abrasion, scuffing or corrosion replace if necessary. If the bore is unserviceable, a new housing must be fitted. Light scuffing in the bore or on the piston can be removed with 600 grade wet and dry paper soaked in brake fluid.

3. Blow through port in bleed screw with compressed air.

4. Inspect the brake shoe lining, if broken away from shoe or not within specified thickness replace the lining / lining and shoe.

Brake Shoe Lining Minimum Thickness:
1.0mm (0.039in)

Check Drum Surface for groove, machine if damaged.
Br018

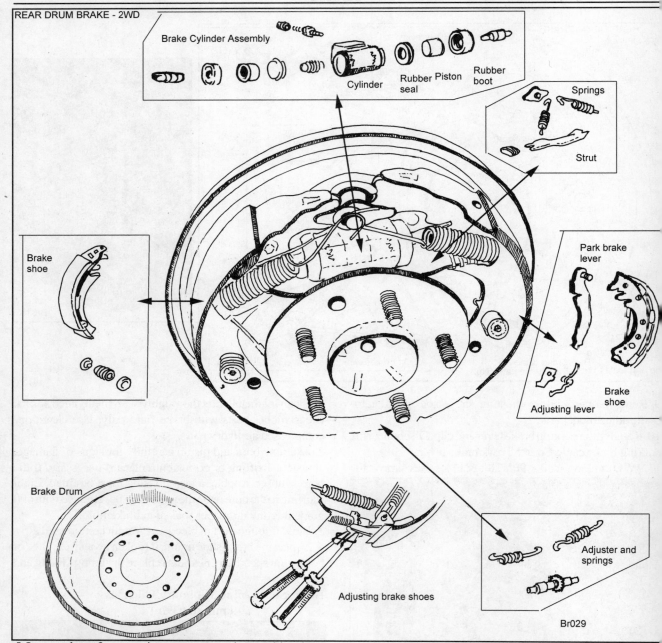

REAR DRUM BRAKE - 2WD

Brake Cylinder Assembly

Cylinder

Rubber Piston seal Piston

Rubber boot

Springs

Strut

Brake shoe

Park brake lever

Adjusting lever

Brake shoe

Brake Drum

Adjuster and springs

Adjusting brake shoes

Br029

5. Inspect drum for corrosion or gouge marks, machine drum if necessary to obtain a good surface.

Install

1. Lubricate cylinder bore and pistons with specified brake fluid.

2. Install the rubber seal to the pistons.

3. Install piston into cylinder.

4. Install rubber boots onto the cylinder and into grove in brake cylinder. Ensure boot flange is squarely and firmly seated in groove.

5. Install brake cylinder to back plate tighten bolts to specification.

Brake Cylinder Bolts Torque
100kg-cm, 7 ft-lb, 10Nm

6. Install brake fluid pipe to the cylinder and tighten to specification.

Brake Pipe Specified Torque:
155kg-cm, 11 ft-lb, 15Nm

7. At the points where the brake shoes contact the backing plate apply a light coating of high temperature grease.

8. At the points where the brake shoes contact the backing plate, shoe adjuster threads, and bell crank parts, apply a light coating of high temperature grease.

9. 4WD models for 80's, to 13's series install the parking brake bell crank, clip and spring to the bell crank bracket. Install the bell crank bracket to the backing plate, tighten to specification.

Parking Brake Bell Crank Bracket Bolt Torque:
130kg-cm, 9 ft-lb, 13Nm

10. Assemble the parking brake lever to the secondary shoe and secure with the spring, before installing the brake shoes

11. Install the shoe adjuster to the front shoe. The adjuster screw must be fitted to the correct brake shoe.

12. Position the brake shoes on the backing plate and secure the assembly with the hold down springs. Ensure the shoes are correctly located into the end of the adjuster, ends of the piston shafts and lower hinge points.

13. Install the automatic brake adjuster and clip to the brake shoe, if not installed. Position the automatic adjuster on the shoe adjuster.

14. Install the return spring to the shoes.

15. 4WD models for 80's, to 13's series adjust the bell crank, pulling out the bell crank lever, and adjust the adjusting bolt so there is no slack in the bell crank movement. Install the bell crank spring.

16. Fit the brake drum, do not damage the brake lining while fitting the brake drum.

17. Adjust brakes as described below.

18. Bleed the brake system as described in this manual.

19. Fit the wheel onto the wheel studs, tighten to specification.

Road Wheel Stud Specification: **100-125Nm**

ADJUSTMENT

* Always adjust both front brakes at the same time.

1. Raise front of vehicle and place on jack stands.

2. Remove wheel and thoroughly clean around the brake adjustment rubber plugs.

3. Remove the adjusting hole cover from the backing plate.

4. Working from the backing plate side, turn the adjusting screw upward to expand the shoes.

5. Expand the shoes until a drag is felt when the drum is rotated

6. Replace the adjusting hole cover from the backing plate.

7. Install wheel and wheel nuts , tighten to specification.

Road Wheel Stud Specification: **100-125Nm**

8. Test drive vehicle.

DISC BRAKE ASSEMBLIES

Disc Brake Model - K [30's & 40's Series]

This procedure refers to front brake pads and front discs.

1. Remove master cylinder cap. Loosen front left wheel brake line connection at master cylinder and allow fluid to bleed down into a container until master cylinder reservoir is approximately 1/3 full. Retighten the connection and refit master cylinder cap.

* Do not remove the brake line or empty the reservoir or it will be necessary to bleed the system.

* Discard the fluid removed.

* Removal of fluid from the reservoir is necessary to prevent reservoir overflow when calliper piston is pushed back in its bore during pad replacement.

* Brake fluid is extremely damaging to paint work.

2. Raise front of vehicle and place on jack stands.

3. Mark relationship of wheel to hub. Remove wheel. Remove the top and lower bolt of the calliper, this will allow you to remove the anti rattle spring, anti squeal shim, support plate and guide plate.

4. Remove the 2 pads.

5. Measure used disc pad wear, replace if not within specification.

Lining Minimum Thickness: **1.0 mm(0.039in)**

6. Remove the cylinder by removing the two attaching bolts.

7. Inspect condition of brake disc, replace if not within specification.

Disc Model - K - 30's & 40's Series Wear specifications

Thickness (New):   **20.0 mm(0.787in)**

Min. Thickness Refaced (overall):   **19.0 mm(0.75in)**

Max. Runout: **0.15 mm(0.006in)**

8. Remove the anchor plate attaching bolts.

9. Remove the front wheel and disc, by removing front wheel bearing cover, then remove split pin and spindle nut.

10. Remove hub/brake disc from knuckle, making sure outer bearing does not fall from hub. Keep dust or mud from falling into or around the bearing.

11. Dismantle Disc Cylinder

a. Remove rubber boot from cylinder.

b. Pack a piece of wood between calliper piston and opposite legs on housing and apply air pressure at brake hose inlet port to eject piston.

Caution: Do not have your fingers inside of the calliper when removing the piston by this method.

c. Remove seal from bore, taking care not to damage bore or seal locating groove.

d. Remove bleeder screw.

Disc Brake Model - S16 [30's & 40's Series]

This procedure refers to front brake pads and front discs.

1. Remove master cylinder cap. Loosen front left wheel brake line connection at master cylinder and allow fluid to bleed down into a container until master cylinder reservoir is approximately 1/3 full. Retighten the connection and refit master cylinder cap.

* Do not remove the brake line or empty the reservoir or it will be necessary to bleed the system.

* Discard the fluid removed.

* Removal of fluid from the reservoir is necessary to prevent reservoir overflow when calliper piston is pushed back in its bore during pad replacement.

* Brake fluid is extremely damaging to paint work.

2. Raise front of vehicle and place on jack stands.

3. Mark relationship of wheel to hub. Remove wheel.

4. Remove the cylinder by removing the two attaching bolts.

5. Remove the clip on the vehicle outside of the calliper, this will allow you to remove the 2 pins.

6. Remove the anti rattle spring.

7. Remove the 2 pads and anti squeal shims.

8. Measure used disc pad wear, replace if not within specification.

Lining Minimum Thickness: **1.0 mm(0.039in)**

9. Using a steel bar or screw driver, force the piston back from the disc.

10. Inspect condition of brake disc, replace if not within specification.

Disc Model S 16 Wear specifications

Thickness (New):   **12.5 mm(0.49in)**

Min. Thickness Refaced (overall): 11.5 mm(0.45in)

Max. Runout: **0.15 mm(0.0059in)**

11. Remove the calliper attaching bolts and calliper.

12. Remove the front wheel and disc, by removing front wheel bearing cover, then remove split pin and spindle nut.

13. Remove hub/brake disc from knuckle, making sure outer bearing does not fall from hub. Keep dust or mud from falling into or around the bearing.

14. Dismantle Disc Cylinder

a. Remove rubber boot from cylinder.

b. Pack a piece of wood between calliper piston and opposite legs on housing and apply air pressure at brake hose inlet port to eject piston.

Caution: Do not have your fingers inside of the calliper when removing the piston by this method.

c. Remove seal from bore, taking care not to damage bore or seal locating groove.

d. Remove bleeder screw.

Disc Brake Model - S12+8 [30's, 40's, 4WD] [50's & 60's 4WD] Series

This procedure refers to front brake pads and front discs.

1. Remove master cylinder cap. Loosen front left wheel brake line connection at master cylinder and allow fluid to bleed down into a container until master cylinder reservoir is approximately 1/3 full. Retighten the connection and refit master cylinder cap.

* Do not remove the brake line or empty the reservoir or it will be necessary to bleed the system.

* Discard the fluid removed.

* Removal of fluid from the reservoir is necessary to prevent reservoir overflow when calliper piston is pushed back in its bore during pad replacement.

* Brake fluid is extremely damaging to paint work.

2. Raise front of vehicle and place on jack stands.

3. Mark relationship of wheel to hub. Remove wheel.

4. Remove the clip on the vehicle inside of the calliper, this will allow you to move the 2 pins.

5. Remove the anti rattle spring.

6. Remove the 2 pads.

7. Measure used disc pad wear, replace if not within specification.

Lining Minimum Thickness: **1.0 mm (0.039in)**

8. Using a steel bar or screw driver, force the piston (4 pistons one at a time) back from the disc.

9. Inspect condition of brake disc, replace if not within specification.

Disc Model S 12+8 Wear specifications

Thickness (New):   **12.5 mm(0.497in)**

Min. Thickness Refaced (overall): 11.5 mm(0.45in)

Max. Runout: **0.15 mm(0.0059in)**

10. Remove the calliper attaching bolts, remove the calliper.

11. Remove the front wheel and disc, by removing front wheel bearing cover, then remove split pin and spindle nut.

12. Remove hub/brake disc from knuckle, making sure outer bearing does not fall from hub. Keep dust or mud from falling into or around the bearing.

13. Dismantle Disc Cylinder.

a. Remove the 4 rubber boot rings and 4 rubber boots from cylinder.

b. Pack a piece of wood between calliper piston and opposite legs on housing and apply air pressure at brake hose inlet port to eject piston.

Caution: Do not have your fingers inside of the calliper when removing the piston by this method.

c. Remove seal from bores, taking care not to damage bore or seal locating groove.

d. Remove bleeder screw.

Disc Brake Model FS 17 [50's & 60's 2WD] Series

Remove

This procedure refers to front brake pads and front discs.

1. Remove master cylinder cap. Loosen front left wheel brake line connection at master cylinder and allow fluid to bleed down into a container until master cylinder reservoir is approximately 1/3 full. Retighten the connection and refit master cylinder cap.

* Do not remove the brake line or empty the reservoir or it will be necessary to bleed the system.

* Discard the fluid removed.

* Removal of fluid from the reservoir is necessary to prevent reservoir overflow when calliper piston is pushed back in its bore during pad replacement.

* Brake fluid is extremely damaging to paint work.

2. Raise front of vehicle and place on jack stands.

3. Mark relationship of wheel to hub. Remove wheel.

4. Remove the cylinder by removing the two attaching bolts.

5. Remove the 2 brake pads, anti squeal shim, 2 brake pad wear plates and 4 brake pad support plates and calliper cylinder.

6. Measure used disc pad wear, replace if not within specification.

Lining New Thickness: **10.0mm(0.393in)**

Lining Minimum Thickness: **1.0 mm(0.039in)**

7. Inspect condition of brake disc, replace if not within specification.

Disc Model FS 17 Wear specifications

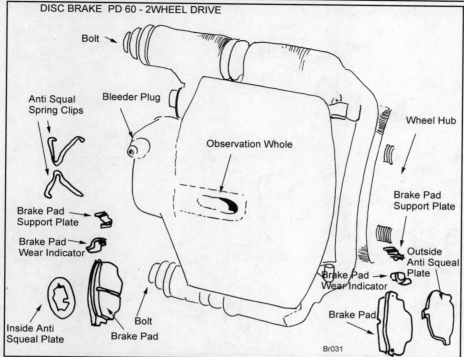

DISC BRAKE PD 60 - 2WHEEL DRIVE

Bolt

Anti Squal Spring Clips

Bleeder Plug

Observation Whole

Wheel Hub

Brake Pad Support Plate

Brake Pad Support Plate

Brake Pad Wear Indicator

Outside Anti Squeal Plate

Brake Pad Wear Indicator

Inside Anti Squeal Plate

Bolt

Brake Pad

Brake Pad

Br031

Thickness (New): 22.0 mm(0.866in)
Min. Thickness Refaced (overall): 21.0 mm(0.827in)
Max. Runout: 0.15 mm(0.0059in)

8. Remove the calliper plate attaching bolts and calliper.

9. Remove the front wheel and disc, by removing front wheel bearing cover, then remove split pin and spindle nut.

10. Remove hub/brake disc from knuckle, making sure outer bearing does not fall from hub. Keep dust or mud from falling into or around the bearing.

11. Dismantle Disc Cylinder.

a. Withdraw 2 bushes and pin boots from cylinder.

b. Remove clip and rubber boot from cylinder.

c. Pack a piece of wood between calliper piston and opposite legs on housing and apply air pressure at brake hose inlet port to eject piston.

Caution: Do not have your fingers inside of the calliper when removing the piston by this method.

d. Remove seal from bore, taking care not to damage bore or seal locating groove.

e. Remove bleeder screw.

Disc Brake Model PD 60 [50's 60's 2WD] [80's 90's 10's & 11's 2WD] Series
Remove

This procedure refers to front brake pads and front discs.

1. Remove master cylinder cap. Loosen front left wheel brake line connection at master cylinder and allow fluid to bleed down into a container until master cylinder reservoir is approximately 1/3 full. Retighten the connection and refit master cylinder cap.

* Do not remove the brake line or empty the reservoir or it will be necessary to bleed the system.

* Discard the fluid removed.

* Removal of fluid from the reservoir is necessary to prevent reservoir overflow when calliper piston is pushed back in its bore during pad replacement.

* Brake fluid is extremely damaging to paint work.

2. Raise front of vehicle and place on jack stands.

3. Mark relationship of wheel to hub. Remove wheel.

4. Remove the cylinder by removing the two attaching bolts.

5. Remove the 2 anti squeal springs, 2 brake pads, 2 anti squeal shims, 2 brake pad wear plates and 4 brake pad support plates and calliper cylinder.

6. Measure used disc pad wear, replace if not within specification.

Lining New Thickness: 9.5mm (0.374in)
Lining Minimum Thickness: 1.0 mm(0.039in)

7. Inspect condition of brake disc, replace if not within specification.

Disc Model PD 60 Wear specifications
Thickness (New): 25.0 mm(0.984in)
Min. Thickness Refaced (overall): 23.0 mm(0.906in)
Max. Runout: 0.09 mm(0.0035in)

8. Remove the anchor plate attaching bolts.

9. Remove the front wheel and disc. Remove front wheel bearing cover, then remove split pin and spindle nut.

10. Remove hub/brake disc from knuckle, making sure outer bearing does not fall from hub. Keep dust or mud from falling into or around the bearing.

11. Dismantle Disc Cylinder

a. Withdraw 2 bushes, 4 dust boots and 2 collars from cylinder.

b. Remove clip and rubber boot from cylinder.

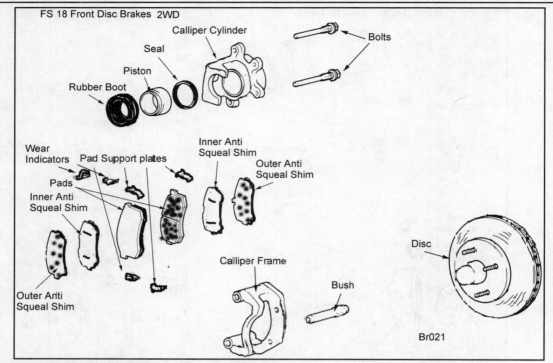

FS 18 Front Disc Brakes 2WD

Calliper Cylinder
Seal
Piston
Rubber Boot
Bolts
Wear Indicators
Pad Support plates
Inner Anti Squeal Shim
Outer Anti Squeal Shim
Pads
Inner Anti Squeal Shim
Calliper Frame
Disc
Bush
Outer Anti Squeal Shim
Br021

c. Pack a piece of wood between calliper piston and opposite legs on housing and apply air pressure at brake hose inlet port to eject piston.

Caution: Do not have your fingers inside of the calliper when removing the piston by this method.

d. Remove seal from bore, taking care not to damage bore or seal locating groove.

e. Remove bleeder screw.

Disc Brake Model FS 18 [80's, 90's 10's and 11's 2WD] Series
Remove

This procedure refers to front brake pads and front discs.

1. Remove master cylinder cap. Loosen front left wheel brake line connection at master cylinder and allow fluid to bleed down into a container until master cylinder reservoir is approximately 1/3 full. Retighten the connection and refit master cylinder cap.

* Do not remove the brake line or empty the reservoir or it will be necessary to bleed the system.

* Discard the fluid removed.

* Removal of fluid from the reservoir is necessary to prevent reservoir overflow when calliper piston is pushed back in its bore during pad replacement.

* Brake fluid is extremely damaging to paint work.

2. Raise front of vehicle and place on jack stands.

3. Mark relationship of wheel to hub. Remove wheel.

4. Remove the cylinder by removing the two attaching bolts.

5. Remove the 2 brake pads, 4 anti squeal shims, 2 brake pad wear plates and 4 brake pad support plates and calliper cylinder.

6. Measure used disc pad wear, replace if not within specifi-

cation.

Lining New Thickness: 10.0mm(0.393in)
Lining Minimum Thickness: 1.0 mm(0.039in)

7. Inspect condition of brake disc, replace if not within specification.

Disc Model FS 18 Wear specifications
Thickness (New):   22.0 mm(0.866in)
Min. Thickness Refaced (overall): 20.0 mm(0.787in)
Max. Runout: 0.09 mm(0.0035in)

8. Remove the anchor plate attaching bolts.

9. Remove the front wheel and disc, by removing front wheel bearing cover, then remove split pin and spindle nut.

10. Remove hub/brake disc from knuckle, making sure outer bearing does not fall from hub. Keep dust or mud from falling into or around the bearing.

11. Dismantle Disc Cylinder.

a. Withdraw 2 bushes, and pin boots from cylinder.

b. Remove clip and rubber boot from cylinder.

c. Pack a piece of wood between calliper piston and opposite legs on housing and apply air pressure at brake hose inlet port to eject piston.

Caution: Do not have your fingers inside of the calliper when removing the piston by this method.

d. Remove seal from bore, taking care not to damage bore or seal locating groove.

e. Remove bleeder screw.

Disc Brake Model - S12+12 [80's, 90's, 10's, 12's & 13's 4WD] Series

This procedure refers to front brake pads and front discs.

1. Remove master cylinder cap. Loosen front left wheel brake line connection at master cylinder and allow fluid to

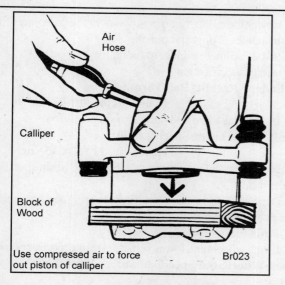

Use compressed air to force
out piston of calliper   Br023

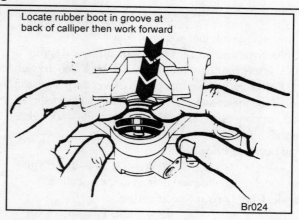

Locate rubber boot in groove at
back of calliper then work forward

Br024

bleed down into a container until master cylinder reservoir is approximately 1/3 full. Retighten the connection and refit master cylinder cap.

* Do not remove the brake line or empty the reservoir or it will be necessary to bleed the system.

* Discard the fluid removed.

* Removal of fluid from the reservoir is necessary to prevent reservoir overflow when calliper piston is pushed back in its bore during pad replacement.

* Brake fluid is extremely damaging to paint work.

2. Raise front of vehicle and place on jack stands.

3. Mark relationship of wheel to hub. Remove wheel.

4. Remove the clip on the vehicle inside of the calliper, this will allow you to move the 2 pins.

5. Remove the anti rattle spring.

6. Remove the 2 pads and anti squeal shims.

7. Measure used disc pad wear, replace if not within specification.

Lining New Thickness: **9.5mm (0.374in)**
Lining Minimum Thickness: **1.0 mm(0.039in)**

8. Using a steel bar or screw driver, force the piston (2 pistons one at a time) back from the disc.

9. Inspect condition of brake disc, replace if not within specification.

Disc Model S 12+12 Wear specifications

Thickness (New):   **20.0 mm(0.787in)**
Min. Thickness Refaced (overall):   **18.0 mm(0.709in)**
Max. Runout: Ind. Front Susp.   **0.09 mm(0.0035in)**
Max. Runout: Leaf Spring Susp.   **0.15 mm(0.0059in)**

10. Remove the anchor plate attaching bolts.

11. Remove the front wheel and disc, by

2WD: Remove front wheel bearing cover, then remove split pin and spindle nut.

4WD: Remove free wheeling hub as described in Front Suspension chapter. Remove nut lock washer and axle nut.

12. Remove hub/brake disc from knuckle, making sure outer bearing does not fall from hub. Keep dust or mud from falling into or around the bearing.

13. Dismantle Disc Cylinder

a. Pack a piece of wood between calliper pistons and opposite legs on housing and apply air pressure at brake hose inlet port to eject pistons.

Caution: Do not have your fingers inside of the calliper when removing the piston by this method.

b. Remove seal from bore, taking care not to damage bore or seal locating groove.

c. Remove bleeder screw.

Disc Brake Model - K [30's & 40's Series]
Install

Disc

1. Replace hub/brake disc to knuckle, making sure outer bearing does not fall from hub.

2. Install wheel bearing nut. Before installing split pin or nut lock washer, adjust wheel bearings as outlined under FRONT WHEEL BEARING ADJUSTMENT Section in Front Suspension Chapter.

3. Replace bearing nut split pin and front wheel bearing cover.

4. Replace torque plate. Replace brake calliper torque plate retaining bolts and washers.

Disc Brake Torque Plate Bolts:
           650 kg-cm, 47ft-lb 64Nm

Calliper Cylinder

1. Apply disc brake grease to rubber components and piston.

2. Lubricate cylinder bore and piston with specified brake fluid.

3. Fit new seal into inner groove of bore. Ensure seal is not twisted and is fully seated in groove.

4. Install piston boot over end of piston.

5. Position piston into calliper housing, seating boot into grove in calliper bore. Ensure boot flange is squarely and firmly seated in groove.

6. Push piston squarely into bore by hand until fully seated. Ensure piston boot is fully seated in piston and calliper bore grooves.

7. Install calliper cylinder to mounting bracket.

Tighten to specification.

Cylinder Attaching Bolt Torque:

500kg-cm, 30 ft-lb, 50Nm

8. Install the pads into position.

9. Install the anti squeal shims and anti squeal spring.

10. Use a G clamp to force the piston back into the calliper.

11. Lower the calliper into position over the pads carefully, install the upper and lower guide plate, support spring and pad support plate. Install retaining bolts and tighten to specification.

Pad Support Plate bolt:

500kg-cm, 30 ft-lb, 50Nm

12. Install brake line and tighten to specification.

Brake Line Torque Specification:

155kg-cm, 11 ft-lb, 15Nm

13. Fill master cylinder to correct level with fresh, specified brake fluid.

14. Depress brake pedal several times to bring pad assemblies into position against disc.

15. Refill master cylinder if necessary.

16. Install wheels and lower vehicle. Torque road wheel nut.

Road Wheel Stud Specification: 100-125Nm

Disc Brake Model - S16 [30's & 40's Series]
Install

Disc

1. Replace hub/brake disc to knuckle, making sure outer bearing does not fall from hub.

2. Install wheel bearing nut. Before installing split pin or nut lock washer, adjust wheel bearings as outlined under FRONT WHEEL BEARING ADJUSTMENT Section in Front Suspension Chapter.

3. Replace bearing nut split pin and front wheel bearing cover.

4. Replace torque plate. Replace brake calliper torque plate retaining bolts and washers.

Disc Brake Torque Plate Bolts:

650 kg-cm, 47ft-lb 64Nm

Calliper Cylinder

1. Apply disc brake grease to rubber components and piston.

2. Lubricate cylinder bore and piston with specified brake fluid.

3. Fit new seal into inner groove of bore. Ensure seal is not twisted and is fully seated in groove.

4. Install piston boot over end of piston.

5. Position pistons into calliper housing, seating boot into grove in calliper bore. Ensure boot flange is squarely and firmly seated in groove.

6. Push pistons squarely into bore by hand until fully seated. Ensure piston boot is fully seated in piston and calliper bore grooves.

7. Install the 2 anti squeal shims, apply brake grease to anti squeal shims only, and new pads.

* Do not get grease on the pad lining.

8. Install the anti rattle spring.

9. Install the pads into position.

10. Use a G clamp to force the piston back into the calliper.

11. Lower the calliper into position over the pads carefully

12. Install the 2 pins and pin clip.

13. Install calliper cylinder to mounting bracket. Tighten to specification.

Cylinder Attaching Bolt Torque:

1,100 kg-cm, 80ft-lb 108Nm

14. Install brake line and tighten to specification.

Brake Line Torque Specification:

155kg-cm, 11 ft-lb, 15Nm

15. Fill master cylinder to correct level with fresh, specified brake fluid.

16. Depress brake pedal several times to bring pad assemblies into position against disc.

17. Refill master cylinder if necessary.

18. Install wheels and lower vehicle. Torque road wheel nut.

Road Wheel Stud Specification: 100-125Nm

Disc Brake Model - S12+8 [30's, 40's, 4WD] [50's & 60's 4WD] Series
Install

Disc

1. Replace hub/brake disc to knuckle, making sure outer bearing does not fall from hub.

2. Install wheel bearing nut. Before installing split pin or nut lock washer, adjust wheel bearings as outlined under FRONT WHEEL BEARING ADJUSTMENT Section in Front Suspension Chapter.

3. Replace bearing nut split pin and front wheel bearing cover.

4. Replace torque plate. Replace brake calliper torque plate retaining bolts and washers.

Disc Brake Torque Plate Bolts:

2WD	**650 kg-cm, 47ft-lb 64Nm**
4WD	**1,100 kg-cm, 80ft-lb 108Nm**

Calliper Cylinder

1. Apply disc brake grease to rubber components and piston.

2. Lubricate cylinder bores and pistons with specified brake fluid.

3. Fit new seal into inner groove of bores. Ensure seal is not twisted and is fully seated in groove.

4. Install piston boot over end of pistons.

5. Position piston into calliper housing, seating boot into grove in calliper bore. Ensure boot flange is squarely and firmly seated in groove.

6. Push piston squarely into bore by hand until fully seated. Ensure piston boot is fully seated in piston and calliper bore grooves.

7. Install calliper cylinder and calliper cylinder attaching bolts, tighten to specification.

Calliper Cylinder Attaching bolts:

900kg-cm, 65 ft-lb, 88Nm

8. Install the new pads.

9. In stall the anti rattle spring.

10. Install the 2 pins and pin clip.

11. Install brake line and tighten to specification.

320

Brake Line Torque Specification:
155kg-cm, 11 ft-lb, 15Nm

12. Fill master cylinder to correct level with fresh, specified brake fluid.

13. Depress brake pedal several times to bring pad assemblies into position against disc.

14. Refill master cylinder if necessary.

15. Install wheels and lower vehicle. Torque road wheel nut.

Road Wheel Stud Specification: **100-125Nm**

Disc Brake Model FS 17 [50's & 60's 2WD] Series
Install
Disc

1. Replace hub/brake disc to knuckle, making sure outer bearing does not fall from hub.

2. Install wheel bearing nut. Before installing split pin or nut lock washer, adjust wheel bearings as outlined under FRONT WHEEL BEARING ADJUSTMENT Section in Front Suspension Chapter.

3. Replace bearing nut split pin and front wheel bearing cover.

4. Replace torque plate. Replace brake calliper torque plate retaining bolts and washers.

Disc Brake Torque Plate Bolts:

2WD	**650 kg-cm, 47ft-lb 64Nm**
4WD	**1,100 kg-cm, 80ft-lb 108Nm**

Calliper Cylinder

1. Apply disc brake grease to rubber components and piston.

2. Lubricate cylinder bore and piston with specified brake fluid.

3. Fit new seal into inner groove of bore. Ensure seal is not twisted and is fully seated in groove.

4. Install piston boot over end of piston.

5. Position piston into calliper housing, seating boot into grove in calliper bore. Ensure boot flange is squarely and firmly seated in groove.

6. Push piston squarely into bore by hand until fully seated. Ensure piston boot is fully seated in piston and calliper bore grooves.

7. Install the dust boots into the calliper support holes.

8. Install the bushes into the pin boots.

9. Install the 4 disc brake support plates.

10. Install the pad wear plates to the pads.

11. Apply disc brake grease to the anti squeal plate ONLY, fit the anti squeal plate to the outside plate pad.

* Do not get grease on the pad lining.

12. Install the pads into position.

13. Use a G clamp to force the piston back into the calliper.

14. Lower the calliper into position over the pads carefully, install the lower sliding sub pin and tighten to specified torque.

FS 17 Calliper Lower Sliding Sub Pin:
900kg-cm, 65 ft-lb, 88Nm

15. Install brake line and tighten to specification.

Brake Line Torque Specification:
155kg-cm, 11 ft-lb, 15Nm

16. Fill master cylinder to correct level with fresh, specified brake fluid.

17. Depress brake pedal several times to bring pad assemblies into position against disc.

18. Refill master cylinder if necessary.

19. Install wheels and lower vehicle. Torque road wheel nut.

Road Wheel Stud Specification: **100-125Nm**

Disc Brake Model PD 60 [50's 60's 2WD] [80's 90's 10's 11's and 12's 2WD] Series
Install
Disc

1. Replace hub/brake disc to knuckle, making sure outer bearing does not fall from hub.

2. Install wheel bearing nut. Before installing split pin or nut lock washer, adjust wheel bearings as outlined under FRONT WHEEL BEARING ADJUSTMENT Section in Front Suspension Chapter.

3. 2WD: Replace bearing nut split pin and front wheel bearing cover.

4WD: Replace nut lock washer and nut. Replace free wheeling hub as described in Front Suspension chapter.

4. Replace torque plate. Replace brake calliper torque plate retaining bolts and washers.

Disc Brake Torque Plate Bolts:

2WD	**650 kg-cm, 47ft-lb 64Nm**
4WD	**1,100 kg-cm, 80ft-lb 108Nm**

Calliper Cylinder

1. Apply disc brake grease to rubber components and piston.

2. Lubricate cylinder bore and piston with specified brake fluid.

3. Fit new seal into inner groove of bore. Ensure seal is not twisted and is fully seated in groove.

4. Install piston boot over end of piston.

5. Position piston into calliper housing, seating boot into grove in calliper bore. Ensure boot flange is squarely and firmly seated in groove.

6. Push piston squarely into bore by hand until fully seated. Ensure piston boot is fully seated in piston and calliper bore grooves.

7. Install the collar, dust boots into the calliper support holes.

8. Install the bushes into the dust boots.

9. Install the 4 disc brake support plates.

10. Install the pad wear plates to the pads.

11. Apply disc brake grease to the anti squeal plates ONLY, fit the anti squeal plates to the pads.

* Do not get grease on the pad lining.

12. Install the pads into position.

13. Use a G clamp to force the piston back into the calliper.

14. Lower the calliper into position over the pads carefully, install the lower sliding sub pin and tighten to specified torque.

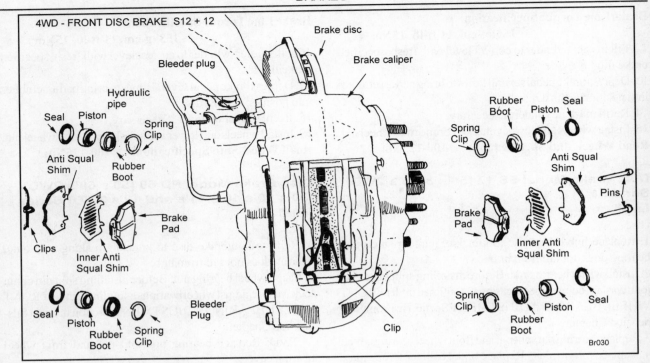

PD 60 Calliper Lower Sliding Sub Pin:
400kg-cm, 24 ft-lb, 39Nm
15. Install brake line and tighten to specification.
Brake Line Torque Specification:
155kg-cm, 11 ft-lb, 15Nm
16. Fill master cylinder to correct level with fresh, specified brake fluid.
17. Depress brake pedal several times to bring pad assemblies into position against disc.
18. Refill master cylinder if necessary.
19. Install wheels and lower vehicle. Torque road wheel nut.
Road Wheel Stud Specification: 100-125N

Disc Brake Model FS 18 [80's, 90's 10's 11's 12's and 13's 2WD] Series
Install
Disc
1. Replace hub/brake disc to knuckle, making sure outer bearing does not fall from hub.
2. Install wheel bearing nut. Before installing split pin or nut lock washer, adjust wheel bearings as outlined under FRONT WHEEL BEARING ADJUSTMENT Section in Front Suspension Chapter.
3. Replace bearing nut split pin and front wheel bearing cover.
4. Replace torque plate. Replace brake calliper torque plate retaining bolts and washers.
Disc Brake Torque Plate Bolts:
650 kg-cm, 47ft-lb 64Nm

Calliper Cylinder
1. Apply disc brake grease to rubber components and piston.
2. Lubricate cylinder bore and piston with specified brake fluid.

3. Fit new seal into inner groove of bore. Ensure seal is not twisted and is fully seated in groove.
4. Install piston boot over end of piston.
5. Position piston into calliper housing, seating boot into grove in calliper bore. Ensure boot flange is squarely and firmly seated in groove.
6. Push piston squarely into bore by hand until fully seated. Ensure piston boot is fully seated in piston and calliper bore grooves.
7. Install the pin boots into the calliper support holes.
8. Install the bushes into the dust boots.
9. Install the 4 disc brake support plates.
10. Install the pad wear plates to the pads.
11. Apply disc brake grease to the 2 inner anti squeal plates ONLY, fit the 4 anti squeal plates to the pads.
* Do not get grease on the pad lining.
12. Install the pads into position.
13. Use a G clamp to force the piston back into the calliper.
14. Lower the calliper into position over the pads carefully, install the lower sliding sub pin and tighten to specified torque.
FS 18 Calliper Lower Sliding Sub Pin:
900kg-cm, 65 ft-lb, 88Nm
15. Install brake line and tighten to specification.
Brake Line Torque Specification:
155kg-cm, 11 ft-lb, 15Nm
16. Fill master cylinder to correct level with fresh, specified brake fluid.
17. Depress brake pedal several times to bring pad assemblies into position against disc.
18. Refill master cylinder if necessary.
19. Install wheels and lower vehicle. Torque road wheel nut.

Road Wheel Stud Specification: 100-125Nm

Disc Brake Model S12+12 [80's, 90's, 10's 11's 12's and 13's 4WD] Series
Install
Disc

1. Replace hub/brake disc to knuckle, making sure outer bearing does not fall from hub. Tighten disc to hub bolts to specification.

Disc To Hub Bolts Torque:
475 kg-cm, 34ft-lb 46Nm

2. Install wheel bearing nut. Before installing split pin or nut lock washer, adjust wheel bearings as outlined under FRONT WHEEL BEARING ADJUSTMENT Section in Front Suspension Chapter.

3. Replace bearing nut split pin and front wheel bearing cover.

4. Replace torque plate. Replace brake calliper torque plate retaining bolts and washers.

Disc Brake Torque Plate Bolts:
1,100 kg-cm, 80ft-lb 108Nm

Calliper Cylinder
1. Apply disc brake grease to rubber components and piston.
2. Lubricate cylinder bore and piston with specified brake fluid.
3. Fit new seal into inner groove of bores. Ensure seal is not twisted and is fully seated in groove.
4. Install piston boot over end of pistons.
5. Position piston into calliper housing, seating boot into grove in calliper bore. Ensure boot flange is squarely and firmly seated in groove.
6. Push piston squarely into bore by hand until fully seated. Ensure piston boot is fully seated in piston and calliper bore grooves.
7. Install calliper and calliper attaching bolts.

Calliper to Torque Plate Bolts Torque:
1,250 kg-cm, 90ft-lb 123Nm

8. Install the new pads.
9. Install the 4 anti squeal shims and new pads.
10. Install the anti rattle spring.
11. Install the 2 pins and pin clip.
12. Install brake line and tighten to specification.

Brake Line Torque Specification:
155kg-cm, 11 ft-lb, 15Nm

13. Fill master cylinder to correct level with fresh, specified brake fluid.
14. Depress brake pedal several times to bring pad assemblies into position against disc.
15. Refill master cylinder if necessary.
16. Install wheels and lower vehicle. Torque road wheel nut.

Road Wheel Stud Specification: 100-125Nm

BRAKE DISC INSPECTION
If disc surface is rusted or lightly scored, resurface disc.

Scores less than 0.4 mm deep will not affect brake performance.

If scoring is deep or if disc parameters are out of specification, the disc must be machined.

* Machine or resurface BOTH sides of disc. Do not machine or resurface one side only.

* After machining, disc finish should be 0.4 to 2.0 microns and should not be circumferential, i.e., disc finish should be non-directional.

* Replace disc if specifications cannot be achieved whilst maintaining minimum disc thickness.

Inspect disc as follows:

1. Mount disc in lathe on bearing cups - do not mount on hub surface.

2. Check that disc surfaces are square with bearing cup centreline with 0.1 mm T.I.R.

3. Check that lateral run-out does not exceed 0.1 mm T.I.R. and that the rate of change does not exceed 0.03 mm in 30°.

4. Check that both surfaces are flat within 0.05 mm T.I.R.

5. Check that disc surfaces are parallel with each other to

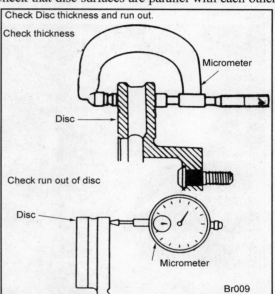

Check Disc thickness and run out.
Check thickness
Micrometer
Disc
Check run out of disc
Disc
Micrometer
Br009

within 0.076 mm T.I.R. when checked readily.

6. Check that total circumferential thickness variation, at any radius, does not exceed 0.013 mm in 360° as disc is rotated.

7. If the disc does not meet specifications replace.

LOAD SENSING PROPORTION VALVE
Remove
1. Disconnect the brake fluid pipes from the valve assembly.
2. Disconnect the lever assembly at the differential.
3. Remove the bolt and nuts attaching the valve to the chassis.
4. Lift the valve and linkage assembly from the vehicle.
5. Remove the bolt and nut at the base of the valve, remove plate and clip from the valve.
6. Mark the valve end of the spring with paint so that during assembly there is no confusion.

323

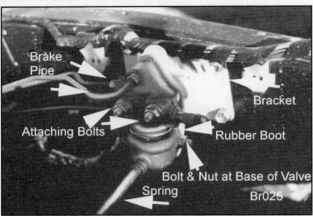

Br025

7. Dismantle the valve spring and lever assembly.

Install

1. Install the valve to the valve support bracket, do not fully tighten the two attaching bolts at this stage.

2. Assemble the valve spring and levers, ensure the long spring is assembled correctly, that is the spring end that was attached to the valve is correct spring end (paint mark during remove).

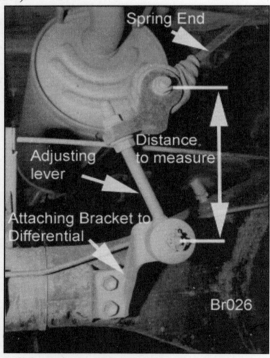

Br026

3. Install the spring and levers to the valve. Replace the plate and clip to the valve. Replace the bolt and nut at the base of the valve, with the nut on the vehicle rear end side of the valve.

4. Position the valve and linkage assembly to the vehicle.

5. Replace the bolt and nuts attaching the valve to the chassis, and tighten to specification.

Load Sensing Proportion Valve Bolts:
195kg-cm, 14ft-lb, 15Nm

6. Connect the lever assembly at the differential.

7. Connect the brake fluid pipes from the valve assembly.

Adjust

1. Adjust the small lever attached to the differential: Lengthening the small lever adjustment will lower the rear brake pressure.

Shortening the small lever adjustment will increase the rear brake pressure.

Standard Rear Brake Pressure:

Xtra Cab

2WD	39-49kg/cm^2, 550-700psi, 3,800-4,800kPa
4WD	45-55kg/cm^2, 640-780psi, 4,400-5,400kPa

Models other than Xtra Cab

2WD	38-48kg/cm^2, 570-730psi, 3,900-4,900kPa
4WD	42-52kg/cm^2, 670-810psi, 4,100-5,100kPa

Standard small lever adjusted length:

2WD	78mm (3.07in)
4WD	120mm (4.72in)

Minimum and Maximum adjustments allowed:

2WD	72-84mm (2.83-3.31in)
4WD	114-126mm (4.49-4.96in)

2. If for some reason the small lever can not be adjusted the load proportioning valve can be adjusted (up for higher pressure or down for lower pressure) on the chassis.

VACUUM PUMP

Remove

1. Disconnect the vacuum hose to the power vacuum brake unit.

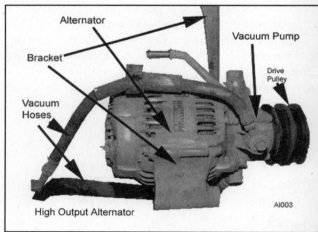

AI003

2. Disconnect the two oil hoses to the vacuum pump, take care not to spill oil over the engine or alternator.

3. Remove the three attaching bolts of the vacuum pump, attaching it to the alternator.

4. Remove the pump and "O" ring.

5. Remove the pump cover by hitting down on the pins with a light hammer, remove the cover and 'O' ring.

6. Inspect the vacuum pump rotor blades for specification, if not within specification replace.

Vacuum Pump Rotor Blades Specification:

Height:	13.3mm 0.524in Min.
Length:	22.98mm 0.9047in Min.
Width:	5.95mm 0.2343in Min.

7. Remove the valve from the vacuum pump and check that air flows only in one direction, that is air should flow from the hose side to the vacuum pump side of the valve only.

Install

1. Install the check valve to the vacuum pump with a new gasket.

2. After checking the vacuum pump rotors as above in point 6. install the pump new "O" and cover, tap in pin.

3. Install the vacuum pump and new "O" ring, to the alternator, install three attaching bolts and tighten to specification.

Vacuum Pump Attaching bolts torque:
      140kg-cm, 10ft-lb, 14Nm

4. Install oil hoses to vacuum pump.

5. Install hose to vacuum power brake unit.

SPECIFICATIONS

BRAKE BOOSTER
Type .... P.B.R Dual Diaphragm
Diaphragm Diameter .... 228 mm
      .... 279 mm

MASTER CYLINDER
Type .... P.B.R Dual Lane (*with 'Fast Fill' Feature)
Main Bore Diameter .... 23.81 mm
Fast Fill Bore Diameter..................................... 31.75 mm

DISC BRAKE CALLIPER (FRONT)
Type .... P.B.R Single Piston Floating Calliper
Bore Diameter .... 60.3 mm
Type .... Girlock Single Piston Floating Calliper
Bore Diameter .... 44.45 mm

DISC BRAKE CALLIPER (REAR)
Type .... P.B.R Single Piston Floating Calliper
Bore Diameter .... 44.45 mm

DISC (FRONT AND REAR)
Type .... Cast Iron - Ventilated
Diameter .... 286 mm
Thickness (New) .... 23.9 mm
Max. Runout .... 0.08 mm
Thickness Variation 0.013mm
Min. Thickness Refaced (overall) .... 22.2 mm
Min. Thickness Refaced (Individual Brake Surfaces)3.2 mm

DISC PADS
Lining Wear Limit .... 1.0 mm

REAR DRUM BRAKES
Drum Diameter (New)................................... 254.0 mm
Drum Diameter (Refinished) .... 255.5 mm

Maximum Runout .... 0.18 mm
Wheel Cylinder Bore .... 20.64 mm
Lining Dimensions .... Primary .... 44.45 x 212.1 mm
      Secondary ..... 44.45 x 273.0 mm
Lining Wear Limit .... 1.0 mm

BRAKE PEDAL HEIGHT
Minimum height without fluid in system and master cylinder bottomed out .... 25 mm

LUBRICATION
High melting point grease - Caltex Thermotex EPI

BRAKE FLUID
Brake fluid spec. .... Heavey Duty Disc Brake Fluid

Torque Specificatioons

Tandem Master Cylinder
Piston Stopper Bolt Specified Torque:
      100kg-cm, 7 ft-lb, 10Nm
Reservoir Internal Mount Nut Torque:
      250kg-cm, 18 ft-lb, 250Nm
Reservoir External Mounting Screw Torque:
      100kg-cm, 7 ft-lb, 10Nm
Master Cylinder Attaching Nuts: 130kg-cm, 9 ft-lb, 13Nm
Booster Attaching Nuts: 130kg-cm, 9 ft-lb, 13Nm
Parking Brake Bell Crank Bracket Bolt Torque:
      130kg-cm, 9 ft-lb, 13Nm
Rear Brake Cylinder Bolts Torque:
      100kg-cm, 7 ft-lb, 10Nm
Front Brake Cylinder Bolts Torque:
      185kg-cm, 13 ft-lb, 18Nm
Brake Hose Specified Torque: 155kg-cm, 11 ft-lb, 15Nm
Road Wheel Stud Specification:
      1,150 kg.cm, (83ft-lb, 113Nm)

Disc Brake Model - K [30's & 40's Series]
Disc Brake Torque Plate Bolts: 650 kg-cm, 47ft-lb 64Nm
Cylinder Attaching Bolt Torque: 500kg-cm, 30 ft-lb, 50Nm
Pad Support Plate bolt: 500kg-cm, 30 ft-lb, 50Nm

Disc Brake Model - S16 [30's & 40's Series]
Disc Brake Torque Plate Bolts: 650 kg-cm, 47ft-lb 64Nm
Cylinder Attaching Bolt Torque: 100kg-cm, 80ft-lb 108Nm

Disc Brake- S12+8
[30's, 40's, 4WD][50's & 60's 4WD] Series
Disc Brake Torque Plate Bolts:
2WD   650 kg-cm, 47ft-lb 64Nm
4WD   1,100 kg-cm, 80ft-lb 108Nm
Calliper Cylinder Attaching bolts:900kg-cm, 65 ft-lb, 88Nm

Disc Brake Model FS 17 [50's & 60's 2WD]Series
Disc Brake Torque Plate Bolts:
2WD   650 kg-cm, 47ft-lb 64Nm
4WD   1,100 kg-cm, 80ft-lb 108Nm
FS 17 Calliper Lower Sliding Sub Pin:
      900kg-cm, 65 ft-lb, 88Nm

Disc Brake Model PD 60 [50's 60's 2WD][80's 90's 10's 11's 12's 2WD] Series

Disc Brake Torque Plate Bolts:

2WD	650 kg-cm, 47ft-lb 64Nm
4WD	1,100 kg-cm, 80ft-lb 108Nm

PD 60 Calliper Lower Sliding Pin: 400kg-cm, 24 ft-lb, 39Nm

Disc Brake Model FS 18
[80's, 90's 10's 11's ans 12's 2WD] Series

Disc Brake Torque Plate Bolts: 650 kg-cm, 47ft-lb 64Nm

FS 18 Calliper Lower Sliding Pin: 900kg-cm, 65 ft-lb, 88Nm

Disc Brake S12+12 [80's, 90's, 10's 11's 12's and 13's 4WD] Series

Disc To Hub Bolts Torque: 475 kg-cm, 34ft-lb 46Nm

Calliper- Torque Plate Bolts Torque:
1,250 kg-cm, 90ft-lb 123Nm

Brake Line Torque Specification: 155kg-cm, 11 ft-lb, 15Nm

Pedal Height from floor Pan
Hi Lux 30's & 40's Series
2WD

All Countries	162.0mm(6.4in) - 172.0mm(6.8in)

4WD

All Countries	162.0mm(6.4in) - 172.0mm(6.8in)

Hi Lux and 4 Runner 50's & 60's Series
2WD

All Countries	151.0mm(5.94in) - 156.0mm(6.14in)

4WD

All Countries	151.0mm(5.94in) - 156.0mm(6.14in)

Hi Lux and 4 Runner 80's, 90's, 100's 11's 12's and 13's Series
2WD

Regular Cab	151.0mm(5.94in) - 156.0mm(6.14in)
Double Cab	151.0mm(5.94in) - 156.0mm(6.14in)
Xtra Cab	148.0mm(5.83in) - 153.0mm(6.02in)

4WD

Australia and Other Countries

Regular Cab	147.0mm(5.79in) - 152.0mm(5.98in)
Double Cab	147.0mm(5.79in) - 152.0mm(5.98in)
Xtra Cab and 4 Runner	145.0mm(5.71in) - 150.0mm(5.91in)

All Countries except Australia

Regular Cab	151.0mm(5.94in) - 156.0mm(6.14in)
Double Cab	151.0mm(5.94in) - 156.0mm(6.14in)
Xtra Cab	148.0mm(5.83in) - 153.0mm(6.02in)

Specified Free Pedal Movement: 3-6mm (0.12-0.24in)

Brake Shoe Lining Minimum Thickness: 1.0mm (0.039in)

Australia and Other Countries

Regular Cab	147.5mm(5.81in) - 152.5mm(6.00in)
Double Cab	148.0mm(5.83in) - 153.0mm(6.02in)
Xtra Cab	148.0mm(5.83in) - 153.0mm(6.02in)

DISC SPECIFICATIONS
Disc Model K Wear specifications

Thickness (New):	20.0 mm(0.787in)
Min. Thickness Refaced (overall):	19.0 mm(0.75in)
Max. Runout:	0.15 mm(0.006in)
Lining Minimum Thickness:	1.0 mm(0.039in)

Disc Model S 16 Wear specifications

Thickness (New):	12.5 mm(0.49in)
Min. Thickness Refaced (overall):	11.5 mm(0.45in)
Max. Runout:	0.15 mm(0.0059in)
Lining Minimum Thickness:	1.0 mm(0.039in)

Disc Model S 12+8 Wear specifications

Thickness (New):	12.5 mm(0.497in)
Min. Thickness Refaced (overall):	11.5 mm(0.45in)
Max. Runout:	0.15 mm(0.0059in)
Lining Minimum Thickness:	1.0 mm(0.039in)

Disc Model FS 17 Wear specifications

Thickness (New):	22.0 mm(0.866in)
Min. Thickness Refaced (overall):	21.0 mm(0.827in)
Max. Runout:	0.15 mm(0.0059in)
Lining New Thickness:	10.0mm(0.393in)
Lining Minimum Thickness:	1.0 mm(0.039in)

Disc Model PD 60 Wear specifications

Thickness (New):	25.0 mm(0.984in)
Min. Thickness Refaced (overall):	23.0 mm(0.906in)
Max. Runout:	0.09 mm(0.0035in)
Lining New Thickness:	9.5mm (0.374in)
Lining Minimum Thickness:	1.0 mm(0.039in)

Disc Model FS 18 Wear specifications

Thickness (New):	22.0 mm(0.866in)
Min. Thickness Refaced (overall):	20.0 mm(0.787in)
Max. Runout:	0.09 mm(0.0035in)
Lining New Thickness:	10.0mm(0.393in)
Lining Minimum Thickness:	1.0 mm(0.039in)

Disc Model S 12+12 Wear specifications

Thickness (New):	20.0 mm(0.787in)
Min. Thickness Refaced (overall):	18.0 mm(0.709in)
Max. Runout: Ind. Front Susp.	0.09 mm(0.0035in)
Max. Runout: Leaf Spring Susp.	0.15 mm(0.0059in
Lining New Thickness:	9.5mm (0.374in)
Lining Minimum Thickness:	1.0 mm(0.039in)

EXHAUST SYSTEM

GENERAL DESCRIPTION

Engines are fitted with a single pipe exhaust system, the engine exhaust manifold is connected to a front pipe. A single resonator or catalytic converter is located between the engine front pipe and the intermediate pipe forward of the muffler assembly.

The pipe in front of the muffler assembly is connected through a slip joint to the rear muffler.

The exhaust system is supported by rubber insulators at the rear end of the muffler and at the rear of the tailpipe.

Exhaust pipe joins and catalytic converter bolts tighten to specification.

Exhaust Pipe Joins Bolt Torque:
450kg-cm, 33ft-lb, 44Nm

SERVICE NOTES

When installing any exhaust system component, care must be taken to install each component in correct order.

Incorrect assembly of exhaust system components can often be the cause of rattles and 'booms' due to incorrect alignment or clearance from body or suspension parts.

While installing the exhaust system, ensure that the correct assembly, installation, tightening sequence and clearance for the system involved are observed. Generally speaking, fit the components closest to the engine first, and work your way back to the rear of the vehicle.

Many vehicles are fitted with a heat shield over the exhaust manifold and catalytic converter, if these heat shields are fitted they must be reinstalled as there could be danger to the vehicle from excess heat.

When exhaust system service work is required, refer to

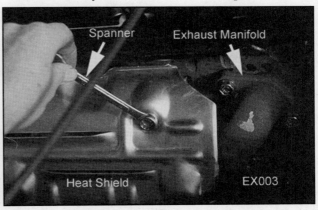

illustrations for necessary information and proper alignment and arrangement of each component position.

Use exhaust sealer on pipe ends to ensure a proper seal which will not leak exhaust gases.

CATALYTIC CONVERTER

The catalytic converter is similar to a muffler in appearance. Inside the steel housing, the converter comprises of ceramic monolith which is surrounded by a mat, this prevents the monolith from contacting the inner casing. The surfaces of the ceramic monolith contain Rhodium, Palladium and Platinum which are exposed to exhaust gases, (this creates the chemical reaction necessary to oxidize carbon monoxide and hydrocarbons to harmless carbon dioxide).

The catalytic converter normally operates at approximately 600°C. The catalytic material is very sensitive to the effects

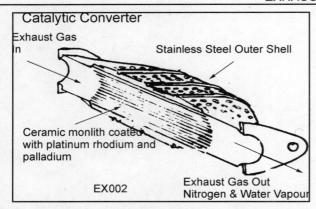

of a rich or lean fuel mixture which causes the temperature of the converter to rise rapidly to the temperature at which the ceramic material melts.

Caution: Excessively rich or lean fuel mixture can cause sudden failure of the catalytic converter.

The catalytic converter is also sensitive to the use of leaded petrol. This causes deposits to form in the converter which restrict the exhaust flow and prevent the catalyst from working.

* The use of unleaded petrol results in black tailpipe deposits rather than the grey colour most people are familiar with. The black colour does not therefore, indicate a state of poor engine tune.

Canadian and USA vehicles between 1980-1984 have a thermo-sensor fitted to the catalytic converter, which is wired back into the vehicle cabin. If replaced tighten bolts to 800kg-cm, 60ft-lb, 80Nm

PROBLEM DIAGNOSIS

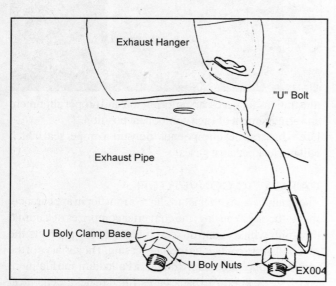

Problem: Leaking exhaust gases!
Possible Causes and Remedies:
* Leaks at pipe joints. Remedy - Torque U-bolt nuts and joint bolts.

* Damaged or improperly installed converter gaskets. Remedy - Replace gasket as necessary.
* Burned or rusted-out exhaust pipe or muffler. Remedy - Replace component as necessary.

Problem: **Exhaust noises!**
Possible Causes and Remedies:
* Leaks at manifold or pipe connections. Remedies - Torque clamps at leaking connections, or replace gasket.
* Burned or blown-out pipe or muffler. Remedy - Replace pipe/muffler assembly as necessary.
* Exhaust manifold cracked or broken. Remedy - Replace manifold.
* Leak between manifold and cylinder head. Remedy - Torque manifold to cylinder head studs.

Problem: **Loss of engine power, hesitation, surging, bad fuel economy, stalling / hard starting!**
Possible Causes and Remedies:
* Clogged catalytic converter (may result from serious engine malfunction or wrong fuel). Remedy - Replace catalytic converter.
* Crushed pipework. Remedy - Replace pipework.

Problem: **Internal rattling in muffler!**
* Dislodged turning tubes and/or baffles in muffler. Remedy - Replace muffler.
* Catalytic converter monolith has crumbled and pieces blown into muffler. Remedy - Replace catalytic converter assembly and affected muffler.

TORQUE WRENCH SPEC

Engine front pipe flange to exhaust manifold flange attaching nuts .... 40 - 55Nm
Exhaust clamp nuts .... 25 - 30Nm
Exhaust manifold to cylinder head studs:
"L" Series 530kg-cm, 38ft-lb, 52Nm
"Y" Series 500kg-cm, 36ft-lb, 49Nm
"R" Series 500kg-cm, 36ft-lb, 49Nm
Rear hanger bracket to tailpipe bracket bolts .... 25 - 30Nm

FUEL TANK & E.F.I. FUEL PUMP

FUEL   TANK & E.F.I. FUEL PUMP

GENERAL INFORMATION

On 80's, 90's 10's 11's 12's & 13's Series models, there are 52, 56, 65 and 73 litre fuel tanks.
Fuel tanks are bolted up to the vehicle frame.

E.F.I. Models (Y series)

E.F.I. vehicle fuel tanks are fitted with a single in-tank fuel feed pump which is a high pressure, two stage roller vane pump.

E.F.I. FUEL PUMP

Roller vane-type fuel feed pump installed integral with the riser pipe and fuel gauge sender unit inside the fuel tank. Station Wagon models use a low pressure priming pump within the fuel tank and an additional high pressure pump in the fuel feed line. The additional external pump is mounted in an insulated bracket to reduce noise transmission. The electrical leads to the tank mounted pump are spliced to accommodate extension leads to the additional pump.

UNLEAD FUEL - FUEL FILLER NECK

Australian and New Zealand vehicles have a fuel filler neck to help prevent the fuel tank being filled with leaded petrol, the fuel filler neck has a built-in restrictor and deflector. The opening in the restrictor will only admit the smaller unleaded petrol nozzle spout and must be fully inserted to by pass the deflector.

Attempted refuelling with a leaded petrol nozzle or failure to fully insert the unleaded petrol nozzle will result in petrol splashing back out of the filler neck.

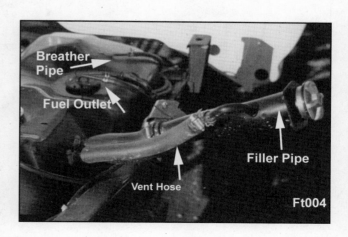

Ft004

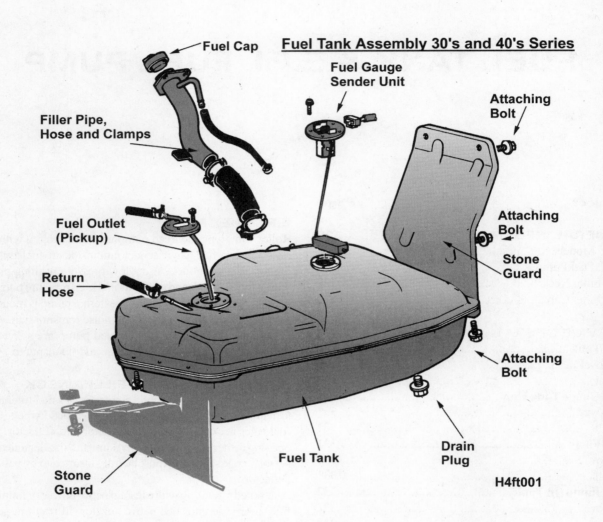

Fuel Tank Assembly 30's and 40's Series

Fuel Cap

Fuel Gauge Sender Unit

Attaching Bolt

Filler Pipe, Hose and Clamps

Fuel Outlet (Pickup)

Return Hose

Attaching Bolt

Stone Guard

Attaching Bolt

Stone Guard

Fuel Tank

Drain Plug

H4ft001

FUEL FILLER CAP

Two types of fuel filler caps are used. One is a conventional push on and turn. The other cap is a "push on" type with a (clicking) feature to lock. When installing the cap, push it until a click sound is heard, which indicates the cap is properly fitted.

SERVICE OPERATIONS

FUEL TANK
Remove

1. Drain the tank from the drain plug in the lower section of the fuel tank.

2. Remove filler neck stoneguard under the fender.

3. Disconnect the fuel line between the fuel gauge tank unit and the fuel feed pipe, then the fuel return line from the tank connection.

4. Disconnect tank vent hoses at filler neck and check for kinks in hoses and replace if necessary.

5. Remove screw attaching filler neck bracket to wheelhouse inner panel.

6. Disconnect electrical connectors from fuel gauge tank unit, then the fuel tank to canister vapour hose from vapour pipe at front of tank.

7. Support fuel tank with suitable jack. Locate a block of

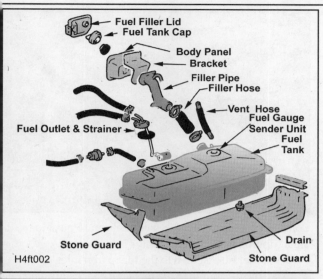

H4ft002

the fuel tank to canister vapour hose from vapour pipe at top of tank.

3. Replace screws attaching filler neck bracket to wheel-house inner panel.

4. Connect tank vent hoses at filler neck and check for kinks in hoses and replace if necessary.

5. Connect the fuel line between the fuel gauge tank unit and the fuel feed pipe, then the fuel return line from the tank connection.

6. Replace filler neck stoneguard under the fender.

7. Replace drain plug in the lower section of the fuel tank.

Drain Plug Specified Torque:
        65kg-cm, 6ft-lb, 7Nm

8. Install the stone guard to the duel tank and tighten bolts to specification.

Stone Guard Specified Torque:
        300kg-cm, 22t-lb, 29Nm

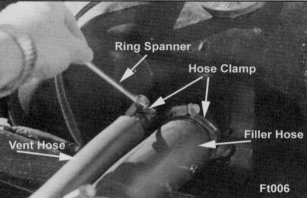

Ft006

wood between the jack and tank to prevent tank damage.

8. Remove the bolts securing the tank to the body and lower tank.

Install

1. Lift the tank into position and install the bolts securing the tank to the body.

Tank Attaching Bolts Torque:

30's & 40's Series   185kg-cm, 13ft-lb, 18Nm

50's & 60's Series   185kg-cm, 13ft-lb, 18Nm

80's, 90's, 10's 11's 12's & 13's Series
        300kg-cm, 22ft-lb, 29Nm

Ft008

2. Connect electrical connectors to fuel gauge tank unit, then

Ft005

FUEL GAUGE TANK UNIT

Remove

1. Remove fuel tank as previously described.

2. Remove the gauge unit mounting screws.

3. Then remove gauge unit and seal from tank.

Install

1. Clean mating surfaces of gauge unit and tank.

2. Install seal to fuel gauge tank unit.

3. Carefully fit fuel gauge tank unit into the tank and tighten screws.

4. Install fuel tank as previously described.

FUEL OUTLET (PICK-UP PIPE) and FILTER

Remove

1. Remove fuel tank as previously described.

2. Remove the pick-up pipe unit mounting screws.

3. Remove pick-up pipe unit and seal from tank.

4. Remove filter from pick-up pipe.

Install

1. Install new filter to pick-up pipe.

2. Clean mating surfaces of pick-up pipe unit and tank.

3. Install seal to pick-up pipe tank unit.

4. Carefully fit fuel pick-up pipe unit into the tank and

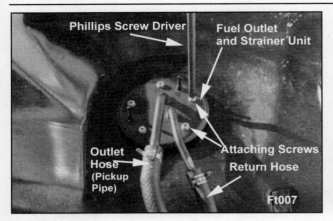

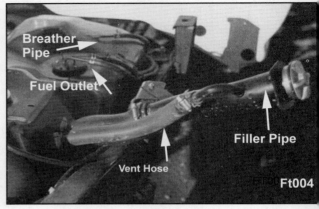

tighten screws.

5. Install fuel tank as previously described.

FUEL PUMP - EFI Models [IN TANK]
Remove

1. Remove fuel tank as previously described.

2. Remove the fuel pump attaching screws and remove the fuel pump.

3. Gently pry the fuel filter screen off the fuel pump inlet fitting with a screwdriver.

4. Disconnect the electrical connector and ease pulsator upwards along the riser pipe until clear of pump outlet fitting.

5. Withdraw pump sideways (clear of pulsator) and remove pump.

6. Remove rubber seats and insulator from pump bracket.

Install

1. Install pump to pump bracket, fit insulators.

2. Connect the electrical connection. Check electrical connec-

tions and connector retainer and make sure pulsator seals engage pump outlet fitting firmly.

3. Fit the fuel filter screen to the fuel pump inlet.

4. Install the fuel pump to the fuel tank and install attaching screws.

5. Install fuel tank as previously described.

TORQUE WRENCH SPEC

Tank Attaching Bolts Torque:

30's & 40's Series	185kg-cm, 13ft-lb, 18Nm
50's & 60's Series	185kg-cm, 13ft-lb, 18Nm
80's, 90's, 10's 11's 12's & 13's Series	300kg-cm, 22ft-lb, 29Nm

Drain Plug Specified Torque:
  65kg-cm, 6ft-lb, 7Nm

Stone Guard Specified Torque:
  300kg-cm, 22t-lb, 29Nm

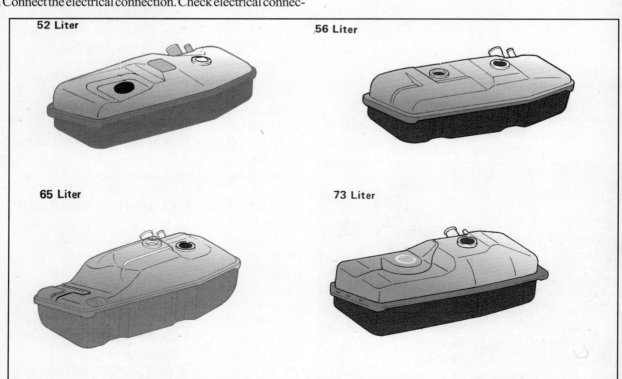

WHEELS AND TYRES

GENERAL INFORMATION.

When installing a wheel ensure that as the road wheel attaching nuts are gradually tightened in the order shown.

Two wheel drive 5 bolt pattern, tighten wheel studs in order shown

W003

Four Wheel Drive - 6 Bolt Pattern

Split Rim Type

W004

Wheel Nut Specified Torque:
    1,000-1,300 kg-cm, 74-92ft-lb, 100-125
Tyre rotation as shown will help correct uneven tyre wear, it is also recommended that the wheels are balanced at the time of tyre rotation.
Tyres should be routinely checked for wear, there are

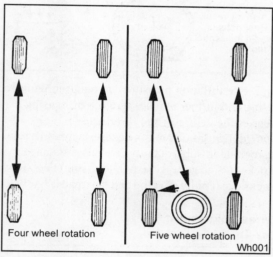

Four wheel rotation   Five wheel rotation

Wh001

special patterns that appear when the tyre tread is low as shown opposite. Also the depth of tread can be checked with a tyre tread depth gauge.

The tyres fitted as original equipment have been selected for safety, handling and comfort characteristics. Therefore when replacing any tyres it must be noted that a tyre of a lesser rating must not be used.

Wheel and tyre specifications are displayed on a decal fitted on the inside of the glove box.

Inflation Pressure

Tyre inflation pressures should be checked with the tyres cold. Never reduce tyre pressure when the tyres are hot.

Low Tyre Pressure

Low tyre pressure is a common fault affecting tyre life. While driving in normal conditions a tyre flexes as it rolls

Tyre pressure that is to low will result in wear on the edges of the tyre

Wh003

along the road and this flexing in turn generates heat. If the tyre is correctly inflated this heat build-up is not detrimental to the tyre. However an under inflated tyre flexes far more than normal resulting in greater heat generation. Under these conditions the temperature of the tyre can rise to a point where the rubber compounds that bind the tyre together are softened and weakened. In extreme conditions this may result in the tread separating from the casing or the plies separating from each other. Under inflation also reduces tyre life by causing excessive wear on the tyre edges.

Overloading has the same effect as under inflation causing excessive tyre flexing and subsequent heat generation. Tyre damage and wear is accelerated if the vehicle is driven at high speed or in an overloaded condition.

High Tyre Pressure

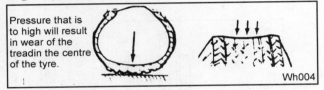

Pressure that is to high will result in wear of the tread in the centre of the tyre.

Wh004

High tyre inflation pressure can result in damage to the casing and further reduces tyre life by causing excessive wear at the centre of the tyre tread.

Very high inflation pressure exerts increased strain on the casing which subsequently reduces resistance to impact shocks. Since the tyre tread is stretched tight, tread cracks can rapidly develop and the tread is likely to crack.

Wheel Alignment
Toe-In

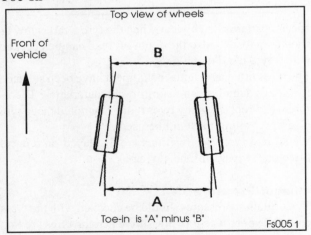

Top view of wheels

Front of vehicle

B

A

Toe-in is "A" minus "B"

Fs005 1

Toe-in setting is an important factor in tyre life. Excessive toe-in results in tapered or feathered wear on the outside edge of the tyre while excessive toe-out has the same result on the inside edge. Under these conditions the tyre is dragged along the road instead of rolling freely.

Check Front Suspension chapter for specifications and the correct procedure for adjusting toe-in.

Camber

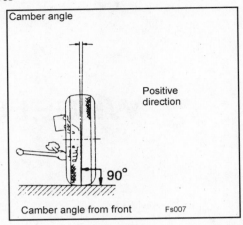

Camber angle

Positive direction

90°

Camber angle from front   Fs007

Excessive wheel camber either positive or negative, results in one side of the tyre wearing faster than the other. Wheel camber is adjustable, the setting may alter as a result of damage to the front end. In this event the damaged components must be replaced, and camber adjusted as described in Front Suspension chapter..

Wheel Balance.

Wheels out of balance can result in cupped or spotted wear around the tyre circumference. Usually an out of balance tyre will vibrate through the steering wheel when driving on smooth surfaces.

Shock Absorbers

Faulty or worn shock absorbers can also result in cupped or spotted wear. Faulty shock absorbers should be replaced in pairs.

It should be noted that in addition to the foregoing factors, driving habits, road conditions and the terrain over which the vehicle is operated will have a direct bearing on tyre life.

Wheels

The road wheels are either a double safety rim type or split rim type They are a steel wheel. It is essential that correct wheel nuts are used at all times.

The wheel nuts are conventional wheel nuts.

Remove
1. Mark the relarionship of the wheel to the drum or hub, this is incase the wheel has been balanced or the vehicle, therefore when the wheel is installed the wheel will still be in balance.
2. Raise vehicle until tyre clears floor and remove the wheel nuts.
3. Remove wheel from hub.

Install
1. Clean dirt from the hub, and position the wheel on the hub, ensure the wheel is in the same position as it was

when removed.

2. Install the wheel nuts and tighten them alternatively as shown previously in order to draw the wheel evenly against the hub.

3. Lower vehicle, and tighten nuts, tighten to specification.

Wheel Nut Specified Torque:
1,000-1,300 kg-cm, 74-92ft-lb, 100-125

Wheel and Tyre Assembly Balancing

Wheel and tyre assemblies should be dynamically balanced. The wheels are balanced on special equipment, whether on the vehicle or mounted onto a wheel balancing machine.

Tyres

Conventional cross ply tyres are fitted as standard equipment. Radial tyres are fitted as optional equipment. Specification and inflation pressure of tyres is shown on a decal on rigth side of door opening.

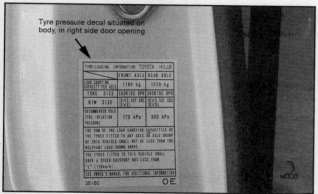

Tyre pressure decal situated on body, in right side door opening

Tyre Care

It is essential that the recommended inflation pressures are always maintained as described previously. Radial ply tyres may appear under-inflated at the correct recommended pressures. This is normal and they should never be inflated beyond the recommended pressures.

Tyre Pressures

The tyre pressures quoted are cold pressures. In this context, the tyre temperature is considered 'hot' after extended motoring at speed. Under certain extreme conditions of operation a tyre may require up to one hour before it can be considered 'cold', i.e. not warm to touch, which is usual after operation.

Tyre Wear

If regular wear is noticed, check the wheel bearings and front suspension ball joints for excess play and also check the front suspension geometry.

Spare Wheel

The spare wheel is located under the rear of the vehicle, whinched up to the chassis, use the jack handle to lower and raise the spare wheel.

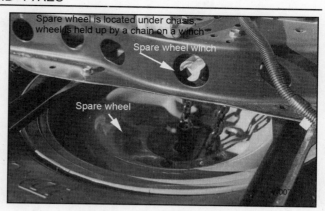

Spare wheel is located under chasis, wheels is held up by a chain on a winch

Spare wheel winch

Spare wheel

Front Wheel, Hub and Bearings

See Front Axle Chapter for replacement and adjusting of wheel bearings.

Removing Tyre From Wheel (Double saftey rim type)

A new snap in valve should be fitted, when fitting a new tubeless tyre. The valve is made to last the life of the tyre, but beyond that time fatigue of the valve body rubber is likely to impair the air seal of the rim hole.

The tyre can be ascended or descended on a machine. A machine should always be used on aluminium alloy wheels. Make sure that the outer side of the wheel is positioned upward.

1. It is OK to use tyre irons on steel wheels using the following operation.

Deflate tyre completely once valve cap and core are deflated, break loose the tyre beads from the wheel, using the bead loosening tool.

2. Remove the wheel weights (if fitted).

* With the outer side of the wheel upward, insert two tyre irons about 200mm apart between the tyre outer bead and the wheel rim. Use only tyre irons with rounded edges or irons designed for dismounting tubeless tyres.

* Lever the tyre bead over the hub cap with one iron and hold it in this position. Pry the rest of the bead over the rim with the over iron. Take small 'bites' with the iron around the tyre in order to avoid damaging the sealing surface on the tyre bead.

* Stand the wheel and tyre upright with the tyre inner bead in the drop centre well at the bottom of the wheel. Position the tyre between the bead and the edge of the wheel rim, and pry the wheel out of the tyre.

SPECIFICATIONS

WHEEL and TYRE DETAILS:
Also see General Information at front of manual.

Tyres	Tyre inflation pressure

50's & 60's Series 2WD

6.00-14-6&8PR	Frt 25 psi, 175 kPa Rr 34 psi, 235 kPa
6.50-14-8PR	Frt 26 psi, 175 kPa Rr 34 psi, 235 kPa
185R-14-8PRLT	Frt 26 psi, 175 kPa Rr 34 psi, 235 kPa
185R14C-8PR	Frt 26 psi, 175 kPa Rr 26 psi, 175 kPa
185SR14	Frt 24 psi, 165 kPa Rr 31 psi, 215 kPa

50's & 60's Series 4WD

7.00-15-6&8PR	Frt 26 psi, 180 kPa Rr 34 psi, 235 kPa
7.00-16-8PR	Frt 34 psi, 235 kPa Rr 43 psi, 295 kPa
205sR 16	Frt 24 psi, 165 kPa Rr 34 psi, 235 kPa
205R 16 C 6PR	Frt 24 psi, 165 kPa Rr 34 psi, 235 kPa

80's, 90's, 10's & 11's Series 2WD Mid East Countries

6.00-14LT-6PR	Frt 23 psi, 160 kPa
6.50-14LT-8PR	Rr 62 psi, 425 kPa
185R-14C-8PR	Frt 26 psi, 180 kPa Rr 65 psi, 450 kPa

80's, 90's, 10's & 11's Series 2WD Other Countries

6.00-14LT-6PR	Frt 25 psi, 170 kPa
6.50-14LT-8PR	Frt 26 psi, 180 kPa Rr 35 psi, 240 kPa
185R-14LT-8PR	Frt 26 psi, 180 kPa Rr 35 psi, 240 kPa
195SR 14	Frt 25 psi, 180 kPa Rr 33 psi, 240 kPa

185R-14C Europe	Frt 26 psi, 180 kPa Rr 26 psi, 180 kPa
185R-14C Other	Frt 26 psi, 180 kPa Rr 65 psi, 450 kPa
195R-14C	Frt 26 psi, 180 kPa Rr 26 psi, 180 kPa

80's, 90's, 10's & 11's Series 4WD [Leaf Spring Frt. Sus.]

7.00-15-6PR	Frt 26 psi 180 kPa
7.00-15-8PR	Rr 62 psi 425 kPa
7.00-16-8PR	Frt 35 psi, 240 kPa Rr 62 psi, 425 kPa
205R 16C-6PR	Frt 25 psi, 170 kPa Rr 44 psi, 300 kPa
205R 16	Frt 25 psi, 170 kPa Rr 35 psi, 240 kPa

80's, 90's, 10's & 11's Series 4WD [Ind. Front Sus.]

205R 16	Frt 25 psi, 170 kPa Rr 35 psi, 240 kPa
205SR 16R	Frt 25 psi, 170 kPa Rr 29 psi, 200 kPa

12's & 13's Series

7.00-15-6.8	Frt 26 psi, 180 kPa Rr 62 psi, 425 kPa
7.00-16-8PR	Frt 35 psi, 240 kPa Rr 62 psi, 425 kPa
205R 16(Radial)	Frt 25 psi, 170 kPa Rr 33 psi, 230 kPa
205R 16C-6PR	Frt 28 psi, 190 kPa Rr 33 psi, 230 kPa
205R 16C-8	Frt 25 psi, 170 kPa Rr 44 psi, 300 kPa
205R 16R/F (Australia)	Frt 25 psi, 170 kPa Rr 35 psi, 240 kPa
205R 16R/F (Europe IFS vehicles)	Frt 25 psi, 170 kPa Rr 38 psi, 260 kPa
205R 16R/F (Europe RFS vehicles)	Frt 25 psi, 170 kPa Rr 44 psi, 300 kPa
215SR 15-6	Frt 28 psi, 190 kPa Rr 33 psi, 230 kPa
265/75R15	Frt 28 psi, 190 kPa Rr 28 psi, 190 kPa

Memo

336

WINDSCREEN WIPERS & WASHERS

DESCRIPTION

The wiper motor is a two speed type and incorporates a parking switch which is activated when wipers are switched off.

The windscreen washer bottle is located in the engine compartment under the bonnet. The washer pump, a centrifugal type driven by an electric motor is mounted to the windscreen wiper motor.

Control switches for high speed, low speed, intermittent operation and the windscreen washer switches are mounted on the side of the steering column.

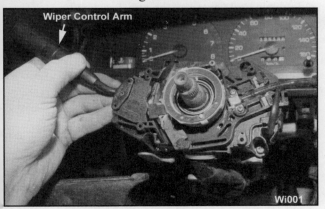

Wiper Control Arm

Wi001

WIPER ARM
Remove

1. The wiper arms are a press on fit then secure with nut.
(a) Remove wiper arm attaching nut cover, then attaching nut.

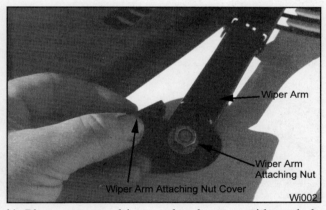

Wiper Arm

Wiper Arm Attaching Nut

Wiper Arm Attaching Nut Cover

Wi002

b) Place a screw driver under the arm with a cloth between the body and screwdriver to prevent damage to paint work, gently lever the arm from the drive shaft, and remove arm.

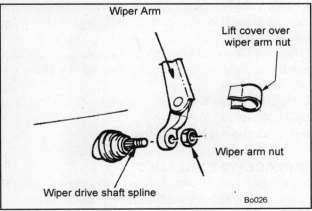

Wiper Arm

Lift cover over wiper arm nut

Wiper arm nut

Wiper drive shaft spline

Bo026

337

3. Remove wiper blade from arm if required.

Remove the wiper blade from the wiper arm on early models remove the two attaching screws. Later models Unclip the wiper locking device, remove the locking block and slide the wiper away from the arm.

Install

1. Install the wiper blade onto the wiper arm.

Clip the wiper onto the arm, or install the blade attaching screws.

2. Install wiper arm assembly onto spline so that the blade is positioned "Normal Stopping Position" as shown on windshield.

3. Press the arm onto the shaft ensuring the arm is fully seated on the shaft in the correct position.

4. Install attaching nut, tighten, then install nut cover which is a push on fit.

WINDSHIELD WIPER MOTOR & LINKAGE
Remove

1. Remove wiper arms from the linkage.

2. From under the instrument panel remove the clip securing the motor driven link to linkage arms.

3. Remove the four bolts securing the wiper motor to the fire wall then remove the motor from inside the engine bay

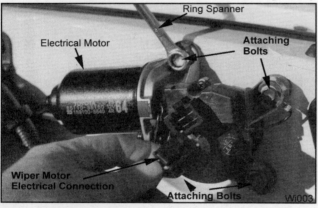

4. Remove the screws securing the linkage assembly.

5. Remove the pivot assembly from inside the body under the dash.

Install

1. Replace the linkage assembly into the vehicle under the instrument panel and then replace and tighten the retaining screws.

2. Replace the motor assembled into the engine bay then install and tighten the four retaining screws under the instrument panel.

3. Install the arm linkage to the motor driven link and replace the retaining clip.

4. Replace the wiper arms to the linkage.

REPLACE WIPER BLADES

Wiper insert rubbers deteriorate as a result of environmental conditions, such as atmospheric pollution and road grime, temperature extremes and natural ageing of rubber.

It is therefore recommended that wiper inserts are replaced every twelve months or as required.

Wiper Blade Insert Assembly (with metal backing)

1. Lift the blade away from the windscreen as far as it will go, so the wiper arm is held into position by its own spring tension.

2. Remove the wiper blade from the wiper arm on early models remove the two attaching screws. Later models

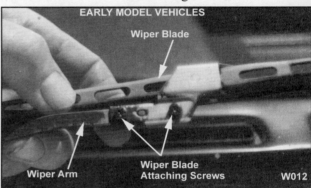

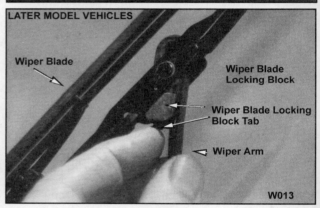

Unclip the wiper locking device, remove the locking block and slide the wiper away from the arm.

3. Remove the retaining clip from the wiper and slide the old rubber blade out from the wiper assembly.

4. Slide the wiper insert assembly into position, install the metal retaining clip.

5. Install the wiper onto the wiper arm.

Clip the wiper onto the arm, or install the blade attaching screws.

Wiper Blade (Rubber insert only)

1. Lift the blade away from the windscreen as far as it will go, so the wiper arm is held into position by its own spring tension.

2. Remove the wiper blade from the wiper arm, on early models remove the two attaching screws. Later models Unclip the wiper locking device, remove the locking block

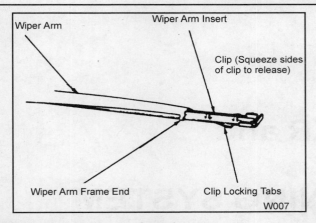

W007

and slide the wiper away from the arm.

3. Remove the retaining clip from the end of the wiper.

4. Pull the rubber away from the wiper arm (retaining clip end) and slide the old blade rubber out from the other end of the wiper.

5. Slide the new rubber wiper insert into position from the end of the retaining clip, install the metal retaining clip.

6. Install the wiper onto the wiper arm. Clip the wiper onto the arm, or install the blade attaching screws.

CHECKING WIPER ARM TO WINDSCREEN ALIGNMENT

This check should be performed if wiper inserts are in good operating condition.

1. Operate wipers and then, by turning ignition switch off, position wipers at approximately 30^0 into the arc of the wiper.

2. Remove wiper blade and check that end of wiper arm

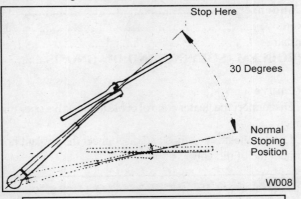

W008

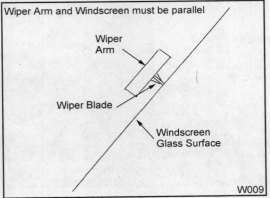

W009

339

is square to windscreen.

3. If arm is not square, gently twist end of arm to achieve correct alignment.

4. Refit wiper blades.

5. Turn ignition switch on and allow wiper arms to return to normal position.

WINDSHIELD WASHER

Don't operate washer motor for more than 20 seconds continuously or when washer bottle is empty as motor or pump could be damaged.

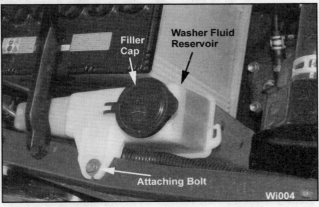

Wi004

Washer Liquid

Fill washer unit with either water or water and a small amount of detergent, this will help remove road grim such as oil and insects.

* *Note: Do not use too much detergent as this will obscure vision on the windscreen.*

Blocked Washer Nozzle

If the nozzles become blocked remove the hose from the back of the washer nozzle and use air pressure to blow the foreign matter from the nozzle. Reconnect the hose to the nozzle and test washer unit.

WASHER NOZZLE ADJUSTMENT

1. Check washer fluid spray pattern is as shown.

2. If adjustment is necessary use a metal wire or pin 1.0 mm or less in diameter inserted in nozzle hole, turn nozzle to direct spray at the desired angle.

3. If insufficient washer fluid is supplied check system for clogged, bent or crushed hoses.

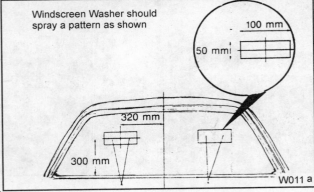

W011 a

HEATER and

AIR CONDITIONING SYSTEM

BLEEDING AIR FROM HEATER CORE

The heater core should bleed air by having the heater turned to fully HOT with the engine operating.

1. Disconnect the heater core outlet hose at the heater control valve connection.

2. Any trapped air should be allowed to flow out.

3. Connect the hose to the heater control valve, when a continuous flow of coolant is obtained from the hose.

HEATER WATER VALVE ASSEMBLY

Remove

1. Disconnect the heater control cable to the valve operating lever.

2. Loosen the hose clamps and disconnect the coolant hose either side of the valve.

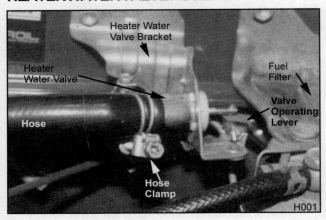

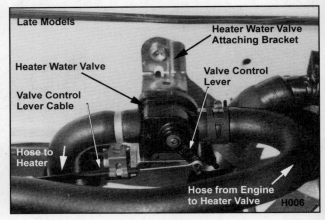

3. Remove the heater water valve attaching screws and valve from the fire wall.

Install

1. Install the heater water valve to the fire wall and attaching screws.

2. Connect the coolant hose either side of the valve, tighten the hose clamps.

3. Connect the heater control cable to the valve operating lever.

HEATER CONTROL SWITCH

See Dash/Instrument Panel in body chapter for more details.

Remove

1. Disconnect the battery.

2. Remove the screw retaining the control knobs and remove the control knobs.

3. Remove the screws retaining the centre facia, then

remove the facia from the vehicle.

4. Remove the screws retaining the control assembly to the instrument panel.

5. Disconnect the wiring connections, and cables from the back of the assembly, it is advisable to label connections for easier installation.

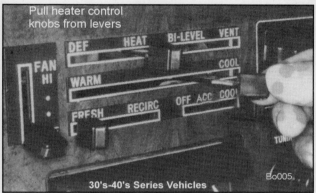

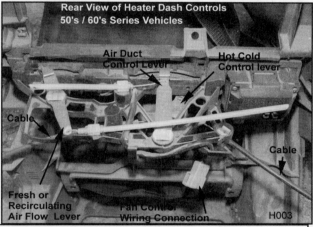

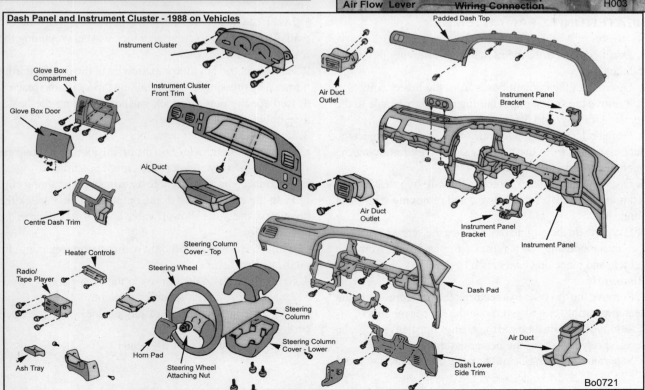

Fan Drum Blade

Heater
Attaching
Bracket

Heater
Fan Motor

Heater
Duct Crank
(Control Lever)

Clip

Heater Case is held together by clips and a screw.

H002

5. Remove the control unit from vehicle.

Install

1. Connect the heater connectors and any vacuum hoses, insert assembly into position and replace the retaining screws.

2. Replace the control cable to the lever and tighten the screw retaining the control cable to the switch lever.

3. Replace the control knobs and tighten securing screws.

4. Reconnect the battery.

HEATER UNIT & FAN ASSEMBLY

Remove

1. Drain coolant from the radiator by removing the lower radiator hose.

2. Disconnect the coolant hoses from the heater core.

3. Remove the spring clip retaining the control cable to the heater assembly, and disconnect the cable.

4. From under the passenger side of the dash disconnect the duct assembly from the heater assembly by removing the retaining nuts and lock washers.

5. Disconnect the heater motor main wire by releasing the retaining tab with a screw driver, and removing wire from connector.

6. From inside the engine bay remove the screws retaining the heater housing, then remove the assembly from the vehicle and place on clean bench.

Dismantle

1. Remove the three screws securing the heater motor to the heater assembly and also remove the rubber mounts.

2. Remove the drain tube and the spring clip, then remove the seven screws securing the heater assembly together.

3. Separate the assembly and remove the heater motor and

the cooler pipe.

Assembly.

1. Replace the cooler pipe and motor assembly into the heater housing, and install the heater housing together tightening the seven retaining screws.

2. Replace the drain tube and the spring clip, then replace the rubber mounts and tighten the screws securing the motor assembly to the heater unit.

Install

1. Install the heater assembly into position against the fire wall, then install the screws and lock washers retaining the assembly to the fire wall.

2. Reconnect the fan motor main wire to the engine wiring harness, by pressing in until retaining tab locks into place.

3. Replace the nuts and lock washers securing the heater assembly to the duct assembly.

3. Reconnect the heater assembly control cable.

a) Position the control lever in the off position, and move the water shut-off valve lever to the closed position.

b) Reconnect the control cable securing with retaining clip.

c) Push the control lever to the on position, and check the position of the water shut-off valve lever, it should be in the open position.

d) If adjustment is required adjust with the spring retaining clip on the control lever.

4. Reconnect the coolant hoses to the heater core.

5. Top up radiator with specified coolant.

6. Bleed the heater system of any air locks, as described earlier in this chapter.

7. Check the operation of the heater.

342

FAN MOTOR ASSEMBLY

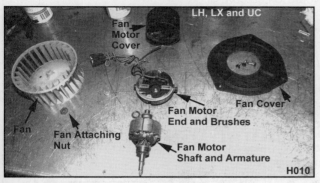

Remove
1. Remove heater assembly as previously described.
2. Disconnect the electrical connections to the fam motor.
3. Remove the screws attaching the fan assembly to the heater case.

Install
1. Position the heater in the heater case and install the attaching screws.

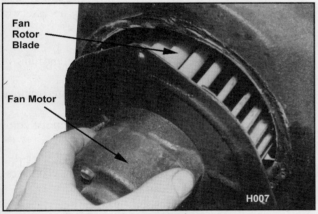

2. Connect the fan wiring connection.
3. Instal the fan assembly as previously described.

PROBLEM SOLVING AND DIAGNOSIS

Condition - Insufficient, No Heat or Demist
CAUSE: Low radiator coolant due to coolant leaks.
ACTION: Check radiator fill if necessary, check for leaks.
CAUSE: Low radiator coolant due to engine overheating.
ACTION: Remove bugs, etc. from radiator. Check for loose drive belt, sticking thermostat, incorrect ignition timing.
CAUSE: Plugged or partially plugged heater core.
ACTION: Clean and back-flush engine cooling system and heater core.
CAUSE: Air flow control doors sticking or blinding.
ACTION: Check control cables.
CAUSE: Blocked air inlet.
ACTION: Check cowl air inlet for leaves etc.

Condition - Too Much Heat
CAUSE: Loose or improperly adjusted control cables.
ACTION: Adjust as specified.
CAUSE: Sticking water valve.
ACTION: Replace if required.

TEST
LOOSE MOTOR FAN TEST
Turn on the fan switch, if only a hum is heard, the fan is loose on the motor.
FAN SWITCH TEST
Substitute a blower switch for the suspected switch.

AIR CONDITIONING

GENERAL INFORMATION
The following information provides basic service operations for the air conditioning system, including the compressor.

REFRIGERANT CIRCUIT
The refrigerant circuit below is schematic of the major components.
A compressor, condenser, expansion tube, evaporator, and an accumulator.
The engine RPM is higher on air conditioned models so as not to drop to low at idle during system operation. When the ignition is turned off and the air conditioning has been operating, a faint sound of liquid flowing for 30-60 seconds maybe heard. This is the refrigerant in the system continuing to flow until high side and low side pressures equalize.

SERVICE OPERATIONS

COMPRESSOR BELT TENSION & ADJUSTMENT
Inspect the condition of the air compressor belt.

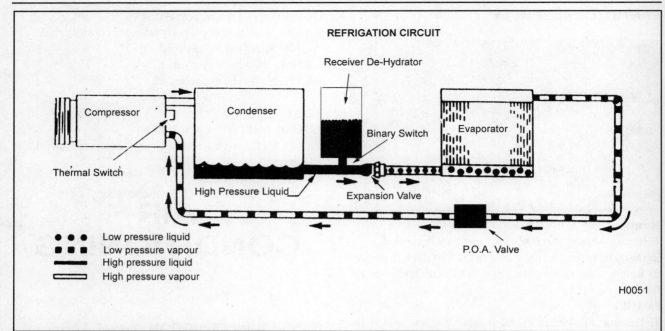

REFRIGATION CIRCUIT

Receiver De-Hydrator

Compressor

Condenser

Binary Switch

Evaporator

Thermal Switch

High Pressure Liquid

Expansion Valve

P.O.A. Valve

- ● ● ● Low pressure liquid
- ■ ■ ■ Low pressure vapour
- ▬ ▬ High pressure liquid
- ▭ High pressure vapour

H0051

COMPRESSOR DRIVE BELT TENSION

NEW	USED
*140 +/- 5 lbs.	*95 +/- 5 lbs.

* Belt deflection in lbs. when a force is applied in the area shown in diagram.

ADJUST.

Using a ring spanner or socket, loosen off the compressor idler pulley assembly. Pull on the idler pulley to tighten the belt, tighten the compressor idler pulley nut.

Torque idler pulley nut to 20-30 lb. ft. when the correct tension has been achieved.

COMPRESSOR

* Where a failure has occurred that may have resulted in foreign material in the system, the system must be flushed using Refrigerant R-12.

* All compressor removal and install operations, except belt replacement, can be performed only after the unit has been discharged.

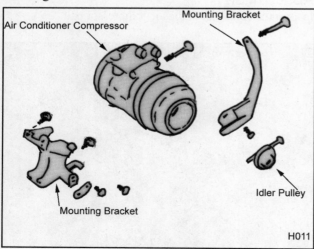

Air Conditioner Compressor

Mounting Bracket

Mounting Bracket

Idler Pulley

H011

Storage of compressor

The port protection plate should be fitted to keep compressor free from moisture and foreign material if it is necessary to store a serviced compressor.

Remove

1. Discharge the air conditioning service system, and remove refrigerant lines from compressor.
2. Loosen compressor mounting bolts, belt adjuster, remove drive belt and disconnect electrical connector.
3. Remove compressor mounting bolts and remove compressor from the vehicle.

Install

1. Install new compressor and fit drive belt. Torque compressor mounting bolts to specification.
2. Adjust drive belt to specification. Install refrigerant hoses, and connect clutch wire.
3. Charge the air conditioning system.

REFRIGERANT (A/C) LINES

Removal

1. Discharge the refrigerant from A/C system following recommended EPA procedure, observing safety precautions.
2. Remove the A/C line using a back-up spanner on each fitting.

Install

1. Install new A/C line with protective caps installed.
2. Using new O-rings lubricated with clean refrigerant oil, connect the A/C line into the system. Use two wrenches when tightening the fittings to specification.
3. To check for leaks, evacuate and charge the refrigerant system following the recommended procedures and safety precautions.

344

EVAPORATOR ASSEMBLY

Remove

1. Discharge refrigerant from air conditioning system and remove the heater assembly as described previously.

2. Disconnect the line for the P.O.A.S.T valve to the compressor, then remove the expansion valve to receiver pipe which also connects the valve to dehydrator.

3. From the heater case mounting frame remove the retaining screws.

4. Disconnect the electrical connections from the resistor and the fan motor, then remove the evaporator assembly.

Install

1. Replace the evaporator assembly into the vehicle and connect the electrical connections.

2. Replace and tighten the heater casing housing mounting frame screws.

3. Reconnect the pipe from the expansion valve to the receiver pipe and the dehydrator, then reconnect the line for the P.O.A.S.T valve to the compressor.

4. Replace the heater assembly as described previously and charge air conditioning system.

CONDENSER

Remove

1. Discharge the refrigerant system and remove the radiator grille as described in Body chapter.

2. Disconnect and cap both the inlet and outlet refrigerant lines.

3. Remove the screws securing the radiator into position, then remove the radiator backwards, then lift out the condenser from the vehicle.

Install

1. Install the condenser into the vehicle.

2. Replace the radiator into position and replace the retaining bolts, then the inlet and outlet lines using new "O" ring seals.

3. Reconnect the refrigerant pipes on the right hand side of the condenser using new oil condenser line 'O' rings and replace the screws securing the right hand side condenser bracket.

4. Replace the radiator grille (as described in body chapter)

Air Conditioner Condensor

Condensor Site Glass

Radiator Grille

H004

5. Evacuate and charge the system with refrigerant.

AIR CONDITIONER CONTROLS

See Heater controls earlier in this chapter.

PROBLEM DIAGNOSIS

COMPRESSOR DIAGNOSIS

Problem: Oil Leaks

Remedy: Inspect for leaks.

Oil leaks do not necessarily indicate leaking refrigerant, check for oil leaks around the following components:
- Shaft seal, leak test see area between clutch and compressor.
- Hose fittings.
- Compressor housing.

Thoroughly clean around compressor and components with detergent and hot water, starting detection procedures. Follow supplier instructions for the proper techniques to be used for 'ELECTRONIC' Leak Detectors.

Another useful test is a soap bubble test. Apply a soapy mixture around all joints or possible leak areas, start air conditioner and turn on to high operation, check for bubbles. If bubbles are found at any section or joint where the soapy solution was applied it will indicate a leak requiring repair.

Problem: Bearing Noise

Remedy: Carry out the following procedure: Remove belt. Disengage clutch. Rotate rotor pulley by hand. Listen for bearing noise. Feel for hard spots. If excessive, repair or replace compressor.

* All compressors have operating noise, this should not be mistaken for a faulty compressor.

Problem: Suspect bearing or seal failure.

Remedy: Discharge the system, disengage clutch, rotate front plate by hand. While rotating, if severe rough spots or 'catches' are felt, repair or replace the compressor.

Problem: Compressor noise.

Remedy: Visual inspection of:

Broken or loose bolts at compressor and engine fixing points - replace and/or torque bolts to specifications.

Loose or bent engine crankshaft pulley - repair or replace.

Broken bracket and/or compressor body mounting - replace broken component.

Oil level - insufficient oil can cause unusual noise.

Drive belt not at correct tension.

Generator bearing noisy - replace.

Water pump bearing noisy - replace.

Loose engine mounting bolts - re-torque.

Low refrigerant charge. Low charge can be determined by low suction pressure together with low head pressure.

LIGHTS, SWITCHES & BATTERY SYSTEMS

BATTERY

GENERAL INFORMATION

Battery acid is highly corrosive which may on contact, cause personal injury or damage paint surfaces. Any spillage must be immediately diluted and flushed away with clean water. The battery electrolyte should be maintained at recommended level by topping up with distilled water.
Clean the battery terminal and the inside of the cable terminal using a suitable tool.

PERIODIC MAINTENANCE

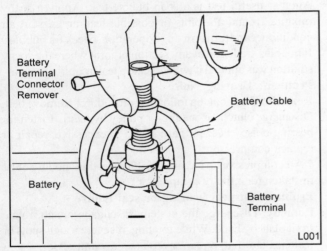

1. Protect paint finish using suitable covers.
2. Disconnect battery cables at battery (negative first).
3. Remove battery hold down clamp and remove battery from vehicle.
4. Inspect battery carrier for acid damage. If necessary remove corrosion by using a solution of bicarbonate of soda in warm water and scrubbing area with a stiff brush, taking care to avoid spreading corrosion residue, and flush area with clean water. Damaged areas should be repainted to avoid further corrosion.
5. Clean battery cover by same method.
* Do not allow any cleaning solution or water to enter battery cells as this will dilute electrolyte.
6. Check battery cables for damage and fraying and replace if necessary.
7. Clean battery terminals. If necessary remove corrosion by using a solution of bicarbonate of soda in warm water and

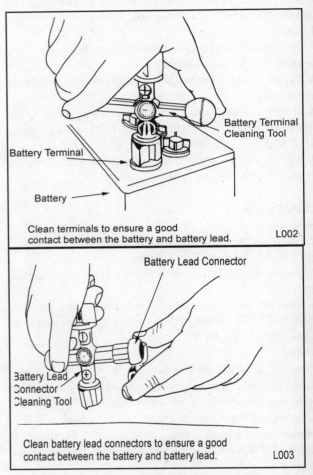

Clean terminals to ensure a good contact between the battery and battery lead. L002

Clean battery lead connectors to ensure a good contact between the battery and battery lead. L003

scrubbing area with a stiff brush, taking care to avoid spreading corrosion residue, and flush area with clean water.
8. Check battery case, cover and vents for damage.
9. Install battery and hold down clamp. Do not overtighten hold down clamp as this could crack case.
10. Connect battery cables and tighten to specifications.
Tighten Battery Terminal: **6-8Nm**
* Ensure battery polarity is not reversed.
11. Coat terminals with light mineral grease to avoid corrosion.

TESTING BATTERY ELECTROLYTE (ACID)

A hydrometer should be used to determine the specific gravity of battery electrolyte. The reading obtained indicates amount of unused sulphuric acid remaining in electrolyte and state of charge of battery.

The reading obtained will vary in relation to the temperature of the electrolyte. As the temperature rises the density of the electrolyte decreases and the specific gravity falls. As the temperature falls the density increases and the specific gravity rises.

USING THE HYDROMETER

1. Liquid level of battery cell should be at normal height and electrolyte should be thoroughly mixed with any battery water which may have just been added by charging battery before taking hydrometer readings.

2. Draw electrolyte in and out of hydrometer barrel several times to bring temperature of hydrometer float to that of the acid in the cell.

3. Draw sufficient electrolyte into hydrometer barrel with the pressure bulb fully expanded to lift float so that it does not touch the sides, bottom or top of barrel.

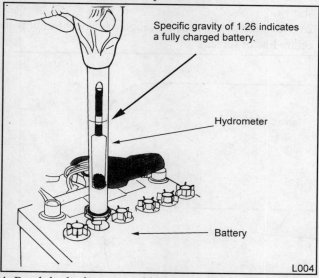

Specific gravity of 1.26 indicates a fully charged battery.

Hydrometer

Battery

L004

4. Read the hydrometer with the hydrometer in a vertical position.

TEST RESULT INDICATIONS

Electrolyte specific gravity	Battery Charge Level.
1.240 to 1.260	100%
1.210 to 1.240	75%
1.180 to 1.210	50%
Below 1.130	Completely discharged.

A battery should be charged if the specific gravity is less than 1.210.

If there is more than 0.25 specific gravity variation between cells then a fault is most likely with the battery itself.

If battery charge is low and battery is serviceable, check alternator operation and all electrical connections.

BATTERY CHARGING

WARNING: When batteries are being charged explosive gas mixture forms beneath the cover of each cell.

* Do not smoke near batteries on charge or which have recently been charged.

* Do not break live circuit at terminals of batteries on charge. A spark will occur where the live circuit is broken. Keep all open flames away from battery.

NB: Fast charging will provide sufficient charge after one hour to enable the battery and alternator to carry electrical load however, whenever possible, slow charging is preferable.

FAST CHARGING

Fast charging a battery in the vehicle is not recommended, however if this procedure is used it is most important that the battery is disconnected.

NB: A battery will be irretrievably damaged if following precautions are not taken.

1. Battery electrolyte temperature must NEVER exceed 45°C.

If this temperature is reached, battery should be cooled by reducing charging rate or remove battery from circuit.

2 . As batteries approach full charge electrolyte in each cell will begin to gas or bubble. Excessive gassing must not be allowed.

3. Do not fast charge longer than one hour. If battery does not show a significant change in specific gravity after one hour of "FAST" charge, the slow charge method should be used.

SLOW CHARGING

Many discharged batteries can be brought back to good condition by slow charging; especially batteries that are sulphated. Battery should be tested with a hydrometer and a record kept of the readings taken at regular intervals throughout the charge. When a cell has a specific gravity reading that is 0.25 or more below other cells, that cell is faulty and battery should be replaced.

Safe slow charging rates can be calculated by allowing one ampere per positive plate per cell i.e. 4 amperes for a 9 plate battery and 5 amperes for an 11 plate battery.

The average time required to charge a battery by the slow charge method at normal rates is from 12 to 16 hours, however, when a battery continues to show an increase in specific gravity, battery charge should be continued even if it takes 24 hours or more. Watch the temperature of batteries carefully and if temperature of any one of them reaches 43°C, lower the charging rate.

Battery will be fully charged when it is gassing freely and when there is no further rise in specific gravity after three successive readings taken at hourly intervals. Make sure hydrometer readings are corrected for temperature.

Many batteries can be brought back to a useful condition by slow charging at half the normal charging rate from 60 to 100 hours. This long charging cycle is necessary to reconvert crystalline lead sulphate in to active materials.

LIGHTS & SWITCHES

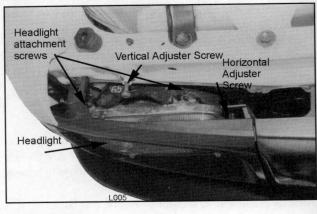

L005

ADJUST HEADLIGHT PATTERN

Always adjust headlight pattern according to the state laws and regulations.

Before adjusting headlight take note of the following procedure:

1. Ensure tyres are inflated correctly.
2. Clean headlight lenses.
3. Check the vehicle is positioned on a level floor.
4. Bounce vehicle to ensure vehicle is at normal height.
5. Place sufficient weight in vehicle to simulate full load conditions (1 litre of fuel = 0.72 kg).

ADJUSTMENT

Adjusting screws are located at the front of headlight assembly between the headlight rim and grille.

Adjust as follows:

VERTICAL

Adjust vertically by turning screw at top of light.

HORIZONTAL

Adjust horizontally by turning screw at the side (vehicle centre side) of the light assembly.

USING A WALL

1. Manufacture an aiming target on a light coloured wall as shown.
2. With vehicle up against wall, align vehicle centre line with centre line of screen.

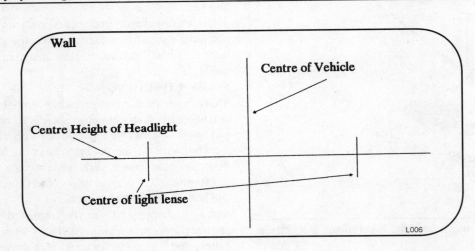

L006

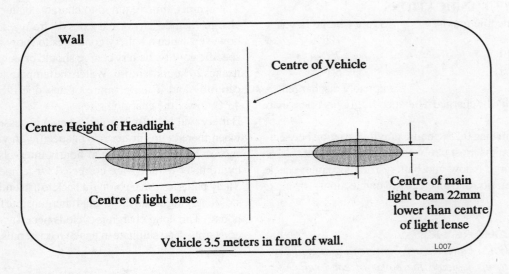

L007

3. With vehicle up against wall, mark head light height and centre of light lens on wall.

4. Place vehicle 3.5 meters in front of screen ensuring the vehicle is aligned with vehicle centre line mark on screen.

5. Switch headlights onto low beam and aim outer lights. To adjust the height of the light beam turn the adjuster screw as shown in the photograph.

6. Switch headlights onto high beam, mask outer lights and aim inner lights.
To adjust the height of the light beam turn the adjuster screw as shown in the photograph.

HEADLIGHT ASSEMBLY

Head Light Replacement

The headlight is a sealed beam unit and must be removed to be replaced.

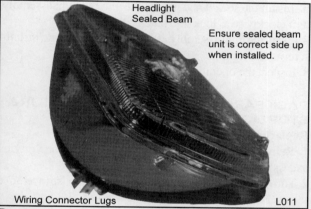

Headlight Sealed Beam

Ensure sealed beam unit is correct side up when installed.

Wiring Connector Lugs — L011

Remove

1. Disconnect the earth lead from the battery.
2. Pull the electrical push-on connection from the back of the headlight sealed beam unit.
3. Remove the headlight trim attaching screws and trim.
4. Remove the four screws from the headlight assembly.
5. Gently remove the light from the body of the car.

Install

1. Install the headlight assembly into the body of the vehicle.
2. Replace the four screws attaching the light assembly.
4. Connect both the headlight wiring loom.
5. Check operation of all the lights.
6. Check headlamp aim.

FRONT TURNING INDICATOR LIGHT ASSEMBLY

Remove

Early Models.

1. Lift bonnet to gain access to the back of the light assembly.
2. Remove the screws attaching the turning indicator light to the body work.
3. Remove the turning indicator light.

Late Models.

1. Remove headlight and indicator light trim attaching screws

and trim.

2. Remove the screws attaching the turning indicator light to the body work.
3. Remove the turning indicator light.

Install

1. Install the turning indicator light to the vehicle and install the attaching screws.

Late Models: Install light surround trim and attaching screws.

2. Connect wiring connectors at back of light assembly.
2. Test operation of all lights and close bonnet.

PARK LIGHT GLOBE

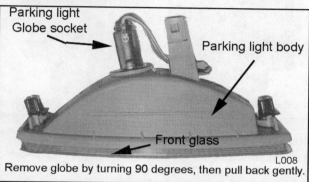

Parking light Globe socket

Parking light body

Front glass

L008

Remove globe by turning 90 degrees, then pull back gently.

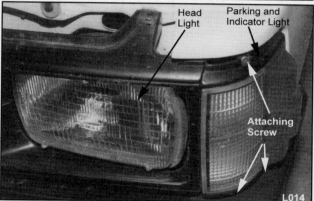

Head Light

Parking and Indicator Light

Attaching Screw

L014

Parking Light

Lense Screw

L015

Replace

1. Remove front glass with phillips screw driver.
2. Remove the parking light globe by turning 90^{0} then pulling back on the globe gently.
3. Replace the globe with a globe of the same wattage.

4. Install the globe into parklight assembly.

5. Replace front glass, take care to align rubber seal correctly so water does not enter light as assembly.

FRONT TURNING INDICATOR LIGHT GLOBE

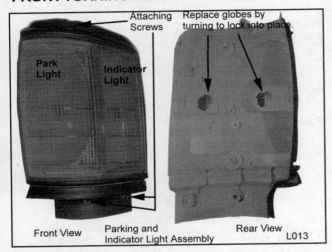

Front View — Parking and Indicator Light Assembly — Rear View   L013

Replace

1. Turn globe and socket anti-clockwise to remove socket from back of light reflector.

2. Remove globe from socket.

3. Replace globe with a similar wattage globe.

4. Install socket, turn clockwise to fix socket into place.

LICENCE PLATE LIGHT

Replacement of Globes

1. Remove the phillips head screws from either end of the light glass lenses.

2. Install new globes of the same wattage if required.

3. Replace the lenses, install the phillips head screws.

Remove

1. Remove the nuts from the licence plate light.

2. Disconnect the wiring loom connectors and remove the light assembly.

Install

1. Install the light assembly to the vehicle, tighten the attaching nuts and screws.

2. Connect the wiring loom.

3. Test operation of light.

BACK PARK LIGHT, TURNING INDICATOR & STOP LIGHT - Tray Truck Models

The light assembly needs to be removed from the vehicle to replace globes.

Replacement of Light and Globes

1. Remove the 4 screws attaching the light to the vehicle.

2. Remove the light assembly from the vehicle.

3. Turn the faulty globe and socket anti-clockwise to remove the socket from the back of the light assembly.

Rear light assembly for tray back Hilux   L009

4. Remove the globe from the light socket.

5. Replace the globe with one of the same wattage.

6. Install the socket and new globe into the light assembly, turn clockwise to lock into place.

7. Install the light assembly to the vehicle bodywork, install 4 screws and tighten.

8. Inspect the operation of lights.

BACK PARK LIGHT, TURNING INDICATOR & STOP LIGHT - Utility and 4 Runner

Replacement of Globes

1. Remove the 4 screws attaching the inside panel giving axcess to the rear of the light assembly.

2. Turn the faulty globe and socket anti-clockwise to remove the socket from the back of the light assembly.

3. Remove the globe from the light socket.

4. Replace the globe with one of the same wattage.

5. Install the socket and new globe into the light assembly, turn clockwise to lock into place.

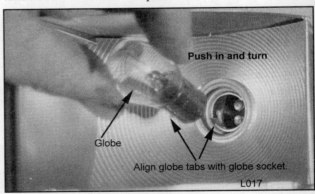

L017

6. Inspect the operation of lights.

7. Install the panel and 4 screws attaching the inside panel giving axcess to the rear of the light assembly.

Remove

1. Remove the 4 screws attaching the light to the vehicle.

2. Partily remove the light assembly from the vehicle.

3. Turn the globe and sockets anti-clockwise to remove the socket from the back of the light assembly.

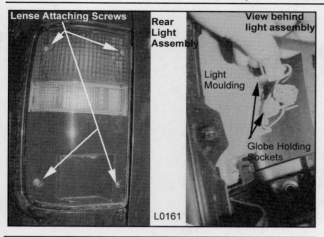

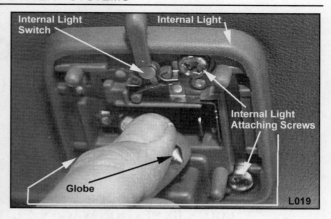

1. Remove the light lens by pressing in on the rear of the lens.
2. Remove globe by levering globe away from the light socket.
3. Remove the 3 or 4 screws attaching the light assembly to the roof panel.

Install

1. Replace light assembly into roof panel, install 3 or 4 screws.
2. Insert new globe if necessary into sockets.
3. Replace light lens.

REAR INTERNAL LIGHT - Station Wagon - Utility

Remove

1. Remove the light lens by using a blade or small screw driver from the passenger side of the vehicle.
2. Remove globe by levering globe away from the light socket.
3. Remove the electrical connections from the light.

Install

1. Replace light assembly into roof panel, install the electrical connections.
2. Insert new globe if necessary into sockets.
3. Replace light and lens into roof by pushing the light into place.

INSTRUMENT CLUSTER AND WARNING LAMP CLUSTER ILLUMINATION

Instrument illumination and warning lamp bulbs are a push fit into sockets which twist.

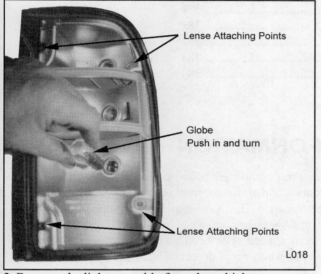

2. Remove the light assembly from the vehicle.

Install

1. Position the light assembly close to the light opening.
2. Install the sockets and globes into the light assembly, turn clockwise to lock into place.
3. Install the light assembly to the vehicle bodywork, install 4 screws and tighten.
4. Inspect the operation of lights.

INTERNAL LIGHT
Remove

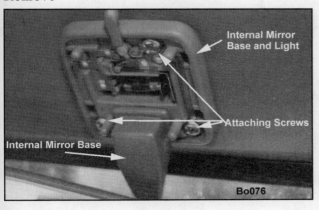

GLOBE SPECIFICATIONS

	Watt
Headlamps	
Hi/Lo beam	60/55
Parking (Front)	5
Turn Signal	21
Reverse Light	21
Stop and Tail Light	21/5
Number Plate Light	5
Instrument Cluster	3.67
Warning Lights	1.2

BODY
INDEX

GENERAL INFORMATION

The body incorporates a driver and passenger compartment then a tray component bolted to a rail chassis.

After a collision it's advisable to check the body alignment. Front section of chassis, front suspension, fenders and body panels ahead of the fire wall are the ones that will most likely be damaged. The front chassis section supports the cabin, the front body panels, engine and transmission as well as the front suspension.

If replacing body panels it is advisable that these panels be perfectly aligned, if they can not be panel beaten or repaired so they align it is advisable that the panels be replaced with another panel either new or second hand in very good repair.

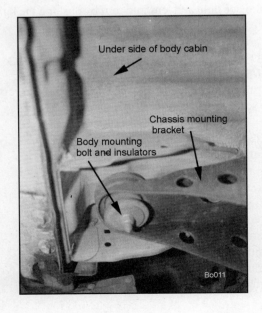

Under side of body cabin

Chassis mounting bracket

Body mounting bolt and insulators

Bo011

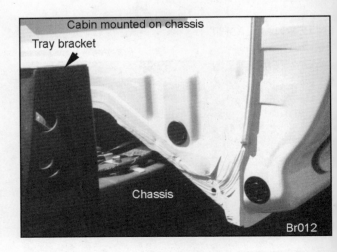

Cabin mounted on chassis

Tray bracket

Chassis

Br012

CHASSIS

CHASSIS ALIGNMENT

Chassis alignment may be checked accurately by the following method:

If damaged has occured mearure from weld joints or from holes centres then compare both sides of vehicle

Bo001

Compare the dimensions made on both sides of vehicle. All dimensions must be measured at the welded joints of the body to ensure uniform measurements or from the centre of holes if measuring from a hole in the body or floor pan / chassis.

FLOOR COVER - INTERNAL
Remove
1. Remove the transmission lever cover trims.
2. Remove the front seat assemblies and rear seat cushion assembly for twin cabs.
3. Remove seat belt securing bolts and remove seat belts.
4. Remove the side panel covers.
5. Lift cover taking care not to damage cover as sealant may need to be worked free.

Install
1. Use a suitable sealant to fix cover into place, carefully replace cover.
2. Replace seat belt anchoring bolts to specified torque.
Seat Belt Anchoring Bolts Torque: **35-70Nm.**
3. Install seat assemblies as described in seat section.
4. Install transmission cover trims.

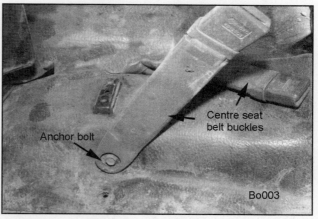

Centre seat belt buckles

Anchor bolt

Bo003

CARPET - 4 Runner Back Section
Remove
Lift the carpet from the vehicle by gently lifting the edges of the carpet towards the centre.

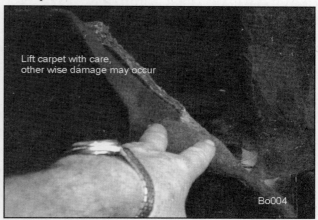

Lift carpet with care, other wise damage may occur

Bo004

Install
Lay carpet out in the correct position and fit carpet to the floor section. Making sure that the carpet fits neatly up against all edges.

TRAY LINER
Replace
Remove screws attaching the liner to the tray and tailgate, lift liner from vehicle. To fit new liner position liner to vehicle, replace attaching screws.

Plastic liner to protect tray and tail gate, liner is attached by screws.

Bo048

DASH/ INSTRUMENT PANEL

of the compartment as shown.

DASH LOWER PANEL - DRIVERS SIDE
Remove
Remove the key barrel cover with a screw driver (80's to 130's Series), remove the screws and bolt, securing the panel to the dash. Pull the panel away and separate the connector.
Install
Fit panel into position, connect the electrical connector and install screws and bolt. Fit key barrel cover.

GLOVE COMPARTMENT 30's & 40's Series
Remove
Open the glove compartment, use a screw driver to remove the glove compartment door hinge screws. Remove the glove compartment door.
Install
Position the glove compartment lid into position and refit the hinge screws. Ensure the glove compartment door fits correctly.

GLOVE COMPARTMENT 50's & 60's Series

To remove glove box remove 2 bolts at arrows

Remove
Remove the two bolts below either side of the glove compartment door. Slide the glove compartment and hinge out from the instrument panel.
Install
Position the glove compartment door into position and refit the two bolts below either side of the glove compartment door. Ensure the glove compartment door fits correctly.

GLOVE COMPARTMENT & TRIM 80's to 130's Series
Remove
Open the glove compartment door. Remove the one bolt and four screws. Slide the glove compartment, door and trim down and out from the instrument panel. The door is hinged by two pins.
Install
Position the glove compartment door into position and refit the two hinge pins. Fit the glove compartment and panel into position, install the one bolt and four screws. Ensure the glove

CENTRE CONSOLE
Remove
Remove the nuts at the base of the consul compartment.
Install
Position the console in place and install the nuts at the base

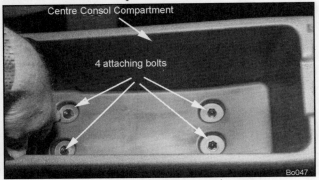

Centre Consol Compartment
4 attaching bolts

354

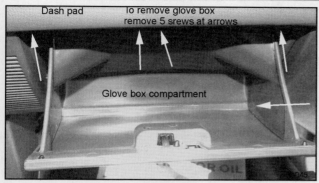

Dash pad To remove glove box remove 5 srews at arrows

Glove box compartment

compartment door fits correctly.

HEATER CONTROLS, RADIO FACIA &CENTRE TRIM 30's & 40's

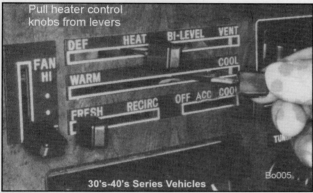

Pull heater control knobs from levers

DEF HEAT BI-LEVEL VENT
FAN HI COOL
WARM
FRESH RECIRC OFF ACC COOL

30's-40's Series Vehicles

Bo005

Remove
1. Disconnect the battery.
2. Remove the heater control knobs by pulling off.
3. Remove the radio control knobs by pulling off.
4. Remove the screws securing the trim to the instrument panel.
5. Pull the centre trim out enough to disconnect the wiring connectors, behind the trim.
6. Remove the trim.

Install
1. Install the centre trim into position, leave it out enough to connect the wiring connectors, behind the trim.
2. Install the screws securing the trim to the instrument panel.
3. Install the radio control knobs by pushing on.
4. Install the heater control knobs by pushing on.
5. Connect battery.

CENTRE CONTROLS, RADIO & TRIM 50's & 60's

Remove
1. Disconnect the battery.
2. Remove the heater control knobs by pulling off.
3. Remove the radio control knobs by pulling off.
4. Remove the centre facia trim by removing the screws.

Install
1. Position the centre facia trim and install the screws.
2. Replace the radio control knobs by pushing on.

3. Replace the heater control knobs by pushing on.
4. Reconnect the battery.

INSTRUMENT PANEL 30's & 40's
Remove
1. Disconnect the battery.
2. Open the glove compartment, use a screw driver to remove the glove compartment door hinge screws. Remove the glove compartment door.
3. Remove the steering column surrounds.
(a) Remove the 4 screws from the lower section of the steering column.
(b) Remove the top plastic section.
(c) Detach column wiring at the multi-pin plugs and tie up out of way.
4. Remove the instrument cluster trim by removing the 5 screws, then lower trim from dash panel.
5. Remove the instrument cluster 4 attaching screws, pull cluster forward enough to disconnect the attaching wires and cable. Remove instrument cluster.
6. Remove the centre trim and radio.
(a) Remove the heater control knobs by pulling off.
(b) Remove the radio control knobs by pulling off.
(c) Remove the screws securing the trim to the instrument panel.
(d) Pull the centre trim out enough to disconnect the wiring connectors, behind the trim.
(e) Remove the trim.
(f) Remove the screws attaching the radio to the dash panel, pull the radio partly out, disconnect the radio wiring.
7. Remove the drivers air duct and side dash trim.
(a) Remove the two screws at the front and one under the trim.
(b) Pull the trim away from the dash.
8. Remove the screw attaching the passenger air duct trim and pull out of dash panel.
9. Remove the safety pad attaching screws either end of the dash panel, lift the safety pad from the top of the dash panel.

Install
1. Lift the safety pad onto the top of the dash panel. Install the safety pad attaching screws either end of the dash panel.
2. Push fit the passenger air duct trim into the dash panel, Install screw.
3. Install the drivers air duct and side dash trim.
(a) Fit the trim into the dash.
(b) Replace the two screws at the front and one under the trim.
4. Install the centre trim and radio.
(a) Fit radio partly in, connect the radio wiring, push the radio all the way into the dash. Install the screws attaching the radio to the dash panel.
(b) Fit the centre trim close enough to connect the wiring connectors, behind the trim.
(c) Install the trim over the radio control shafts, and heater control levers.

Dash Pad and Instruments - 30's and 40's Series Vehicles

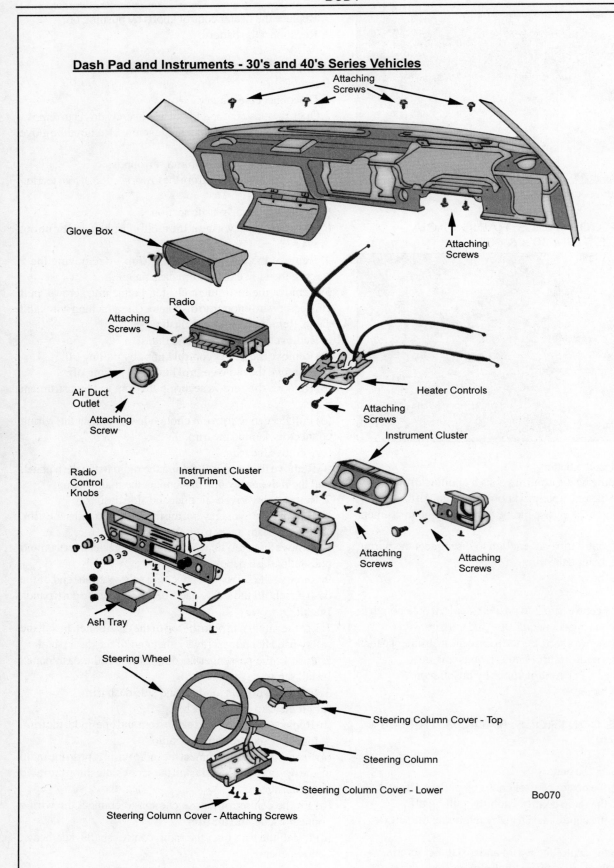

Attaching Screws

Glove Box

Attaching Screws

Radio

Attaching Screws

Air Duct Outlet

Attaching Screw

Heater Controls

Attaching Screws

Instrument Cluster

Radio Control Knobs

Instrument Cluster Top Trim

Attaching Screws

Attaching Screws

Ash Tray

Steering Wheel

Steering Column Cover - Top

Steering Column

Steering Column Cover - Lower

Steering Column Cover - Attaching Screws

Bo070

356

Dash Panel and Instrument Cluster - 50's and 60's Series Vehicles

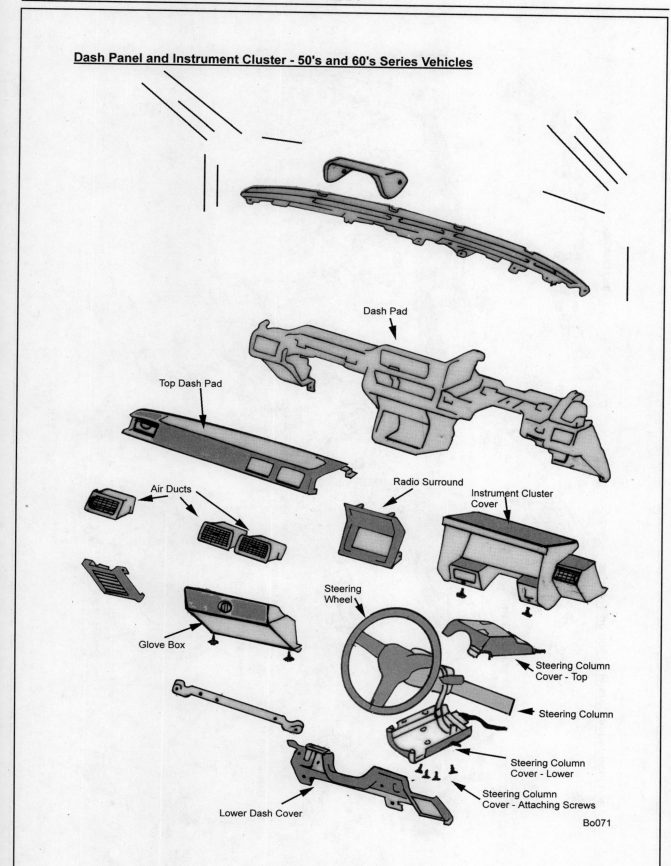

Dash Pad

Top Dash Pad

Air Ducts

Radio Surround

Instrument Cluster Cover

Glove Box

Steering Wheel

Steering Column Cover - Top

Steering Column

Steering Column Cover - Lower

Steering Column Cover - Attaching Screws

Lower Dash Cover

Bo071

Bo072

Dash Panel and Instrument Cluster - 1988 on Vehicles

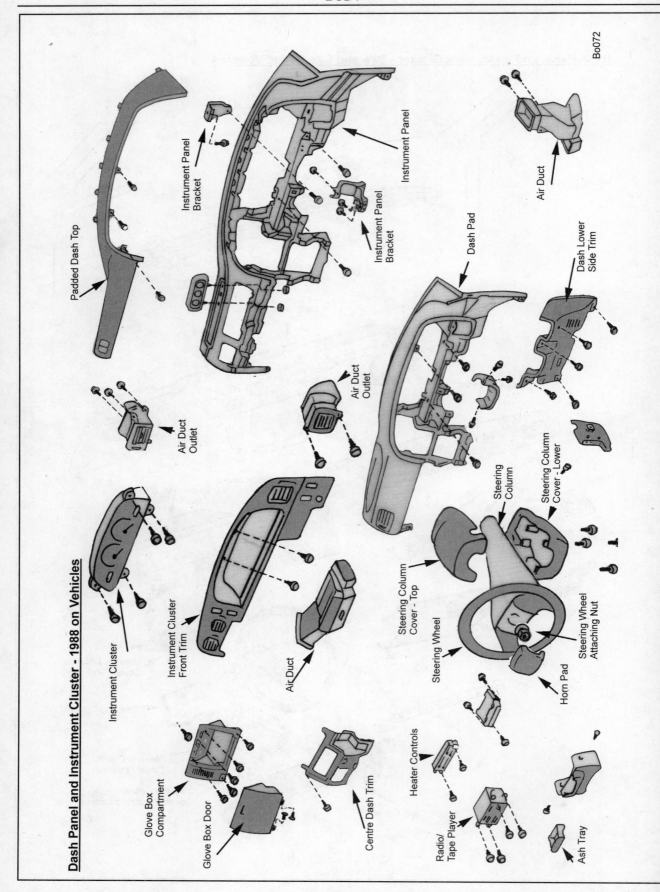

Padded Dash Top

Instrument Panel Bracket

Instrument Panel

Instrument Panel Bracket

Air Duct

Dash Pad

Dash Lower Side Trim

Air Duct Outlet

Air Duct Outlet

Steering Column

Steering Column Cover - Lower

Steering Column Cover - Top

Steering Wheel

Steering Wheel Attaching Nut

Horn Pad

Instrument Cluster

Instrument Cluster Front Trim

Air Duct

Glove Box Compartment

Glove Box Door

Centre Dash Trim

Heater Controls

Radio/ Tape Player

Ash Tray

(d) Replace the screws securing the trim to the instrument panel.

(e) Replace the radio control knobs by pushing on.

(f) Replace the heater control knobs by pushing on.

5. Install the instrument cluster close enough to connect the attaching wires and cable. Replace the instrument cluster 4 attaching screws. Install the instrument cluster trim and secure by replacing the 5 screws.

6. Install the steering column surrounds.

(a) Connect column wiring at the multi-pin plugs.

(b) Replace the top plastic section.

(c) Replace the 4 screws into the lower section of the steering column.

7. Fit the glove compartment, use a screw driver to replace the glove compartment door hinge screws.

8. Connect the battery.

INSTRUMENT PANEL 50's & 60's

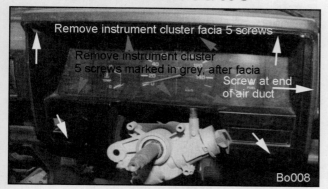

Remove instrument cluster facia 5 screws

Remove instrument cluster 5 screws marked in grey, after facia

Screw at end of air duct

Bo008

Remove

1. Disconnect the battery.

2. Remove the glove compartment, use a socket spanner to remove the four bolts securing the glove compartment and the glove compartment door.

3. Remove the steering column surrounds.

(a) Remove the screws from the lower section of the steering column.

(b) Remove the top plastic section.

(c) Detach column wiring at the multi-pin plugs and tie up out of way.

4. Remove the instrument cluster trim by removing the 5 screws, (4 screws at front, 1 at side of drivers air duct). Then lower trim from dash panel.

5. Remove the instrument cluster 4 attaching screws, pull cluster forward enough to disconnect the attaching wires and cable. Remove instrument cluster.

6. Remove the centre trim and radio.

(a) Remove the heater control knobs by pulling off.

(b) Remove the radio control knobs by pulling off.

(c) Remove the screws securing the trim to the instrument panel.

(d) Pull the centre trim out enough to disconnect the wiring connectors, behind the trim.

(e) Remove the trim.

(f) Remove the screws attaching the radio to the dash panel, pull the radio partly out, disconnect the radio wiring.

7. Remove the passenger air duct from the dash pad by prying the air duct out with a screw driver.

8. Remove the safety pad by removing the 6 screws and 2 nuts, lift the safety pad from the top of the dash panel.

Install

1. Lift the safety pad onto the top of the dash panel. Install the safety pad 6 attaching screws and 2 nuts around the safety pad of the dash panel.

2. Push fit the passenger air duct trim into the dash panel.

3. Install the centre trim and radio.

(a) Fit radio partly in, connect the radio wiring, push the radio all the way into the dash. Install the screws attaching the radio to the dash panel.

(b) Fit the centre trim close enough to connect the wiring connectors, behind the trim.

(c) Install the trim over the radio control shafts, and heater control levers.

(d) Replace the screws securing the trim to the instrument panel.

(e) Replace the radio control knobs by pushing on.

(f) Replace the heater control knobs by pushing on.

4. Install the instrument cluster close enough to connect the attaching wires and cable. Replace the instrument cluster 4 attaching screws. Install the instrument cluster trim and secure by replacing the 5 screws (4 screws at front, 1 at side of drivers air duct).

5. Install the steering column surrounds.

(a) Connect column wiring at the multi-pin plugs.

(b) Replace the top plastic section.

(c) Replace the screws into the lower section of the steering column.

6. Fit the glove compartment, use a socket spanner to replace the four bolts securing the glove compartment and the glove compartment door.

7. Connect the battery.

INSTRUMENT PANEL 80's to 130's Series

Remove

1. Disconnect the battery.

2. Remove the glove compartment, use a socket spanner and phillips screw driver to remove the five screws and bolts securing the glove compartment and the pins hinging the glove compartment door.

3. Remove the steering column surrounds.

(a) Prise the steering wheel centre pad from the steering wheel.

(b) Remove the nut securing the steering wheel to the steering shaft.

(c) Remove the steering wheel with a puller that bolts to the steering wheel.

(d) Remove the screws from the lower section of the steering

BODY

column.

(e) Remove the top plastic section.

(f) Detach column wiring at the multi-pin plugs and tie up out of way.

4. Remove the screws securing the bonnet release lever.

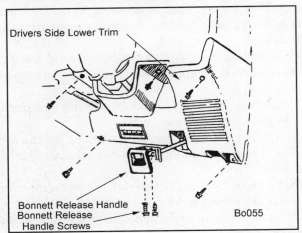

Drivers Side Lower Trim

Bonnett Release Handle
Bonnett Release
Handle Screws

Bo055

5. Vehicles fitted with a trim between the transmission tunnel and dash, remove the 2 clips and lift the trim away.

6. Remove the side cowl trim on the drivers side, secured by a nut.

7. Remove the drivers side air duct, attached by 2 phillips screws.

8. Remove the heater centre trim.

(a) Remove the heater control knobs by pulling off.

Radio, Heater control facia & centre trim   !1988 on

Pull off heater control knobs

Trim

Lower right trim

H006   PRESS BUTTON & TURN   Bo006

(b) Remove the air conditioner control knob by pulling out.

(c) Remove the trim by prising away the trim from the instrument panel with a screw driver.

(d) If clock fitted disconnect wiring.

(e) Remove the trim.

9. Remove the heater controls by removing the attaching screws.

10. Remove the drivers side lower dash panel. Remove the key barrel cover with a screw driver, remove the screws and bolt, securing the panel to the dash. Pull the panel away and separate the connector.

11. Remove the instrument cluster trim by removing the 2 screws, then lower trim from dash panel. Some models have

Radio heater control facia, centre trim

Remove scrwew here

Trim

These screws are removed when lower right trim is removed

Bo007

Remove instrument cluster facia
2 screws after lower trims are removed
there is no need to remove steering wheel

Remove instrument cluster
4 screws marked in grey, after facia

Bo009

a cover over the instrument cluster, remove this if fitted.

12. Remove the instrument cluster air duct, attached by 2 phillips screws.

13. Remove the instrument cluster 4 attaching screws, pull cluster forward enough to disconnect the attaching wires and cable. Remove instrument cluster.

14. Remove the centre lower radio trim, some models have a screw above the radio, prise the trim out from the dash.

15. Remove the radio by removing the 4 bolts securing the radio into the steel bracket, disconnect the wiring at the rear of the radio.

16. Remove the safety pad by removing the 3 bolts, lift the safety pad from the top of the dash panel, there are lugs at the back of the safety pad.

17. Remove the instrument panel frame by removing the bracket bolts high on the fire wall, in the centre down near floor level, some vehicles have brackets on the fire wall passenger side. The panel frame is fitted into the side of the vehicle body, lift the panel up on an angle to free the panel.

Install

1. Install the panel frame, it fits into the side of the vehicle body, slide the panel down at an angle to install the panel. Install the instrument panel frame by replacing the bracket bolts high on the fire wall, in the centre down near floor level, some vehicles have brackets on the fire wall passenger side.

2. Install the safety pad, lift the safety pad onto the top of the dash panel, there are lugs at the back of the safety pad. Install the safety pad securing 3 bolts.

3. Install the radio, connect the wiring at the rear of the radio. Fit the 4 bolts securing the radio into the steel bracket

4. Install the centre lower radio trim, some models have a

screw above the radio, the trim clip into the dash.

5. Fit the instrument cluster close enough to connect the attaching wires and cable. Install the instrument cluster and 4 attaching screws.

6. Install the instrument cluster (cover if one fitted) trim and secure by replacing the 2 screws.

Bo0091

7. Install the instrument cluster air duct, attached by 2 phillips screws.

8. Install the drivers side lower dash panel, connect the wiring connectors. Replace the key barrel cover, push in fit, replace the screws and bolt, securing the panel to the dash.

9. Install the heater controls by fitting the controls into the steel frame and replacing the attaching screws.

10. Replace the heater centre trim if clock fitted connect wiring.

(a) Replace the heater control knobs by pushing on.

(b) Replace the air conditioner control knob by pushing into place.

11. Replace the drivers side air duct, attached by 2 phillips screws.

12. Replace the side cowl trim on the drivers side, secured by a nut.

13. Vehicles fitted with a trim between the transmission tunnel and dash, fit the trim replace the 2 clips.

14. Replace the bonnet release lever by fitting the attaching screws.

15. Replace the steering column and surrounds.

(a) Lift the steering column up to the dash panel, install and tighten bolt to specification.

Steering Column Support Bolts
        260kg-cm, 19ft-lb, 25Nm

(b) Connect the steering column wiring at the multi-pin plugs.

(c) Replace the top plastic section.

(d) Replace the screws attaching the lower section of the steering column cover to the top cover.

(e) Replace the steering wheel, ensure the wheels and the steering wheel are at the straight ahead position.

(f) Install the nut securing the steering wheel to the steering shaft, tighten to specification.

Steering Wheel Attaching Nut:
        350kg-cm, 25ft-lb, 34Nm

(g) Push fit the steering wheel centre pad onto the steering wheel.

16. Install the glove compartment, use a socket spanner and phillips screw driver to replace the five screws and bolts securing the glove compartment and the pins hinging the glove compartment door.

17. Connect the battery.

INSTRUMENT CLUSTER & SURROUND
80's to 130's Series

Bo010

Remove

1. Disconnect the battery.

(a) Remove the screws from the lower section of the steering column.

(b) Remove the top plastic section.

2. Remove the screws securing the bonnet release lever.

3. Remove the drivers side lower dash panel. Remove the key barrel cover with a screw driver, remove the screws and bolt, securing the panel to the dash. Pull the panel away and separate the connector.

4. Remove the instrument cluster trim by removing the 2 screws, then lower trim from dash panel. Some models have a cover over the instrument cluster, remove this if fitted.

5. Remove the instrument cluster 4 attaching screws, pull cluster forward enough to disconnect the attaching wires and cable. Remove instrument cluster.

Install

1. Fit the instrument cluster close enough to connect the attaching wires and cable. Install the instrument cluster and 4 attaching screws.

2. Install the instrument cluster (cover if one fitted) trim and secure by replacing the 2 screws.

3. Install the instrument cluster air duct, attached by 2 phillips screws.

4. Install the drivers side lower dash panel, connect the wiring connectors. Replace the key barrel cover, push in fit, replace the screws and bolt, securing the panel to the dash.

5. Replace the steering column and surrounds.

6. Connect the battery.

DOOR ASSEMBLIES

MAINTENANCE

Description

Doors consist of a pressed inner door panel and an outer panel which is spot welded and folded on to the inner panel.

A mechanical lever system of the window regulator, which is attached to the glass lifter channel and door inner panels operate the front and rear door sliding windows.

Door locks are activated by lifting an external lever that is recessed into the door panel for safety reasons. The handles operate the fork type door locks in conjunction with door lock striker bolts.

The drivers door has an external key lock, and a lock internally for all doors.

Drain holes are located on the underside of the all doors, these drain water away from the door to stop rust, these holes should be checked and cleared periodically.

DOORS

Remove

1. If required, remove the door and window handles, remove the door trim and disconnect the wiring loom connectors that may be present for such items as radio speakers, electric mirrors, electric windows and electric door locks.
2. Support the door with an assistant or a car jack with soft padding support the base of the door.
3. Remove the door hinge bolts either on the door or body.

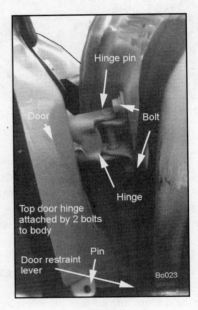

Top door hinge attached by 2 bolts to body. Hinge pin, Door, Bolt, Hinge, Door restraint lever, Pin. Bo023

Install

1. If the hinge is removed, install the hinge. Install the door onto the hinges and tighten the attaching bolts only firmly.
2. Support the door with an assistant or use wood blocks or car jacks with soft padding support the base of the door.
3. Replace the door hinge bolts to the body
4. Align the door to the body and tighten the hinge attaching bolts to specification.

Door Hinge Bolt specified torque:
        350kg-cm, 25ft-lb, 34Nm

5. If required, reconnect the wiring loom connectors that may be present for such items as radio speakers, electric mirrors, electric windows and electric door locks, replace the door trim and replace the door and window handles

DOOR ALIGNMENT

The door hinges provide enough adjustment to correct a lot of misalignment conditions. Loosen the door hinge attaching bolts slightly and arrange the door so that it is centred in the door opening whilst closed. Then, tighten the hinge joining the bolts to specification.

Door Hinge Bolt specified torque :
        350kg-cm, 25ft-lb, 34Nm

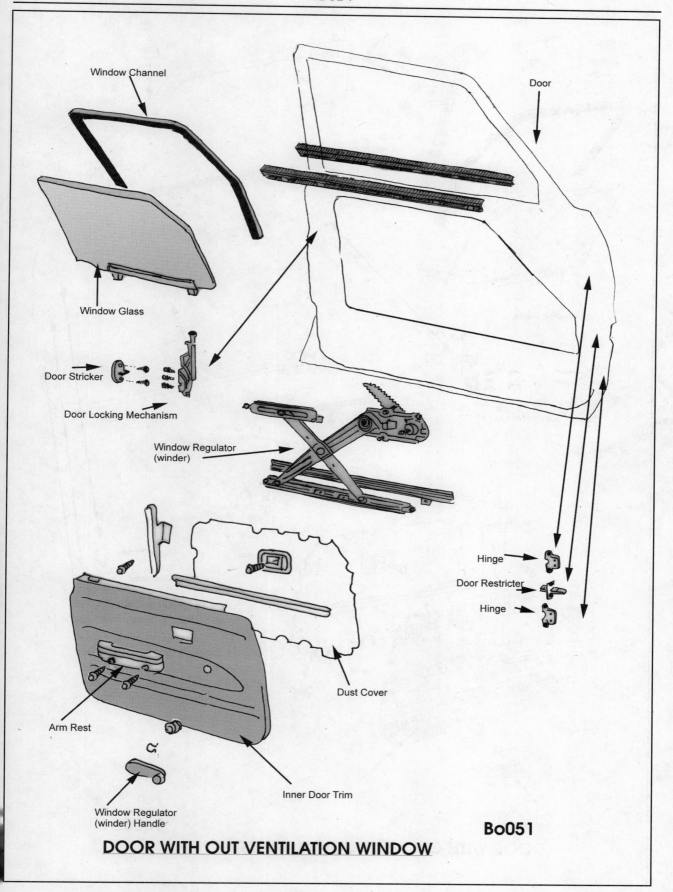

Window Channel

Door

Window Glass

Door Stricker

Door Locking Mechanism

Window Regulator
(winder)

Hinge

Door Restricter

Hinge

Dust Cover

Arm Rest

Inner Door Trim

Window Regulator
(winder) Handle

Bo051

DOOR WITH OUT VENTILATION WINDOW

BODY

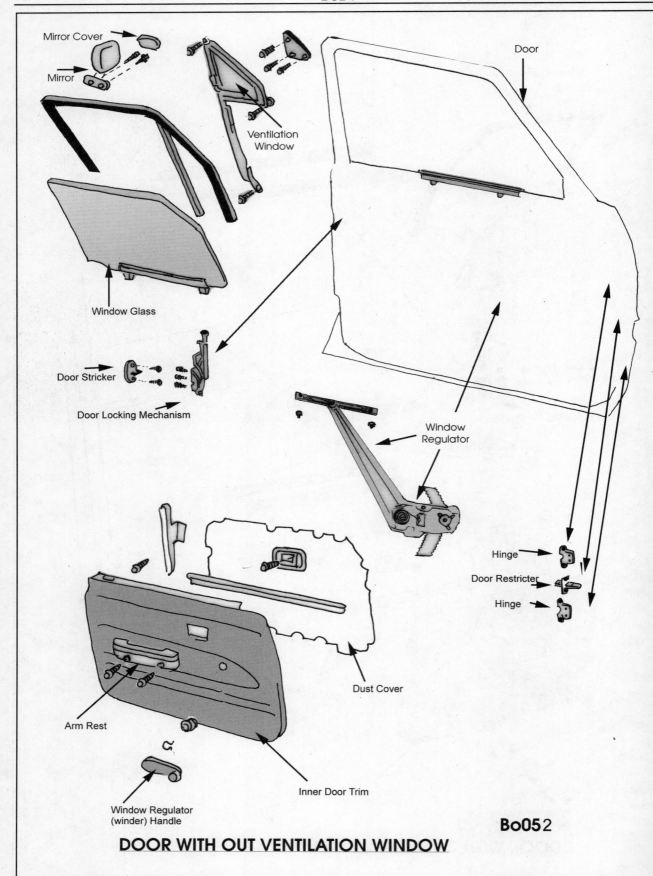

Mirror Cover

Mirror

Ventilation Window

Door

Window Glass

Door Stricker

Door Locking Mechanism

Window Regulator

Hinge

Door Restricter

Hinge

Arm Rest

Dust Cover

Inner Door Trim

Window Regulator (winder) Handle

Bo052

DOOR WITH OUT VENTILATION WINDOW

The door to the body alignment is set accordingly and maintained at the lock striker adjustment as described later in this section.

To correct door sag the lock striker can be adjusted.

WINDOW REGULATOR HANDLE

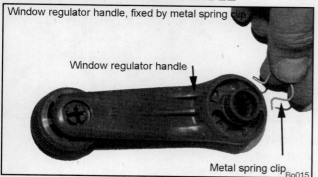

Window regulator handle, fixed by metal spring clip

Window regulator handle

Metal spring clip Bo015

Remove

1. Use a piece of cloth under the window handle, working the cloth to either side to remove the window handle spring clip. If there is difficulty using the cloth make a special tool as shown, to push in behind the handle, then force the metal spring clip back to allow the handle to be removed.

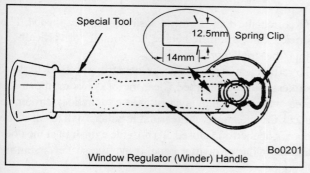

Special Tool

12.5mm Spring Clip

14mm

Window Regulator (Winder) Handle   Bo0201

2. Remove the handle, taking care not to loose the spring clip, backing material or spring.

Install

1. Position the spring and backing plate over the regulator spline shaft.

2. Install the spring clip on the handle.

3. With the window wound fully up:

Front Doors: Position handle so it is pointing down towards the bottom front corner of the door.

Rear Doors: Position the handle horizontally, so it is pointing towards the front of the vehicle.

4. Firmly push the window regulator handle on to the spline so the spring clip locks the handle into position.

ARM REST

Remove

Remove the two phillip screws, remove the arm rest.

Install

Position the arm rest against the door trim and install the two phillip head screws.

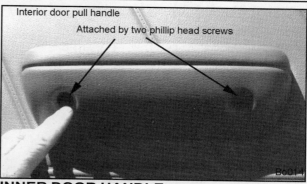

Interior door pull handle

Attached by two phillip head screws

Bo014

INNER DOOR HANDLE

Remove

1. Remove the phillip screw, to remove trim in behind door handle.

2. Pull the pull handle out partly so the connecting lever can be disconnected.

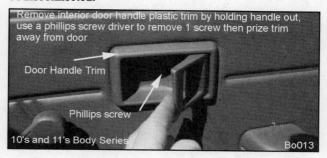

Remove interior door handle plastic trim by holding handle out, use a phillips screw driver to remove 1 screw then prize trim away from door

Door Handle Trim

Phillips screw

10's and 11's Body Series   Bo013

3. Remove the inner door handle.

Install

1. Position the door handle so the connecting lever can be connected to the door handle.

2. Fit the door handle into the door trim.

3. Install the back trim and phillip screw.

INNER TRIM PANEL

Remove

1. Remove window handle, previously described.

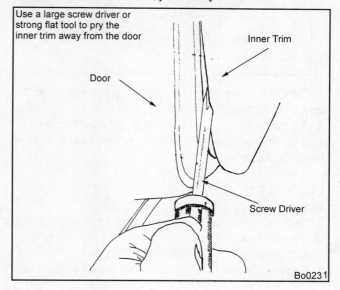

Use a large screw driver or strong flat tool to pry the inner trim away from the door

Inner Trim

Door

Screw Driver

Bo0231

2. Remove the arm rest as previously described.

3. Remove the inner door handle as previously described.

4. Remove the door lock knob by unscrewing the knob from the control lever.

5. Prise the door trim away from the door with a screw driver or strong flat tool.

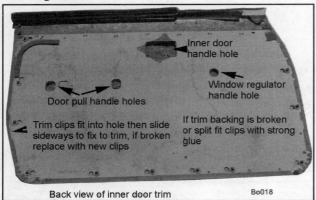

Back view of inner door trim   Bo018

Install

1. Carefully position the door trim on the door aligning retainers with the retainer holes in the door steel panel.

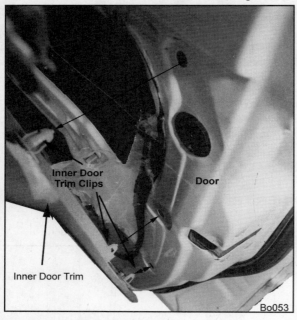

Bo053

2. If any of the inner door trim retainers come away from the trim, glue the retainers back to the door trim.

3. Once the door trim is in position fit the attachments back, such as window regulator handle, inner door lock, inner door handle and arm rest.

LOCK STRICKER
Remove

1. Mark the striker position on the body panel with a pencil or felt pen, this will help when installing the striker to its correct position.

2. Remove the attaching screws and remove the striker

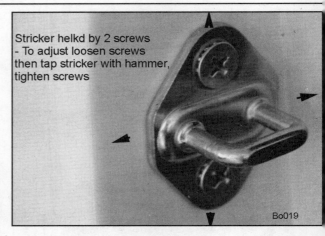

Stricker helkd by 2 screws - To adjust loosen screws then tap stricker with hammer, tighten screws

Bo019

assembly taking care not to loose any shims that may be under the stricker.

Install

1. Place the stricker and shims against the body panel aligning the stricker with the pen marks from the removal.

2. Install the attaching screws and tighten to specification.

Stricker Attaching Screw specified torque:
100kg-cm, 7ft-lb, 10Nm

3. Check adjustment of the stricker.

Adjust

To correct the door sag the lock striker can be adjusted. The stricker can be adjusted either horizontally or vertically to align the stricker with the lock.

To get the clearance between the lock striker and lock the lock striker should be shimmed. Clean the lock jaws and the striker area and apply a thin layer of grease to the lock striker, to check this clearance. A measurable pattern will result as the door is opened and closed. To provide a flush fit at the door and the pillar or quarter panel move the striker assembly laterally.

FRONT DOOR LOCK & DOOR HANDLE
Remove

1. Remove the arm rest as previously described.

2. Remove the window regulator handle as previously described.

3. Remove the door lock knob by unscrewing the knob from the control lever.

4. Remove the inner door handle as previously described.

5. Prise the door trim away from the door with a screw driver

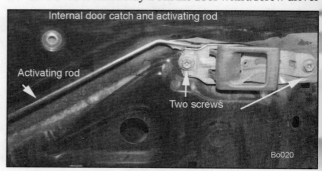

Internal door catch and activating rod

Activating rod

Two screws

Bo020

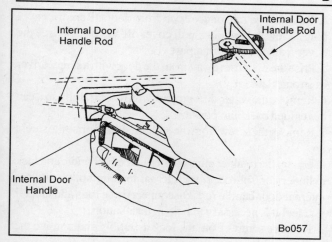

Internal Door Handle Rod

Internal Door Handle Rod

Internal Door Handle

Bo057

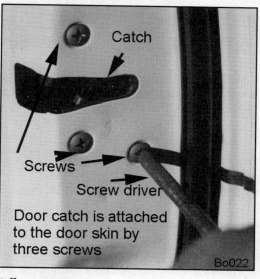

Catch

Screws

Screw driver

Door catch is attached to the door skin by three screws

Bo022

or strong flat tool.

6. Remove the water/dust protection cover carefully so it can be reglued back into position.

7. Unclip the retainer clips on the outer door handle and lock cylinder control rod, from internal locking button and the internal door handle rod. Disconnect these rods and label if you feel it is necessary to help in installation.

8. Remove three screws from the lock assembly and remove the lock assembly.

9. Remove the two bolts securing the outside door handle with key cylinder lock.

10. Remove the lock activating rod from the barrel lock assembly.

11. Remove "C" clip from rear of exterior door handle.

12. Remove the barrel cylinder.

Install

1. Fit lock cylinder or barrel into the outer door handle and fit "C" clip.

2. Connect the rod to the door lock assembly rod.

3. Fit outer door handle and lock cylinder to the door and install the two bolts.

4. Install the lock assembly to the door, tighten the three attaching screws.

5. Fit and clip the retainer clips on the rod from internal locking button and the internal door handle rod.

6. Replace the water/dust protection cover carefully, reglue back into position if necessary.

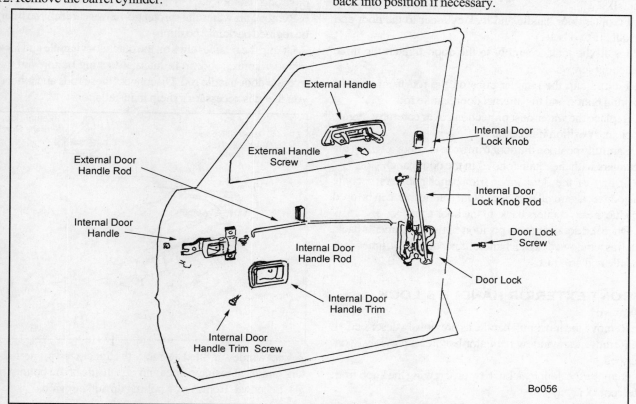

External Handle

External Handle Screw

Internal Door Lock Knob

External Door Handle Rod

Internal Door Lock Knob Rod

Internal Door Handle

Internal Door Handle Rod

Door Lock Screw

Internal Door Handle Trim

Door Lock

Internal Door Handle Trim Screw

Bo056

367

7. Carefully position the door trim on to the door aligning the retainers with the retainer holes in the door panel.

8. If any of the door inner trim panel retainers become dislodged, a general purpose hot melt adhesive, can be used to glue these retainers back to the door trim.

9. Once the door trim is in position fit the attachments back, such as window regulator handle, inner door lock, inner door handle and arm rest.

REAR DOOR HANDLE & DOOR LOCK
Remove

1. Remove the arm rest as previously described.

2. Remove the window regulator handle as previously described.

3. Remove the door lock knob by unscrewing the knob from the control lever.

4. Remove the inner door handle as previously described.

5. Prise the door trim away from the door with a screw driver or strong flat tool.

6. Remove the water/dust protection cover carefully so it can be reglued back into position.

7. Unclip the retainer clips on the outer door handle and lock cylinder control rod, from internal locking button and the internal door handle rod. Disconnect these rods and label if you feel it is necessary to help in installation.

8. Remove three screws from the lock assembly and remove the lock assembly.

9. Remove the two bolts securing the outside door handle with key cylinder lock.

Install

1. Fit outer door handle and lock cylinder to the door and install the two bolts.

2. Install the lock assembly to the door, tighten the three attaching screws.

3. Fit and clip the retainer clips on the rod from internal locking button and the internal door handle rod.

4. Replace the water/dust protection cover carefully, reglue back into position if necessary.

5. Carefully position the door trim on to the door aligning the retainers with the retainer holes in the door panel.

6. If any of the door inner trim panel retainers become dislodged, a general purpose hot melt adhesive, can be used to glue these retainers back to the door trim.

7. Once the door trim is in position fit the attachments back, such as window regulator handle, inner door lock, inner door handle and arm rest.

FRONT EXTERIOR HANDLE & LOCK
Remove

1. Remove the inner pull handle as previously described.

2. Remove the window regulator handle as previously described.

3. Remove the door lock knob by unscrewing the knob from the control lever.

4. Remove the mirror cover on front doors. Remove cover plug, screw behind plug, pull cover off and back to free the cover from the centre support.

5. Prise the door trim away from the door with a screw driver or strong flat tool.

6. Remove the water/dust protection cover carefully so it can be reglued back into position.

7. Remove the screw from the lock shield and prise the shield up.

8. Unclip the retainer clips on the outer door handle and lock cylinder control rod, from internal locking button and the internal door handle rod. Disconnect these rods and label if you feel it is necessary to help in installation.

9. Remove screws from the lock assembly and remove the lock assembly.

10. Inside the door at the back of the exterior door handle, pull the slide attaching clip to the centre of the door to free the external door handle.

FRONT DOOR WINDOW GLASS
See previous illustration.
Remove

1. Remove the arm rest as previously described.

2. Remove the window regulator handle as previously described.

3. Remove the door lock knob by unscrewing the knob from the control lever.

4. Remove the inner door handle as previously described.

5. Prise the door trim away from the door with a screw driver or strong flat tool.

6. Remove the water/dust protection cover carefully so it can be reglued back into position.

7. Unclip the retainer clips on the outer door handle and lock cylinder control rod, from internal locking button and the internal door handle rod. Disconnect these rods and label if you feel it is necessary to help in installation.

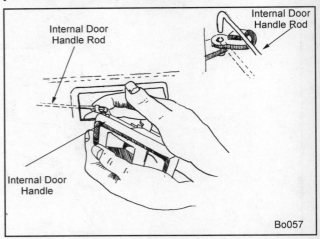

Internal Door Handle Rod

Internal Door Handle Rod

Internal Door Handle

Bo057

8. Vent window if fitted. Remove the three screws, one at the top, one front inside corner and one inside at the bottom of glass channel. Remove by pulling up and outwards.

9. Remove the lower glass channel and one bolt.

10. Remove three screws from the lock assembly and remove the lock assembly.

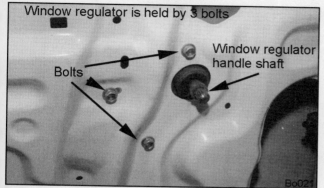

11. Remove the two bolts securing the outside door handle with key cylinder lock.

12. Lower the window and remove the two low front window channel bolts. Lift the glass from the channel and leave in the door.

13. Remove the three bolts attaching the window regulator to the inner door panel.

14. Remove the two bolts attaching the regulator cross over arm to the inner door panel.

15. Remove the window regulator from the inner door panel.

16. Tilt the glass forward and remove the glass upwards through the glass opening, from the outside of the door.

Install

1. Install the glass in through the glass opening, from outside of the door, tilt the glass forward and slide down.

2. Place the window regulator into the inner door panel.

3. Install the two bolts attaching the regulator cross over arm to the inner door panel.

4. Install the three bolts attaching the window regulator to the inner door panel.

5. Lift the glass from the inner door to the window regulator, fit the two bolts.

6. Vent window if fitted. Install by sliding down into the door. Replace the three screws, one at the top, one front inside corner and one inside at the bottom of glass channel.

7. Fit the lower glass channel and one bolt.

8. Check that the glass runs freely in runs.

Adjustment: First pull the glass tightly into the window rear run channel, to adjust the window glass. Then moving the window regulator cam down to remove excess clearance and at the same time maintaining a horizontal attitude, tighten the adjusting screws. Remove any excess clearance that may be apparent in the front window run channel by moving the run channel towards the window glass.

9. Replace the water/dust protection cover, carefully reglue back into position if necessary.

10. Carefully position the door trim on to the door aligning the retainers with the retainer holes in the door steel panel

11. If any of the door inner trim panel retainers become

dislodged, a general purpose hot melt adhesive, can be used to glue these retainers back to the door trim.

12. Once the door trim is in position fit the attachments back, such as window regulator handle, inner door lock, inner door handle and arm rest.

REAR DOOR WINDOW GLASS
See Front Door Window Glass

REAR DOOR FIXED WINDOW GLASS
Remove

1. Remove the inner handle as previously described.

2. Remove the inner arm rest as previously described.

3. Remove the window regulator handle as previously described.

4. Remove the door lock knob by unscrewing the knob from the control lever.

5. Prise the door trim away from the door with a screw driver or strong flat tool.

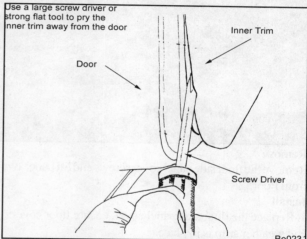

6. Remove the water/dust protection cover, carefully so it can be reglued back into position.

7. Remove the weather strips from the door.

8. Remove the rear window channel.

9. With the window wound down manoeuvre the rear glass channel forwards at the top (it may be necessary to completely remove the channel).

10. Remove or ease forward the rubber seal between the back fixed glass and the moved window channel.

11. Prise out the fixed glass panel.

Install

1. Slide the glass into position, gently tap the glass home with a rubber mullet.

2. Replace the rubber seal between the fixed glass and the window channel.

3. Replace the window into its original position.

4. Replace the rear window channel.

5. Check that the glass runs freely in runs.

Adjustment: First pull the glass tightly into the window rear run channel, to adjust the window glass. Then moving the window regulator cam down to remove excess clearance and at the same time maintaining a horizontal attitude, tighten the adjusting screws. Remove any excess clearance that may be apparent in the front window run channel by moving the run channel towards the window glass.

6. Replace the weather strips to the door frame.

7. Replace the water/dust protection cover, carefully reglue back into position if necessary.

8. Carefully position the door trim on to the door aligning the retainers with the retainer holes in the door steel panel

9. If any of the door inner trim panel retainers become dislodged, a general purpose hot melt adhesive, can be used to glue these retainers back to the door trim.

10. Once the door trim is in position fit the attachments back, such as window handle, door handle and screw on moulding.

FLOOR SIDE PANEL

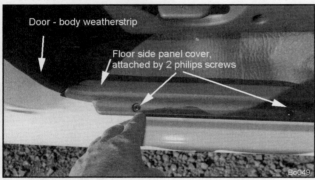

Bo049

Remove
Remove the floor side panel cover screws and lift panel away from floor.

Install
1. Replace the floor side panel cover, ensure floor covering and weather strip is in place.

2. Install screws attaching the panel.

DOOR BODY WEATHERSTRIP
Remove
1. Remove the floor side panel cover screws and lift panel away from floor.

2. Remove the weatherstrip, from around the body panels in the door openings.

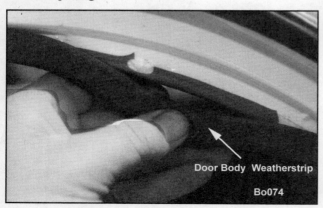

Bo074

Install
1. Replace the weatherstrip, pushing the finishing lace and weatherstrip into the door opening.

2. Replace the floor side panel cover.

REAR VIEW MIRROR
Type A

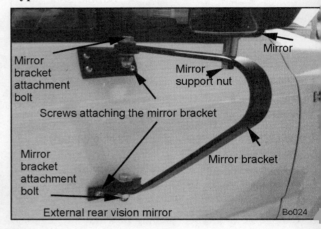

Bo024

Remove
1. Remove the mirror support bracket bolts. Hold the mirror otherwise damage may occur to the body panel.

2. Unscrew the screws attaching the mirror support bracket to the door or in some cases the front mudguard.

Install
1. Position mirror bracket supports to body panel, tighten screws.

2. Attach the mirror and bracket to the bracket support plates then tighten bolts and nuts.

Type B

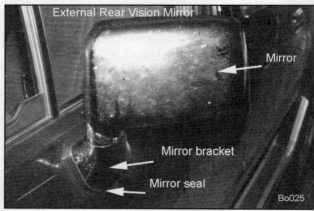

Bo025

Remove
1. Remove the door internal trim as previously described.

2. Remove the mirror attaching nuts from inside the door skin

3. Remove the mirror assembly from the door.

Install
1. Replace the seal to the door frame if it is damaged.

2. Install the mirror assembly to the front door.

3. Replace the nuts securing the mirror to the door.

4. Replace the inner door trim.

TAILGATE

TAILGATE

Bo060

Remove

1. Remove bolt attaching the support stay each side of the tailgate to the body.

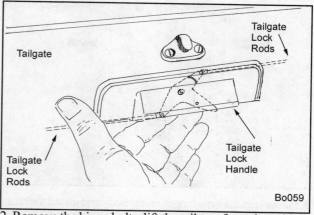

Bo059

2. Remove the hinge bolts, lift the tailgate from the vehicle.

Install

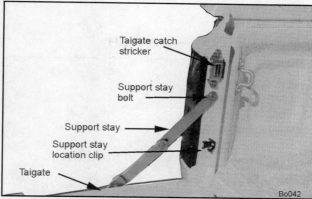

Bo042

<u>**TAILGATE**</u>

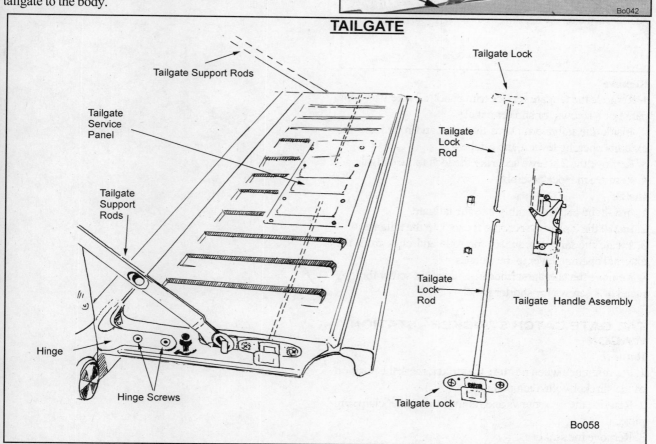

Bo058

371

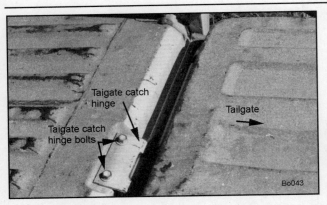

1. Position the tailgate hinges on the body and install the hinge bolts.
2. Replace bolt attaching the support stay each side of the tailgate to the body.

TAILGATE LOCK and CATCH

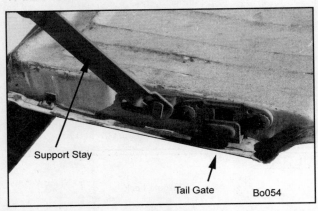

Remove
1. Remove the tailgate service trim panel, 12 screw for long panel or 8 screws for shorter panel.
2. Inside the tailgate remove the clips and rods from the external opening lever to the catches.
3. Remove the 2 screws securing the lock to the tailgate.
4. Remove the lock assembly.

Install
1. Install the catch assembly into the tailgate.
2. Install the 2 screws securing the lock to the tailgate.
3. Inside the tailgate connect the rods and clips from the external opening lever to the catches.
4. Remove the tailgate service trim panel, 12 screw for long panel or 8 screws for shorter panel.

TAILGATE CATCH STRICKER - STATION WAGON

Remove
1. For reference when refitting the striker, mark the position of the striker with a felt pen.
2. Remove the two screws and remove the striker clamping plate.
3. Remove the striker.

Install
1. Replace the striker taking note of the position of the felt pen markings made during removal.
2. Install the stricker plate and screws and tighten.

FUEL TANK CAP LID

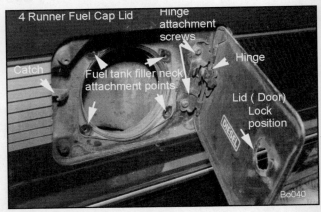

Remove
Open the fuel tank cap lid, take the hinge out, remove the screws and remove the cap lid.

Install
Install the fuel tank cap lid and hinge into the correct position, fit and tighten the securing screws.

FIXED WINDOW GLASS

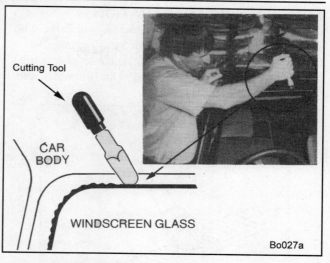

Bo027a

GENERAL INFORMATION

The windscreen is a laminated type of glass which has a plastic lamination between two layers of safety glass. If struck hard enough it will crack into a large section enabling the driver to stop the vehicle safely.

The vehicle manufacture fitted windscreen and rear windows are held in position by a compound adhesive. Service kits for replacement windows use a thermo electric butyl tape.

WINDSCREEN
REMOVE

1. Remove windscreen wiper arms.
2. Remove sun visors, interior rear vision mirror.
3. Remove outside windscreen moulding with a screwdriver.
4. Remove the body cowl in front of the windshield.
5. Apply cloth tape around opening perimeter of windscreen

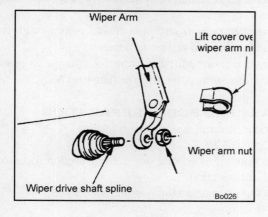

Bo026

to protect paint finish.

6. Using a sharp bladed instrument such as BTB Windscreen removal blade. Lubricate the blade with soapy water, cut the urethane from centre top inside the vehicle. These blades can be used with an air tool or manual handle, it may be necessary to use long blades to work down behind the dash panel.
7. Cutting from the top, then down each side, easing glass forward to an upright position and cutting through bottom material.
8. If glass is to be reused, remove old adhesive with a suitable knife being careful not to damage glass surface.
9. Trim excess sealant from the external edge of the windscreen
10. Cut sealant away from the pinchweld, so the new glass and sealant has an even surface to bond too.

Remove as much adhesive, from body flange as possible without damaging paint finish or flange on body..

GLASS PREPARATION

1. Degrease glass bonding surface 20 mm around perimeter of glass, using an oil free cleaning solvent.
2. Apply a thin coating of glass primer around glass on bonding surface. Allow to dry for 10-15 minutes.
NB: The primed surface must not be touched, if this occurs it must be primed again.
3. Bare end of butyl tape to copper wire core for 30 to 40 mm. Remove cloth only for a further 30 to 40 mm.
4. Starting in bottom corner of glass, position tape with cloth facing inwards.
NB: Excessive deformation of butyl tape is to be avoided.
5. With butyl tape positioned around window bare copper wire and remove cloth as previously described.
6. Position ends of tape together and keep copper wires well separated. Don't twist two ends of tape together, they must be pressed against each other.

BODY OPENING PREPARATION

1. Clean fence flange and any remaining adhesive with cleaning solvent and allow to dry for 5 to 10 minutes.
2. Apply body primer over metal flange to give a total "blacked-out" appearance. Allow to dry for 10 minutes, refer below.

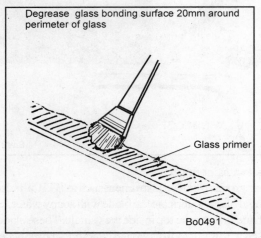

Degrease glass bonding surface 20mm around perimeter of glass

Glass primer

Bo0491

3. Fit moulding retainers.

GLASS FITMENT

1. Centrally locate windscreen in opening on spacer blocks.
2. Connect ends of copper wire to a 32 volt, 10 amp transformer for 5 minutes ensuring electrical connections are not in contact with and hence damaging, the paint finish. The above stated time is for an ambient temperature of 20° to 25°. For lower temperatures it is necessary to apply power for a longer time to allow tape to soften.
NB: If a 32 volt transformer isn't available, two fully charged 12 volt vehicle batteries connected in series for 6 to 7 minutes, can be used.
3. As butyl tape softens, apply even pressure over glass to compress tape to approximately 6 mm, refer below.
NB: If tape isn't softened sufficiently excess pressure required to ensure sealing could lead to bowing of screen and cracking of outer lamination of glass.
4. Disconnect electrical supply and allow tape to cool.
5. Water test windscreen and note position of any leaks.
6. Remedy any leaks by thoroughly washing and drying screen and either reheating and repressurising or by secondary sealing with sealant.
NB: Bad or large leaks due to tape misplacement will necessitate removal and refitment of screen.

Installing Windscreen using Sealant

1. Using a flat blade or automatic applicator, apply a smooth continuous bead of urethane/silicon adhesive, between the centre and outer edge, around contact area of the entire perimeter of the body opening. The silicon should have an average size of 6mm in diameter.
* There are urethane window replacement kits for various windows. Follow the steps provided with the replacement kits.
2. Install the windshield, using small blocks of wood or plastic to help keep the glass at the correct height. When the glass is in the correct position, masking tape can be used to hold the glass in position. Press windshield gently until the glass is fitted into the correct position.
3. If any areas have gaps or the sealant is not visible. Apply extra sealant using a trowel or flat blade knife, or smooth existing sealant.
4. After the sealant has partly dried, $^3/_4$ to $1^1/_2$ hours depending on conditions. Test the glass perimeter for leaks with a low pressure water hose. If any leaks are found, apply extra sealant using a trowel or flat blade knife, or smooth existing sealant.
5. Clean off any excess urethane/silicon using commercial cleaning fluid or methylated spirits.

INSTALL WINDSCREEN COMPONENTS

Install the windscreen components in the following order.
- Windscreen moulding.
- Interior rear vision mirror.
- Sunvisor.
- Windscreen wiper arms.
- Body cowl.

REAR WINDOW
Remove

1. Apply cloth tape around opening perimeter of windscreen to protect paint finish.
2. Remove the weather strip using a screw driver.
3. Using a sharp bladed instrument such as BTB Windscreen removal blade. Lubricate the blade with soapy water, cut the urethane from centre top inside the vehicle. These blades can be used with an air tool or manual handle, it may be necessary to use long blades to work down behind the dash panel.
4. Cutting from the top, then down each side, easing glass forward to an upright position and cutting through bottom material.
5. If glass is to be reused, remove old adhesive with a suitable knife being careful not to damage glass surface.
6. Trim excess sealant from the external edge of the windscreen
7. Cut sealant away from the pinchweld, so the new glass and sealant has an even surface to bond too.
Remove as much adhesive, from body flange as possible without damaging paint finish or flange on body..

GLASS AND BODY PREPARATION

Procedure is same as windscreen section.
GLASS FITMENT
Glass bonding is carried out using procedure detailed in Windscreen section.
Press fit the weather strip over the rubber seal.

XTRA CAB Quarter Window

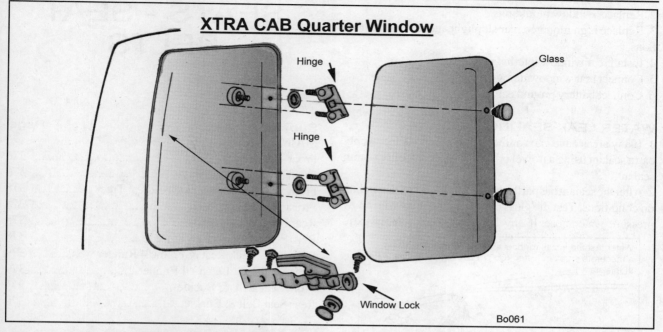

Hinge

Hinge

Glass

Window Lock

Bo061

REAR DOOR FIXED WINDOW GLASS
See Door Section.

QUARTER WINDOW - 4 RUNNER
Remove

1. Apply cloth tape around opening perimeter of windscreen to protect paint finish.

2. Remove the weather strip using a screw driver.

3. Using a sharp bladed instrument such as BTB Windscreen removal blade. Lubricate the blade with soapy water, cut the urethane from centre top inside the vehicle. These blades can be used with an air tool or manual handle, it may be necessary to use long blades to work down behind the dash panel.

4. Cutting from the top, then down each side, easing glass forward to an upright position and cutting through bottom material.

5. If glass is to be reused, remove old adhesive with a suitable knife being careful not to damage glass surface.

6. Trim excess sealant from the external edge of the windscreen

7. Cut sealant away from the pinchweld, so the new glass and sealant has an even surface to bond too.

Remove as much adhesive, from body flange as possible without damaging paint finish or flange on body..

GLASS AND BODY PREPARATION

Procedure is same as windscreen section.

GLASS FITMENT

Glass bonding is carried out using procedure detailed in Windscreen section.

Press fit the weather strip over the rubber seal.

QUARTER WINDOW - XTRA CAB

1. Remove the cabin back panel, which is attached by 3 screws, also remove the back panel trims.

2. Remove the 3 screws securing the quarter window lock to the back of the body.

3. Remove the rear quarter side trim by removing the seat belt anchor bolts, 4 bolts, one screw and hook.

4. Remove the two rear quarter window hinges securing nuts.

5. Carefully remove the glass from the vehicle.

6. To ensure that no surface irregularities exist, thoroughly check rear quarter window pinchweld flange.

Install

1. Carefully position the glass into the vehicle.

2. Install the rear quarter window retaining nuts.

3. Replace the rear quarter side trim by installing the seat belt anchor bolts, 4 bolts, one screw and hook.

4. Install the quarter window lock 3 screws to the back of the body and window.

5. Install the cabin back panel, which is attached by 3 screws, also remove the back panel trims by pushing on.

TAILGATE WINDOW - 4 RUNNER
Remove

1. Remove tail gate window wiper arm and blade assembly.

2. Remove high mounted rear stop light and wiring connections, if fitted.

3. Disconnect rear window defogger wiring.

4. Remove rear window internal moulding.

5. Remove window mouldings.

6. Carefully cut out the tailgate window.

* It is not necessary to remove all traces of original urethane. However, any original urethane remaining must be smooth and firm.

Glass installation procedure

See "Windscreen Install" for installation procedure.

Install

1. Replace tail gate window wiper arm and blade assembly.

2. Replace window mouldings.

3. Replace high mounted rear stoplight and wiring connections.

4. Install rear window internal moulding.

5. Connect rear window defogger wiring.

6. Connect battery ground cable.

WATER LEAK SEALING

1. If any areas have gaps or the sealant is not visible. Apply extra sealant using a trowel or flat blade, or smooth existing sealant.

2. After the sealant has partly dried, $^3/_4$ to $1^1/_2$ hours depending on conditions. Test the glass perimeter for leaks with a low pressure water hose. If any leaks are found, apply extra

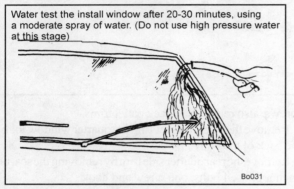

Water test the install window after 20-30 minutes, using a moderate spray of water. (Do not use high pressure water at this stage)

Bo031

sealant using a trowel or flat blade knife, or smooth existing sealant.

3. Clean off any excess urethane/silicon using commercial cleaning fluid or methylated spirits.

INTERIOR MIRROR

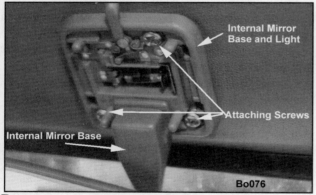

Internal Mirror Base and Light

Attaching Screws

Internal Mirror Base

Bo076

Remove

1. Remove the screws from the internal mirror base, later models remove internal light cover.

2. Remove the mirror.

Install

1. Install the mirror to the head lining position.

2. Replace and tighten the screws attaching the mirror to the head lining and roof, and install internal light cover on later models.

SEATS - SEAT BELTS

Maintenance

FRONT SEATS
Remove

1. Remove the bolts attaching the front end and rear end of the seat frame to floor.

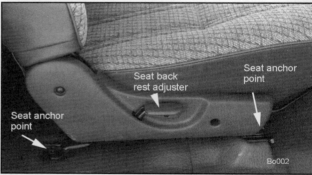

Seat back rest adjuster

Seat anchor point

Seat anchor point

Bo002

2. Remove the seat taking care not to damage any of the internal upholstery or internal lining.

Install

1. Install the seat taking care not to damage any of the internal upholstery or internal lining.

2. Install the seat and frame, tightening the attaching bolts to specification.

Seat Anchor Bolts Specified Torque:
185kg-cm, 13ft-lb, 18Nm

FRONT SEAT HEAD SUPPORTS

Front seat head supports are retained by spring steel clips located in the sleeve which holds one of the head rest legs.

Remove

1. Push in on the head rest support sleeve which has a spring

Front Bucket Seat

Bucket Seat and Half Bench Seat

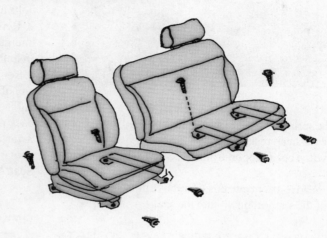

Bench Seat

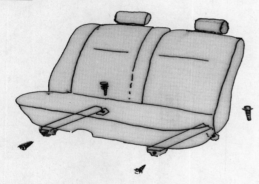

Rear Bench Seat

Xtra Rear Seat

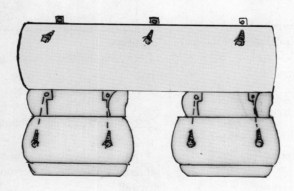

Bo062

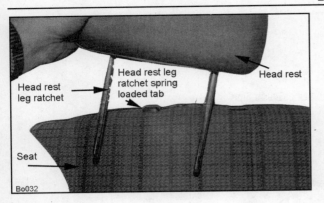

loaded tab.

2. Push the spring loaded tab in towards the head rest support to release the head rest.

3. Remove the head support from the seat back by pulling up.

Install

Place the head restraint into position above the seat, and push the legs of the support down into the seat.

FRONT SEAT FORWARD & BACK ADJUST TRACK

Remove

1. Remove the front seat and frame as described above, taking care not to damage any of the internal upholstery or internal lining.

2. Remove the side plastic trim 3 screws.

3. Remove the 4 screws, 2 nuts securing the adjustment tracks to the seat frame.

Install

1. Replace the adjustment tracks, 4 screws and 2 nuts.

2. Replace the side plastic trim 3 screws.

3. Install the seat taking care not to damage any of the internal upholstery or internal lining.

4. Install the seat assembly, tightening the attaching bolts to specification.

Seat Anchor Bolts specified torque: 25-35 Nm.

FRONT SEAT RECLINER

Remove

1. Remove the front seat and frame as described above, taking care not to damage any of the internal upholstery or internal lining.

2. Remove the side plastic trim 2 screws.

3. Remove the seat recliner knob.

4. Remove the recliner assembly.

Install

1. Replace the recliner assembly.

2. Push the recliner control insert and knob back into place. Fit the back of the seat into place.

3. Replace the side plastic trim and 2 screws.

4. Install the seat taking care not to damage any of the internal upholstery or internal lining.

5. Install the seat assembly, tightening the attaching bolts to

specification.

Seat Anchor Bolts specified torque: -   25-35 Nm.

REAR SEAT - Xtra Cab

Remove

1. Remove the four bolts below the back rest, remove the 3 bolts above the back rest.

2. Remove the seat taking care not to damage any of the internal upholstery or internal lining.

Install

1. Replace the seat into the vehicle taking care not to damage any of the internal upholstery or internal lining.

2. Fit the seat into place with the back of the seat against the back of the cabin.

3. Install the four bolts below the back rest, install the 3 bolts above the back rest. Tighten bolts to specification.

Seat Anchor Bolts Specified Torque:
185kg-cm, 13ft-lb, 18Nm

REAR SEAT - Double Cab

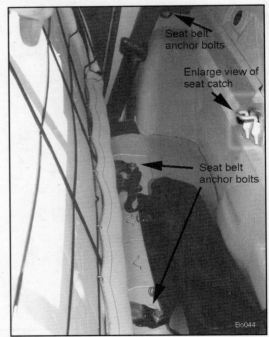

Remove

1. Remove the 2 bolts attaching the front of the seat to the floor pan.

2. Fold the back rest forward to gain access to the back of the seat frame..

3. Remove the 2 bolts attaching the back of the seat to the floor pan.

4. Remove the seat taking care not to damage any of the internal upholstery or internal lining.

Install

1. Replace the seat into the vehicle taking care not to damage any of the internal upholstery or internal lining.

2. Fit seat frame to the retaining brackets attached to the rear

floor pan panel.

3. Install two bolts securing the back of the seat frame to the rear floor pan.

4. Install two bolts securing the front of the seat frame to the floor pan.

5. Tighten bolts to specification.

Seat Anchor Bolts Specified Torque:
185kg-cm, 13ft-lb, 18Nm

REAR SEAT BACK REST & FRAME-Station Wagon - 4 Runner

Remove

1. Remove the cushion as described above.

2. Push in the locking buttons on top of the back rest to release the back rest from the top anchor points.

3. Remove the bolts attaching the back rest to the floor pan and bracket.

4. Remove the seat taking care not to damage any of the internal upholstery or internal lining.

Install

1. Replace the seat into the vehicle taking care not to damage any of the internal upholstery or internal lining.

2. Fit seat frame to the brackets on the floor pan install the attaching bolts.

3. Push the back rest back into position, press the locking buttons to lock the back rest into place if necessary.

4. Fit the cushion section into place with the back of the cushion in under the back section.

5. Push down hard on the front of the cushion and force back, this will clip the seat frame under the seat bracket and force the cushion back further under the back section.

REAR SEAT BACK LATCH - 4 Runner

Remove

1. Remove the seat back from the vehicle as previously described.

2. Pull back the seat back covering from seat frame.

3. Remove latch from either side of the seat back and the connecting rods from the lever to the latch/lock.

4. Remove the lever attaching nut and spring from the lever, remove lever.

Install

1. Position the latch into the seat frame, engage the rods and spring.

2. Work the back rest cover and foam back into position, glue if necessary.

3. Replace the back rest into the vehicle as described above.

FRONT SEAT BELT AND BUCKLE

Remove

1. Remove seat as previously described.

2. Remove the plastic bolt cover from the bolt securing the seat belt to side of the cabin, remove the bolt and belt upper support.

3. Remove the lower bolt securing the seat belt to side of the cabin.

4. Remove the seat belt retractor by removing the attaching bolt to the side of the cabin. Remove the retractor and belt.

5. Remove seat belt buckle and support belt or cable, by removing the attaching bolt to the floor pan.

Install

1. Install bolt securing front seat belt retractor to centre pillar.

Seat Belt Anchor Bolts Specified Torque:
440kg-cm, 32ft-lb, 43Nm

2. Replace lower bolt and seat belt anchor attachment to side of cabin.

Seat Belt Anchor Bolts Specified Torque:
440kg-cm, 32ft-lb, 43Nm

3. Install the bolt and belt upper support, Fit the plastic bolt cover to the bolt securing the seat belt to side of the cabin,

Seat Belt Anchor Bolts Specified Torque:
440kg-cm, 32ft-lb, 43Nm

4. Install bolt securing rear seat belt buckle and belt to the floor pan of the vehicle.

Seat Belt Anchor Bolts Specified Torque:
440kg-cm, 32ft-lb, 43Nm

5. Replace the seat as previously described.

REAR SEAT BELT AND BUCKLE

Remove

1. Remove rear seat cushion and back rest as described above.

2. Remove the plastic bolt cover from the bolt securing the seat belt to the upper anchor point, remove the bolt and belt upper support.

3. Remove the lower bolt securing the seat belt to floor pan of the cabin.

4. Remove the seat belt retractor assembly from the quarter panel, remove the retractor bolt. Remove the belt and retractor from the vehicle.

5. Remove bolt securing rear seat belt buckle and belt to the floor pan of the vehicle.

Install

1. Replace bolts securing rear seat belt lower attachments to floor pan. Replace the bolt securing rear seat belt retractor assembly to quarter inner panel.

Seat Belt Anchor Bolts Specified Torque:
440kg-cm, 32ft-lb, 43Nm

2. Replace sash guide and bolt securing upper seat belt attachment to quarter panel, fit plastic cover.

Seat Belt Anchor Bolts Specified Torque:
440kg-cm, 32ft-lb, 43Nm

3. Install bolt securing rear seat belt buckle and belt to the floor pan of the vehicle.

Seat Belt Anchor Bolts Specified Torque:
440kg-cm, 32ft-lb, 43Nm

4. Replace rear seat cushion and back assemblies as described above.

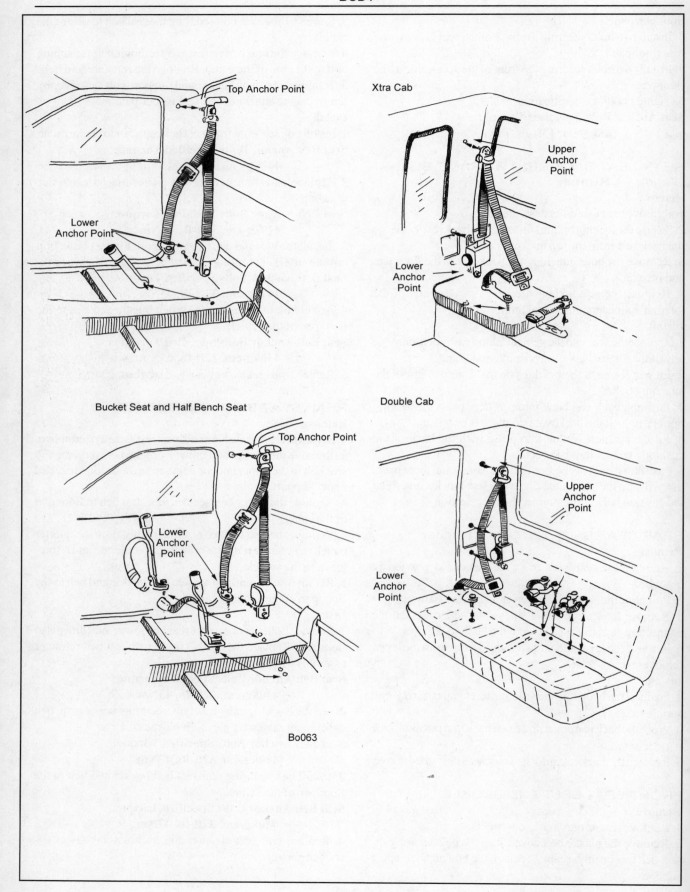

Top Anchor Point

Lower
Anchor Point

Xtra Cab

Upper
Anchor
Point

Lower
Anchor
Point

Bucket Seat and Half Bench Seat

Top Anchor Point

Lower
Anchor
Point

Double Cab

Upper
Anchor
Point

Lower
Anchor
Point

Bo063

PAINT & EXTERIOR BADGES

BODY MAINTENANCE
EXTERNAL PAINT
Acrylic Enamel Paints

This range of paints have a harder surface, and hold a higher gloss surface for metallic colours than the ordinary enamels, provided the paint surface is maintained. This enamel also has the property of good smoothness.

Below are repair guide lines for acrylic enamel paints:

Polishing Paint:

Minor paint runs, scratches, dry over spray and orange peel can be eradicated by machine or hand polishing or by both sanding and polishing without the necessity of repainting. If repairing this type of defect treat the entire panel as, spot repairs will leave a blemish appearance and should be attempted only in areas that do not have large areas of paint. When polishing follow the guide lines below.

Lightly sanding using 1200 wet and dry paper with water or mineral spirits as a lubricant removing the defect. Using a brush apply medium grit machine polishing compound to the painted surface. Use a polisher or drill and polishing wheel and woollen pad, polish the entire panel, do not hold the polisher in the one position as this will leave cut marks in the paint surface. Change woollen pad, then with a clean lambs wool pad buff the entire panel.

Acrylic enamel paints need a light polishing to improve their gloss, as age and weathering can remove the lustre from the paint surface.

Painting Panels:

Painting with either conventional air drying or low bake enamels, or with acrylic lacquers acrylic enamels can be used to repair damage to panels. Often a better colour match can be obtained by repainting metallic colours with acrylic lacquer, both the original paint surface and the repaired surface can be polished at the same time to provide a good surface. Air dry acrylic lacquer will provide better service-ability than air dry enamels.

Remove wax, polish or grease with a silicone remover when using any one of the three types of repair materials over acrylic enamel. Using No. 800 grit paper thoroughly sand off the original finish. If trims and mouldings are not removed, care should be taken to ensure that paint surfaces near trim and mouldings, are thoroughly sanded in order to provide adhesion of the repair top coat. Areas sanded to the base metal should be treated with an acid cleaner to give a good surface.

If panels have been damaged, the paint should be removed, the damaged section panel beaten to the correct shape. Body filler and putty are applied, then the repaired section sanded back with coarse paper such as No 120 grit paper to start

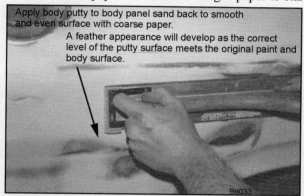

Apply body putty to body panel sand back to smooth and even surface with coarse paper.

A feather appearance will develop as the correct level of the putty surface meets the original paint and body surface.

Bo033

with. Then use No 360 or 420 grit paper before moving to No 600 grit paper to obtain a good finish.

After sanding, apply a primer to any bare metal that has been exposed. Sand the primer surfaces with No. 800 wet and dry paper with water before applying paint. The lacquer or enamel used should be thinned with thinners as recommended by the supplier of the paint.

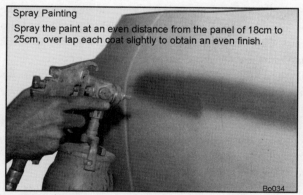

Spray Painting

Spray the paint at an even distance from the panel of 18cm to 25cm, over lap each coat slightly to obtain an even finish.

Bo034

CLEANING

Regular maintenance throughout the life of a car, is recommended to help the appearance of the paint surface and the general appearance of the vehicle. The following steps are suggested as a guide for regular body maintenance:

1. Wash the car, chamois dry exterior and vacuum the interior thoroughly.

2. Inspect openings for water leaks and seal where necessary. Repair all loose weatherstrips which are still useable.

3. Replace any door or boot lid weatherstrips which are unfit for service. Apply silicone lubricant to the weatherstripping.

4. Replace all cracked, fogged, or chipped glass, the effectiveness of the lights and windows will be impaired.

5. Inspect the windshield wiper blades and replace them if necessary.

6. Clean the seats, door trim panels and headlining.

Exterior Cleaning

The outside of the vehicle should be kept clean by washing. Never wipe the painted surface with a dry cloth. Do not dust the finish when it is dry because this will rub the dust and dirt into the baked enamel, and it leaves a sandpaper effect on the surface. To keep the finish bright and attractive and eliminate the necessity of using polish, wash the car whenever it has accumulated a moderate amount of dirt and road grime.

Trim and Mouldings

Bo065

Trim mouldings and name badges are held into place by clips, fasteners, retainers, bushes, nuts and contact adhesive. When removing or installing exterior mouldings, care should be exercised. Finishes adjacent to the moulding should be covered with masking tape to prevent damage. Holes in body panels for screws, bolts, clips, etc; that could permit water entry into the body must be adequately sealed with non hardening sealer or presealed screws, nuts or clips.

The body side mouldings are secured to the front fender and front and rear doors with double sided adhesive tape and urethane adhesive.

If replacing moulding clips drill a small hole in the panel next to the original weld stud location. Insert a self-sealing screw through original clip and into outer panel, or replace damaged weld stud with self-sealing screw-type weld stud.

Bonded adhesive nameplates and emblems are more easily removed with the use of heat lamps positioned adjacent to the part to be removed.

* Ensure that the heat lamps are not too close or the heat too intense to adversely effect paint finish.

When installing these adhesive bonded trims and mouldings to the panel, thoroughly clean the panel and ensure the panel temperature is at least 21 degrees Celsius otherwise the bonding may not be satisfactory.

FRONT GRILLE

Remove

Bo035

1. Prop the bonnet open.
2. Remove the screws around the grille moulding assembly.

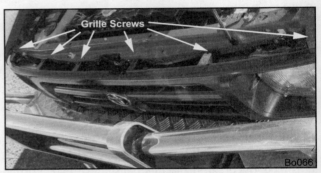

Bo066

3. Pull the grille out, to disengage the moulded prongs of the grille from around the lights etc.

Install

1. Position the grille on top of the bumper bar, slide in and around the lights to locate the prongs to the front panel.
2. Replace the screws into the grille moulding assembly, and tighten.
3. Close the bonnet.

FRONT FENDERS & BONNET

The floor pan and cabin, is bolted to the chassis to make a very strong structure, therefore front and back panels are either bolted or welded to this structure.

Panels that are attached to the front consist of engine bonnet, front fender and front end panel, into which, headlights are fitted. The engine bonnet assembly is hinged from the fire wall and is supported in the open position by a support rod attached to the front radiator support panel. The bonnet lock release lever mounted beneath the instrument panel, controls the bonnet lock release spring. The engine bonnet, when released from the locked position, engages in a secondary safety catch which can be released by inserting fingers beneath the leading edge of the engine bonnet.

FRONT FENDER
Remove

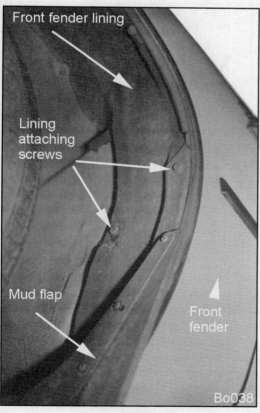

Front fender lining

Lining attaching screws

Mud flap

Front fender

Bo038

1. Remove the radio antenna if one is fitted.
2. Remove the front bumper bar assembly.
3. The front fenders are attached by self tapper bolts to the fire wall panel, engine compartment panel and front chassis assembly. Take care and remove the fender, do not let the fender drop and damage.

Installation
1. Place the front fender into position insert the bolt and washer assemblies to secure the lower and upper part of the fender then the rear section of the fender. Do not tighten the screws until the fender has been aligned so that it fits into the correct position with the other body panels.
2. Install the front bumper bar assembly.
3. Replace the radio antenna if one is fitted.

Bonnet
Remove
1. Prop the bonnet open. For reference when refitting the hinge, mark the hinge position with a felt pen.

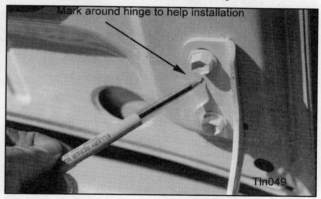

Mark around hinge to help installation

Tln049

2. Place a cover on the front fenders to prevent damage.
3. Disconnect windshield washer tube.
4. Remove the hinge to the bonnet bolts.
5. Remove the bonnet.
6. If the hinges are to be removed the cowl panel will need to be removed. Remove the hinge attaching bolts and remove hinge.

Install
1. Replace the hinge. Replace the hinge attaching bolts and tighten to specification. Replace the cowl panel.

Hinge to Body attaching bolts specified torque:
220kg-cm, 16ft-lb, 21Nm

2. Install the bonnet to the hinge, taking note of the felt marks made during removal. Install bolts to specification.

Hinge to Bonnet bolts specified torque:
220kg-cm, 16ft-lb, 21Nm

3. Reconnect the hose to the windscreen washer.
4. Take the bonnet safety prop and the protection cover off. Close the bonnet and check alignment. After any necessary adjustments tighten the hinge attaching nuts.

Adjust
1. Loosen slightly the hinge to bonnet bolts, gently close the

bonnet and check the surrounding edges of the bonnet.

2. There should be an even gap on all sides of the bonnet.

3. If not raise bonnet and firmly but carefully move the bonnet on the hinges, correct the position of the bonnet.

4. Lower bonnet, check clearance gaps, if correct lift bonnet and tighten the bolts to specification.

Hinge to Boot Lid bolts specified torque:

220kg-cm, 16ft-lb, 21Nm

5. Adjust the height of the bonnet at the front by adjusting bonnet support bolts either side at the front. Turn clockwise to lower bonnet, turn anticlockwise to raise the bonnet.

Bonnet Catch

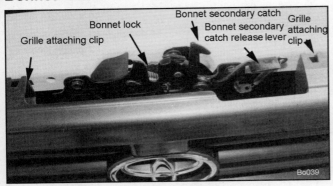

Bo039

Remove

1. Lift bonnet and clip in bonnet support.

2. For reference when refitting the catch, mark the catch position with a felt pen.

3. Remove three catch attaching bolts.

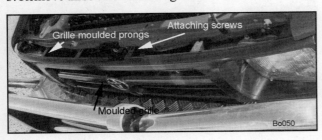

Bo050

Install

1. Replace the spring and catch in the correct position, taking note of the felt marks made during removal. Install bolts to specification.

Catch Attaching bolts specified torque:

220kg-cm, 16ft-lb, 21Nm.

2. Lower bonnet and check operation of catch.

Adjust

1. Loosen slightly the catch bolts, gently close the bonnet and check the alignment of the catch to the bonnet.

BUMPER BARS

FRONT BUMPER BAR

Front Bumper

Bo067

Remove

1. Remove the bolts attaching the bumper support bars to the front chassis rail, it may be necessary to use an assistant to hold the bumper bar.

2. Remove the front bumper bar assembly.

Install

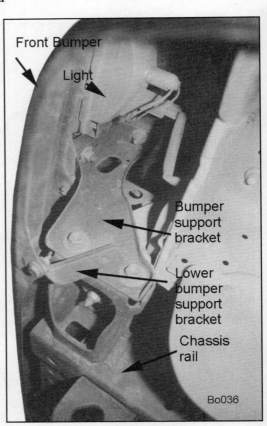

Bo036

1. Position the front bumper bar assembly onto the front of the vehicle, it may be necessary to use an assistant to hold the bumper bar.

2. Install the bolts attaching the bumper support bars to the front chassis rail.

REAR BUMPER BAR

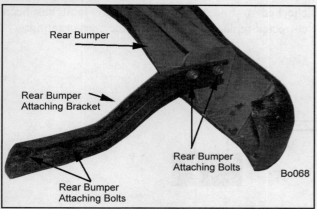

Rear Bumper

Rear Bumper Attaching Bracket

Rear Bumper Attaching Bolts

Rear Bumper Attaching Bolts

Bo068

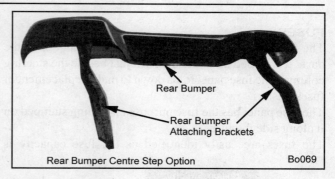

Rear Bumper

Rear Bumper Attaching Brackets

Rear Bumper Attaching Brackets

Rear Bumper Centre Step Option

Bo069

Remove

1. Remove the number plate light from the rear bumper bar with a screw driver. Remove electrical connectors.

2. Remove the bolts attaching the bumper support bars to the rear chassis panels, it may be necessary to use an assistant to hold the bumper bar.

3. Remove the rear bumper bar assembly.

Install

1. Position the rear bumper bar assembly onto the rear of the vehicle, it may be necessary to use an assistant.

2. Install the bolts attaching the bumper support bars to the rear chassis panel.

3. Replace the number plate light to the rear bumper bar, push fit. Replace the electrical connectors.

4. Lower vehicle from support stands.

Memo

ELECTRICAL WIRING & FUSES ETC

FUSES

The fuse box is either located under the bonnet or in the dash, it is folded up under the dash just beside the steering column. The fuse panel folds down to make replacement of fuses easier.

The fuse panel has the fuse purpose and rating stamped on it along side the fuses.

The fuses are easily identified as the fuse capacity is stamped on the fuse.

Inspection of fuses is achieved by removing the suspected fuse and examine the element in the fuse for a break.

* Always replace blown fuses with fuses of the same rating, if another fuse failure occurs, the circuit must be checked to find the fault, once the fault has been corrected replace the fuse, with the correct rating.

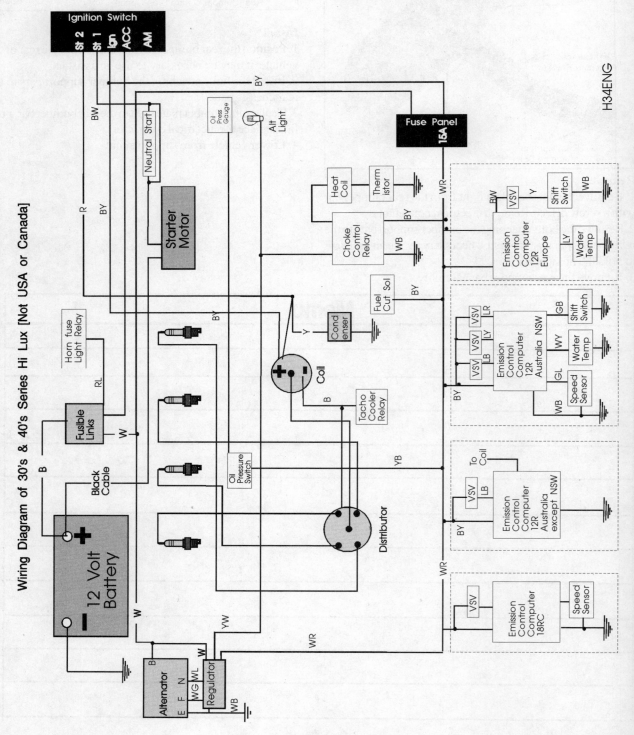

Wiring Diagram of 30's & 40's Series Hi Lux [Not USA or Canada]

386

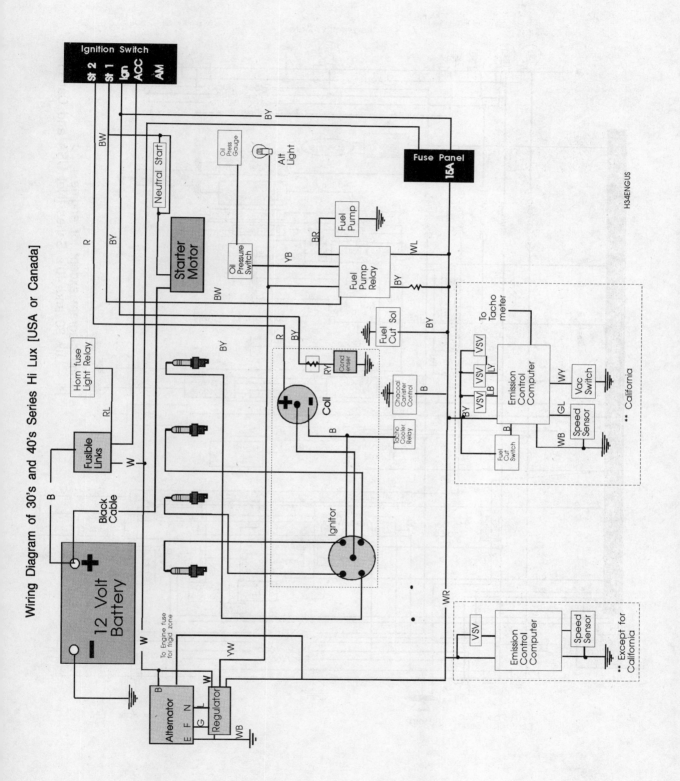

Wiring Diagram of 30's and 40's Series Hi Lux [USA or Canada]

H34ENGUS

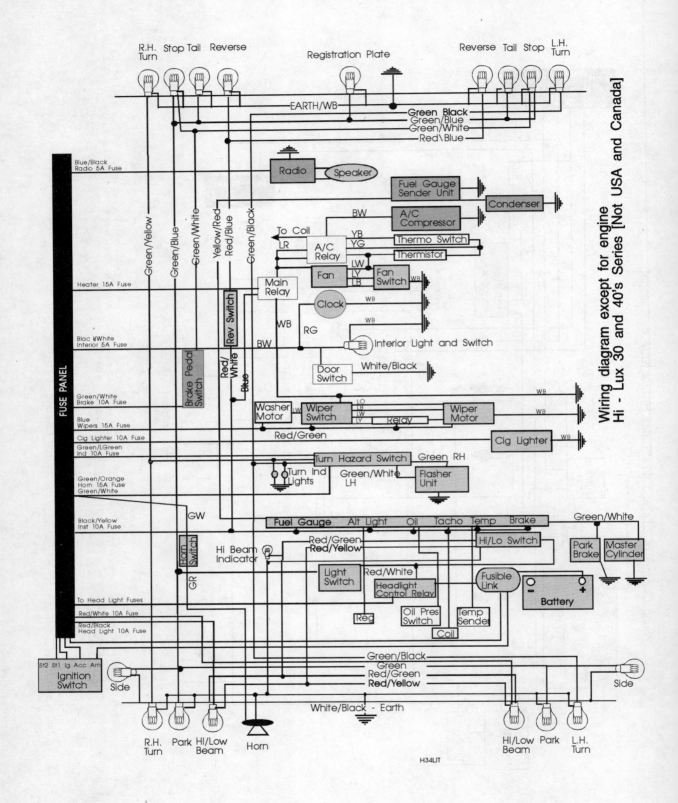

Wiring diagram except for engine
Hi - Lux 30 and 40's Series [Not USA and Canada]

H34LIT

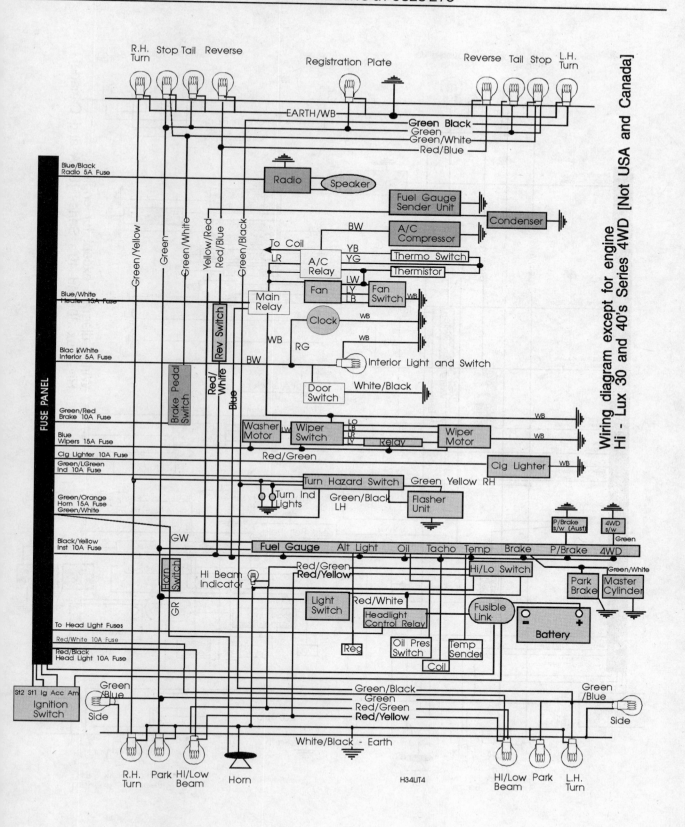

H34LIT4

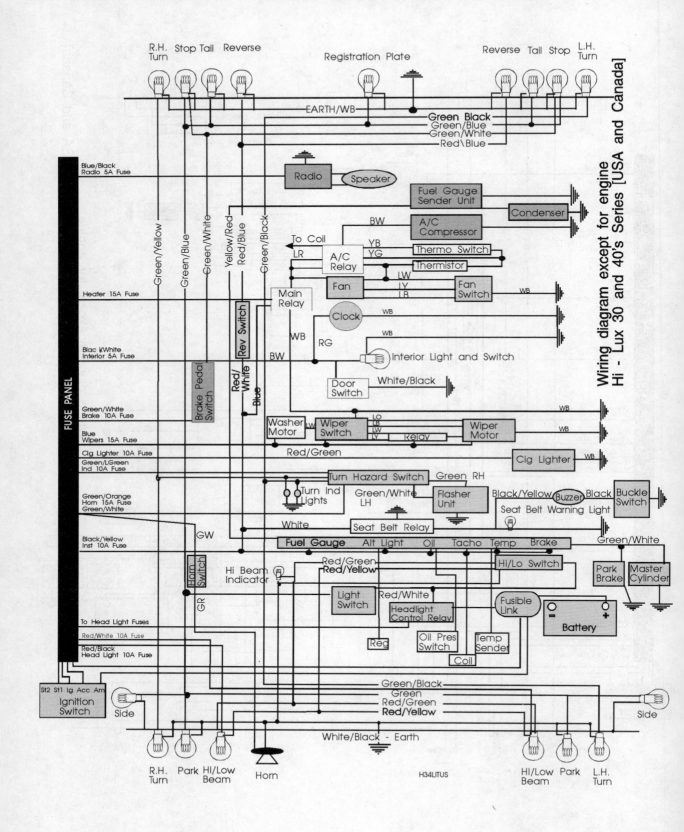

H34LITUS

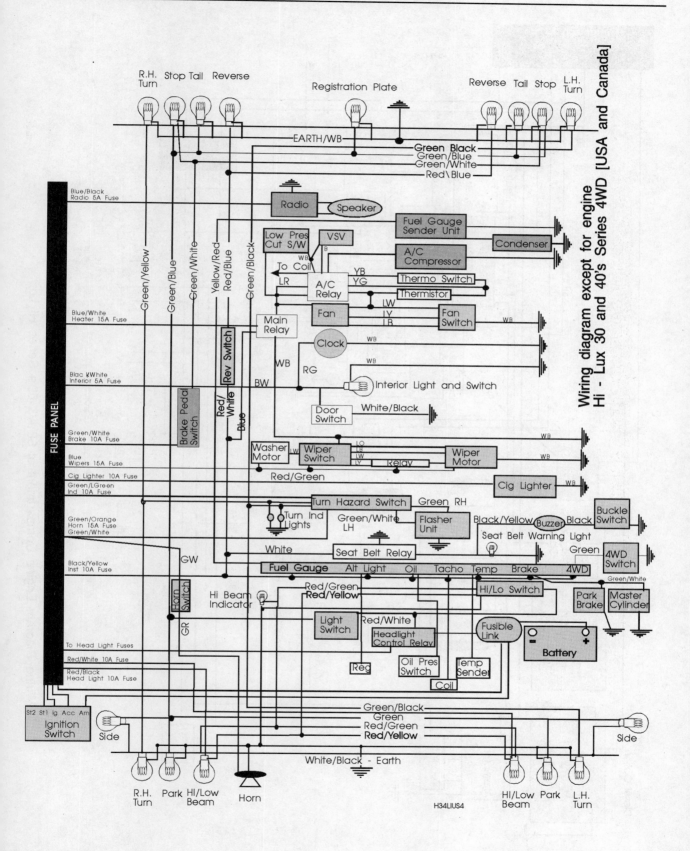

Wiring diagram except for engine
Hi - Lux 30 and 40's Series 4WD [USA and Canada]

H34LIUS4

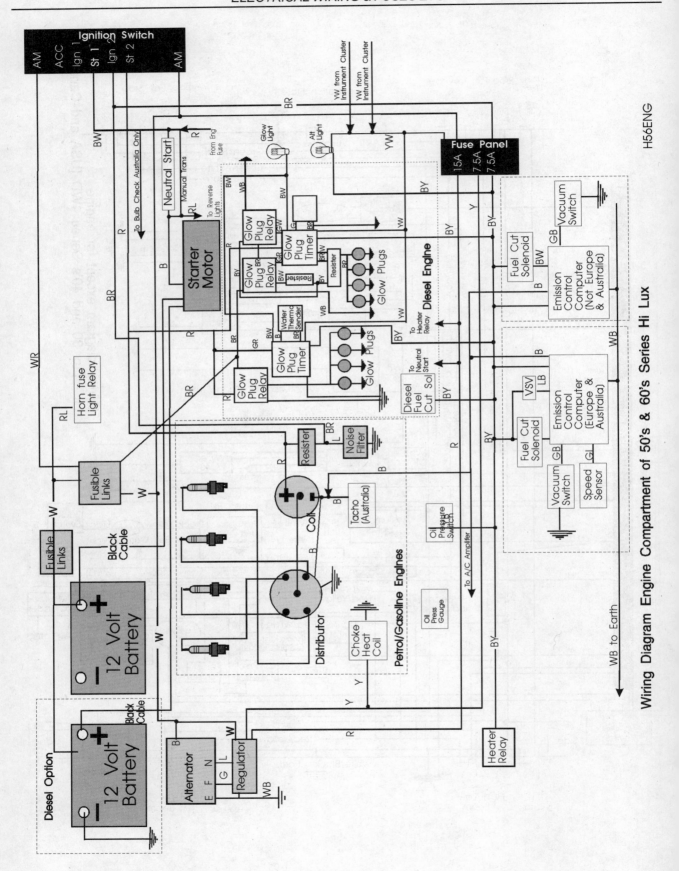

Wiring Diagram Engine Compartment of 50's & 60's Series Hi Lux

H56ENG

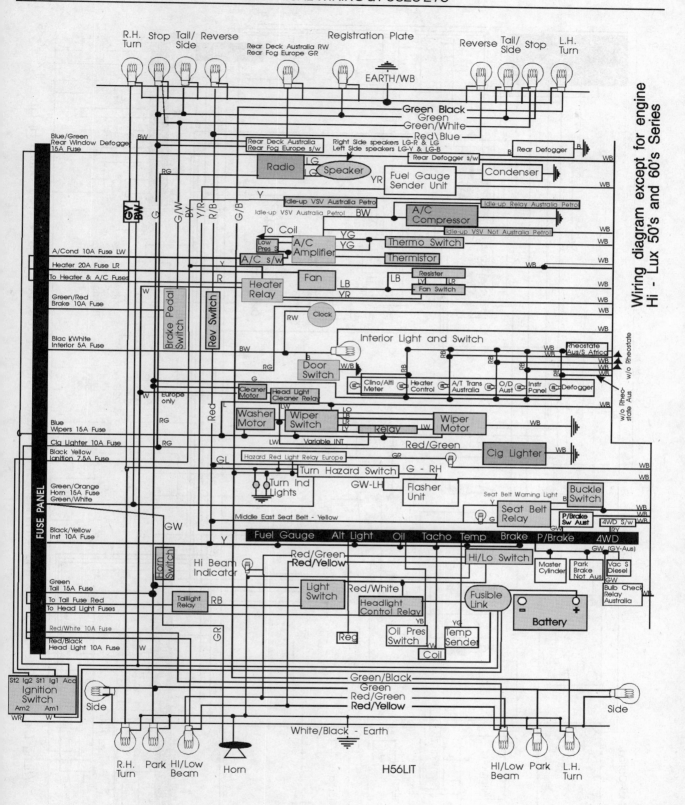

ELECTRICAL WIRING & FUSES ETC

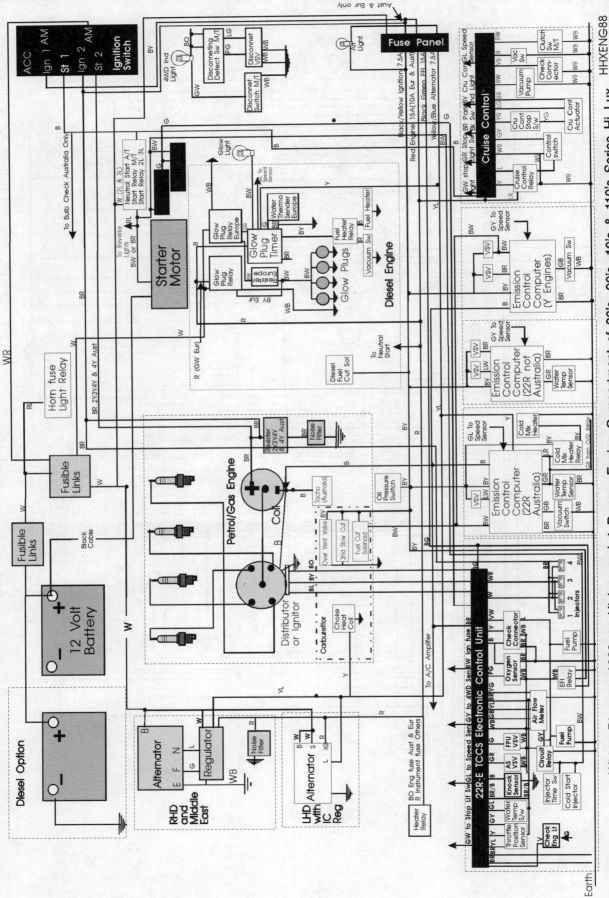

Wiring Diagram 1988 on Hi Lux and 4 Runner Engine Compartment of 80's, 90's, 10's & 110's Series Hi Lux

HHXENG88

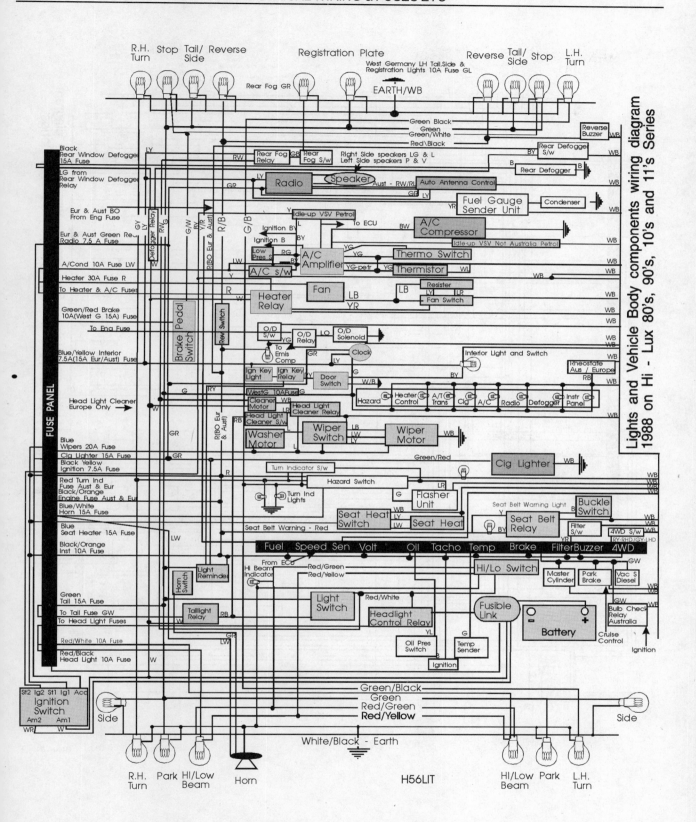

Lights and Vehicle Body components wiring diagram
1988 on Hi - Lux 80's, 90's, 10's and 11's Series

H56LIT

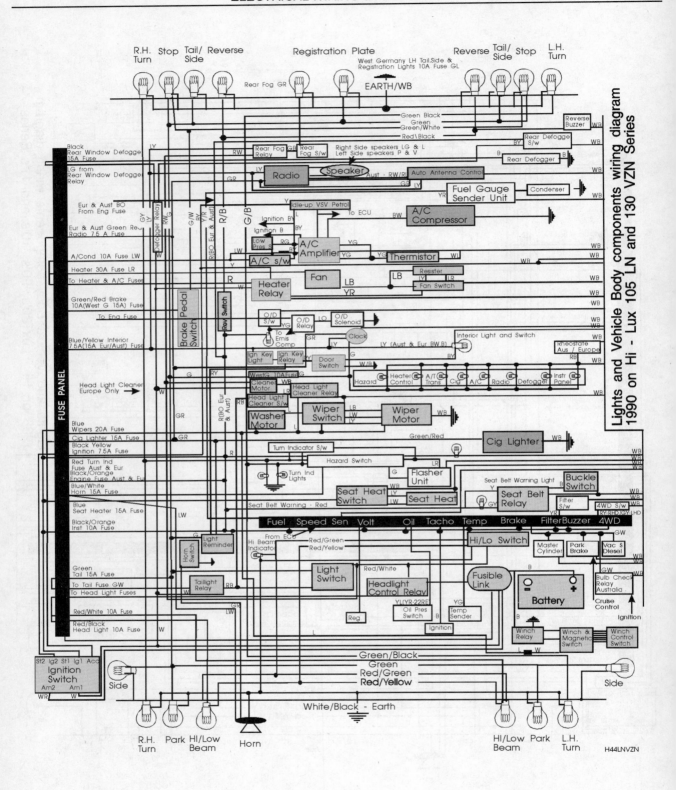

Lights and Vehicle Body components wiring diagram
1990 on Hi - Lux 105 LN and 130 VZN Series

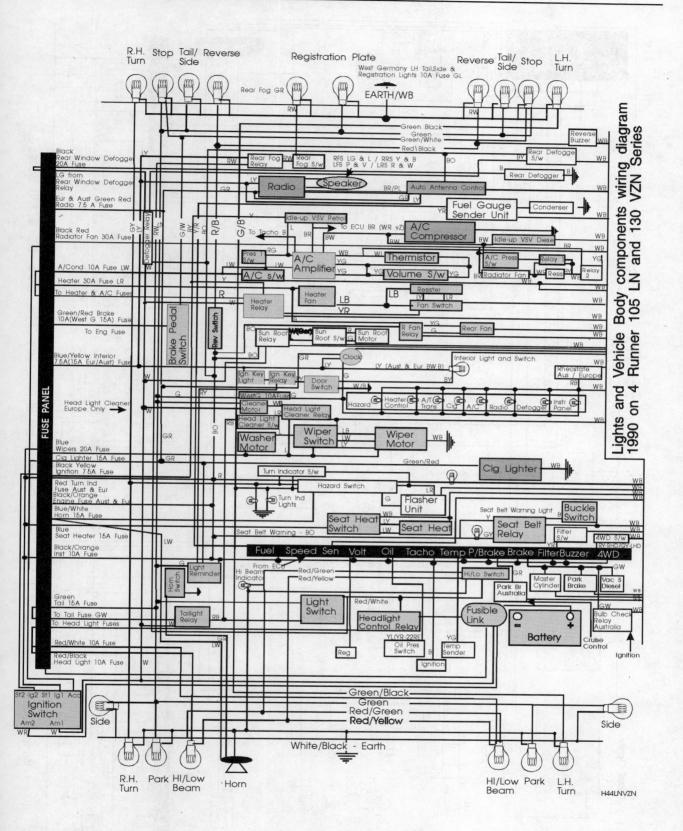

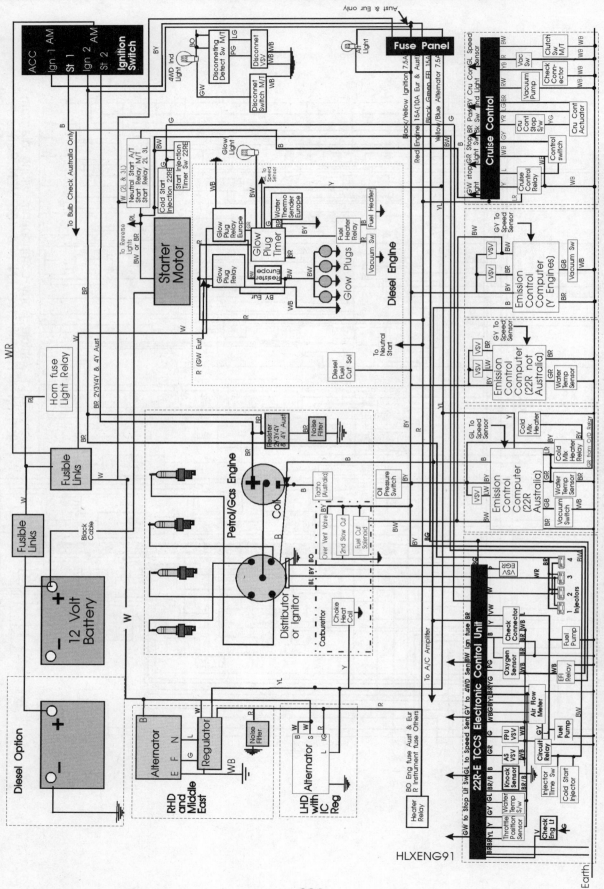

Wiring Diagram 1991- 1993 Hi Lux Engine Compartment of 80's, 90's, 10's, 110's, 125 & 130 Series

HLXENG91

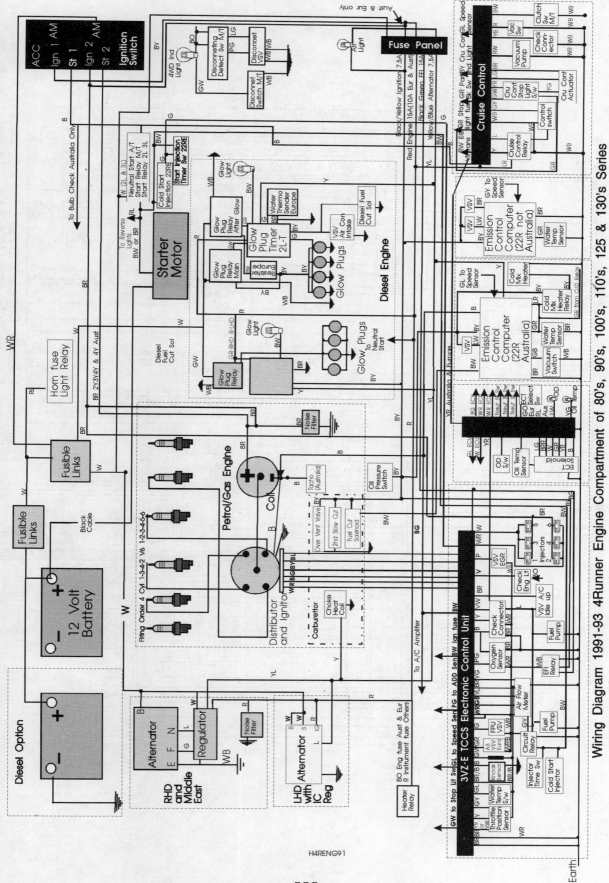

Wiring Diagram 1991-93 4Runner Engine Compartment of 80's, 90's, 100's, 110's, 125 & 130's Series

H4RENG91

ELECTRICAL WIRING & FUSES ETC

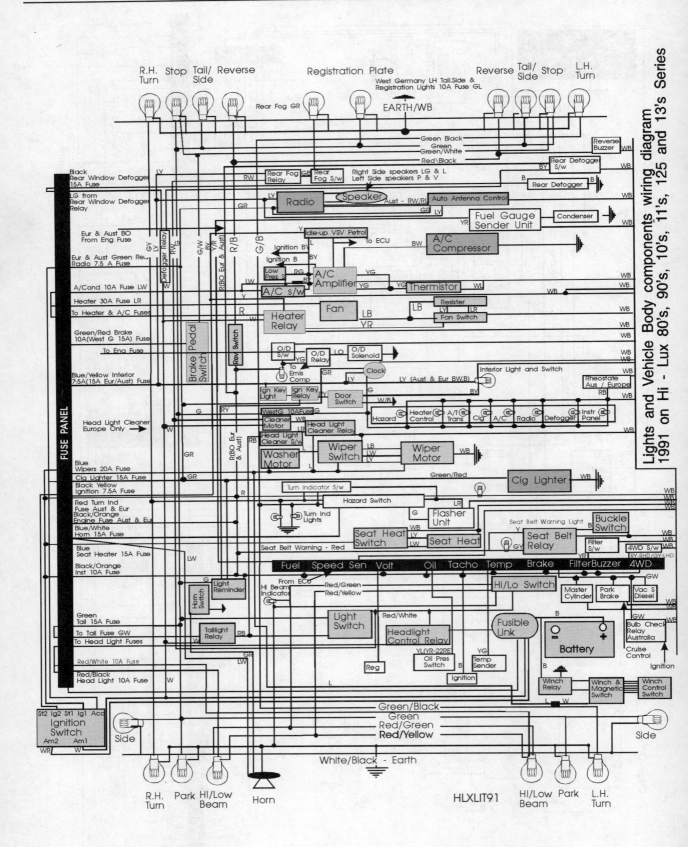

Lights and Vehicle Body components wiring diagram
1991 on Hi - Lux 80's, 90's, 10's, 11's, 125 and 13's Series

HLXLIT91

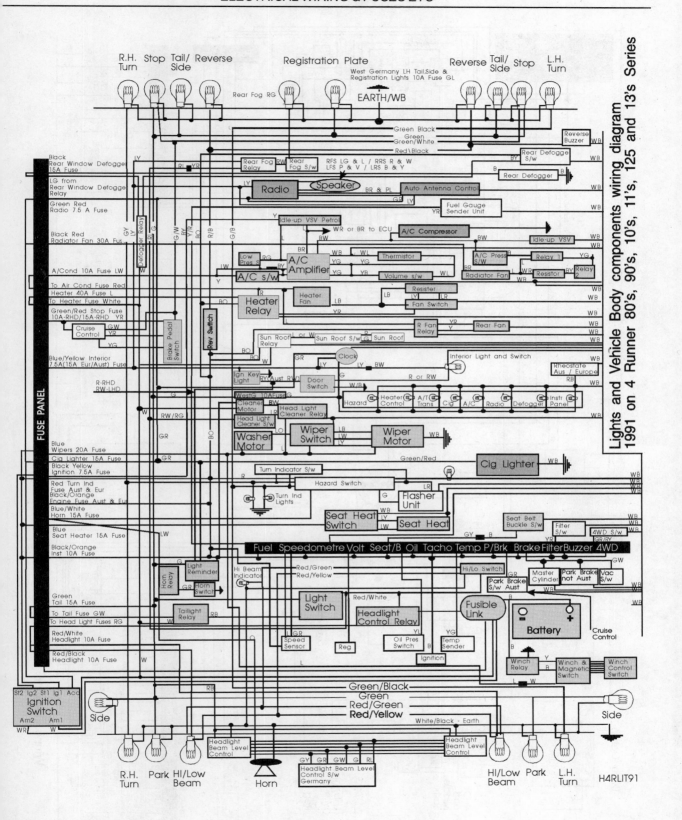

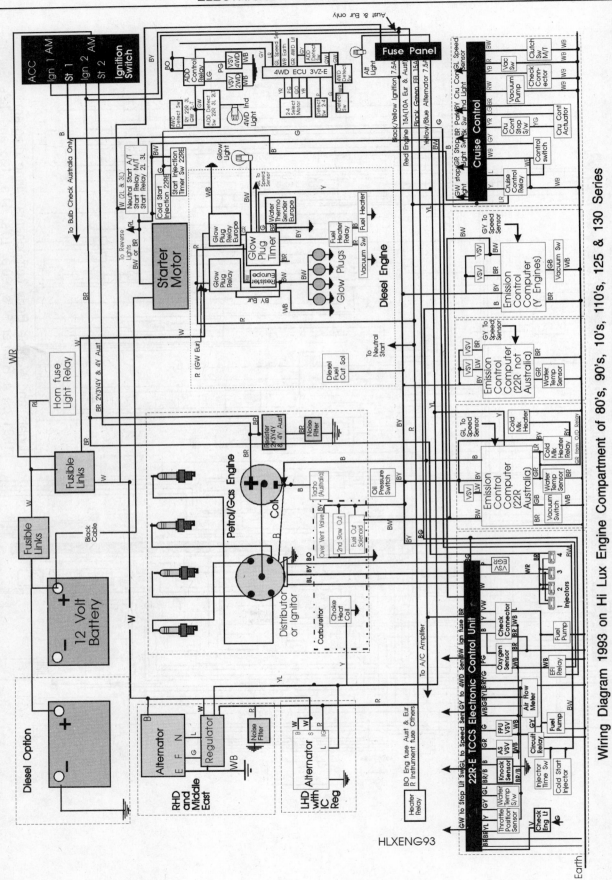

Wiring Diagram 1993 on Hi Lux Engine Compartment of 80's, 90's, 10's, 110's, 125 & 130 Series

HLXENG93

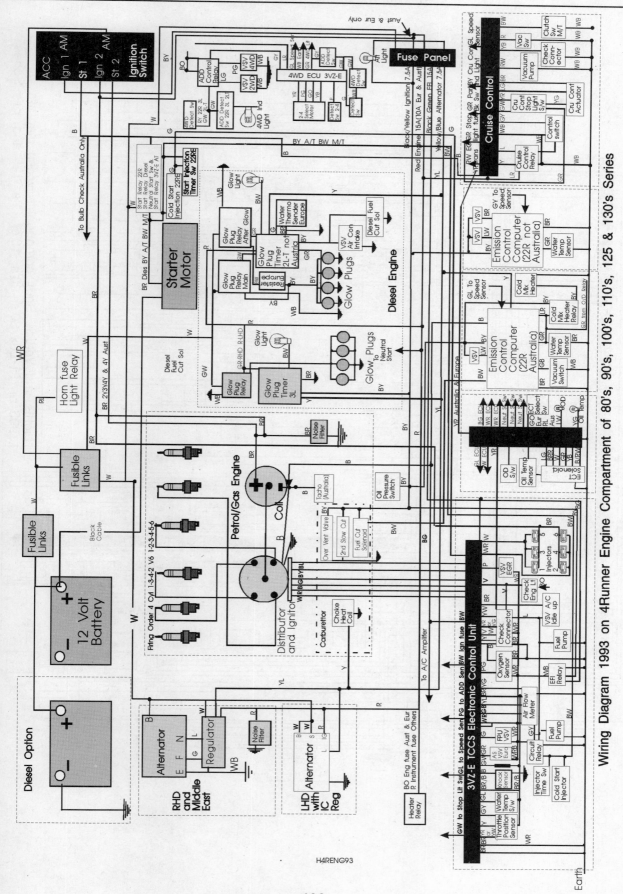

Wiring Diagram 1993 on 4Runner Engine Compartment of 80's, 90's, 100's, 110's, 125 & 130's Series

H4RENG93

ELECTRICAL WIRING & FUSES ETC

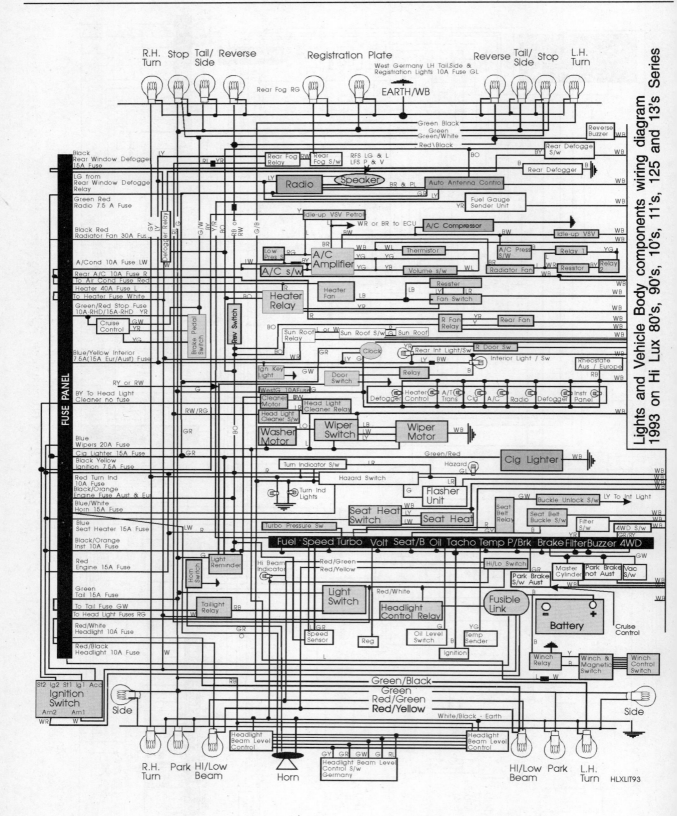

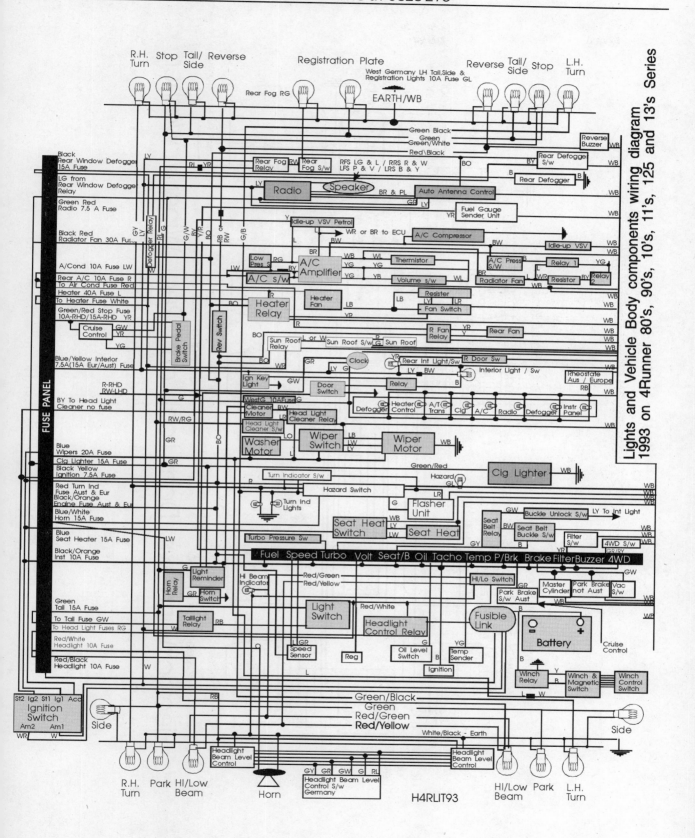

Lights and Vehicle Body components wiring diagram
1993 on 4Runner 80's, 90's, 10's, 11's, 125 and 13's Series

H4RLIT93

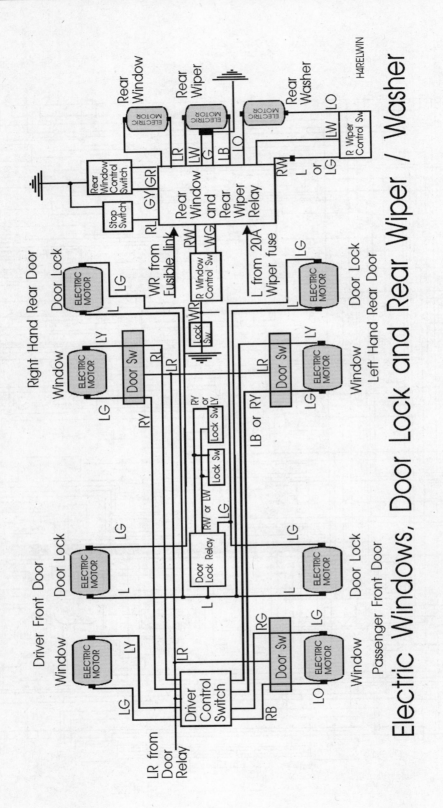

Electric Windows, Door Lock and Rear Wiper / Washer

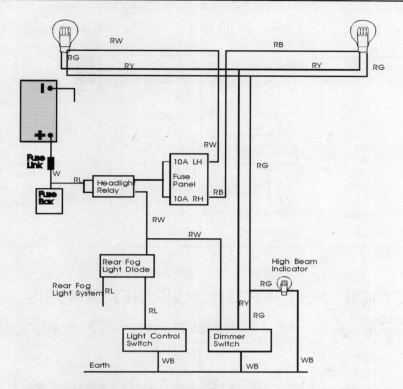

Headlights - Europe No Day Time Headlight

HHDLIGHT

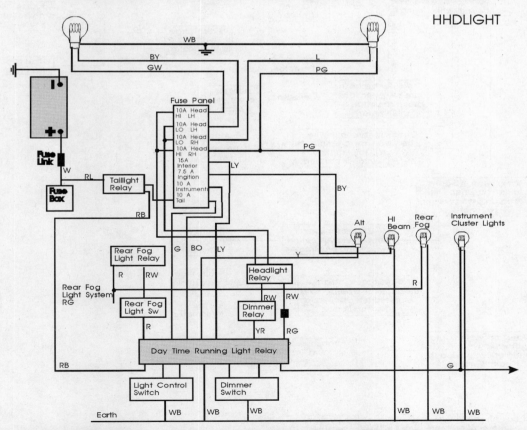

Headlights - Europe With Day Time Headlight

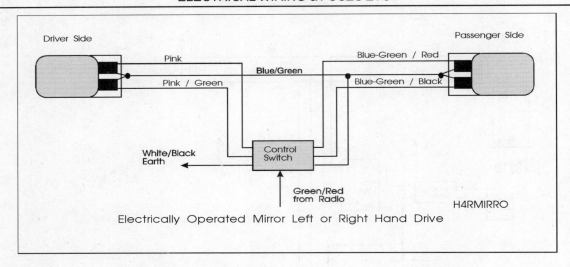

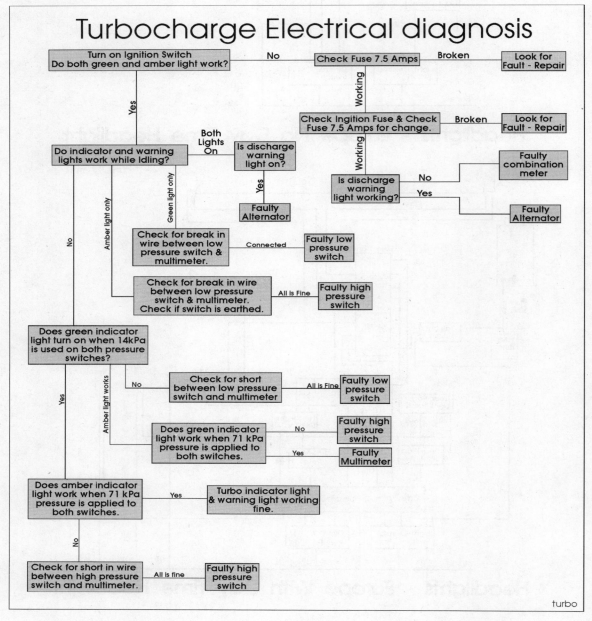

Turbocharge Electrical diagnosis

ADDENDUM: FLUID CAPACITIES Toyota Hi-Lux / 4 Runner 1979-1997

YEAR	MODEL	ENGINE TYPE	CRANKCASE LITRES	MANUAL TRANS. LITRES	AUTOMATIC TRANS. T/REFILL	DIFFERENTIAL LITRES	RADIATOR LITRES
81-83	Hilux 4x4 LN46	2L Diesel	4.8	1.9		2.2 (15)	
	4WD Transfer & Differential			1.6		2.3	
83-88	Hilux 4x4 LN65	2L Diesel	4.8, 5.8*	3.9		2.2 (15)	9.8
	4WD Transfer & Differential			1.6		2.3	
88-97	Hilux 4x4 LN106	3L Diesel	4.3., 5.3*	3.9		2.2 (15)	9.8
	4WD Transfer & Differential			1.6		2.3	
79-83	Hilux 4x4 RN36, RN46	18R-C Eng	3.8	1.9		2.0 (15)	
	4WD Transfer & Differential			1.6		1.9	
88-97	Hilux 4x4 RN105	22R Eng	3.8, 4.3*	3.9		2.2 (15)	8.4
	4WD Transfer & Differential			1.6		2.3	
88-97	Hilux 4x4 SR5, LN107, LN111	3L Diesel	4.3, 5.3*	3.9		2.2 (15)	9.8
	4WD Transfer & Differential			1.1		1.9	
88-97	Hilux 4x4 SR5, RN106, RN110	22R Eng	3.8, 4.3*	3.9		2.2 (15)	
	4WD Transfer & Differential			1.1		1.9	
83-85	Hilux 4x4 YN65	3Y-C Eng	3.5	3.9		2.2 (15)	
	4WD Transfer & Differential			1.6		2.3	
85-88	Hilux 4x4 YN67	4Y-C Eng	3.5	3.9	4.5	2.2 (15)	7.4
	4WD Transfer & Differential			1.6 (23)		2.3	
80-84	Hilux LN40, LN55	L Diesel	4.8	1.9		1.8	
84-88	Hilux LN56	2L Diesel	4.8	2.2	2.4	1.8	9.8
88-91	Hilux LN85	2L Diesel	4.8, 5.8*	2.2	2.4	1.8	9.8
91-97	Hilux LN86	3L Diesel	4.8, 5.8*	2.2	2.4	1.8	9.8
71-78	Hilux RN20, RN25	12R Eng	3.5	1.9		1.2	
77-83	Hilux RN27, RN31, RN41	18R-C Eng	3.8	1.9		1.8	
79-83	Hilux RN30, RN40	12R Eng	3.5	1.9		1.8	
88-97	Hilux RN85, RN90	22R Eng	3.8, 4.3*	2.2	2.4	1.8	8.4
79-83	Hilux SR5, RN41	18R-C Eng	3.8	2.6		1.8	
83-87	Hilux YN55	1Y-C Eng	3.0	1.9		1.8	7.7
87-88	Hilux YN56	2Y-C Eng	3.0	1.9		1.8	7.3
84-87	Hilux YN57 (inc SR5)	3Y/3Y-C Eng	3.0	2.6	2.4	1.8	7.4
87-88	Hilux YN58	4Y-C Eng	3.0	2.6	2.4	1.8	7.4
88-97	Hilux YN85	2Y-C Eng	3.0, 3.5*	1.9		1.8	7.0
89-96	4Runner 4x4 (inc SR5) RN130	22R Eng	3.8, 4.3*	3.9		2.2 (15)	8.4
	4WD Transfer & Differential			1.1		1.6 (78)	
84-85	4Runner 4x4 LN60	2L Diesel	4.8, 5.8*	3.9		2.2 (15)	
	4WD Transfer & Differential			1.6		2.3	
85-89	4Runner 4x4 LN61	2L Diesel	4.8, 5.8*	3.9		2.2 (15)	
	4WD Transfer & Differential			1.6		1.6	
89-96	4Runner 4x4 LN130	2L Diesel	4.3, 5.3*	3.9		2.2 (15)	9.8
	4WD Transfer & Differential			1.1		1.6	
90-96	4Runner 4x4 RV6, SR5	3VZ-E Eng	4.0, 4.3*	3	4.5	2.2 (15)	8.5
	4WD Transfer & Differential			1.1 (23)		1.6 (78)	
84-85	4Runner 4x4 YN60	3Y-C Eng	3.5	3.9		2.2 (15)	
	4WD Transfer & Differential			1.6		2.3	
85-89	4Runner 4x4 YN63	4Y-C/4Y-EC Eng	3.5	3.9	4.5	2.2 (15)	
	4WD Transfer & Differential			1.6 (80)		1.6	
89-90	4Runner 4x4 YN130	4Y-C Eng	3.5, 4.0*		4.5	2.2 (15)	
	4WD Transfer & Differential			0.8		1.6, 1.9	

*INCLUDES OIL FILTER
Fluid levels SHOULD ALWAYS be checked with the dipstick or level plug